W9-AFM-717

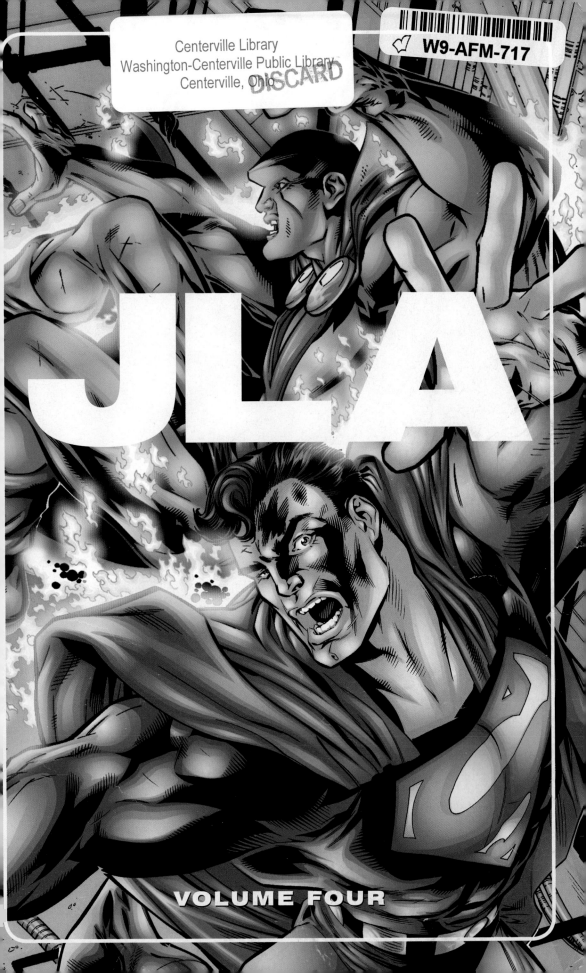

JLA

VOLUME FOUR

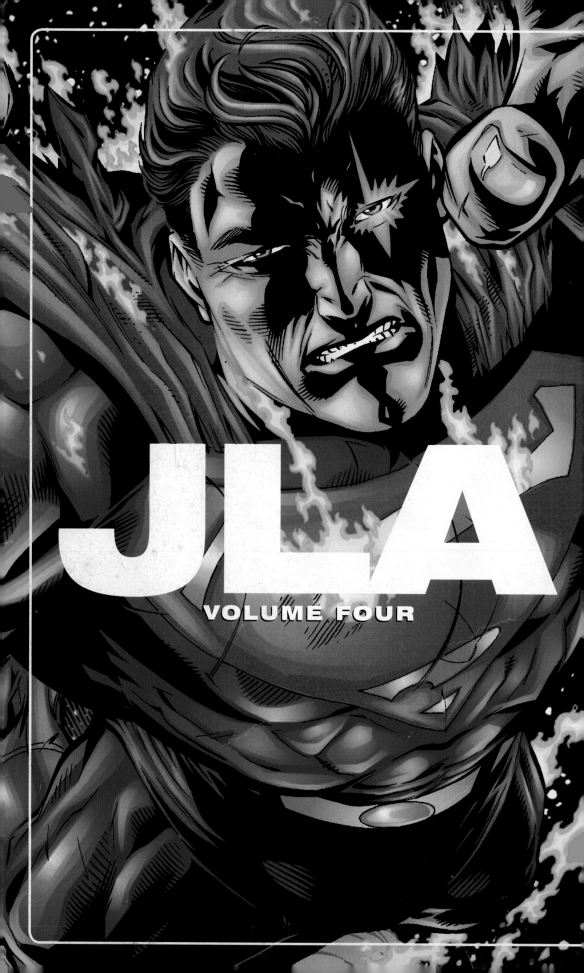

JLA

VOLUME FOUR

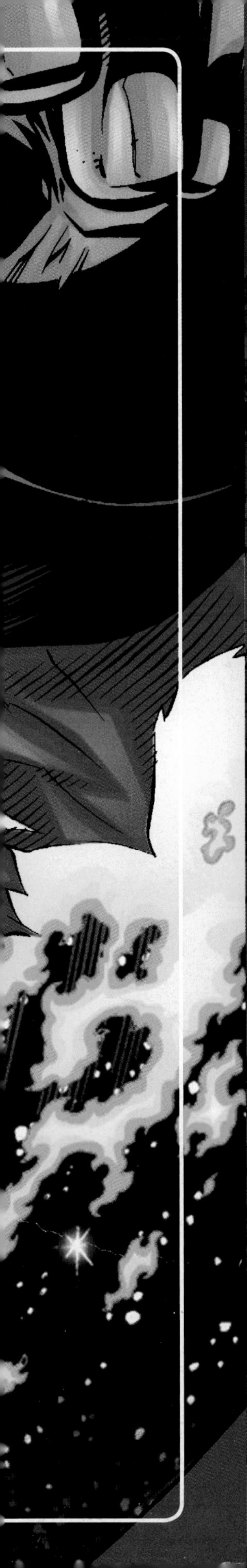

GRANT MORRISON
MARK WAID
DAN CURTIS JOHNSON
J.M. DeMATTEIS
DEVIN GRAYSON
writers

HOWARD PORTER
MARK PAJARILLO
STEVE SCOTT
pencillers

DREW GERACI
JOHN DELL
WALDEN WONG
MARK PROPST
inkers

PAT GARRAHY
JOHN KALISZ
colorists

KEN LOPEZ
letterer

HOWARD PORTER
WITH MOOSE BAUMANN
collection cover artists

Superman created by
JERRY SIEGEL & JOE SHUSTER
By special arrangement with the
Jerry Siegel family

DAN RASPLER Editor – Original Series TONY BEDARD Associate Editor – Original Series
ROBIN WILDMAN Editor ROBBIN BROSTERMAN Design Director – Books

BOB HARRAS Senior VP – Editor-in-Chief, DC Comics

DIANE NELSON President DAN DIDIO & JIM LEE Co-Publishers GEOFF JOHNS Chief Creative Officer
JOHN ROOD Executive VP – Sales, Marketing and Business Development AMY GENKINS Senior VP – Business & Legal Affairs
NAIRI GARDINER Senior VP – Finance JEFF BOISON VP – Publishing Planning MARK CHIARELLO VP – Art Direction & Design
JOHN CUNNINGHAM VP – Marketing TERRI CUNNINGHAM VP – Editorial Administration
ALISON GILL Senior VP – Manufacturing & Operations HANK KANALZ Senior VP – Vertigo & Integrated Publishing
JAY KOGAN VP – Business & Legal Affairs, Publishing JACK MAHAN VP – Business Affairs, Talent
NICK NAPOLITANO VP – Manufacturing Administration SUE POHJA VP – Book Sales
COURTNEY SIMMONS Senior VP – Publicity BOB WAYNE Senior VP – Sales

Interior color separations by Heroic Age

Library of Congress Cataloging-in-Publication Data

Morrison, Grant.
JLA. Volume four / Grant Morrison, Mark Waid ; [illustrated by] Howard Porter, Mark Pajarillo.
    pages cm
    Summary: "In this latest trade paperback collecting JLA #32–46, the team is up against a new, deadly Injustice Gang led by Lex
Luthor. With Prometheus, the man who almost single-handedly defeated the JLA, as well as the General and Queen Bee. It looks as if
the Justice League may lose even if they win." Provided by publisher.
    ISBN 978-1-4012-4385-2 (pbk.)
    1. Graphic novels. I. Waid, Mark. II. Porter, Howard. III. Pajarillo, Mark. IV. Title.
    PN6728.J87M69633 2014
    741.5'973—dc23
                                                                                                    2013039778

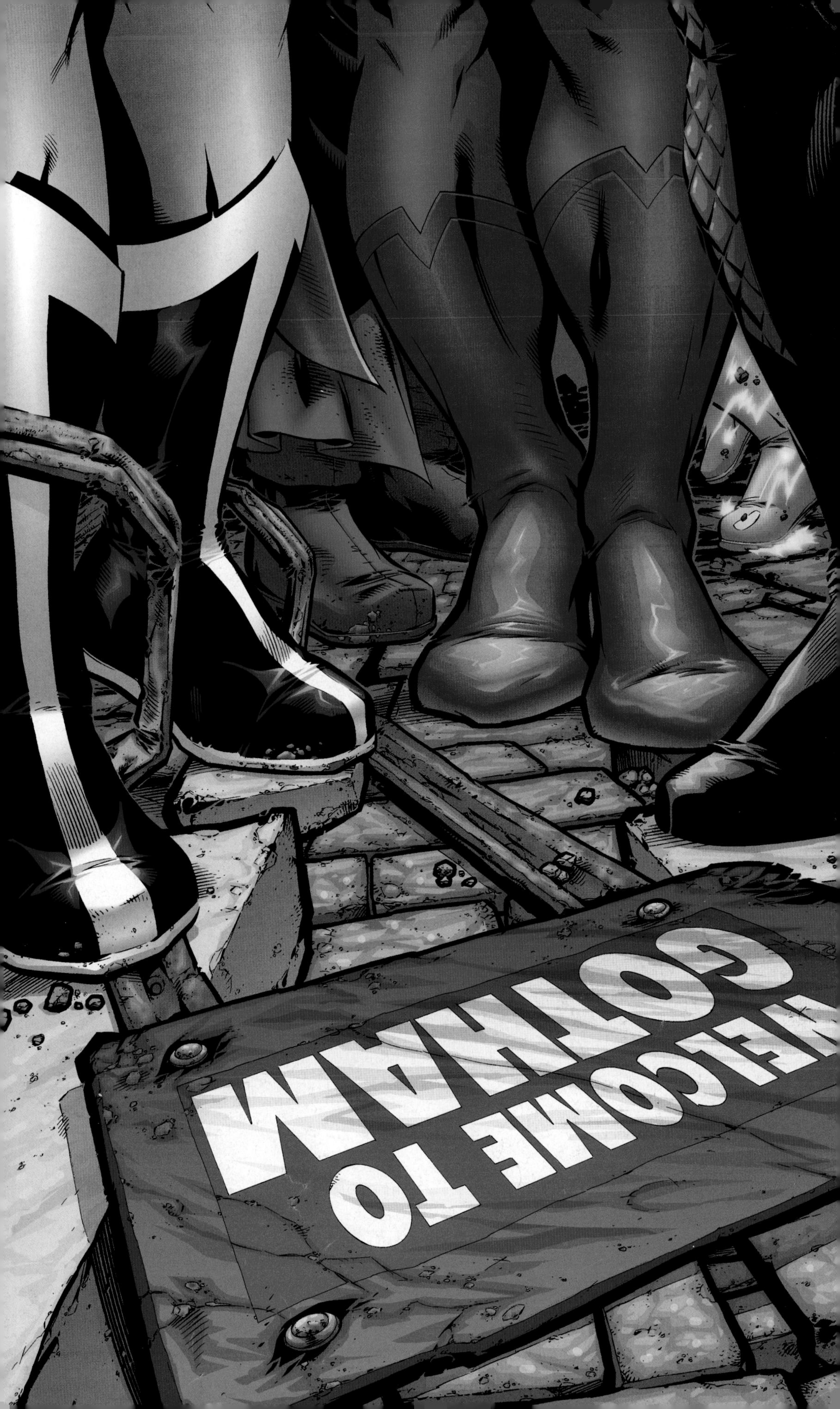
WELCOME TO
GOTHAM

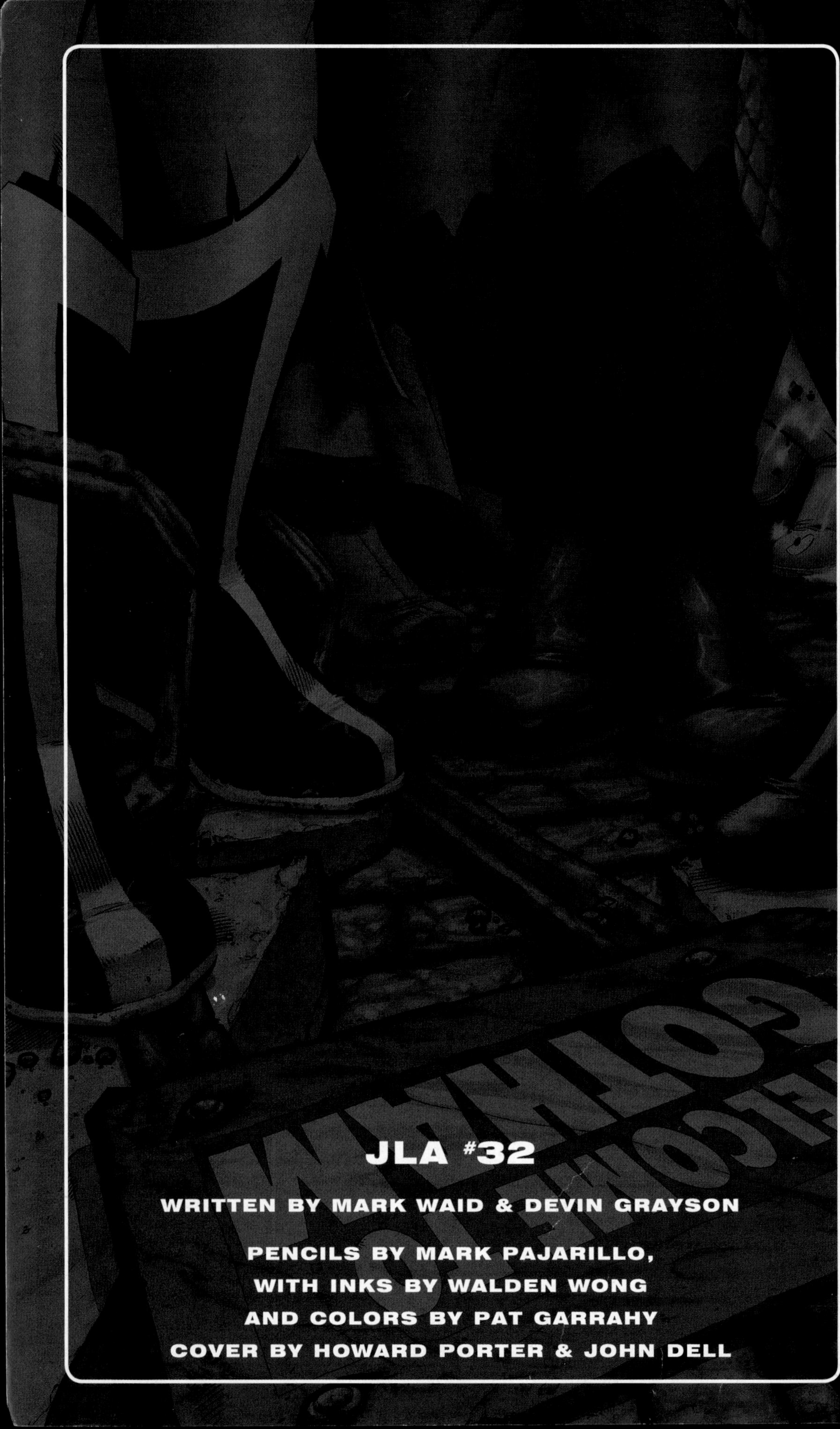

JLA #32

WRITTEN BY MARK WAID & DEVIN GRAYSON

PENCILS BY MARK PAJARILLO,
WITH INKS BY WALDEN WONG
AND COLORS BY PAT GARRAHY
COVER BY HOWARD PORTER & JOHN DELL

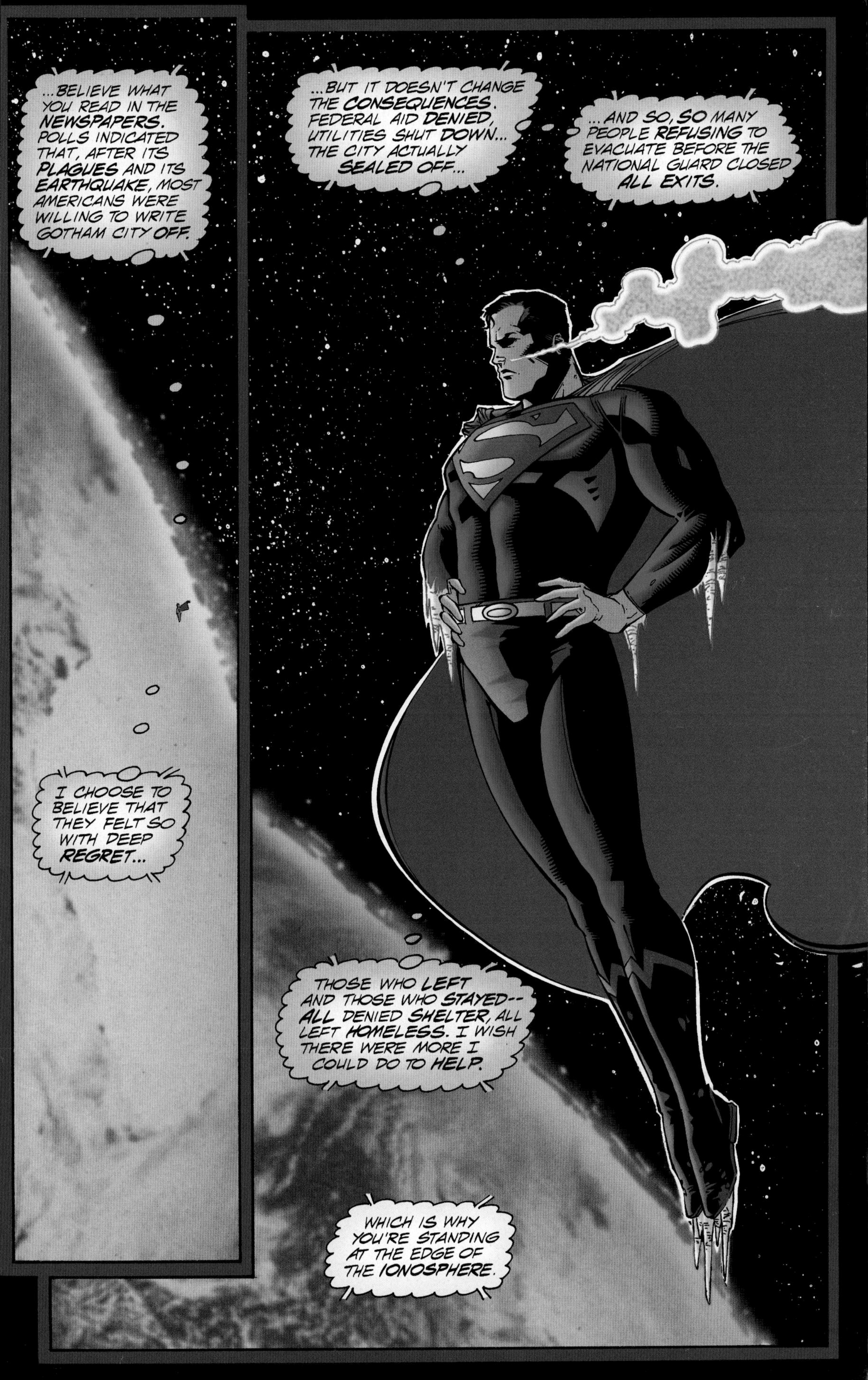
...BELIEVE WHAT YOU READ IN THE NEWSPAPERS. POLLS INDICATED THAT, AFTER ITS PLAGUES AND ITS EARTHQUAKE, MOST AMERICANS WERE WILLING TO WRITE GOTHAM CITY OFF.
I CHOOSE TO BELIEVE THAT THEY FELT SO WITH DEEP REGRET...
...BUT IT DOESN'T CHANGE THE CONSEQUENCES. FEDERAL AID DENIED, UTILITIES SHUT DOWN... THE CITY ACTUALLY SEALED OFF...
...AND SO, SO MANY PEOPLE REFUSING TO EVACUATE BEFORE THE NATIONAL GUARD CLOSED ALL EXITS.
THOSE WHO LEFT AND THOSE WHO STAYED-- ALL DENIED SHELTER, ALL LEFT HOMELESS. I WISH THERE WERE MORE I COULD DO TO HELP.
WHICH IS WHY YOU'RE STANDING AT THE EDGE OF THE IONOSPHERE.

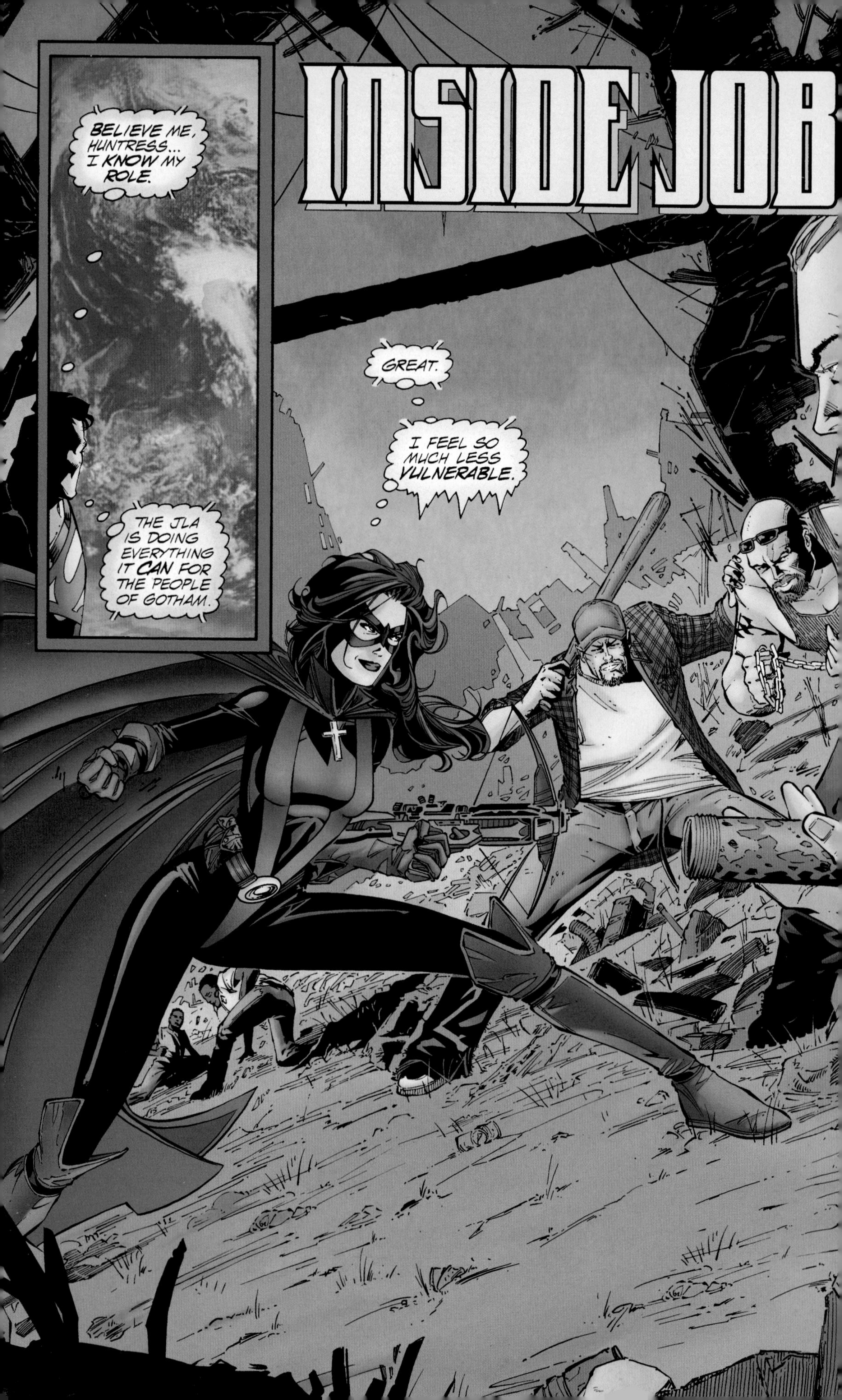
INSIDE JOB
BELIEVE ME, HUNTRESS... I KNOW MY ROLE.
THE JLA IS DOING EVERYTHING IT CAN FOR THE PEOPLE OF GOTHAM.
GREAT.
I FEEL SO MUCH LESS VULNERABLE.

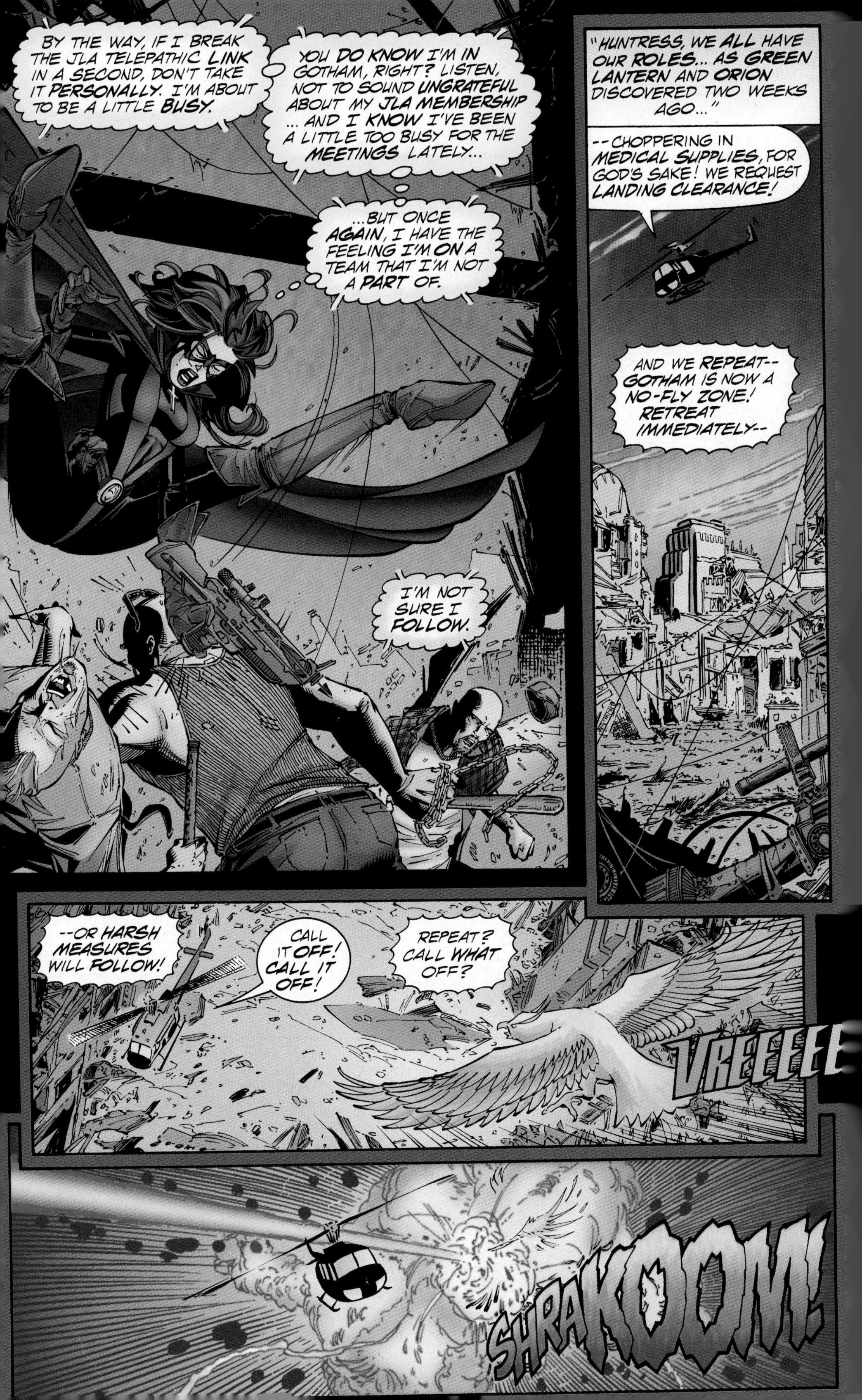
BY THE WAY, IF I BREAK THE JLA TELEPATHIC LINK IN A SECOND, DON'T TAKE IT PERSONALLY. I'M ABOUT TO BE A LITTLE BUSY.
YOU DO KNOW I'M IN GOTHAM, RIGHT? LISTEN, NOT TO SOUND UNGRATEFUL ABOUT MY JLA MEMBERSHIP ... AND I KNOW I'VE BEEN A LITTLE TOO BUSY FOR THE MEETINGS LATELY...
...BUT ONCE AGAIN, I HAVE THE FEELING I'M ON A TEAM THAT I'M NOT A PART OF.
I'M NOT SURE I FOLLOW.
"HUNTRESS, WE ALL HAVE OUR ROLES... AS GREEN LANTERN AND ORION DISCOVERED TWO WEEKS AGO..."
--CHOPPERING IN MEDICAL SUPPLIES, FOR GOD'S SAKE! WE REQUEST LANDING CLEARANCE!
AND WE REPEAT-- GOTHAM IS NOW A NO-FLY ZONE! RETREAT IMMEDIATELY--
--OR HARSH MEASURES WILL FOLLOW!
CALL IT OFF! CALL IT OFF!
REPEAT? CALL WHAT OFF?
VREEEEE
SHRAKOOM!

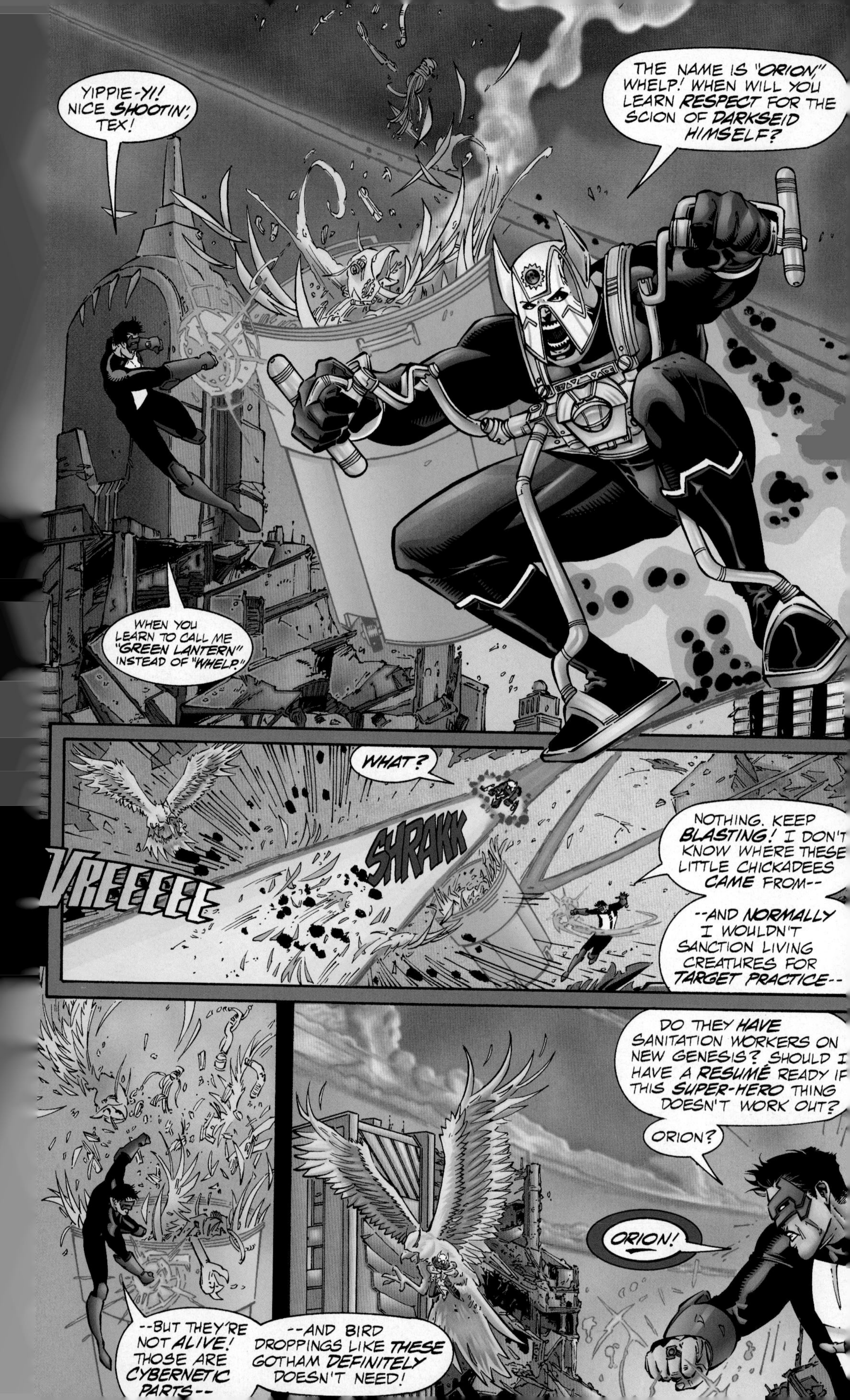
YIPPIE-YI! NICE SHOOTIN', TEX!
THE NAME IS "ORION," WHELP! WHEN WILL YOU LEARN RESPECT FOR THE SCION OF DARKSEID HIMSELF?
WHEN YOU LEARN TO CALL ME "GREEN LANTERN" INSTEAD OF "WHELP."
WHAT?
VREEEEE
SHRAKK
NOTHING. KEEP BLASTING! I DON'T KNOW WHERE THESE LITTLE CHICKADEES CAME FROM--
--AND NORMALLY I WOULDN'T SANCTION LIVING CREATURES FOR TARGET PRACTICE--
--BUT THEY'RE NOT ALIVE! THOSE ARE CYBERNETIC PARTS--
--AND BIRD DROPPINGS LIKE THESE GOTHAM DEFINITELY DOESN'T NEED!
DO THEY HAVE SANITATION WORKERS ON NEW GENESIS? SHOULD I HAVE A RESUMÉ READY IF THIS SUPER-HERO THING DOESN'T WORK OUT?
ORION?
ORION!

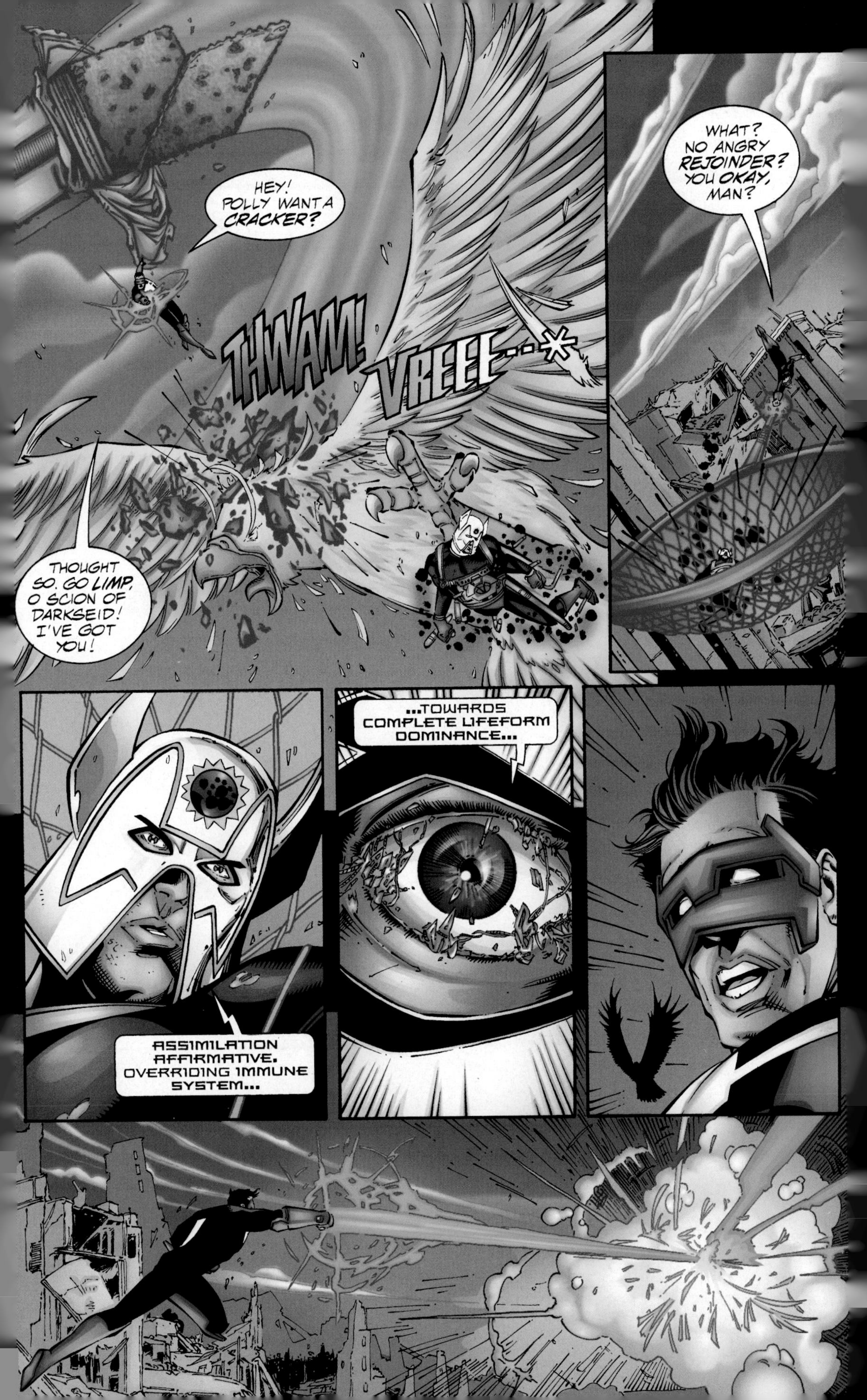
HEY! POLLY WANT A CRACKER?
THWAM!
VREEE..
THOUGHT SO. GO LIMP, O SCION OF DARKSEID! I'VE GOT YOU!
WHAT? NO ANGRY REJOINDER? YOU OKAY, MAN?
ASSIMILATION AFFIRMATIVE. OVERRIDING IMMUNE SYSTEM...
...TOWARDS COMPLETE LIFEFORM DOMINANCE...

ARTIFICIAL LIFE...

...IN THE FORM OF A MECHANICAL VIRUS.

GENANITE TECHNOLOGY.

EXCUSE ME?

MICROSCOPIC *NANITES* GENETICALLY ENGINEERED TO TRANSFOR[M] ORGANIC CELLS INTO *MACHINE* CELLS ON *CONTACT*--PRESUMA[BLY] TURNING THOSE *AFFECTED* INTO *DRONES.*

IN ORION'S CASE, WE CAUGHT IT *QUICKLY* ENOU[GH] TO *TREAT* IT--AND ONLY *THEN* BECAUSE OF HIS *EXTRATERRESTRIAL PHYSIOLOGY.* THE GOTHA[M]ITES WOULD NOT HAVE BEEN SO *FORTUNATE.*

CLEARLY, THE BIRDS WERE DESIGNED AS *CARRIERS* FOR A *GENGINEERED DISEASE...* AND THE *IMPLICATION* IS *STAGGERING.*

LOCUS.

AGAIN... EXCUSE ME?

"*LOCUS.* A ROGUE GROUP OF *GENETICISTS* THE JLA FOUGHT LONG BEFORE YOUR *TIME.* * APPARENTLY, THEY'RE UP AND *RUNNING AGAIN--*

"--BECAUSE THE *YELLOW BIRDS* ARE *THEIRS*--AN AVIAN MAPPED FROM *ALIEN DNA.*"

SO NOW THAT GOTHAM'S BEEN *SEVERED* FROM THE MAINLAND, THEY SEE IT AS ONE BIG *PETRI DISH?*

PERHAPS...OR PERHAPS THE *REVERSE.* DID THEY *SEE* IT AS A POTENTIAL LABORATORY-- AND HAVE IT QUARANTINED BY THE GOVERNMENT?

*JLA: YEAR ONE --DAN.

NO *WAY!* YOU'RE SAYING THIS *"NO MAN'S LAND"* LEGISLATION IS *THEIR...*

DOES LOCUS *OWN* THE SENATORS IT WOULD *TAKE* TO PULL SOMETHING LIKE THAT OFF?

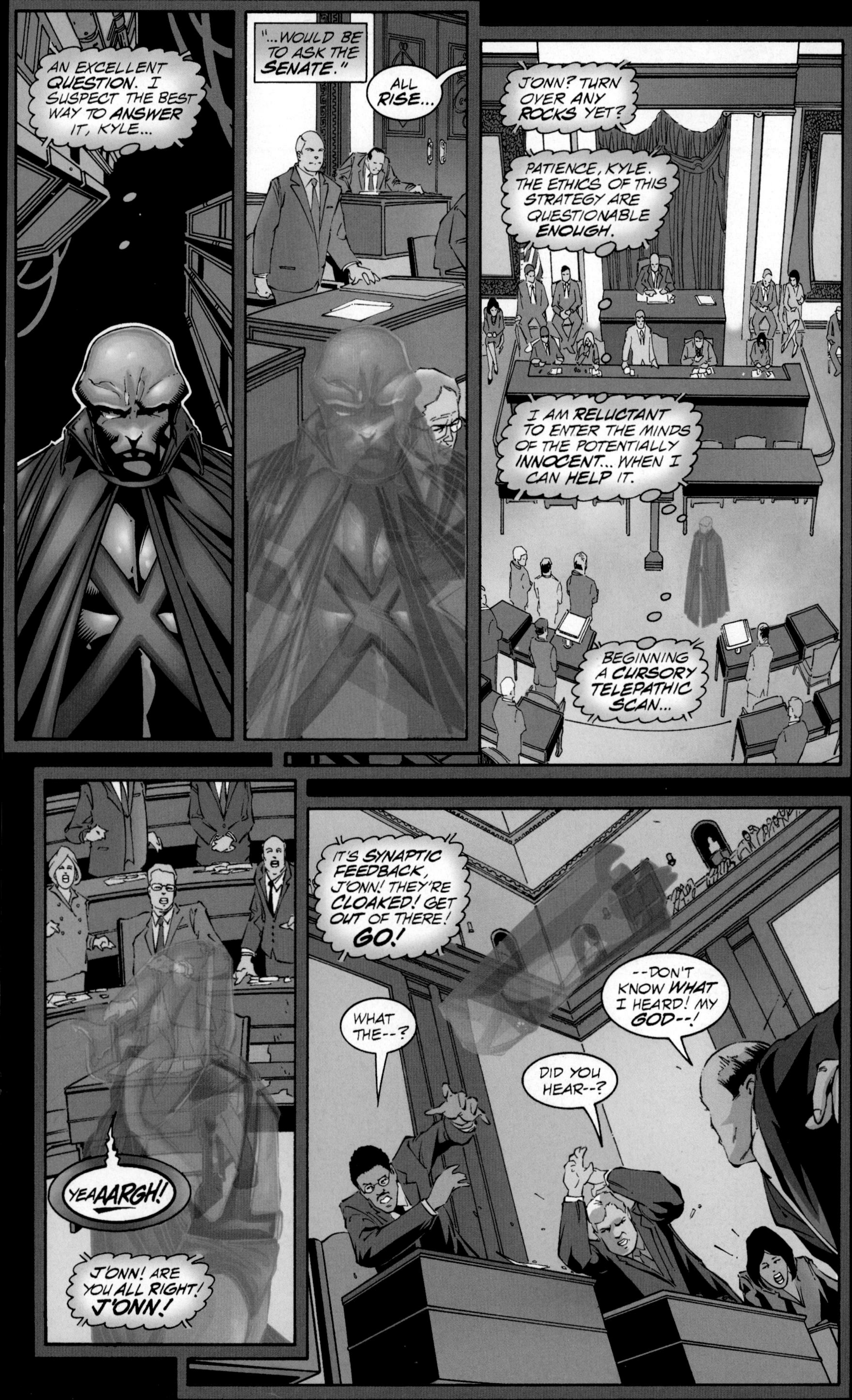
AN EXCELLENT QUESTION. I SUSPECT THE BEST WAY TO ANSWER IT, KYLE...
"...WOULD BE TO ASK THE SENATE."
ALL RISE...
J'ONN? TURN OVER ANY ROCKS YET?
PATIENCE, KYLE. THE ETHICS OF THIS STRATEGY ARE QUESTIONABLE ENOUGH.
I AM RELUCTANT TO ENTER THE MINDS OF THE POTENTIALLY INNOCENT... WHEN I CAN HELP IT.
BEGINNING A CURSORY TELEPATHIC SCAN...
YEAAARGH!
J'ONN! ARE YOU ALL RIGHT! J'ONN!
IT'S SYNAPTIC FEEDBACK, J'ONN! THEY'RE CLOAKED! GET OUT OF THERE! GO!
WHAT THE--?
DID YOU HEAR--?
--DON'T KNOW WHAT I HEARD! MY GOD--!

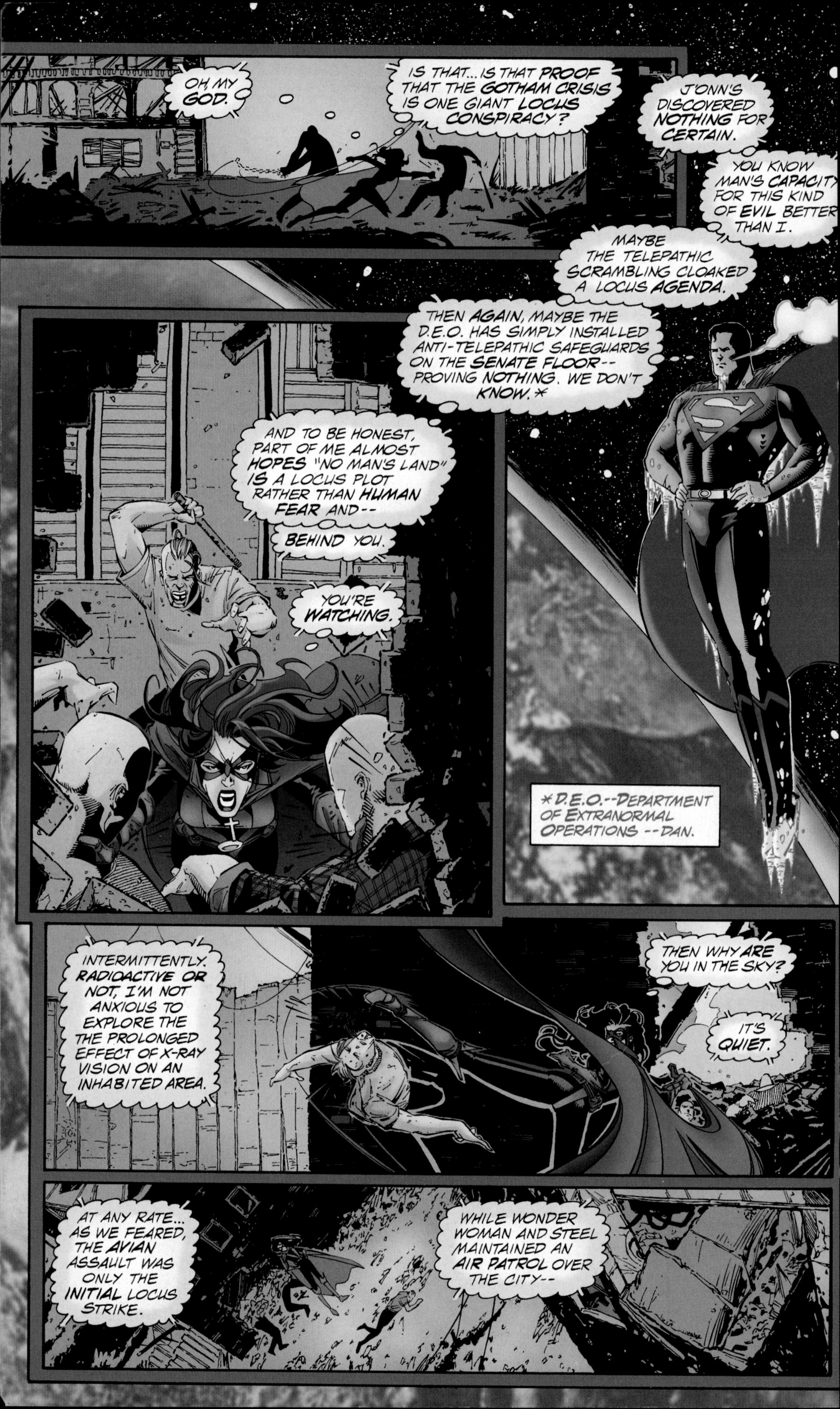
OH MY GOD.
IS THAT... IS THAT PROOF THAT THE GOTHAM CRISIS IS ONE GIANT LOCUS CONSPIRACY?
J'ONN'S DISCOVERED NOTHING FOR CERTAIN.
YOU KNOW MAN'S CAPACITY FOR THIS KIND OF EVIL BETTER THAN I.
MAYBE THE TELEPATHIC SCRAMBLING CLOAKED A LOCUS AGENDA.
THEN AGAIN, MAYBE THE D.E.O. HAS SIMPLY INSTALLED ANTI-TELEPATHIC SAFEGUARDS ON THE SENATE FLOOR-- PROVING NOTHING. WE DON'T KNOW.*
AND TO BE HONEST, PART OF ME ALMOST HOPES "NO MAN'S LAND" IS A LOCUS PLOT RATHER THAN HUMAN FEAR AND--
BEHIND YOU.
YOU'RE WATCHING.
*D.E.O.--DEPARTMENT OF EXTRANORMAL OPERATIONS --DAN.
INTERMITTENTLY. RADIOACTIVE OR NOT, I'M NOT ANXIOUS TO EXPLORE THE THE PROLONGED EFFECT OF X-RAY VISION ON AN INHABITED AREA.
THEN WHY ARE YOU IN THE SKY?
IT'S QUIET.
AT ANY RATE... AS WE FEARED, THE AVIAN ASSAULT WAS ONLY THE INITIAL LOCUS STRIKE.
WHILE WONDER WOMAN AND STEEL MAINTAINED AN AIR PATROL OVER THE CITY--

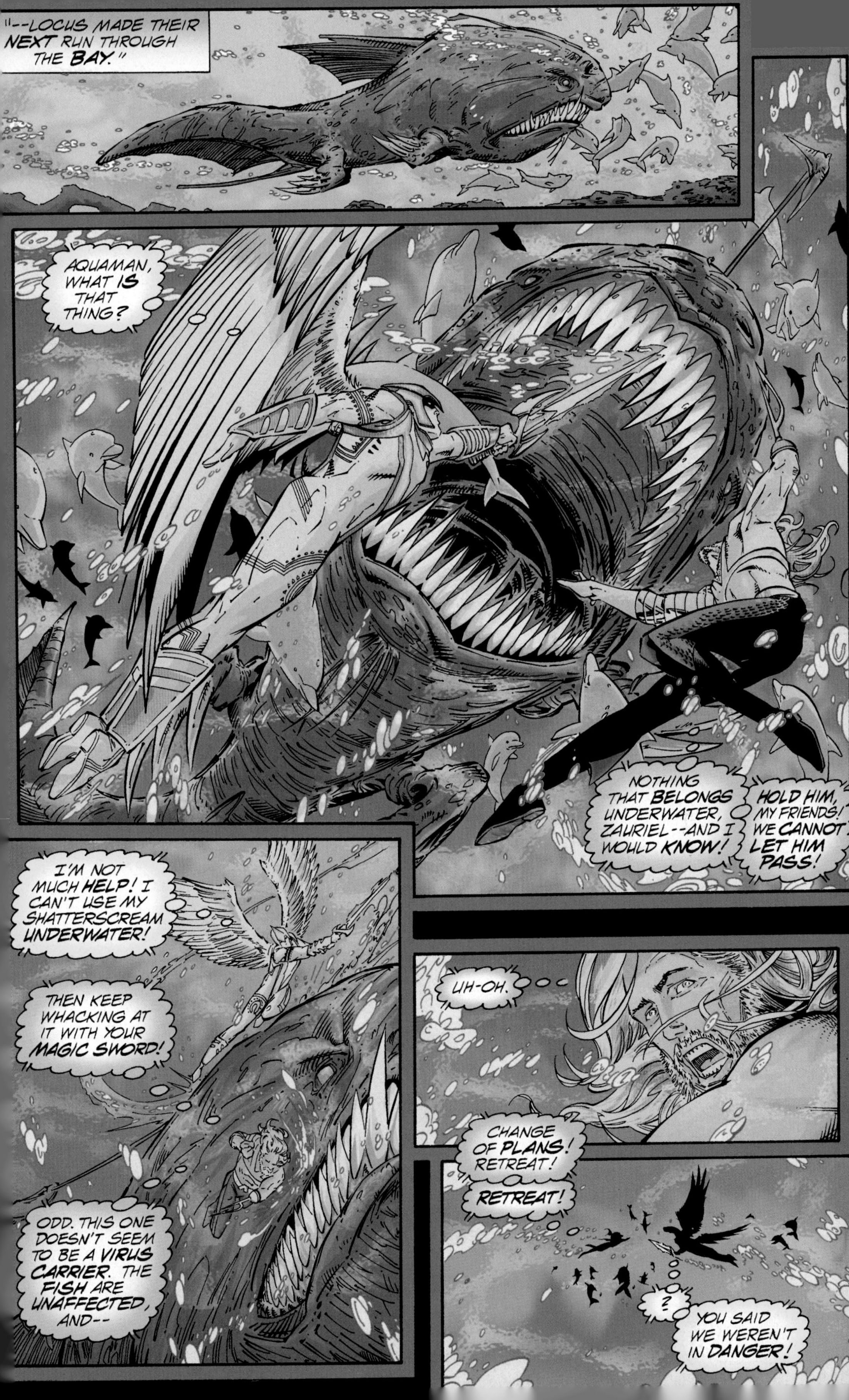
"--LOCUS MADE THEIR NEXT RUN THROUGH THE BAY."
AQUAMAN, WHAT IS THAT THING?
NOTHING THAT BELONGS UNDERWATER, ZAURIEL--AND I WOULD KNOW!
HOLD HIM, MY FRIENDS! WE CANNOT LET HIM PASS!
I'M NOT MUCH HELP! I CAN'T USE MY SHATTERSCREAM UNDERWATER!
THEN KEEP WHACKING AT IT WITH YOUR MAGIC SWORD!
ODD. THIS ONE DOESN'T SEEM TO BE A VIRUS CARRIER. THE FISH ARE UNAFFECTED, AND--
UH-OH.
CHANGE OF PLANS! RETREAT!
RETREAT!
?
YOU SAID WE WEREN'T IN DANGER!

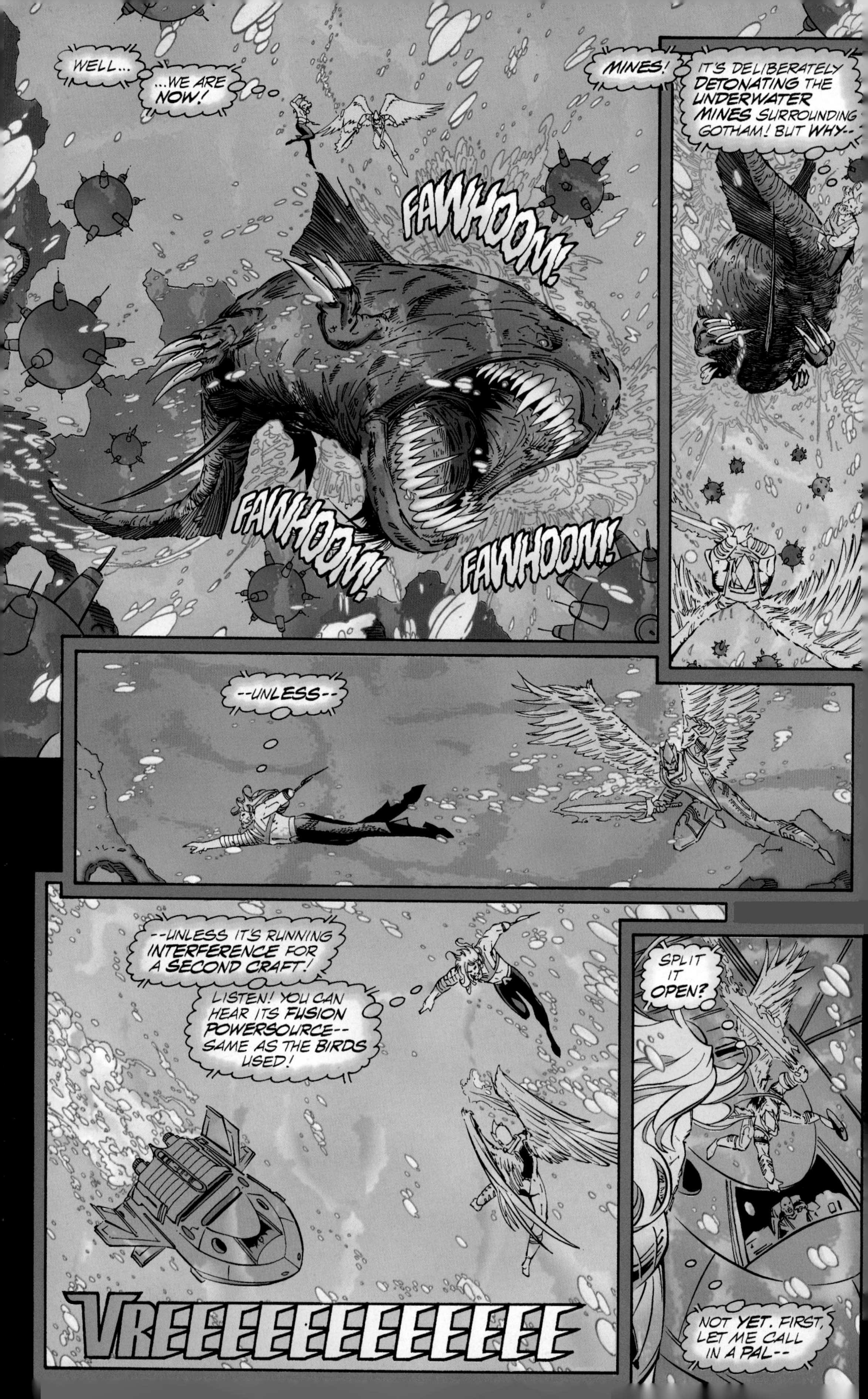
WELL...
...WE ARE NOW!
FAWHOOM!
FAWHOOM!
FAWHOOM!
MINES!
IT'S DELIBERATELY DETONATING THE UNDERWATER MINES SURROUNDING GOTHAM! BUT WHY--
--UNLESS--
--UNLESS IT'S RUNNING INTERFERENCE FOR A SECOND CRAFT!
LISTEN! YOU CAN HEAR ITS FUSION POWERSOURCE-- SAME AS THE BIRDS USED!
VREEEEEEEEEEEEE
SPLIT IT OPEN?
NOT YET. FIRST, LET ME CALL IN A PAL--

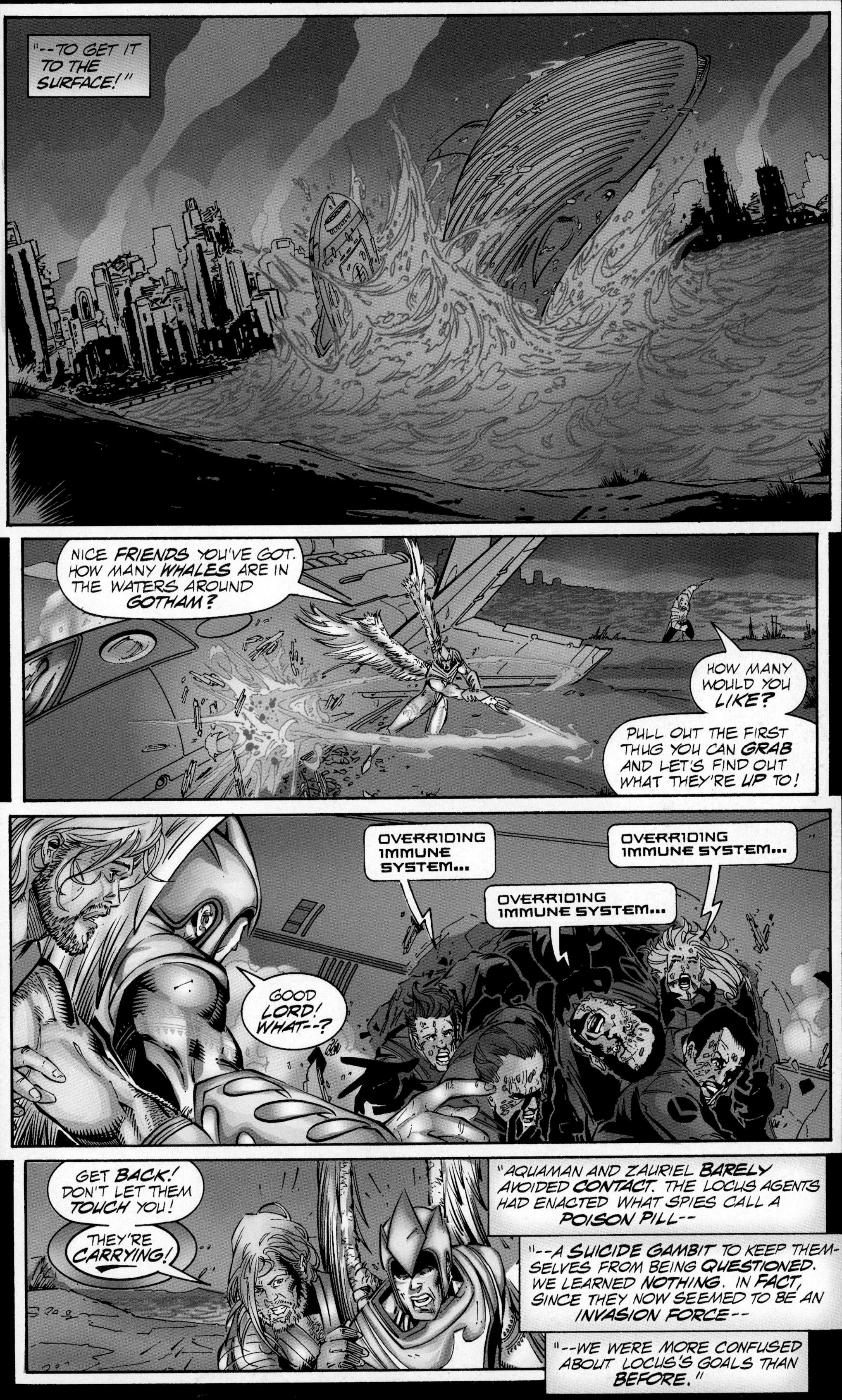
"--TO GET IT TO THE SURFACE!"
NICE FRIENDS YOU'VE GOT. HOW MANY WHALES ARE IN THE WATERS AROUND GOTHAM?
HOW MANY WOULD YOU LIKE?
PULL OUT THE FIRST THUG YOU CAN GRAB AND LET'S FIND OUT WHAT THEY'RE UP TO!
OVERRIDING IMMUNE SYSTEM...
OVERRIDING IMMUNE SYSTEM...
OVERRIDING IMMUNE SYSTEM...
GOOD LORD! WHAT--?
GET BACK! DON'T LET THEM TOUCH YOU!
THEY'RE CARRYING!
"AQUAMAN AND ZAURIEL BARELY AVOIDED CONTACT. THE LOCUS AGENTS HAD ENACTED WHAT SPIES CALL A POISON PILL--
"--A SUICIDE GAMBIT TO KEEP THEMSELVES FROM BEING QUESTIONED. WE LEARNED NOTHING. IN FACT, SINCE THEY NOW SEEMED TO BE AN INVASION FORCE--
"--WE WERE MORE CONFUSED ABOUT LOCUS'S GOALS THAN BEFORE."

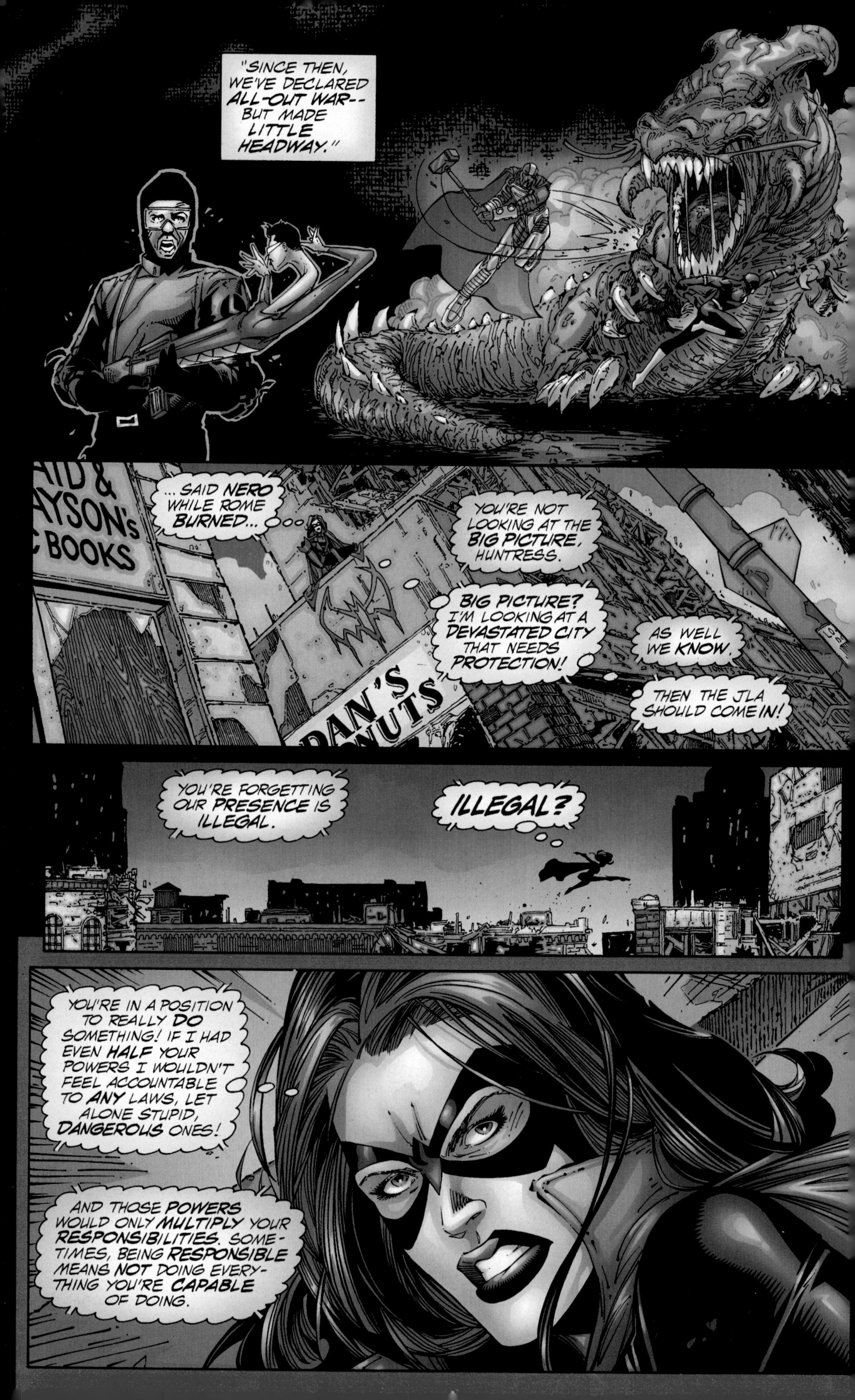
"SINCE THEN, WE'VE DECLARED ALL-OUT WAR-- BUT MADE LITTLE HEADWAY."
...SAID NERO WHILE ROME BURNED...
YOU'RE NOT LOOKING AT THE BIG PICTURE, HUNTRESS.
BIG PICTURE? I'M LOOKING AT A DEVASTATED CITY THAT NEEDS PROTECTION!
AS WELL WE KNOW.
THEN THE JLA SHOULD COME IN!
YOU'RE FORGETTING OUR PRESENCE IS ILLEGAL.
ILLEGAL?
YOU'RE IN A POSITION TO REALLY DO SOMETHING! IF I HAD EVEN HALF YOUR POWERS I WOULDN'T FEEL ACCOUNTABLE TO ANY LAWS, LET ALONE STUPID, DANGEROUS ONES!
AND THOSE POWERS WOULD ONLY MULTIPLY YOUR RESPONSIBILITIES. SOMETIMES, BEING RESPONSIBLE MEANS NOT DOING EVERYTHING YOU'RE CAPABLE OF DOING.

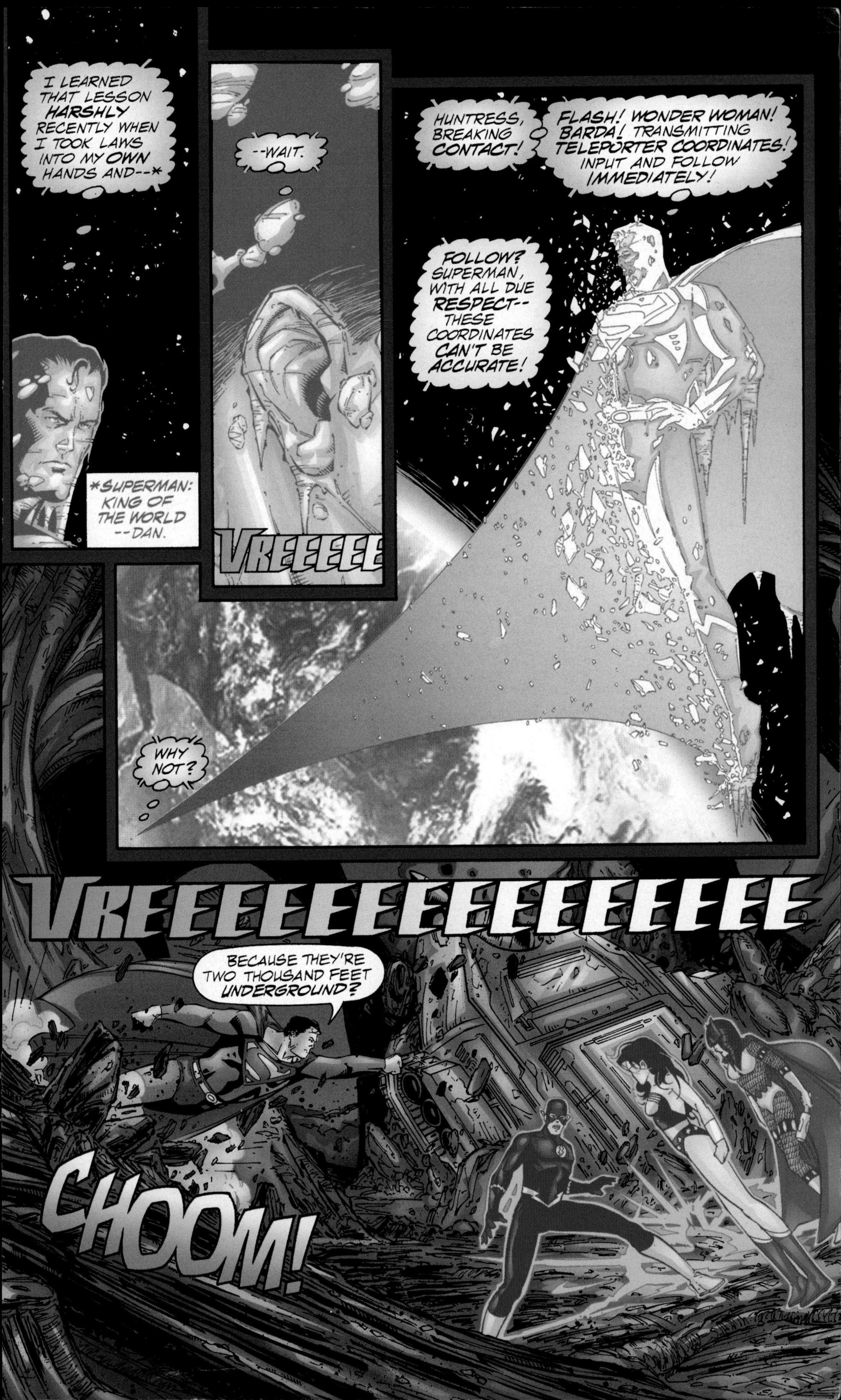

I LEARNED THAT LESSON HARSHLY RECENTLY WHEN I TOOK LAWS INTO MY OWN HANDS AND--*
*SUPERMAN: KING OF THE WORLD --DAN.
--WAIT.
VREEEEE
HUNTRESS, BREAKING CONTACT!
FLASH! WONDER WOMAN! BARDA! TRANSMITTING TELEPORTER COORDINATES! INPUT AND FOLLOW IMMEDIATELY!
FOLLOW? SUPERMAN, WITH ALL DUE RESPECT--THESE COORDINATES CAN'T BE ACCURATE!
WHY NOT?
VREEEEEEEEEEEEEEE
BECAUSE THEY'RE TWO THOUSAND FEET UNDERGROUND?
CHOOM!

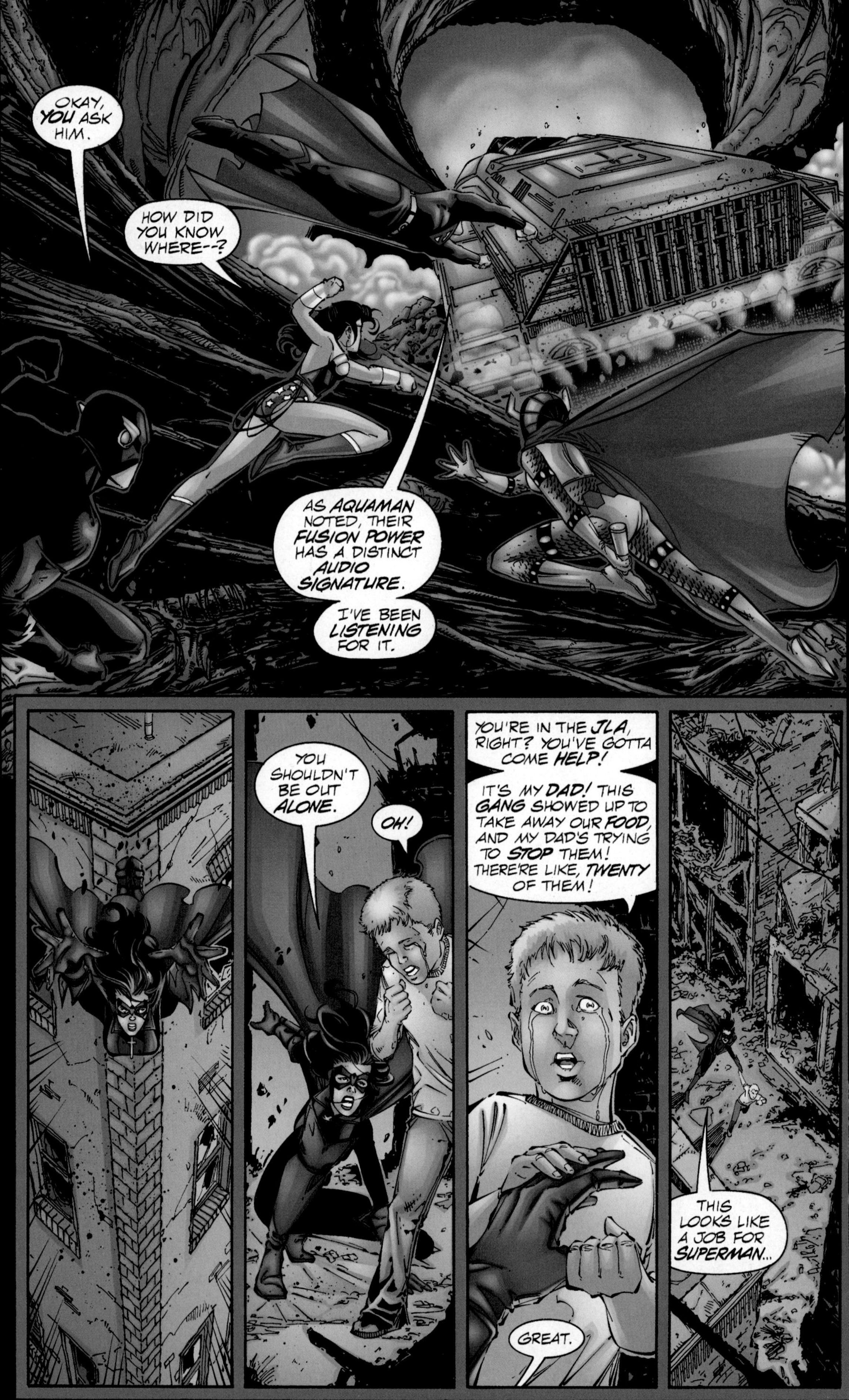
OKAY, YOU ASK HIM.
HOW DID YOU KNOW WHERE--?
AS AQUAMAN NOTED, THEIR FUSION POWER HAS A DISTINCT AUDIO SIGNATURE.
I'VE BEEN LISTENING FOR IT.
YOU SHOULDN'T BE OUT ALONE.
OH!
YOU'RE IN THE JLA, RIGHT? YOU'VE GOTTA COME HELP!
IT'S MY DAD! THIS GANG SHOWED UP TO TAKE AWAY OUR FOOD, AND MY DAD'S TRYING TO STOP THEM! THERE'RE LIKE, TWENTY OF THEM!
GREAT.
THIS LOOKS LIKE A JOB FOR SUPERMAN...

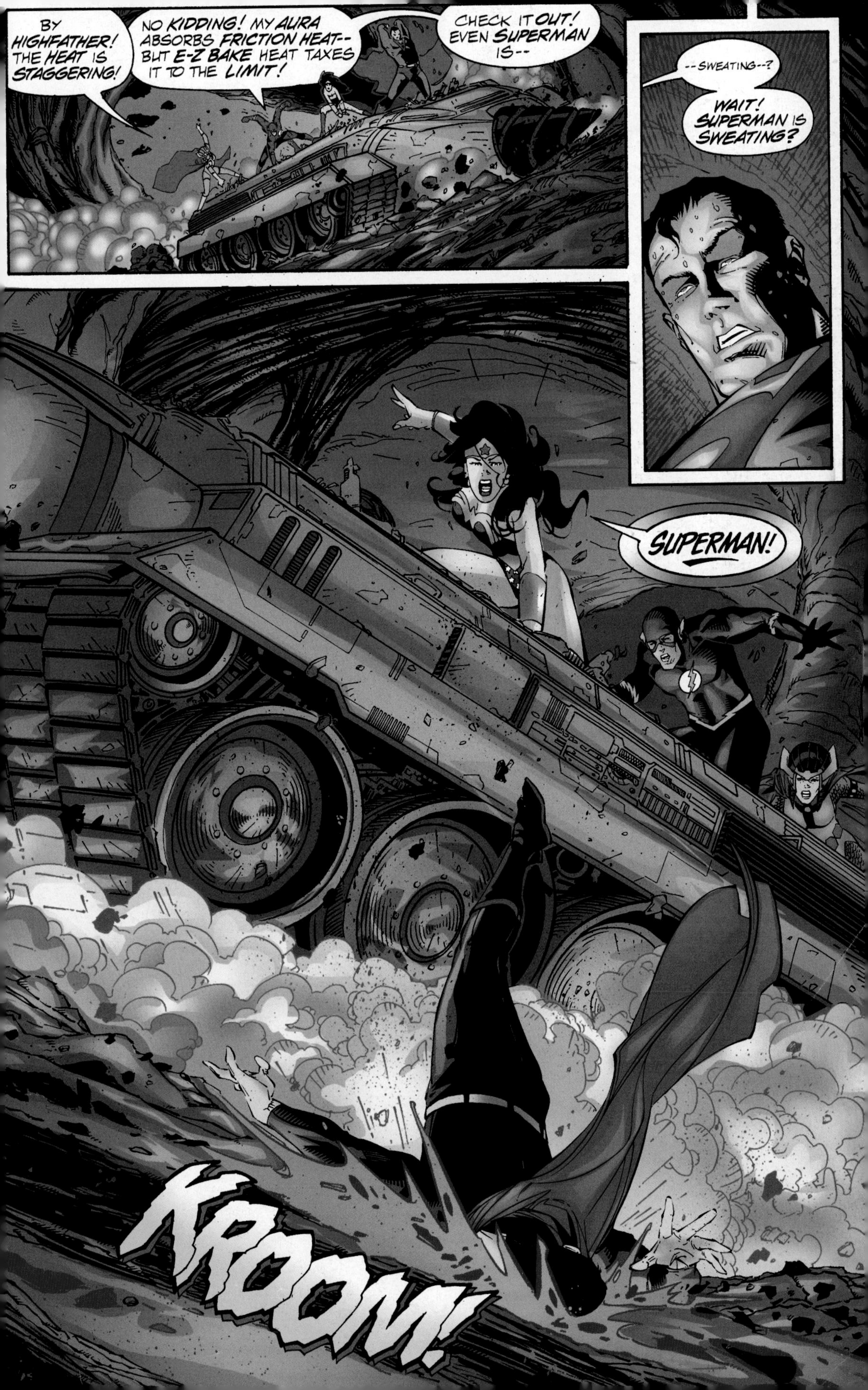
BY HIGHFATHER! THE HEAT IS STAGGERING!
NO KIDDING! MY AURA ABSORBS FRICTION HEAT-- BUT E-Z BAKE HEAT TAXES IT TO THE LIMIT!
CHECK IT OUT! EVEN SUPERMAN IS--
--SWEATING--?
WAIT! SUPERMAN IS SWEATING?
SUPERMAN!
KROOM!

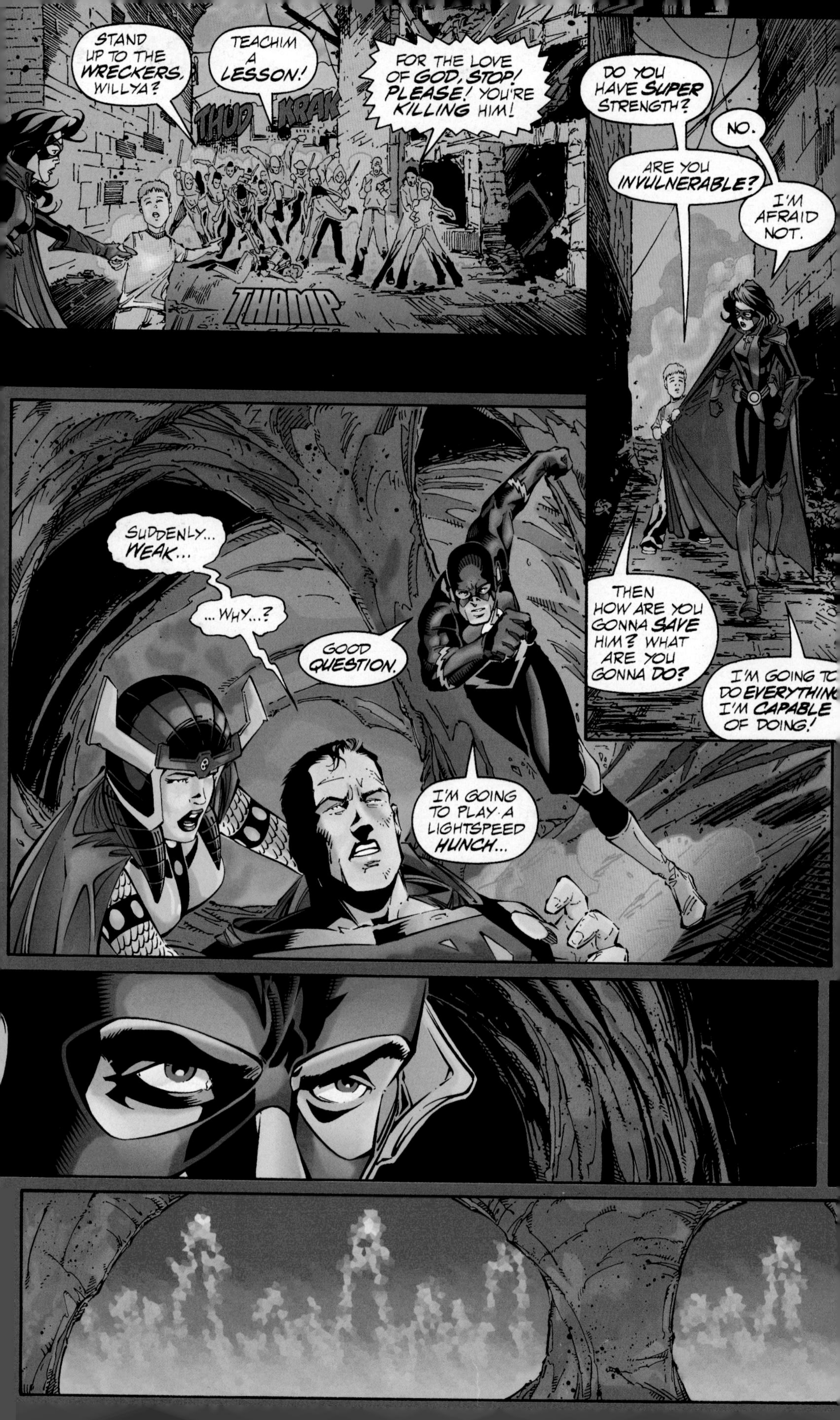

STAND UP TO THE WRECKERS, WILLYA?
TEACHIM A LESSON!
FOR THE LOVE OF GOD, STOP! PLEASE! YOU'RE KILLING HIM!
THUD
KRAK
THAMP
DO YOU HAVE SUPER STRENGTH?
NO.
ARE YOU INVULNERABLE?
I'M AFRAID NOT.
THEN HOW ARE YOU GONNA SAVE HIM? WHAT ARE YOU GONNA DO?
I'M GOING TO DO EVERYTHING I'M CAPABLE OF DOING!
SUDDENLY... WEAK...
...WHY...?
GOOD QUESTION.
I'M GOING TO PLAY A LIGHTSPEED HUNCH...

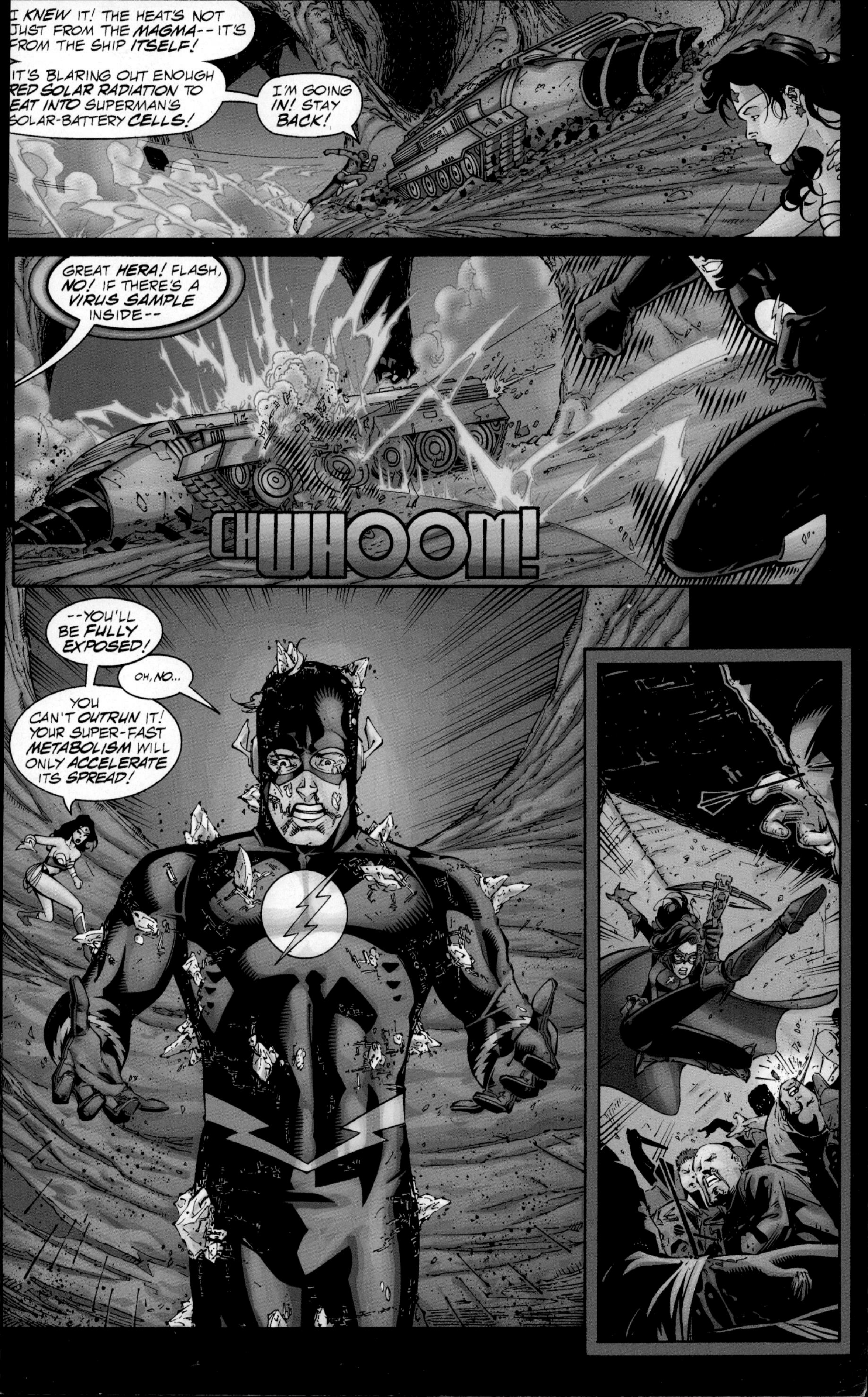
I KNEW IT! THE HEAT'S NOT JUST FROM THE MAGMA-- IT'S FROM THE SHIP ITSELF!
IT'S BLARING OUT ENOUGH RED SOLAR RADIATION TO EAT INTO SUPERMAN'S SOLAR-BATTERY CELLS!
I'M GOING IN! STAY BACK!
GREAT HERA! FLASH, NO! IF THERE'S A VIRUS SAMPLE INSIDE--
CHWHOOM!
--YOU'LL BE FULLY EXPOSED!
OH, NO...
YOU CAN'T OUTRUN IT! YOUR SUPER-FAST METABOLISM WILL ONLY ACCELERATE ITS SPREAD!

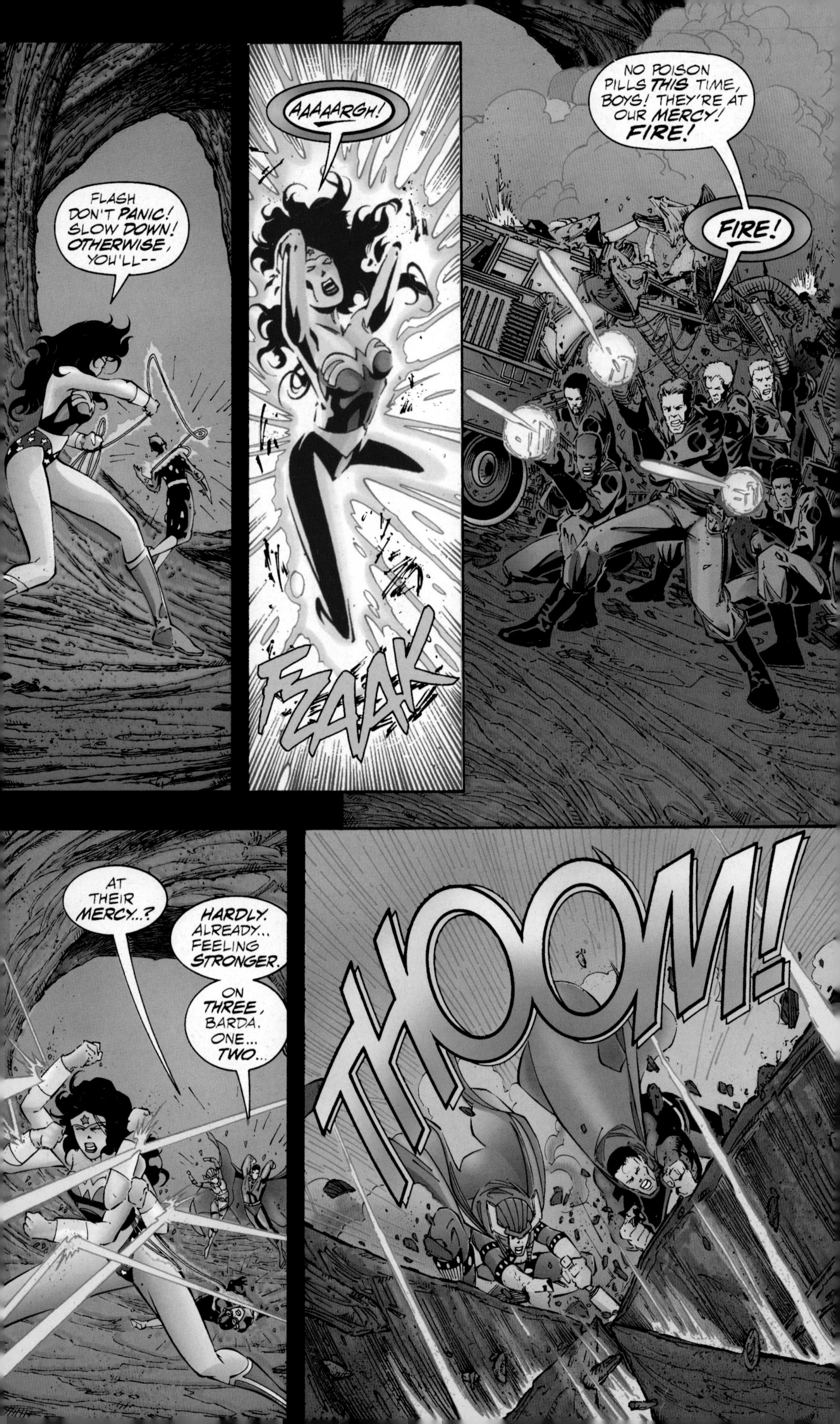
FLASH DON'T PANIC! SLOW DOWN! OTHERWISE, YOU'LL--
AAAAARGH!
FZAAK
NO POISON PILLS THIS TIME, BOYS! THEY'RE AT OUR MERCY! FIRE!
FIRE!
AT THEIR MERCY...?
HARDLY. ALREADY... FEELING STRONGER.
ON THREE, BARDA. ONE... TWO...
THOOM!

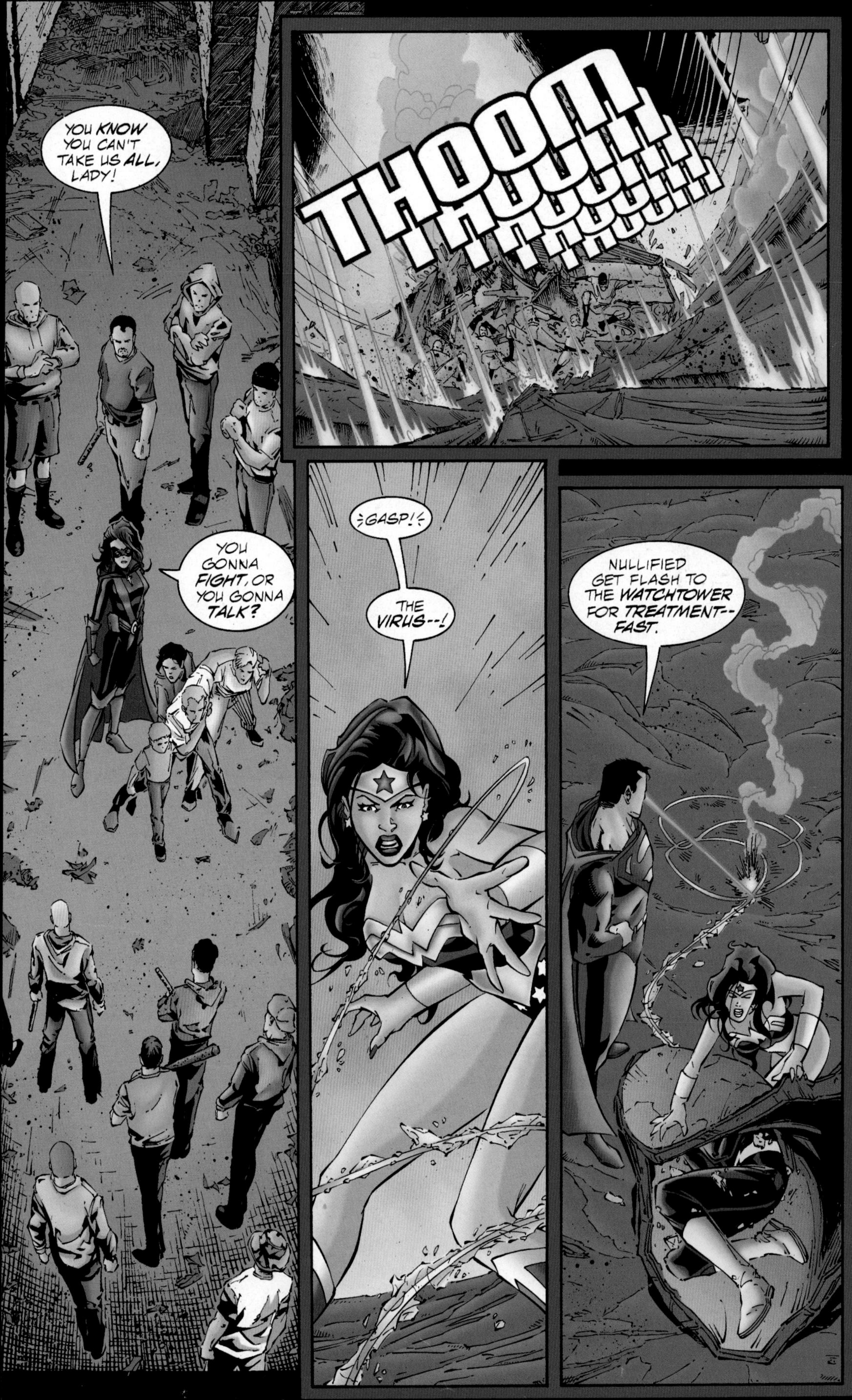
YOU KNOW YOU CAN'T TAKE US ALL, LADY!
YOU GONNA FIGHT, OR YOU GONNA TALK?
THOOM
THOOM
THOOM
GASP!
THE VIRUS--!
NULLIFIED GET FLASH TO THE WATCHTOWER FOR TREATMENT-- FAST.

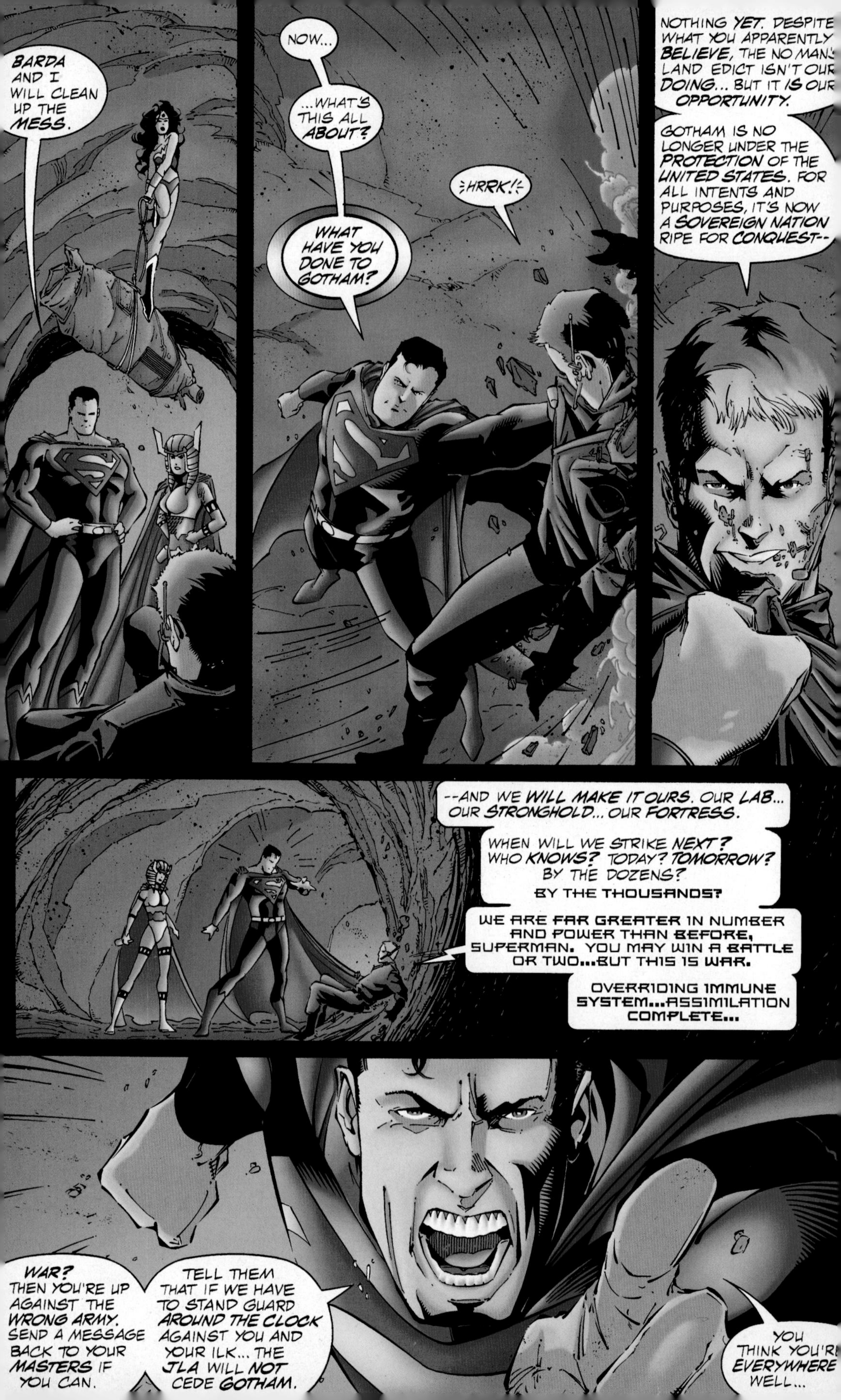

BARDA AND I WILL CLEAN UP THE MESS.
NOW...
...WHAT'S THIS ALL ABOUT?
WHAT HAVE YOU DONE TO GOTHAM?
HRRK!
NOTHING YET. DESPITE WHAT YOU APPARENTLY BELIEVE, THE NO MAN'S LAND EDICT ISN'T OUR DOING... BUT IT IS OUR OPPORTUNITY.
GOTHAM IS NO LONGER UNDER THE PROTECTION OF THE UNITED STATES. FOR ALL INTENTS AND PURPOSES, IT'S NOW A SOVEREIGN NATION RIPE FOR CONQUEST--
--AND WE WILL MAKE IT OURS. OUR LAB... OUR STRONGHOLD... OUR FORTRESS.
WHEN WILL WE STRIKE NEXT? WHO KNOWS? TODAY? TOMORROW? BY THE DOZENS?
BY THE THOUSANDS?
WE ARE FAR GREATER IN NUMBER AND POWER THAN BEFORE, SUPERMAN. YOU MAY WIN A BATTLE OR TWO...BUT THIS IS WAR.
OVERRIDING IMMUNE SYSTEM...ASSIMILATION COMPLETE...
WAR? THEN YOU'RE UP AGAINST THE WRONG ARMY. SEND A MESSAGE BACK TO YOUR MASTERS IF YOU CAN.
TELL THEM THAT IF WE HAVE TO STAND GUARD AROUND THE CLOCK AGAINST YOU AND YOUR ILK... THE JLA WILL NOT CEDE GOTHAM.

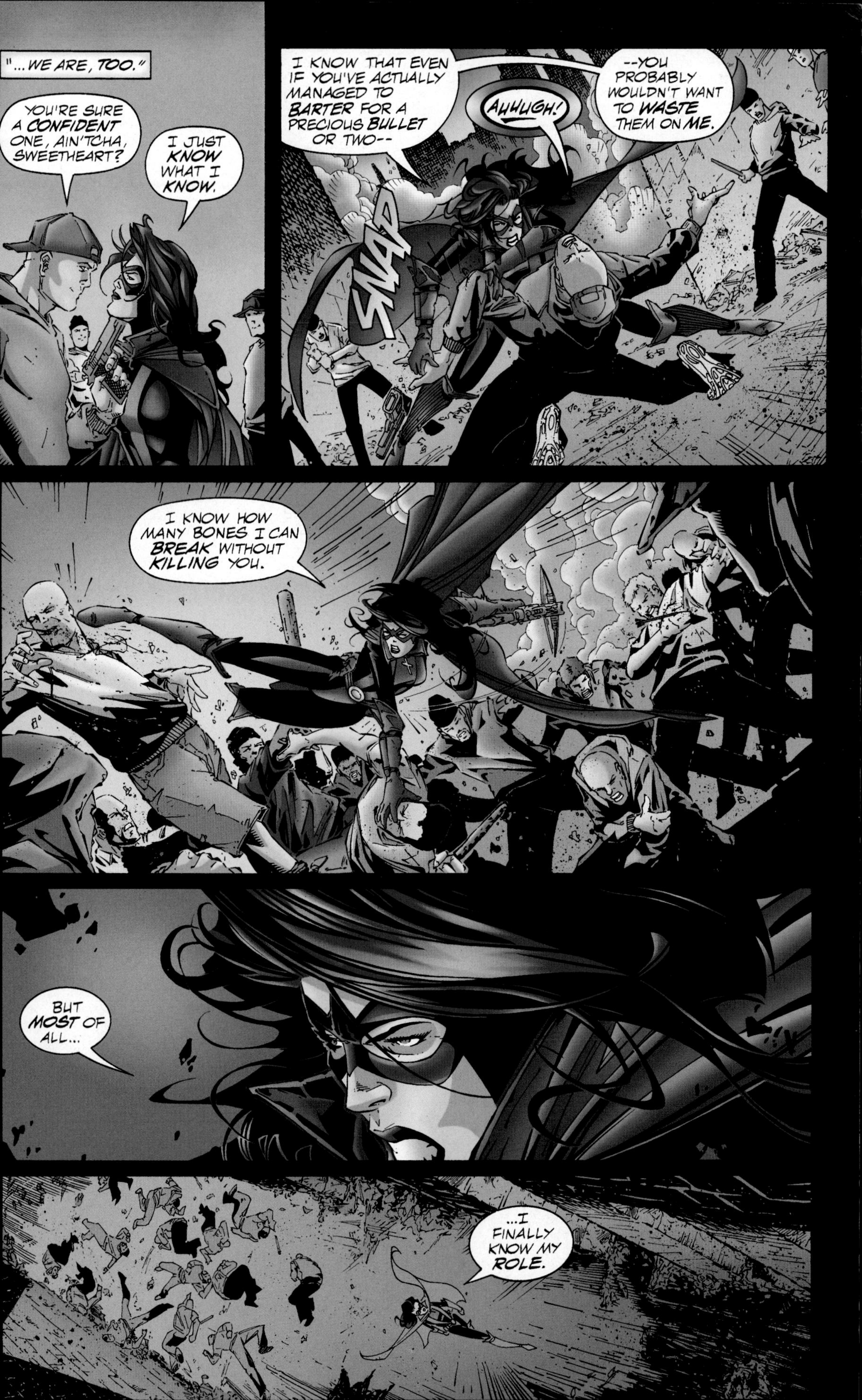
"...WE ARE, TOO."
YOU'RE SURE A CONFIDENT ONE, AIN'TCHA, SWEETHEART?
I JUST KNOW WHAT I KNOW.
I KNOW THAT EVEN IF YOU'VE ACTUALLY MANAGED TO BARTER FOR A PRECIOUS BULLET OR TWO--
SNAP
AHHUGH!
--YOU PROBABLY WOULDN'T WANT TO WASTE THEM ON ME.
I KNOW HOW MANY BONES I CAN BREAK WITHOUT KILLING YOU.
BUT MOST OF ALL...
...I FINALLY KNOW MY ROLE.

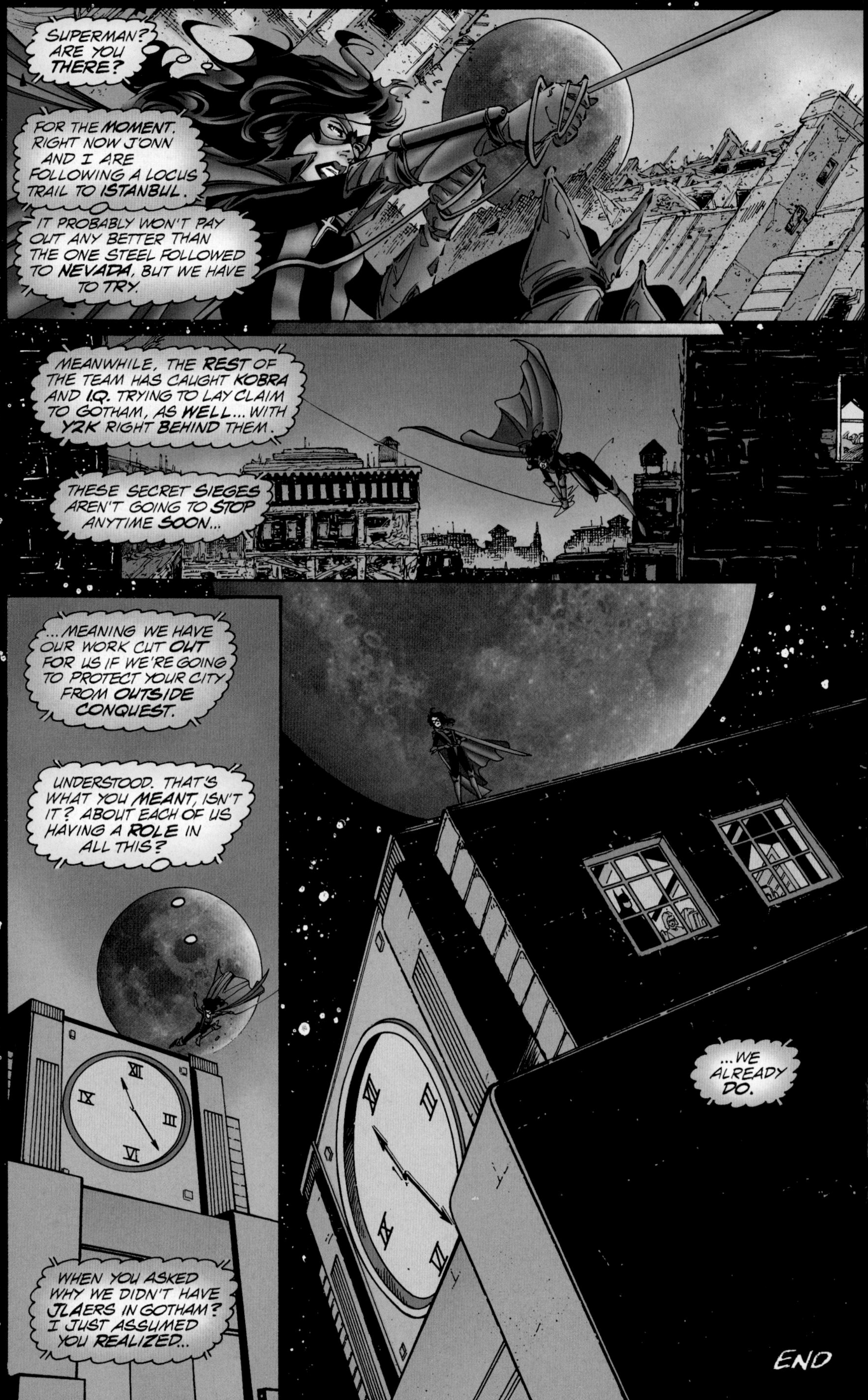
SUPERMAN? ARE YOU THERE?
FOR THE MOMENT. RIGHT NOW J'ONN AND I ARE FOLLOWING A LOCUS TRAIL TO ISTANBUL.
IT PROBABLY WON'T PAY OUT ANY BETTER THAN THE ONE STEEL FOLLOWED TO NEVADA, BUT WE HAVE TO TRY.
MEANWHILE, THE REST OF THE TEAM HAS CAUGHT KOBRA AND I.Q. TRYING TO LAY CLAIM TO GOTHAM, AS WELL... WITH Y2K RIGHT BEHIND THEM.
THESE SECRET SIEGES AREN'T GOING TO STOP ANYTIME SOON...
...MEANING WE HAVE OUR WORK CUT OUT FOR US IF WE'RE GOING TO PROTECT YOUR CITY FROM OUTSIDE CONQUEST.
UNDERSTOOD. THAT'S WHAT YOU MEANT, ISN'T IT? ABOUT EACH OF US HAVING A ROLE IN ALL THIS?
WHEN YOU ASKED WHY WE DIDN'T HAVE JLAERS IN GOTHAM? I JUST ASSUMED YOU REALIZED...
...WE ALREADY DO.
END

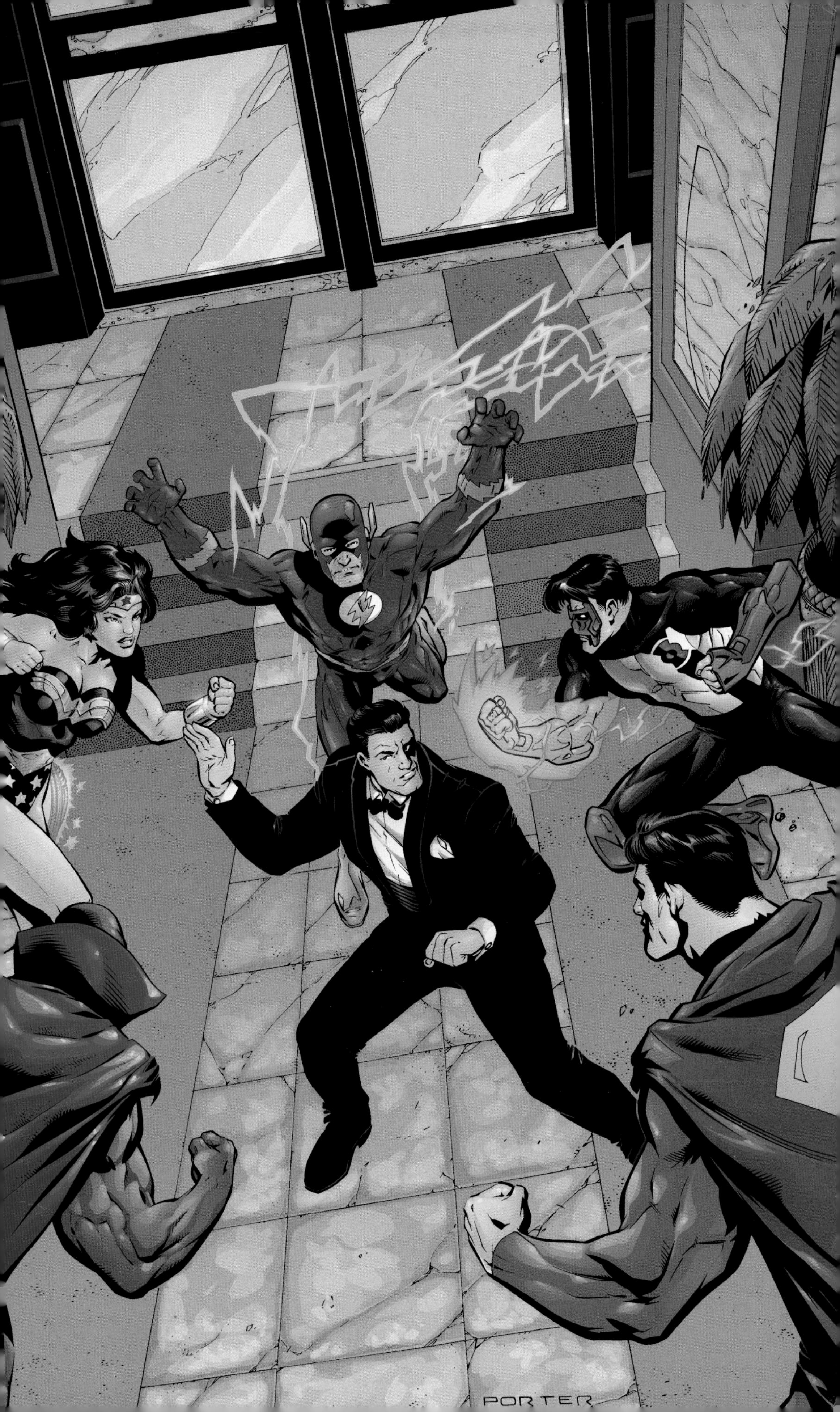
PORTER

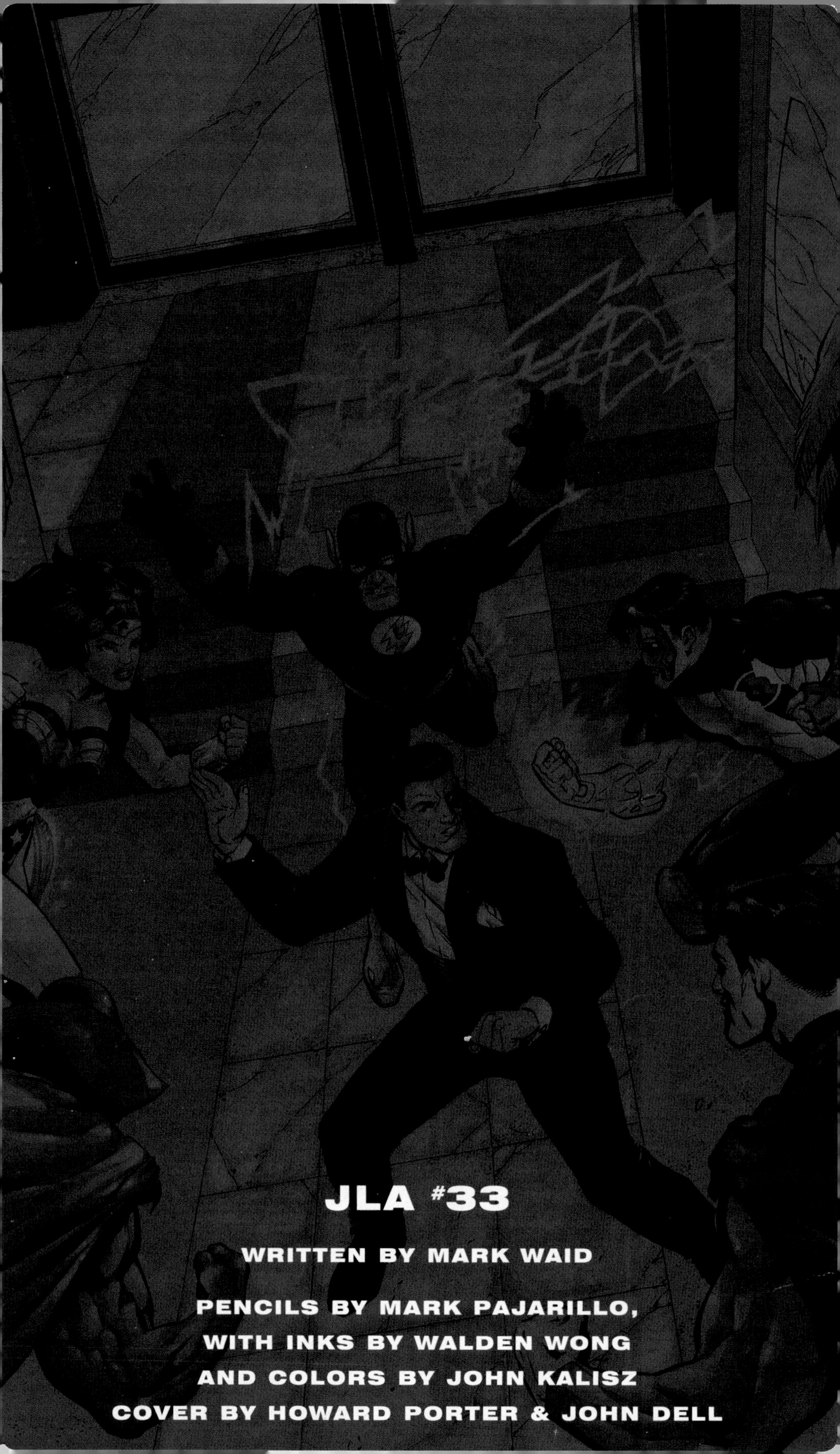

JLA #33

WRITTEN BY MARK WAID

PENCILS BY MARK PAJARILLO,
WITH INKS BY WALDEN WONG
AND COLORS BY JOHN KALISZ
COVER BY HOWARD PORTER & JOHN DELL

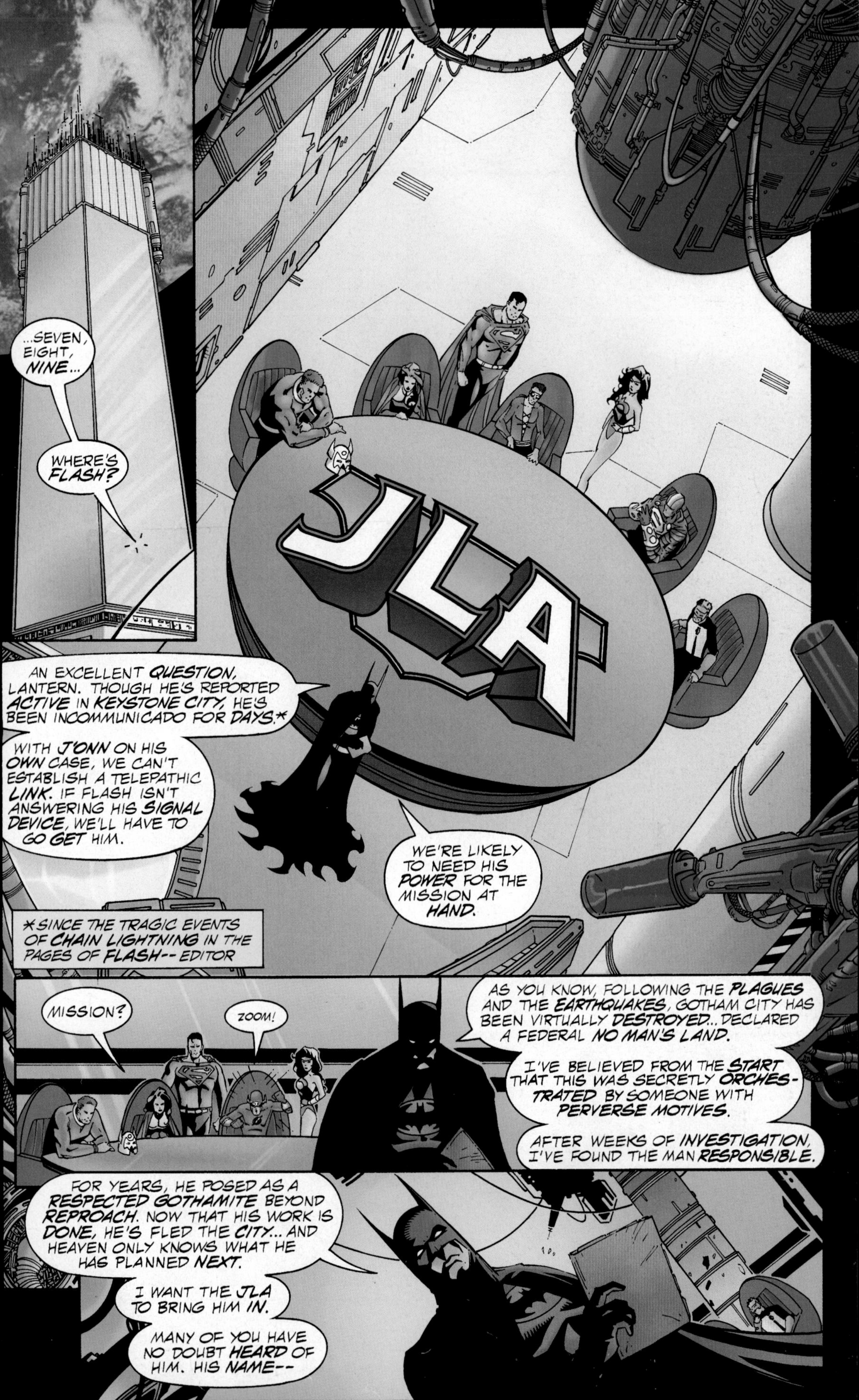
...SEVEN, EIGHT, NINE...
WHERE'S FLASH?
AN EXCELLENT QUESTION, LANTERN. THOUGH HE'S REPORTED ACTIVE IN KEYSTONE CITY, HE'S BEEN INCOMMUNICADO FOR DAYS.*
WITH J'ONN ON HIS OWN CASE, WE CAN'T ESTABLISH A TELEPATHIC LINK. IF FLASH ISN'T ANSWERING HIS SIGNAL DEVICE, WE'LL HAVE TO GO GET HIM.
WE'RE LIKELY TO NEED HIS POWER FOR THE MISSION AT HAND.
*SINCE THE TRAGIC EVENTS OF CHAIN LIGHTNING IN THE PAGES OF FLASH-- EDITOR
MISSION?
ZOOM!
AS YOU KNOW, FOLLOWING THE PLAGUES AND THE EARTHQUAKES, GOTHAM CITY HAS BEEN VIRTUALLY DESTROYED... DECLARED A FEDERAL NO MAN'S LAND.
I'VE BELIEVED FROM THE START THAT THIS WAS SECRETLY ORCHESTRATED BY SOMEONE WITH PERVERSE MOTIVES.
AFTER WEEKS OF INVESTIGATION, I'VE FOUND THE MAN RESPONSIBLE.
FOR YEARS, HE POSED AS A RESPECTED GOTHAMITE BEYOND REPROACH. NOW THAT HIS WORK IS DONE, HE'S FLED THE CITY... AND HEAVEN ONLY KNOWS WHAT HE HAS PLANNED NEXT.
I WANT THE JLA TO BRING HIM IN.
MANY OF YOU HAVE NO DOUBT HEARD OF HIM. HIS NAME--

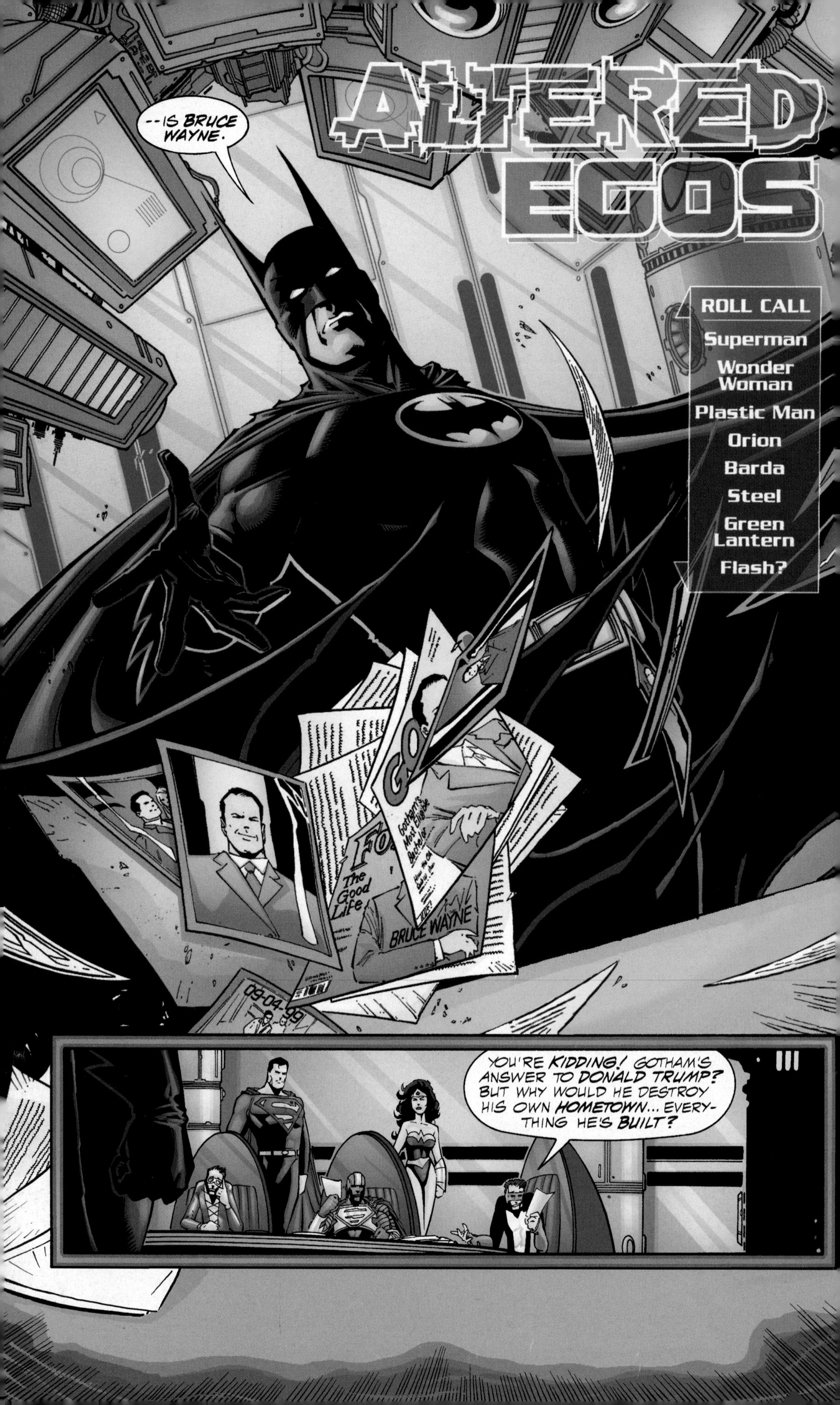
--IS BRUCE WAYNE.
ALTERED EGOS
ROLL CALL
Superman
Wonder Woman
Plastic Man
Orion
Barda
Steel
Green Lantern
Flash?
The Good Life
Gotham's Most Eligible Bachelor
BRUCE WAYNE
09-04-99
YOU'RE KIDDING! GOTHAM'S ANSWER TO DONALD TRUMP? BUT WHY WOULD HE DESTROY HIS OWN HOMETOWN... EVERYTHING HE'S BUILT?

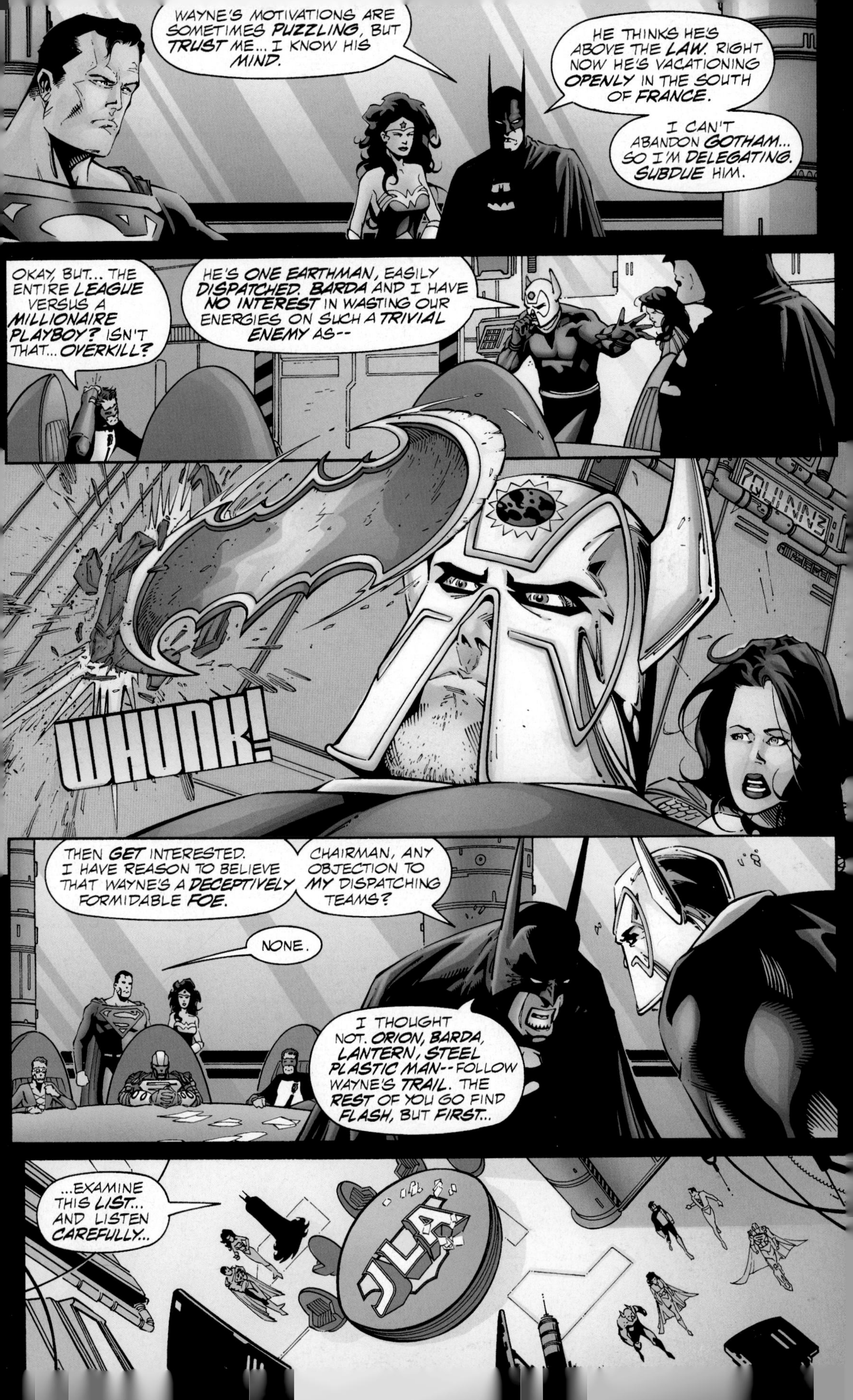

WAYNE'S MOTIVATIONS ARE SOMETIMES PUZZLING, BUT TRUST ME... I KNOW HIS MIND.
HE THINKS HE'S ABOVE THE LAW. RIGHT NOW HE'S VACATIONING OPENLY IN THE SOUTH OF FRANCE.
I CAN'T ABANDON GOTHAM... SO I'M DELEGATING. SUBDUE HIM.
OKAY, BUT... THE ENTIRE LEAGUE VERSUS A MILLIONAIRE PLAYBOY? ISN'T THAT... OVERKILL?
HE'S ONE EARTHMAN, EASILY DISPATCHED. BARDA AND I HAVE NO INTEREST IN WASTING OUR ENERGIES ON SUCH A TRIVIAL ENEMY AS--
WHUNK!
THEN GET INTERESTED. I HAVE REASON TO BELIEVE THAT WAYNE'S A DECEPTIVELY FORMIDABLE FOE.
CHAIRMAN, ANY OBJECTION TO MY DISPATCHING TEAMS?
NONE.
I THOUGHT NOT. ORION, BARDA, LANTERN, STEEL PLASTIC MAN--FOLLOW WAYNE'S TRAIL. THE REST OF YOU GO FIND FLASH, BUT FIRST...
...EXAMINE THIS LIST... AND LISTEN CAREFULLY...
JLA

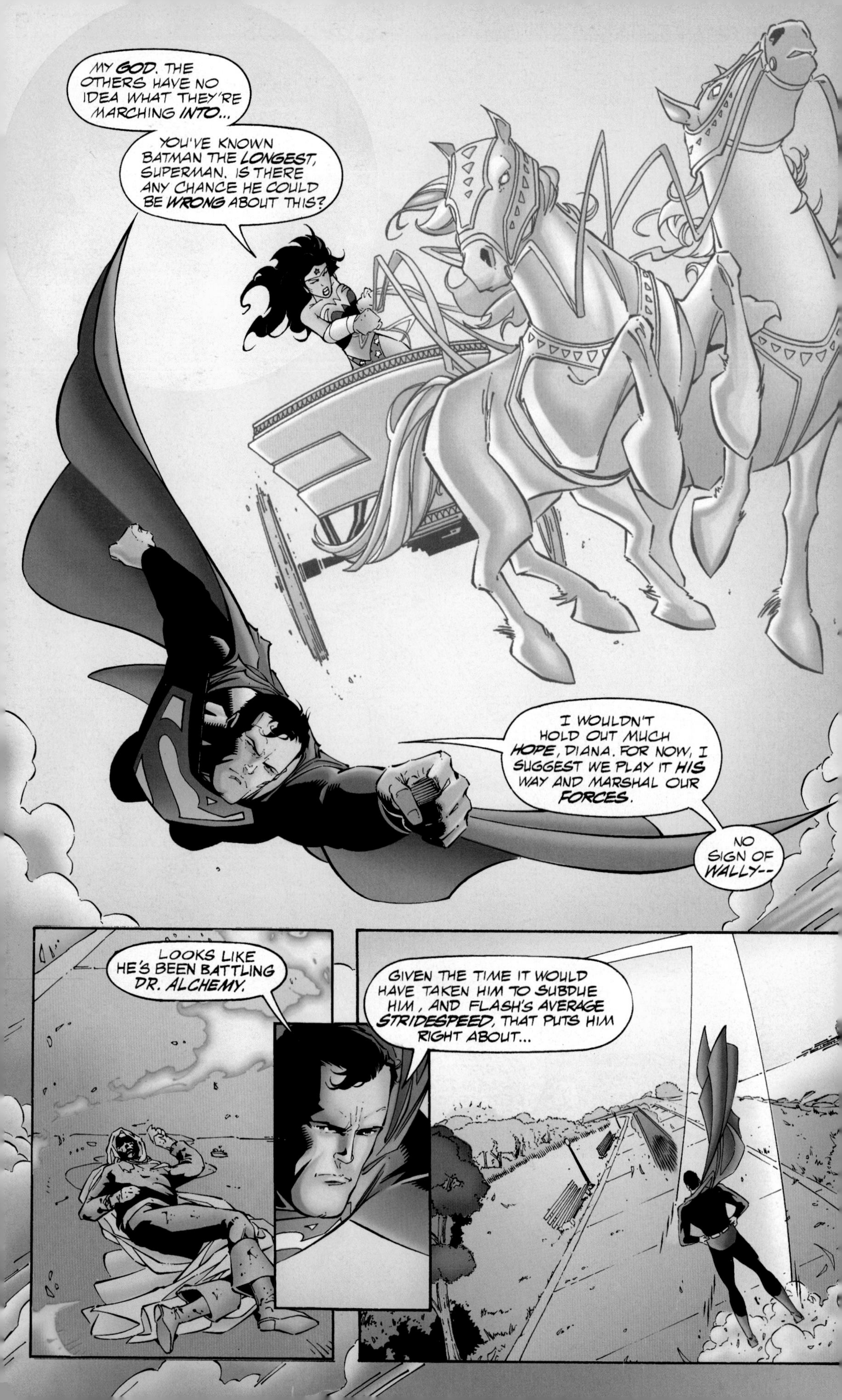
MY GOD. THE OTHERS HAVE NO IDEA WHAT THEY'RE MARCHING INTO...
YOU'VE KNOWN BATMAN THE LONGEST, SUPERMAN. IS THERE ANY CHANCE HE COULD BE WRONG ABOUT THIS?
I WOULDN'T HOLD OUT MUCH HOPE, DIANA. FOR NOW, I SUGGEST WE PLAY IT HIS WAY AND MARSHAL OUR FORCES.
NO SIGN OF WALLY--
LOOKS LIKE HE'S BEEN BATTLING DR. ALCHEMY.
GIVEN THE TIME IT WOULD HAVE TAKEN HIM TO SUBDUE HIM, AND FLASH'S AVERAGE STRIDESPEED, THAT PUTS HIM RIGHT ABOUT...

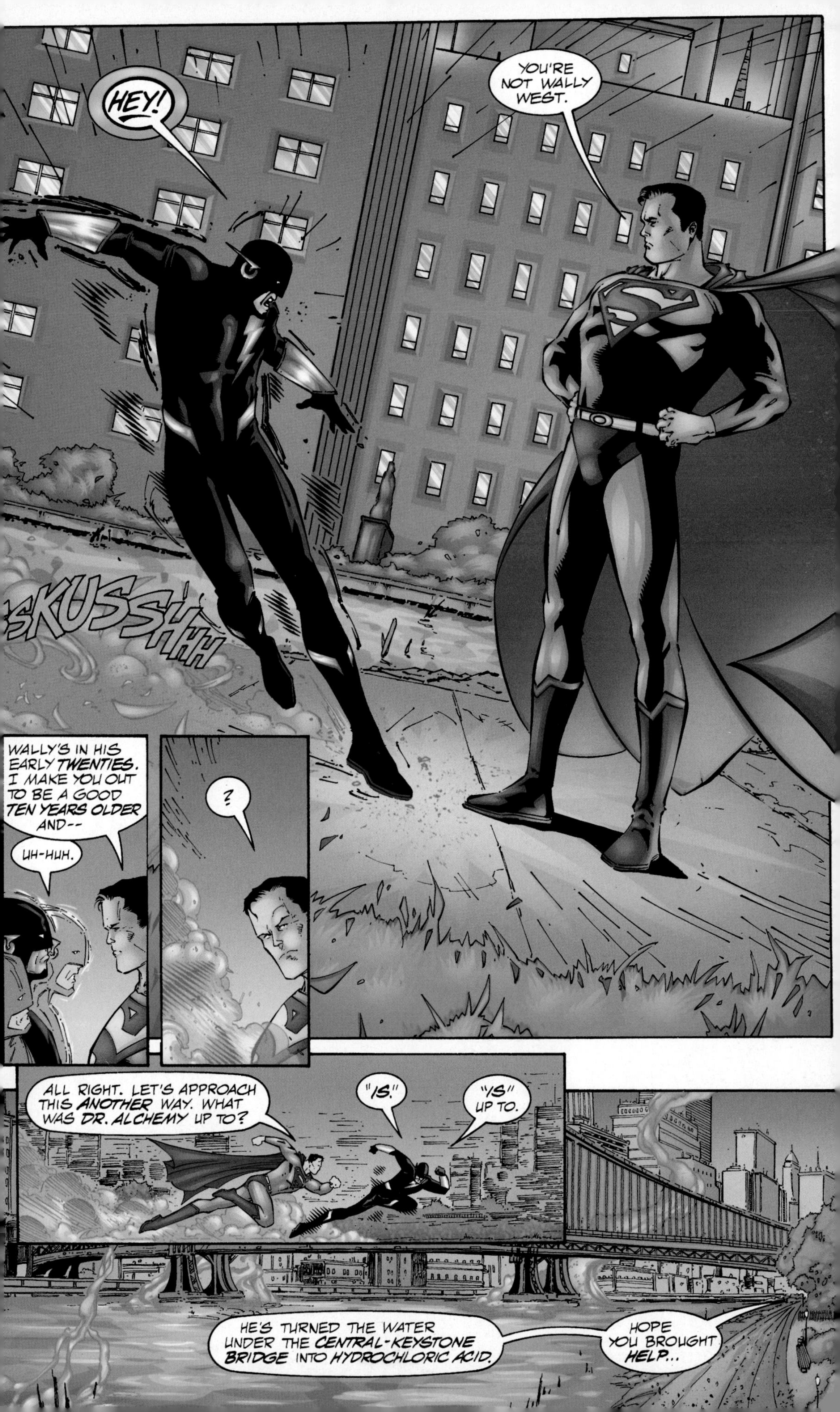
HEY!
YOU'RE NOT WALLY WEST.
SKUSSHHH
WALLY'S IN HIS EARLY TWENTIES. I MAKE YOU OUT TO BE A GOOD TEN YEARS OLDER AND--
UH-HUH.
?
ALL RIGHT. LET'S APPROACH THIS ANOTHER WAY. WHAT WAS DR. ALCHEMY UP TO?
"IS."
"IS" UP TO.
HE'S TURNED THE WATER UNDER THE CENTRAL-KEYSTONE BRIDGE INTO HYDROCHLORIC ACID.
HOPE YOU BROUGHT HELP...

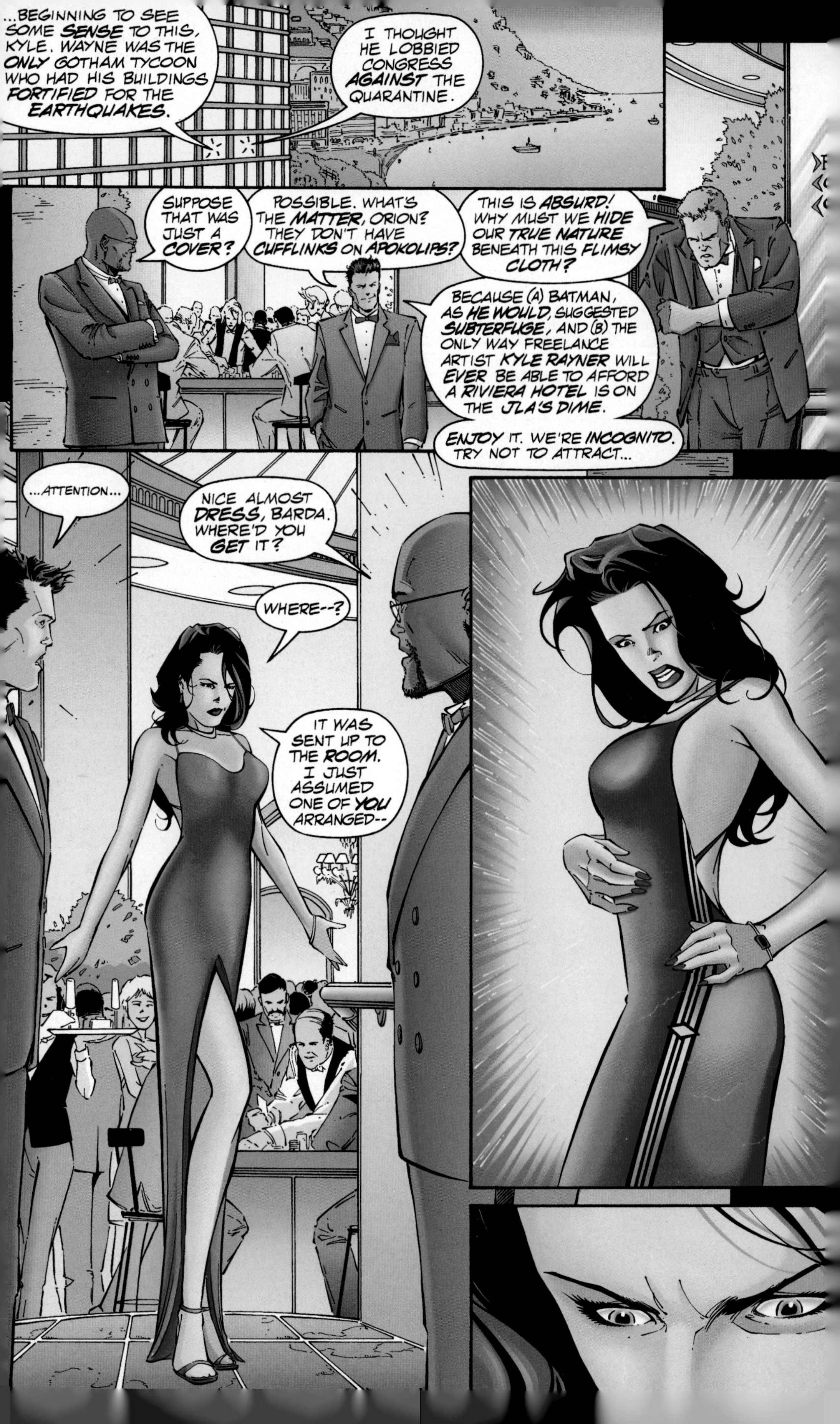
...BEGINNING TO SEE SOME SENSE TO THIS, KYLE. WAYNE WAS THE ONLY GOTHAM TYCOON WHO HAD HIS BUILDINGS FORTIFIED FOR THE EARTHQUAKES.
I THOUGHT HE LOBBIED CONGRESS AGAINST THE QUARANTINE.
SUPPOSE THAT WAS JUST A COVER?
POSSIBLE. WHAT'S THE MATTER, ORION? THEY DON'T HAVE CUFFLINKS ON APOKOLIPS?
THIS IS ABSURD! WHY MUST WE HIDE OUR TRUE NATURE BENEATH THIS FLIMSY CLOTH?
BECAUSE (A) BATMAN, AS HE WOULD, SUGGESTED SUBTERFUGE, AND (B) THE ONLY WAY FREELANCE ARTIST KYLE RAYNER WILL EVER BE ABLE TO AFFORD A RIVIERA HOTEL IS ON THE JLA'S DIME.
ENJOY IT. WE'RE INCOGNITO. TRY NOT TO ATTRACT...
...ATTENTION...
NICE ALMOST DRESS, BARDA. WHERE'D YOU GET IT?
WHERE--?
IT WAS SENT UP TO THE ROOM. I JUST ASSUMED ONE OF YOU ARRANGED--

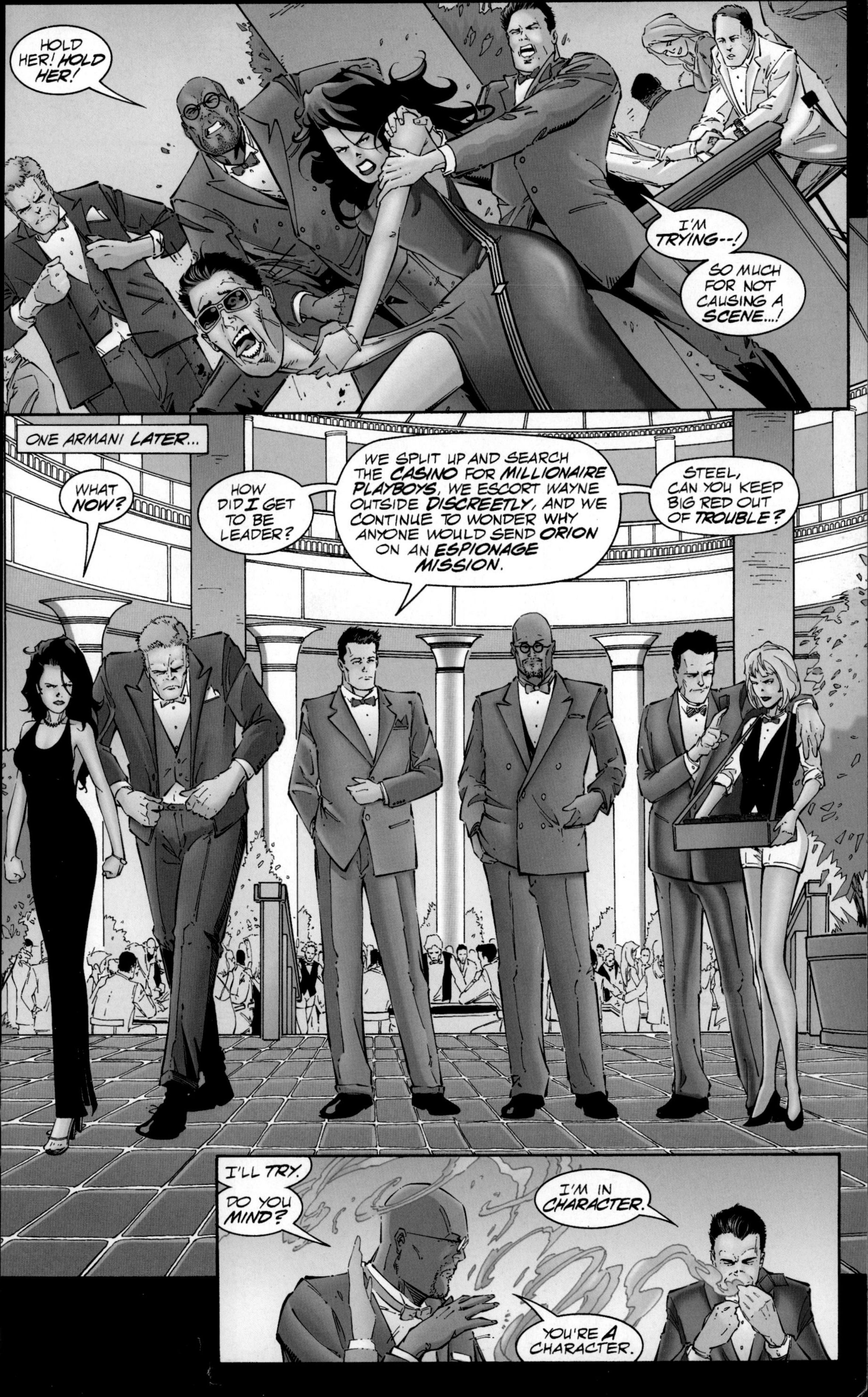
HOLD HER! HOLD HER!
I'M TRYING--!
SO MUCH FOR NOT CAUSING A SCENE...!
ONE ARMANI LATER...
WHAT NOW?
HOW DID I GET TO BE LEADER?
WE SPLIT UP AND SEARCH THE CASINO FOR MILLIONAIRE PLAYBOYS, WE ESCORT WAYNE OUTSIDE DISCREETLY, AND WE CONTINUE TO WONDER WHY ANYONE WOULD SEND ORION ON AN ESPIONAGE MISSION.
STEEL, CAN YOU KEEP BIG RED OUT OF TROUBLE?
I'LL TRY.
DO YOU MIND?
I'M IN CHARACTER.
YOU'RE A CHARACTER.

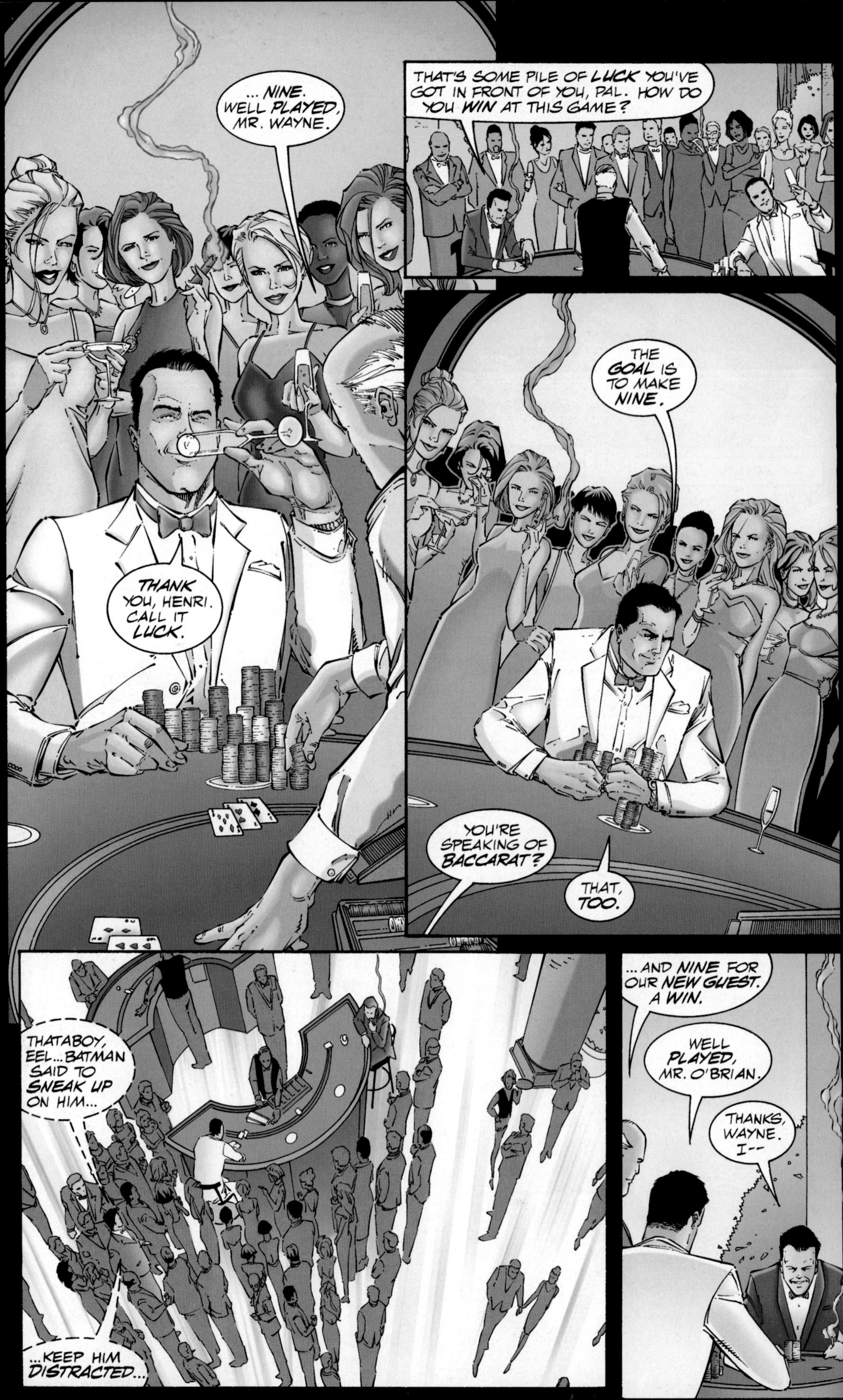
...NINE. WELL PLAYED, MR. WAYNE.
THANK YOU, HENRI. CALL IT LUCK.
THAT'S SOME PILE OF LUCK YOU'VE GOT IN FRONT OF YOU, PAL. HOW DO YOU WIN AT THIS GAME?
THE GOAL IS TO MAKE NINE.
YOU'RE SPEAKING OF BACCARAT?
THAT, TOO.
THATABOY, EEL...BATMAN SAID TO SNEAK UP ON HIM...
...KEEP HIM DISTRACTED...
...AND NINE FOR OUR NEW GUEST. A WIN.
WELL PLAYED, MR. O'BRIAN.
THANKS, WAYNE. I--

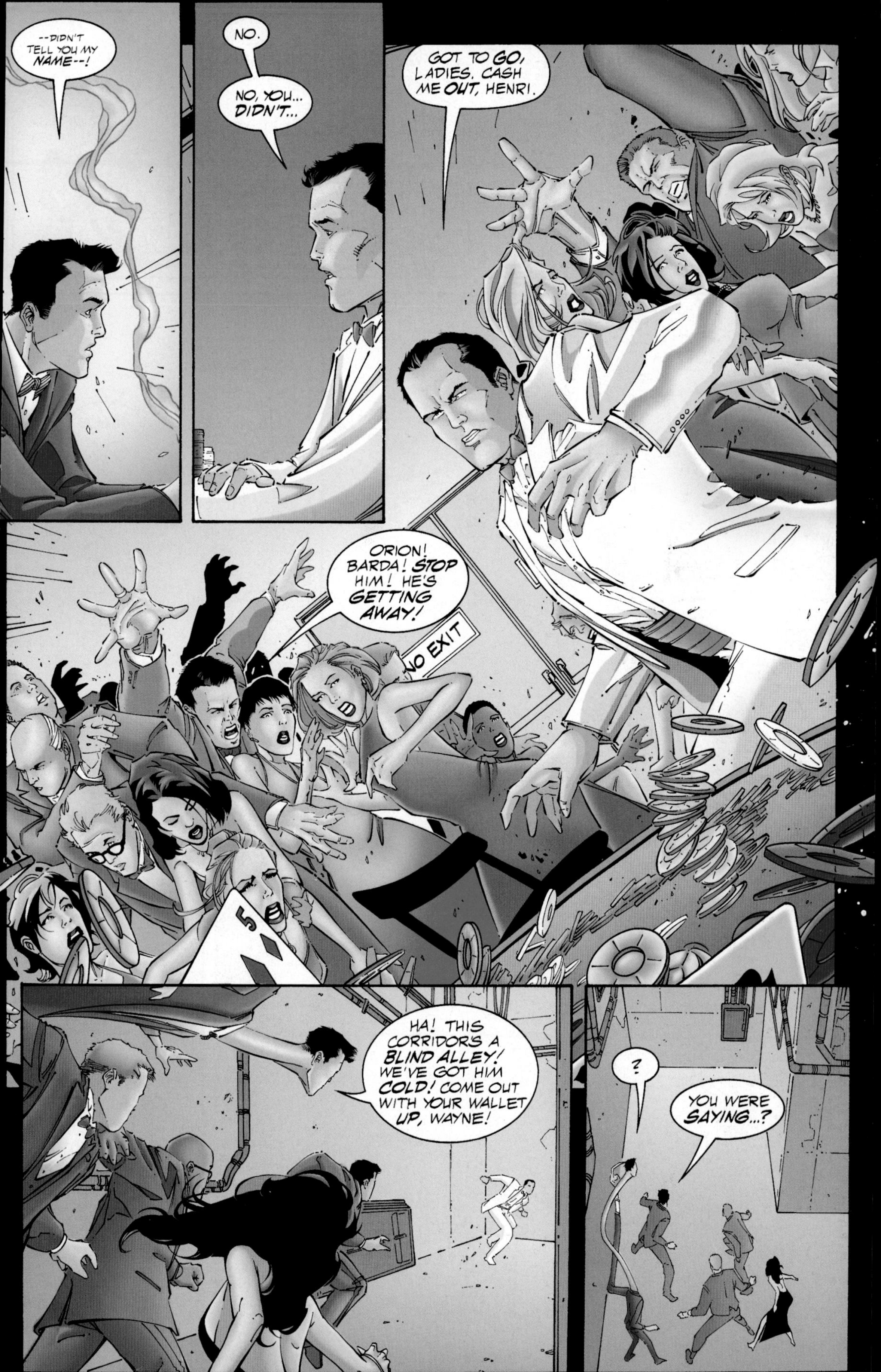
--DIDN'T TELL YOU MY NAME--!
NO.
NO, YOU... DIDN'T...
GOT TO GO, LADIES. CASH ME OUT, HENRI.
ORION! BARDA! STOP HIM! HE'S GETTING AWAY!
NO EXIT
HA! THIS CORRIDOR'S A BLIND ALLEY! WE'VE GOT HIM COLD! COME OUT WITH YOUR WALLET UP, WAYNE!
?
YOU WERE SAYING...?

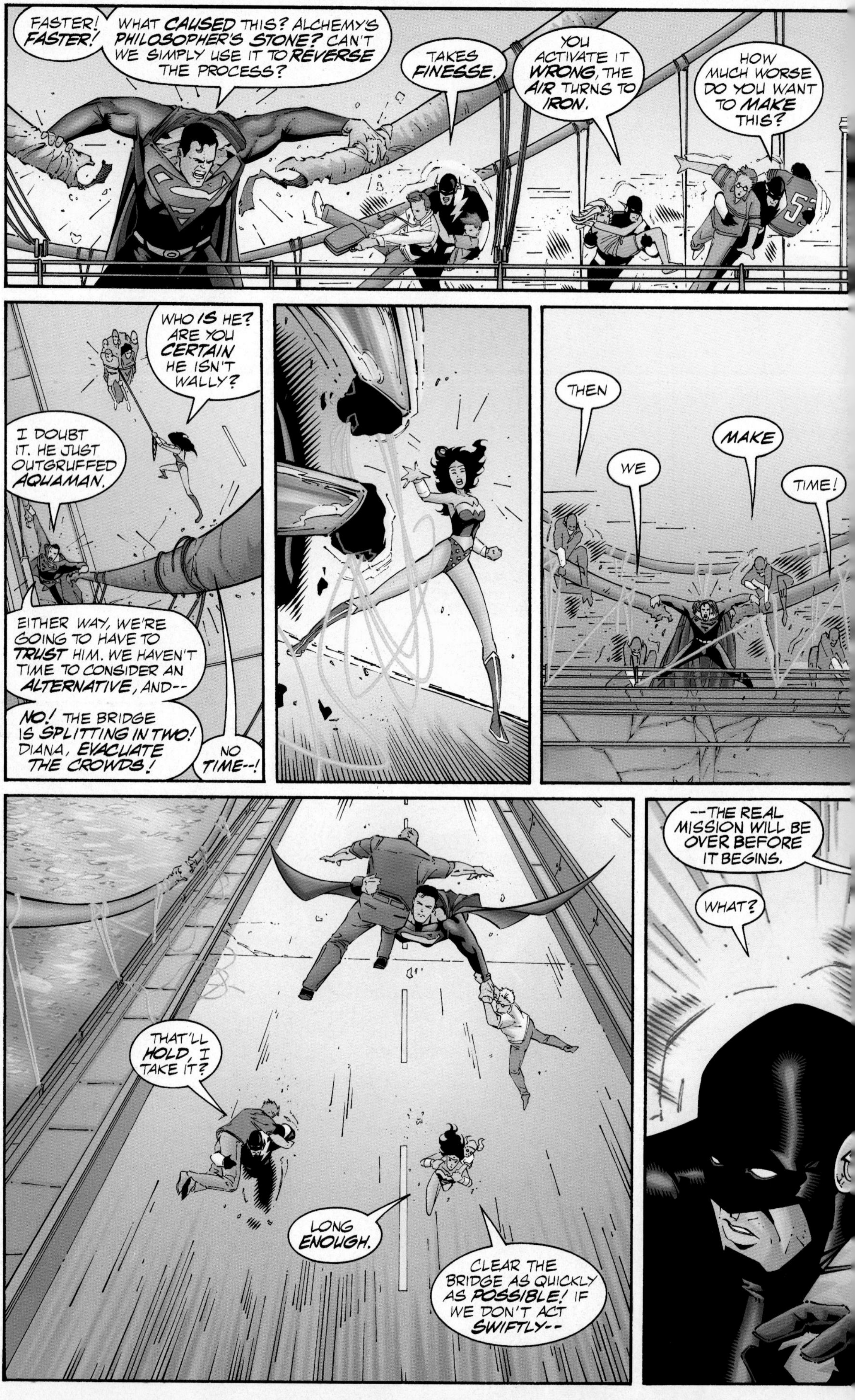
FASTER! FASTER!
WHAT CAUSED THIS? ALCHEMY'S PHILOSOPHER'S STONE? CAN'T WE SIMPLY USE IT TO REVERSE THE PROCESS?
TAKES FINESSE.
YOU ACTIVATE IT WRONG, THE AIR TURNS TO IRON.
HOW MUCH WORSE DO YOU WANT TO MAKE THIS?
WHO IS HE? ARE YOU CERTAIN HE ISN'T WALLY?
I DOUBT IT. HE JUST OUTGRUFFED AQUAMAN.
EITHER WAY, WE'RE GOING TO HAVE TO TRUST HIM. WE HAVEN'T TIME TO CONSIDER AN ALTERNATIVE, AND--
NO! THE BRIDGE IS SPLITTING IN TWO! DIANA, EVACUATE THE CROWDS!
NO TIME--!
THEN
WE
MAKE
TIME!
THAT'LL HOLD, I TAKE IT?
LONG ENOUGH.
CLEAR THE BRIDGE AS QUICKLY AS POSSIBLE! IF WE DON'T ACT SWIFTLY--
--THE REAL MISSION WILL BE OVER BEFORE IT BEGINS.
WHAT?

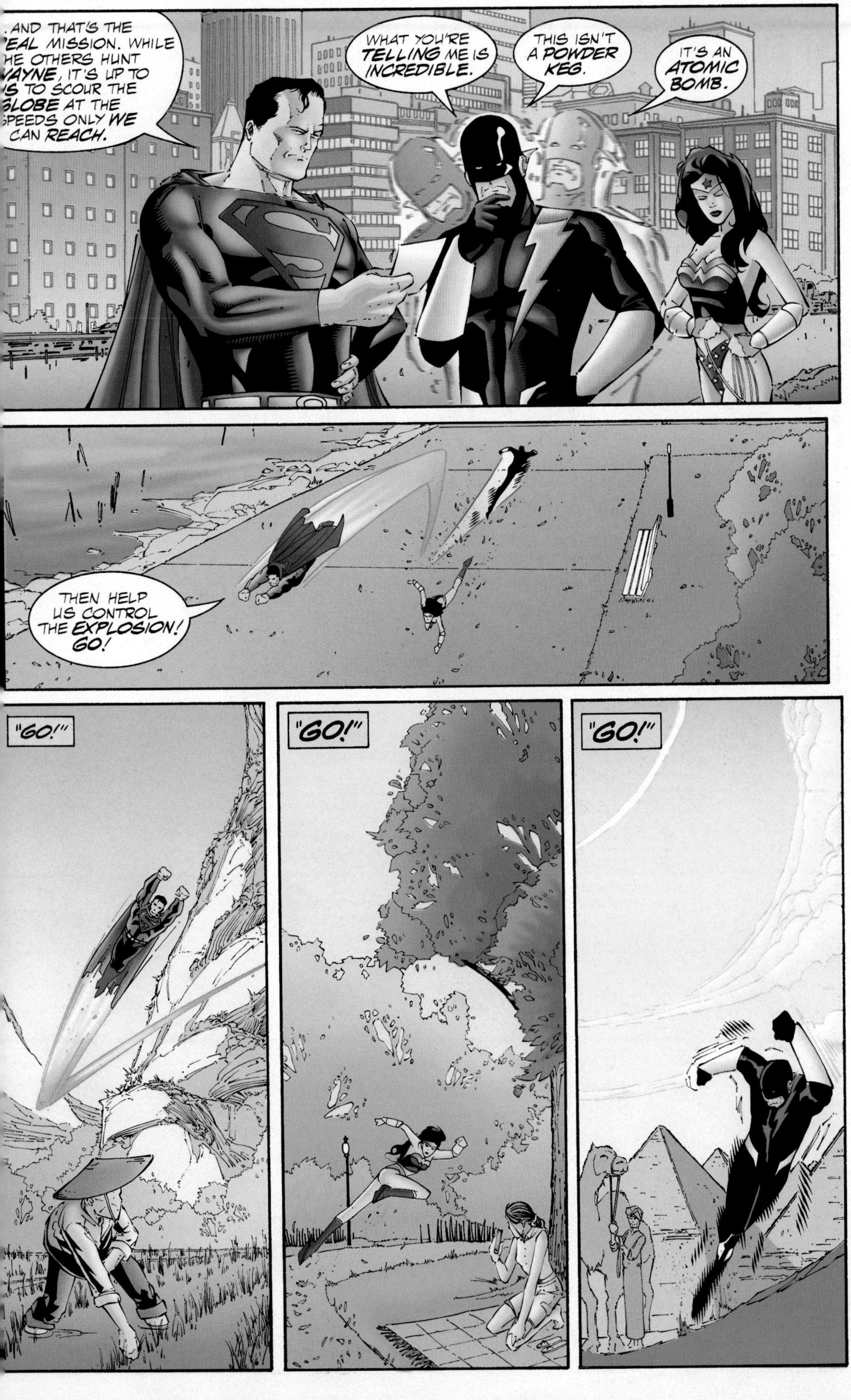

...AND THAT'S THE REAL MISSION. WHILE THE OTHERS HUNT WAYNE, IT'S UP TO US TO SCOUR THE GLOBE AT THE SPEEDS ONLY WE CAN REACH.
WHAT YOU'RE TELLING ME IS INCREDIBLE.
THIS ISN'T A POWDER KEG.
IT'S AN ATOMIC BOMB.
THEN HELP US CONTROL THE EXPLOSION! GO!
"GO!"
"GO!"
"GO!"

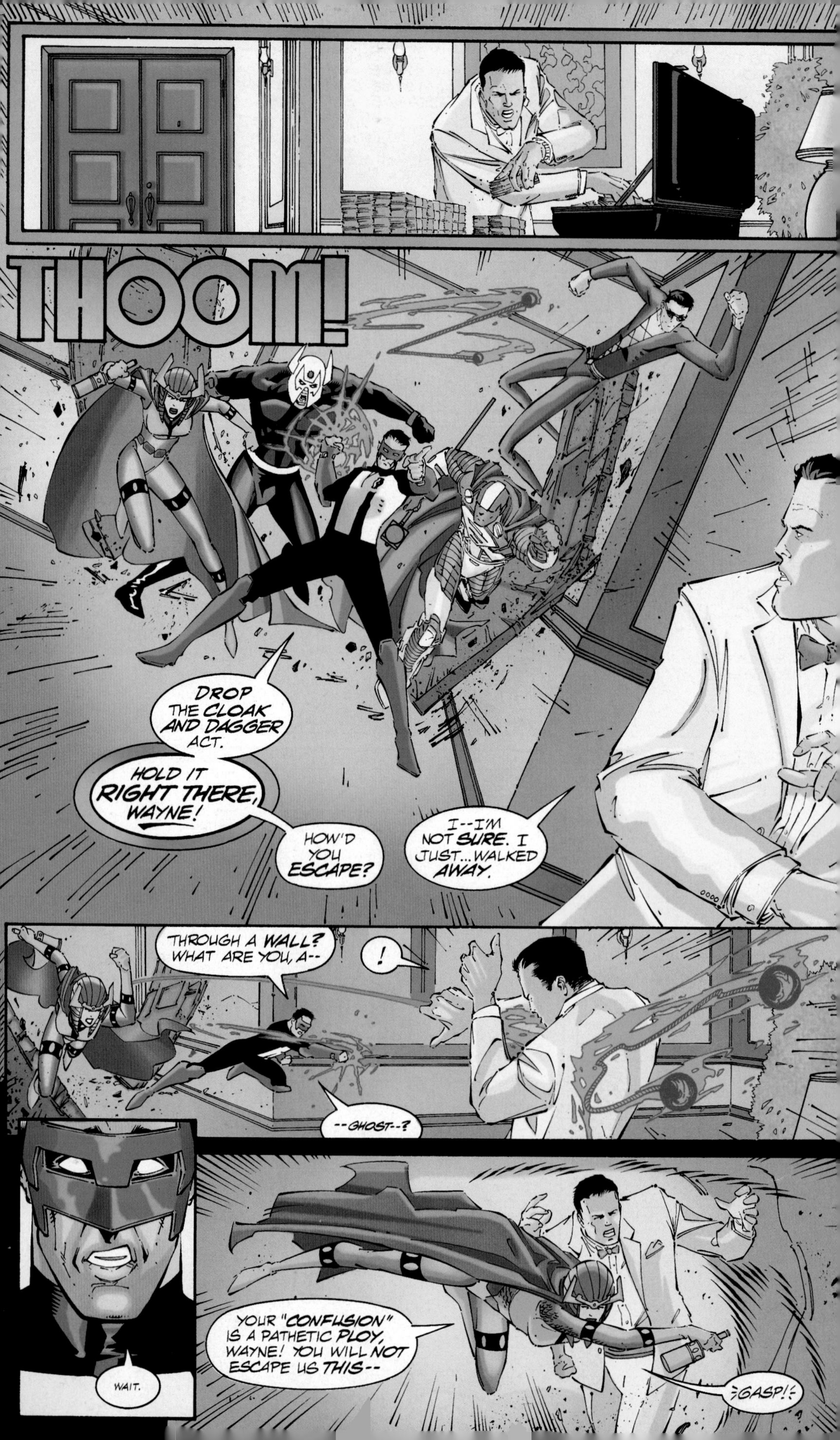
THOOM!
DROP THE CLOAK AND DAGGER ACT.
HOLD IT RIGHT THERE, WAYNE!
HOW'D YOU ESCAPE?
I--I'M NOT SURE. I JUST...WALKED AWAY.
THROUGH A WALL? WHAT ARE YOU, A--
!
--GHOST--?
WAIT.
YOUR "CONFUSION" IS A PATHETIC PLOY, WAYNE! YOU WILL NOT ESCAPE US THIS--
GASP!

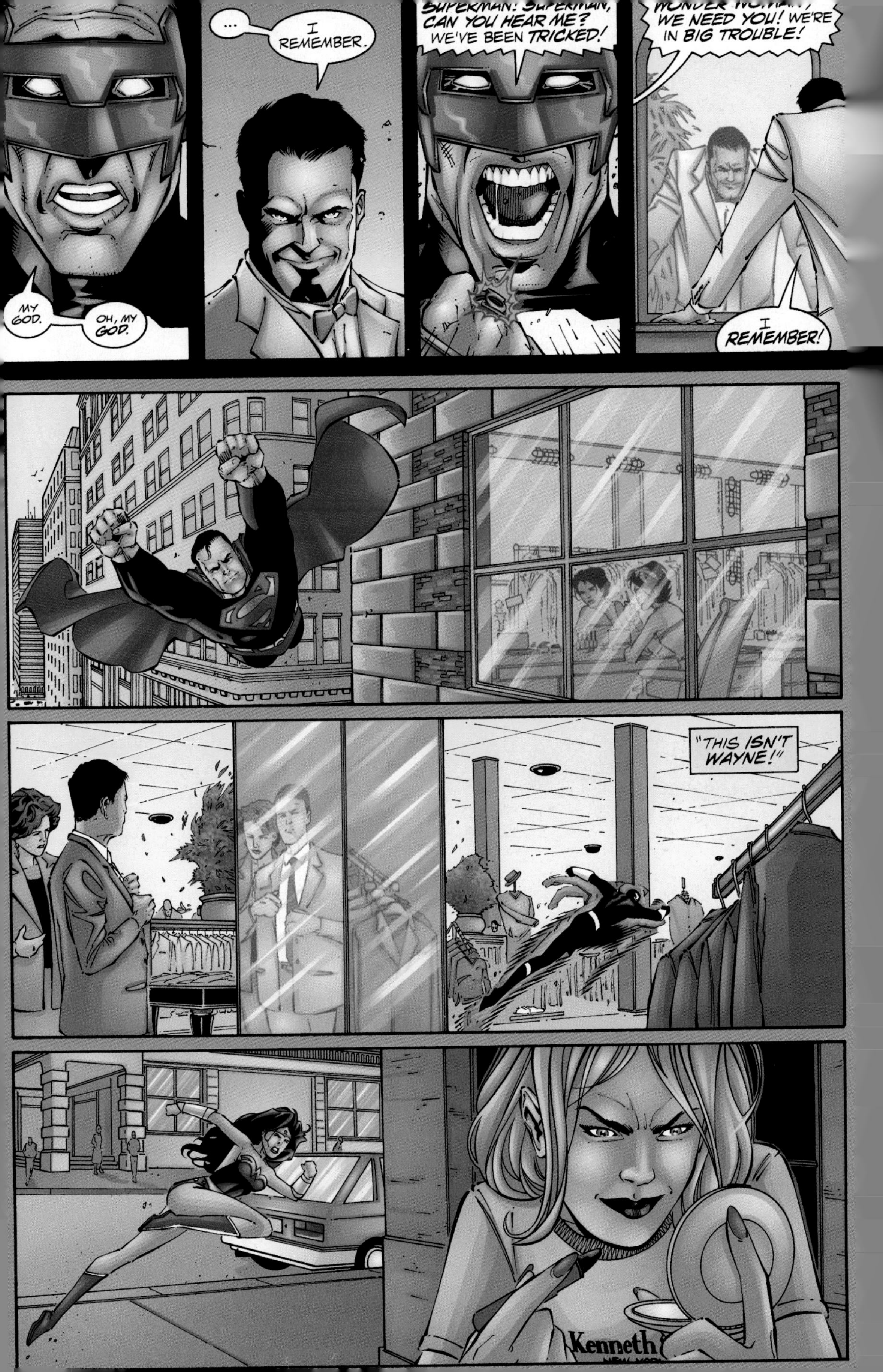
MY GOD.
OH, MY GOD.
...
I REMEMBER.
SUPERMAN! SUPERMAN, CAN YOU HEAR ME? WE'VE BEEN TRICKED!
WE NEED YOU! WE'RE IN BIG TROUBLE!
I REMEMBER!
"THIS ISN'T WAYNE!"
Kenneth

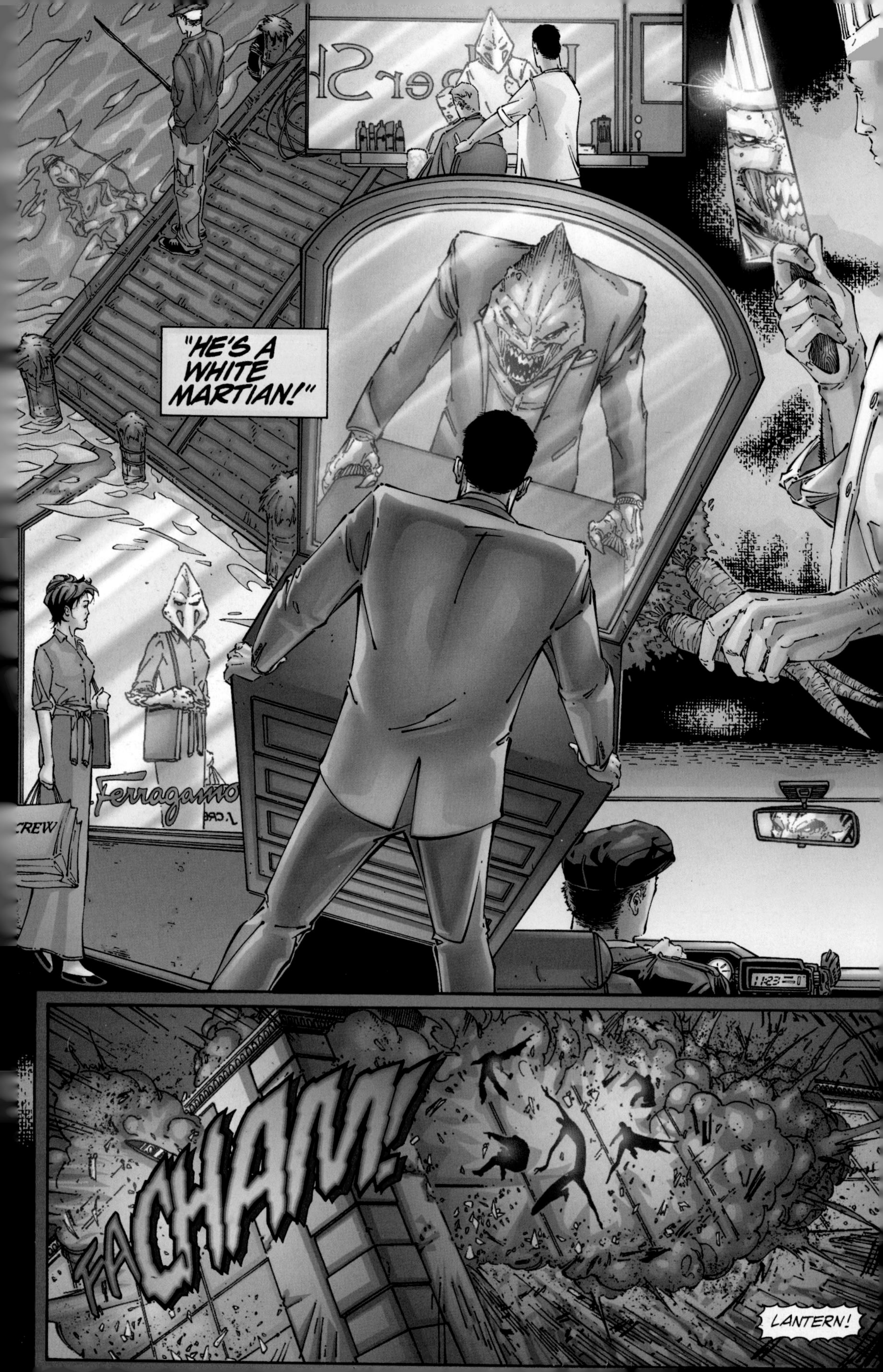
"HE'S A WHITE MARTIAN!"
Ferragamo
CREW
11:23
FACHAM!
LANTERN!

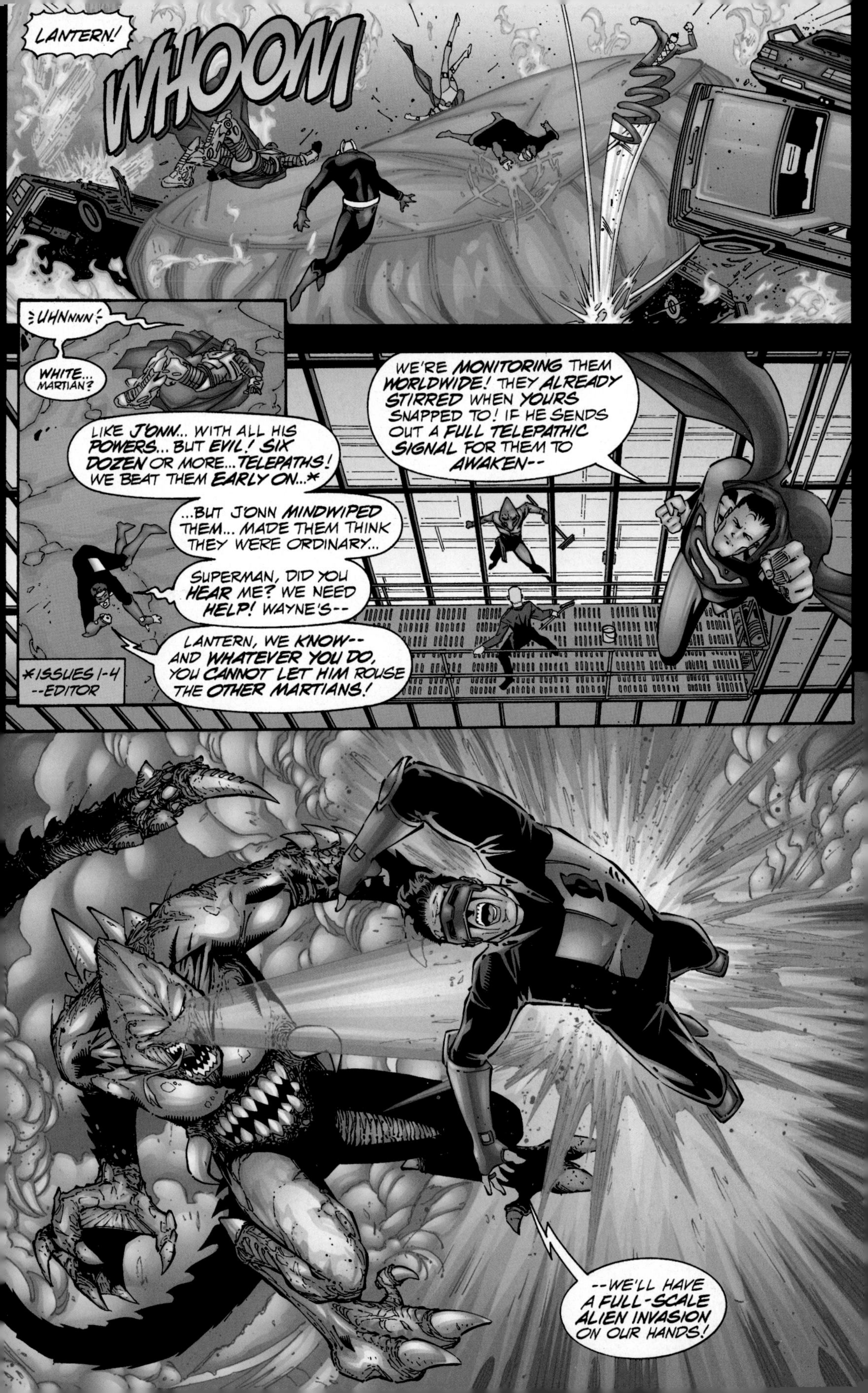
LANTERN!
WHOOM
UHNNNN
WHITE... MARTIAN?
LIKE J'ONN... WITH ALL HIS POWERS... BUT EVIL! SIX DOZEN OR MORE... TELEPATHS! WE BEAT THEM EARLY ON...*
...BUT J'ONN MINDWIPED THEM... MADE THEM THINK THEY WERE ORDINARY...
SUPERMAN, DID YOU HEAR ME? WE NEED HELP! WAYNE'S--
*ISSUES 1-4 --EDITOR
WE'RE MONITORING THEM WORLDWIDE! THEY ALREADY STIRRED WHEN YOURS SNAPPED TO! IF HE SENDS OUT A FULL TELEPATHIC SIGNAL FOR THEM TO AWAKEN--
LANTERN, WE KNOW-- AND WHATEVER YOU DO, YOU CANNOT LET HIM ROUSE THE OTHER MARTIANS!
--WE'LL HAVE A FULL-SCALE ALIEN INVASION ON OUR HANDS!

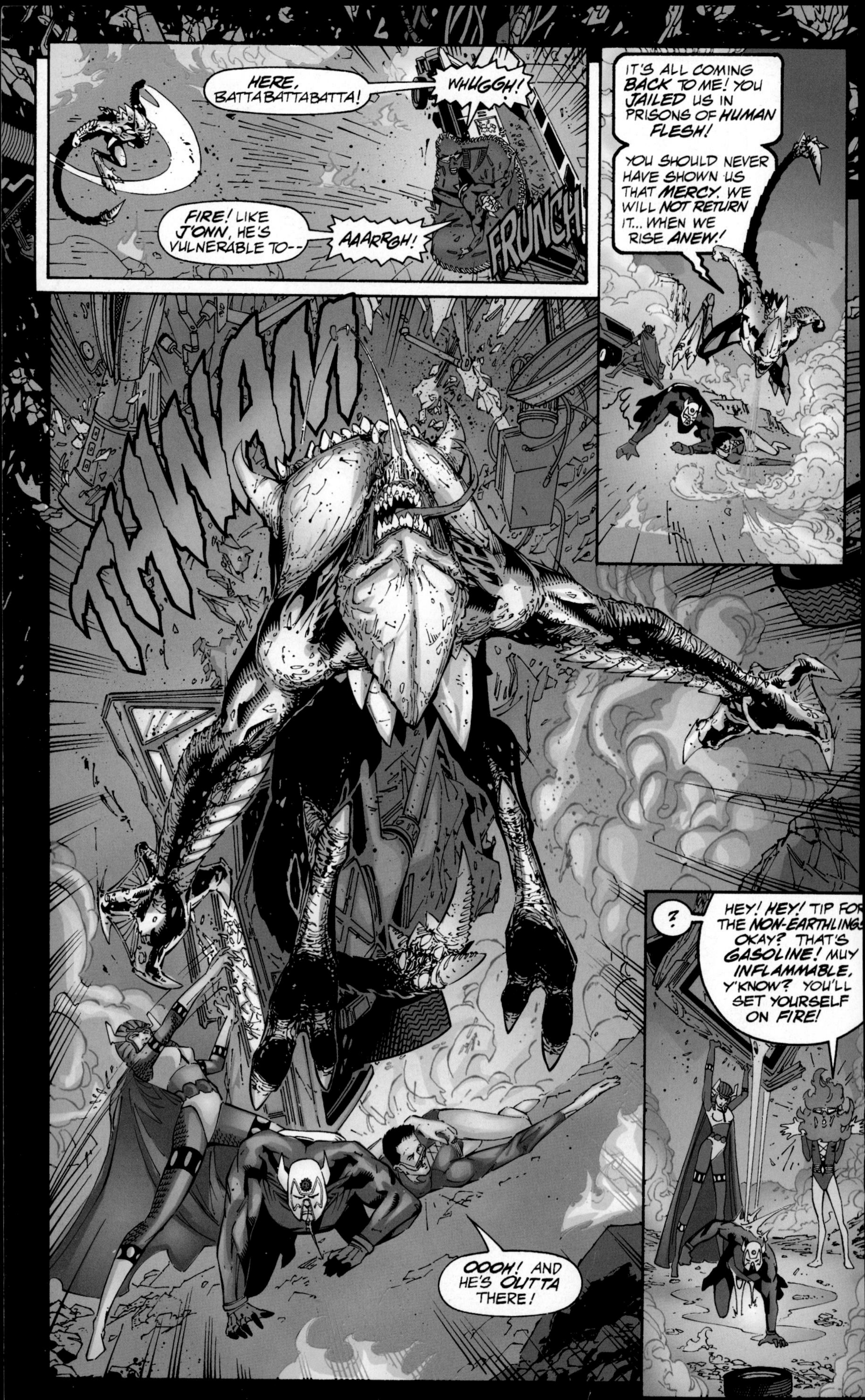

HERE, BATTABATTABATTA!
WHUGGH!
FIRE! LIKE J'ONN, HE'S VULNERABLE TO--
AAARRGH!
FRUNCH
IT'S ALL COMING BACK TO ME! YOU JAILED US IN PRISONS OF HUMAN FLESH!
YOU SHOULD NEVER HAVE SHOWN US THAT MERCY. WE WILL NOT RETURN IT... WHEN WE RISE ANEW!
THWAM
OOOH! AND HE'S OUTTA THERE!
?
HEY! HEY! TIP FOR THE NON-EARTHLINGS, OKAY? THAT'S GASOLINE! MUY INFLAMMABLE, Y'KNOW? YOU'LL SET YOURSELF ON FIRE!

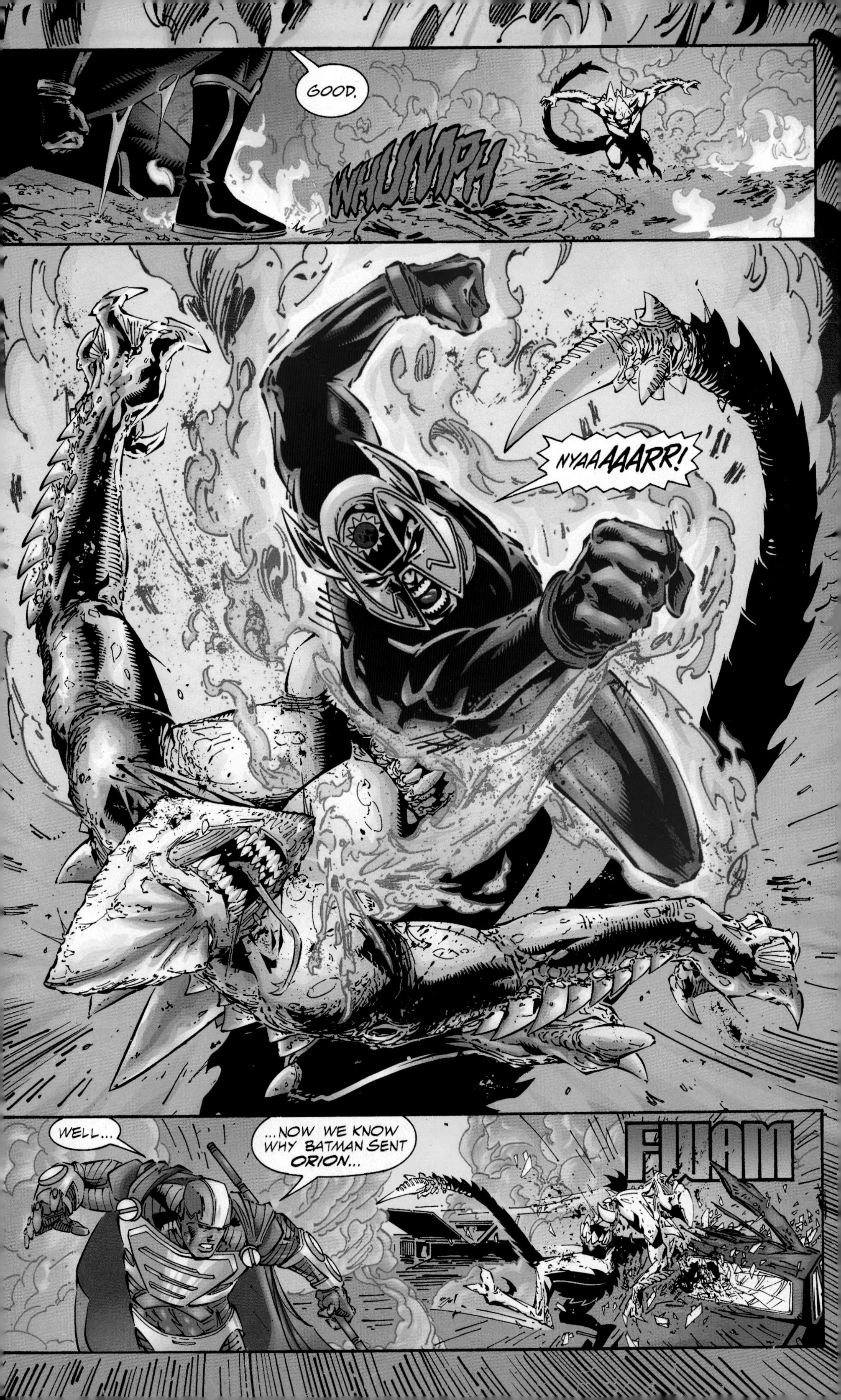
GOOD.
WHUMPH
NYAAAAARR!
WELL...
...NOW WE KNOW WHY BATMAN SENT ORION...
FWAM

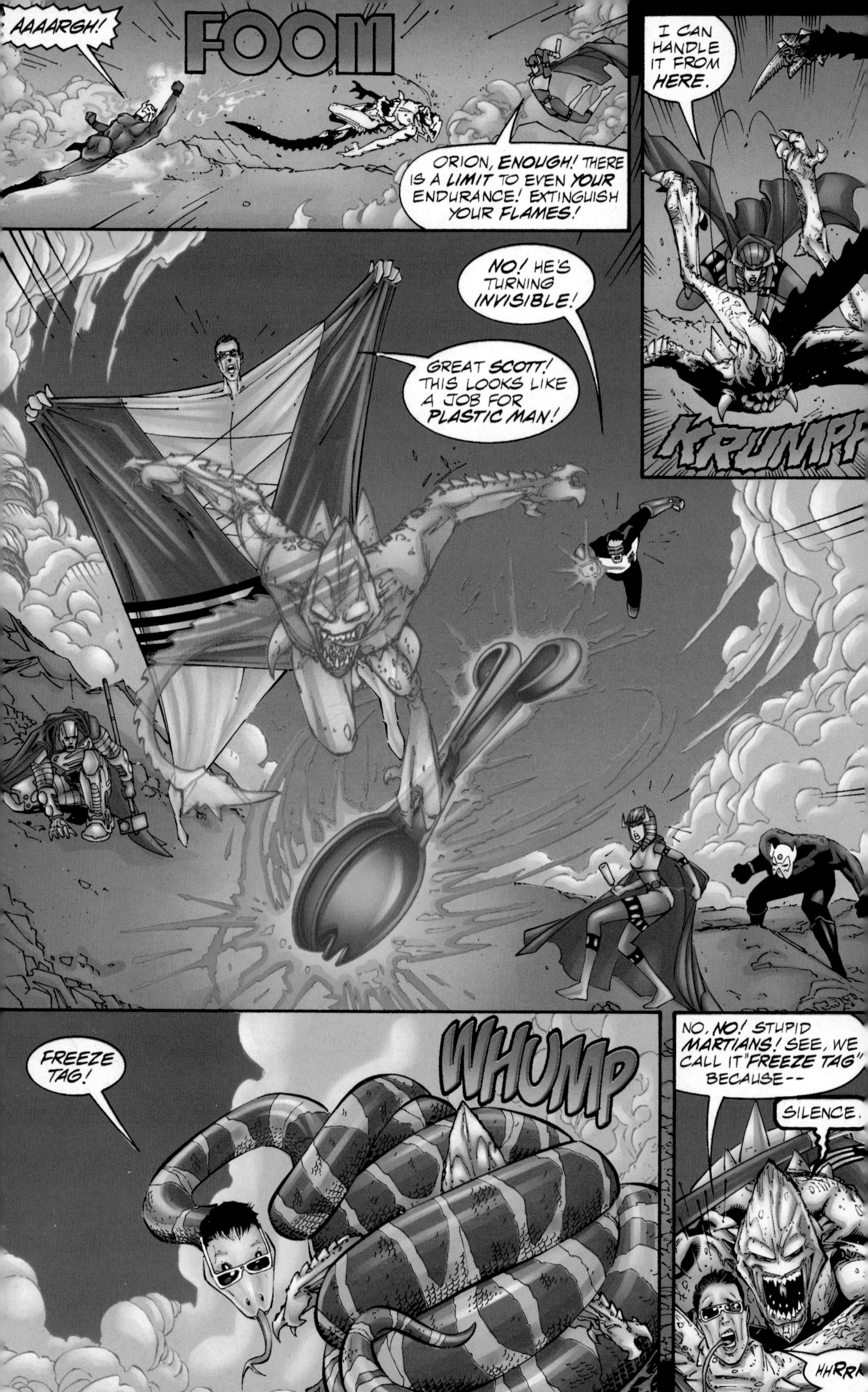
AAAARGH!
FOOM
ORION, ENOUGH! THERE IS A LIMIT TO EVEN YOUR ENDURANCE! EXTINGUISH YOUR FLAMES!
I CAN HANDLE IT FROM HERE.
NO! HE'S TURNING INVISIBLE!
GREAT SCOTT! THIS LOOKS LIKE A JOB FOR PLASTIC MAN!
FREEZE TAG!
WHUMP
NO, NO! STUPID MARTIANS! SEE, WE CALL IT "FREEZE TAG" BECAUSE--
SILENCE.
NECK.

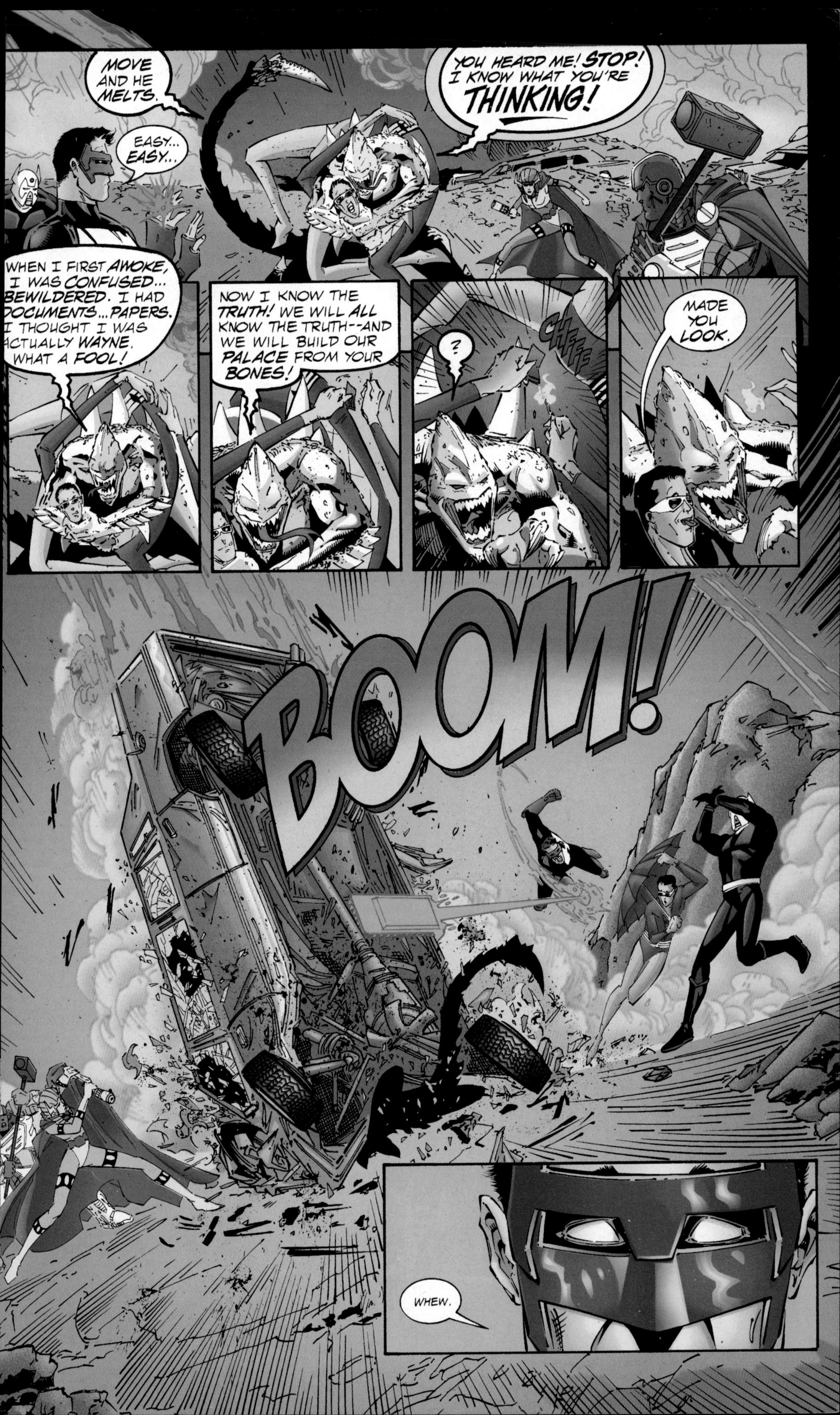
MOVE AND HE MELTS.
EASY... EASY...
YOU HEARD ME! STOP! I KNOW WHAT YOU'RE THINKING!
WHEN I FIRST AWOKE, I WAS CONFUSED... BEWILDERED. I HAD DOCUMENTS...PAPERS. I THOUGHT I WAS ACTUALLY WAYNE. WHAT A FOOL!
NOW I KNOW THE TRUTH! WE WILL ALL KNOW THE TRUTH--AND WE WILL BUILD OUR PALACE FROM YOUR BONES!
?
CHFFF
MADE YOU LOOK.
BOOM!
WHEW.

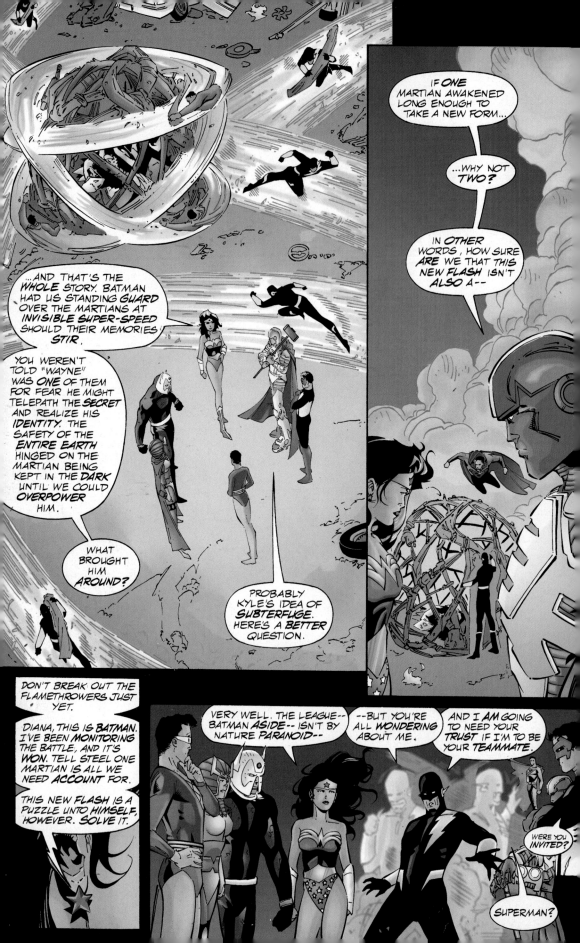

...AND THAT'S THE *WHOLE* STORY. BATMAN HAD US STANDING *GUARD* OVER THE MARTIANS AT *INVISIBLE SUPER-SPEED* SHOULD THEIR MEMORIES *STIR.*

YOU WEREN'T TOLD "WAYNE" WAS *ONE* OF THEM FOR FEAR HE MIGHT TELEPATH THE *SECRET* AND REALIZE HIS *IDENTITY.* THE SAFETY OF THE *ENTIRE EARTH* HINGED ON THE MARTIAN BEING KEPT IN THE *DARK* UNTIL WE COULD *OVERPOWER* HIM.

WHAT BROUGHT HIM *AROUND?*

PROBABLY *KYLE'S* IDEA OF *SUBTERFUGE.* HERE'S A *BETTER* QUESTION.

IF *ONE* MARTIAN AWAKENED LONG ENOUGH TO TAKE A NEW FORM...

...WHY NOT *TWO?*

IN *OTHER* WORDS, HOW SURE *ARE* WE THAT *THIS* NEW FLASH ISN'T ALSO A--

DON'T BREAK OUT THE FLAMETHROWERS JUST YET.

DIANA, THIS IS *BATMAN.* I'VE BEEN *MONITORING* THE BATTLE, AND IT'S *WON.* TELL STEEL ONE MARTIAN IS ALL WE NEED *ACCOUNT* FOR.

THIS NEW *FLASH* IS A *PUZZLE* UNTO HIMSELF, HOWEVER. *SOLVE* IT.

VERY WELL. THE LEAGUE-- BATMAN *ASIDE*-- ISN'T BY NATURE *PARANOID*--

--BUT YOU'RE ALL *WONDERING* ABOUT ME.

AND I *AM* GOING TO NEED YOUR *TRUST* IF I'M TO BE YOUR *TEAMMATE.*

WERE YOU *INVITED?*

SUPERMAN?

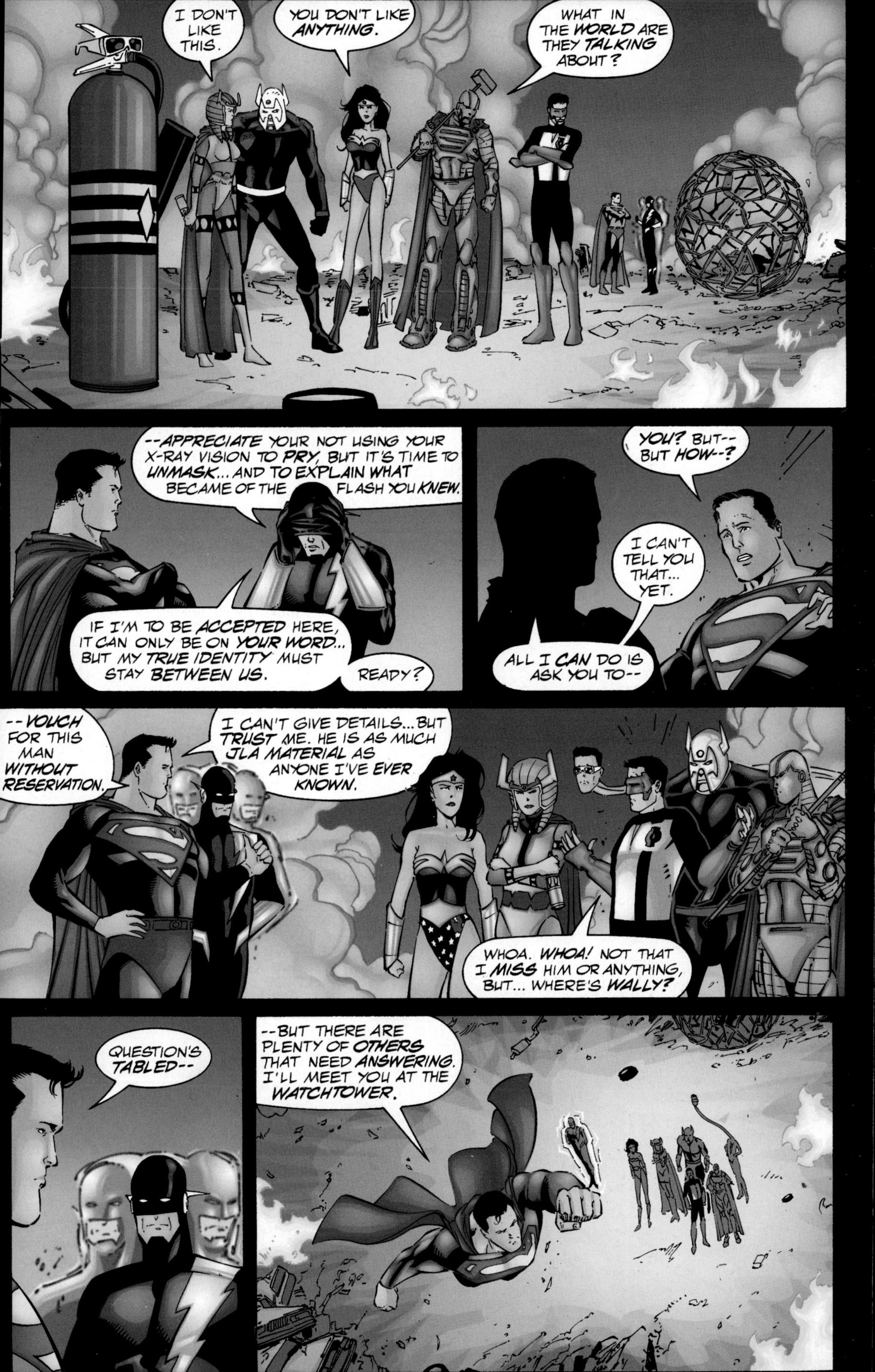

I DON'T LIKE THIS.
YOU DON'T LIKE ANYTHING.
WHAT IN THE WORLD ARE THEY TALKING ABOUT?
--APPRECIATE YOUR NOT USING YOUR X-RAY VISION TO PRY, BUT IT'S TIME TO UNMASK... AND TO EXPLAIN WHAT BECAME OF THE FLASH YOU KNEW.
IF I'M TO BE ACCEPTED HERE, IT CAN ONLY BE ON YOUR WORD... BUT MY TRUE IDENTITY MUST STAY BETWEEN US.
READY?
YOU? BUT-- BUT HOW--?
I CAN'T TELL YOU THAT... YET.
ALL I CAN DO IS ASK YOU TO--
--VOUCH FOR THIS MAN WITHOUT RESERVATION.
I CAN'T GIVE DETAILS... BUT TRUST ME. HE IS AS MUCH JLA MATERIAL AS ANYONE I'VE EVER KNOWN.
WHOA. WHOA! NOT THAT I MISS HIM OR ANYTHING, BUT... WHERE'S WALLY?
QUESTION'S TABLED--
--BUT THERE ARE PLENTY OF OTHERS THAT NEED ANSWERING. I'LL MEET YOU AT THE WATCHTOWER.

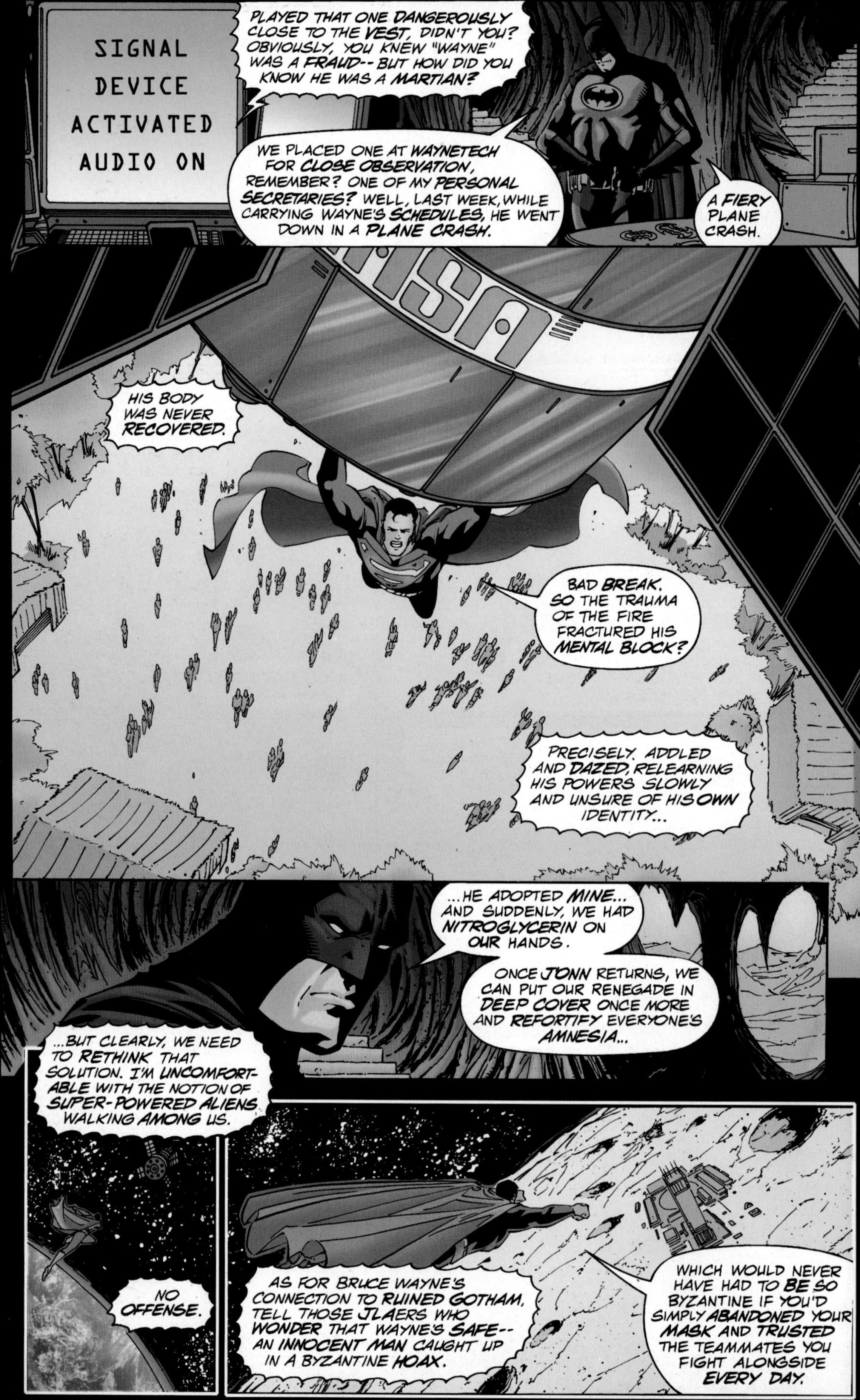
SIGNAL DEVICE ACTIVATED AUDIO ON
PLAYED THAT ONE DANGEROUSLY CLOSE TO THE VEST, DIDN'T YOU? OBVIOUSLY, YOU KNEW "WAYNE" WAS A FRAUD-- BUT HOW DID YOU KNOW HE WAS A MARTIAN?
WE PLACED ONE AT WAYNETECH FOR CLOSE OBSERVATION, REMEMBER? ONE OF MY PERSONAL SECRETARIES? WELL, LAST WEEK, WHILE CARRYING WAYNE'S SCHEDULES, HE WENT DOWN IN A PLANE CRASH.
A FIERY PLANE CRASH.
HIS BODY WAS NEVER RECOVERED.
BAD BREAK. SO THE TRAUMA OF THE FIRE FRACTURED HIS MENTAL BLOCK?
PRECISELY. ADDLED AND DAZED, RELEARNING HIS POWERS SLOWLY AND UNSURE OF HIS OWN IDENTITY...
...HE ADOPTED MINE... AND SUDDENLY, WE HAD NITROGLYCERIN ON OUR HANDS.
ONCE J'ONN RETURNS, WE CAN PUT OUR RENEGADE IN DEEP COVER ONCE MORE AND REFORTIFY EVERYONE'S AMNESIA...
...BUT CLEARLY, WE NEED TO RETHINK THAT SOLUTION. I'M UNCOMFORTABLE WITH THE NOTION OF SUPER-POWERED ALIENS WALKING AMONG US.
NO OFFENSE.
AS FOR BRUCE WAYNE'S CONNECTION TO RUINED GOTHAM, TELL THOSE JLAERS WHO WONDER THAT WAYNE'S SAFE-- AN INNOCENT MAN CAUGHT UP IN A BYZANTINE HOAX.
WHICH WOULD NEVER HAVE HAD TO BE SO BYZANTINE IF YOU'D SIMPLY ABANDONED YOUR MASK AND TRUSTED THE TEAMMATES YOU FIGHT ALONGSIDE EVERY DAY.

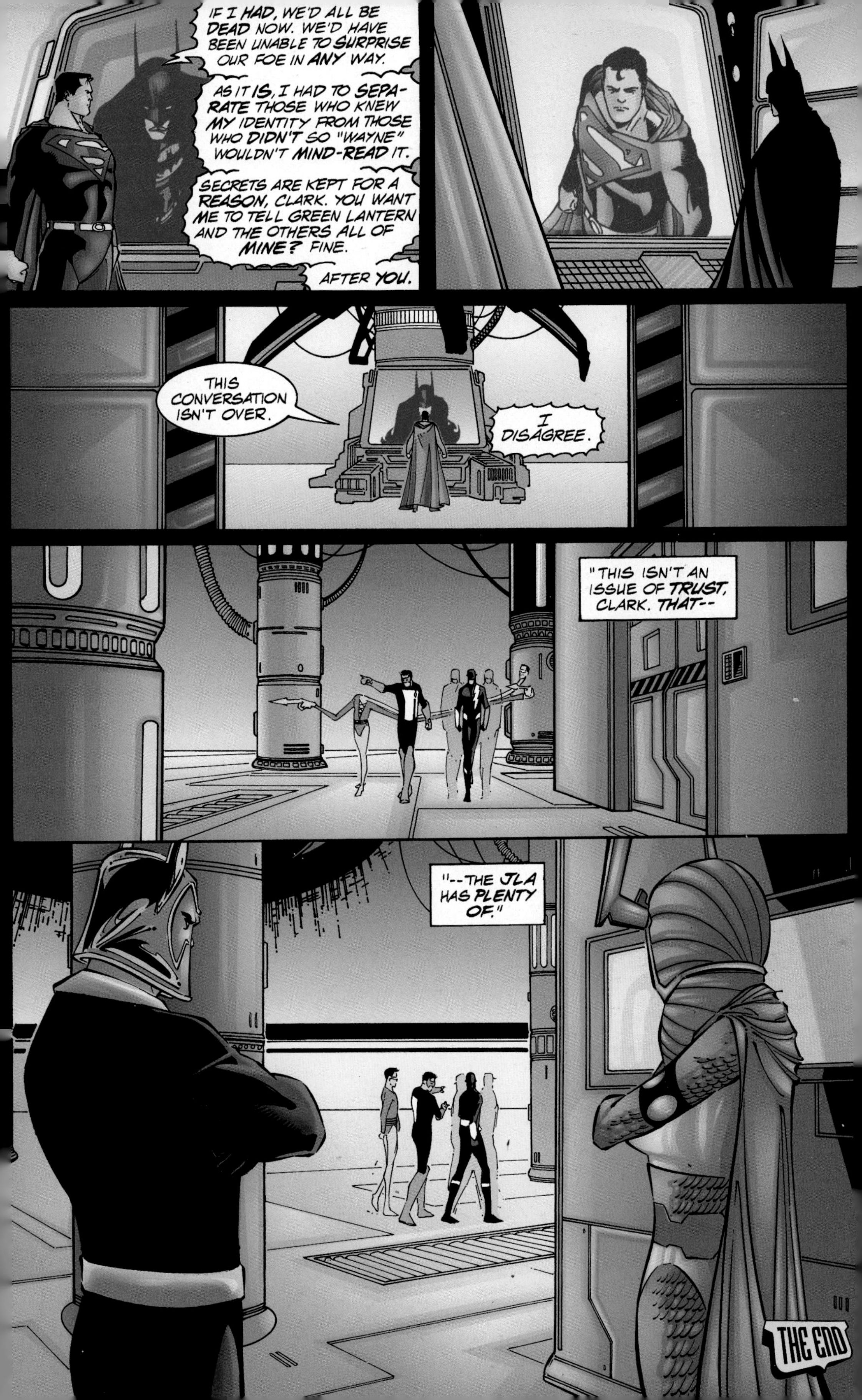
IF I HAD, WE'D ALL BE DEAD NOW. WE'D HAVE BEEN UNABLE TO SURPRISE OUR FOE IN ANY WAY.
AS IT IS, I HAD TO SEPARATE THOSE WHO KNEW MY IDENTITY FROM THOSE WHO DIDN'T SO "WAYNE" WOULDN'T MIND-READ IT.
SECRETS ARE KEPT FOR A REASON, CLARK. YOU WANT ME TO TELL GREEN LANTERN AND THE OTHERS ALL OF MINE? FINE.
AFTER YOU.
THIS CONVERSATION ISN'T OVER.
I DISAGREE.
"THIS ISN'T AN ISSUE OF TRUST, CLARK. THAT--
"--THE JLA HAS PLENTY OF."
THE END

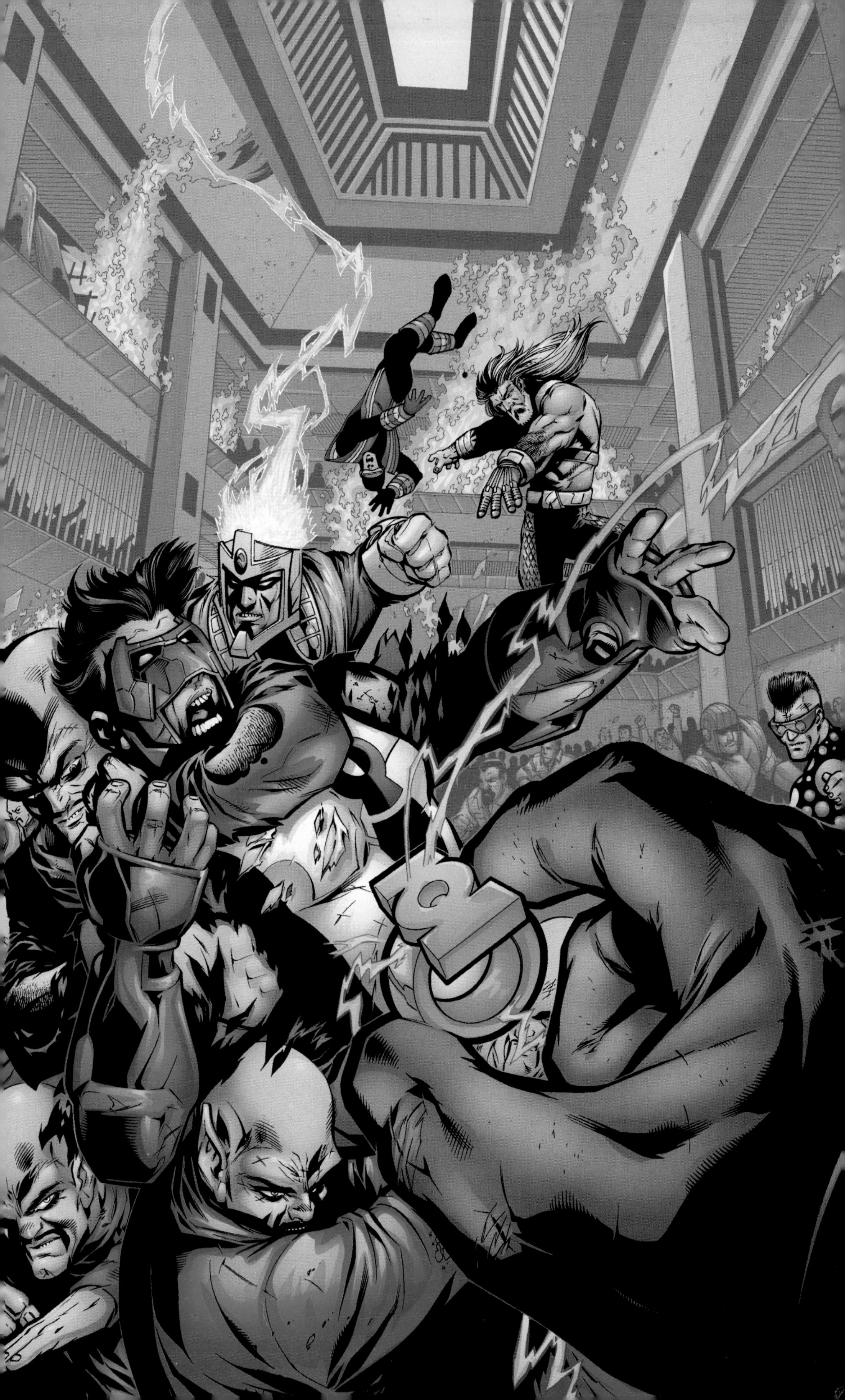

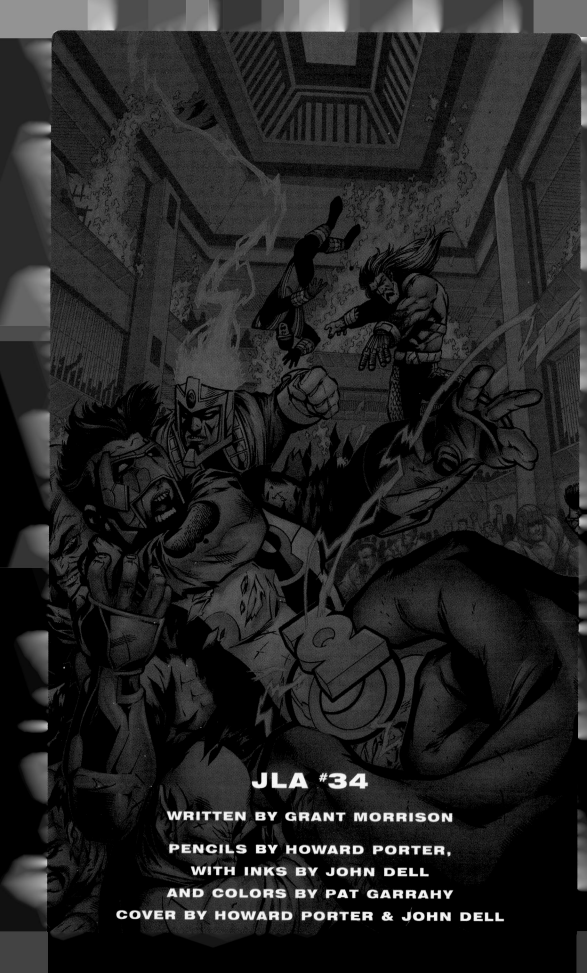

JLA #34

WRITTEN BY GRANT MORRISON

PENCILS BY HOWARD PORTER,
WITH INKS BY JOHN DELL
AND COLORS BY PAT GARRAHY
COVER BY HOWARD PORTER & JOHN DELL

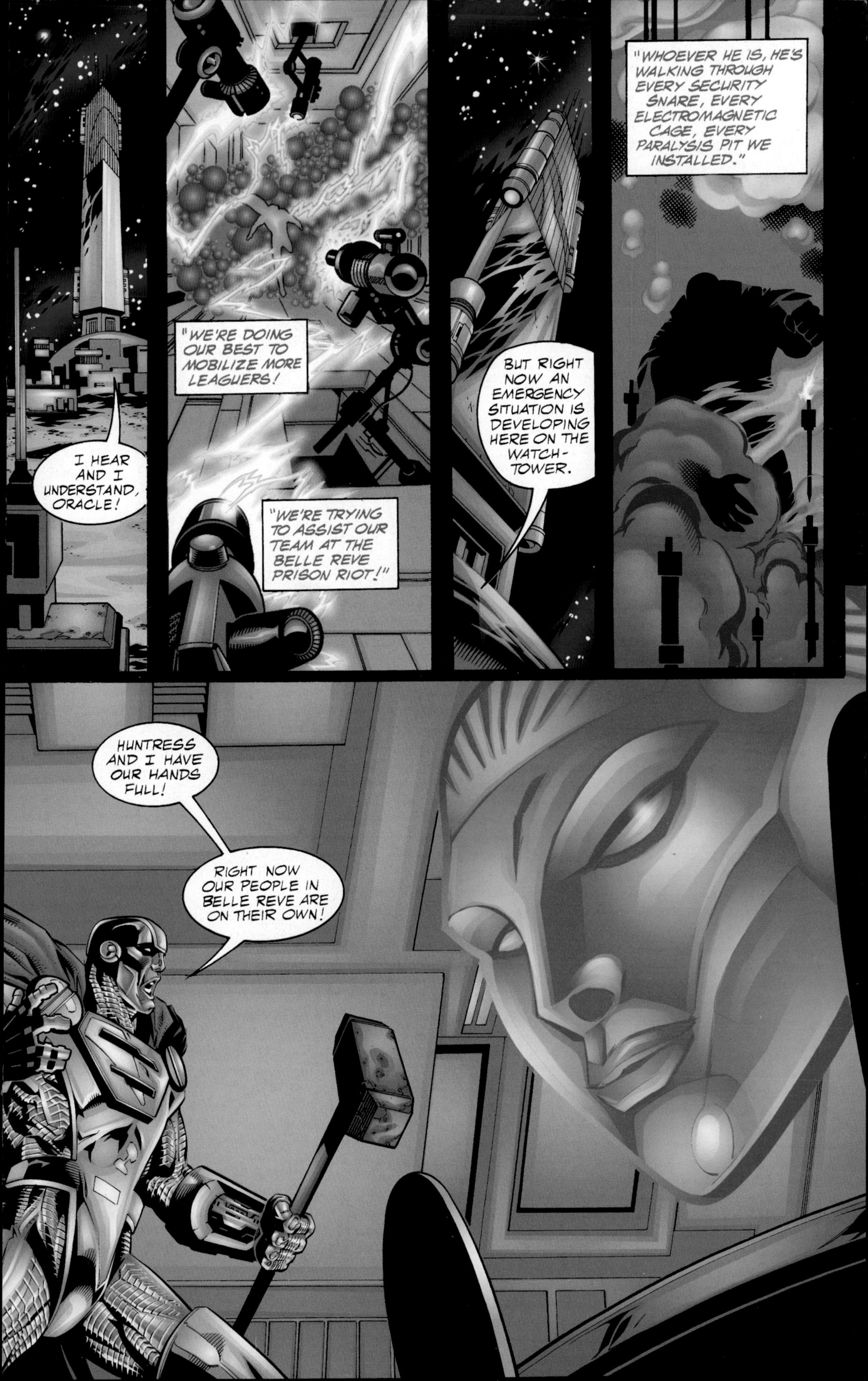
I HEAR AND I UNDERSTAND, ORACLE!
"WE'RE DOING OUR BEST TO MOBILIZE MORE LEAGUERS!
"WE'RE TRYING TO ASSIST OUR TEAM AT THE BELLE REVE PRISON RIOT!"
BUT RIGHT NOW AN EMERGENCY SITUATION IS DEVELOPING HERE ON THE WATCH-TOWER.
"WHOEVER HE IS, HE'S WALKING THROUGH EVERY SECURITY SNARE, EVERY ELECTROMAGNETIC CAGE, EVERY PARALYSIS PIT WE INSTALLED."
HUNTRESS AND I HAVE OUR HANDS FULL!
RIGHT NOW OUR PEOPLE IN BELLE REVE ARE ON THEIR OWN!

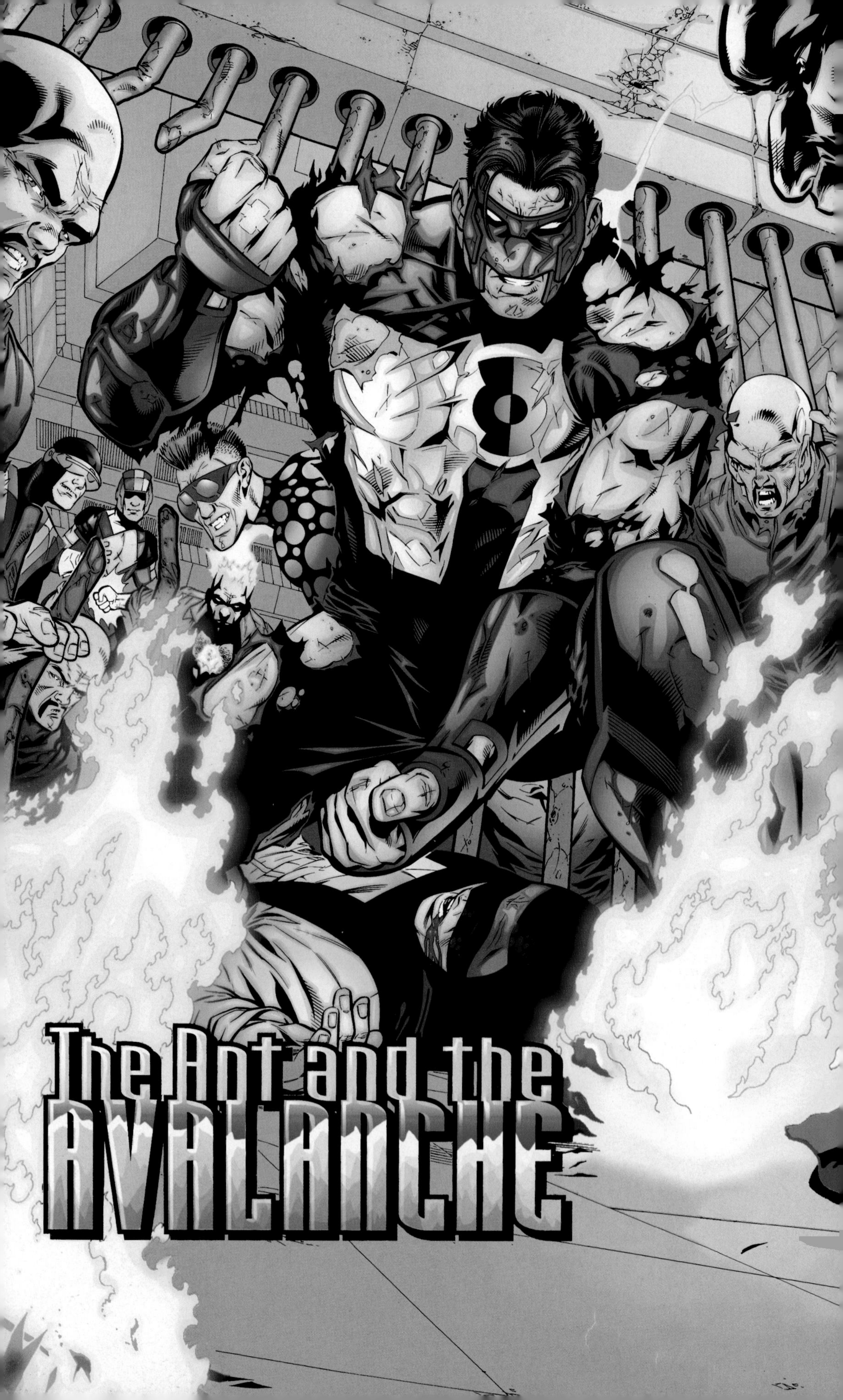
The Ant and the
AVALANCHE

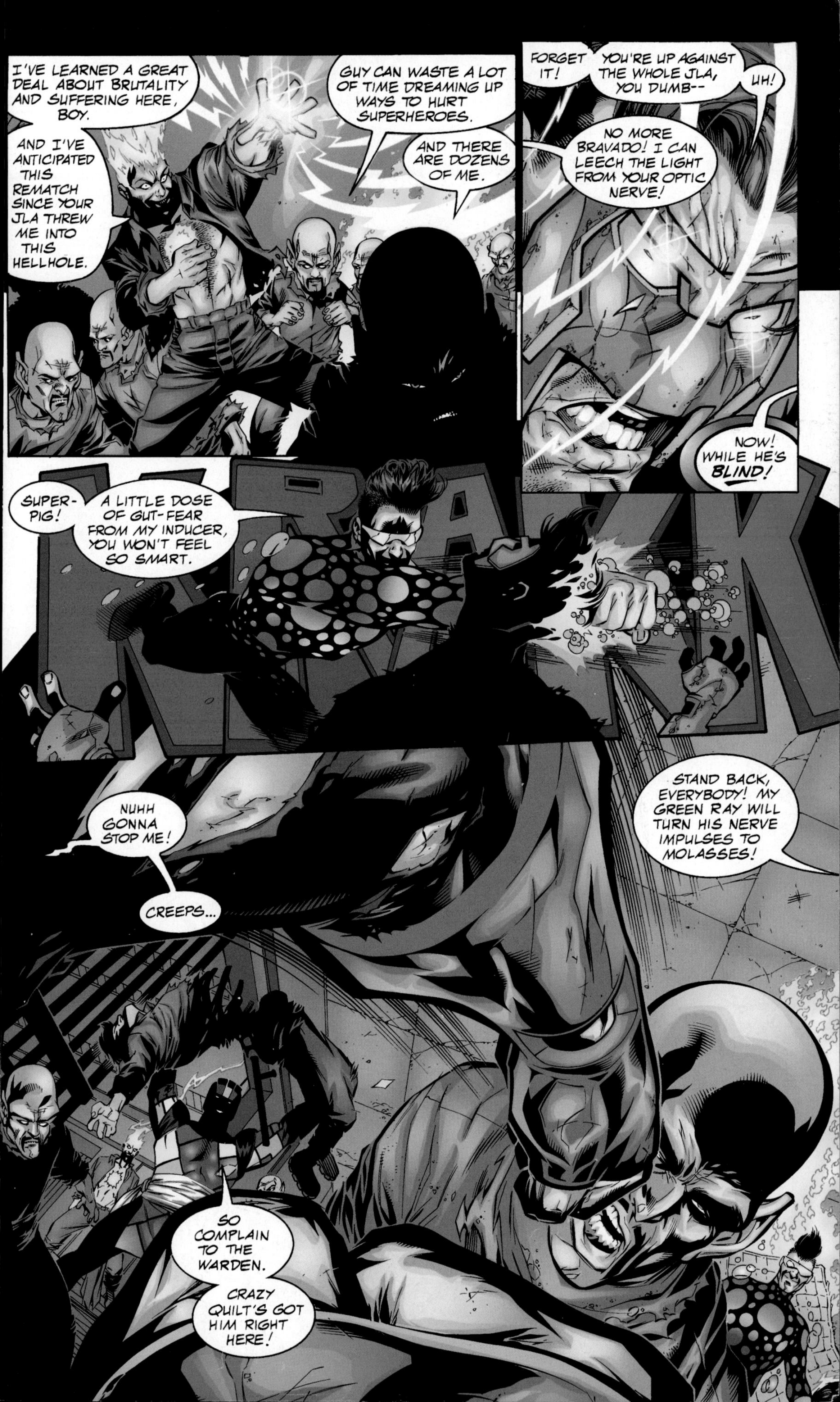

I'VE LEARNED A GREAT DEAL ABOUT BRUTALITY AND SUFFERING HERE, BOY.
AND I'VE ANTICIPATED THIS REMATCH SINCE YOUR JLA THREW ME INTO THIS HELLHOLE.
GUY CAN WASTE A LOT OF TIME DREAMING UP WAYS TO HURT SUPERHEROES.
AND THERE ARE DOZENS OF ME.
FORGET IT!
YOU'RE UP AGAINST THE WHOLE JLA, YOU DUMB--
UH!
NO MORE BRAVADO! I CAN LEECH THE LIGHT FROM YOUR OPTIC NERVE!
NOW! WHILE HE'S BLIND!
SUPER-PIG!
A LITTLE DOSE OF GUT-FEAR FROM MY INDUCER, YOU WON'T FEEL SO SMART.
NUHH GONNA STOP ME!
CREEPS...
STAND BACK, EVERYBODY! MY GREEN RAY WILL TURN HIS NERVE IMPULSES TO MOLASSES!
SO COMPLAIN TO THE WARDEN.
CRAZY QUILT'S GOT HIM RIGHT HERE!

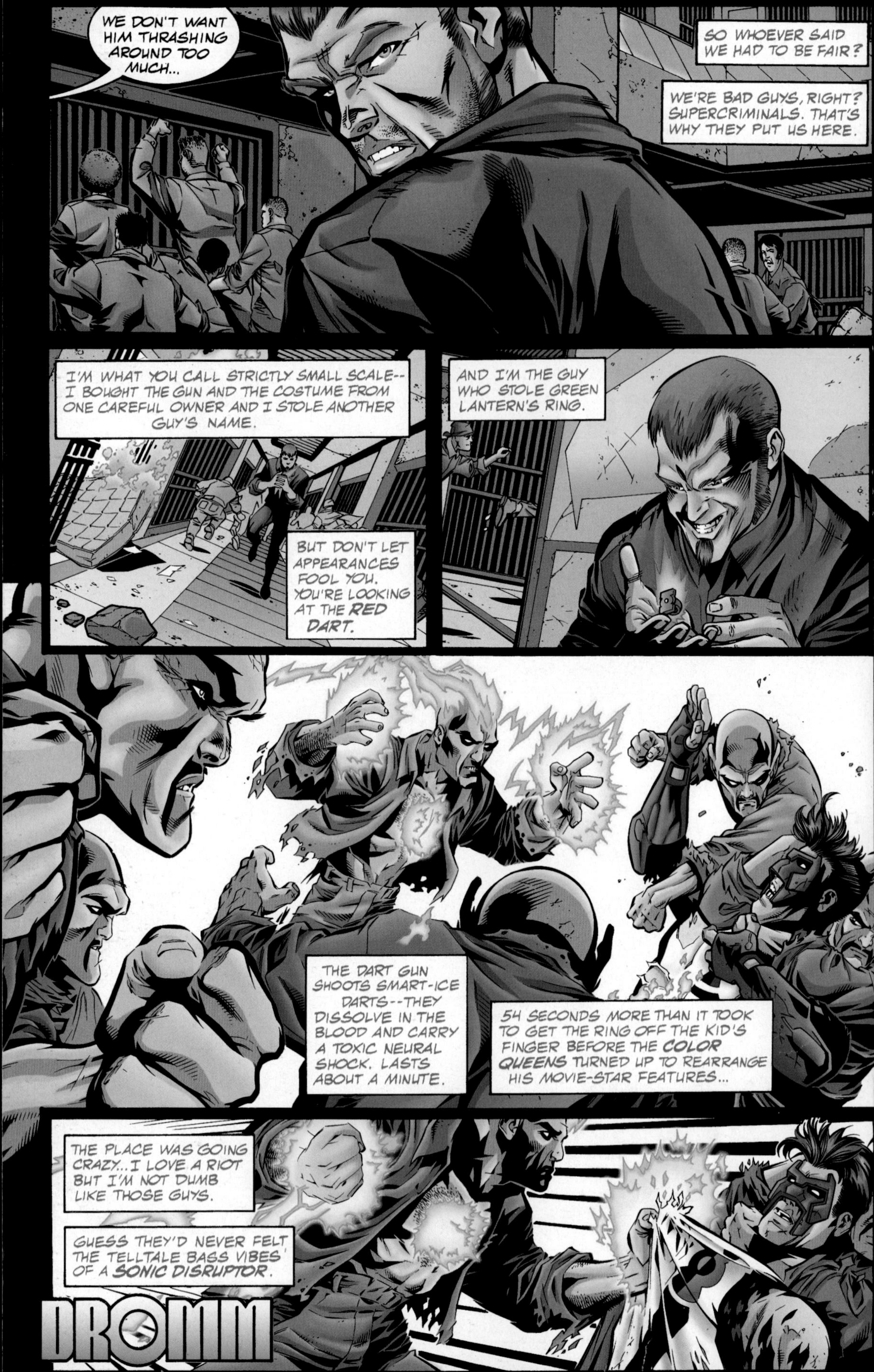
WE DON'T WANT HIM THRASHING AROUND TOO MUCH...
SO WHOEVER SAID WE HAD TO BE FAIR?
WE'RE BAD GUYS, RIGHT? SUPERCRIMINALS. THAT'S WHY THEY PUT US HERE.
I'M WHAT YOU CALL STRICTLY SMALL SCALE-- I BOUGHT THE GUN AND THE COSTUME FROM ONE CAREFUL OWNER AND I STOLE ANOTHER GUY'S NAME.
BUT DON'T LET APPEARANCES FOOL YOU. YOU'RE LOOKING AT THE RED DART.
AND I'M THE GUY WHO STOLE GREEN LANTERN'S RING.
THE DART GUN SHOOTS SMART-ICE DARTS--THEY DISSOLVE IN THE BLOOD AND CARRY A TOXIC NEURAL SHOCK. LASTS ABOUT A MINUTE.
54 SECONDS MORE THAN IT TOOK TO GET THE RING OFF THE KID'S FINGER BEFORE THE COLOR QUEENS TURNED UP TO REARRANGE HIS MOVIE-STAR FEATURES...
THE PLACE WAS GOING CRAZY... I LOVE A RIOT BUT I'M NOT DUMB LIKE THOSE GUYS.
GUESS THEY'D NEVER FELT THE TELLTALE BASS VIBES OF A SONIC DISRUPTOR.
DROMM

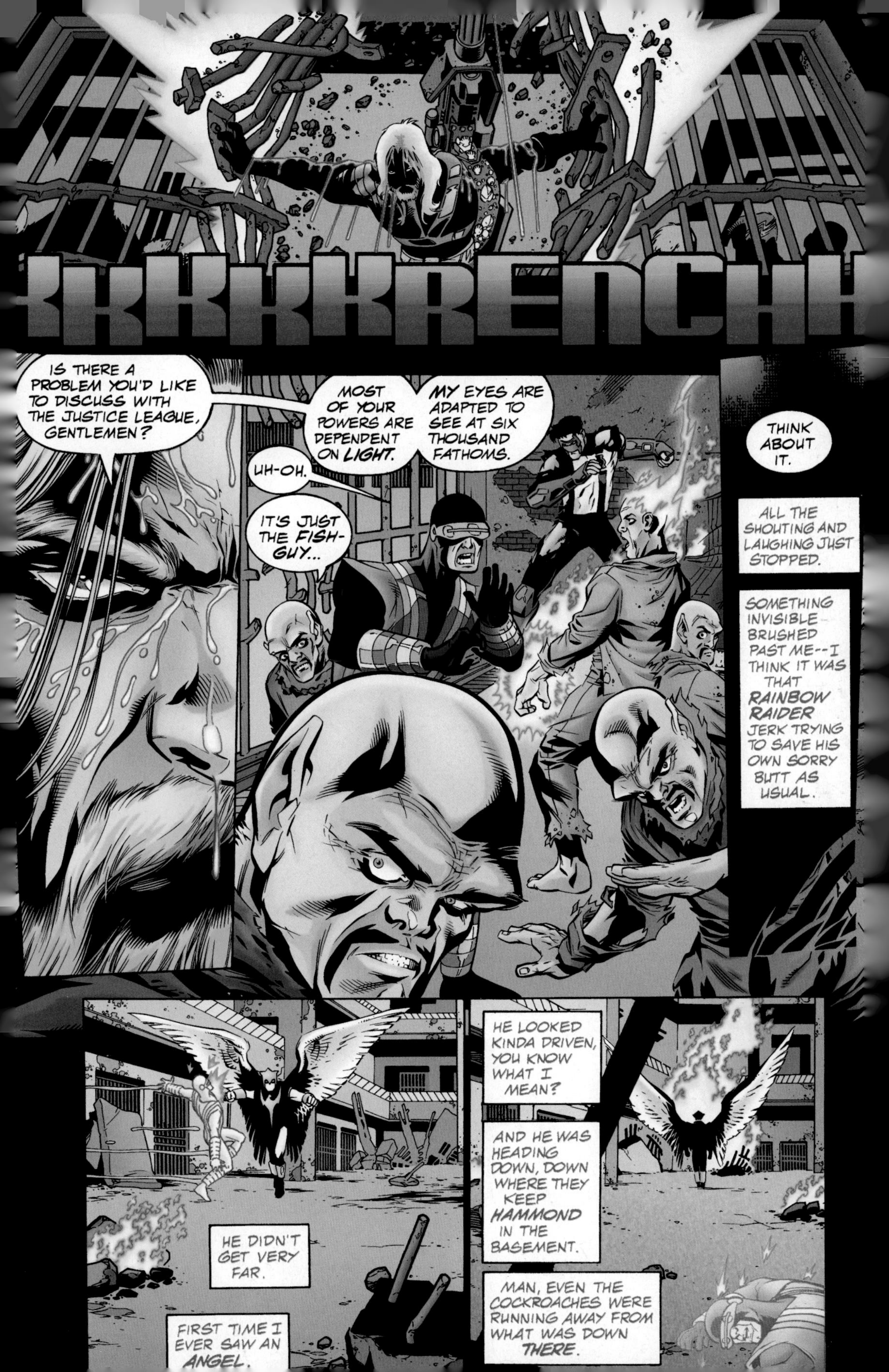
KKKKKRENCHH
IS THERE A PROBLEM YOU'D LIKE TO DISCUSS WITH THE JUSTICE LEAGUE, GENTLEMEN?
MOST OF YOUR POWERS ARE DEPENDENT ON LIGHT.
MY EYES ARE ADAPTED TO SEE AT SIX THOUSAND FATHOMS.
UH-OH.
IT'S JUST THE FISH-GUY...
THINK ABOUT IT.
ALL THE SHOUTING AND LAUGHING JUST STOPPED.
SOMETHING INVISIBLE BRUSHED PAST ME--I THINK IT WAS THAT RAINBOW RAIDER JERK TRYING TO SAVE HIS OWN SORRY BUTT AS USUAL.
HE DIDN'T GET VERY FAR.
FIRST TIME I EVER SAW AN ANGEL.
HE LOOKED KINDA DRIVEN, YOU KNOW WHAT I MEAN?
AND HE WAS HEADING DOWN, DOWN WHERE THEY KEEP HAMMOND IN THE BASEMENT.
MAN, EVEN THE COCKROACHES WERE RUNNING AWAY FROM WHAT WAS DOWN THERE.

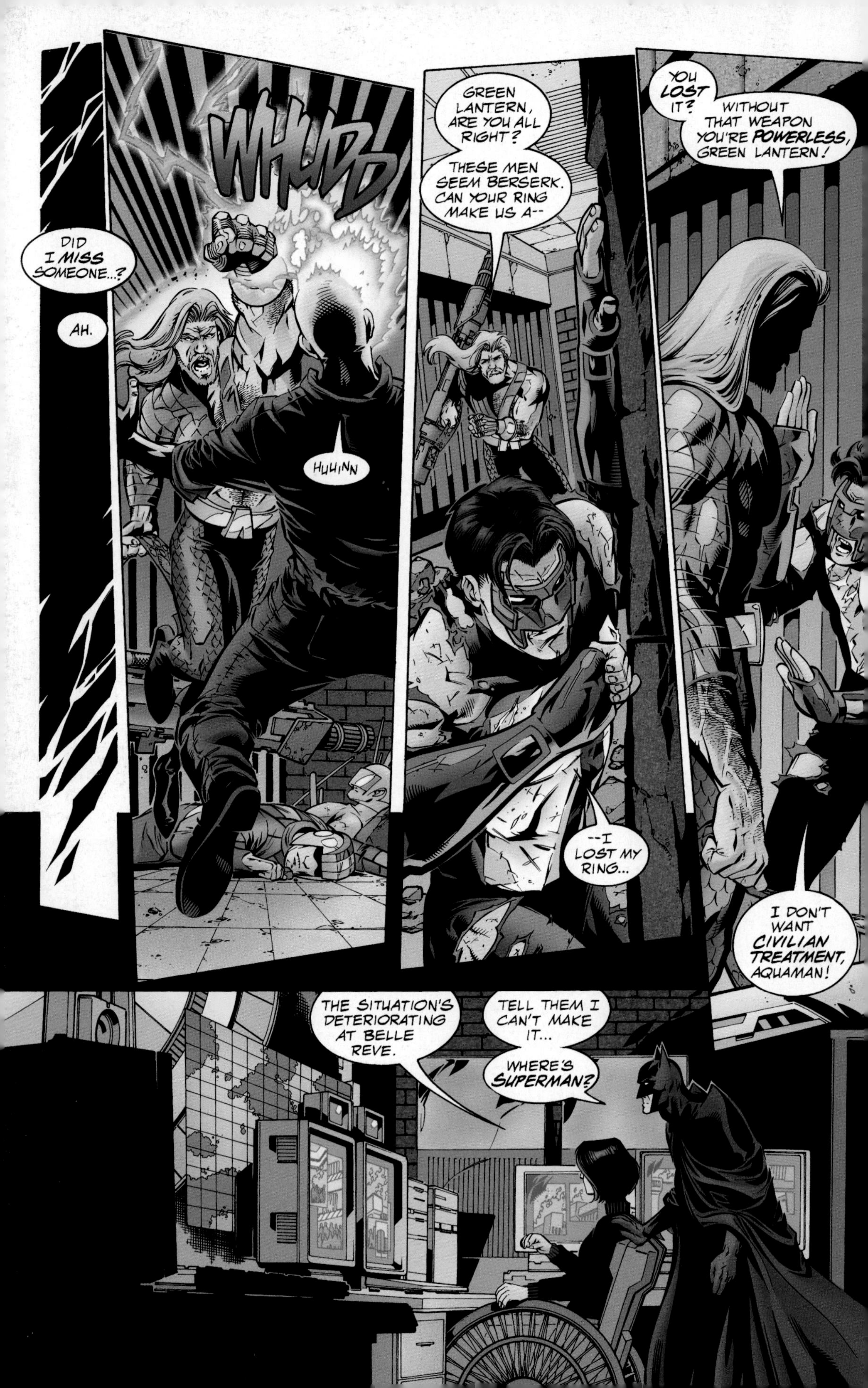
WHUDD
DID I MISS SOMEONE..?
AH.
HUHINN
GREEN LANTERN, ARE YOU ALL RIGHT?
THESE MEN SEEM BERSERK. CAN YOUR RING MAKE US A--
--I LOST MY RING...
YOU LOST IT?
WITHOUT THAT WEAPON YOU'RE POWERLESS, GREEN LANTERN!
I DON'T WANT CIVILIAN TREATMENT, AQUAMAN!
THE SITUATION'S DETERIORATING AT BELLE REVE.
TELL THEM I CAN'T MAKE IT...
WHERE'S SUPERMAN?

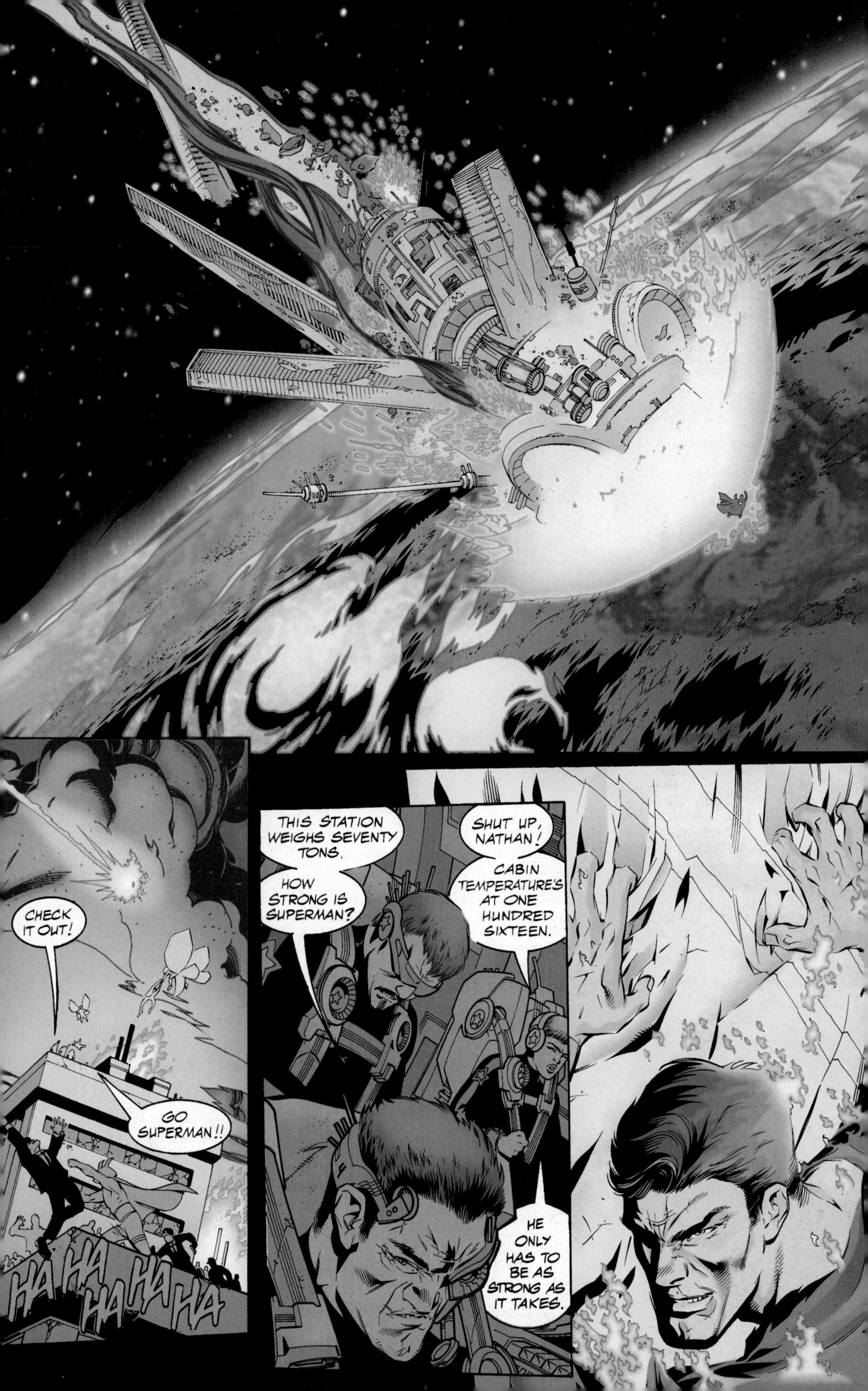
CHECK IT OUT!
GO SUPERMAN!!
HA HA HA HA HA HA HA
THIS STATION WEIGHS SEVENTY TONS.
HOW STRONG IS SUPERMAN?
SHUT UP, NATHAN!
CABIN TEMPERATURE'S AT ONE HUNDRED SIXTEEN.
HE ONLY HAS TO BE AS STRONG AS IT TAKES.

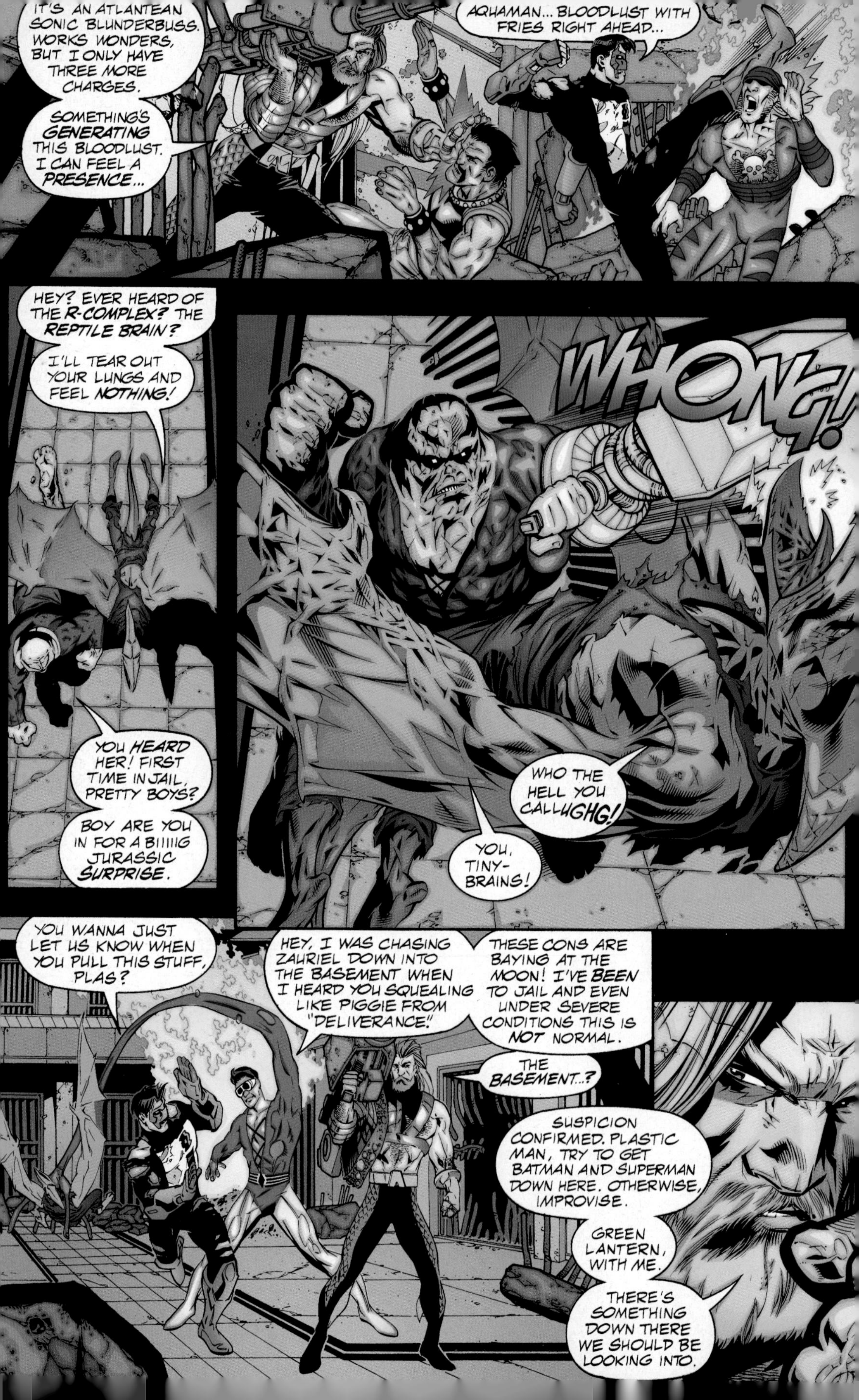
IT'S AN ATLANTEAN SONIC BLUNDERBUSS. WORKS WONDERS, BUT I ONLY HAVE THREE MORE CHARGES.
SOMETHING'S GENERATING THIS BLOODLUST. I CAN FEEL A PRESENCE...
AQUAMAN... BLOODLUST WITH FRIES RIGHT AHEAD...
HEY? EVER HEARD OF THE R-COMPLEX? THE REPTILE BRAIN?
I'LL TEAR OUT YOUR LUNGS AND FEEL NOTHING!
YOU HEARD HER! FIRST TIME IN JAIL, PRETTY BOYS?
BOY ARE YOU IN FOR A BIIIIG JURASSIC SURPRISE.
WHONG!
WHO THE HELL YOU CALLUGHG!
YOU, TINY-BRAINS!
YOU WANNA JUST LET US KNOW WHEN YOU PULL THIS STUFF, PLAS?
HEY, I WAS CHASING ZAURIEL DOWN INTO THE BASEMENT WHEN I HEARD YOU SQUEALING LIKE PIGGIE FROM "DELIVERANCE."
THESE CONS ARE BAYING AT THE MOON! I'VE BEEN TO JAIL AND EVEN UNDER SEVERE CONDITIONS THIS IS NOT NORMAL.
THE BASEMENT...?
SUSPICION CONFIRMED. PLASTIC MAN, TRY TO GET BATMAN AND SUPERMAN DOWN HERE. OTHERWISE, IMPROVISE.
GREEN LANTERN, WITH ME.
THERE'S SOMETHING DOWN THERE WE SHOULD BE LOOKING INTO.

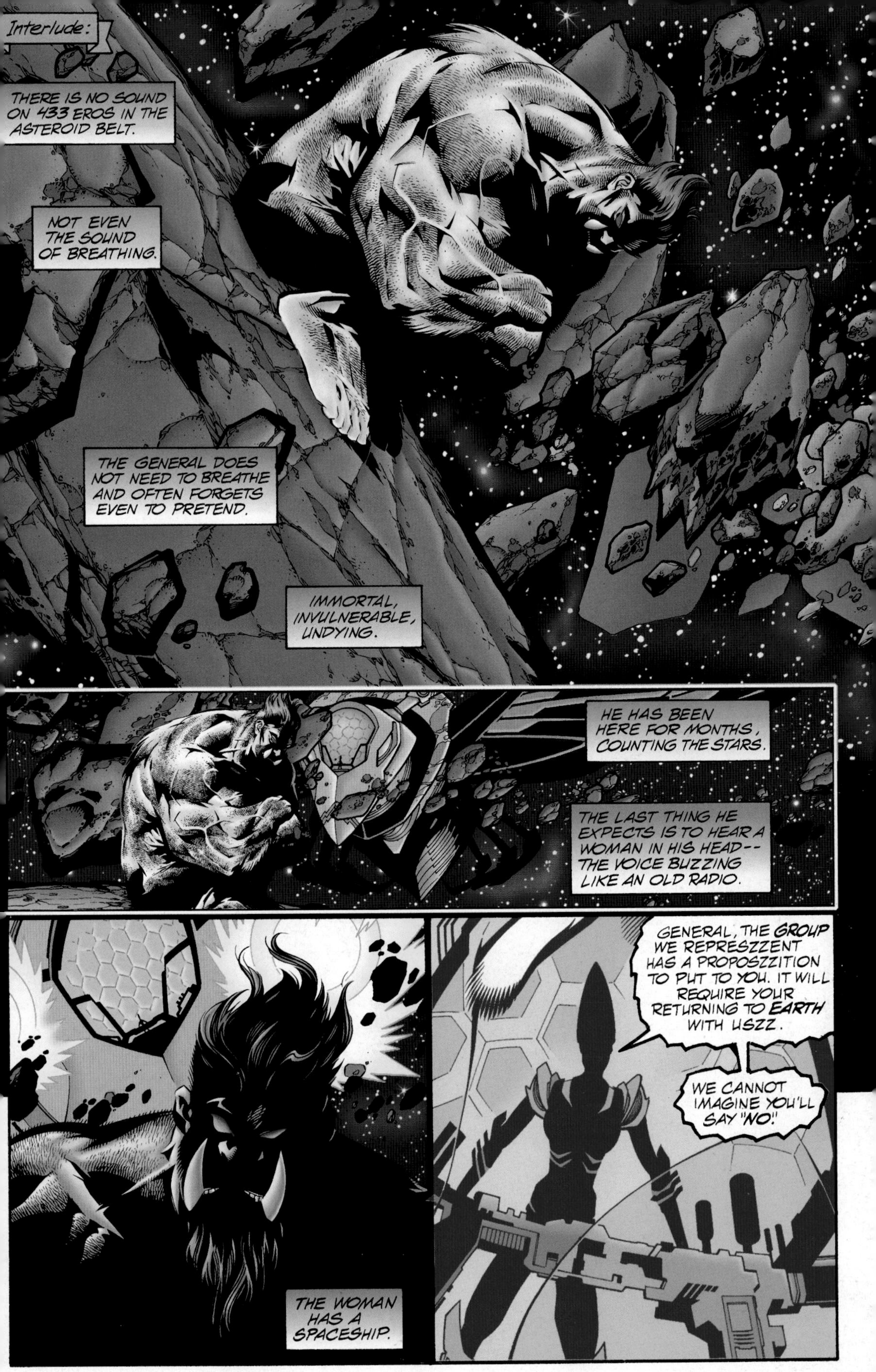
Interlude:
THERE IS NO SOUND ON 433 EROS IN THE ASTEROID BELT.
NOT EVEN THE SOUND OF BREATHING.
THE GENERAL DOES NOT NEED TO BREATHE AND OFTEN FORGETS EVEN TO PRETEND.
IMMORTAL, INVULNERABLE, UNDYING.
HE HAS BEEN HERE FOR MONTHS, COUNTING THE STARS.
THE LAST THING HE EXPECTS IS TO HEAR A WOMAN IN HIS HEAD-- THE VOICE BUZZING LIKE AN OLD RADIO.
THE WOMAN HAS A SPACESHIP.
GENERAL, THE GROUP WE REPRESZZENT HAS A PROPOSZZITION TO PUT TO YOU. IT WILL REQUIRE YOUR RETURNING TO EARTH WITH USZZ.
WE CANNOT IMAGINE YOU'LL SAY "NO!"

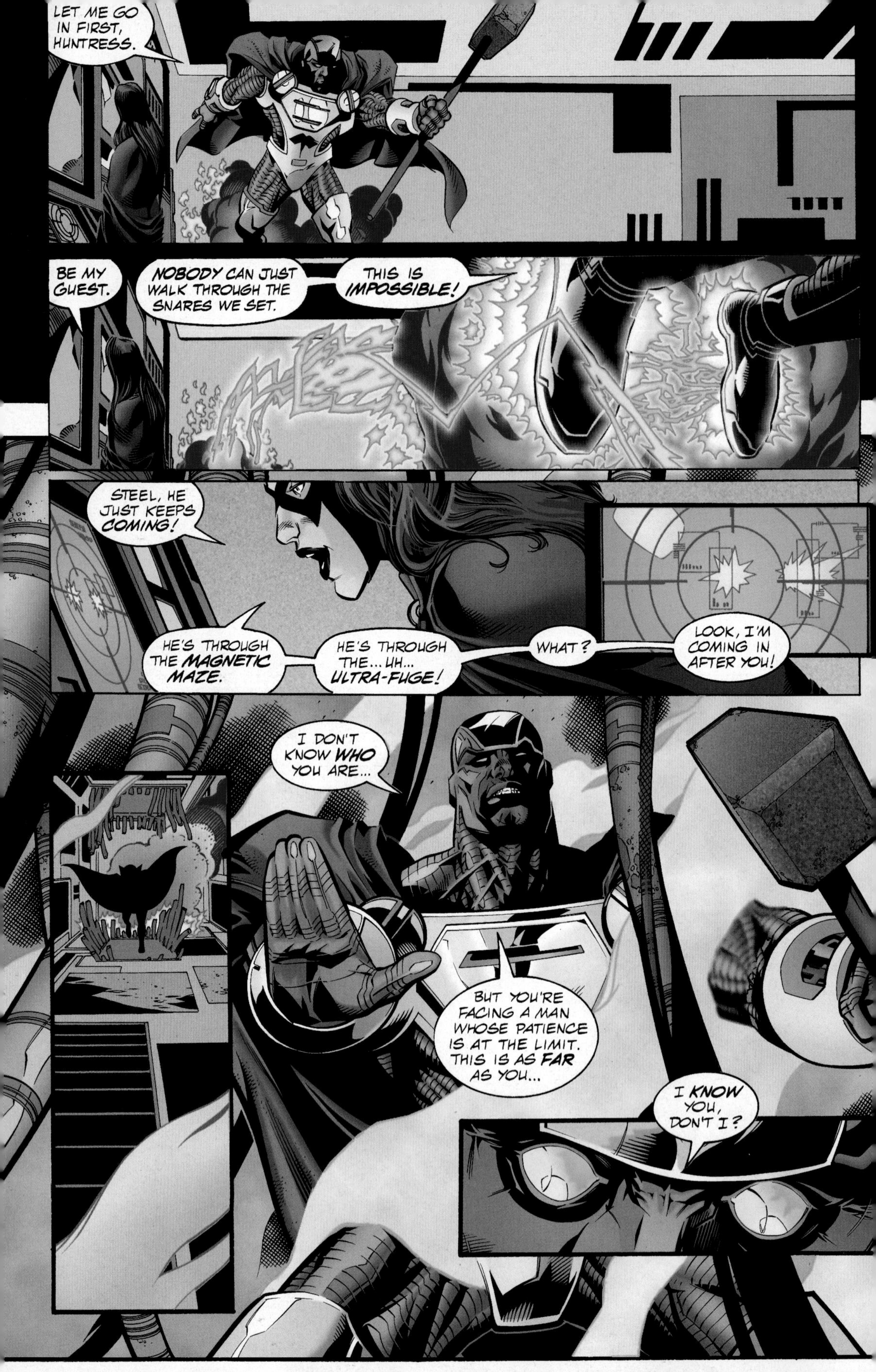
LET ME GO IN FIRST, HUNTRESS.
BE MY GUEST.
NOBODY CAN JUST WALK THROUGH THE SNARES WE SET.
THIS IS IMPOSSIBLE!
STEEL, HE JUST KEEPS COMING!
HE'S THROUGH THE MAGNETIC MAZE.
HE'S THROUGH THE... UH... ULTRA-FUGE!
WHAT?
LOOK, I'M COMING IN AFTER YOU!
I DON'T KNOW WHO YOU ARE...
BUT YOU'RE FACING A MAN WHOSE PATIENCE IS AT THE LIMIT. THIS IS AS FAR AS YOU...
I KNOW YOU, DON'T I?

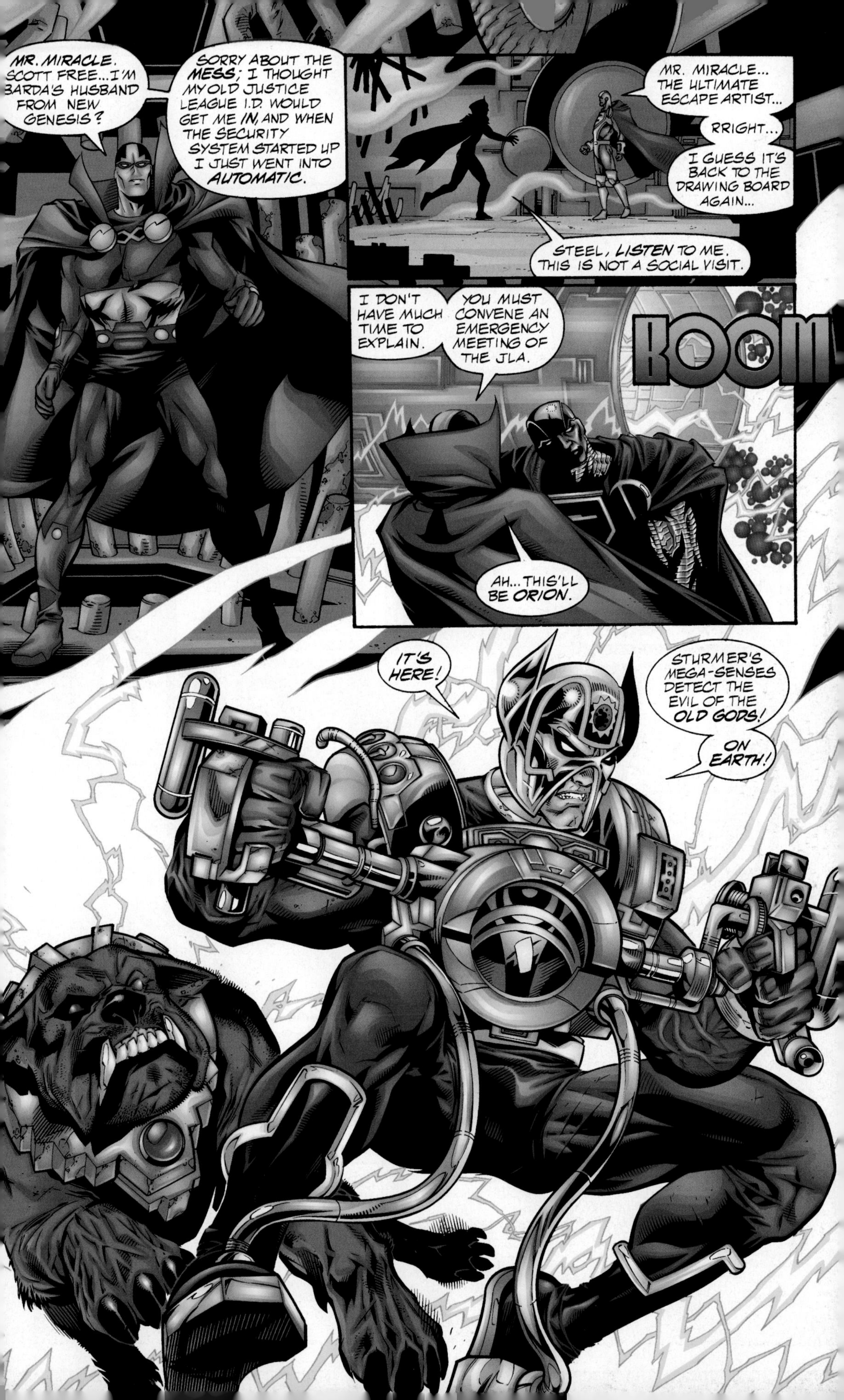
MR. MIRACLE. SCOTT FREE...I'M BARDA'S HUSBAND FROM NEW GENESIS?
SORRY ABOUT THE MESS; I THOUGHT MY OLD JUSTICE LEAGUE I.D. WOULD GET ME IN, AND WHEN THE SECURITY SYSTEM STARTED UP I JUST WENT INTO AUTOMATIC.
MR. MIRACLE... THE ULTIMATE ESCAPE ARTIST...
RRIGHT...
I GUESS IT'S BACK TO THE DRAWING BOARD AGAIN...
STEEL, LISTEN TO ME. THIS IS NOT A SOCIAL VISIT.
I DON'T HAVE MUCH TIME TO EXPLAIN.
YOU MUST CONVENE AN EMERGENCY MEETING OF THE JLA.
BOOM
AH...THIS'LL BE ORION.
IT'S HERE!
STURMER'S MEGA-SENSES DETECT THE EVIL OF THE OLD GODS!
ON EARTH!

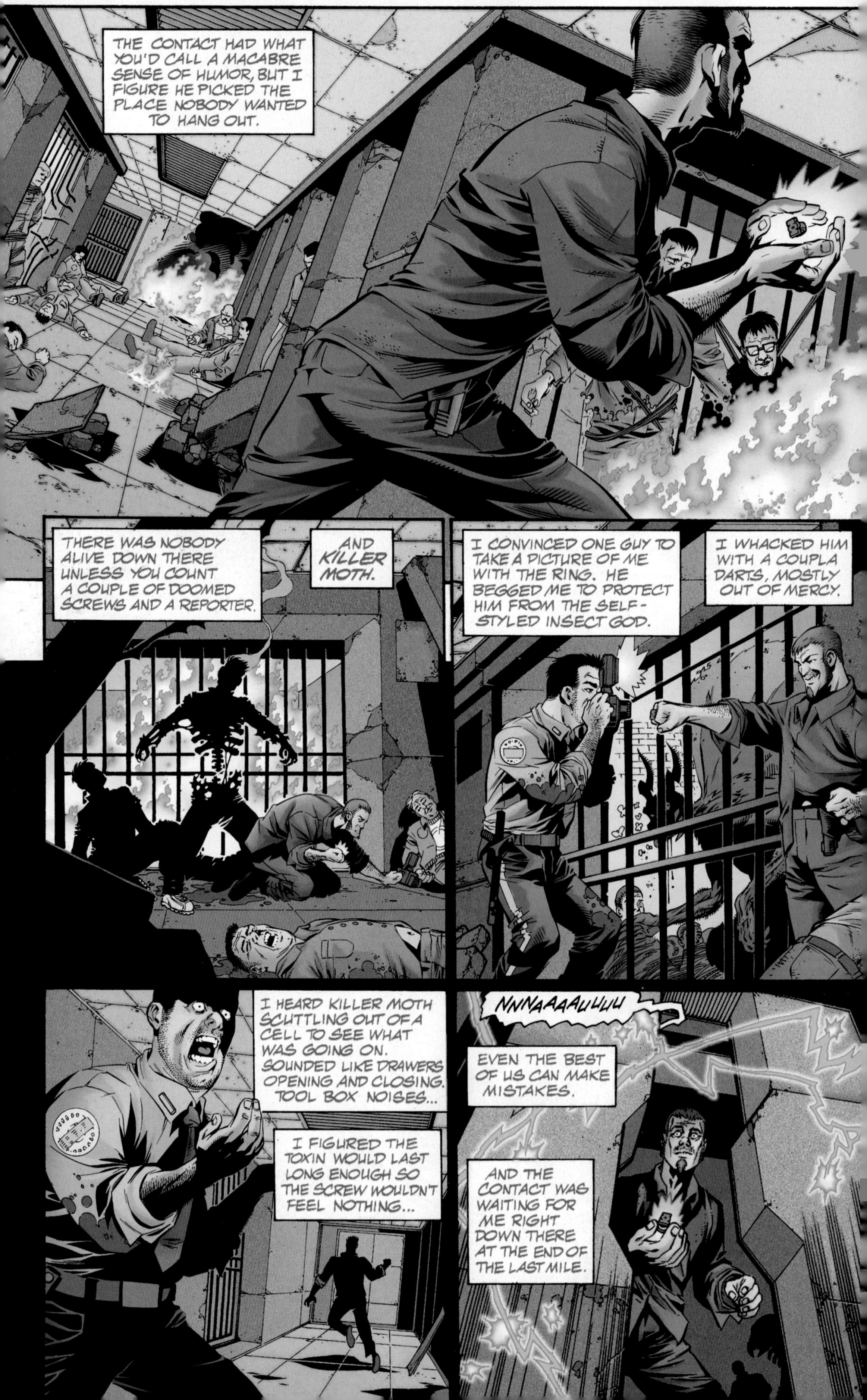
THE CONTACT HAD WHAT YOU'D CALL A MACABRE SENSE OF HUMOR, BUT I FIGURE HE PICKED THE PLACE NOBODY WANTED TO HANG OUT.
THERE WAS NOBODY ALIVE DOWN THERE UNLESS YOU COUNT A COUPLE OF DOOMED SCREWS AND A REPORTER.
AND KILLER MOTH.
I CONVINCED ONE GUY TO TAKE A PICTURE OF ME WITH THE RING. HE BEGGED ME TO PROTECT HIM FROM THE SELF-STYLED INSECT GOD.
I WHACKED HIM WITH A COUPLA DARTS, MOSTLY OUT OF MERCY.
I HEARD KILLER MOTH SCUTTLING OUT OF A CELL TO SEE WHAT WAS GOING ON. SOUNDED LIKE DRAWERS OPENING AND CLOSING. TOOL BOX NOISES...
I FIGURED THE TOXIN WOULD LAST LONG ENOUGH SO THE SCREW WOULDN'T FEEL NOTHING...
NNNAAAAULUU
EVEN THE BEST OF US CAN MAKE MISTAKES.
AND THE CONTACT WAS WAITING FOR ME RIGHT DOWN THERE AT THE END OF THE LAST MILE.

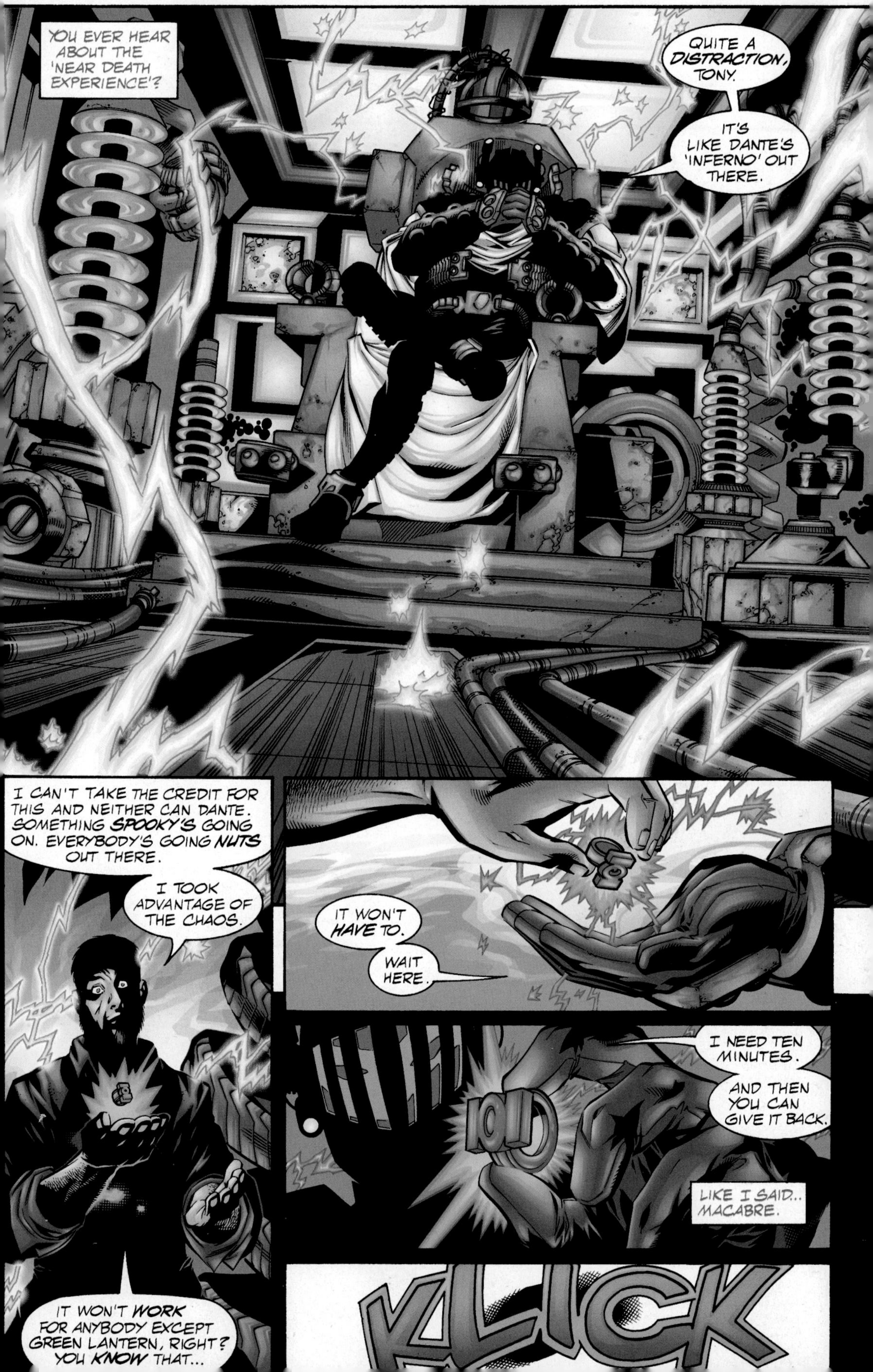
YOU EVER HEAR ABOUT THE 'NEAR DEATH EXPERIENCE'?
QUITE A DISTRACTION, TONY.
IT'S LIKE DANTE'S 'INFERNO' OUT THERE.
I CAN'T TAKE THE CREDIT FOR THIS AND NEITHER CAN DANTE. SOMETHING SPOOKY'S GOING ON. EVERYBODY'S GOING NUTS OUT THERE.
I TOOK ADVANTAGE OF THE CHAOS.
IT WON'T WORK FOR ANYBODY EXCEPT GREEN LANTERN, RIGHT? YOU KNOW THAT...
IT WON'T HAVE TO.
WAIT HERE.
I NEED TEN MINUTES.
AND THEN YOU CAN GIVE IT BACK.
LIKE I SAID... MACABRE.
KLICK

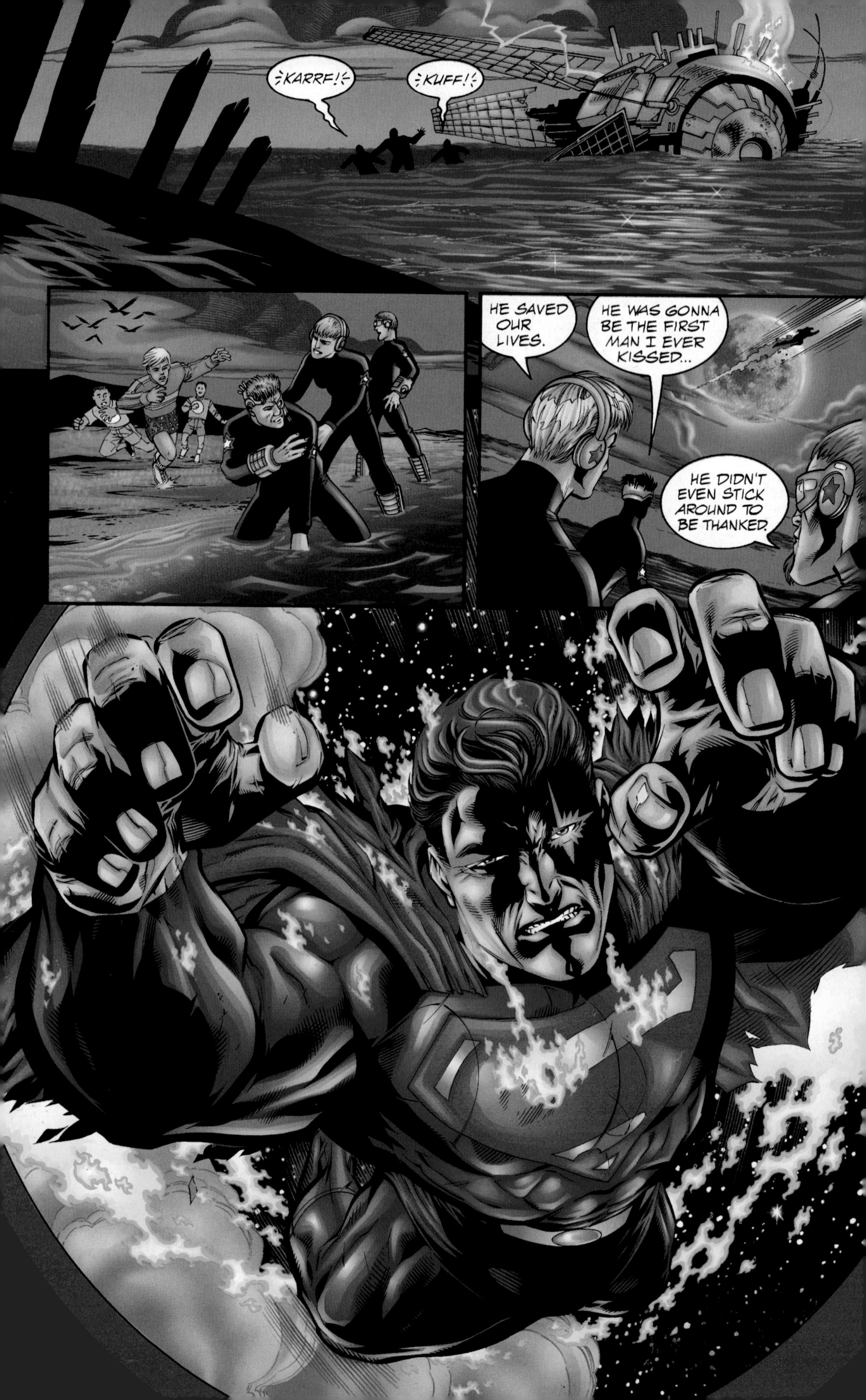
KARRF!
KUFF!
HE SAVED OUR LIVES.
HE WAS GONNA BE THE FIRST MAN I EVER KISSED...
HE DIDN'T EVEN STICK AROUND TO BE THANKED.

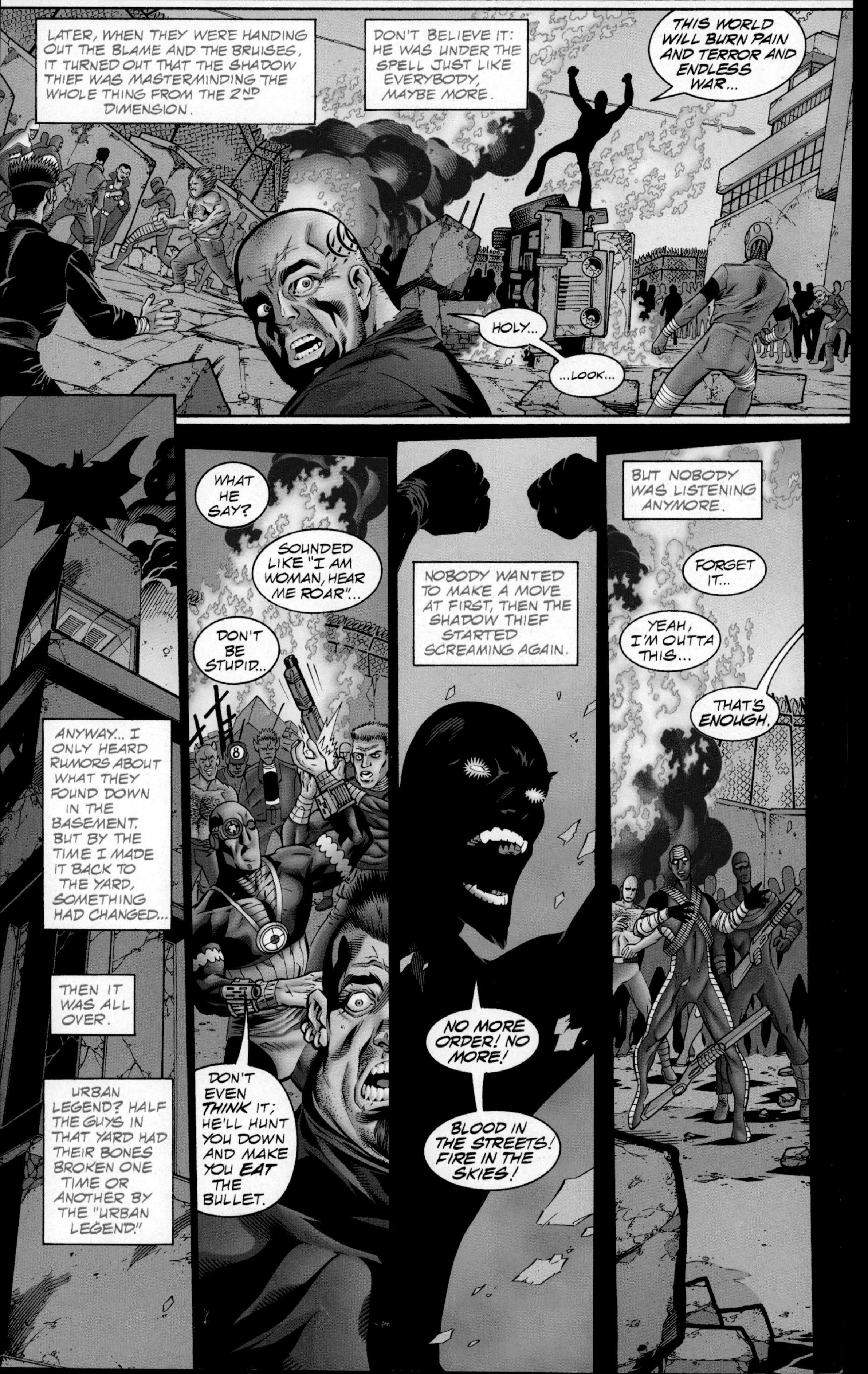

LATER, WHEN THEY WERE HANDING OUT THE BLAME AND THE BRUISES, IT TURNED OUT THAT THE SHADOW THIEF WAS MASTERMINDING THE WHOLE THING FROM THE 2ND DIMENSION.
DON'T BELIEVE IT: HE WAS UNDER THE SPELL JUST LIKE EVERYBODY, MAYBE MORE.
THIS WORLD WILL BURN PAIN AND TERROR AND ENDLESS WAR...
HOLY...
...LOOK...
ANYWAY... I ONLY HEARD RUMORS ABOUT WHAT THEY FOUND DOWN IN THE BASEMENT, BUT BY THE TIME I MADE IT BACK TO THE YARD, SOMETHING HAD CHANGED...
THEN IT WAS ALL OVER.
URBAN LEGEND? HALF THE GUYS IN THAT YARD HAD THEIR BONES BROKEN ONE TIME OR ANOTHER BY THE "URBAN LEGEND."
WHAT HE SAY?
SOUNDED LIKE "I AM WOMAN, HEAR ME ROAR"...
DON'T BE STUPID...
DON'T EVEN THINK IT; HE'LL HUNT YOU DOWN AND MAKE YOU EAT THE BULLET.
NOBODY WANTED TO MAKE A MOVE AT FIRST, THEN THE SHADOW THIEF STARTED SCREAMING AGAIN.
NO MORE ORDER! NO MORE!
BLOOD IN THE STREETS! FIRE IN THE SKIES!
BUT NOBODY WAS LISTENING ANYMORE.
FORGET IT...
YEAH, I'M OUTTA THIS...
THAT'S ENOUGH.

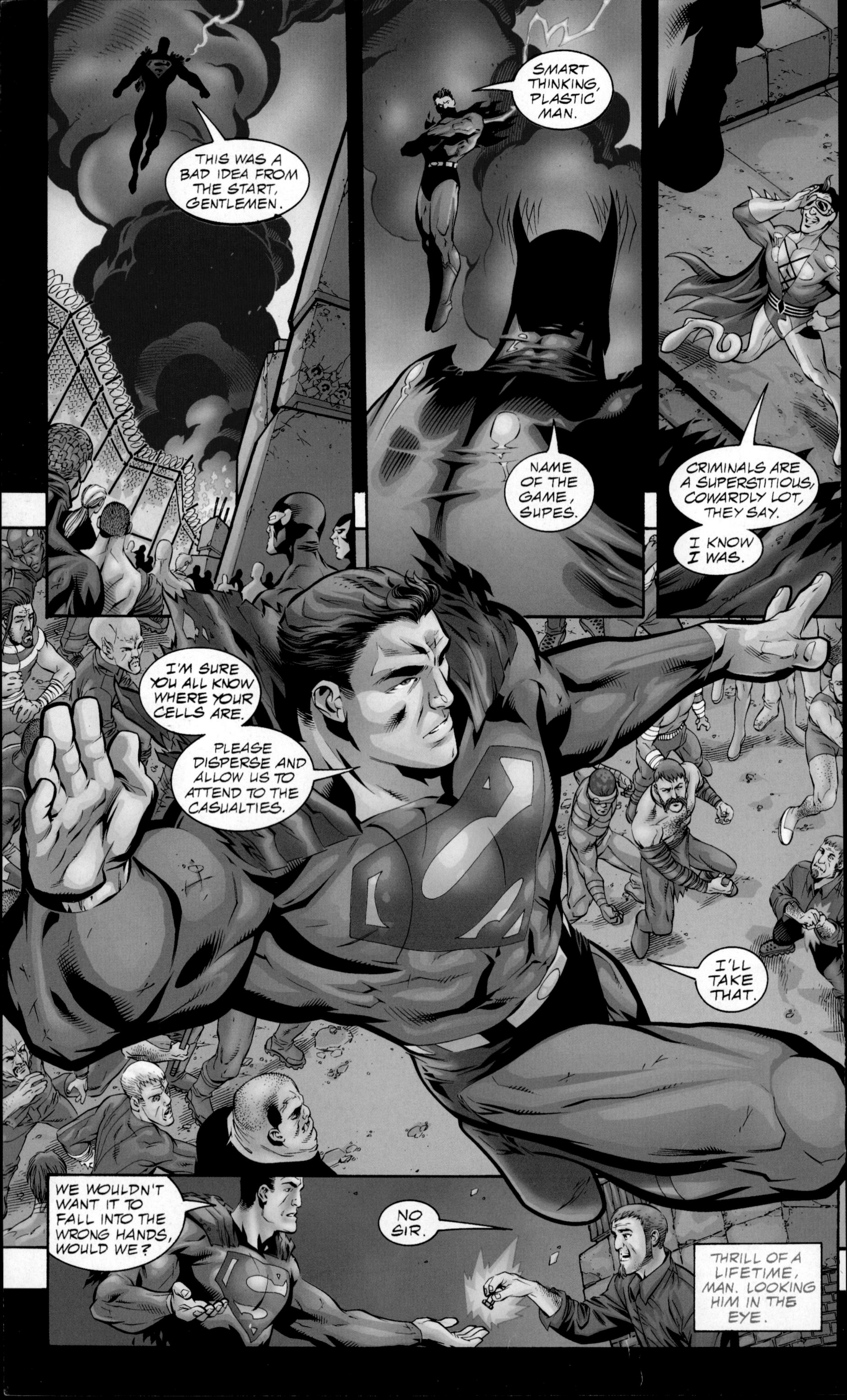
THIS WAS A BAD IDEA FROM THE START, GENTLEMEN.
SMART THINKING, PLASTIC MAN.
NAME OF THE GAME, SUPES.
CRIMINALS ARE A SUPERSTITIOUS, COWARDLY LOT, THEY SAY.
I KNOW I WAS.
I'M SURE YOU ALL KNOW WHERE YOUR CELLS ARE.
PLEASE DISPERSE AND ALLOW US TO ATTEND TO THE CASUALTIES.
I'LL TAKE THAT.
WE WOULDN'T WANT IT TO FALL INTO THE WRONG HANDS, WOULD WE?
NO SIR.
THRILL OF A LIFETIME, MAN. LOOKING HIM IN THE EYE.

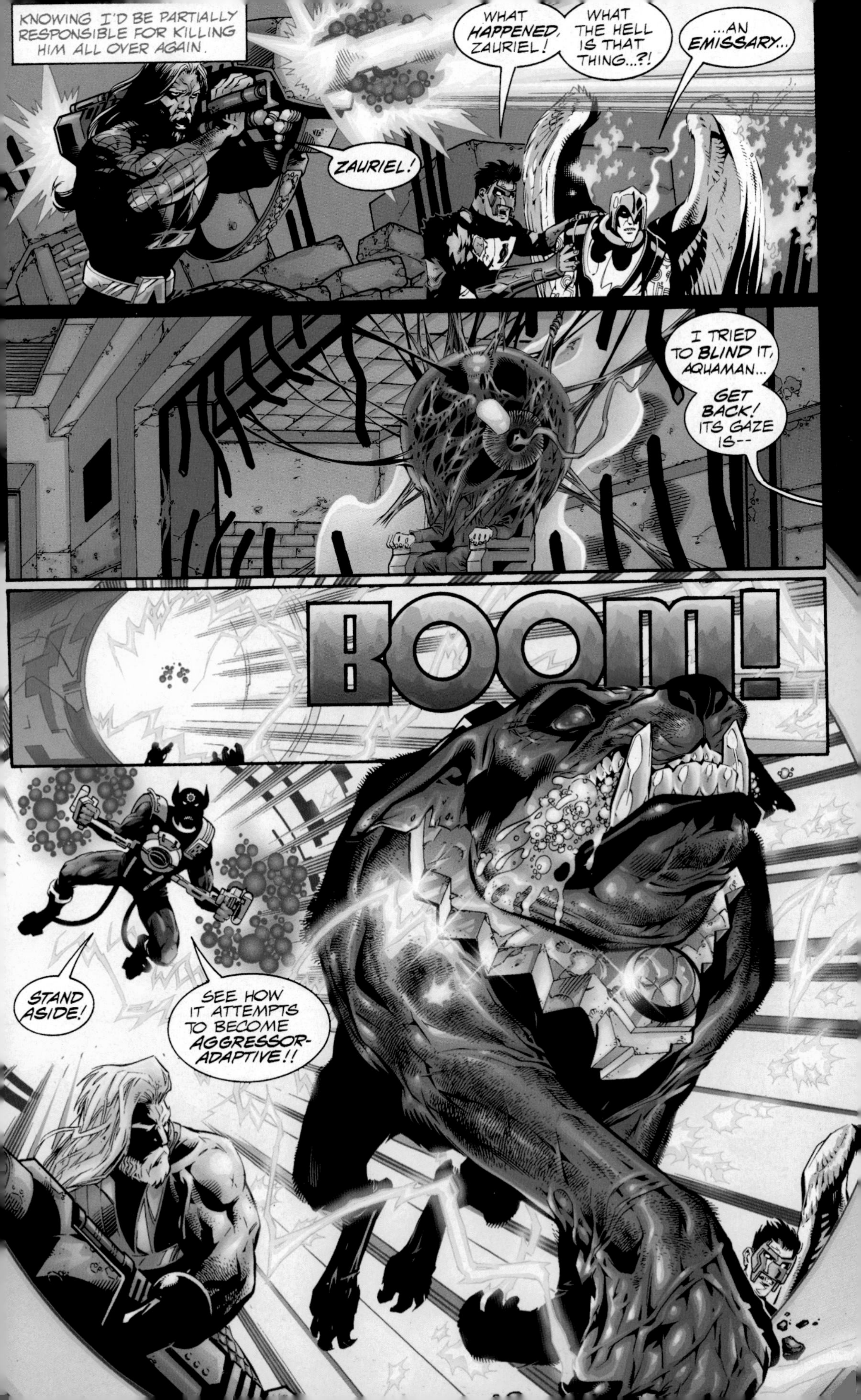
KNOWING I'D BE PARTIALLY RESPONSIBLE FOR KILLING HIM ALL OVER AGAIN.
WHAT HAPPENED, ZAURIEL!
WHAT THE HELL IS THAT THING...?!
...AN EMISSARY...
ZAURIEL!
I TRIED TO BLIND IT, AQUAMAN...
GET BACK! ITS GAZE IS--
BOOM!
STAND ASIDE!
SEE HOW IT ATTEMPTS TO BECOME AGGRESSOR-ADAPTIVE!!

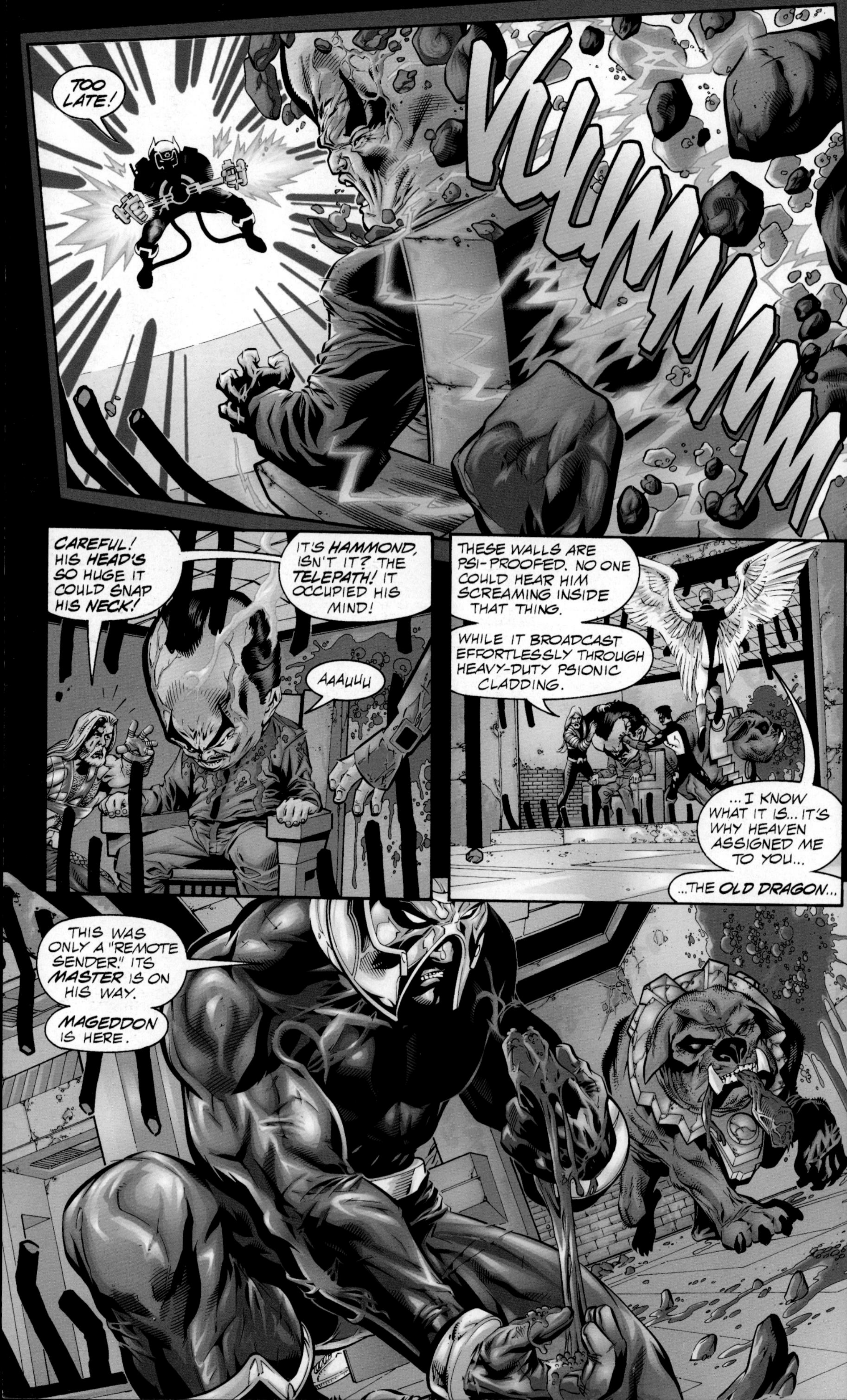

TOO LATE!
VVUUMMMMMM
CAREFUL! HIS HEAD'S SO HUGE IT COULD SNAP HIS NECK!
IT'S HAMMOND, ISN'T IT? THE TELEPATH! IT OCCUPIED HIS MIND!
AAAUUU
THESE WALLS ARE PSI-PROOFED. NO ONE COULD HEAR HIM SCREAMING INSIDE THAT THING.
WHILE IT BROADCAST EFFORTLESSLY THROUGH HEAVY-DUTY PSIONIC CLADDING.
...I KNOW WHAT IT IS... IT'S WHY HEAVEN ASSIGNED ME TO YOU...
...THE OLD DRAGON...
THIS WAS ONLY A "REMOTE SENDER." ITS MASTER IS ON HIS WAY.
MAGEDDON IS HERE.

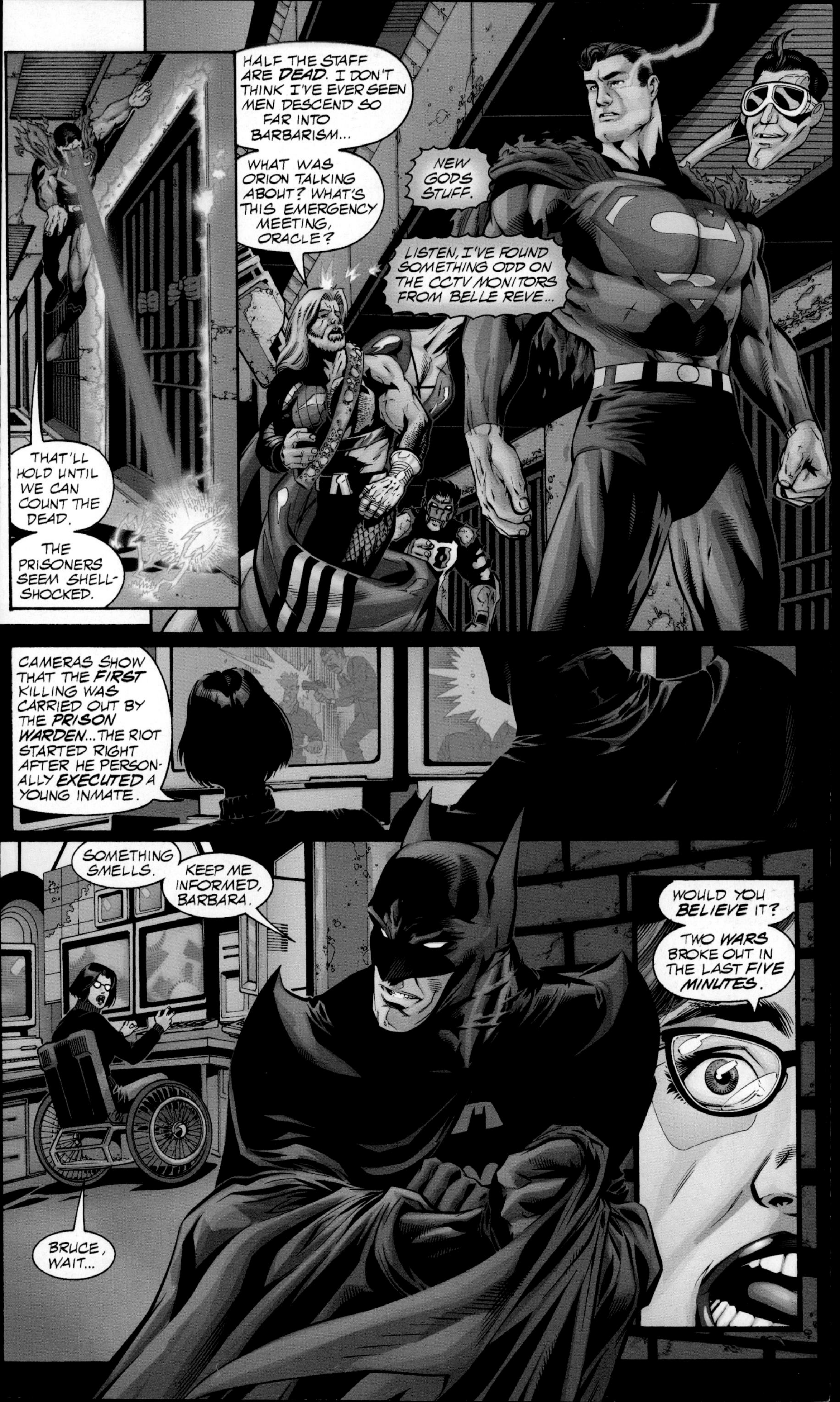

THAT'LL HOLD UNTIL WE CAN COUNT THE DEAD.
THE PRISONERS SEEM SHELL-SHOCKED.
HALF THE STAFF ARE DEAD. I DON'T THINK I'VE EVER SEEN MEN DESCEND SO FAR INTO BARBARISM...
WHAT WAS ORION TALKING ABOUT? WHAT'S THIS EMERGENCY MEETING, ORACLE?
NEW GODS STUFF.
LISTEN, I'VE FOUND SOMETHING ODD ON THE CCTV MONITORS FROM BELLE REVE...
CAMERAS SHOW THAT THE FIRST KILLING WAS CARRIED OUT BY THE PRISON WARDEN... THE RIOT STARTED RIGHT AFTER HE PERSONALLY EXECUTED A YOUNG INMATE.
SOMETHING SMELLS.
KEEP ME INFORMED, BARBARA.
BRUCE, WAIT...
WOULD YOU BELIEVE IT?
TWO WARS BROKE OUT IN THE LAST FIVE MINUTES.

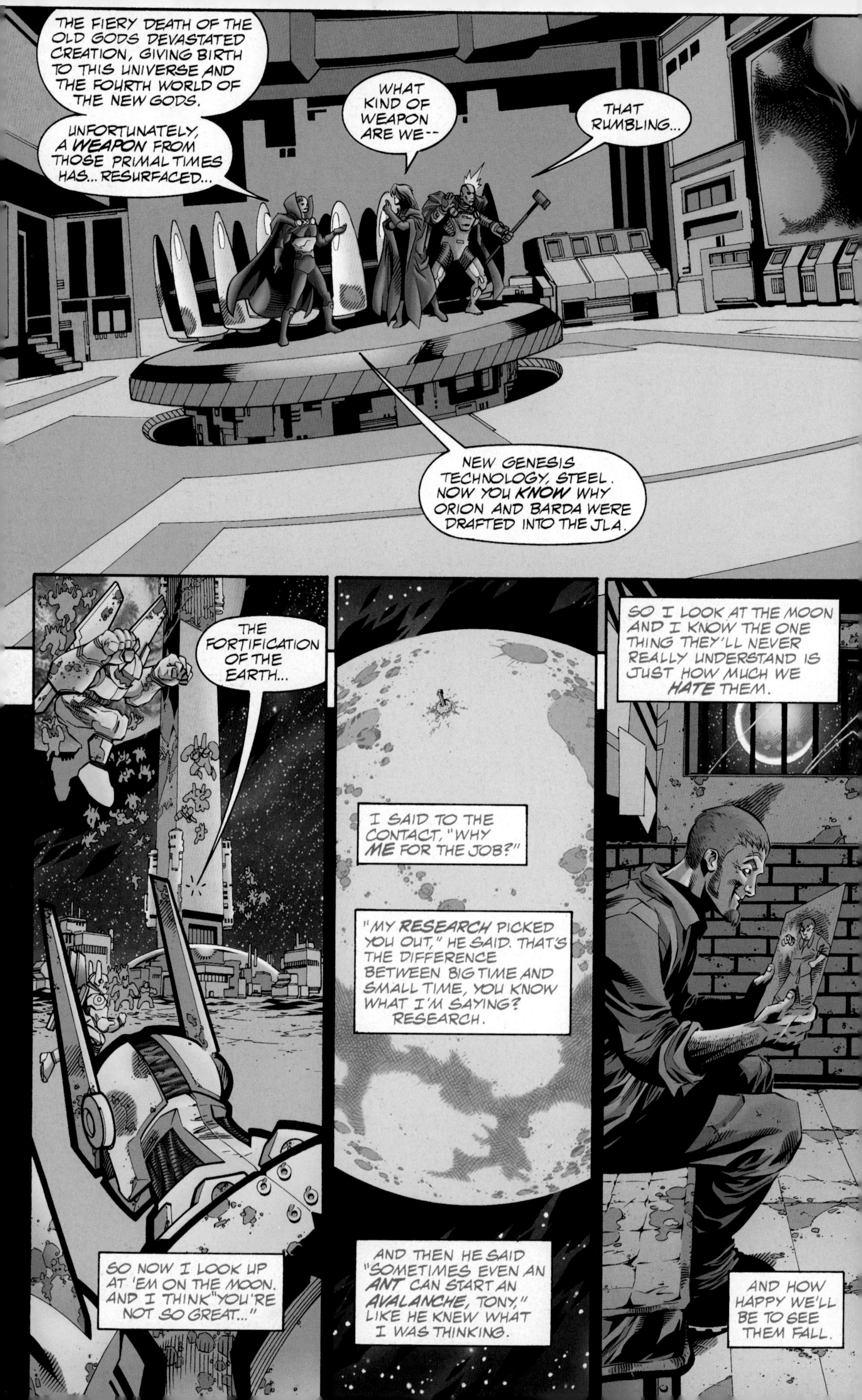

THE FIERY DEATH OF THE OLD GODS DEVASTATED CREATION, GIVING BIRTH TO THIS UNIVERSE AND THE FOURTH WORLD OF THE NEW GODS.
UNFORTUNATELY, A WEAPON FROM THOSE PRIMAL TIMES HAS... RESURFACED...
WHAT KIND OF WEAPON ARE WE--
THAT RUMBLING...
NEW GENESIS TECHNOLOGY, STEEL. NOW YOU KNOW WHY ORION AND BARDA WERE DRAFTED INTO THE JLA.
THE FORTIFICATION OF THE EARTH...
SO NOW I LOOK UP AT 'EM ON THE MOON. AND I THINK "YOU'RE NOT SO GREAT..."
I SAID TO THE CONTACT, "WHY ME FOR THE JOB?"
"MY RESEARCH PICKED YOU OUT," HE SAID. THAT'S THE DIFFERENCE BETWEEN BIG TIME AND SMALL TIME, YOU KNOW WHAT I'M SAYING? RESEARCH.
AND THEN HE SAID "SOMETIMES EVEN AN ANT CAN START AN AVALANCHE, TONY," LIKE HE KNEW WHAT I WAS THINKING.
SO I LOOK AT THE MOON AND I KNOW THE ONE THING THEY'LL NEVER REALLY UNDERSTAND IS JUST HOW MUCH WE HATE THEM.
AND HOW HAPPY WE'LL BE TO SEE THEM FALL.

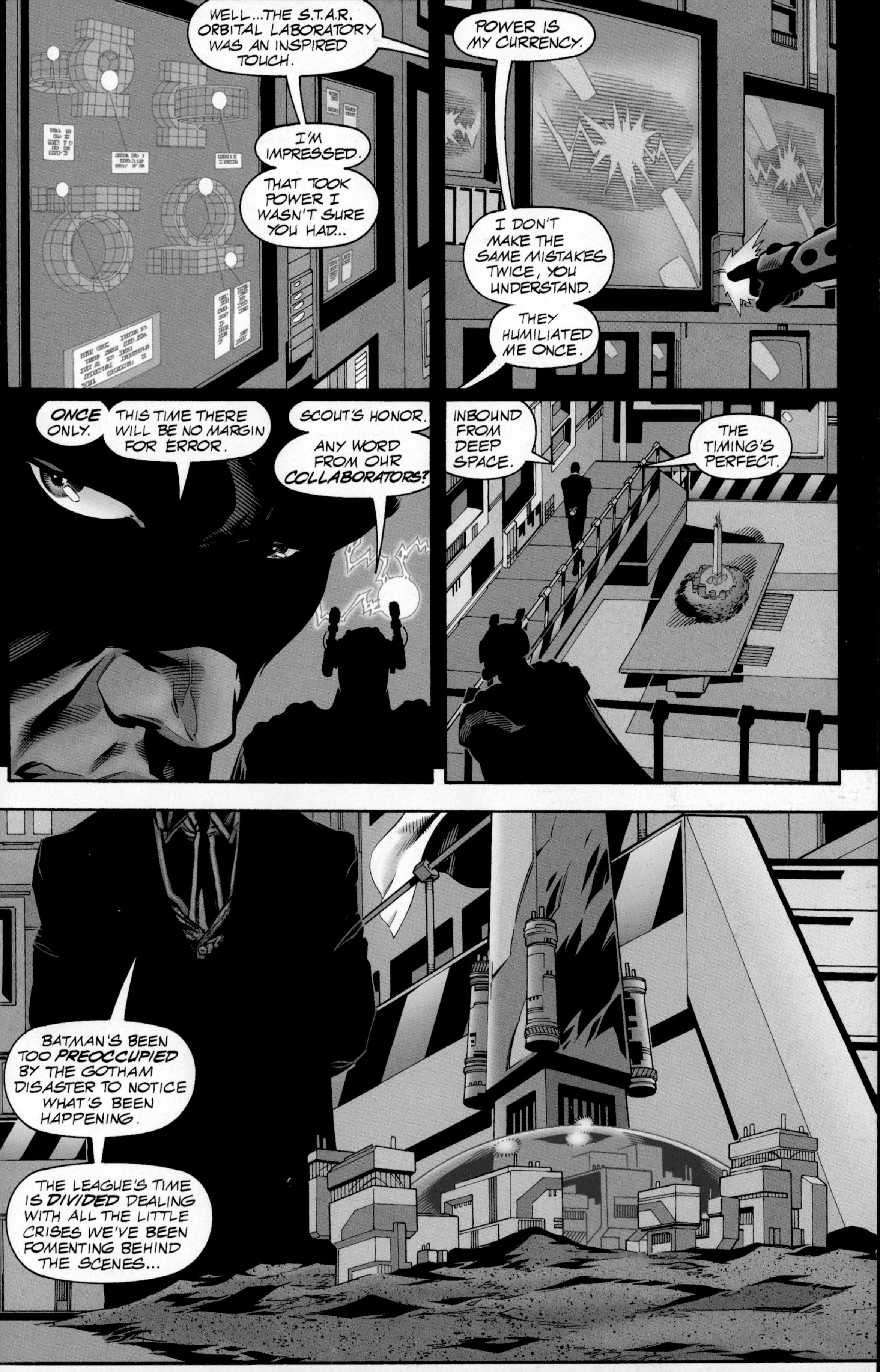
WELL...THE S.T.A.R. ORBITAL LABORATORY WAS AN INSPIRED TOUCH.
I'M IMPRESSED.
THAT TOOK POWER I WASN'T SURE YOU HAD...
POWER IS MY CURRENCY.
I DON'T MAKE THE SAME MISTAKES TWICE, YOU UNDERSTAND.
THEY HUMILIATED ME ONCE.
ONCE ONLY.
THIS TIME THERE WILL BE NO MARGIN FOR ERROR.
SCOUT'S HONOR.
ANY WORD FROM OUR COLLABORATORS?
INBOUND FROM DEEP SPACE.
THE TIMING'S PERFECT.
BATMAN'S BEEN TOO PREOCCUPIED BY THE GOTHAM DISASTER TO NOTICE WHAT'S BEEN HAPPENING.
THE LEAGUE'S TIME IS DIVIDED DEALING WITH ALL THE LITTLE CRISES WE'VE BEEN FOMENTING BEHIND THE SCENES...

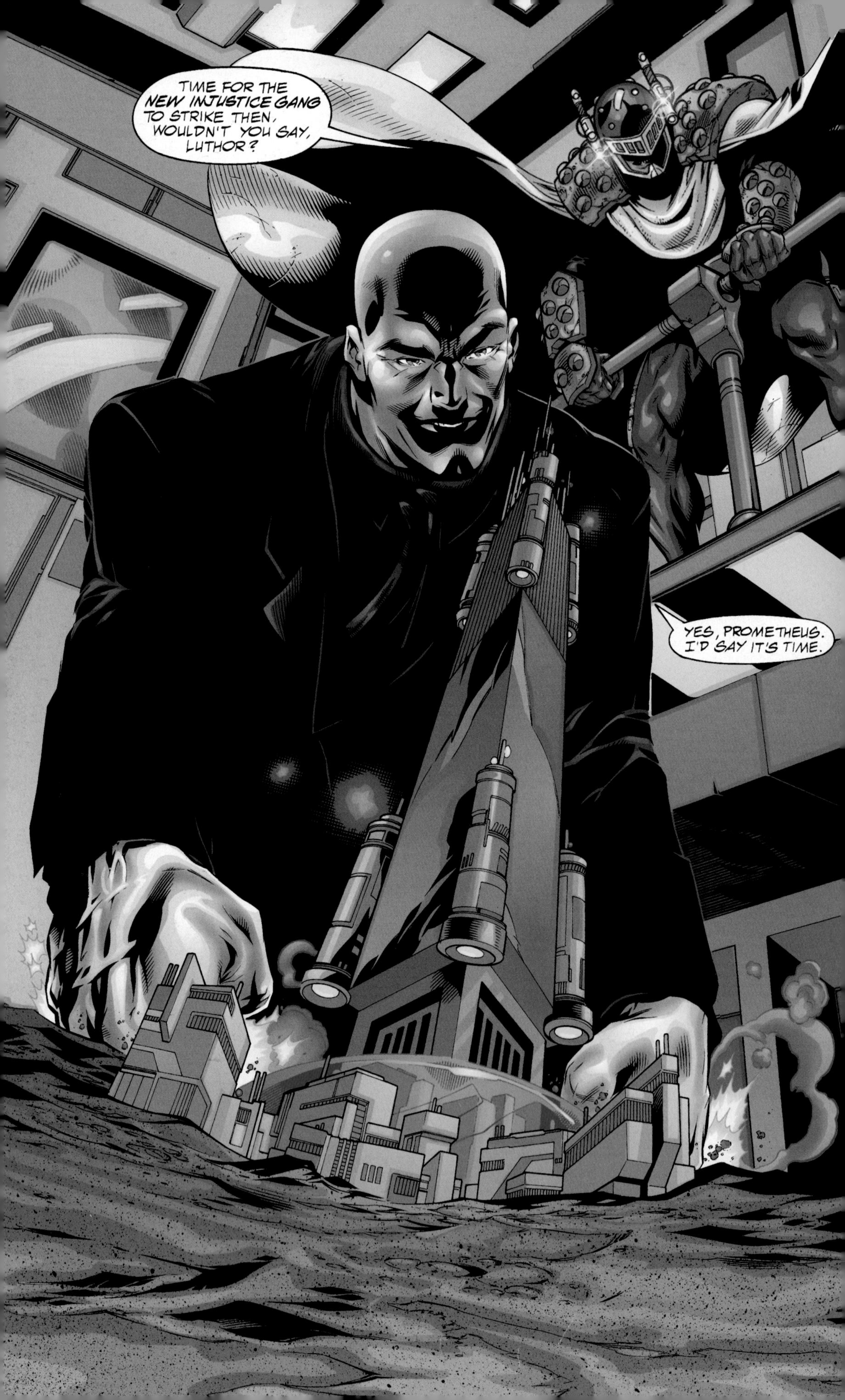
TIME FOR THE NEW INJUSTICE GANG TO STRIKE THEN, WOULDN'T YOU SAY, LUTHOR?
YES, PROMETHEUS. I'D SAY IT'S TIME.

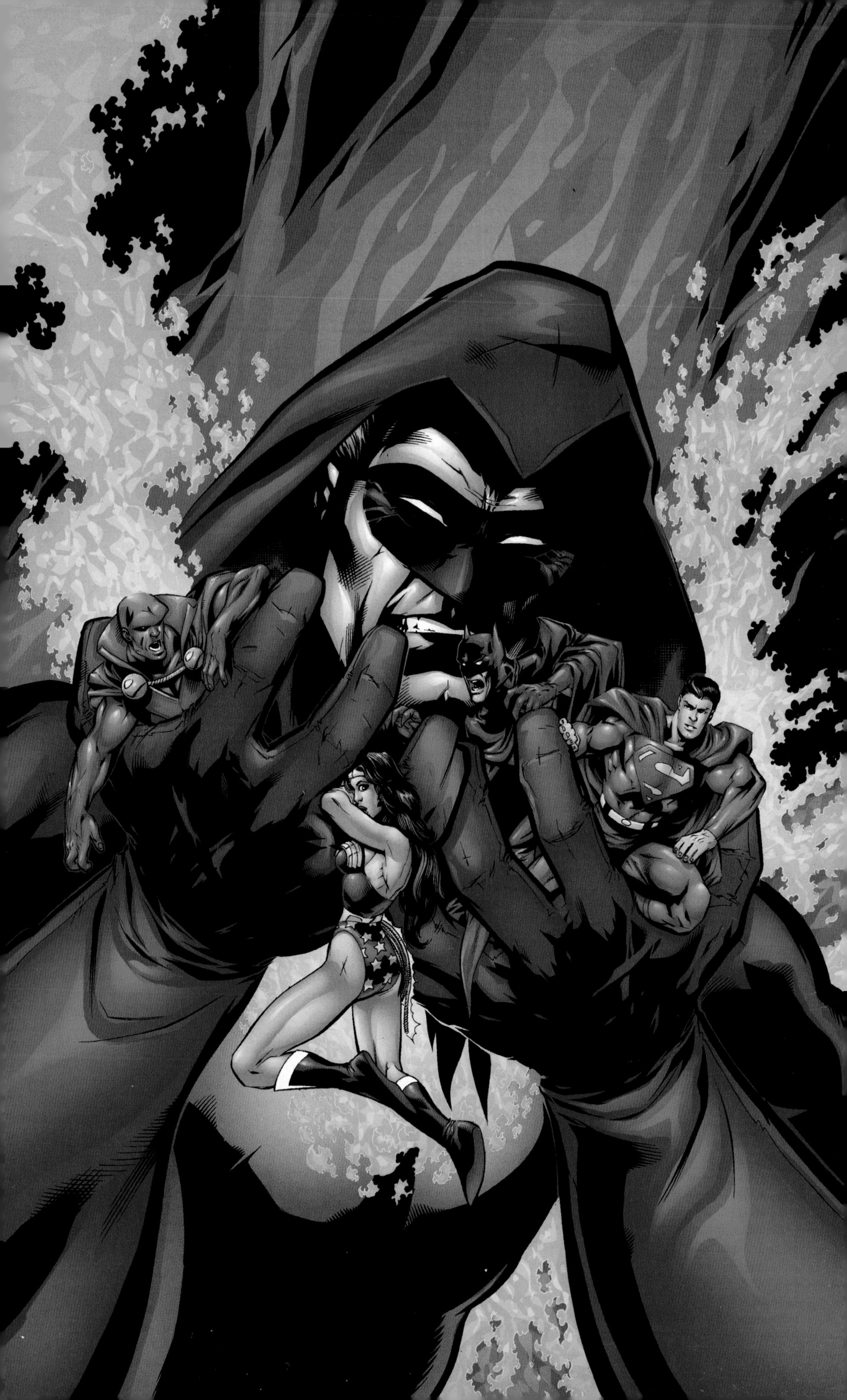

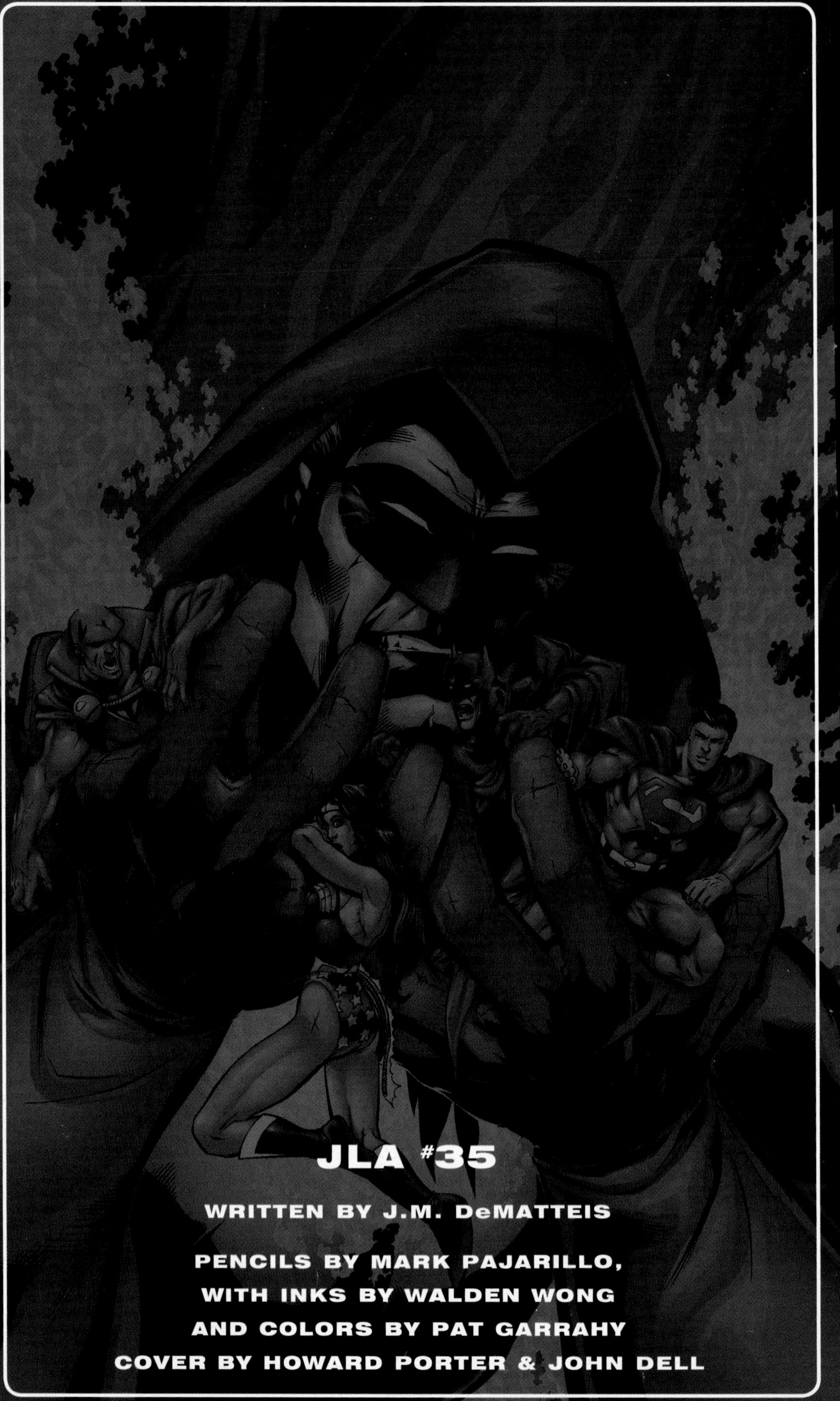

JLA #35

WRITTEN BY J.M. DeMATTEIS

**PENCILS BY MARK PAJARILLO,
WITH INKS BY WALDEN WONG
AND COLORS BY PAT GARRAHY
COVER BY HOWARD PORTER & JOHN DELL**

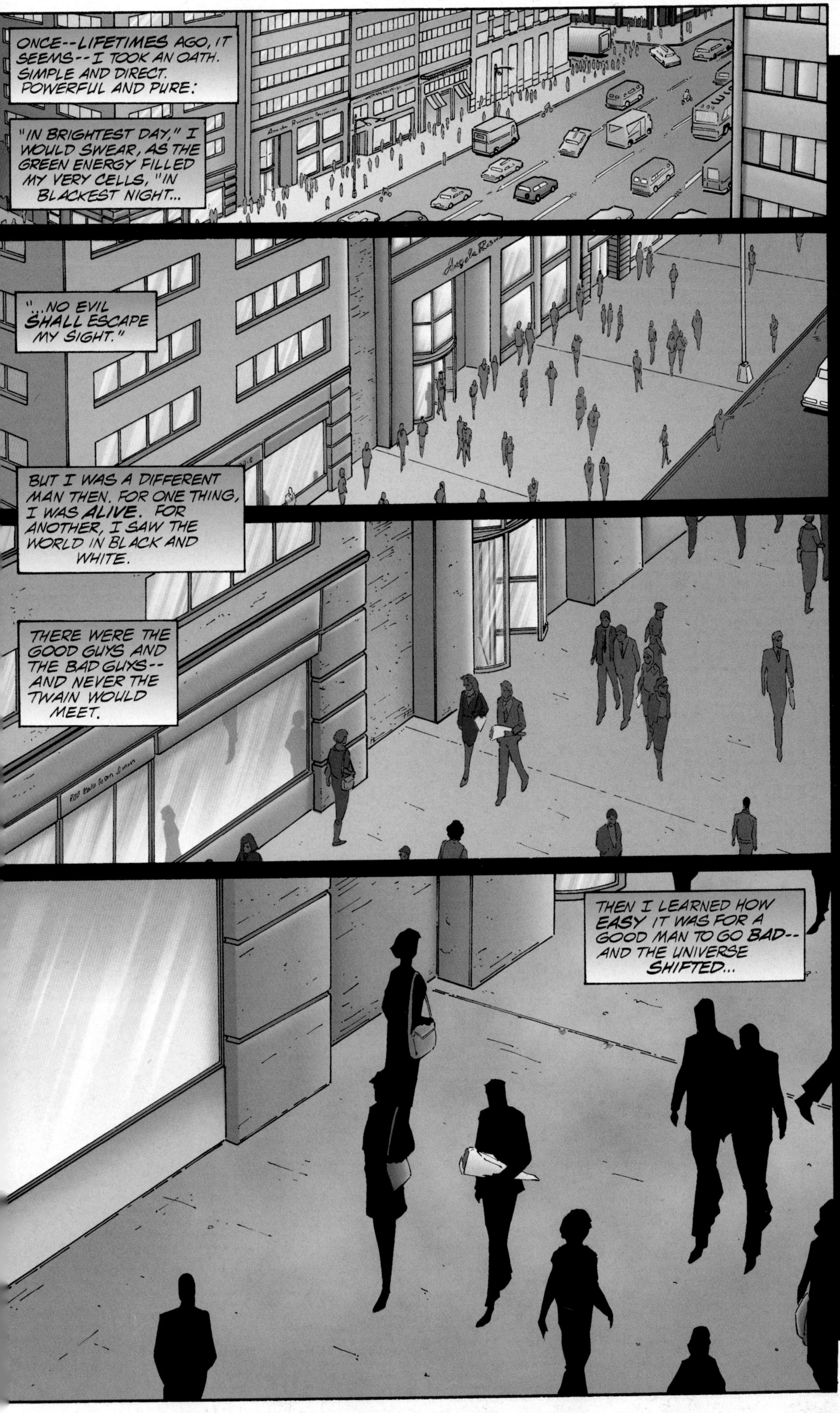
ONCE--LIFETIMES AGO, IT SEEMS--I TOOK AN OATH. SIMPLE AND DIRECT. POWERFUL AND PURE:
"IN BRIGHTEST DAY," I WOULD SWEAR, AS THE GREEN ENERGY FILLED MY VERY CELLS, "IN BLACKEST NIGHT...
"...NO EVIL SHALL ESCAPE MY SIGHT."
BUT I WAS A DIFFERENT MAN THEN. FOR ONE THING, I WAS ALIVE. FOR ANOTHER, I SAW THE WORLD IN BLACK AND WHITE.
THERE WERE THE GOOD GUYS AND THE BAD GUYS--AND NEVER THE TWAIN WOULD MEET.
THEN I LEARNED HOW EASY IT WAS FOR A GOOD MAN TO GO BAD--AND THE UNIVERSE SHIFTED...

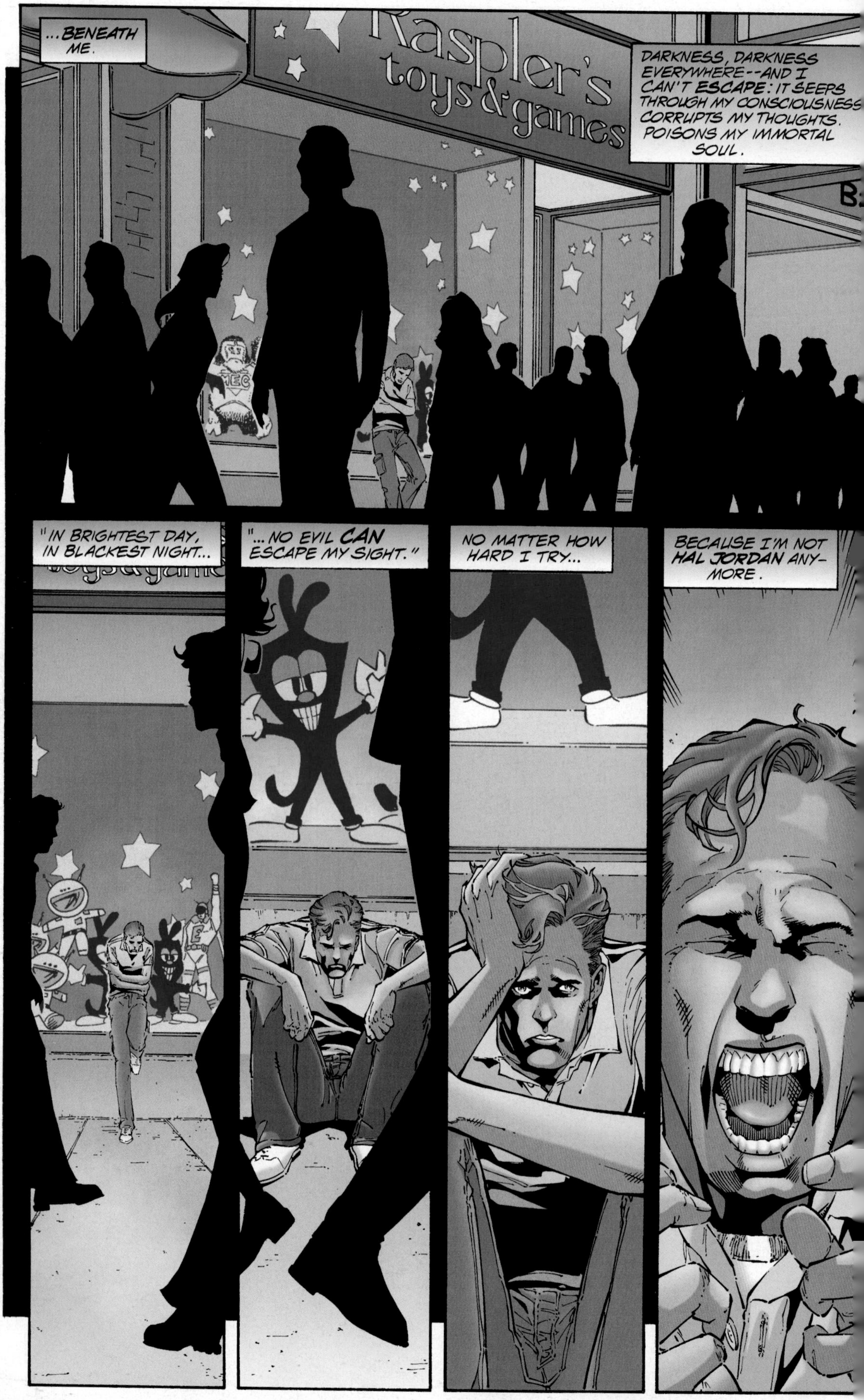

...BENEATH ME.
Raspler's toys & games
DARKNESS, DARKNESS EVERYWHERE--AND I CAN'T ESCAPE: IT SEEPS THROUGH MY CONSCIOUSNESS. CORRUPTS MY THOUGHTS. POISONS MY IMMORTAL SOUL.
"IN BRIGHTEST DAY, IN BLACKEST NIGHT...
"...NO EVIL CAN ESCAPE MY SIGHT."
NO MATTER HOW HARD I TRY...
BECAUSE I'M NOT HAL JORDAN ANY-MORE.

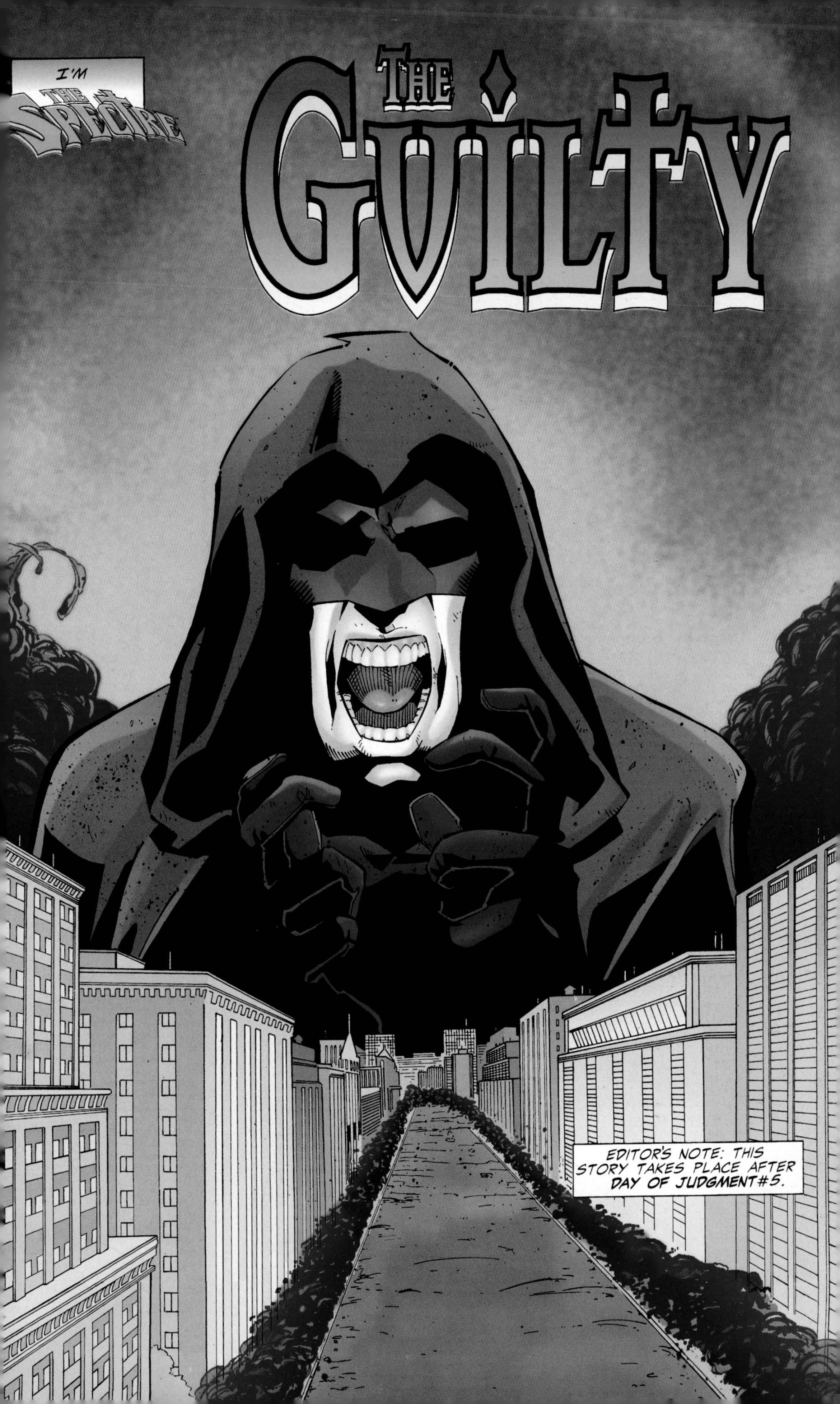
I'M
THE SPECTRE
THE GUILTY
EDITOR'S NOTE: THIS STORY TAKES PLACE AFTER DAY OF JUDGMENT #5.

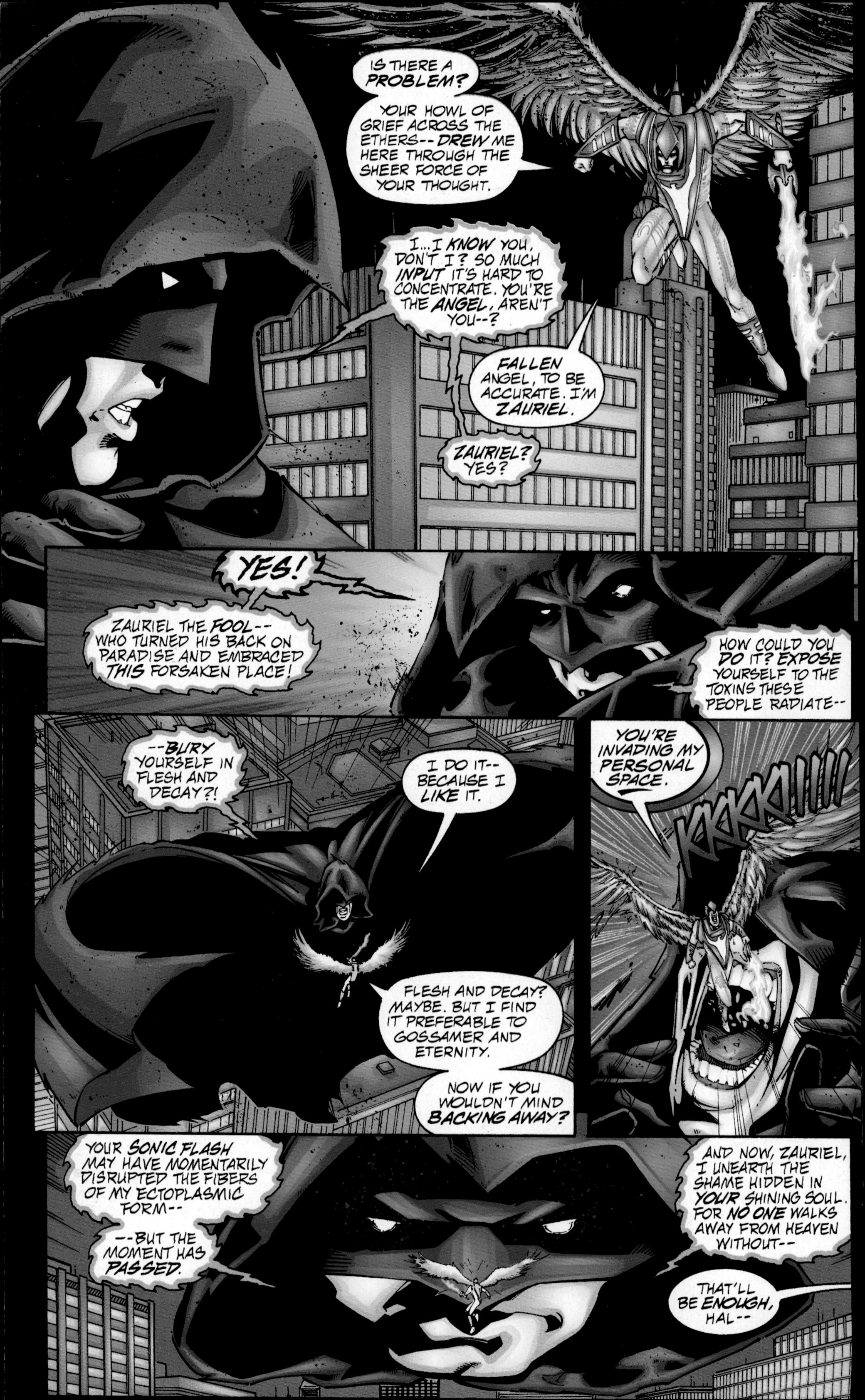

IS THERE A PROBLEM?
YOUR HOWL OF GRIEF ACROSS THE ETHERS--DREW ME HERE THROUGH THE SHEER FORCE OF YOUR THOUGHT.
I...I KNOW YOU, DON'T I? SO MUCH INPUT IT'S HARD TO CONCENTRATE. YOU'RE THE ANGEL, AREN'T YOU--?
FALLEN ANGEL, TO BE ACCURATE. I'M ZAURIEL.
ZAURIEL? YES?
YES!
ZAURIEL THE FOOL--WHO TURNED HIS BACK ON PARADISE AND EMBRACED THIS FORSAKEN PLACE!
HOW COULD YOU DO IT? EXPOSE YOURSELF TO THE TOXINS THESE PEOPLE RADIATE--
--BURY YOURSELF IN FLESH AND DECAY?!
I DO IT--BECAUSE I LIKE IT.
FLESH AND DECAY? MAYBE. BUT I FIND IT PREFERABLE TO GOSSAMER AND ETERNITY.
NOW IF YOU WOULDN'T MIND BACKING AWAY?
YOU'RE INVADING MY PERSONAL SPACE.
KKKKKIIIIII
YOUR SONIC FLASH MAY HAVE MOMENTARILY DISRUPTED THE FIBERS OF MY ECTOPLASMIC FORM--
--BUT THE MOMENT HAS PASSED.
AND NOW, ZAURIEL, I UNEARTH THE SHAME HIDDEN IN YOUR SHINING SOUL. FOR NO ONE WALKS AWAY FROM HEAVEN WITHOUT--
THAT'LL BE ENOUGH, HAL--

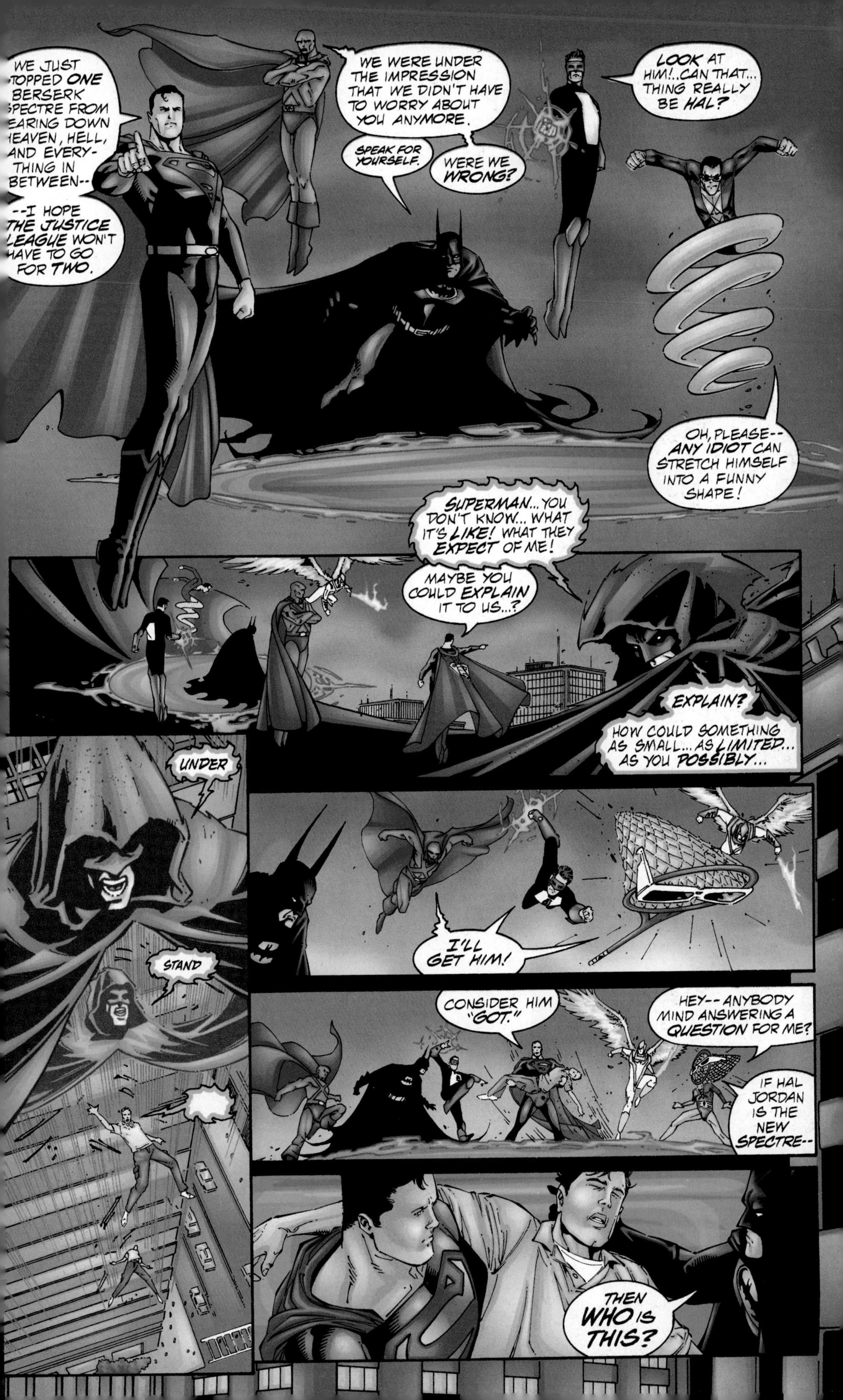
WE JUST STOPPED ONE BERSERK SPECTRE FROM TEARING DOWN HEAVEN, HELL, AND EVERY-THING IN BETWEEN--
--I HOPE THE JUSTICE LEAGUE WON'T HAVE TO GO FOR TWO.
WE WERE UNDER THE IMPRESSION THAT WE DIDN'T HAVE TO WORRY ABOUT YOU ANYMORE.
SPEAK FOR YOURSELF.
WERE WE WRONG?
LOOK AT HIM!..CAN THAT... THING REALLY BE HAL?
OH, PLEASE-- ANY IDIOT CAN STRETCH HIMSELF INTO A FUNNY SHAPE!
SUPERMAN... YOU DON'T KNOW... WHAT IT'S LIKE! WHAT THEY EXPECT OF ME!
MAYBE YOU COULD EXPLAIN IT TO US...?
EXPLAIN?
HOW COULD SOMETHING AS SMALL... AS LIMITED... AS YOU POSSIBLY...
UNDER
STAND
I'LL GET HIM!
CONSIDER HIM "GOT."
HEY-- ANYBODY MIND ANSWERING A QUESTION FOR ME?
IF HAL JORDAN IS THE NEW SPECTRE--
THEN WHO IS THIS?

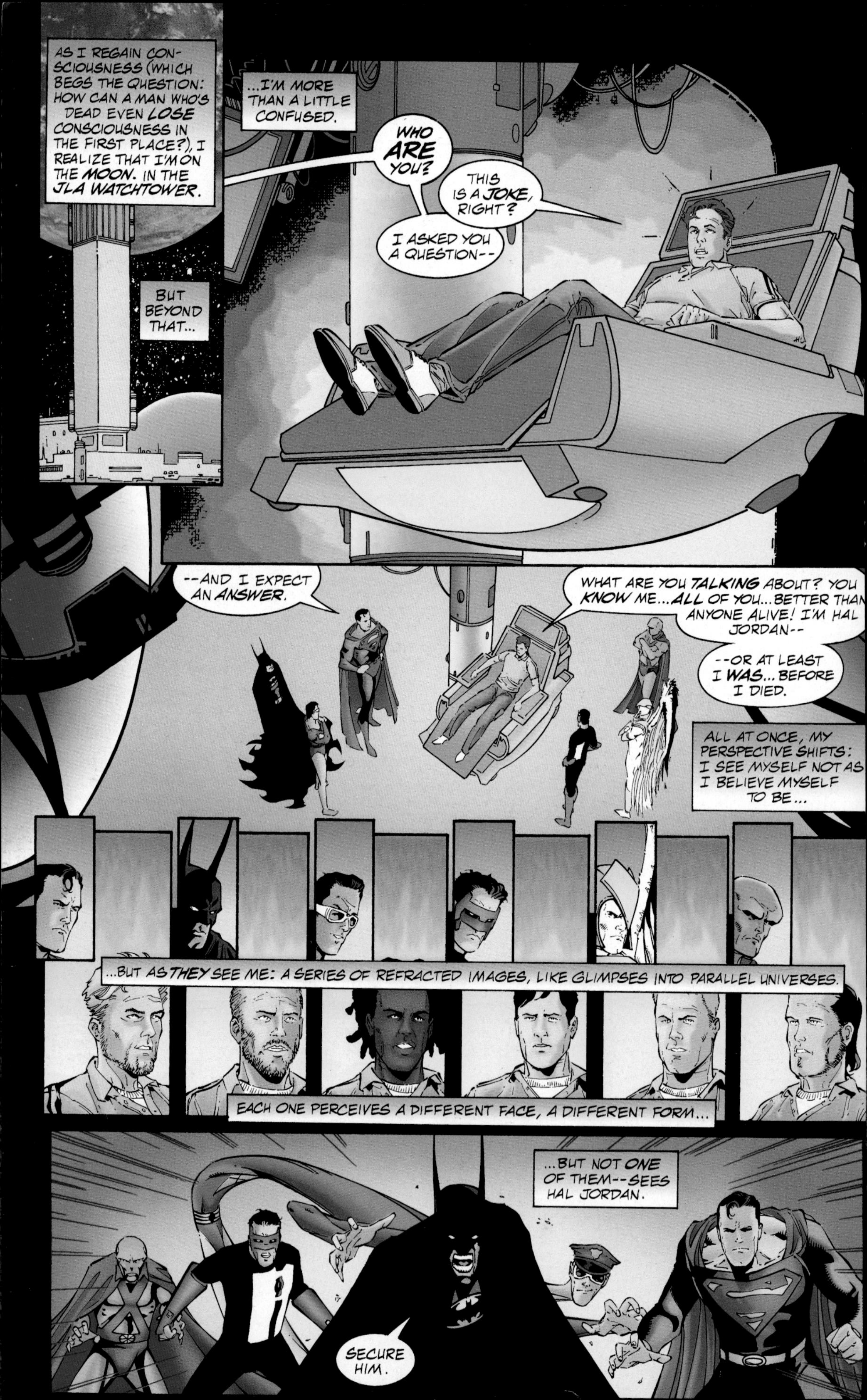

AS I REGAIN CONSCIOUSNESS (WHICH BEGS THE QUESTION: HOW CAN A MAN WHO'S DEAD EVEN LOSE CONSCIOUSNESS IN THE FIRST PLACE?), I REALIZE THAT I'M ON THE MOON. IN THE JLA WATCHTOWER.
BUT BEYOND THAT...
...I'M MORE THAN A LITTLE CONFUSED.
WHO ARE YOU?
THIS IS A JOKE, RIGHT?
I ASKED YOU A QUESTION--
--AND I EXPECT AN ANSWER.
WHAT ARE YOU TALKING ABOUT? YOU KNOW ME...ALL OF YOU...BETTER THAN ANYONE ALIVE! I'M HAL JORDAN--
--OR AT LEAST I WAS... BEFORE I DIED.
ALL AT ONCE, MY PERSPECTIVE SHIFTS: I SEE MYSELF NOT AS I BELIEVE MYSELF TO BE...
...BUT AS THEY SEE ME: A SERIES OF REFRACTED IMAGES, LIKE GLIMPSES INTO PARALLEL UNIVERSES.
EACH ONE PERCEIVES A DIFFERENT FACE, A DIFFERENT FORM...
...BUT NOT ONE OF THEM--SEES HAL JORDAN.
SECURE HIM.

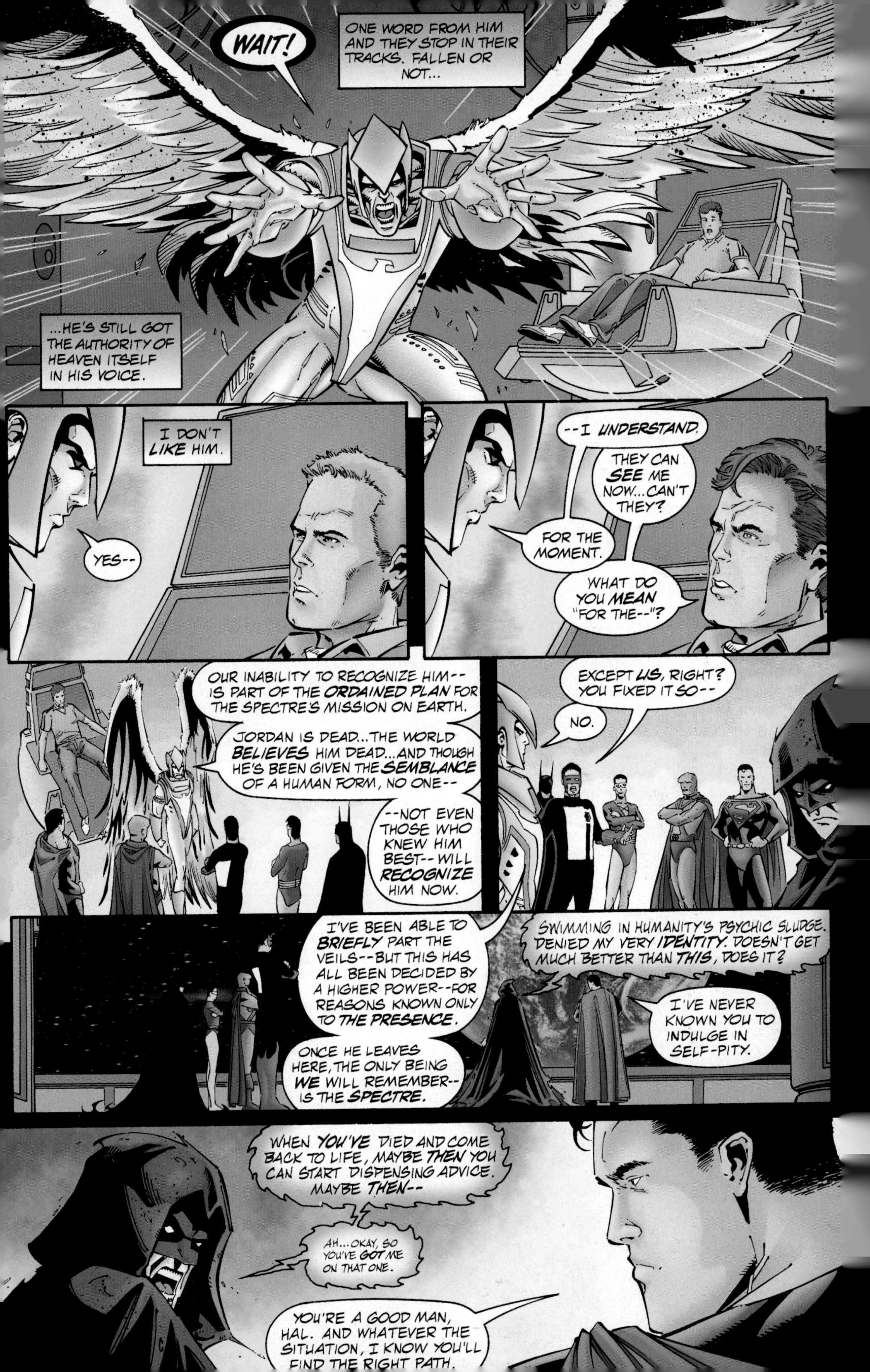
WAIT!
ONE WORD FROM HIM AND THEY STOP IN THEIR TRACKS. FALLEN OR NOT...
...HE'S STILL GOT THE AUTHORITY OF HEAVEN ITSELF IN HIS VOICE.
I DON'T LIKE HIM.
YES--
--I UNDERSTAND.
THEY CAN SEE ME NOW...CAN'T THEY?
FOR THE MOMENT.
WHAT DO YOU MEAN "FOR THE--"?
OUR INABILITY TO RECOGNIZE HIM-- IS PART OF THE ORDAINED PLAN FOR THE SPECTRE'S MISSION ON EARTH.
JORDAN IS DEAD...THE WORLD BELIEVES HIM DEAD...AND THOUGH HE'S BEEN GIVEN THE SEMBLANCE OF A HUMAN FORM, NO ONE--
--NOT EVEN THOSE WHO KNEW HIM BEST-- WILL RECOGNIZE HIM NOW.
EXCEPT US, RIGHT? YOU FIXED IT SO--
NO.
I'VE BEEN ABLE TO BRIEFLY PART THE VEILS--BUT THIS HAS ALL BEEN DECIDED BY A HIGHER POWER--FOR REASONS KNOWN ONLY TO THE PRESENCE.
ONCE HE LEAVES HERE, THE ONLY BEING WE WILL REMEMBER-- IS THE SPECTRE.
SWIMMING IN HUMANITY'S PSYCHIC SLUDGE. DENIED MY VERY IDENTITY. DOESN'T GET MUCH BETTER THAN THIS, DOES IT?
I'VE NEVER KNOWN YOU TO INDULGE IN SELF-PITY.
WHEN YOU'VE DIED AND COME BACK TO LIFE, MAYBE THEN YOU CAN START DISPENSING ADVICE. MAYBE THEN--
AH...OKAY, SO YOU'VE GOT ME ON THAT ONE.
YOU'RE A GOOD MAN, HAL. AND WHATEVER THE SITUATION, I KNOW YOU'LL FIND THE RIGHT PATH.

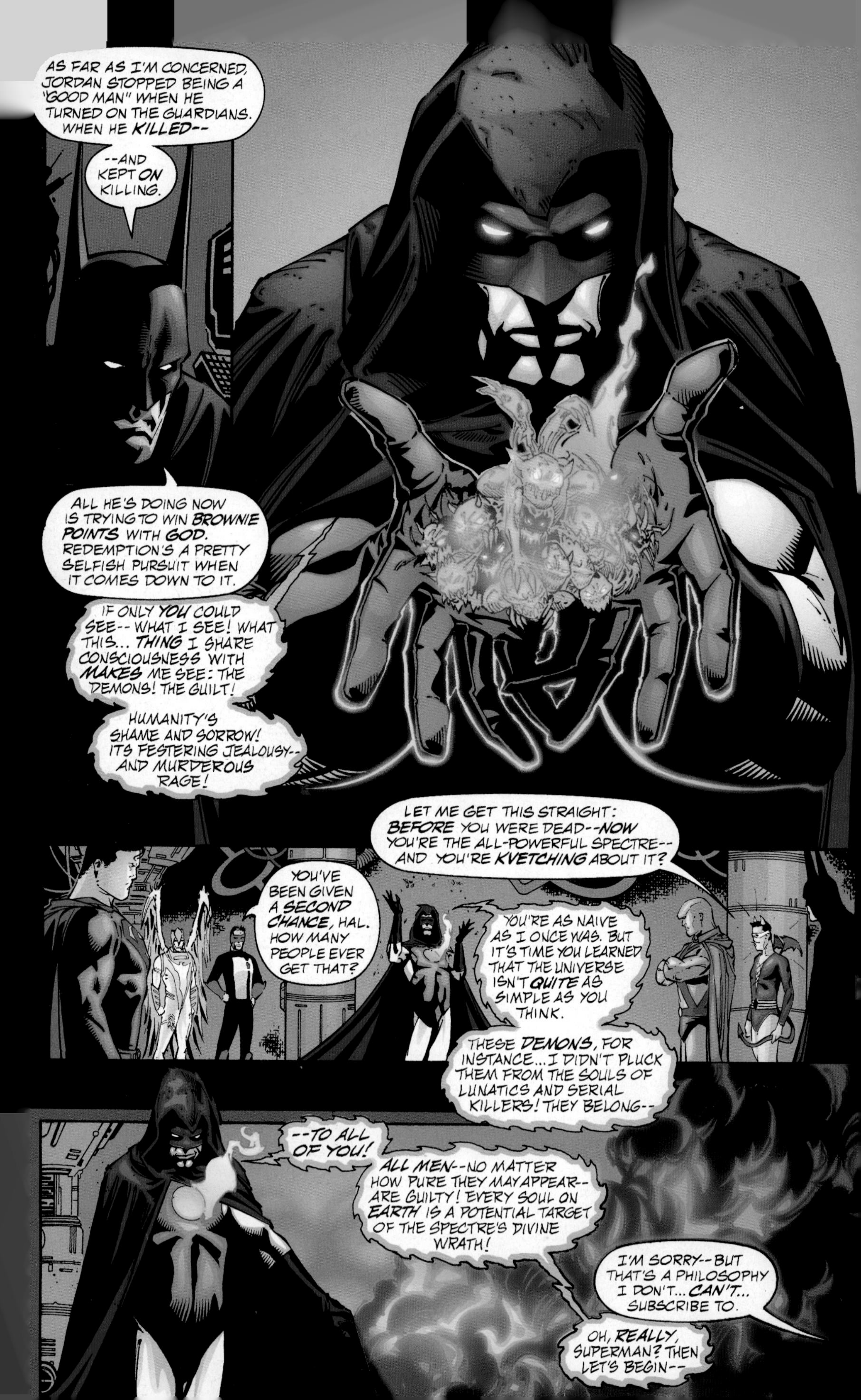
AS FAR AS I'M CONCERNED, JORDAN STOPPED BEING A "GOOD MAN" WHEN HE TURNED ON THE GUARDIANS. WHEN HE KILLED--
--AND KEPT ON KILLING.
ALL HE'S DOING NOW IS TRYING TO WIN BROWNIE POINTS WITH GOD. REDEMPTION'S A PRETTY SELFISH PURSUIT WHEN IT COMES DOWN TO IT.
IF ONLY YOU COULD SEE-- WHAT I SEE! WHAT THIS... THING I SHARE CONSCIOUSNESS WITH MAKES ME SEE: THE DEMONS! THE GUILT!
HUMANITY'S SHAME AND SORROW! ITS FESTERING JEALOUSY--AND MURDEROUS RAGE!
LET ME GET THIS STRAIGHT: BEFORE YOU WERE DEAD--NOW YOU'RE THE ALL-POWERFUL SPECTRE--AND YOU'RE KVETCHING ABOUT IT?
YOU'VE BEEN GIVEN A SECOND CHANCE, HAL. HOW MANY PEOPLE EVER GET THAT?
YOU'RE AS NAIVE AS I ONCE WAS. BUT IT'S TIME YOU LEARNED THAT THE UNIVERSE ISN'T QUITE AS SIMPLE AS YOU THINK.
THESE DEMONS, FOR INSTANCE... I DIDN'T PLUCK THEM FROM THE SOULS OF LUNATICS AND SERIAL KILLERS! THEY BELONG--
--TO ALL OF YOU!
ALL MEN--NO MATTER HOW PURE THEY MAY APPEAR--ARE GUILTY! EVERY SOUL ON EARTH IS A POTENTIAL TARGET OF THE SPECTRE'S DIVINE WRATH!
I'M SORRY--BUT THAT'S A PHILOSOPHY I DON'T... CAN'T... SUBSCRIBE TO.
OH, REALLY, SUPERMAN? THEN LET'S BEGIN--

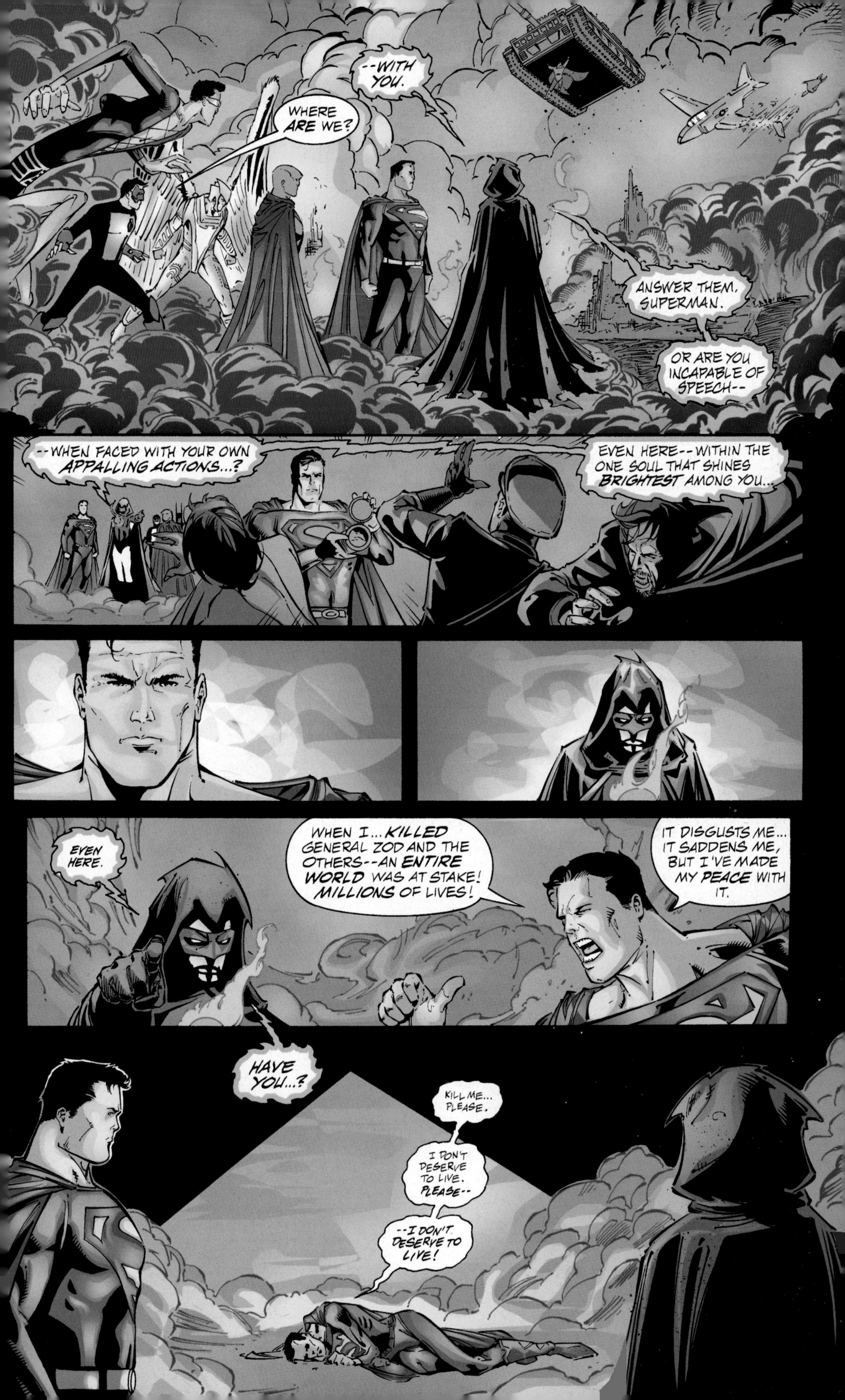
--WITH YOU.
WHERE ARE WE?
ANSWER THEM, SUPERMAN.
OR ARE YOU INCAPABLE OF SPEECH--
--WHEN FACED WITH YOUR OWN APPALLING ACTIONS...?
EVEN HERE--WITHIN THE ONE SOUL THAT SHINES BRIGHTEST AMONG YOU...
EVEN HERE.
WHEN I...KILLED GENERAL ZOD AND THE OTHERS--AN ENTIRE WORLD WAS AT STAKE! MILLIONS OF LIVES!
IT DISGUSTS ME... IT SADDENS ME, BUT I'VE MADE MY PEACE WITH IT.
HAVE YOU...?
KILL ME... PLEASE.
I DON'T DESERVE TO LIVE. PLEASE--
--I DON'T DESERVE TO LIVE!

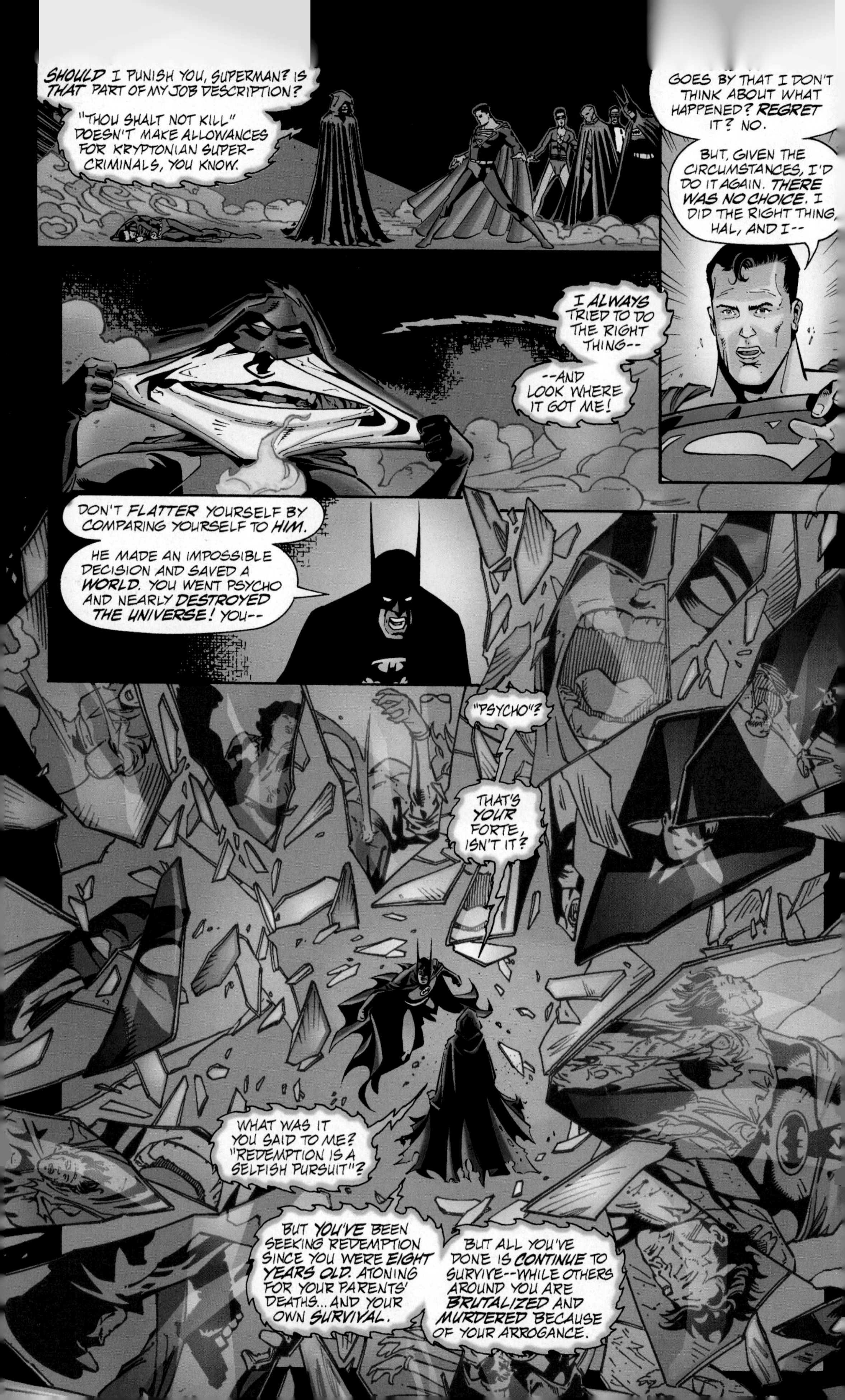
SHOULD I PUNISH YOU, SUPERMAN? IS THAT PART OF MY JOB DESCRIPTION?
"THOU SHALT NOT KILL" DOESN'T MAKE ALLOWANCES FOR KRYPTONIAN SUPER-CRIMINALS, YOU KNOW.
GOES BY THAT I DON'T THINK ABOUT WHAT HAPPENED? REGRET IT? NO.
BUT, GIVEN THE CIRCUMSTANCES, I'D DO IT AGAIN. THERE WAS NO CHOICE. I DID THE RIGHT THING, HAL, AND I--
I ALWAYS TRIED TO DO THE RIGHT THING--
--AND LOOK WHERE IT GOT ME!
DON'T FLATTER YOURSELF BY COMPARING YOURSELF TO HIM.
HE MADE AN IMPOSSIBLE DECISION AND SAVED A WORLD. YOU WENT PSYCHO AND NEARLY DESTROYED THE UNIVERSE! YOU--
"PSYCHO"?
THAT'S YOUR FORTE, ISN'T IT?
WHAT WAS IT YOU SAID TO ME? "REDEMPTION IS A SELFISH PURSUIT"?
BUT YOU'VE BEEN SEEKING REDEMPTION SINCE YOU WERE EIGHT YEARS OLD. ATONING FOR YOUR PARENTS' DEATHS... AND YOUR OWN SURVIVAL.
BUT ALL YOU'VE DONE IS CONTINUE TO SURVIVE--WHILE OTHERS AROUND YOU ARE BRUTALIZED AND MURDERED BECAUSE OF YOUR ARROGANCE.

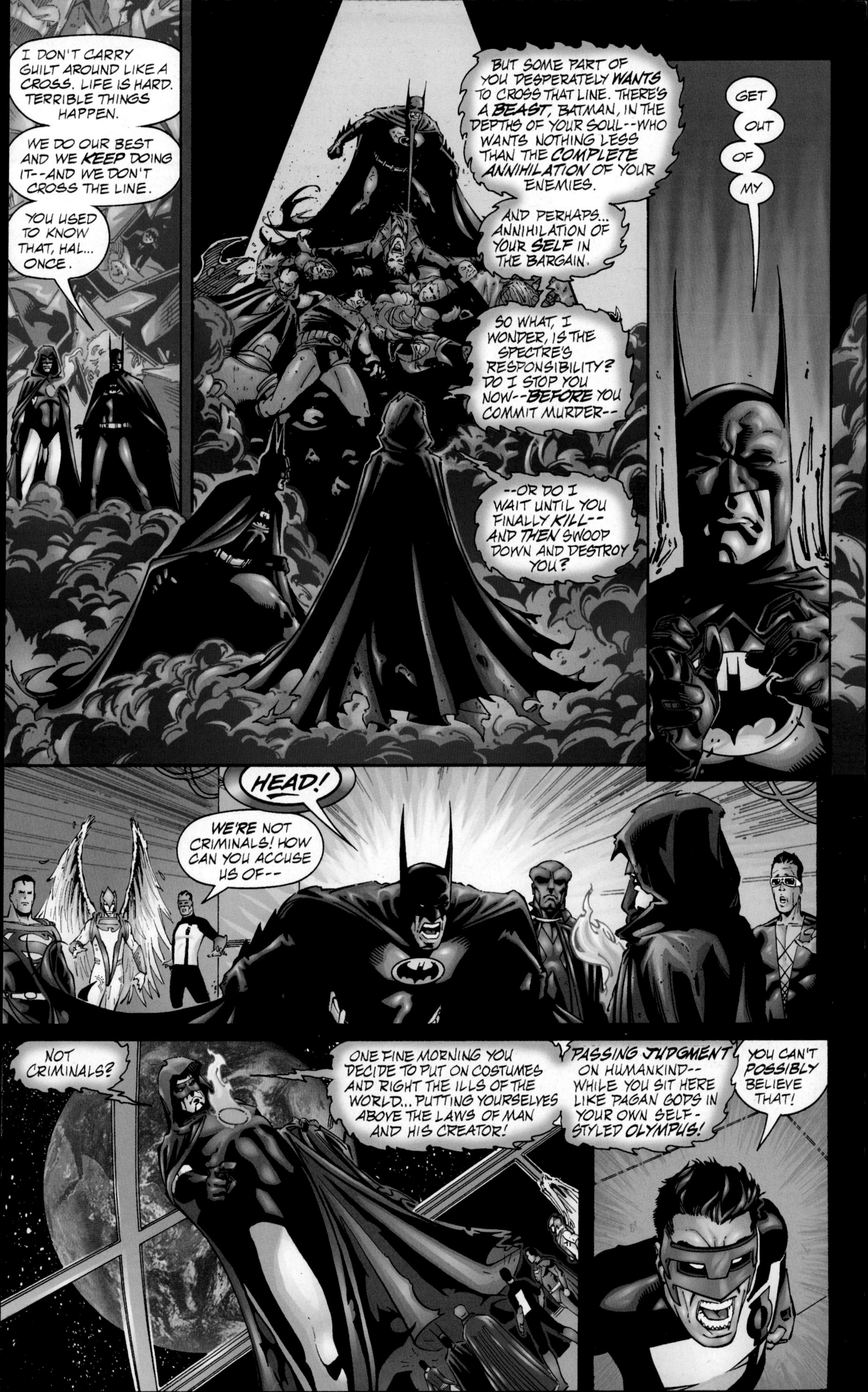
I DON'T CARRY GUILT AROUND LIKE A CROSS. LIFE IS HARD. TERRIBLE THINGS HAPPEN.
WE DO OUR BEST AND WE KEEP DOING IT--AND WE DON'T CROSS THE LINE.
YOU USED TO KNOW THAT, HAL... ONCE.
BUT SOME PART OF YOU DESPERATELY WANTS TO CROSS THAT LINE. THERE'S A BEAST, BATMAN, IN THE DEPTHS OF YOUR SOUL--WHO WANTS NOTHING LESS THAN THE COMPLETE ANNIHILATION OF YOUR ENEMIES.
AND PERHAPS... ANNIHILATION OF YOUR SELF IN THE BARGAIN.
SO WHAT, I WONDER, IS THE SPECTRE'S RESPONSIBILITY? DO I STOP YOU NOW--BEFORE YOU COMMIT MURDER--
--OR DO I WAIT UNTIL YOU FINALLY KILL--AND THEN SWOOP DOWN AND DESTROY YOU?
GET OUT OF MY
HEAD!
WE'RE NOT CRIMINALS! HOW CAN YOU ACCUSE US OF--
NOT CRIMINALS?
ONE FINE MORNING YOU DECIDE TO PUT ON COSTUMES AND RIGHT THE ILLS OF THE WORLD... PUTTING YOURSELVES ABOVE THE LAWS OF MAN AND HIS CREATOR!
PASSING JUDGMENT ON HUMANKIND--WHILE YOU SIT HERE LIKE PAGAN GODS IN YOUR OWN SELF-STYLED OLYMPUS!
YOU CAN'T POSSIBLY BELIEVE THAT!

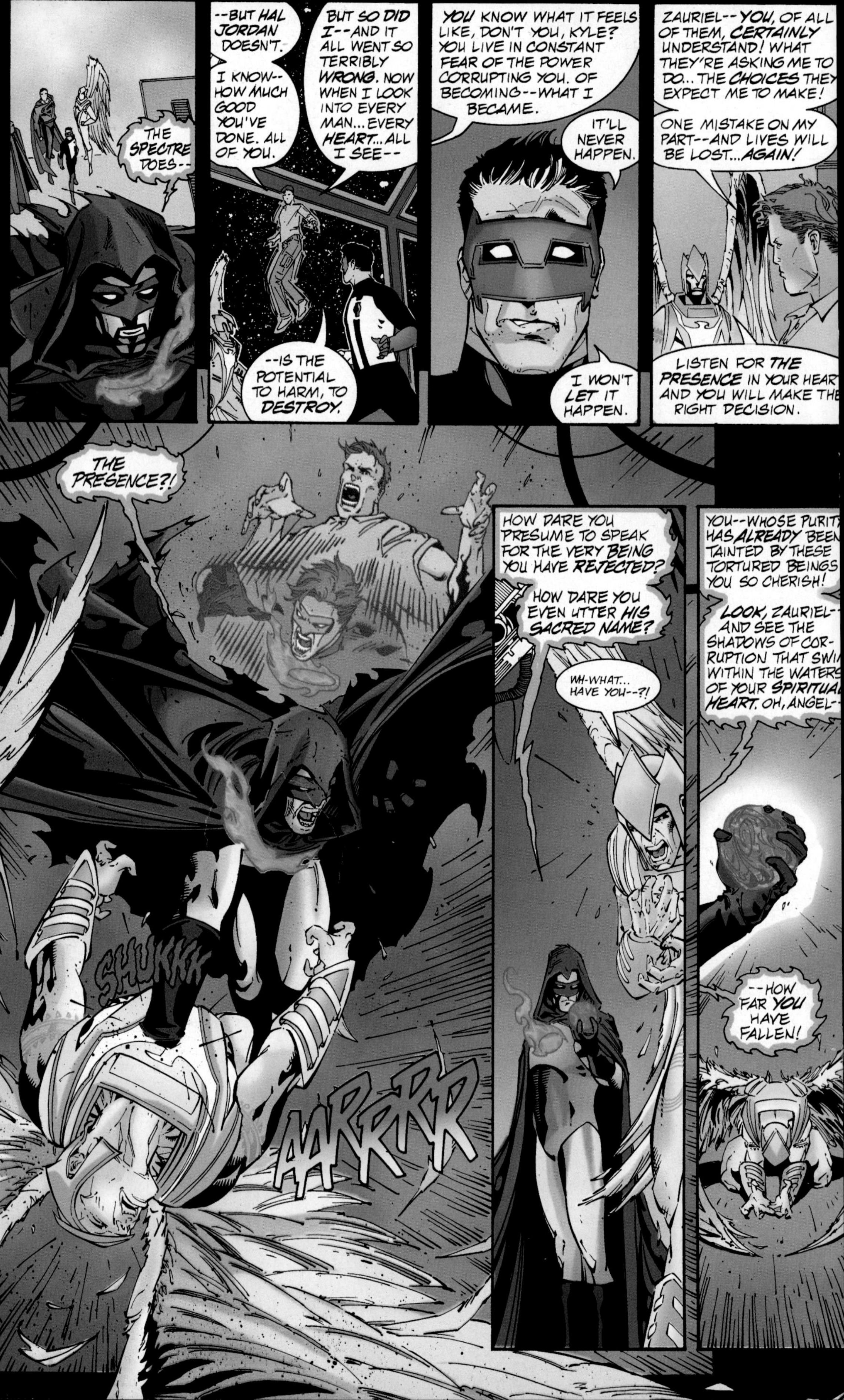

THE SPECTRE DOES--
--BUT HAL JORDAN DOESN'T.
I KNOW-- HOW MUCH GOOD YOU'VE DONE. ALL OF YOU.
BUT SO DID I--AND IT ALL WENT SO TERRIBLY WRONG. NOW WHEN I LOOK INTO EVERY MAN... EVERY HEART... ALL I SEE--
--IS THE POTENTIAL TO HARM, TO DESTROY.
YOU KNOW WHAT IT FEELS LIKE, DON'T YOU, KYLE? YOU LIVE IN CONSTANT FEAR OF THE POWER CORRUPTING YOU. OF BECOMING--WHAT I BECAME.
IT'LL NEVER HAPPEN.
I WON'T LET IT HAPPEN.
ZAURIEL--YOU, OF ALL OF THEM, CERTAINLY UNDERSTAND! WHAT THEY'RE ASKING ME TO DO... THE CHOICES THEY EXPECT ME TO MAKE!
ONE MISTAKE ON MY PART--AND LIVES WILL BE LOST...AGAIN!
LISTEN FOR THE PRESENCE IN YOUR HEART AND YOU WILL MAKE THE RIGHT DECISION.
THE PRESENCE?!
SHUKKK
AARRRR
HOW DARE YOU PRESUME TO SPEAK FOR THE VERY BEING YOU HAVE REJECTED?
HOW DARE YOU EVEN UTTER HIS SACRED NAME?
WH-WHAT... HAVE YOU--?!
YOU--WHOSE PURITY HAS ALREADY BEEN TAINTED BY THESE TORTURED BEINGS YOU SO CHERISH!
LOOK, ZAURIEL--AND SEE THE SHADOWS OF CORRUPTION THAT SWIM WITHIN THE WATERS OF YOUR SPIRITUAL HEART. OH, ANGEL--
--HOW FAR YOU HAVE FALLEN!

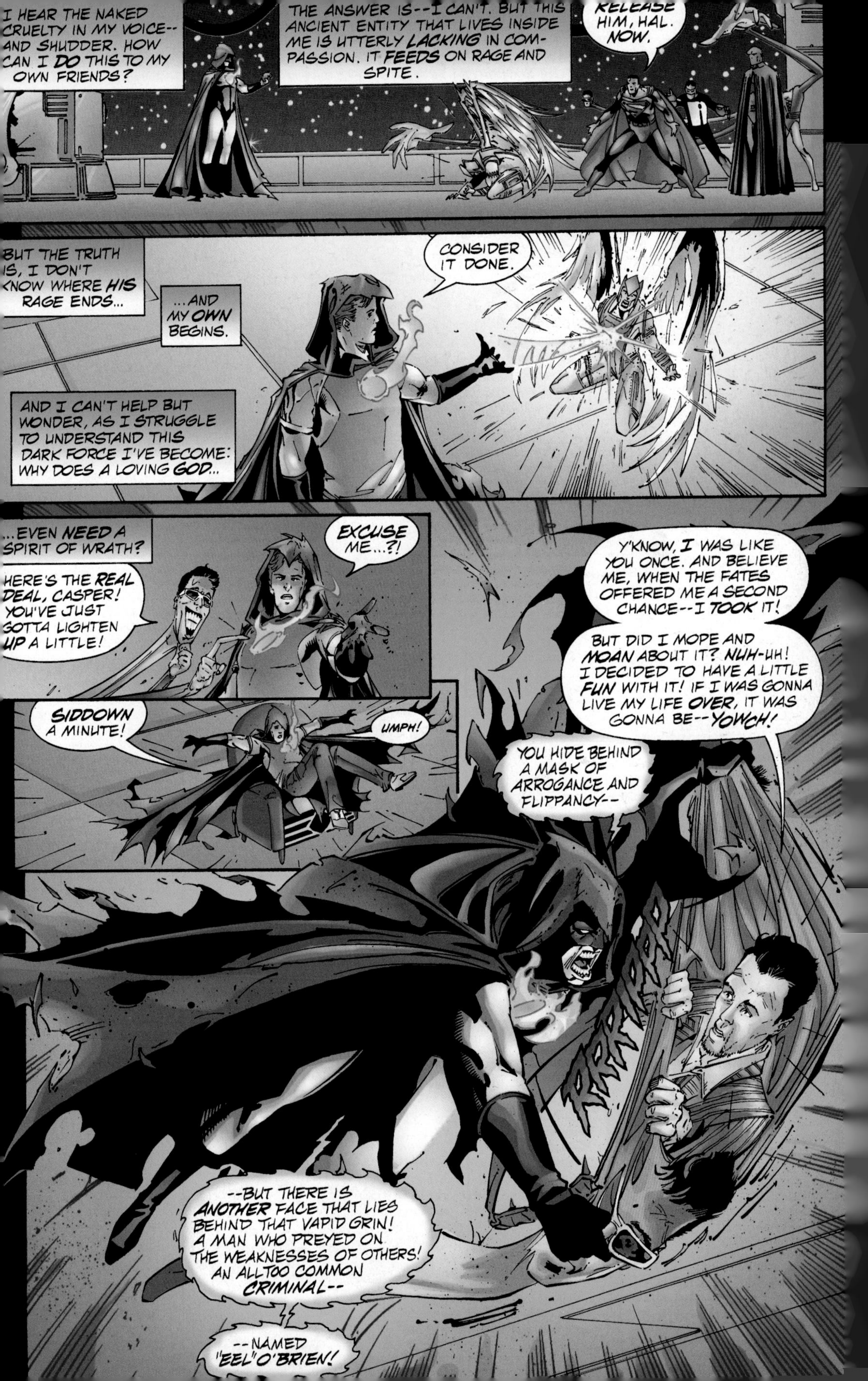

I HEAR THE NAKED CRUELTY IN MY VOICE-- AND SHUDDER. HOW CAN I DO THIS TO MY OWN FRIENDS?
THE ANSWER IS--I CAN'T. BUT THIS ANCIENT ENTITY THAT LIVES INSIDE ME IS UTTERLY LACKING IN COMPASSION. IT FEEDS ON RAGE AND SPITE.
RELEASE HIM, HAL. NOW.
BUT THE TRUTH IS, I DON'T KNOW WHERE HIS RAGE ENDS...
...AND MY OWN BEGINS.
CONSIDER IT DONE.
AND I CAN'T HELP BUT WONDER, AS I STRUGGLE TO UNDERSTAND THIS DARK FORCE I'VE BECOME: WHY DOES A LOVING GOD...
...EVEN NEED A SPIRIT OF WRATH?
HERE'S THE REAL DEAL, CASPER! YOU'VE JUST GOTTA LIGHTEN UP A LITTLE!
EXCUSE ME...?!
SIDDOWN A MINUTE!
UMPH!
Y'KNOW, I WAS LIKE YOU ONCE. AND BELIEVE ME, WHEN THE FATES OFFERED ME A SECOND CHANCE--I TOOK IT!
BUT DID I MOPE AND MOAN ABOUT IT? NUH-UH! I DECIDED TO HAVE A LITTLE FUN WITH IT! IF I WAS GONNA LIVE MY LIFE OVER, IT WAS GONNA BE--YOWCH!
YOU HIDE BEHIND A MASK OF ARROGANCE AND FLIPPANCY--
--BUT THERE IS ANOTHER FACE THAT LIES BEHIND THAT VAPID GRIN! A MAN WHO PREYED ON THE WEAKNESSES OF OTHERS! AN ALLTOO COMMON CRIMINAL--
--NAMED "EEL" O'BRIEN!

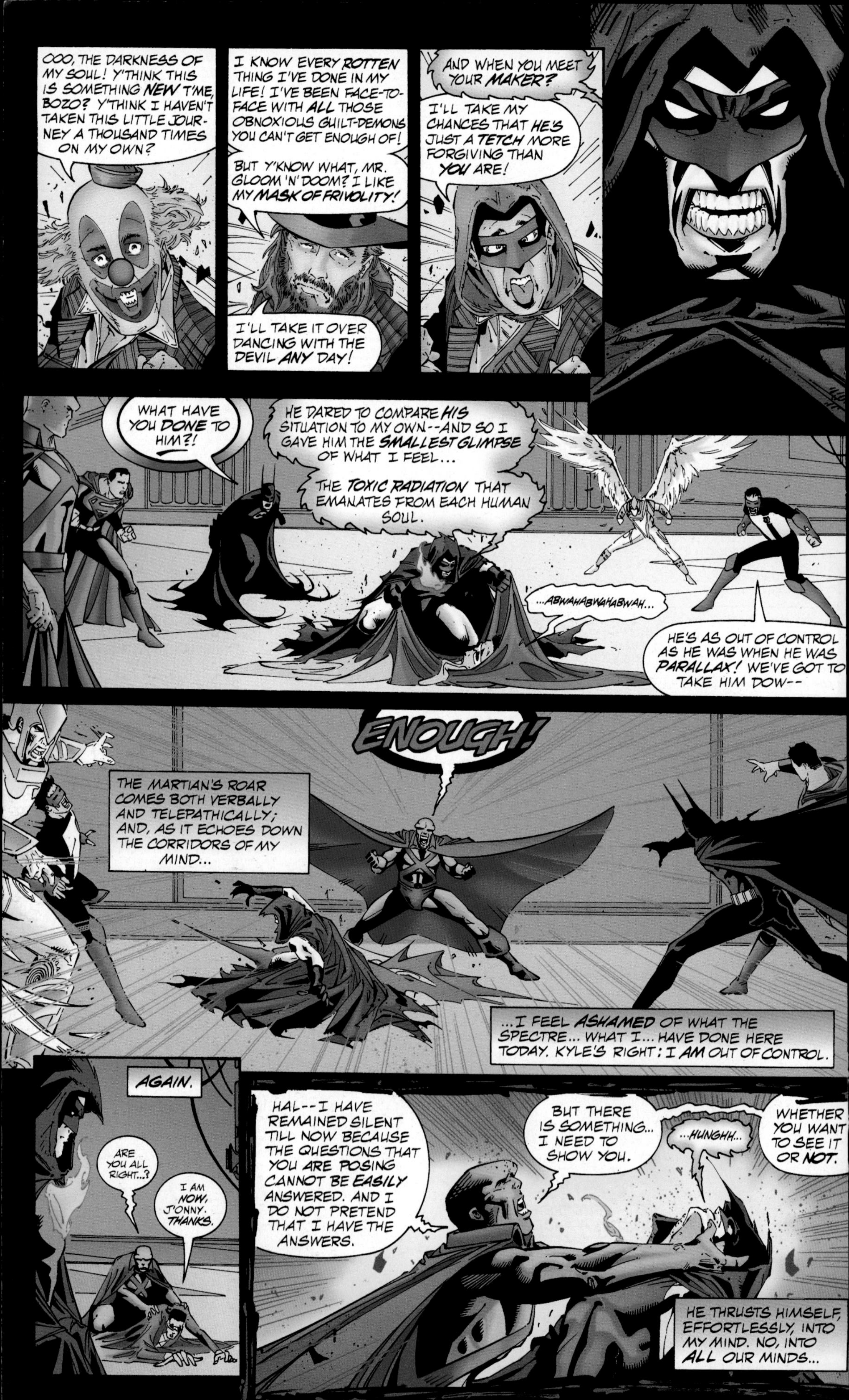
OOO, THE DARKNESS OF MY SOUL! Y'THINK THIS IS SOMETHING NEW T'ME, BOZO? Y'THINK I HAVEN'T TAKEN THIS LITTLE JOURNEY A THOUSAND TIMES ON MY OWN?
I KNOW EVERY ROTTEN THING I'VE DONE IN MY LIFE! I'VE BEEN FACE-TO-FACE WITH ALL THOSE OBNOXIOUS GUILT-DEMONS YOU CAN'T GET ENOUGH OF!
BUT Y'KNOW WHAT, MR. GLOOM 'N' DOOM? I LIKE MY MASK OF FRIVOLITY!
I'LL TAKE IT OVER DANCING WITH THE DEVIL ANY DAY!
AND WHEN YOU MEET YOUR MAKER?
I'LL TAKE MY CHANCES THAT HE'S JUST A TETCH MORE FORGIVING THAN YOU ARE!
WHAT HAVE YOU DONE TO HIM?!
HE DARED TO COMPARE HIS SITUATION TO MY OWN--AND SO I GAVE HIM THE SMALLEST GLIMPSE OF WHAT I FEEL...
THE TOXIC RADIATION THAT EMANATES FROM EACH HUMAN SOUL.
...ABWAHABWAHABWAH...
HE'S AS OUT OF CONTROL AS HE WAS WHEN HE WAS PARALLAX! WE'VE GOT TO TAKE HIM DOW--
ENOUGH!
THE MARTIAN'S ROAR COMES BOTH VERBALLY AND TELEPATHICALLY; AND, AS IT ECHOES DOWN THE CORRIDORS OF MY MIND...
...I FEEL ASHAMED OF WHAT THE SPECTRE... WHAT I... HAVE DONE HERE TODAY. KYLE'S RIGHT: I AM OUT OF CONTROL.
AGAIN.
ARE YOU ALL RIGHT...?
I AM NOW, J'ONNY. THANKS.
HAL--I HAVE REMAINED SILENT TILL NOW BECAUSE THE QUESTIONS THAT YOU ARE POSING CANNOT BE EASILY ANSWERED. AND I DO NOT PRETEND THAT I HAVE THE ANSWERS.
BUT THERE IS SOMETHING... I NEED TO SHOW YOU.
...HUNGHH...
WHETHER YOU WANT TO SEE IT OR NOT.
HE THRUSTS HIMSELF, EFFORTLESSLY, INTO MY MIND. NO, INTO ALL OUR MINDS...

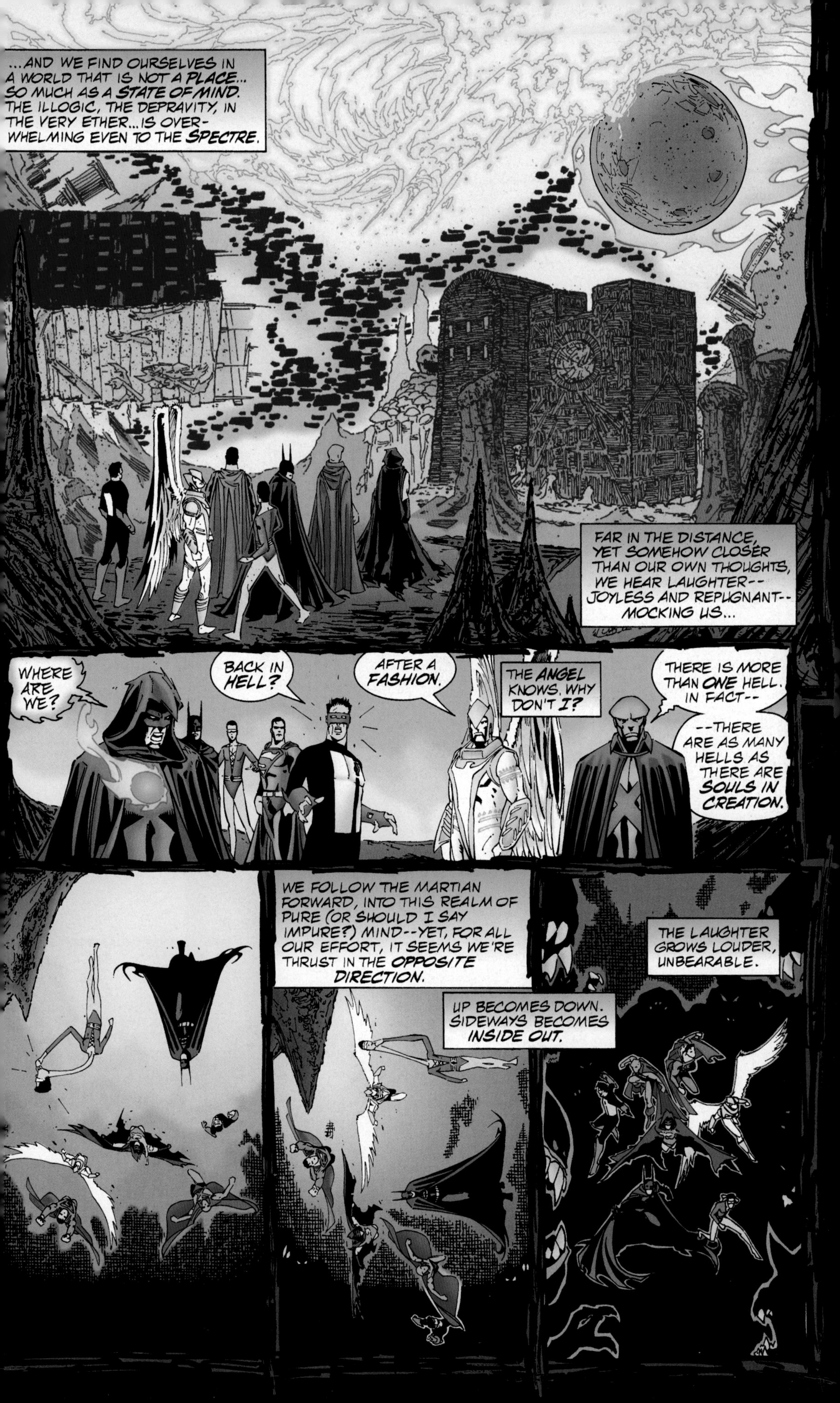
...AND WE FIND OURSELVES IN A WORLD THAT IS NOT A PLACE... SO MUCH AS A STATE OF MIND. THE ILLOGIC, THE DEPRAVITY, IN THE VERY ETHER...IS OVER-WHELMING EVEN TO THE SPECTRE.
FAR IN THE DISTANCE, YET SOMEHOW CLOSER THAN OUR OWN THOUGHTS, WE HEAR LAUGHTER-- JOYLESS AND REPUGNANT-- MOCKING US...
WHERE ARE WE?
BACK IN HELL?
AFTER A FASHION.
THE ANGEL KNOWS. WHY DON'T I?
THERE IS MORE THAN ONE HELL. IN FACT--
--THERE ARE AS MANY HELLS AS THERE ARE SOULS IN CREATION.
WE FOLLOW THE MARTIAN FORWARD, INTO THIS REALM OF PURE (OR SHOULD I SAY IMPURE?) MIND--YET, FOR ALL OUR EFFORT, IT SEEMS WE'RE THRUST IN THE OPPOSITE DIRECTION.
UP BECOMES DOWN. SIDEWAYS BECOMES INSIDE OUT.
THE LAUGHTER GROWS LOUDER, UNBEARABLE.

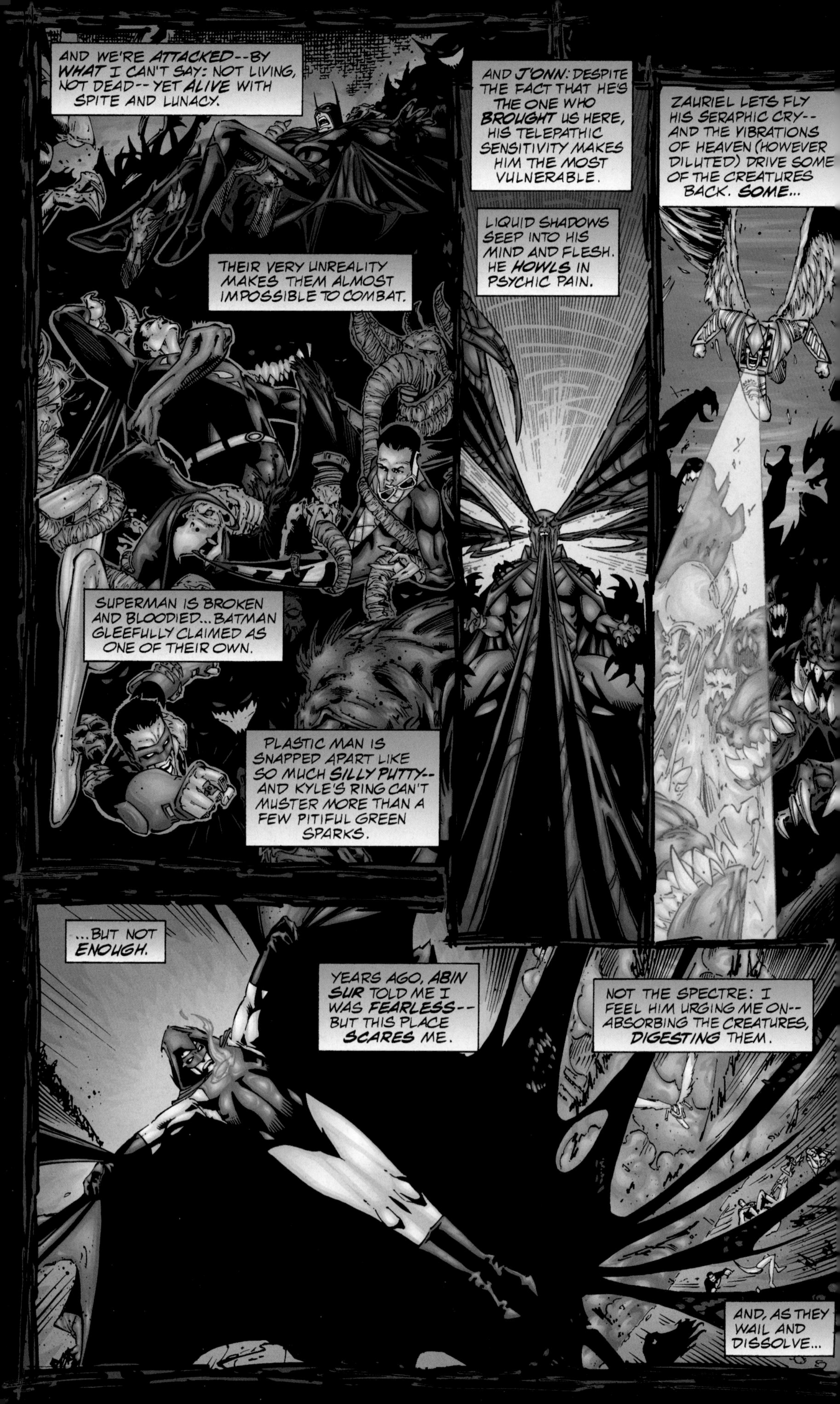
AND WE'RE ATTACKED--BY WHAT I CAN'T SAY: NOT LIVING, NOT DEAD--YET ALIVE WITH SPITE AND LUNACY.
THEIR VERY UNREALITY MAKES THEM ALMOST IMPOSSIBLE TO COMBAT.
SUPERMAN IS BROKEN AND BLOODIED...BATMAN GLEEFULLY CLAIMED AS ONE OF THEIR OWN.
PLASTIC MAN IS SNAPPED APART LIKE SO MUCH SILLY PUTTY--AND KYLE'S RING CAN'T MUSTER MORE THAN A FEW PITIFUL GREEN SPARKS.
AND J'ONN: DESPITE THE FACT THAT HE'S THE ONE WHO BROUGHT US HERE, HIS TELEPATHIC SENSITIVITY MAKES HIM THE MOST VULNERABLE.
LIQUID SHADOWS SEEP INTO HIS MIND AND FLESH. HE HOWLS IN PSYCHIC PAIN.
ZAURIEL LETS FLY HIS SERAPHIC CRY--AND THE VIBRATIONS OF HEAVEN (HOWEVER DILUTED) DRIVE SOME OF THE CREATURES BACK. SOME...
...BUT NOT ENOUGH.
YEARS AGO, ABIN SUR TOLD ME I WAS FEARLESS--BUT THIS PLACE SCARES ME.
NOT THE SPECTRE: I FEEL HIM URGING ME ON--ABSORBING THE CREATURES, DIGESTING THEM.
AND, AS THEY WAIL AND DISSOLVE...

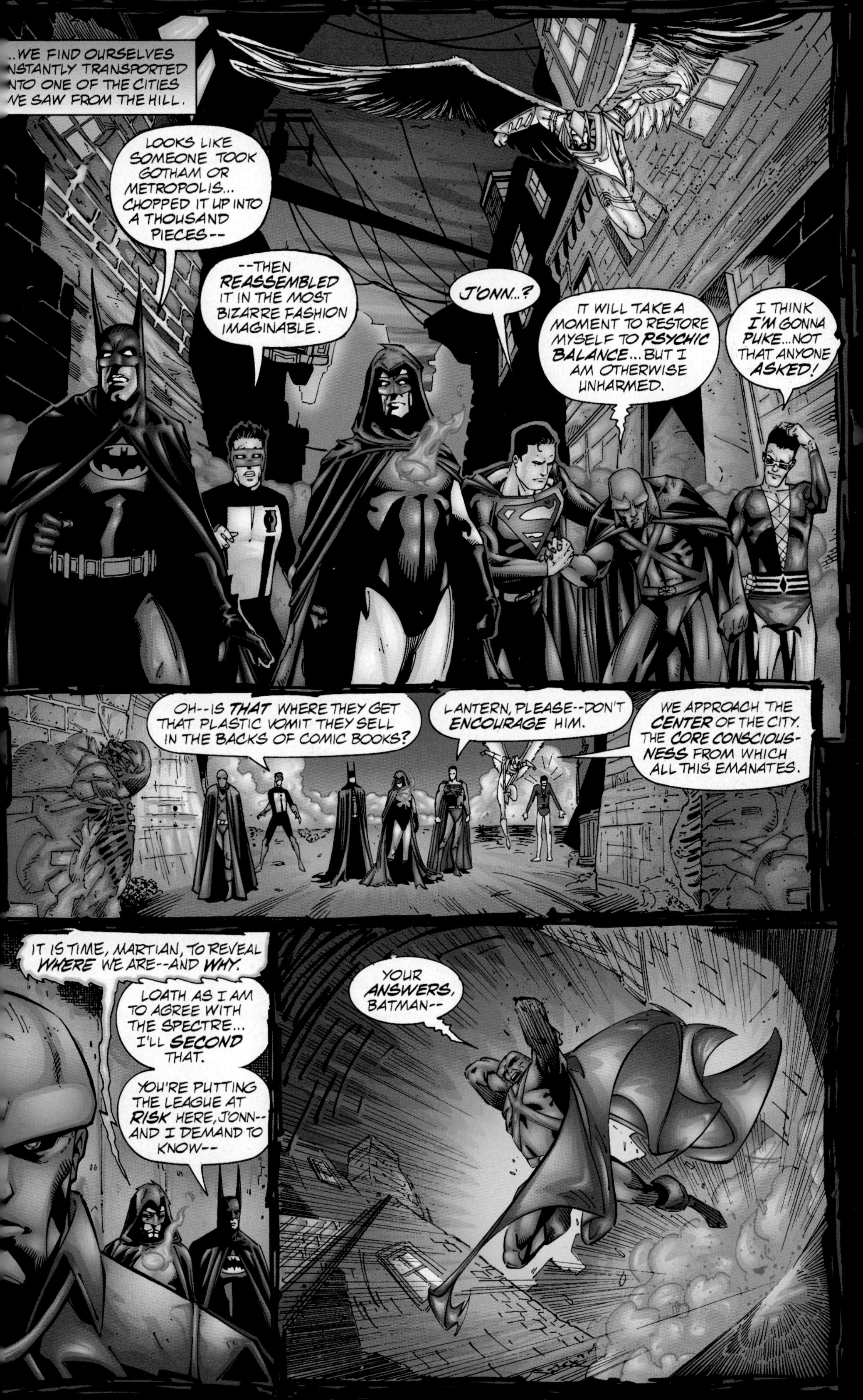
..WE FIND OURSELVES INSTANTLY TRANSPORTED INTO ONE OF THE CITIES WE SAW FROM THE HILL.
LOOKS LIKE SOMEONE TOOK GOTHAM OR METROPOLIS... CHOPPED IT UP INTO A THOUSAND PIECES--
--THEN REASSEMBLED IT IN THE MOST BIZARRE FASHION IMAGINABLE.
J'ONN..?
IT WILL TAKE A MOMENT TO RESTORE MYSELF TO PSYCHIC BALANCE... BUT I AM OTHERWISE UNHARMED.
I THINK I'M GONNA PUKE...NOT THAT ANYONE ASKED!
OH--IS THAT WHERE THEY GET THAT PLASTIC VOMIT THEY SELL IN THE BACKS OF COMIC BOOKS?
LANTERN, PLEASE--DON'T ENCOURAGE HIM.
WE APPROACH THE CENTER OF THE CITY. THE CORE CONSCIOUSNESS FROM WHICH ALL THIS EMANATES.
IT IS TIME, MARTIAN, TO REVEAL WHERE WE ARE--AND WHY.
LOATH AS I AM TO AGREE WITH THE SPECTRE... I'LL SECOND THAT.
YOU'RE PUTTING THE LEAGUE AT RISK HERE, J'ONN--AND I DEMAND TO KNOW--
YOUR ANSWERS, BATMAN--

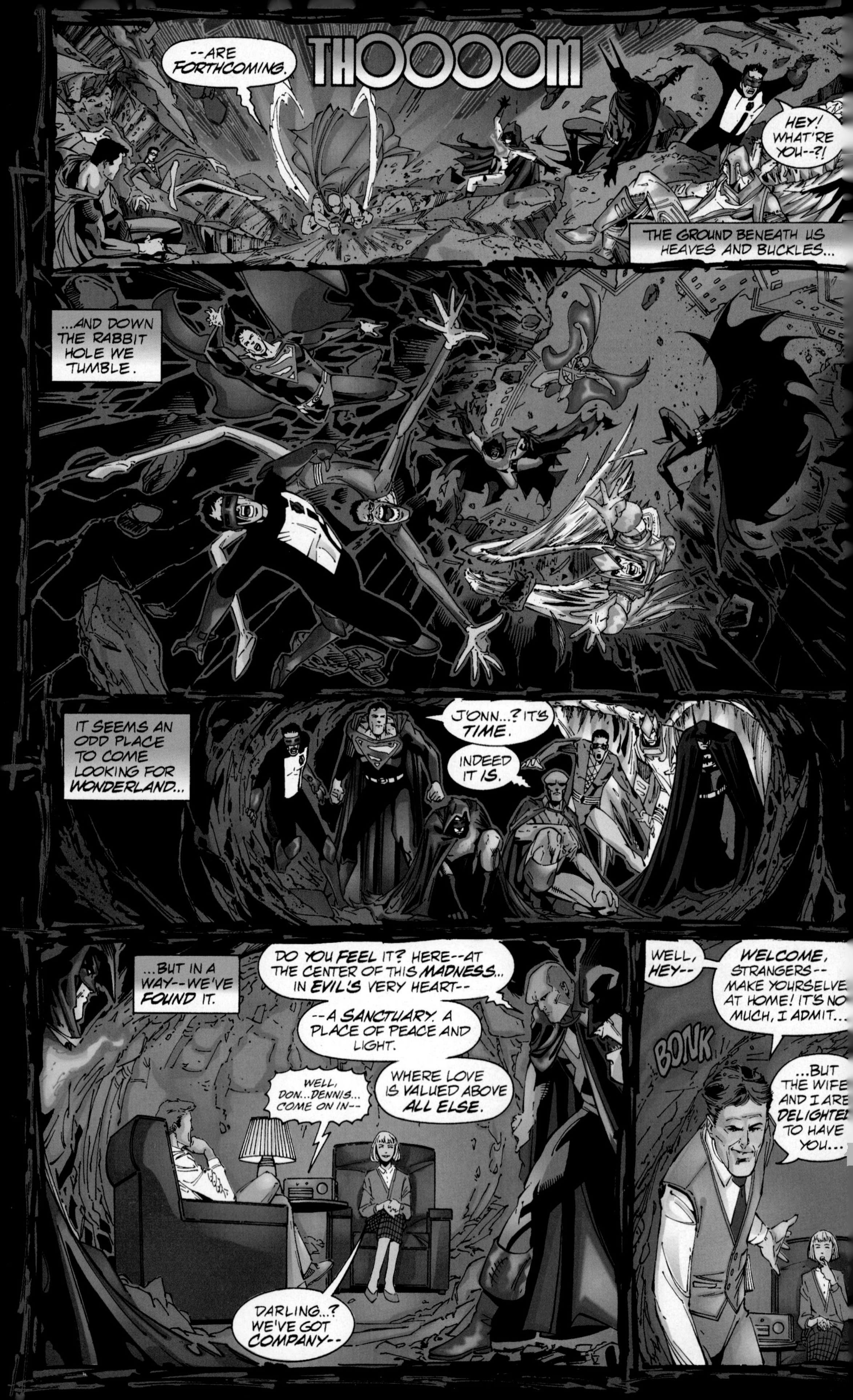
--ARE FORTHCOMING.
THOOOOM
HEY! WHAT'RE YOU--?!
THE GROUND BENEATH US HEAVES AND BUCKLES...
...AND DOWN THE RABBIT HOLE WE TUMBLE.
IT SEEMS AN ODD PLACE TO COME LOOKING FOR WONDERLAND...
J'ONN...? IT'S TIME.
INDEED IT IS.
...BUT IN A WAY--WE'VE FOUND IT.
DO YOU FEEL IT? HERE--AT THE CENTER OF THIS MADNESS... IN EVIL'S VERY HEART--
--A SANCTUARY. A PLACE OF PEACE AND LIGHT.
WHERE LOVE IS VALUED ABOVE ALL ELSE.
WELL, DON...DENNIS... COME ON IN--
DARLING...? WE'VE GOT COMPANY--
WELL, HEY--
BONK
WELCOME, STRANGERS--MAKE YOURSELVE AT HOME! IT'S NO MUCH, I ADMIT...
...BUT THE WIFE AND I ARE DELIGHTED TO HAVE YOU...

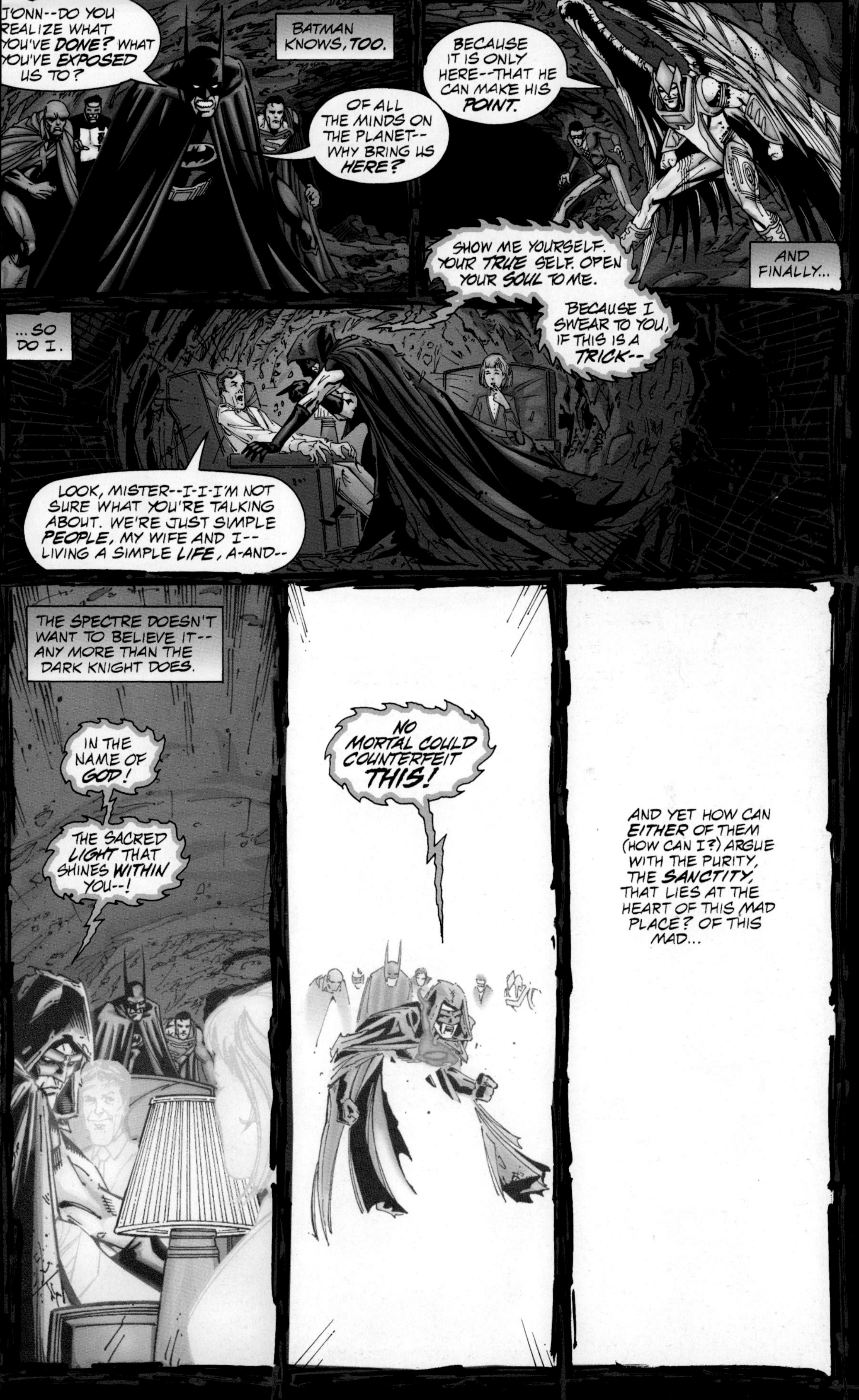
J'ONN--DO YOU REALIZE WHAT YOU'VE DONE? WHAT YOU'VE EXPOSED US TO?
BATMAN KNOWS, TOO.
OF ALL THE MINDS ON THE PLANET--WHY BRING US HERE?
BECAUSE IT IS ONLY HERE--THAT HE CAN MAKE HIS POINT.
AND FINALLY...
SHOW ME YOURSELF. YOUR TRUE SELF. OPEN YOUR SOUL TO ME.
...SO DO I.
BECAUSE I SWEAR TO YOU, IF THIS IS A TRICK--
LOOK, MISTER--I-I-I'M NOT SURE WHAT YOU'RE TALKING ABOUT. WE'RE JUST SIMPLE PEOPLE, MY WIFE AND I--LIVING A SIMPLE LIFE, A-AND--
THE SPECTRE DOESN'T WANT TO BELIEVE IT--ANY MORE THAN THE DARK KNIGHT DOES.
IN THE NAME OF GOD!
THE SACRED LIGHT THAT SHINES WITHIN YOU--!
NO MORTAL COULD COUNTERFEIT THIS!
AND YET HOW CAN EITHER OF THEM (HOW CAN I?) ARGUE WITH THE PURITY, THE SANCTITY, THAT LIES AT THE HEART OF THIS MAD PLACE? OF THIS MAD...

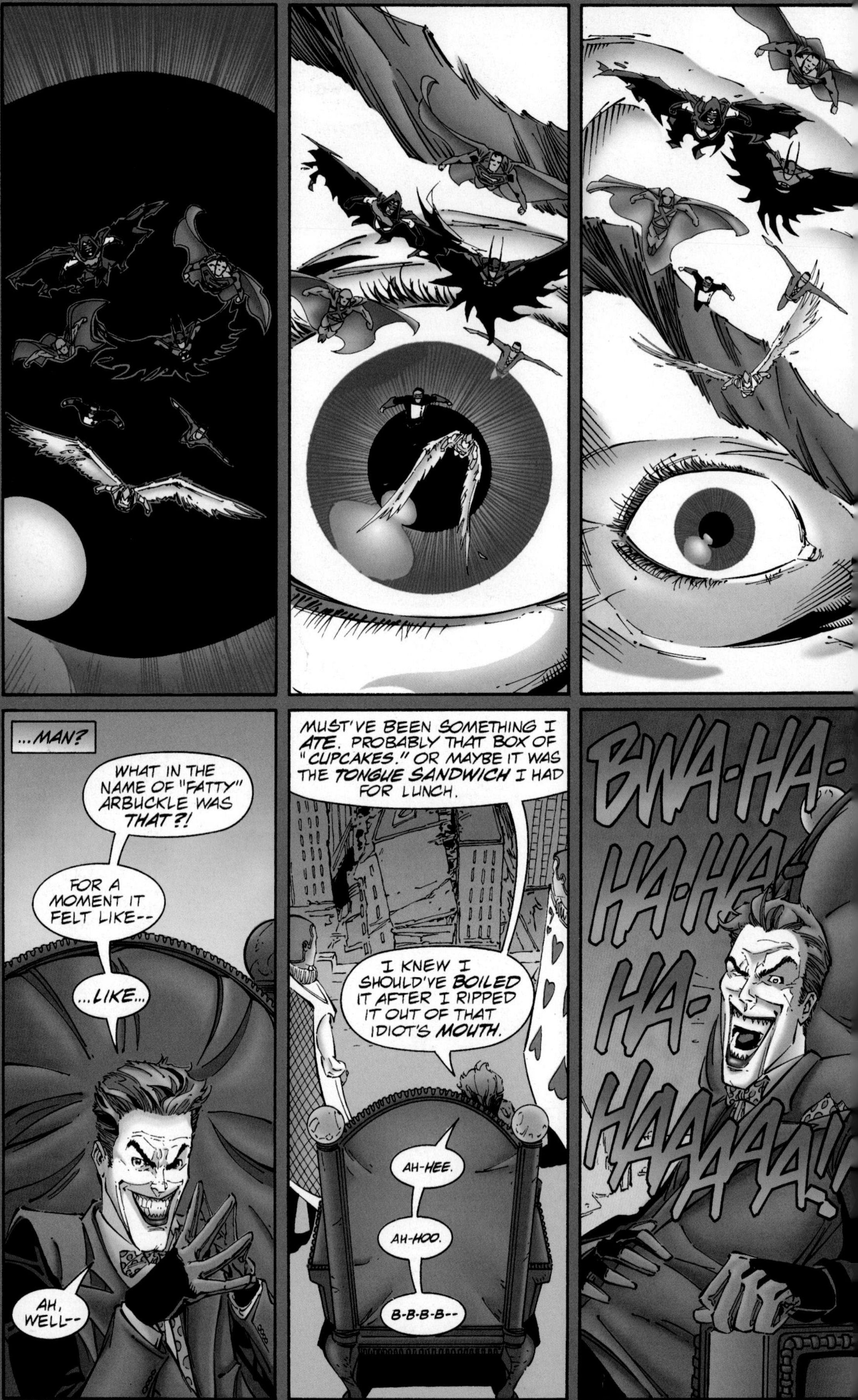
...MAN?
WHAT IN THE NAME OF "FATTY" ARBUCKLE WAS THAT?!
FOR A MOMENT IT FELT LIKE--
...LIKE...
AH, WELL--
MUST'VE BEEN SOMETHING I ATE. PROBABLY THAT BOX OF "CUPCAKES." OR MAYBE IT WAS THE TONGUE SANDWICH I HAD FOR LUNCH.
I KNEW I SHOULD'VE BOILED IT AFTER I RIPPED IT OUT OF THAT IDIOT'S MOUTH.
AH-HEE.
AH-HOO.
B-B-B-B--
BWA-HA-HA-HA-HA-HAAAAA!!

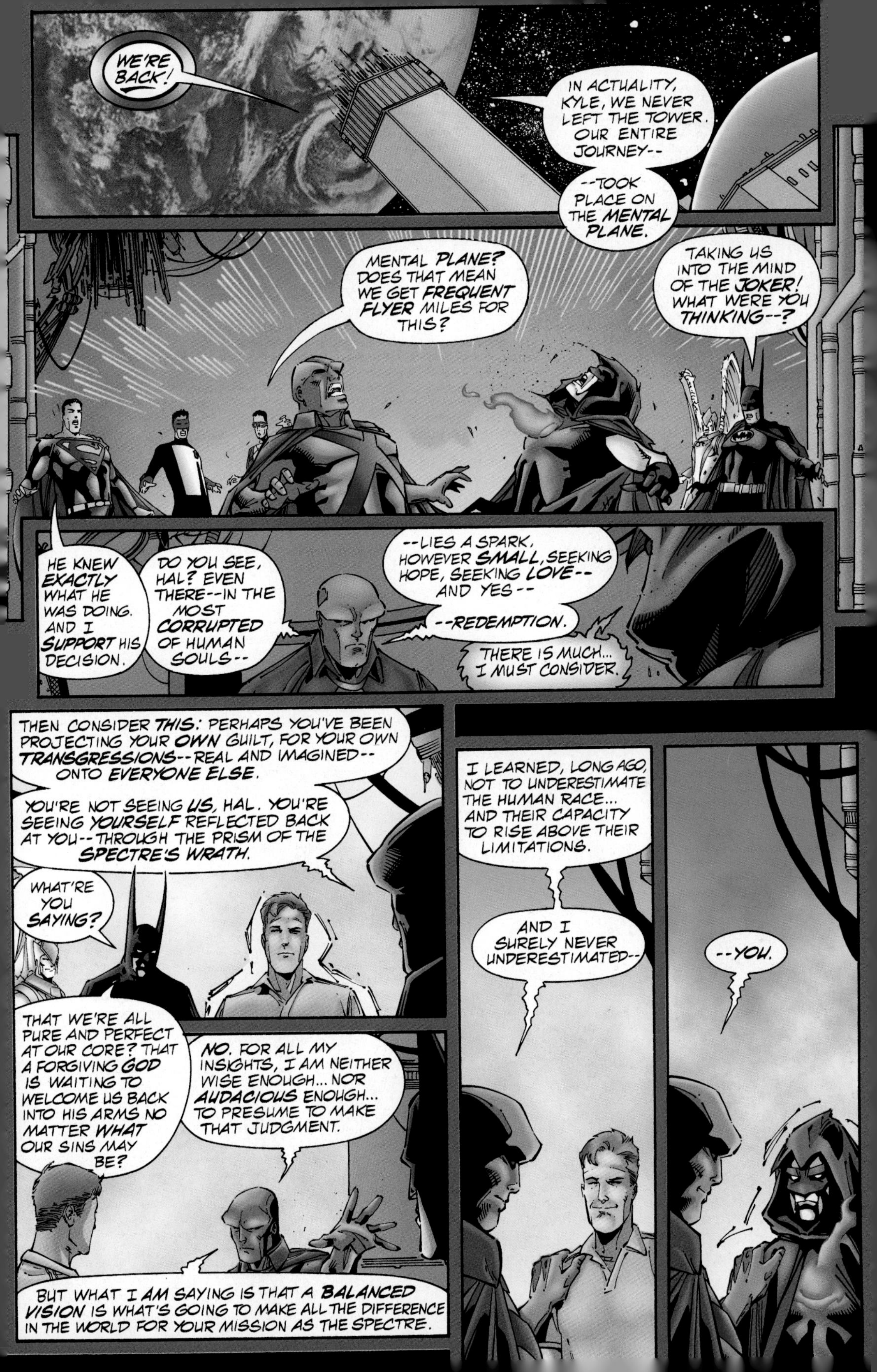
WE'RE BACK!
IN ACTUALITY, KYLE, WE NEVER LEFT THE TOWER. OUR ENTIRE JOURNEY--
--TOOK PLACE ON THE MENTAL PLANE.
MENTAL PLANE? DOES THAT MEAN WE GET FREQUENT FLYER MILES FOR THIS?
TAKING US INTO THE MIND OF THE JOKER! WHAT WERE YOU THINKING--?
HE KNEW EXACTLY WHAT HE WAS DOING. AND I SUPPORT HIS DECISION.
DO YOU SEE, HAL? EVEN THERE--IN THE MOST CORRUPTED OF HUMAN SOULS--
--LIES A SPARK, HOWEVER SMALL, SEEKING HOPE, SEEKING LOVE-- AND YES--
--REDEMPTION.
THERE IS MUCH... I MUST CONSIDER.
THEN CONSIDER THIS: PERHAPS YOU'VE BEEN PROJECTING YOUR OWN GUILT, FOR YOUR OWN TRANSGRESSIONS--REAL AND IMAGINED-- ONTO EVERYONE ELSE.
YOU'RE NOT SEEING US, HAL. YOU'RE SEEING YOURSELF REFLECTED BACK AT YOU--THROUGH THE PRISM OF THE SPECTRE'S WRATH.
WHAT'RE YOU SAYING?
THAT WE'RE ALL PURE AND PERFECT AT OUR CORE? THAT A FORGIVING GOD IS WAITING TO WELCOME US BACK INTO HIS ARMS NO MATTER WHAT OUR SINS MAY BE?
NO. FOR ALL MY INSIGHTS, I AM NEITHER WISE ENOUGH... NOR AUDACIOUS ENOUGH... TO PRESUME TO MAKE THAT JUDGMENT.
BUT WHAT I AM SAYING IS THAT A BALANCED VISION IS WHAT'S GOING TO MAKE ALL THE DIFFERENCE IN THE WORLD FOR YOUR MISSION AS THE SPECTRE.
I LEARNED, LONG AGO, NOT TO UNDERESTIMATE THE HUMAN RACE... AND THEIR CAPACITY TO RISE ABOVE THEIR LIMITATIONS.
AND I SURELY NEVER UNDERESTIMATED--
--YOU.

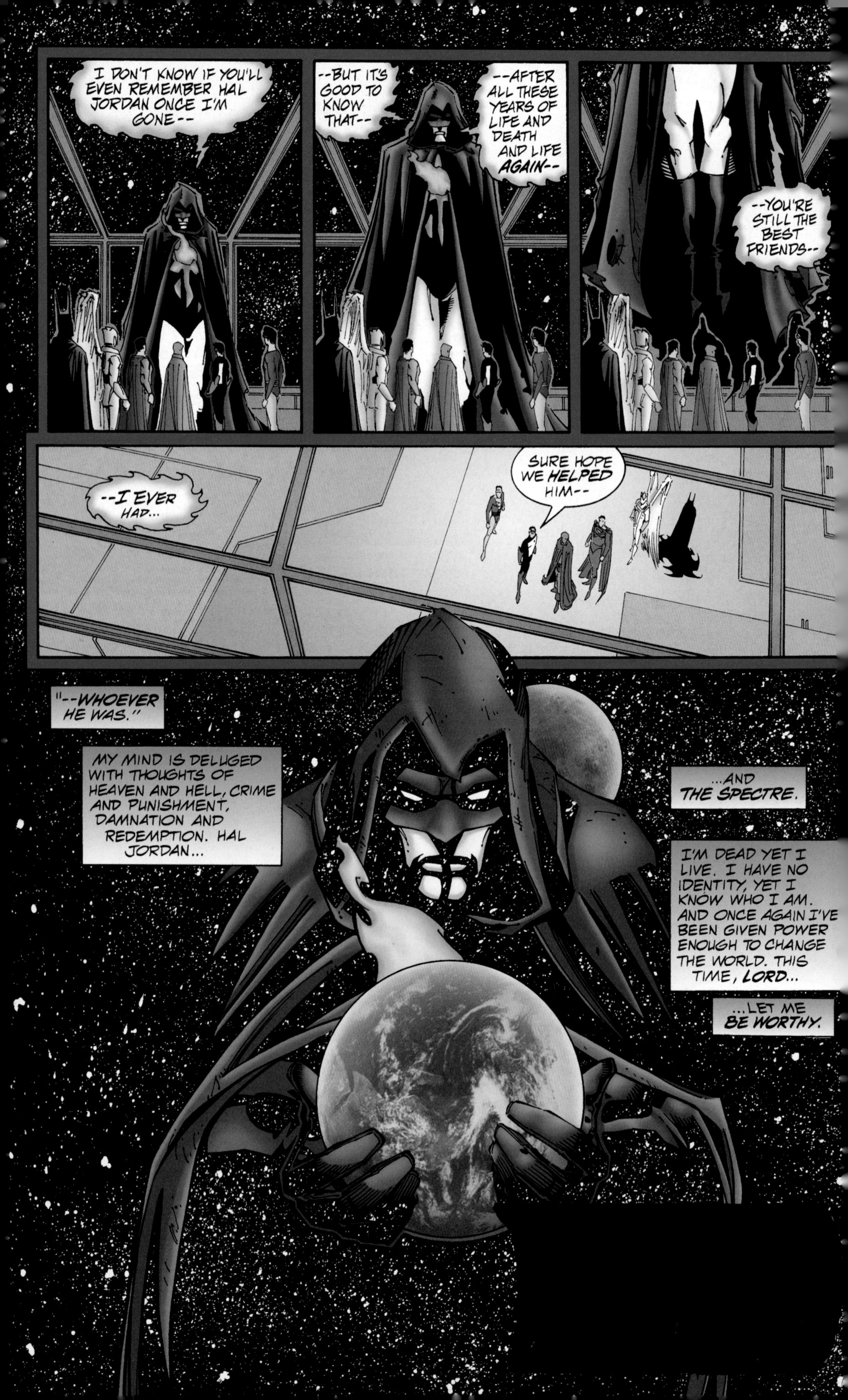
I DON'T KNOW IF YOU'LL EVEN REMEMBER HAL JORDAN ONCE I'M GONE--
--BUT IT'S GOOD TO KNOW THAT--
--AFTER ALL THESE YEARS OF LIFE AND DEATH AND LIFE AGAIN--
--YOU'RE STILL THE BEST FRIENDS--
--I EVER HAD...
SURE HOPE WE HELPED HIM--
"--WHOEVER HE WAS."
MY MIND IS DELUGED WITH THOUGHTS OF HEAVEN AND HELL, CRIME AND PUNISHMENT, DAMNATION AND REDEMPTION. HAL JORDAN...
...AND THE SPECTRE.
I'M DEAD YET I LIVE. I HAVE NO IDENTITY, YET I KNOW WHO I AM. AND ONCE AGAIN I'VE BEEN GIVEN POWER ENOUGH TO CHANGE THE WORLD. THIS TIME, LORD...
...LET ME BE WORTHY.

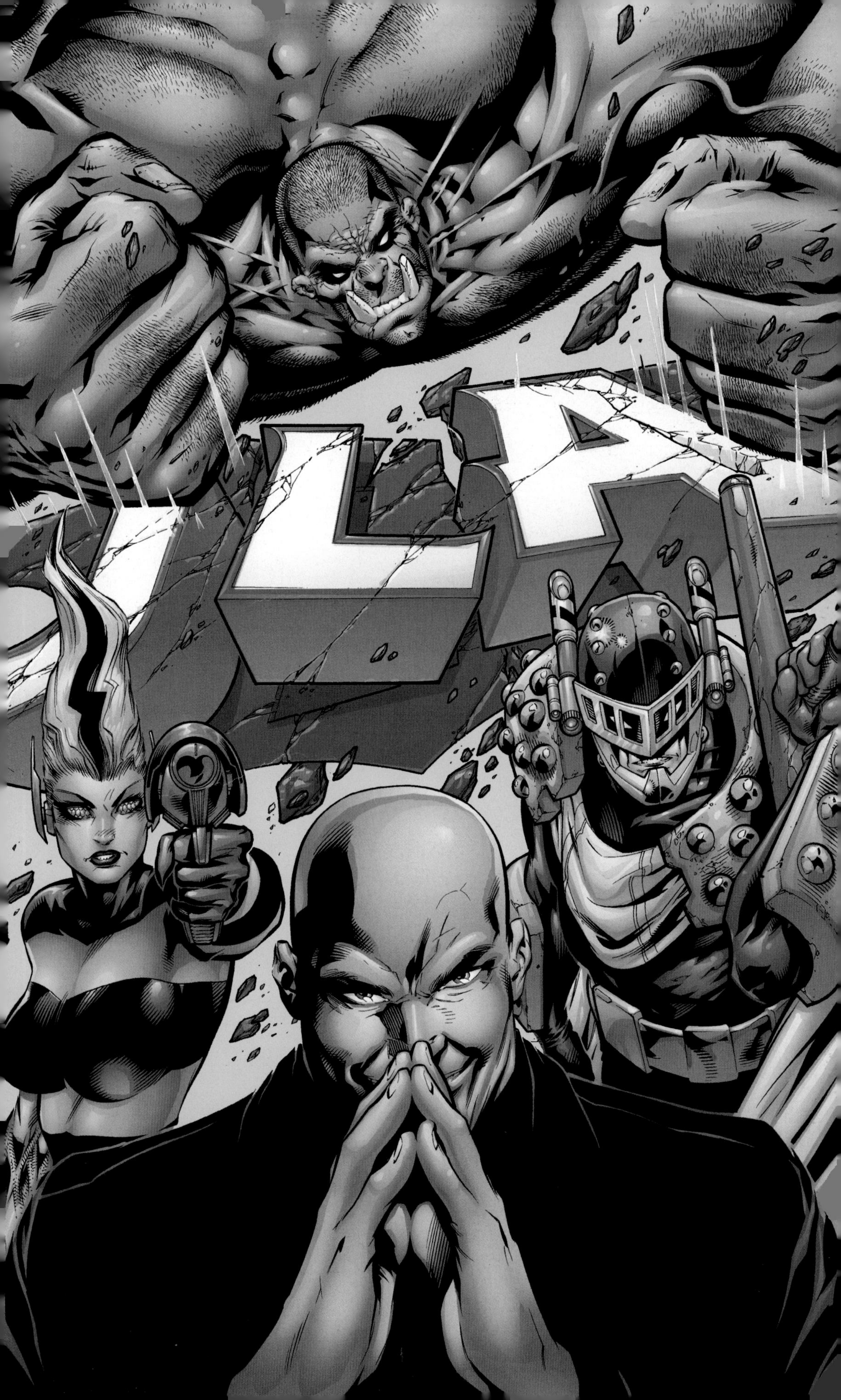

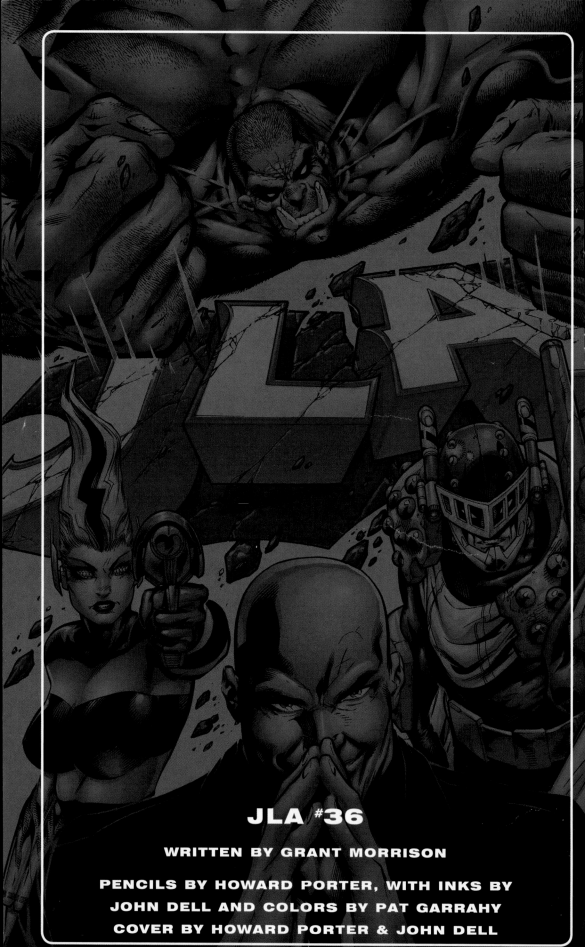

JLA #36

WRITTEN BY GRANT MORRISON

PENCILS BY HOWARD PORTER, WITH INKS BY
JOHN DELL AND COLORS BY PAT GARRAHY
COVER BY HOWARD PORTER & JOHN DELL

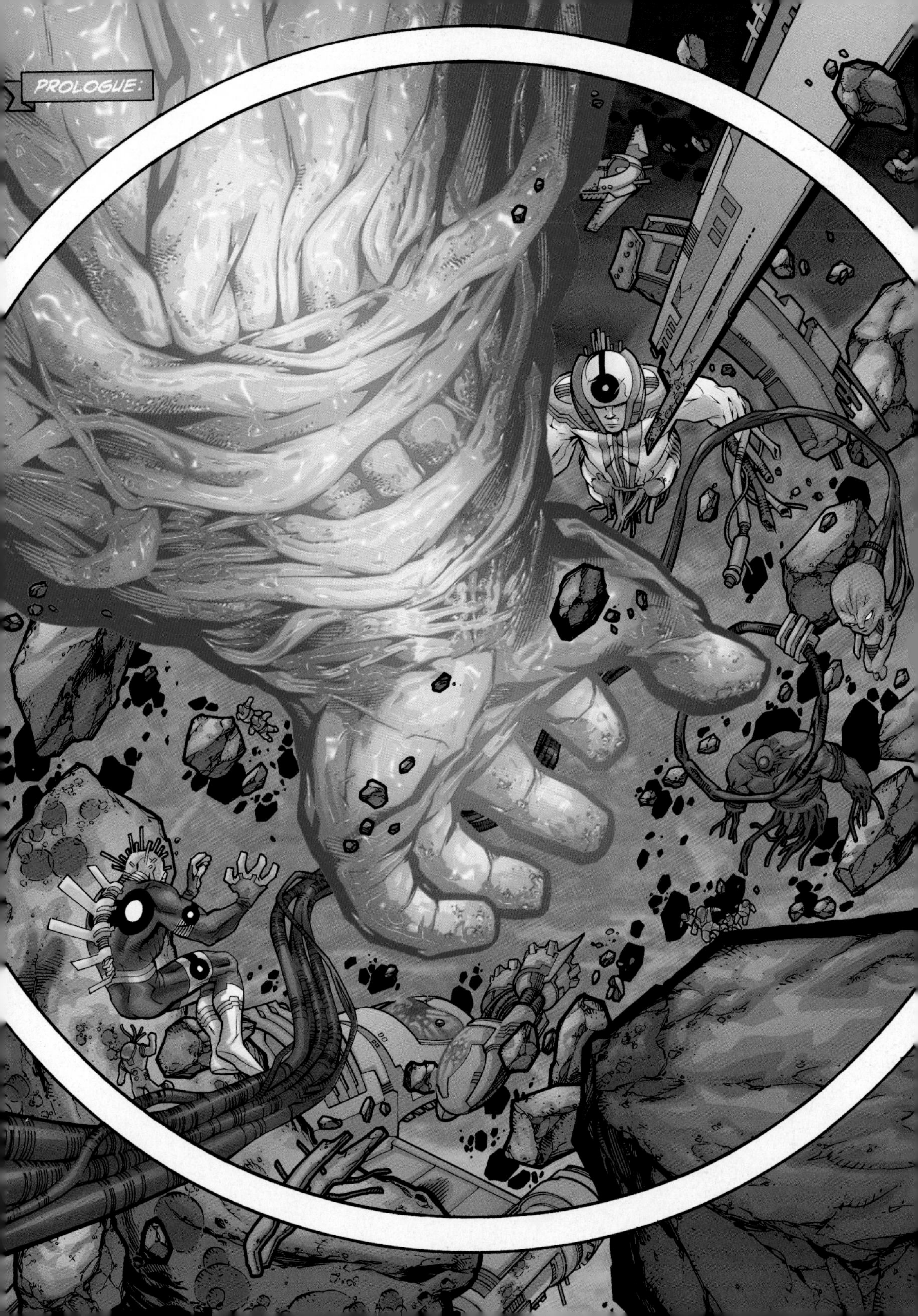
PROLOGUE:

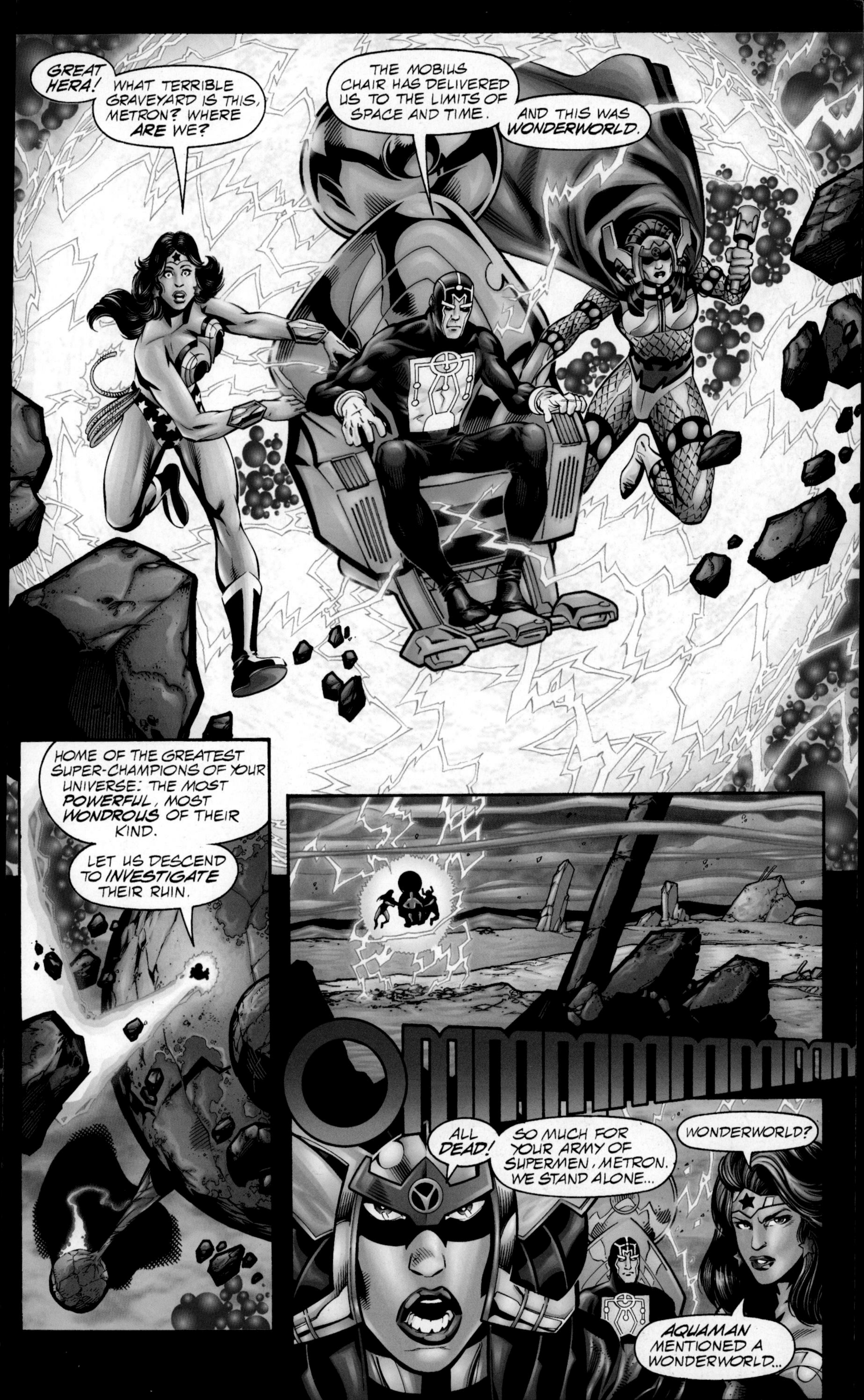
GREAT HERA! WHAT TERRIBLE GRAVEYARD IS THIS, METRON? WHERE ARE WE?
THE MOBIUS CHAIR HAS DELIVERED US TO THE LIMITS OF SPACE AND TIME.
AND THIS WAS WONDERWORLD.
HOME OF THE GREATEST SUPER-CHAMPIONS OF YOUR UNIVERSE: THE MOST POWERFUL, MOST WONDROUS OF THEIR KIND.
LET US DESCEND TO INVESTIGATE THEIR RUIN.
OMMMMMMMMMM
ALL DEAD!
SO MUCH FOR YOUR ARMY OF SUPERMEN, METRON. WE STAND ALONE...
WONDERWORLD?
AQUAMAN MENTIONED A WONDERWORLD...

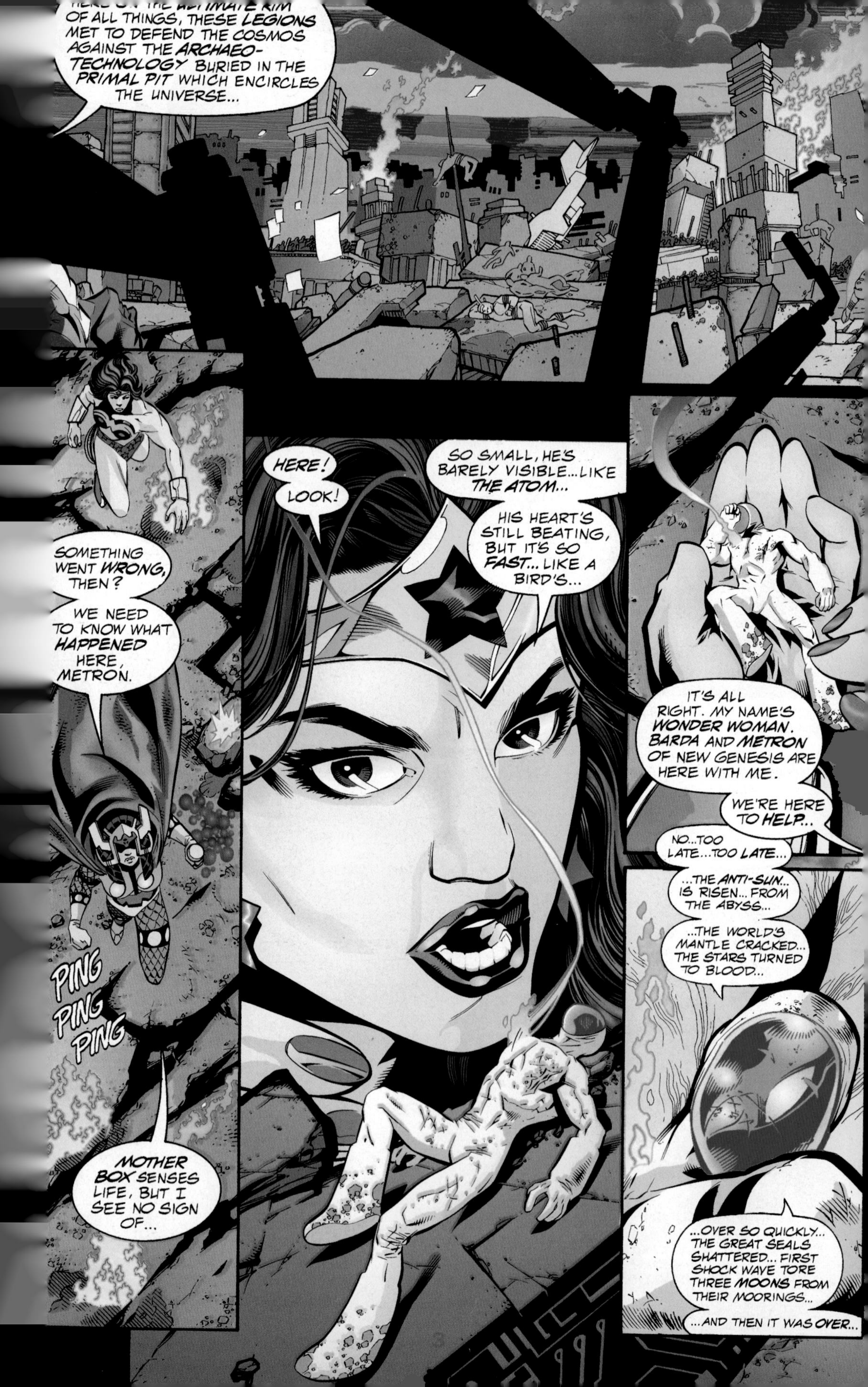
OF ALL THINGS, THESE LEGIONS MET TO DEFEND THE COSMOS AGAINST THE ARCHAEO-TECHNOLOGY BURIED IN THE PRIMAL PIT WHICH ENCIRCLES THE UNIVERSE...
SOMETHING WENT WRONG, THEN?
WE NEED TO KNOW WHAT HAPPENED HERE, METRON.
PING PING PING
MOTHER BOX SENSES LIFE, BUT I SEE NO SIGN OF...
HERE!
LOOK!
SO SMALL, HE'S BARELY VISIBLE...LIKE THE ATOM...
HIS HEART'S STILL BEATING, BUT IT'S SO FAST... LIKE A BIRD'S...
IT'S ALL RIGHT. MY NAME'S WONDER WOMAN. BARDA AND METRON OF NEW GENESIS ARE HERE WITH ME.
WE'RE HERE TO HELP...
NO...TOO LATE...TOO LATE...
...THE ANTI-SUN... IS RISEN... FROM THE ABYSS...
...THE WORLD'S MANTLE CRACKED... THE STARS TURNED TO BLOOD...
...OVER SO QUICKLY... THE GREAT SEALS SHATTERED... FIRST SHOCK WAVE TORE THREE MOONS FROM THEIR MOORINGS...
...AND THEN IT WAS OVER...

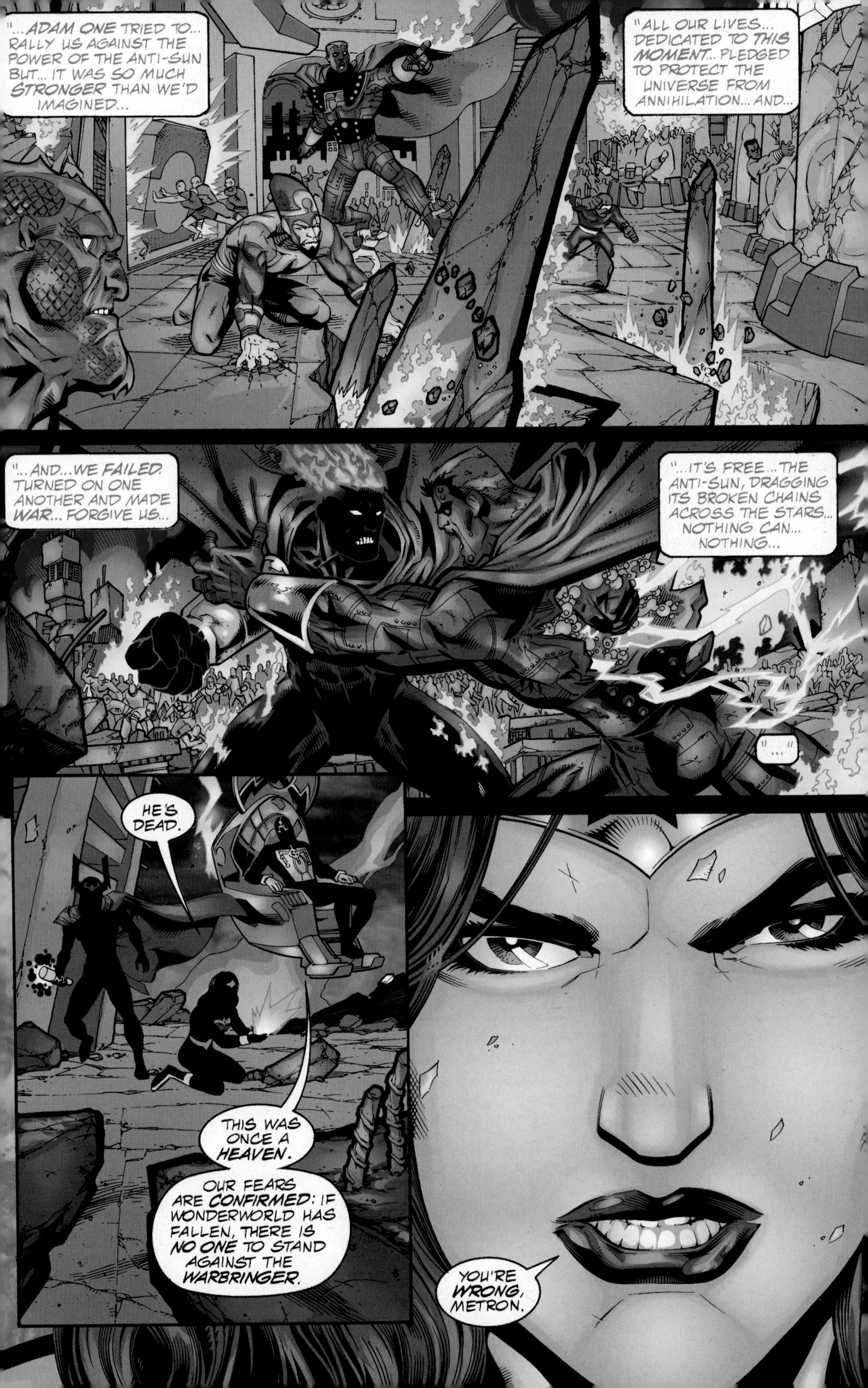
"...ADAM ONE TRIED TO... RALLY US AGAINST THE POWER OF THE ANTI-SUN BUT... IT WAS SO MUCH STRONGER THAN WE'D IMAGINED...
"ALL OUR LIVES... DEDICATED TO THIS MOMENT... PLEDGED TO PROTECT THE UNIVERSE FROM ANNIHILATION... AND...
"...AND... WE FAILED. TURNED ON ONE ANOTHER AND MADE WAR... FORGIVE US...
"...IT'S FREE... THE ANTI-SUN, DRAGGING ITS BROKEN CHAINS ACROSS THE STARS... NOTHING CAN... NOTHING...
"..."
HE'S DEAD.
THIS WAS ONCE A HEAVEN.
OUR FEARS ARE CONFIRMED: IF WONDERWORLD HAS FALLEN, THERE IS NO ONE TO STAND AGAINST THE WARBRINGER.
YOU'RE WRONG, METRON.

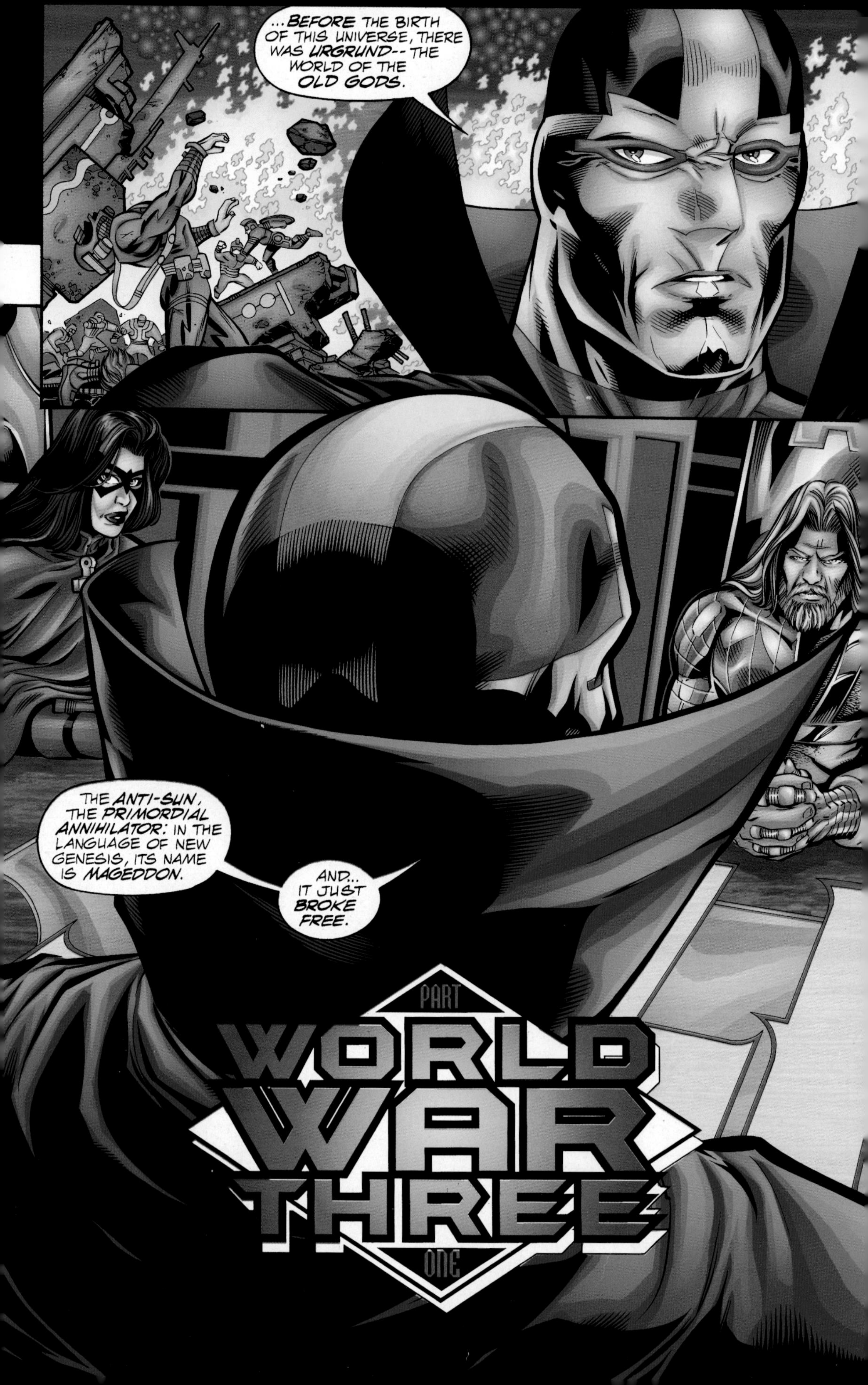
...BEFORE THE BIRTH OF THIS UNIVERSE, THERE WAS URGRUND-- THE WORLD OF THE OLD GODS.
THE ANTI-SUN, THE PRIMORDIAL ANNIHILATOR: IN THE LANGUAGE OF NEW GENESIS, ITS NAME IS MAGEDDON.
AND... IT JUST BROKE FREE.
PART
WORLD WAR THREE
ONE

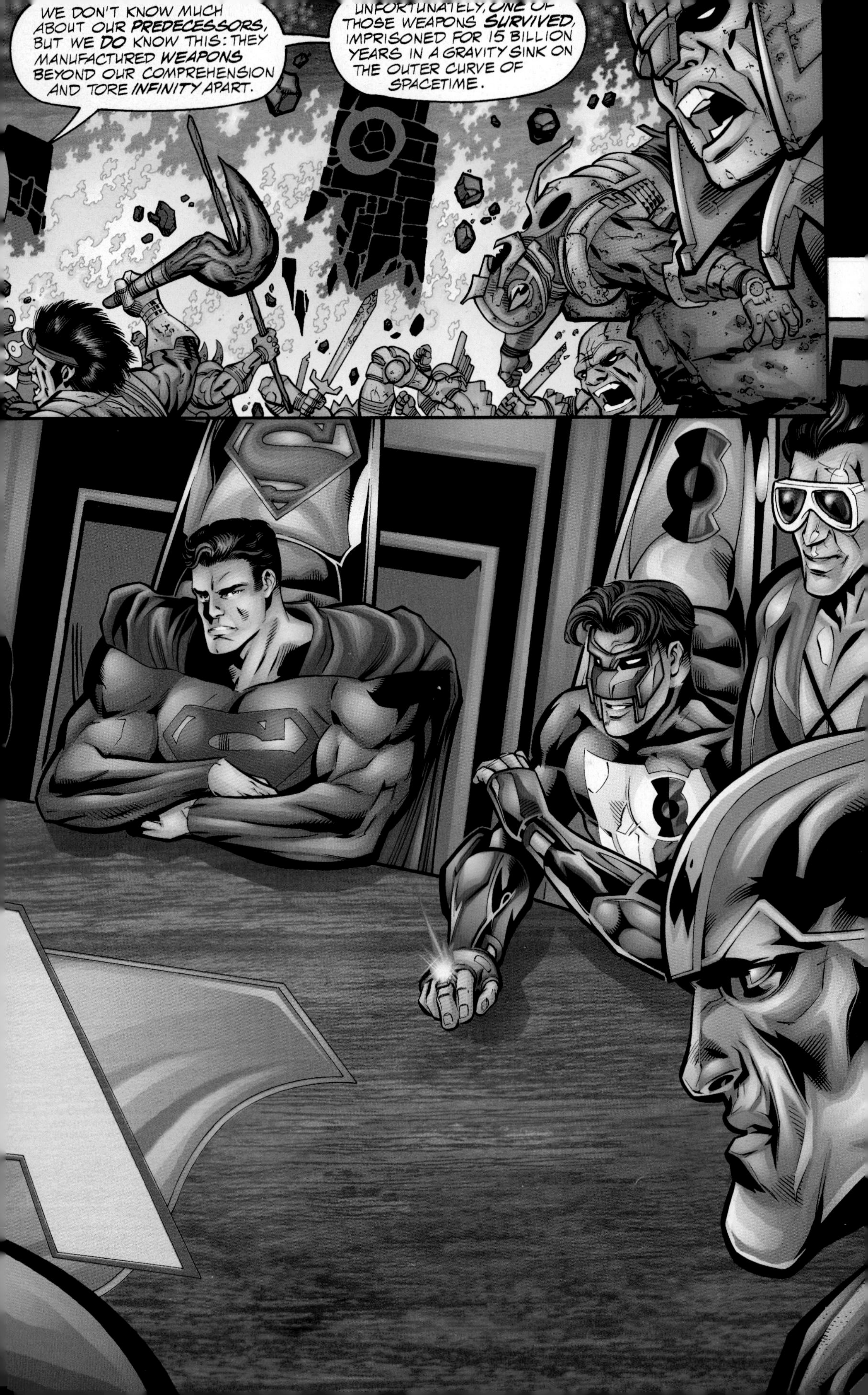
WE DON'T KNOW MUCH ABOUT OUR PREDECESSORS, BUT WE DO KNOW THIS: THEY MANUFACTURED WEAPONS BEYOND OUR COMPREHENSION AND TORE INFINITY APART.
UNFORTUNATELY, ONE OF THOSE WEAPONS SURVIVED, IMPRISONED FOR 15 BILLION YEARS IN A GRAVITY SINK ON THE OUTER CURVE OF SPACETIME.

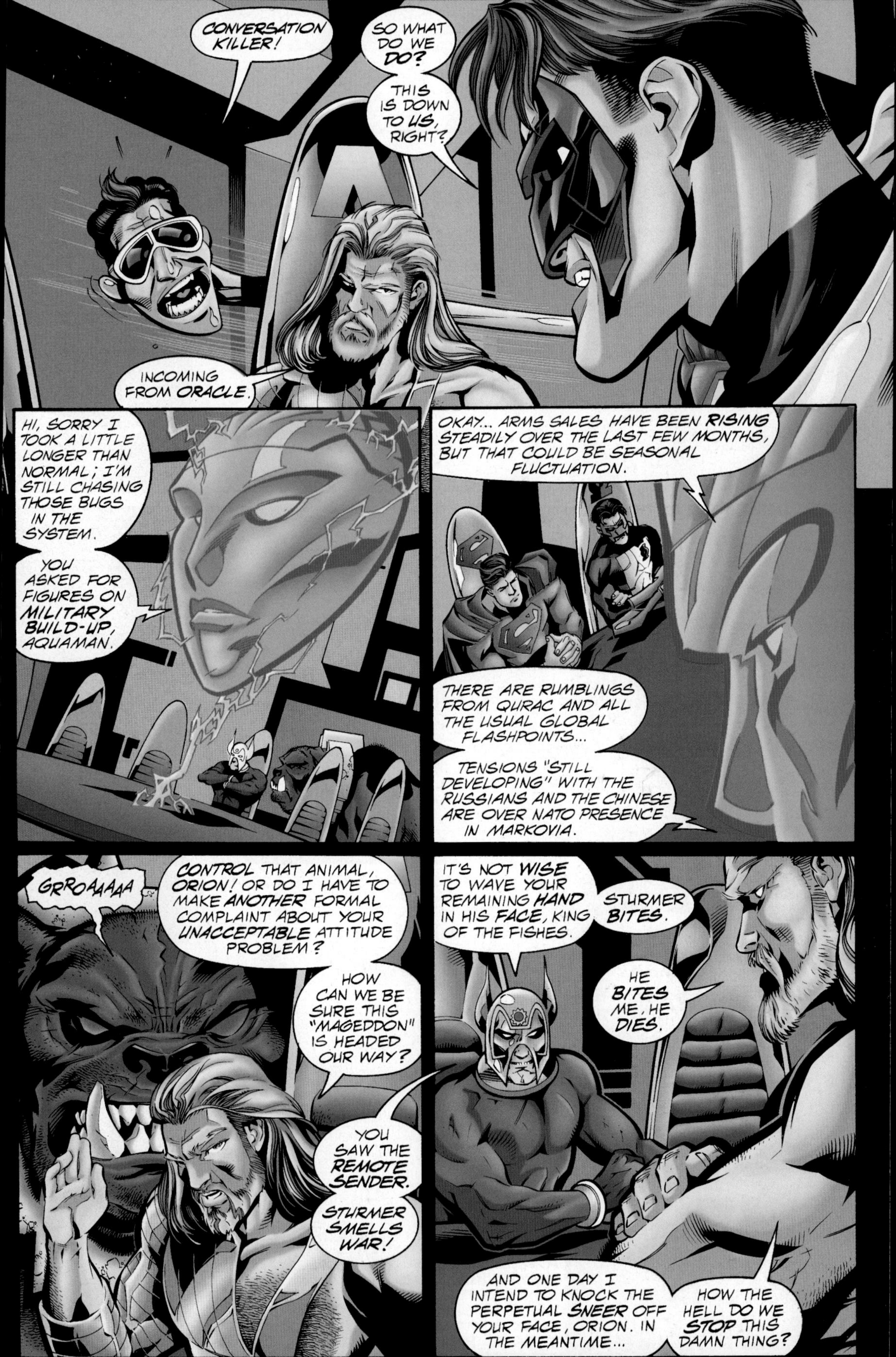
CONVERSATION KILLER!
SO WHAT DO WE DO?
THIS IS DOWN TO US, RIGHT?
INCOMING FROM ORACLE.
HI, SORRY I TOOK A LITTLE LONGER THAN NORMAL; I'M STILL CHASING THOSE BUGS IN THE SYSTEM.
YOU ASKED FOR FIGURES ON MILITARY BUILD-UP, AQUAMAN.
OKAY... ARMS SALES HAVE BEEN RISING STEADILY OVER THE LAST FEW MONTHS, BUT THAT COULD BE SEASONAL FLUCTUATION.
THERE ARE RUMBLINGS FROM QURAC AND ALL THE USUAL GLOBAL FLASHPOINTS...
TENSIONS "STILL DEVELOPING" WITH THE RUSSIANS AND THE CHINESE ARE OVER NATO PRESENCE IN MARKOVIA.
GRROAAAAA
CONTROL THAT ANIMAL, ORION! OR DO I HAVE TO MAKE ANOTHER FORMAL COMPLAINT ABOUT YOUR UNACCEPTABLE ATTITUDE PROBLEM?
HOW CAN WE BE SURE THIS "MAGEDDON" IS HEADED OUR WAY?
YOU SAW THE REMOTE SENDER.
STURMER SMELLS WAR!
IT'S NOT WISE TO WAVE YOUR REMAINING HAND IN HIS FACE, KING OF THE FISHES.
STURMER BITES.
HE BITES ME, HE DIES.
AND ONE DAY I INTEND TO KNOCK THE PERPETUAL SNEER OFF YOUR FACE, ORION. IN THE MEANTIME...
HOW THE HELL DO WE STOP THIS DAMN THING?

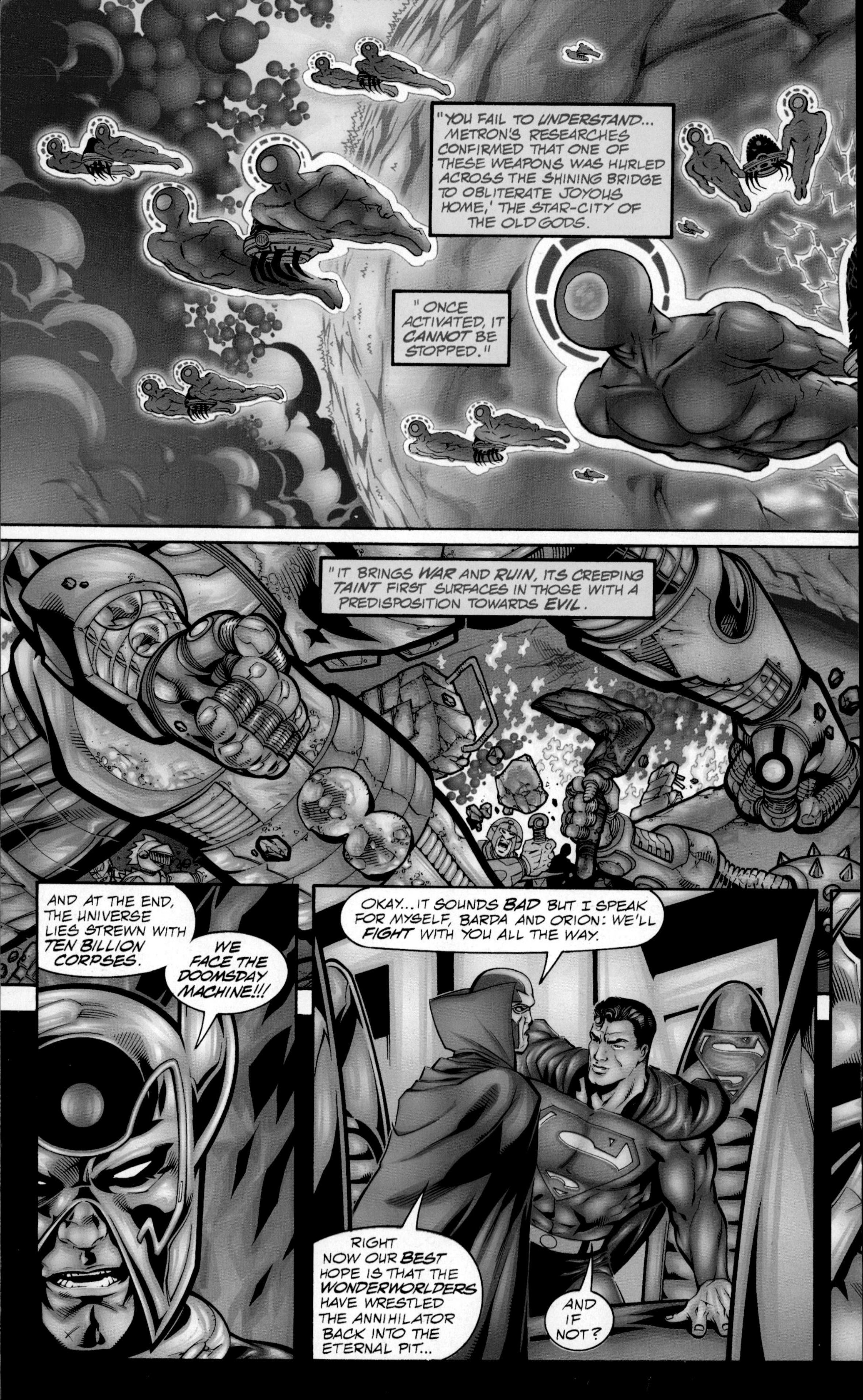
"YOU FAIL TO UNDERSTAND... METRON'S RESEARCHES CONFIRMED THAT ONE OF THESE WEAPONS WAS HURLED ACROSS THE SHINING BRIDGE TO OBLITERATE JOYOUS HOME,' THE STAR-CITY OF THE OLD GODS.
"ONCE ACTIVATED, IT CANNOT BE STOPPED."
"IT BRINGS WAR AND RUIN, ITS CREEPING TAINT FIRST SURFACES IN THOSE WITH A PREDISPOSITION TOWARDS EVIL.
AND AT THE END, THE UNIVERSE LIES STREWN WITH TEN BILLION CORPSES.
WE FACE THE DOOMSDAY MACHINE!!!
OKAY... IT SOUNDS BAD BUT I SPEAK FOR MYSELF, BARDA AND ORION: WE'LL FIGHT WITH YOU ALL THE WAY.
RIGHT NOW OUR BEST HOPE IS THAT THE WONDERWORLDERS HAVE WRESTLED THE ANNIHILATOR BACK INTO THE ETERNAL PIT...
AND IF NOT?

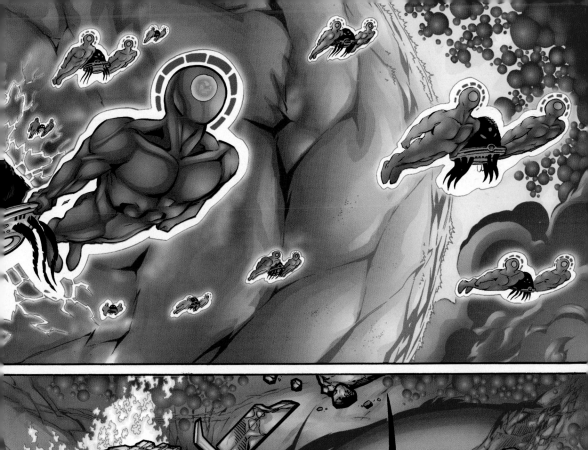

"THEN, AS IT COMES *CLOSER,* ALL THE SOLDIERS OF *CHAOS* BESET THE FORCES OF *ORDER.*

"FINALLY THE *MAGEDDON* WARHEAD MANIFESTS IN THE HEAVENS. BROTHER *MURDERS* BROTHER... THE STARS *DIE...*"

THEN HOPE IS *LOST* AND WE MUST CONFRONT *COSMIC APOCALYPSE* AS BEST WE CAN.

ORACLE, ALERT *EVERY* LEAGUER, PAST AND PRESENT.

EVERYONE.

HOW *LONG* DO WE HAVE?

AAAOOOOOOO

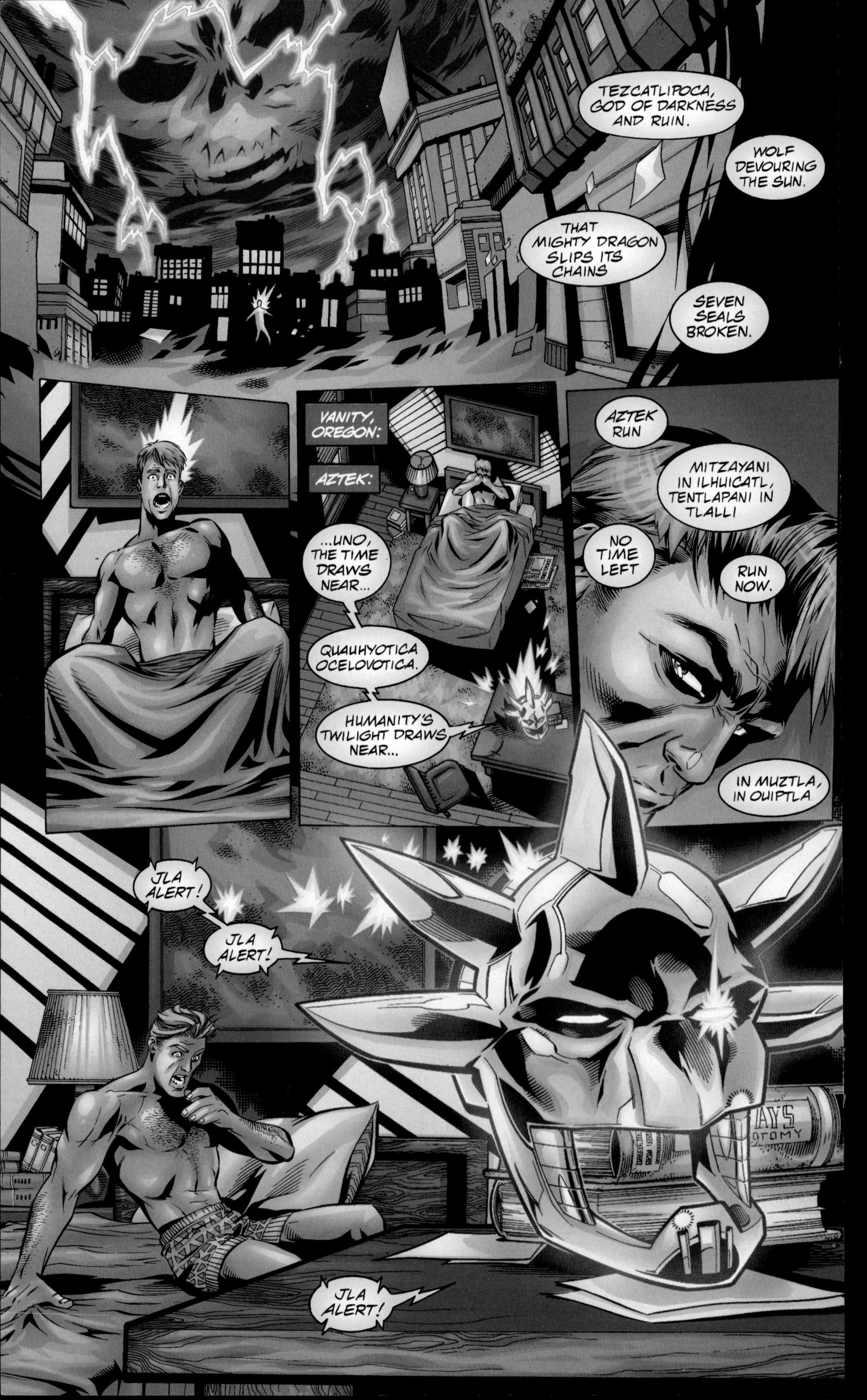
TEZCATLIPOCA, GOD OF DARKNESS AND RUIN.
WOLF DEVOURING THE SUN.
THAT MIGHTY DRAGON SLIPS ITS CHAINS
SEVEN SEALS BROKEN.
VANITY, OREGON:
AZTEK:
...UNO, THE TIME DRAWS NEAR...
QUAUHYOTICA OCELOVOTICA.
HUMANITY'S TWILIGHT DRAWS NEAR...
AZTEK RUN
MITZAYANI IN ILHUICATL, TENTLAPANI IN TLALLI
NO TIME LEFT
RUN NOW.
IN MUZTLA, IN OUIPTLA
JLA ALERT!
JLA ALERT!
JLA ALERT!

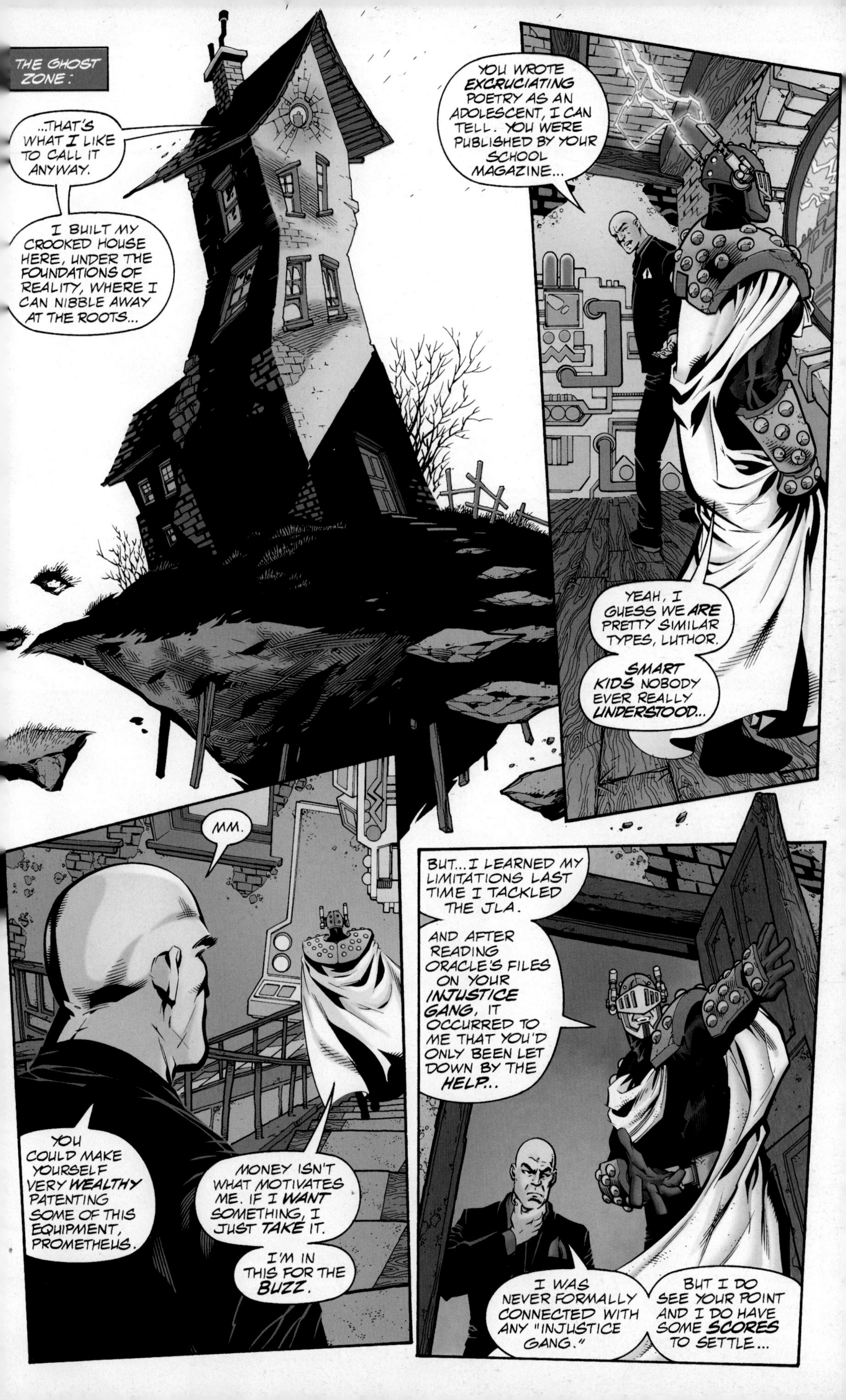
THE GHOST ZONE:
...THAT'S WHAT I LIKE TO CALL IT ANYWAY.
I BUILT MY CROOKED HOUSE HERE, UNDER THE FOUNDATIONS OF REALITY, WHERE I CAN NIBBLE AWAY AT THE ROOTS...
YOU WROTE EXCRUCIATING POETRY AS AN ADOLESCENT, I CAN TELL. YOU WERE PUBLISHED BY YOUR SCHOOL MAGAZINE...
YEAH, I GUESS WE ARE PRETTY SIMILAR TYPES, LUTHOR.
SMART KIDS NOBODY EVER REALLY UNDERSTOOD...
MM.
YOU COULD MAKE YOURSELF VERY WEALTHY PATENTING SOME OF THIS EQUIPMENT, PROMETHEUS.
MONEY ISN'T WHAT MOTIVATES ME. IF I WANT SOMETHING, I JUST TAKE IT.
I'M IN THIS FOR THE BUZZ.
BUT... I LEARNED MY LIMITATIONS LAST TIME I TACKLED THE JLA.
AND AFTER READING ORACLE'S FILES ON YOUR INJUSTICE GANG, IT OCCURRED TO ME THAT YOU'D ONLY BEEN LET DOWN BY THE HELP...
I WAS NEVER FORMALLY CONNECTED WITH ANY "INJUSTICE GANG."
BUT I DO SEE YOUR POINT AND I DO HAVE SOME SCORES TO SETTLE...

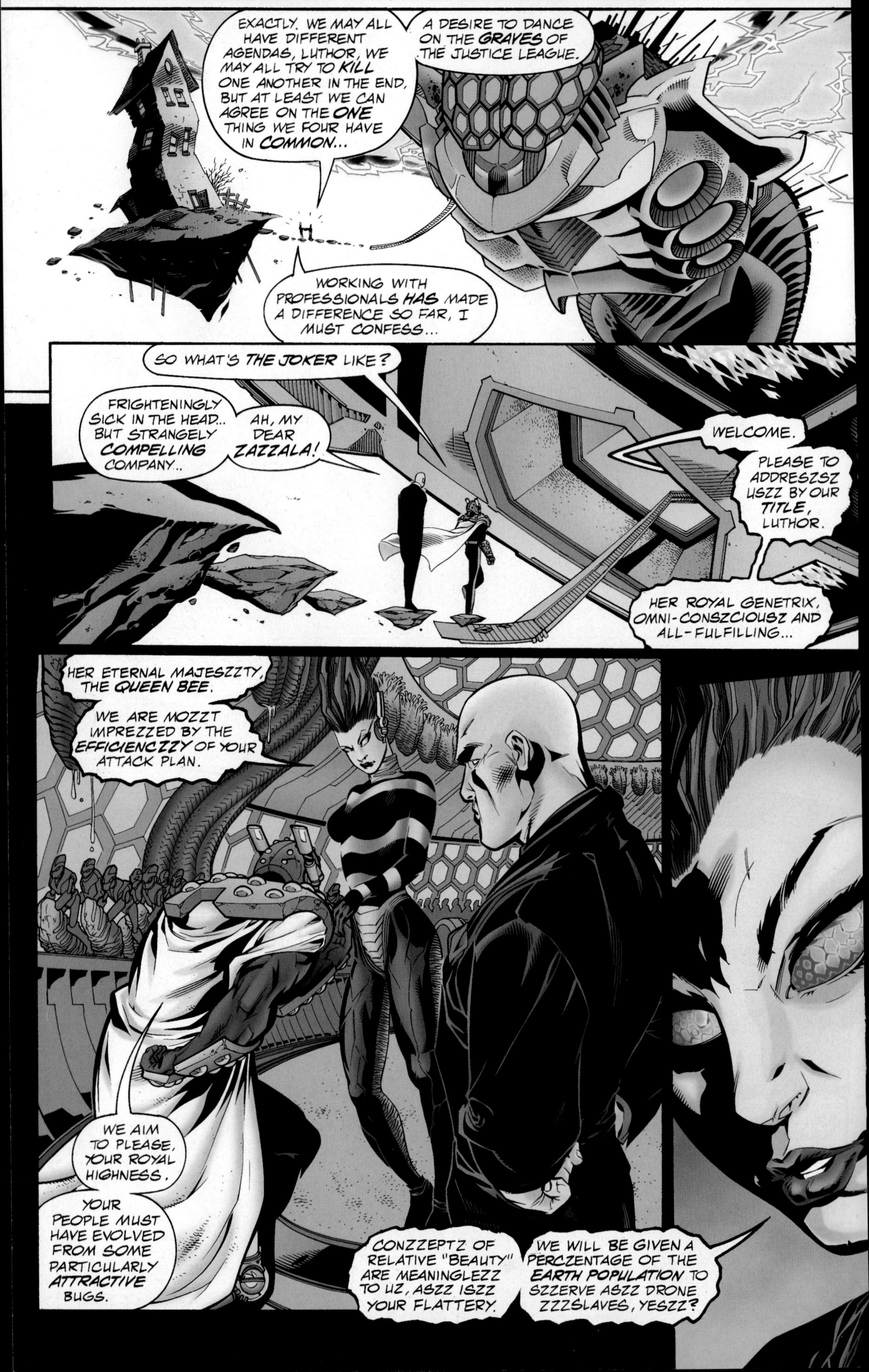
EXACTLY. WE MAY ALL HAVE DIFFERENT AGENDAS, LUTHOR, WE MAY ALL TRY TO KILL ONE ANOTHER IN THE END, BUT AT LEAST WE CAN AGREE ON THE ONE THING WE FOUR HAVE IN COMMON...
A DESIRE TO DANCE ON THE GRAVES OF THE JUSTICE LEAGUE.
WORKING WITH PROFESSIONALS HAS MADE A DIFFERENCE SO FAR, I MUST CONFESS...
SO WHAT'S THE JOKER LIKE?
FRIGHTENINGLY SICK IN THE HEAD... BUT STRANGELY COMPELLING COMPANY...
AH, MY DEAR ZAZZALA!
WELCOME.
PLEASE TO ADDRESZSZ USZZ BY OUR TITLE, LUTHOR.
HER ROYAL GENETRIX, OMNI-CONSZCIOUSZ AND ALL-FULFILLING...
HER ETERNAL MAJESZZTY, THE QUEEN BEE.
WE ARE MOZZT IMPREZZED BY THE EFFICIENCZZY OF YOUR ATTACK PLAN.
WE AIM TO PLEASE, YOUR ROYAL HIGHNESS.
YOUR PEOPLE MUST HAVE EVOLVED FROM SOME PARTICULARLY ATTRACTIVE BUGS.
CONZZEPTZ OF RELATIVE "BEAUTY" ARE MEANINGLEZZ TO UZ, ASZZ ISZZ YOUR FLATTERY.
WE WILL BE GIVEN A PERCZENTAGE OF THE EARTH POPULATION TO SZZERVE ASZZ DRONE ZZZSLAVES, YESZZ?

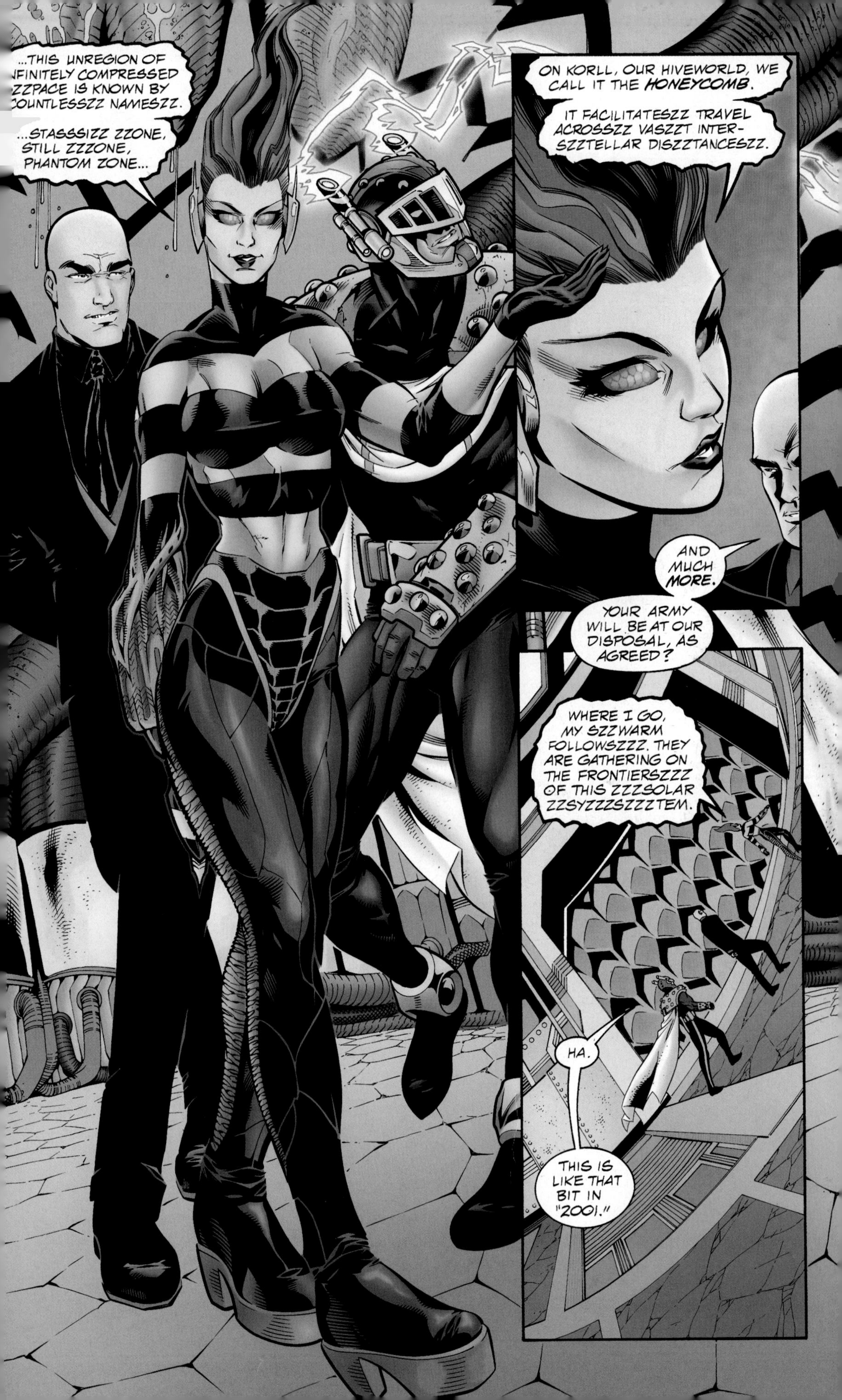
...THIS UNREGION OF INFINITELY COMPRESSED ZZPACE IS KNOWN BY COUNTLESSZZ NAMESZZ.
...STASSSIZZ ZZONE, STILL ZZZONE, PHANTOM ZONE...
ON KORLL, OUR HIVEWORLD, WE CALL IT THE *HONEYCOMB*.
IT FACILITATESZZ TRAVEL ACROSSZZ VASZZT INTER-SZZTELLAR DISZZTANCESZZ.
AND MUCH *MORE*.
YOUR ARMY WILL BE AT OUR DISPOSAL, AS AGREED?
WHERE I GO, MY SZZWARM FOLLOWSZZZ. THEY ARE GATHERING ON THE FRONTIERSZZZ OF THIS ZZZSOLAR ZZSYZZZSZZZTEM.
HA.
THIS IS LIKE THAT BIT IN "2001."

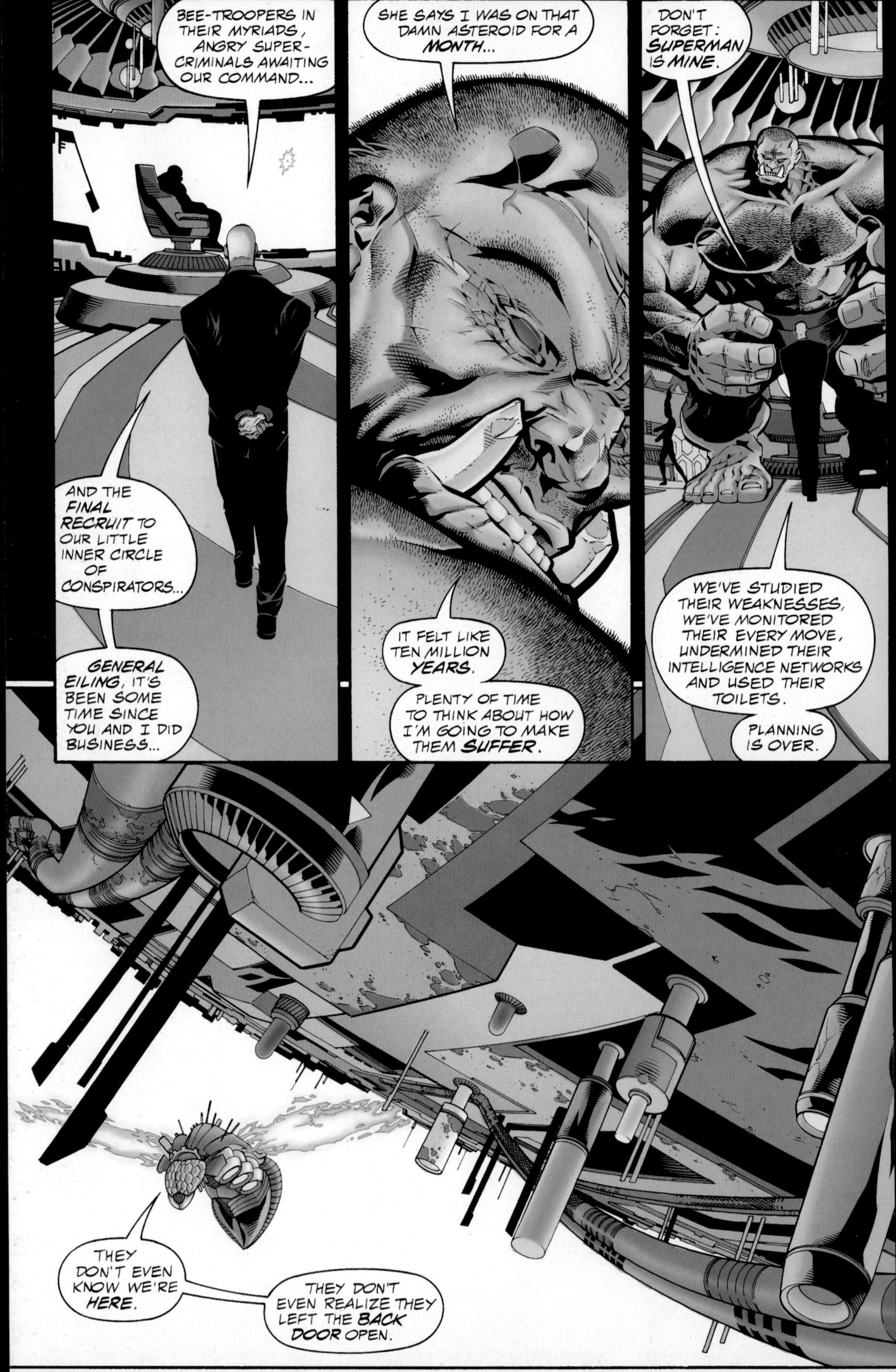
BEE-TROOPERS IN THEIR MYRIADS, ANGRY SUPER-CRIMINALS AWAITING OUR COMMAND...
AND THE FINAL RECRUIT TO OUR LITTLE INNER CIRCLE OF CONSPIRATORS...
GENERAL EILING, IT'S BEEN SOME TIME SINCE YOU AND I DID BUSINESS...
SHE SAYS I WAS ON THAT DAMN ASTEROID FOR A MONTH...
IT FELT LIKE TEN MILLION YEARS.
PLENTY OF TIME TO THINK ABOUT HOW I'M GOING TO MAKE THEM SUFFER.
DON'T FORGET: SUPERMAN IS MINE.
WE'VE STUDIED THEIR WEAKNESSES, WE'VE MONITORED THEIR EVERY MOVE, UNDERMINED THEIR INTELLIGENCE NETWORKS AND USED THEIR TOILETS.
PLANNING IS OVER.
THEY DON'T EVEN KNOW WE'RE HERE.
THEY DON'T EVEN REALIZE THEY LEFT THE BACK DOOR OPEN.

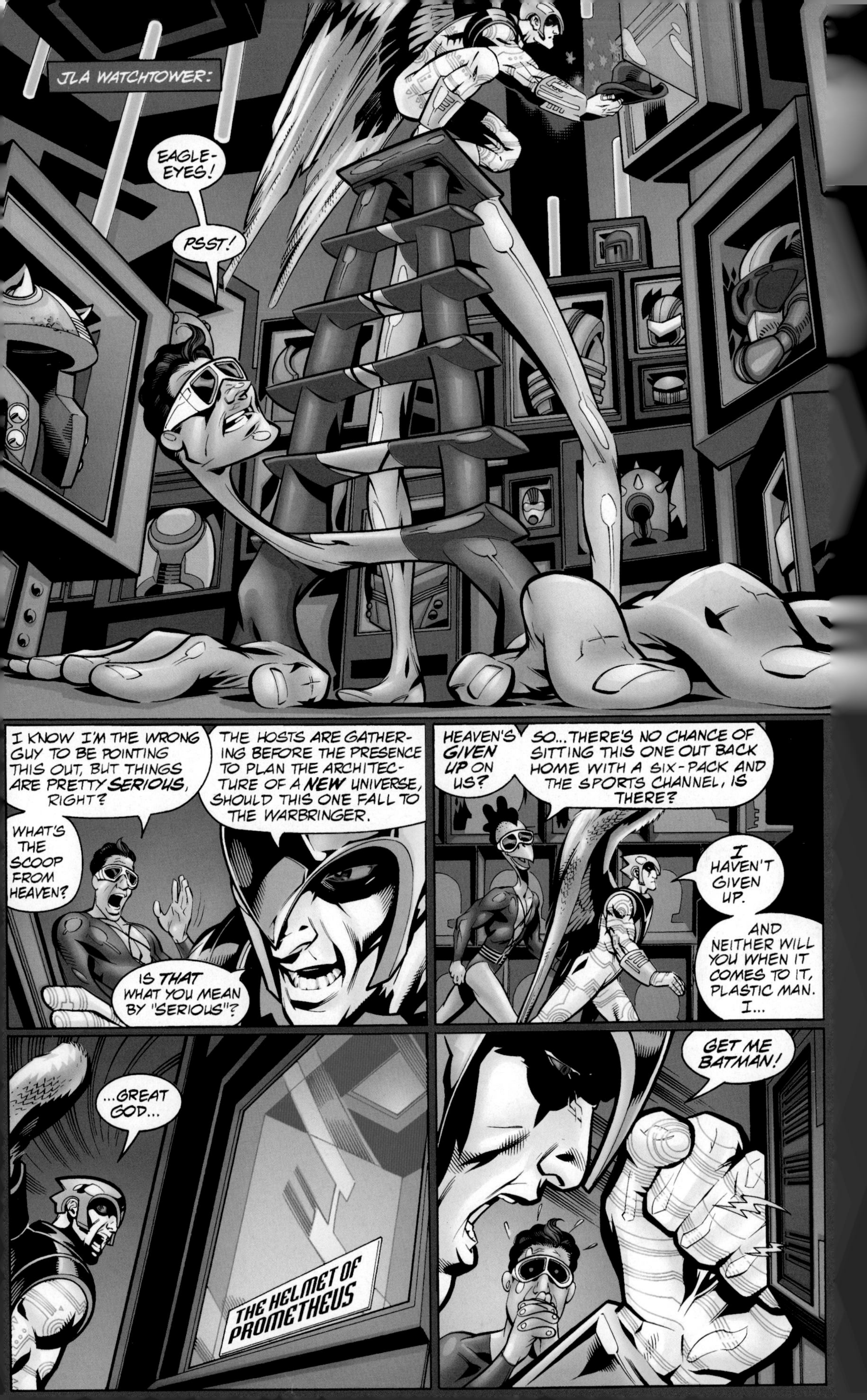

JLA WATCHTOWER:
EAGLE-EYES!
PSST!
I KNOW I'M THE WRONG GUY TO BE POINTING THIS OUT, BUT THINGS ARE PRETTY SERIOUS, RIGHT?
WHAT'S THE SCOOP FROM HEAVEN?
THE HOSTS ARE GATHERING BEFORE THE PRESENCE TO PLAN THE ARCHITECTURE OF A NEW UNIVERSE, SHOULD THIS ONE FALL TO THE WARBRINGER.
IS THAT WHAT YOU MEAN BY "SERIOUS"?
HEAVEN'S GIVEN UP ON US?
SO...THERE'S NO CHANCE OF SITTING THIS ONE OUT BACK HOME WITH A SIX-PACK AND THE SPORTS CHANNEL, IS THERE?
I HAVEN'T GIVEN UP.
AND NEITHER WILL YOU WHEN IT COMES TO IT, PLASTIC MAN. I...
...GREAT GOD...
THE HELMET OF PROMETHEUS
GET ME BATMAN!

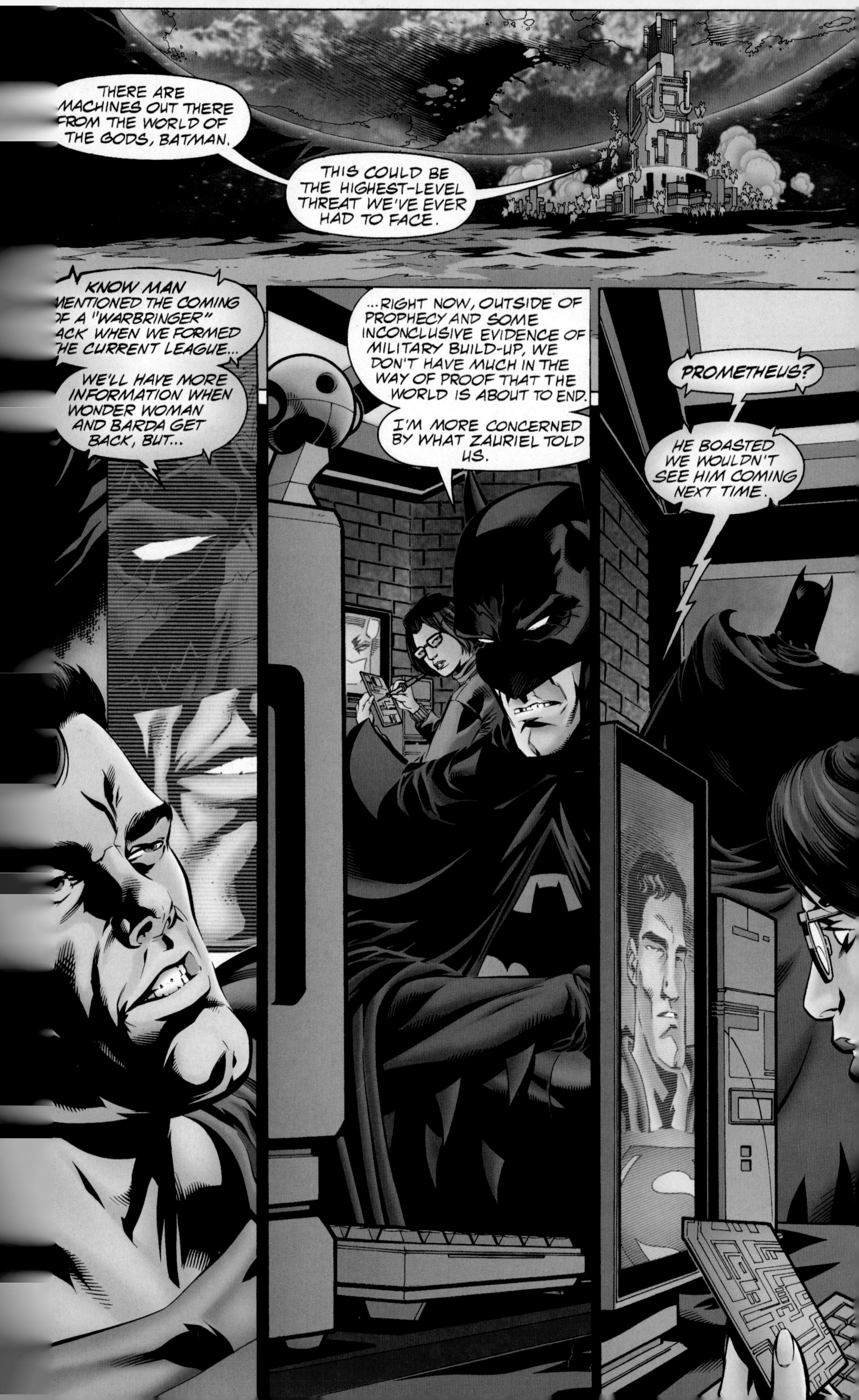
THERE ARE MACHINES OUT THERE FROM THE WORLD OF THE GODS, BATMAN.
THIS COULD BE THE HIGHEST-LEVEL THREAT WE'VE EVER HAD TO FACE.
KNOW MAN MENTIONED THE COMING OF A "WARBRINGER" BACK WHEN WE FORMED THE CURRENT LEAGUE...
WE'LL HAVE MORE INFORMATION WHEN WONDER WOMAN AND BARDA GET BACK, BUT...
...RIGHT NOW, OUTSIDE OF PROPHECY AND SOME INCONCLUSIVE EVIDENCE OF MILITARY BUILD-UP, WE DON'T HAVE MUCH IN THE WAY OF PROOF THAT THE WORLD IS ABOUT TO END.
I'M MORE CONCERNED BY WHAT ZAURIEL TOLD US.
PROMETHEUS?
HE BOASTED WE WOULDN'T SEE HIM COMING NEXT TIME.

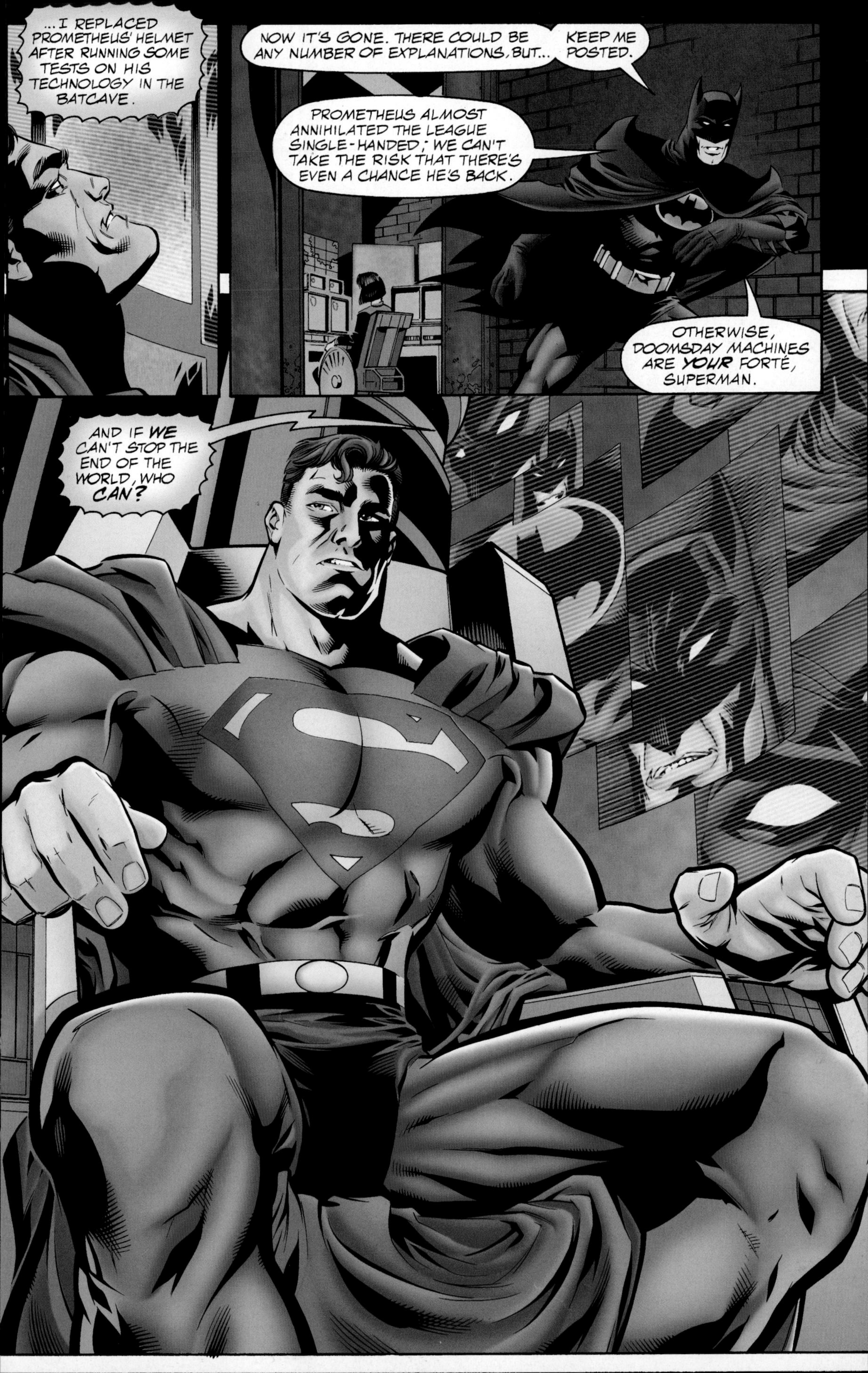
...I REPLACED PROMETHEUS' HELMET AFTER RUNNING SOME TESTS ON HIS TECHNOLOGY IN THE BATCAVE.
NOW IT'S GONE. THERE COULD BE ANY NUMBER OF EXPLANATIONS, BUT...
KEEP ME POSTED.
PROMETHEUS ALMOST ANNIHILATED THE LEAGUE SINGLE-HANDED; WE CAN'T TAKE THE RISK THAT THERE'S EVEN A CHANCE HE'S BACK.
OTHERWISE, DOOMSDAY MACHINES ARE YOUR FORTÉ, SUPERMAN.
AND IF WE CAN'T STOP THE END OF THE WORLD, WHO CAN?

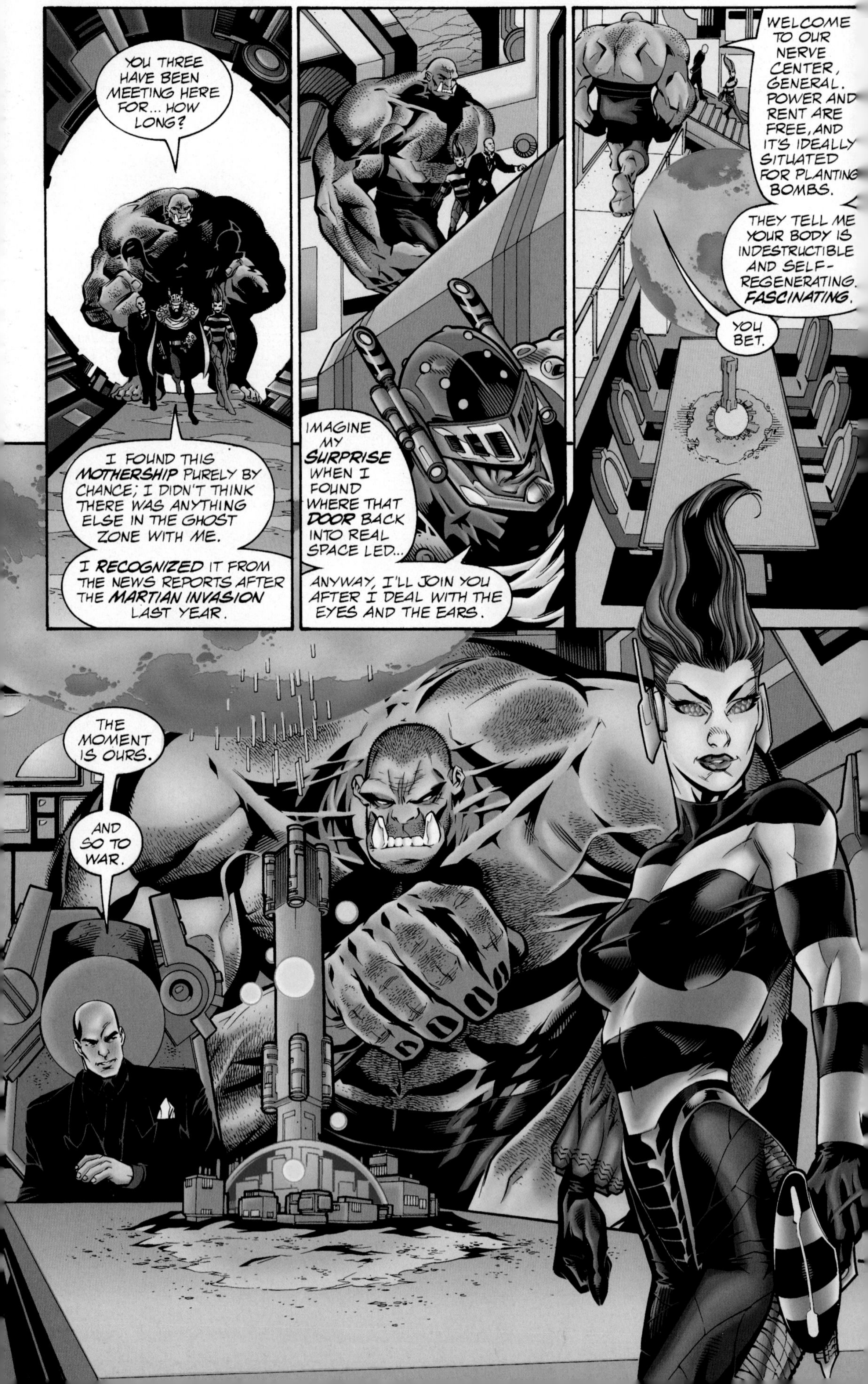
YOU THREE HAVE BEEN MEETING HERE FOR... HOW LONG?
I FOUND THIS MOTHERSHIP PURELY BY CHANCE; I DIDN'T THINK THERE WAS ANYTHING ELSE IN THE GHOST ZONE WITH ME.
I RECOGNIZED IT FROM THE NEWS REPORTS AFTER THE MARTIAN INVASION LAST YEAR.
IMAGINE MY SURPRISE WHEN I FOUND WHERE THAT DOOR BACK INTO REAL SPACE LED...
ANYWAY, I'LL JOIN YOU AFTER I DEAL WITH THE EYES AND THE EARS.
WELCOME TO OUR NERVE CENTER, GENERAL. POWER AND RENT ARE FREE, AND IT'S IDEALLY SITUATED FOR PLANTING BOMBS.
THEY TELL ME YOUR BODY IS INDESTRUCTIBLE AND SELF-REGENERATING. FASCINATING.
YOU BET.
THE MOMENT IS OURS.
AND SO TO WAR.

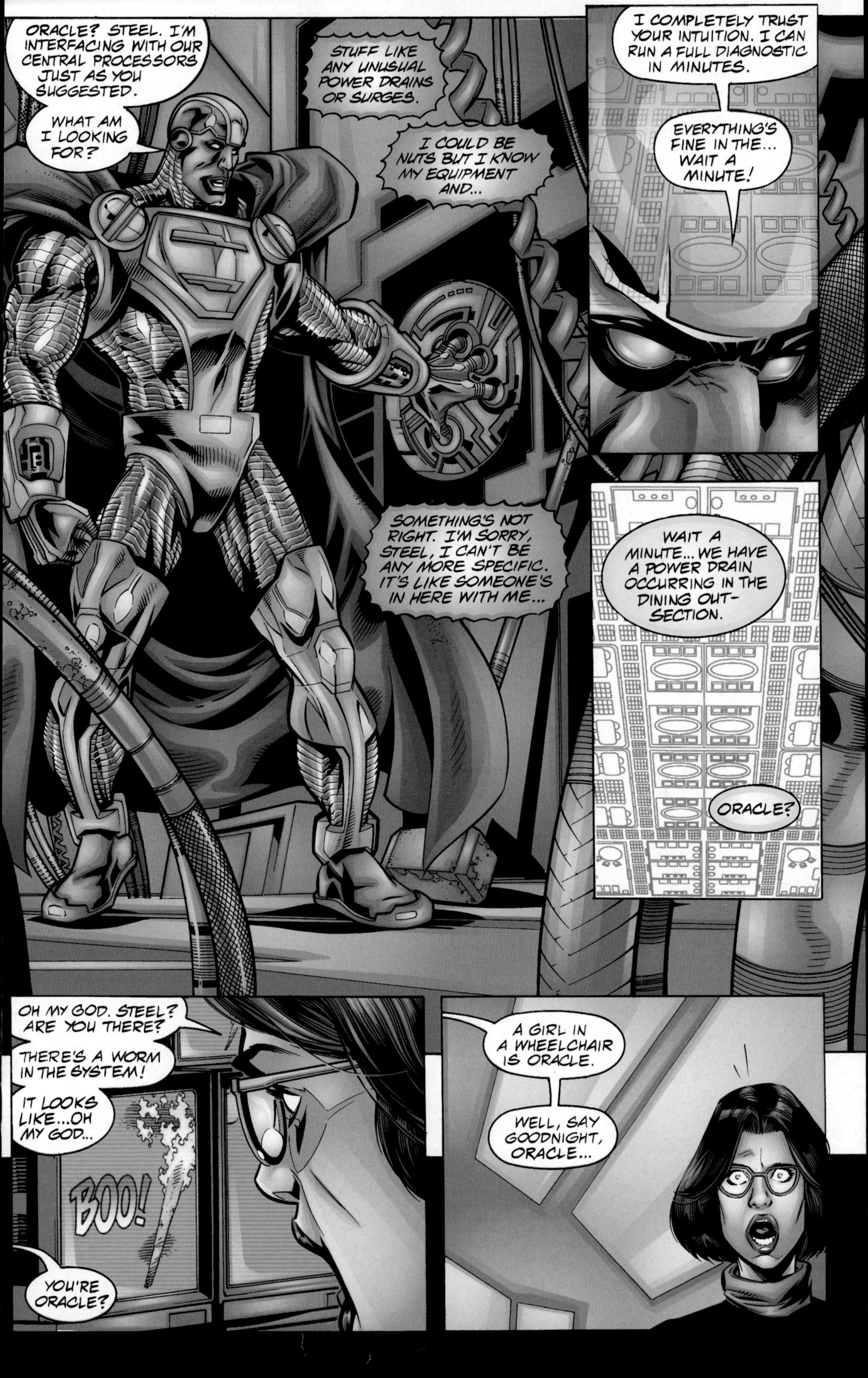
ORACLE? STEEL. I'M INTERFACING WITH OUR CENTRAL PROCESSORS JUST AS YOU SUGGESTED.
WHAT AM I LOOKING FOR?
STUFF LIKE ANY UNUSUAL POWER DRAINS OR SURGES.
I COULD BE NUTS BUT I KNOW MY EQUIPMENT AND...
SOMETHING'S NOT RIGHT. I'M SORRY, STEEL, I CAN'T BE ANY MORE SPECIFIC. IT'S LIKE SOMEONE'S IN HERE WITH ME...
I COMPLETELY TRUST YOUR INTUITION. I CAN RUN A FULL DIAGNOSTIC IN MINUTES.
EVERYTHING'S FINE IN THE... WAIT A MINUTE!
WAIT A MINUTE... WE HAVE A POWER DRAIN OCCURRING IN THE DINING OUT-SECTION.
ORACLE?
OH MY GOD. STEEL? ARE YOU THERE?
THERE'S A WORM IN THE SYSTEM!
IT LOOKS LIKE...OH MY GOD...
BOO!
YOU'RE ORACLE?
A GIRL IN A WHEELCHAIR IS ORACLE.
WELL, SAY GOODNIGHT, ORACLE...

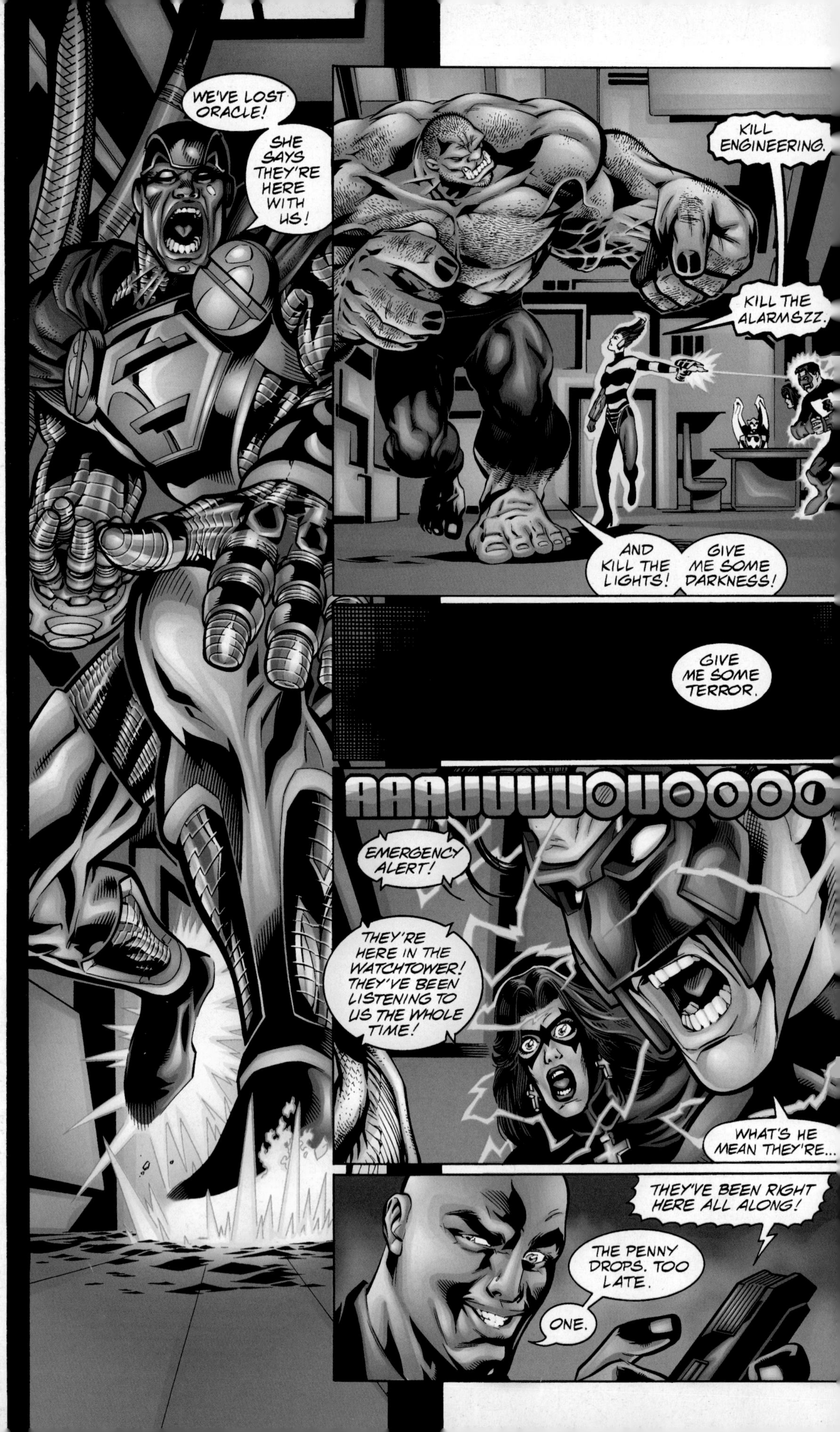
WE'VE LOST ORACLE!
SHE SAYS THEY'RE HERE WITH US!
KILL ENGINEERING.
KILL THE ALARMSZZ.
AND KILL THE LIGHTS!
GIVE ME SOME DARKNESS!
GIVE ME SOME TERROR.
AAAUUUUUOUOOOO
EMERGENCY ALERT!
THEY'RE HERE IN THE WATCHTOWER! THEY'VE BEEN LISTENING TO US THE WHOLE TIME!
WHAT'S HE MEAN THEY'RE...
THEY'VE BEEN RIGHT HERE ALL ALONG!
THE PENNY DROPS. TOO LATE.
ONE.

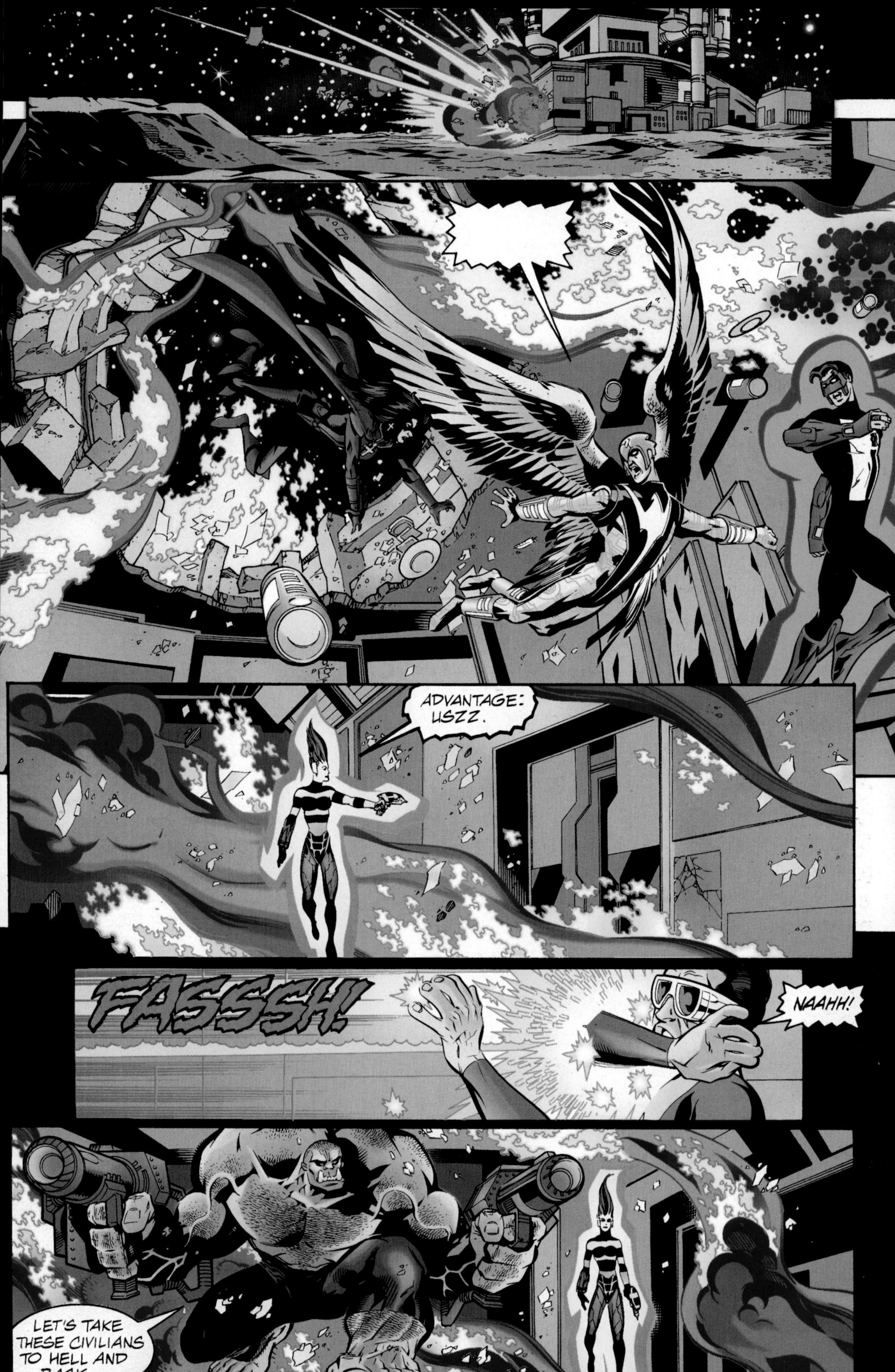
ADVANTAGE: USZZ.
FASSSH!
NAAHH!
LET'S TAKE THESE CIVILIANS TO HELL AND BACK.

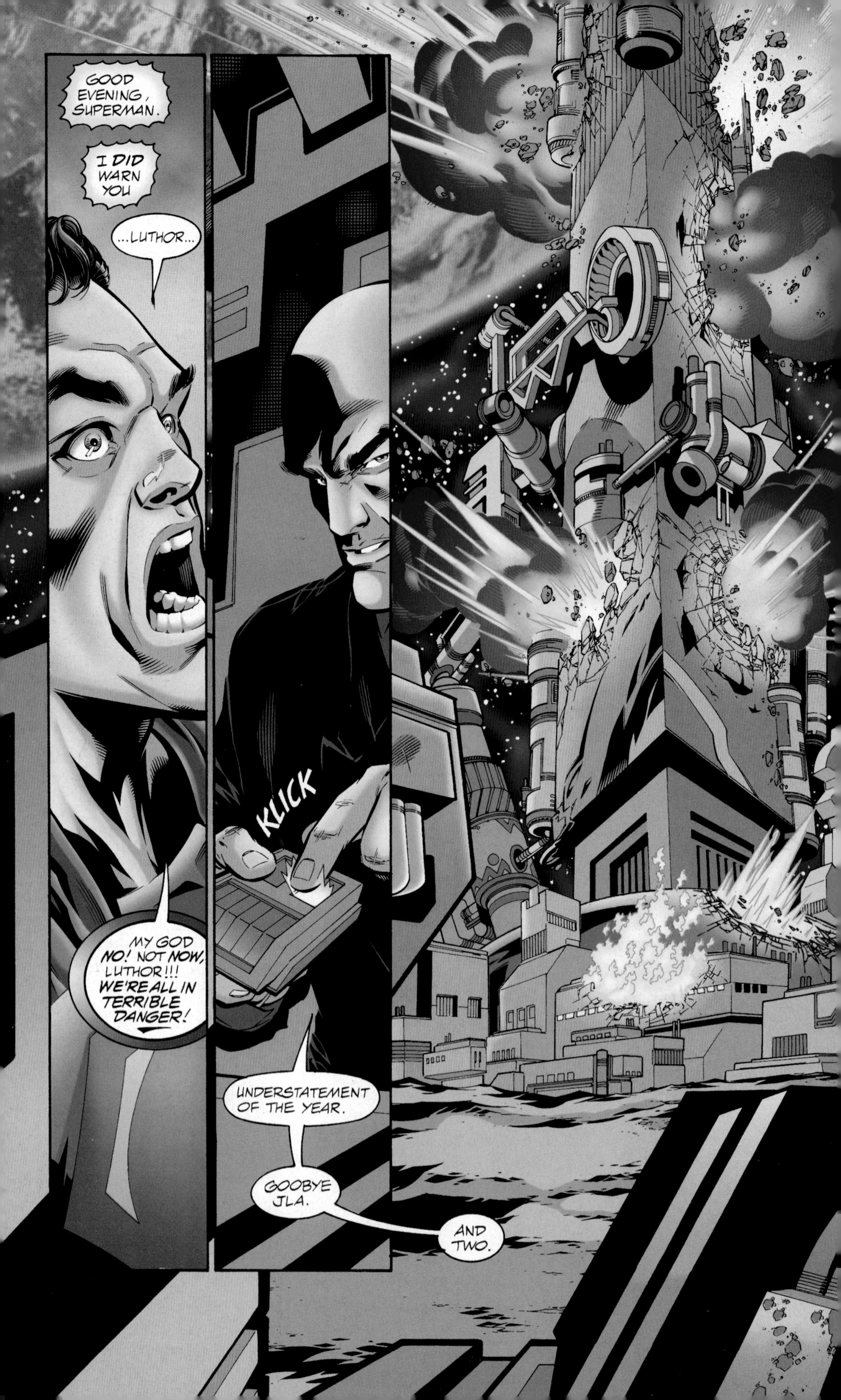

GOOD EVENING, SUPERMAN.
I DID WARN YOU
...LUTHOR...
MY GOD NO! NOT NOW, LUTHOR!!! WE'RE ALL IN TERRIBLE DANGER!
KLICK
UNDERSTATEMENT OF THE YEAR.
GOOBYE JLA.
AND TWO.

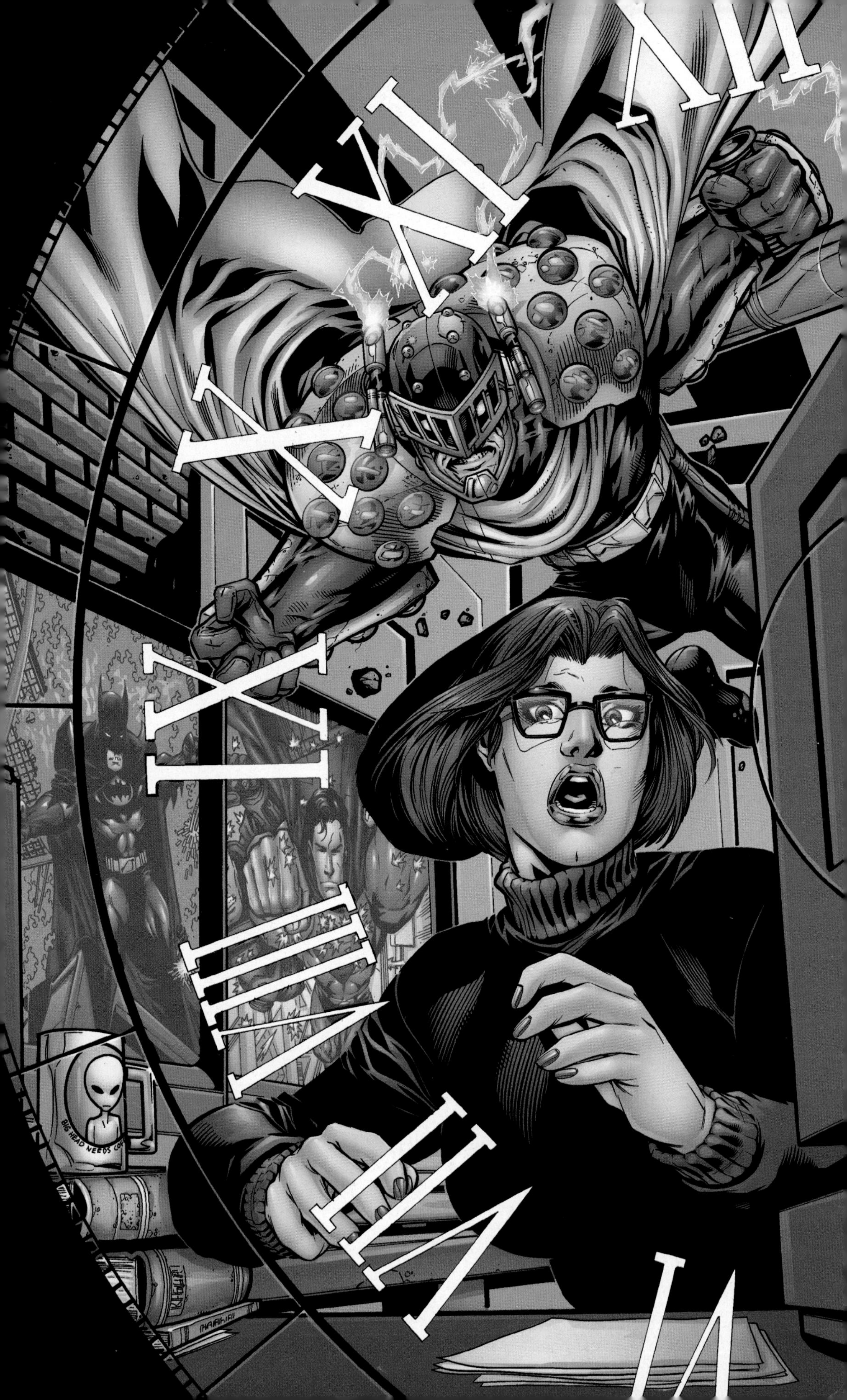
XII
XI
X
IX
VIII
VII
VI

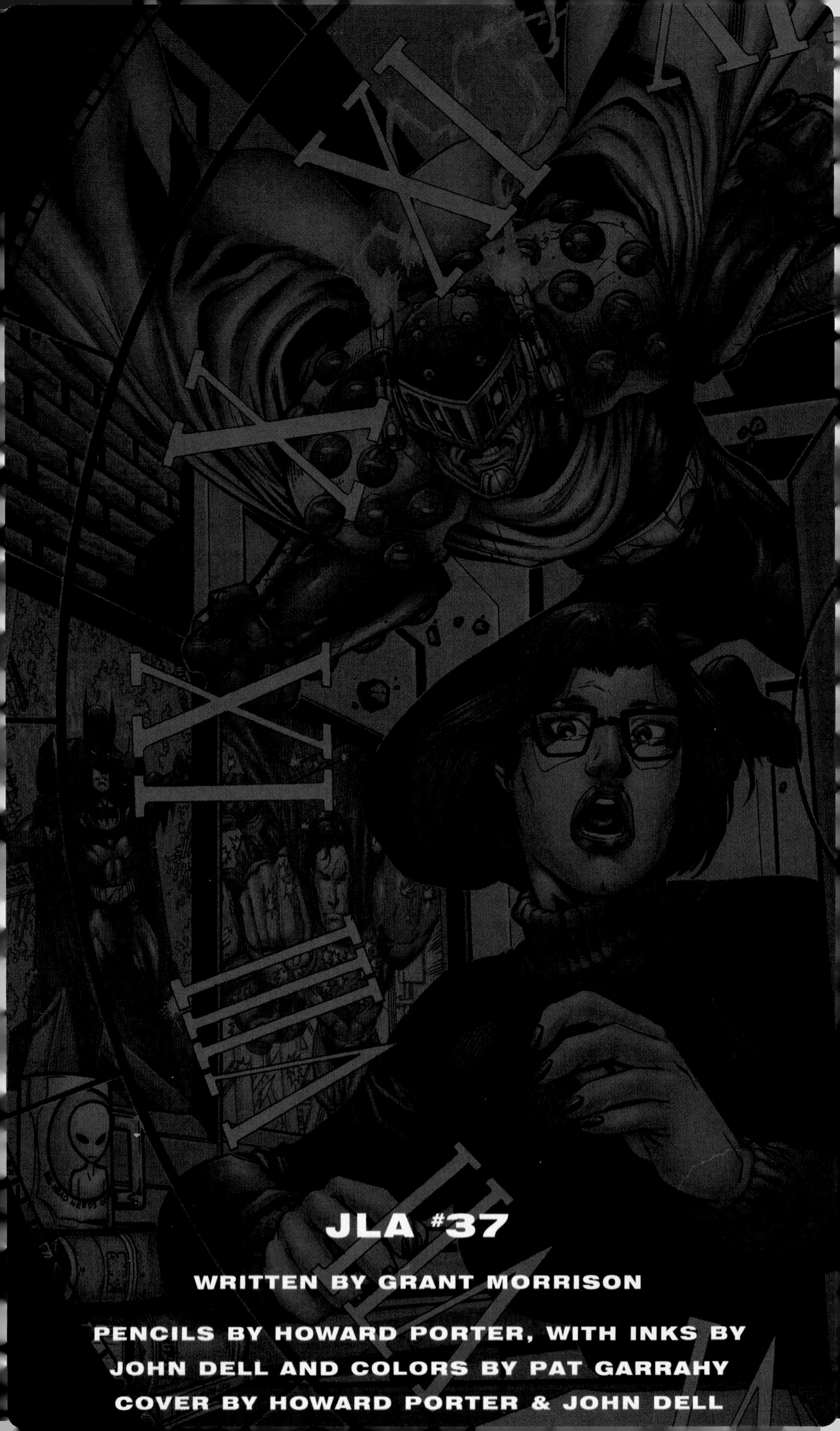

JLA #37

WRITTEN BY GRANT MORRISON

PENCILS BY HOWARD PORTER, WITH INKS BY JOHN DELL AND COLORS BY PAT GARRAHY

COVER BY HOWARD PORTER & JOHN DELL

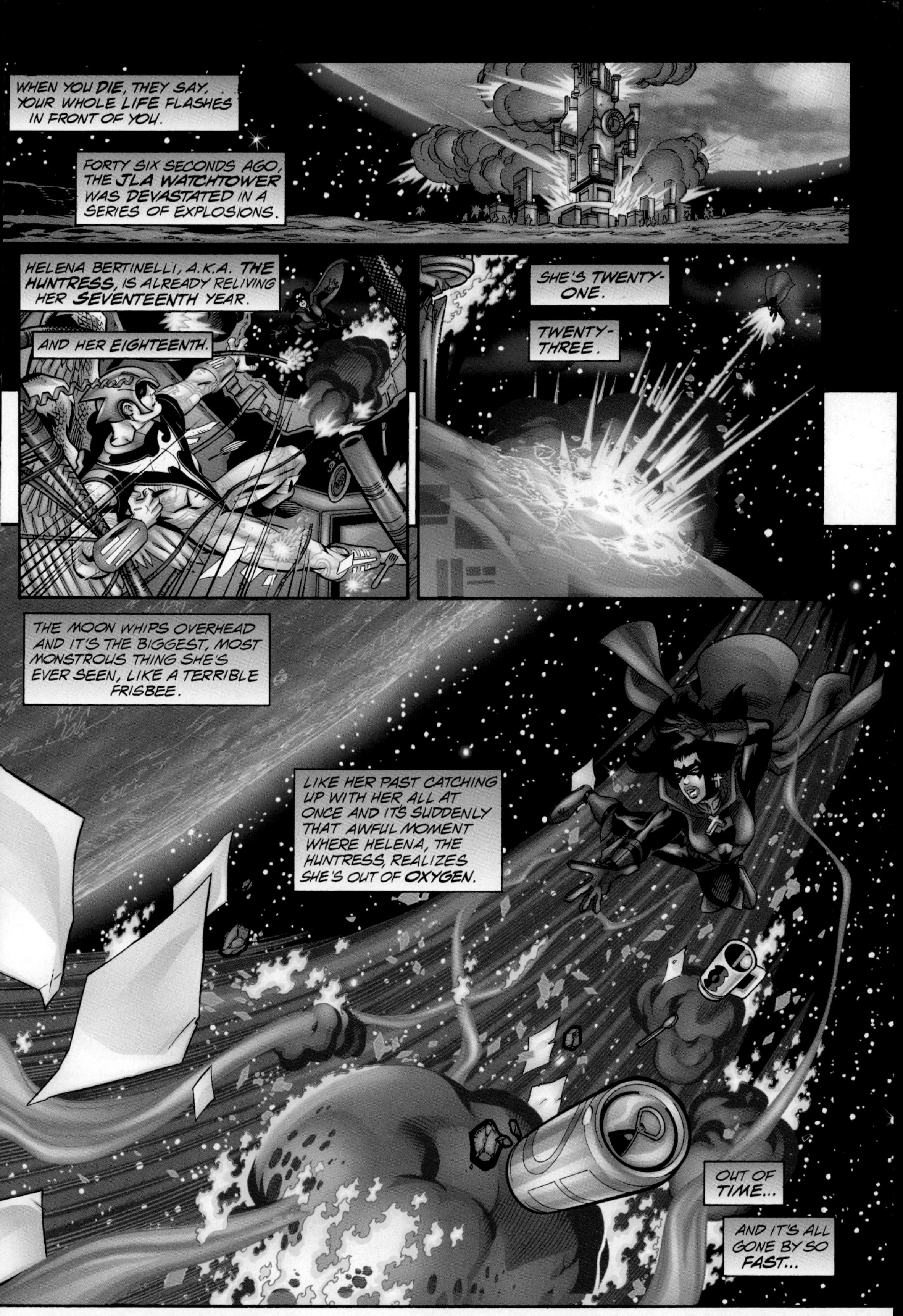
WHEN YOU DIE, THEY SAY, YOUR WHOLE LIFE FLASHES IN FRONT OF YOU.
FORTY SIX SECONDS AGO, THE JLA WATCHTOWER WAS DEVASTATED IN A SERIES OF EXPLOSIONS.
HELENA BERTINELLI, A.K.A. THE HUNTRESS, IS ALREADY RELIVING HER SEVENTEENTH YEAR.
AND HER EIGHTEENTH.
SHE'S TWENTY-ONE.
TWENTY-THREE.
THE MOON WHIPS OVERHEAD AND IT'S THE BIGGEST, MOST MONSTROUS THING SHE'S EVER SEEN, LIKE A TERRIBLE FRISBEE.
LIKE HER PAST CATCHING UP WITH HER ALL AT ONCE AND IT'S SUDDENLY THAT AWFUL MOMENT WHERE HELENA, THE HUNTRESS, REALIZES SHE'S OUT OF OXYGEN.
OUT OF TIME...
AND IT'S ALL GONE BY SO FAST...

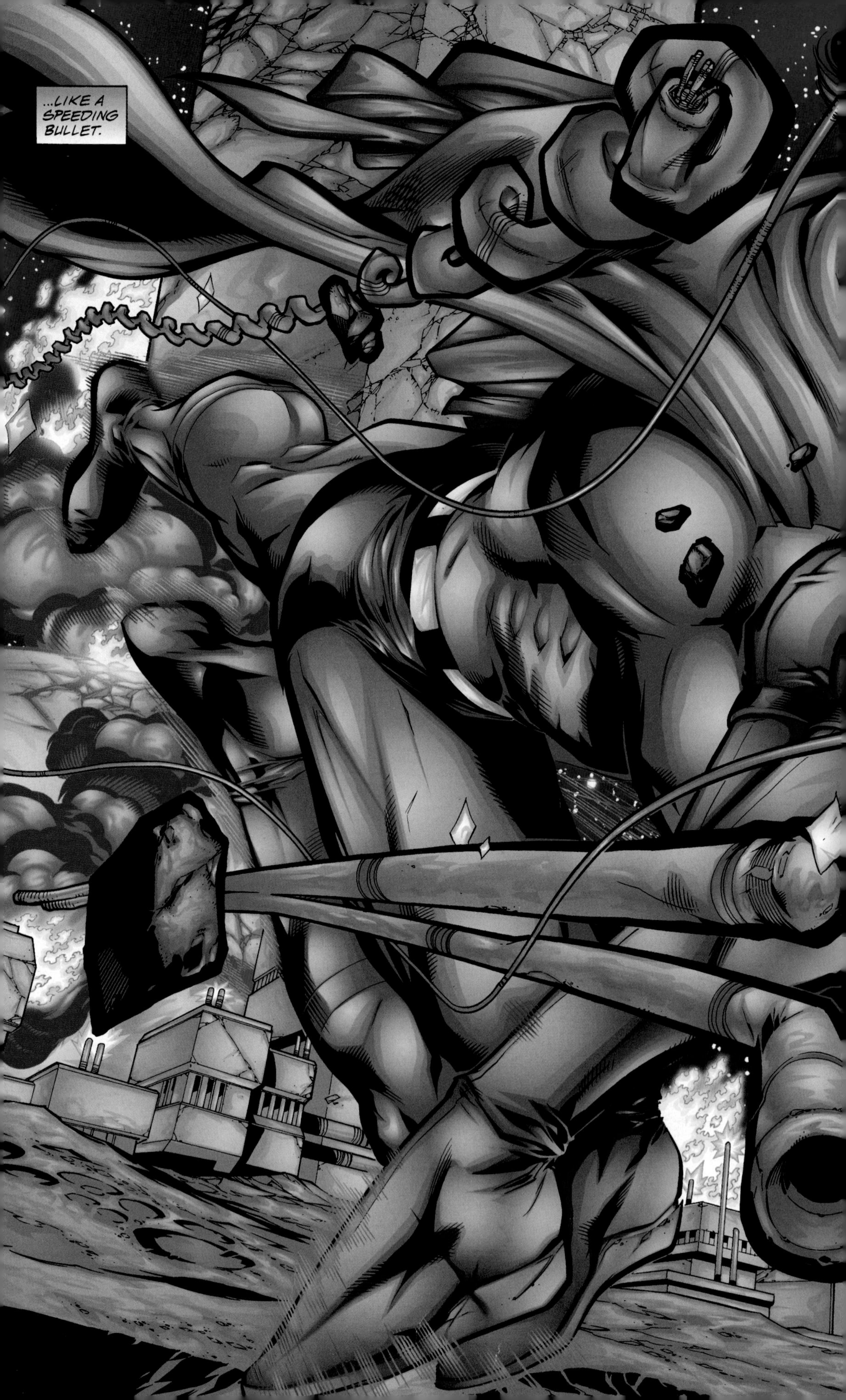
...LIKE A SPEEDING BULLET.

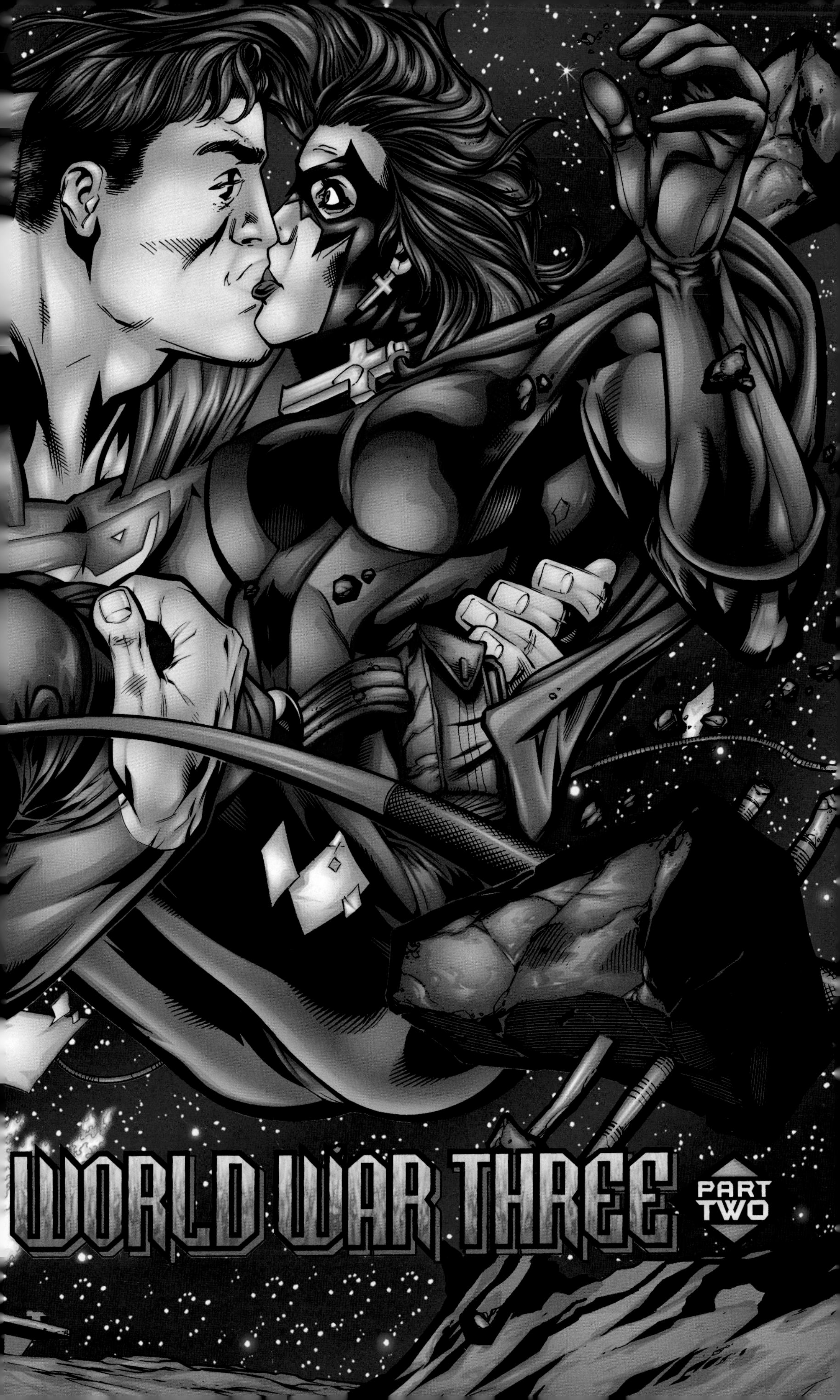
WORLD WAR THREE
PART TWO

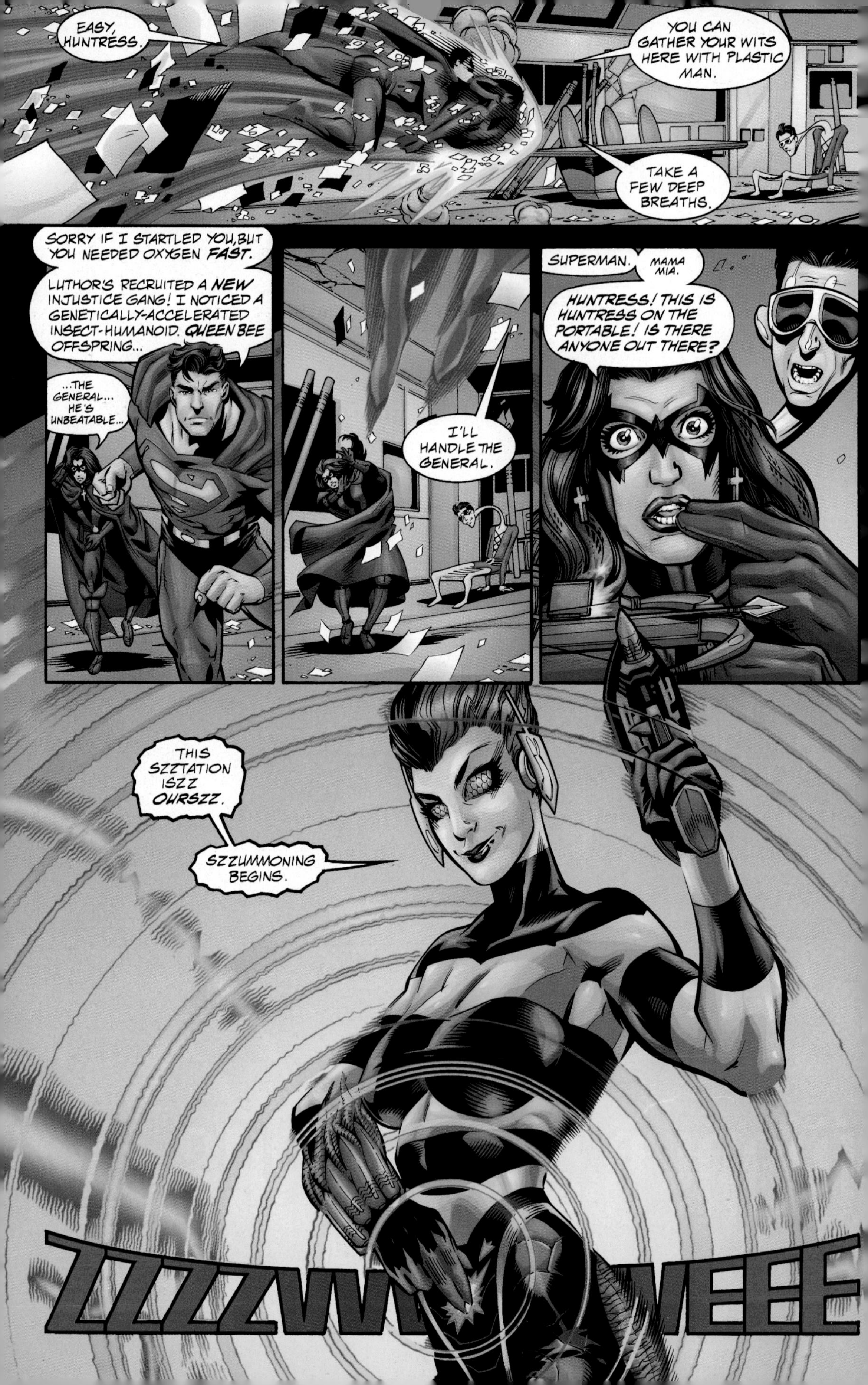
EASY, HUNTRESS.
YOU CAN GATHER YOUR WITS HERE WITH PLASTIC MAN.
TAKE A FEW DEEP BREATHS.
SORRY IF I STARTLED YOU, BUT YOU NEEDED OXYGEN FAST.
LUTHOR'S RECRUITED A NEW INJUSTICE GANG! I NOTICED A GENETICALLY-ACCELERATED INSECT-HUMANOID. QUEEN BEE OFFSPRING...
...THE GENERAL... HE'S UNBEATABLE...
I'LL HANDLE THE GENERAL.
SUPERMAN.
MAMA MIA.
HUNTRESS! THIS IS HUNTRESS ON THE PORTABLE! IS THERE ANYONE OUT THERE?
THIS SZZTATION ISZZ OURSZZ.
SZZZUMMONING BEGINS.
ZZZZVVV
EEE

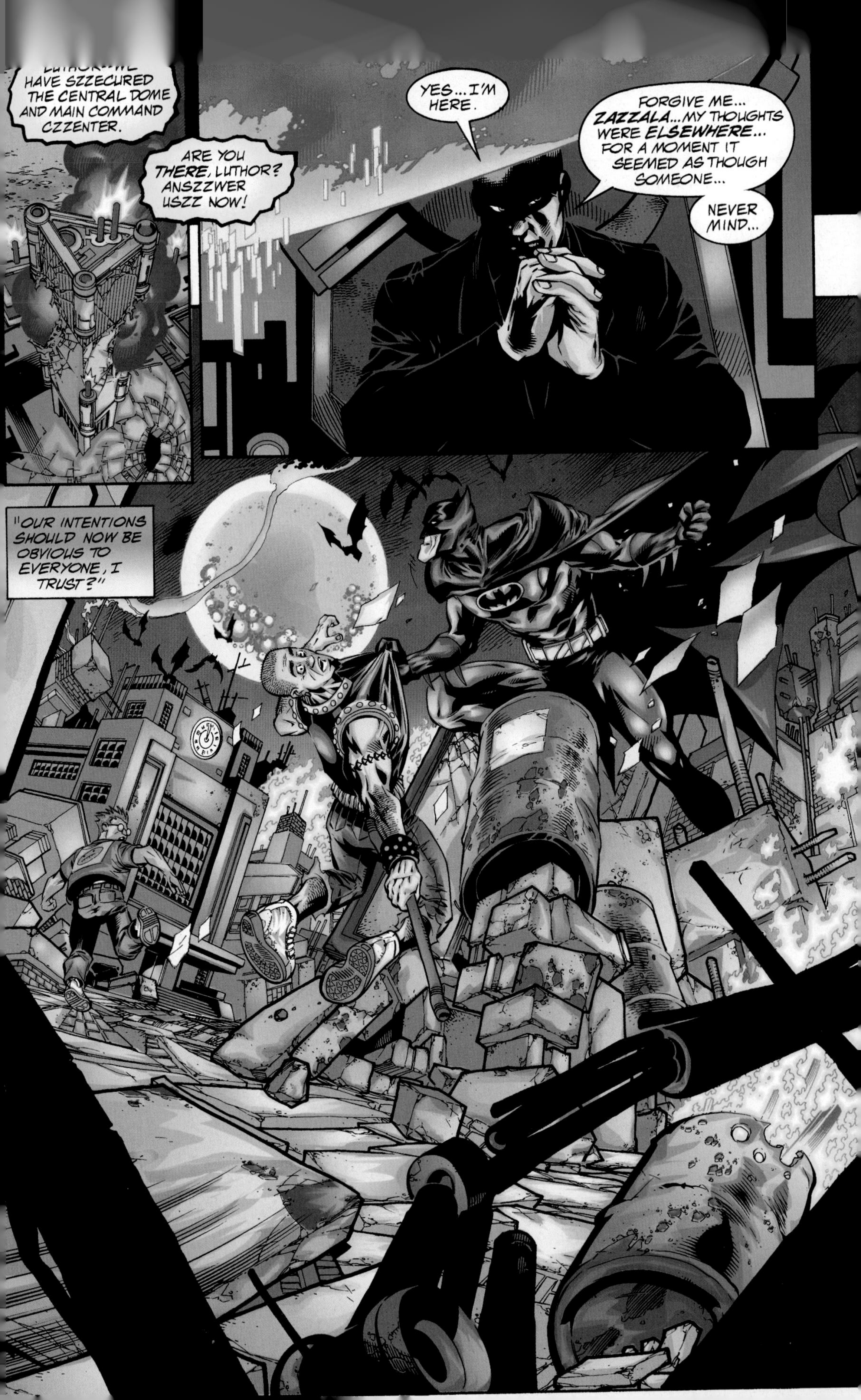
HAVE SZZECURED THE CENTRAL DOME AND MAIN COMMAND CZZENTER.
ARE YOU THERE, LUTHOR? ANSZZWER USZZ NOW!
YES... I'M HERE.
FORGIVE ME... ZAZZALA... MY THOUGHTS WERE ELSEWHERE... FOR A MOMENT IT SEEMED AS THOUGH SOMEONE...
NEVER MIND...
"OUR INTENTIONS SHOULD NOW BE OBVIOUS TO EVERYONE, I TRUST?"

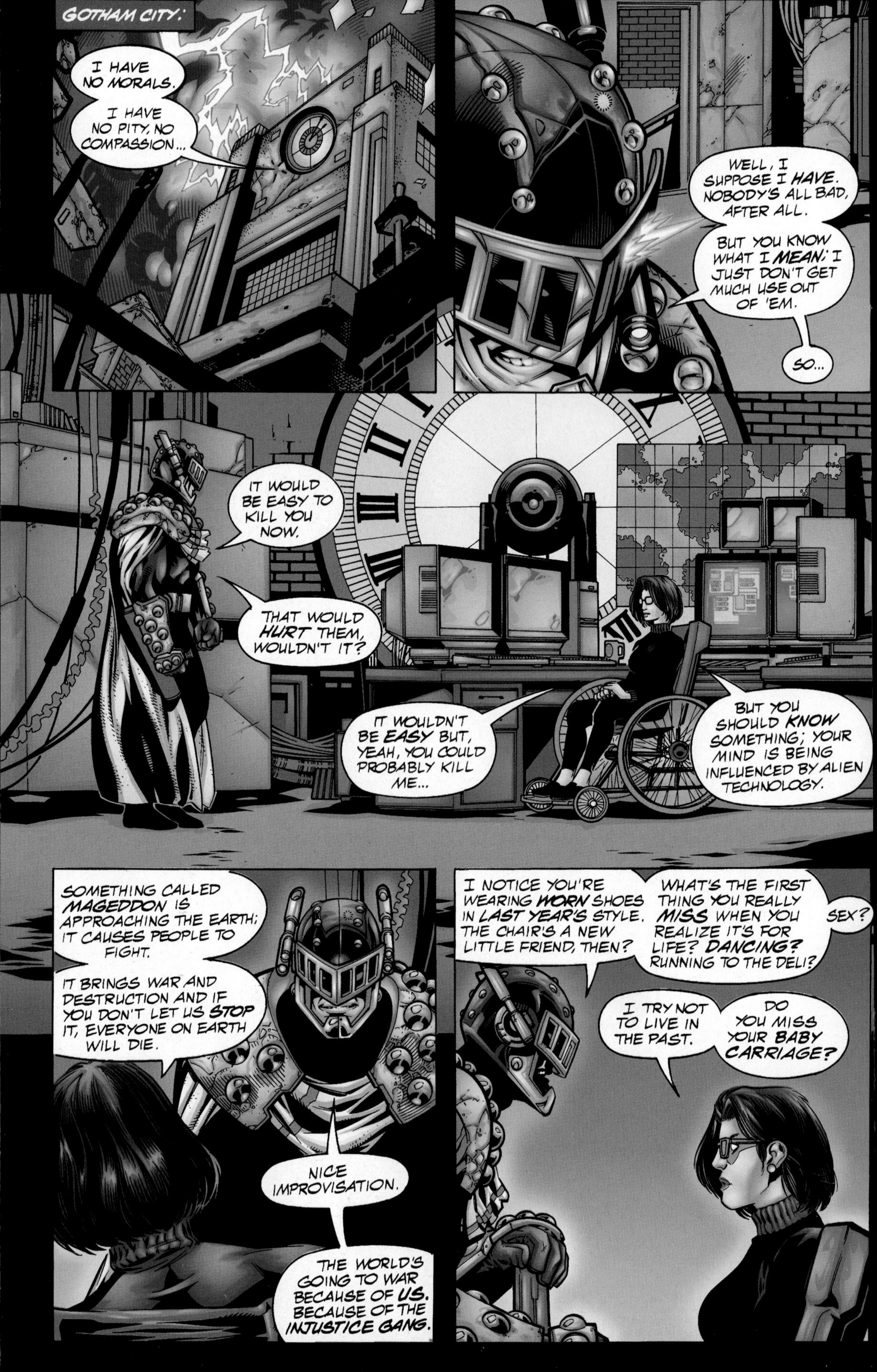
GOTHAM CITY:
I HAVE NO MORALS.
I HAVE NO PITY, NO COMPASSION...
WELL, I SUPPOSE I HAVE. NOBODY'S ALL BAD, AFTER ALL.
BUT YOU KNOW WHAT I MEAN; I JUST DON'T GET MUCH USE OUT OF 'EM.
SO...
IT WOULD BE EASY TO KILL YOU NOW.
THAT WOULD HURT THEM, WOULDN'T IT?
IT WOULDN'T BE EASY BUT, YEAH, YOU COULD PROBABLY KILL ME...
BUT YOU SHOULD KNOW SOMETHING; YOUR MIND IS BEING INFLUENCED BY ALIEN TECHNOLOGY.
SOMETHING CALLED MAGEDDON IS APPROACHING THE EARTH; IT CAUSES PEOPLE TO FIGHT.
IT BRINGS WAR AND DESTRUCTION AND IF YOU DON'T LET US STOP IT, EVERYONE ON EARTH WILL DIE.
NICE IMPROVISATION.
THE WORLD'S GOING TO WAR BECAUSE OF US. BECAUSE OF THE INJUSTICE GANG.
I NOTICE YOU'RE WEARING WORN SHOES IN LAST YEAR'S STYLE. THE CHAIR'S A NEW LITTLE FRIEND, THEN?
WHAT'S THE FIRST THING YOU REALLY MISS WHEN YOU REALIZE IT'S FOR LIFE? DANCING? RUNNING TO THE DELI?
SEX?
I TRY NOT TO LIVE IN THE PAST.
DO YOU MISS YOUR BABY CARRIAGE?

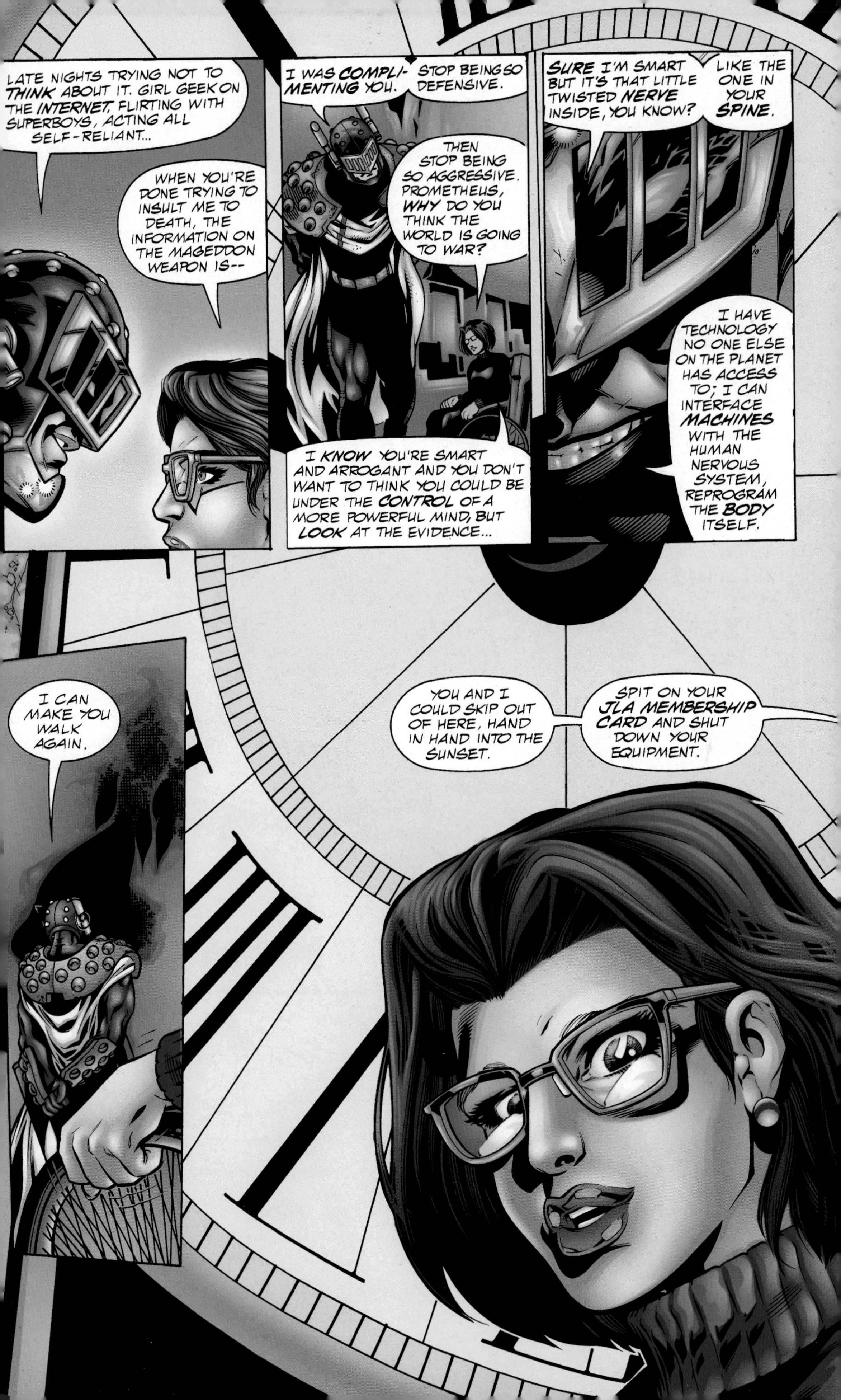

LATE NIGHTS TRYING NOT TO THINK ABOUT IT. GIRL GEEK ON THE INTERNET, FLIRTING WITH SUPERBOYS, ACTING ALL SELF-RELIANT...
WHEN YOU'RE DONE TRYING TO INSULT ME TO DEATH, THE INFORMATION ON THE MAGEDDON WEAPON IS--
I WAS COMPLIMENTING YOU.
STOP BEING SO DEFENSIVE.
THEN STOP BEING SO AGGRESSIVE. PROMETHEUS, WHY DO YOU THINK THE WORLD IS GOING TO WAR?
I KNOW YOU'RE SMART AND ARROGANT AND YOU DON'T WANT TO THINK YOU COULD BE UNDER THE CONTROL OF A MORE POWERFUL MIND, BUT LOOK AT THE EVIDENCE...
SURE I'M SMART BUT IT'S THAT LITTLE TWISTED NERVE INSIDE, YOU KNOW?
LIKE THE ONE IN YOUR SPINE.
I HAVE TECHNOLOGY NO ONE ELSE ON THE PLANET HAS ACCESS TO; I CAN INTERFACE MACHINES WITH THE HUMAN NERVOUS SYSTEM, REPROGRAM THE BODY ITSELF.
I CAN MAKE YOU WALK AGAIN.
YOU AND I COULD SKIP OUT OF HERE, HAND IN HAND INTO THE SUNSET.
SPIT ON YOUR JLA MEMBERSHIP CARD AND SHUT DOWN YOUR EQUIPMENT.

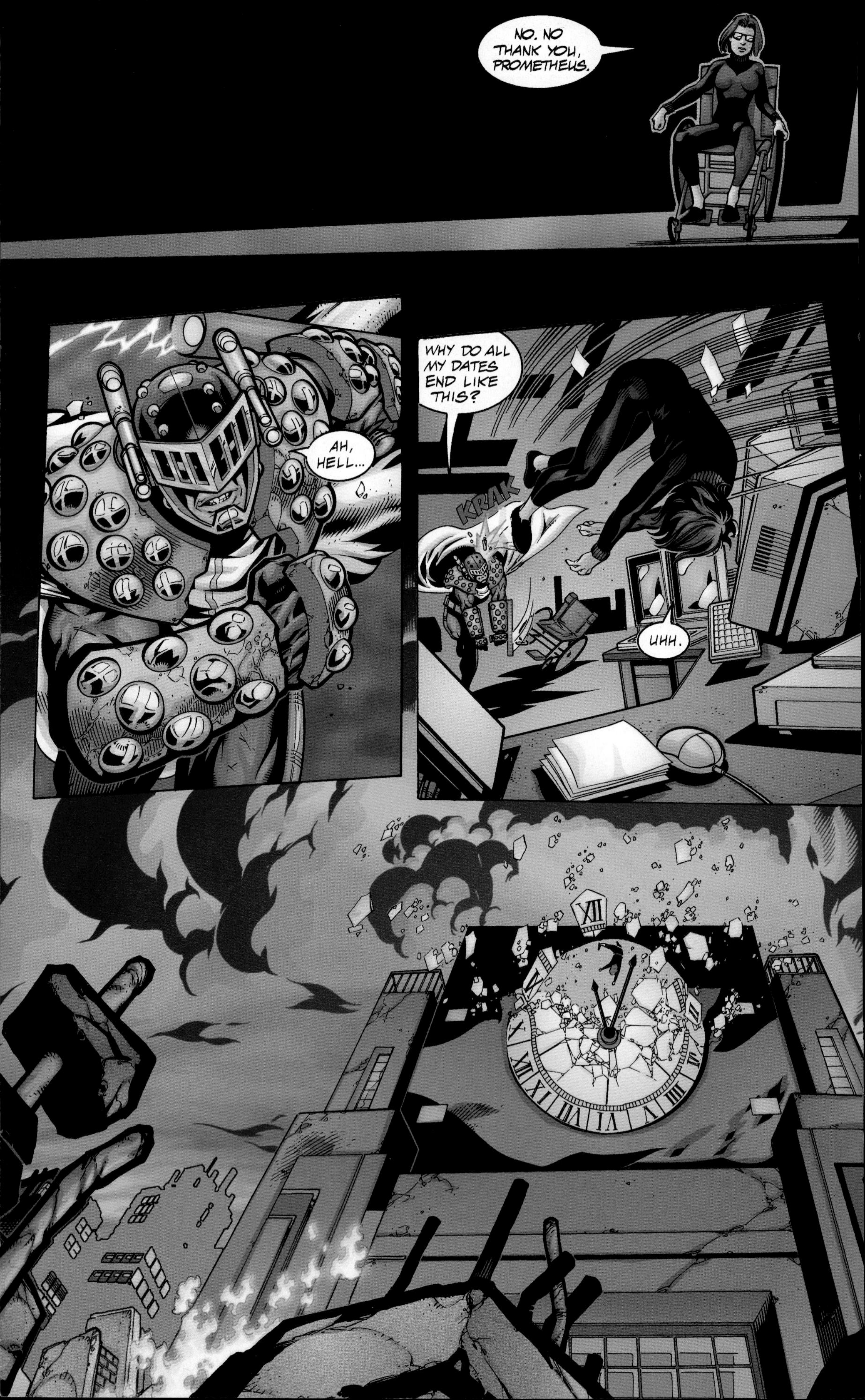
NO. NO THANK YOU, PROMETHEUS.
AH, HELL...
WHY DO ALL MY DATES END LIKE THIS?
KRAK
UHH.

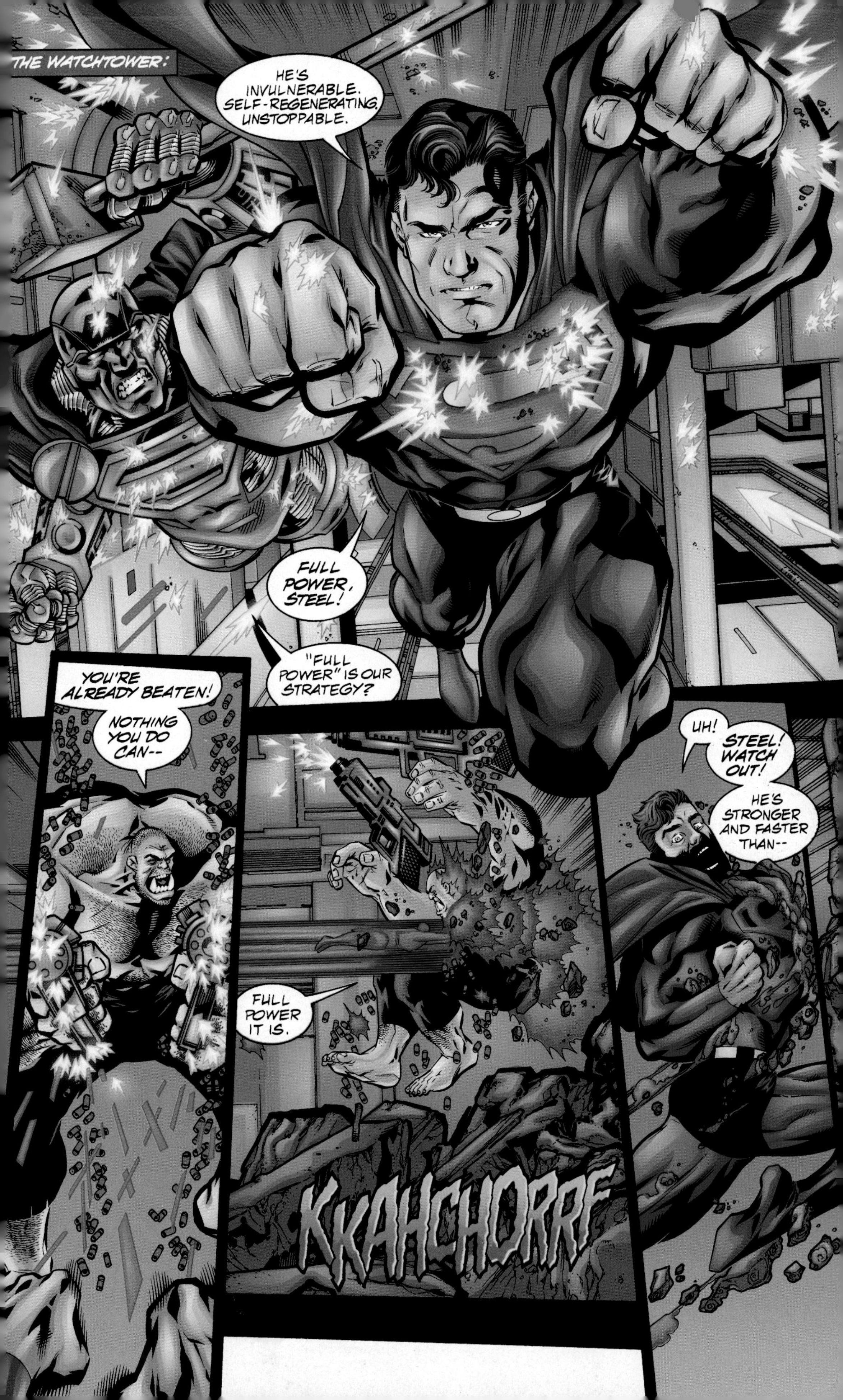
THE WATCHTOWER:
HE'S INVULNERABLE. SELF-REGENERATING. UNSTOPPABLE.
FULL POWER, STEEL!
"FULL POWER" IS OUR STRATEGY?
YOU'RE ALREADY BEATEN!
NOTHING YOU DO CAN--
FULL POWER IT IS.
KKAHCHORRF
UH!
STEEL! WATCH OUT!
HE'S STRONGER AND FASTER THAN--

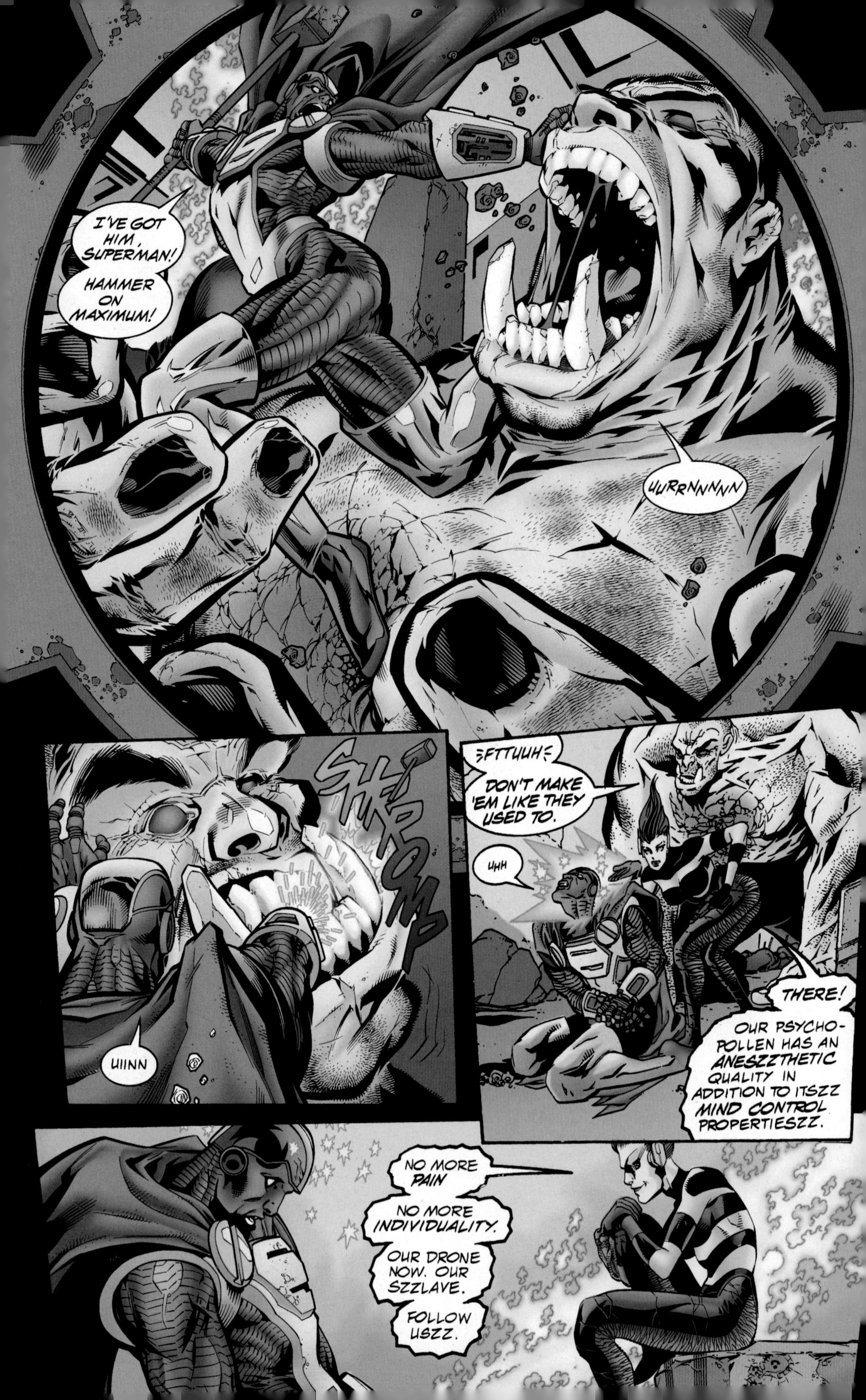
I'VE GOT HIM, SUPERMAN!
HAMMER ON MAXIMUM!
UURRNNNNN
SHRROOM
UIINN
FTTUUH
DON'T MAKE 'EM LIKE THEY USED TO.
UHH
THERE!
OUR PSYCHO-POLLEN HAS AN ANESZZTHETIC QUALITY IN ADDITION TO ITSZZ MIND CONTROL PROPERTIESZZ.
NO MORE PAIN
NO MORE INDIVIDUALITY.
OUR DRONE NOW. OUR SZZLAVE.
FOLLOW USZZ.

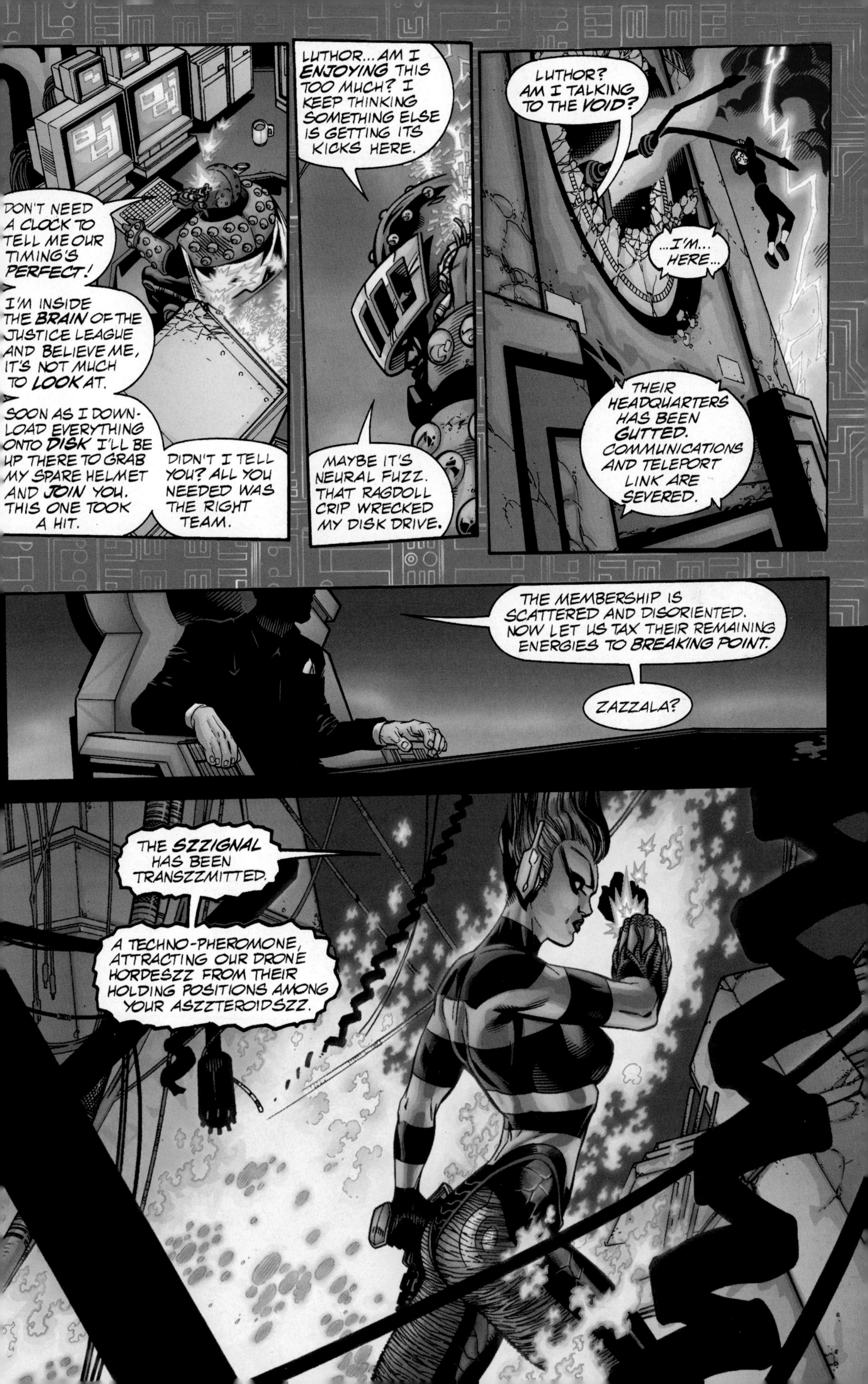
DON'T NEED A CLOCK TO TELL ME OUR TIMING'S PERFECT! I'M INSIDE THE BRAIN OF THE JUSTICE LEAGUE AND BELIEVE ME, IT'S NOT MUCH TO LOOK AT. SOON AS I DOWN-LOAD EVERYTHING ONTO DISK I'LL BE UP THERE TO GRAB MY SPARE HELMET AND JOIN YOU. THIS ONE TOOK A HIT.
DIDN'T I TELL YOU? ALL YOU NEEDED WAS THE RIGHT TEAM.
LUTHOR... AM I ENJOYING THIS TOO MUCH? I KEEP THINKING SOMETHING ELSE IS GETTING ITS KICKS HERE.
MAYBE IT'S NEURAL FUZZ. THAT RAGDOLL CRIP WRECKED MY DISK DRIVE.
LUTHOR? AM I TALKING TO THE VOID?
...I'M... HERE...
THEIR HEADQUARTERS HAS BEEN GUTTED. COMMUNICATIONS AND TELEPORT LINK ARE SEVERED.
THE MEMBERSHIP IS SCATTERED AND DISORIENTED. NOW LET US TAX THEIR REMAINING ENERGIES TO BREAKING POINT.
ZAZZALA?
THE SZZIGNAL HAS BEEN TRANSZZMITTED.
A TECHNO-PHEROMONE, ATTRACTING OUR DRONE HORDESZZ FROM THEIR HOLDING POSITIONS AMONG YOUR ASZZTEROIDSZZ.

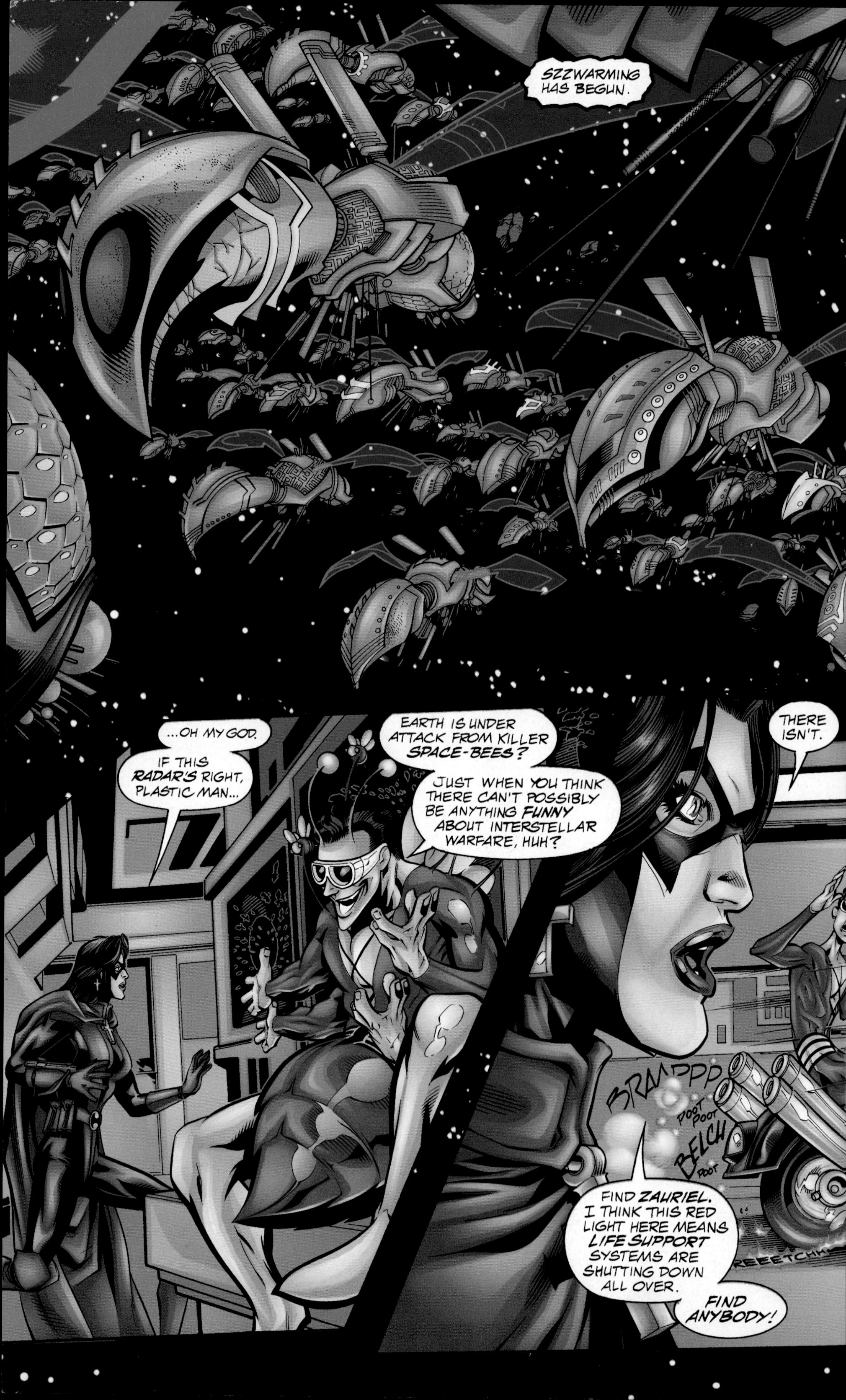
SZZWARMING HAS BEGUN.
...OH MY GOD.
IF THIS RADAR'S RIGHT, PLASTIC MAN...
EARTH IS UNDER ATTACK FROM KILLER SPACE-BEES?
JUST WHEN YOU THINK THERE CAN'T POSSIBLY BE ANYTHING FUNNY ABOUT INTERSTELLAR WARFARE, HUH?
THERE ISN'T.
BRAAPPP
POOT POOT
BELCH
POOT
FIND ZAURIEL. I THINK THIS RED LIGHT HERE MEANS LIFE SUPPORT SYSTEMS ARE SHUTTING DOWN ALL OVER.
FIND ANYBODY!

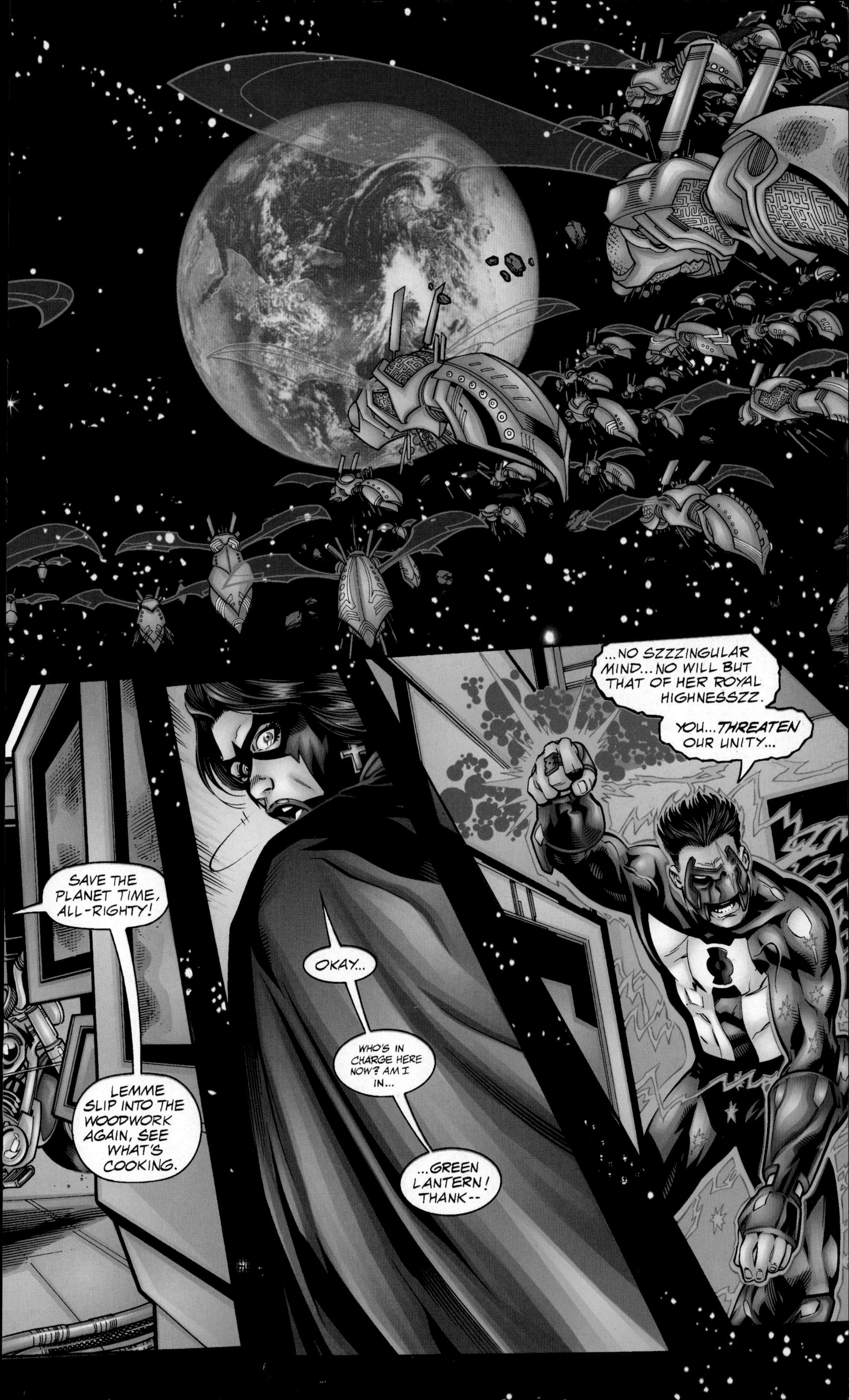
...NO SZZZINGULAR MIND... NO WILL BUT THAT OF HER ROYAL HIGHNESSZZ.
YOU... THREATEN OUR UNITY...
SAVE THE PLANET TIME, ALL-RIGHTY!
LEMME SLIP INTO THE WOODWORK AGAIN, SEE WHAT'S COOKING.
OKAY...
WHO'S IN CHARGE HERE NOW? AM I IN...
...GREEN LANTERN! THANK--

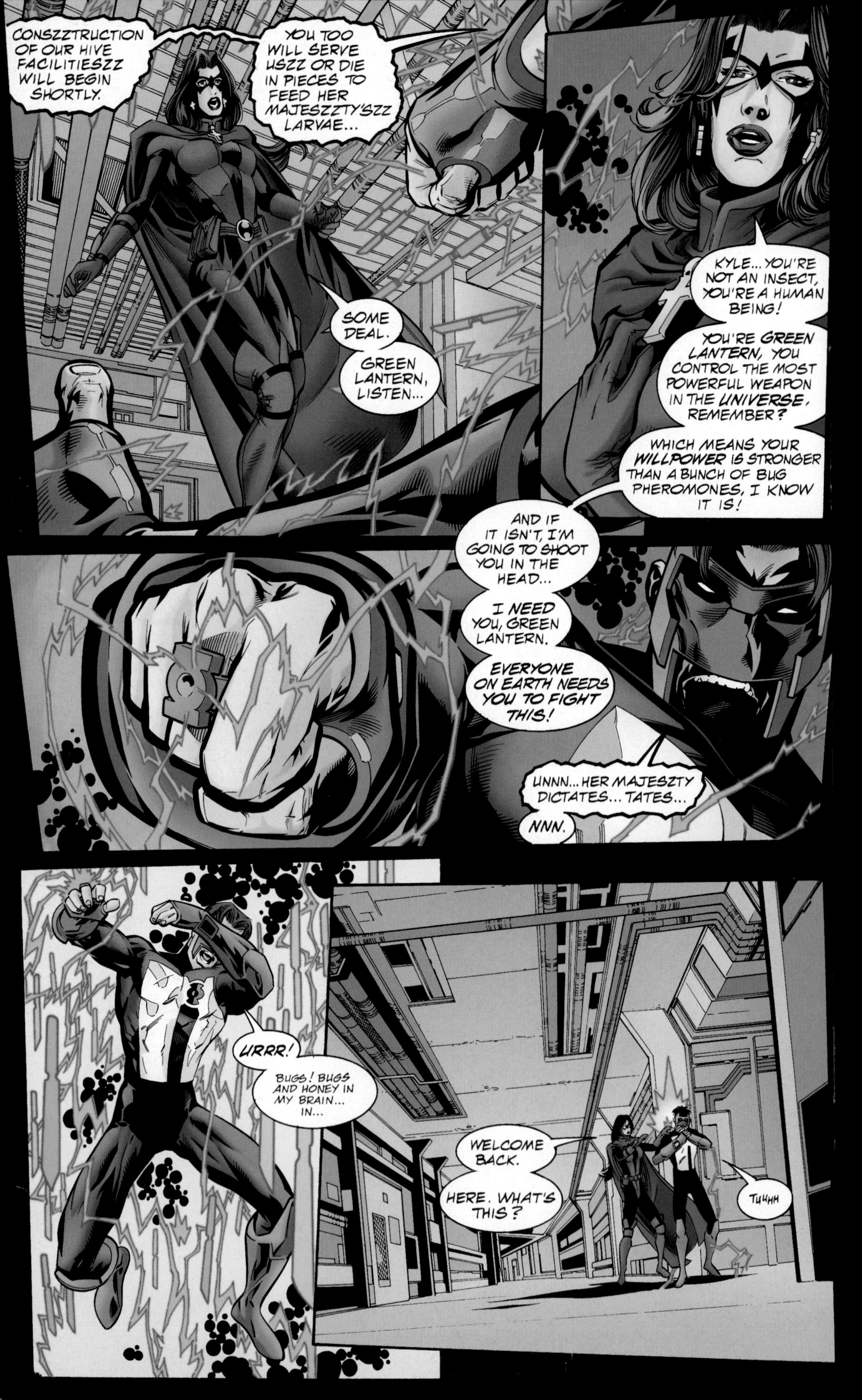

CONSZZTRUCTION OF OUR HIVE FACILITIESZZ WILL BEGIN SHORTLY.
YOU TOO WILL SERVE USZZ OR DIE IN PIECES TO FEED HER MAJESZZTY'SZZ LARVAE...
SOME DEAL.
GREEN LANTERN, LISTEN...
KYLE... YOU'RE NOT AN INSECT, YOU'RE A HUMAN BEING!
YOU'RE GREEN LANTERN, YOU CONTROL THE MOST POWERFUL WEAPON IN THE UNIVERSE, REMEMBER?
WHICH MEANS YOUR WILLPOWER IS STRONGER THAN A BUNCH OF BUG PHEROMONES, I KNOW IT IS!
AND IF IT ISN'T, I'M GOING TO SHOOT YOU IN THE HEAD...
I NEED YOU, GREEN LANTERN.
EVERYONE ON EARTH NEEDS YOU TO FIGHT THIS!
UNNN... HER MAJESZTY DICTATES... TATES...
NNN.
URRR!
BUGS! BUGS AND HONEY IN MY BRAIN... IN...
WELCOME BACK.
HERE. WHAT'S THIS?
TUHHH

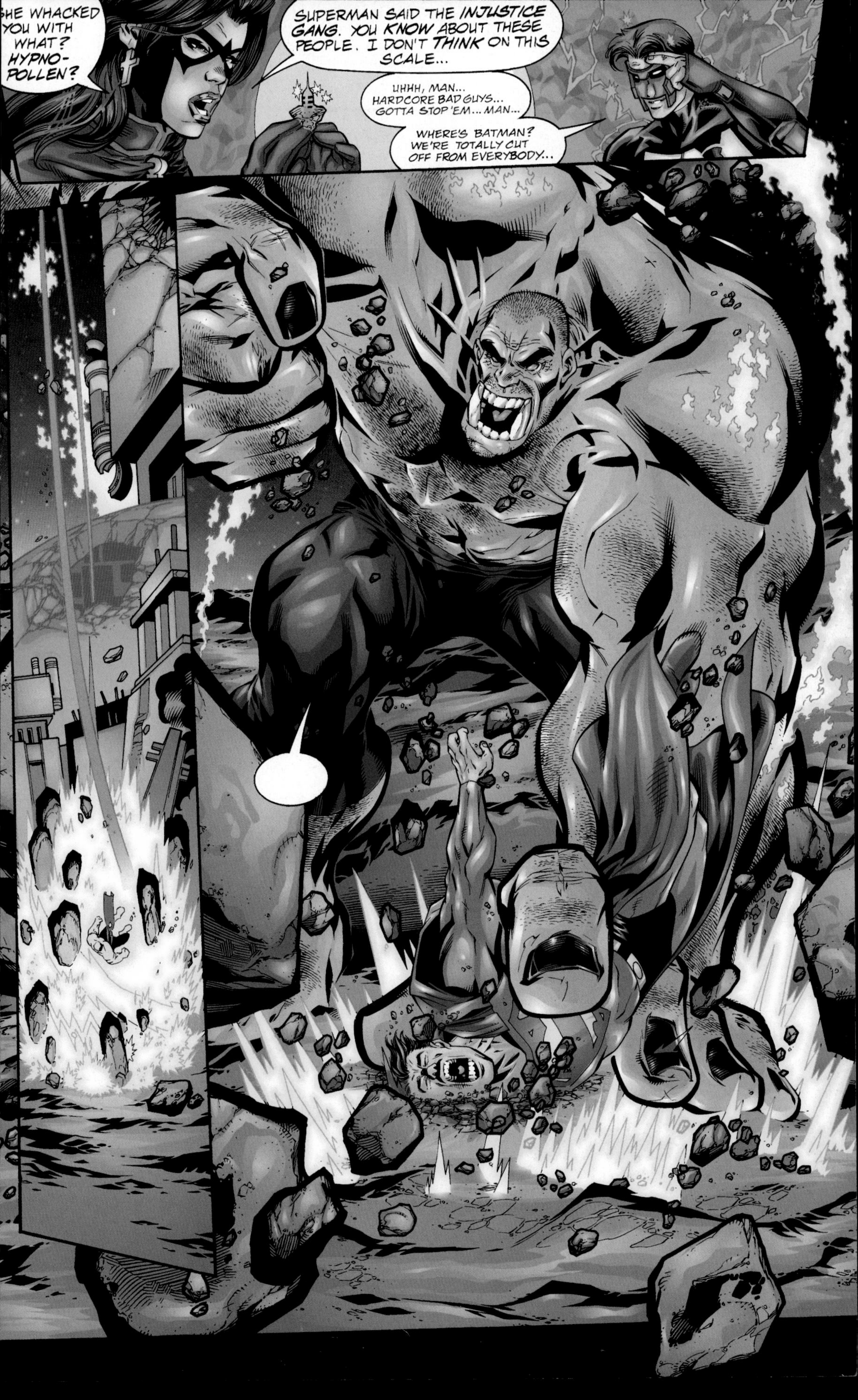
SHE WHACKED YOU WITH WHAT? HYPNO-POLLEN?
SUPERMAN SAID THE INJUSTICE GANG. YOU KNOW ABOUT THESE PEOPLE. I DON'T THINK ON THIS SCALE...
UHHH, MAN... HARDCORE BAD GUYS... GOTTA STOP 'EM... MAN...
WHERE'S BATMAN? WE'RE TOTALLY CUT OFF FROM EVERYBODY...

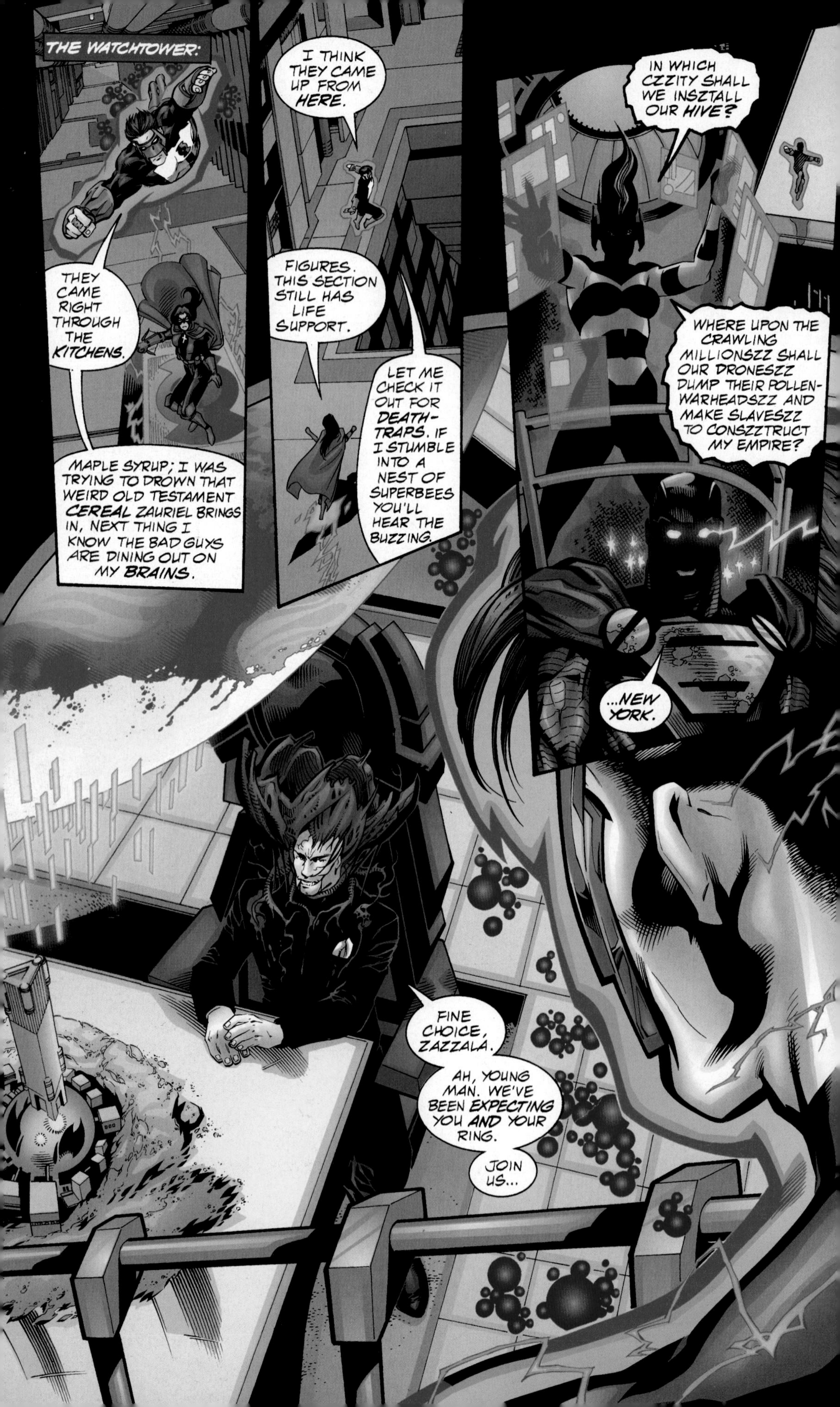
THE WATCHTOWER:
THEY CAME RIGHT THROUGH THE KITCHENS.
MAPLE SYRUP; I WAS TRYING TO DROWN THAT WEIRD OLD TESTAMENT CEREAL ZAURIEL BRINGS IN, NEXT THING I KNOW THE BAD GUYS ARE DINING OUT ON MY BRAINS.
I THINK THEY CAME UP FROM HERE.
FIGURES. THIS SECTION STILL HAS LIFE SUPPORT.
LET ME CHECK IT OUT FOR DEATH-TRAPS. IF I STUMBLE INTO A NEST OF SUPERBEES YOU'LL HEAR THE BUZZING.
IN WHICH CZZITY SHALL WE INSZTALL OUR HIVE?
WHERE UPON THE CRAWLING MILLIONSZZ SHALL OUR DRONESZZ DUMP THEIR POLLEN-WARHEADSZZ AND MAKE SLAVESZZ TO CONSZZTRUCT MY EMPIRE?
...NEW YORK.
FINE CHOICE, ZAZZALA.
AH, YOUNG MAN. WE'VE BEEN EXPECTING YOU AND YOUR RING.
JOIN US...

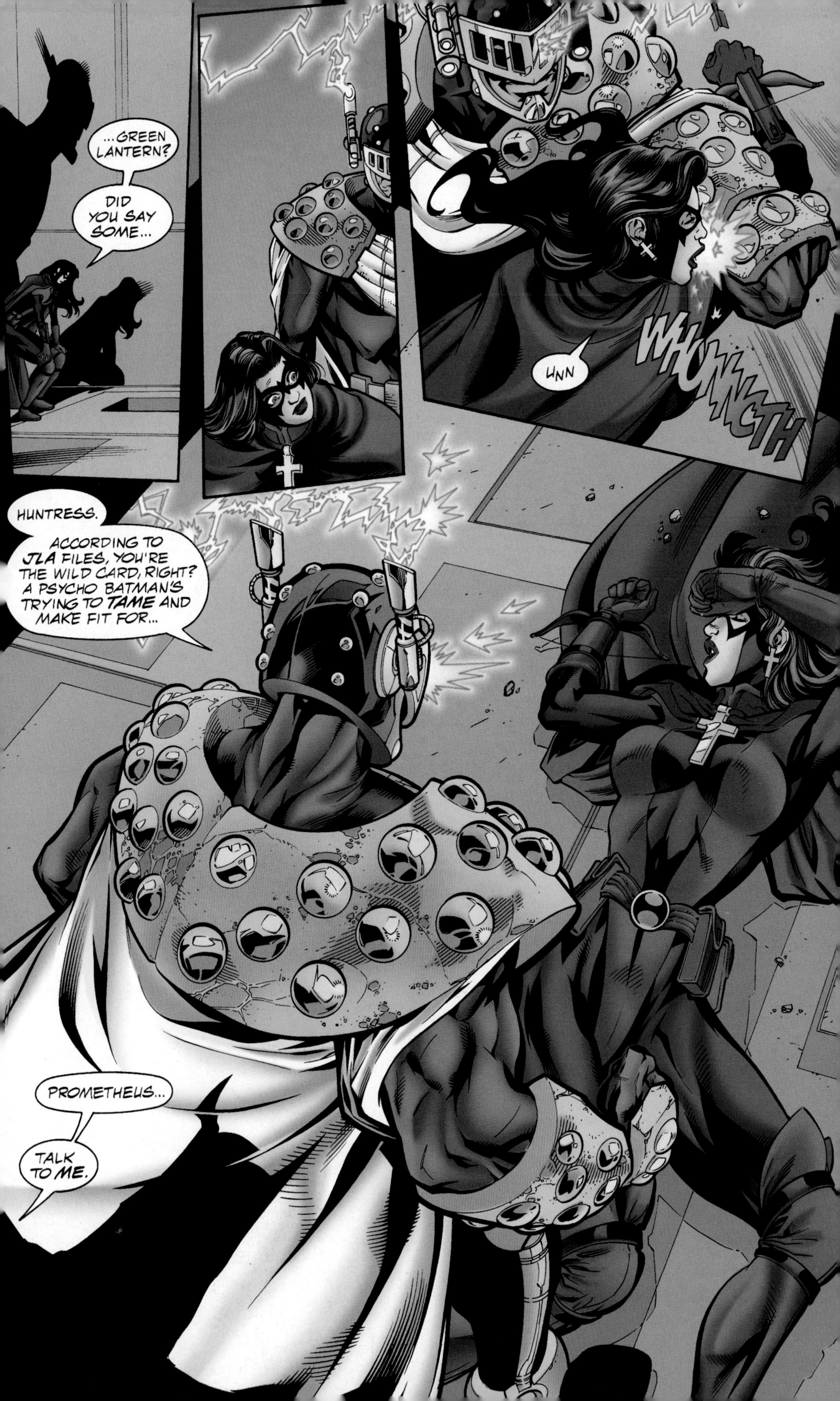
...GREEN LANTERN?
DID YOU SAY SOME...
UNN
WHUNNCTH
HUNTRESS.
ACCORDING TO JLA FILES, YOU'RE THE WILD CARD, RIGHT? A PSYCHO BATMAN'S TRYING TO TAME AND MAKE FIT FOR...
PROMETHEUS...
TALK TO ME.

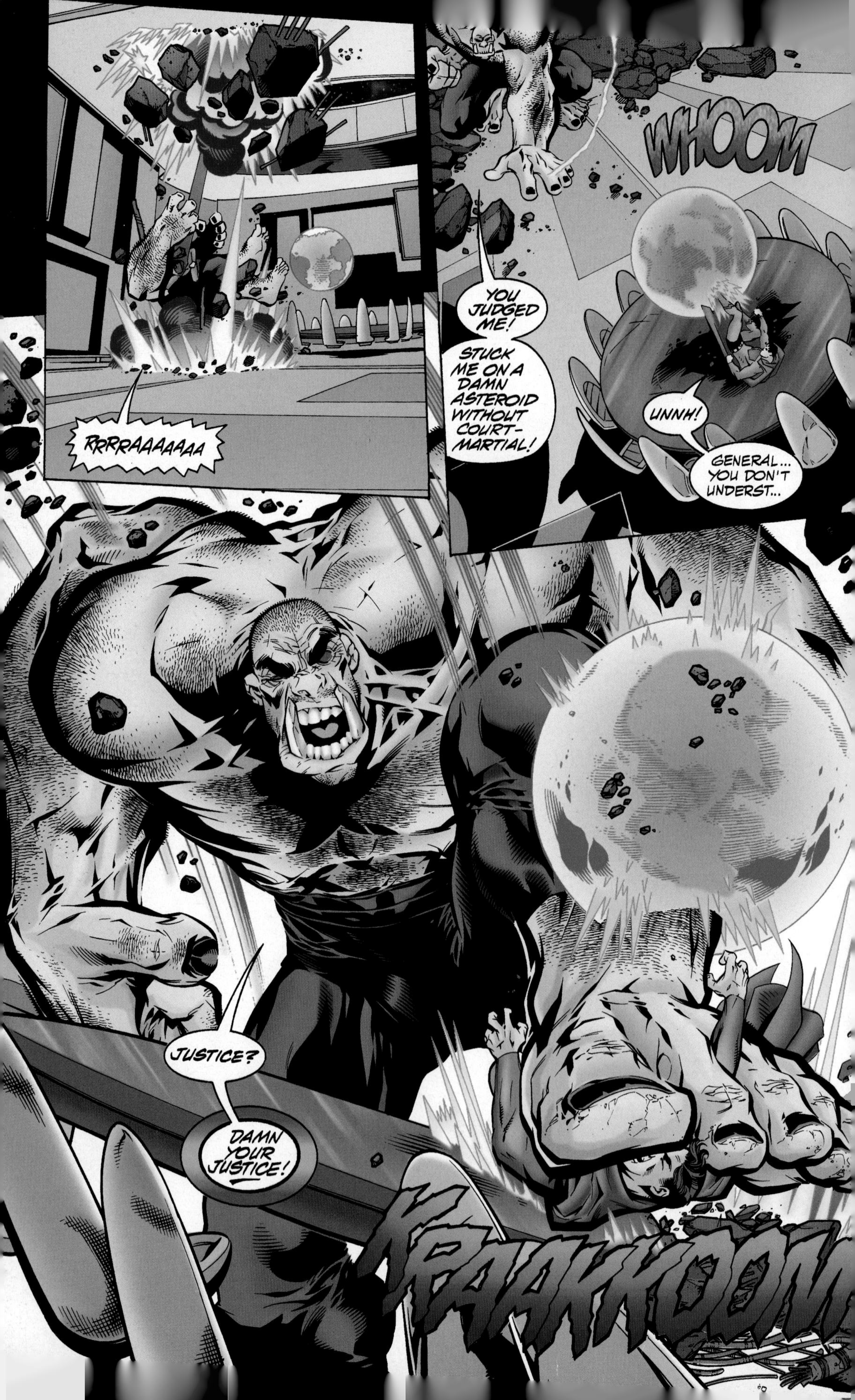
RRRRAAAAAAAA
WHOOM
YOU JUDGED ME!
STUCK ME ON A DAMN ASTEROID WITHOUT COURT-MARTIAL!
UNNH!
GENERAL... YOU DON'T UNDERST...
JUSTICE?
DAMN YOUR JUSTICE!
KRAAKKOOM

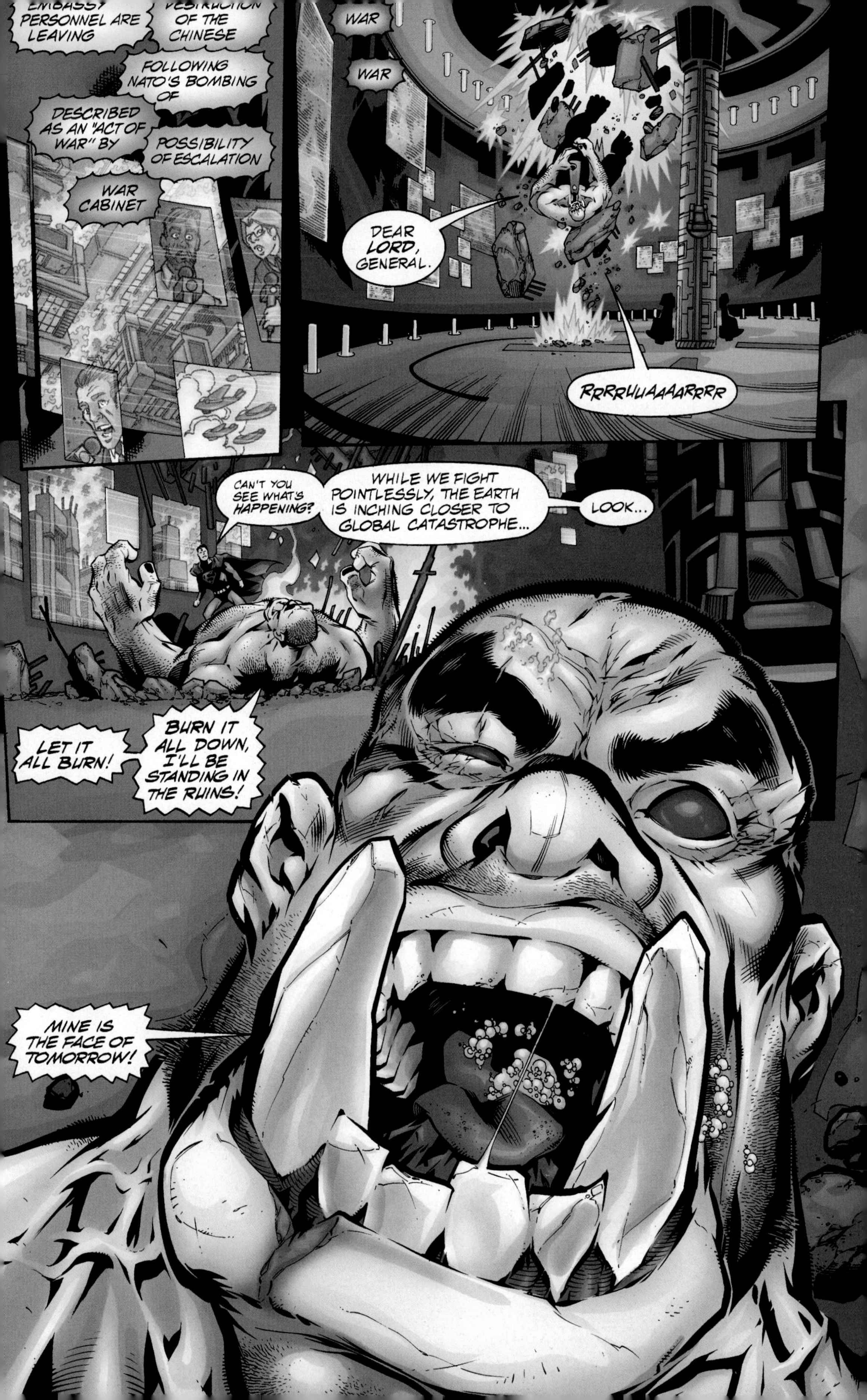
EMBASSY PERSONNEL ARE LEAVING
DESTRUCTION OF THE CHINESE
FOLLOWING NATO'S BOMBING OF
DESCRIBED AS AN "ACT OF WAR" BY
POSSIBILITY OF ESCALATION
WAR CABINET
WAR
WAR
DEAR LORD, GENERAL.
RRRRUUAAAARRRR
CAN'T YOU SEE WHAT'S HAPPENING?
WHILE WE FIGHT POINTLESSLY, THE EARTH IS INCHING CLOSER TO GLOBAL CATASTROPHE...
LOOK...
LET IT ALL BURN!
BURN IT ALL DOWN, I'LL BE STANDING IN THE RUINS!
MINE IS THE FACE OF TOMORROW!

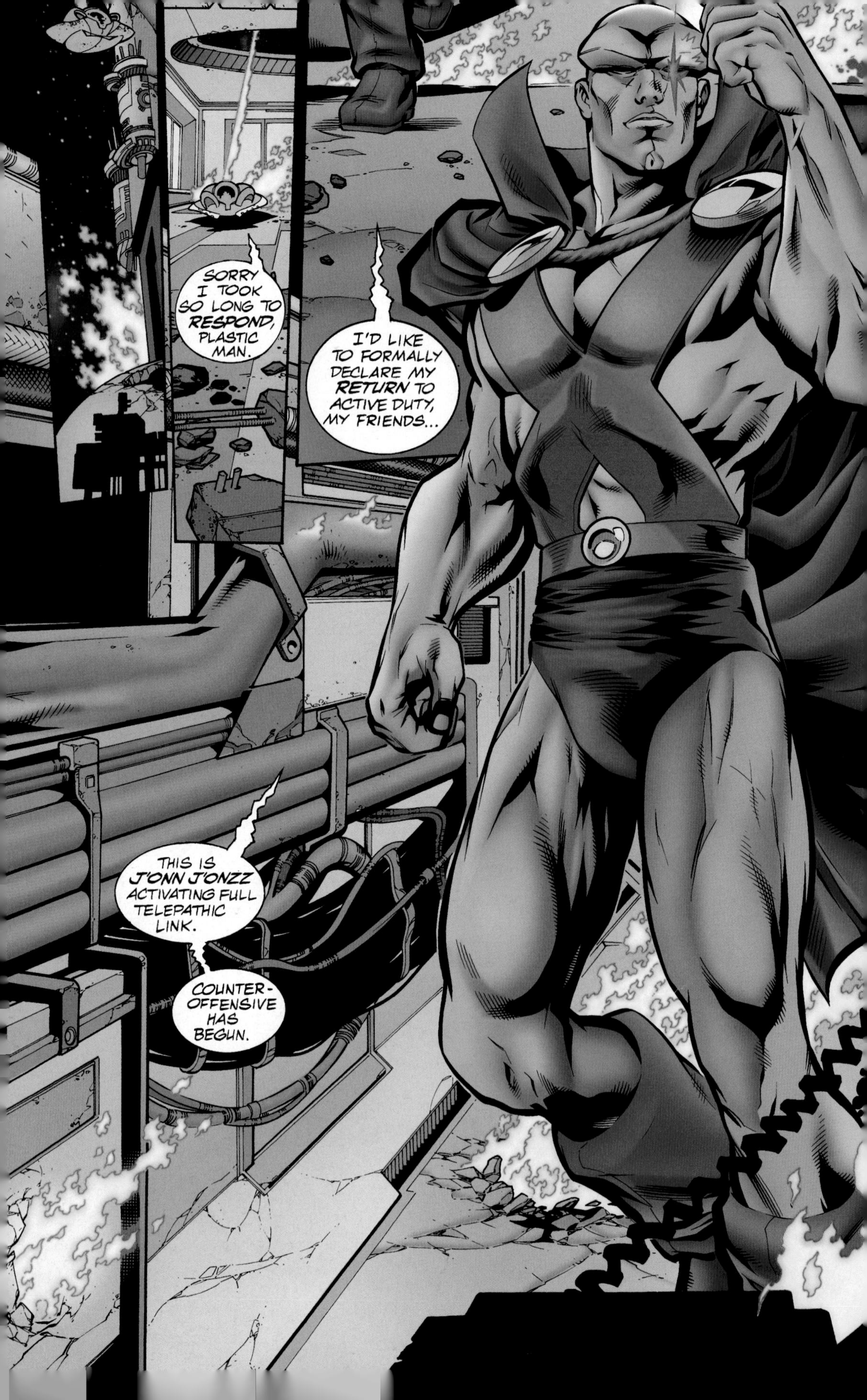
SORRY I TOOK SO LONG TO RESPOND, PLASTIC MAN.
I'D LIKE TO FORMALLY DECLARE MY RETURN TO ACTIVE DUTY, MY FRIENDS...
THIS IS J'ONN J'ONZZ ACTIVATING FULL TELEPATHIC LINK.
COUNTER-OFFENSIVE HAS BEGUN.

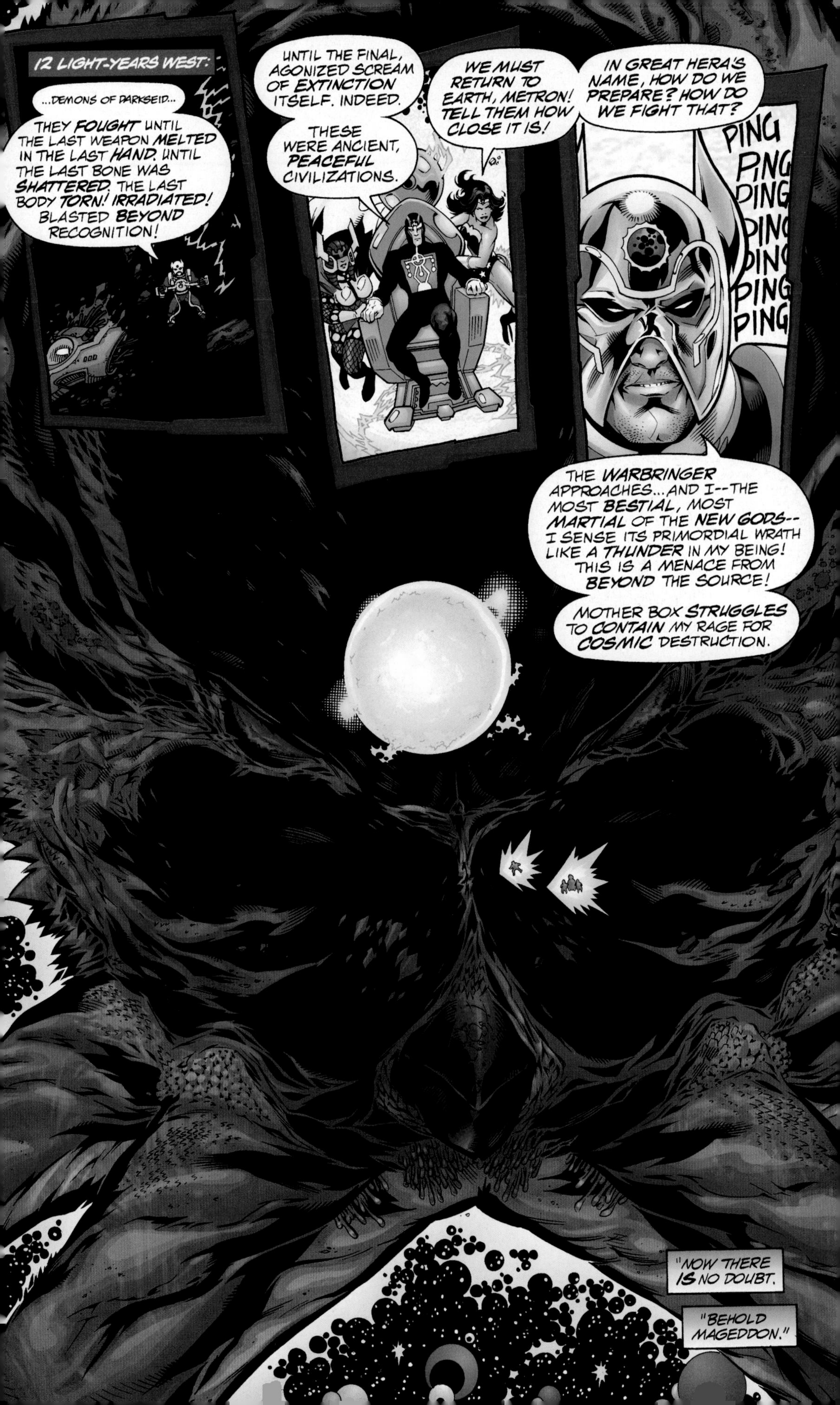
12 LIGHT-YEARS WEST:
...DEMONS OF DARKSEID...
THEY FOUGHT UNTIL THE LAST WEAPON MELTED IN THE LAST HAND. UNTIL THE LAST BONE WAS SHATTERED. THE LAST BODY TORN! IRRADIATED! BLASTED BEYOND RECOGNITION!
UNTIL THE FINAL, AGONIZED SCREAM OF EXTINCTION ITSELF. INDEED.
THESE WERE ANCIENT, PEACEFUL CIVILIZATIONS.
WE MUST RETURN TO EARTH, METRON! TELL THEM HOW CLOSE IT IS!
IN GREAT HERA'S NAME, HOW DO WE PREPARE? HOW DO WE FIGHT THAT?
PING PING PING PING PING PING PING PING
THE WARBRINGER APPROACHES... AND I--THE MOST BESTIAL, MOST MARTIAL OF THE NEW GODS-- I SENSE ITS PRIMORDIAL WRATH LIKE A THUNDER IN MY BEING! THIS IS A MENACE FROM BEYOND THE SOURCE!
MOTHER BOX STRUGGLES TO CONTAIN MY RAGE FOR COSMIC DESTRUCTION.
"NOW THERE IS NO DOUBT.
"BEHOLD MAGEDDON."

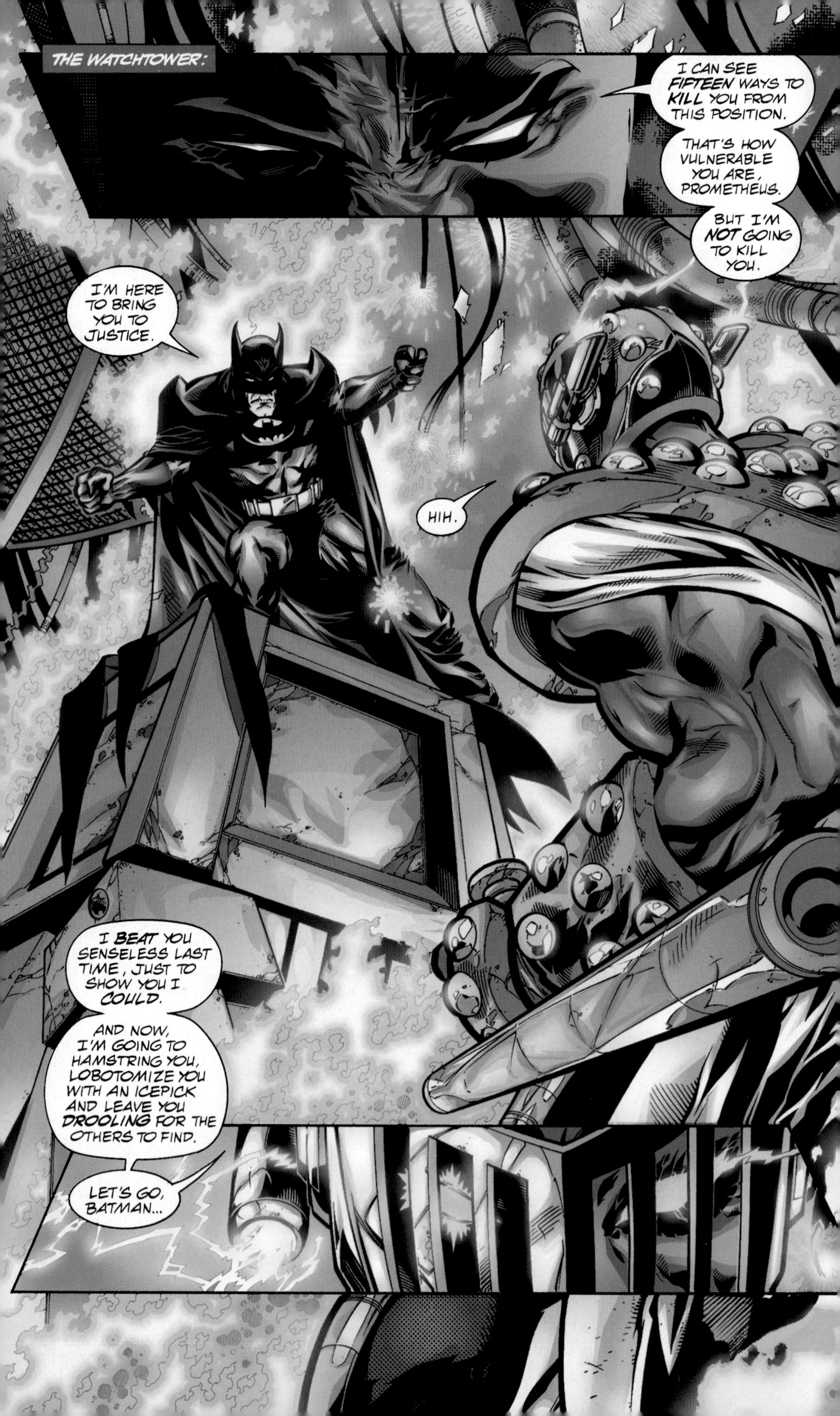
THE WATCHTOWER:
I CAN SEE FIFTEEN WAYS TO KILL YOU FROM THIS POSITION.
THAT'S HOW VULNERABLE YOU ARE, PROMETHEUS.
BUT I'M NOT GOING TO KILL YOU.
I'M HERE TO BRING YOU TO JUSTICE.
HIH.
I BEAT YOU SENSELESS LAST TIME, JUST TO SHOW YOU I COULD.
AND NOW, I'M GOING TO HAMSTRING YOU, LOBOTOMIZE YOU WITH AN ICEPICK AND LEAVE YOU DROOLING FOR THE OTHERS TO FIND.
LET'S GO, BATMAN...

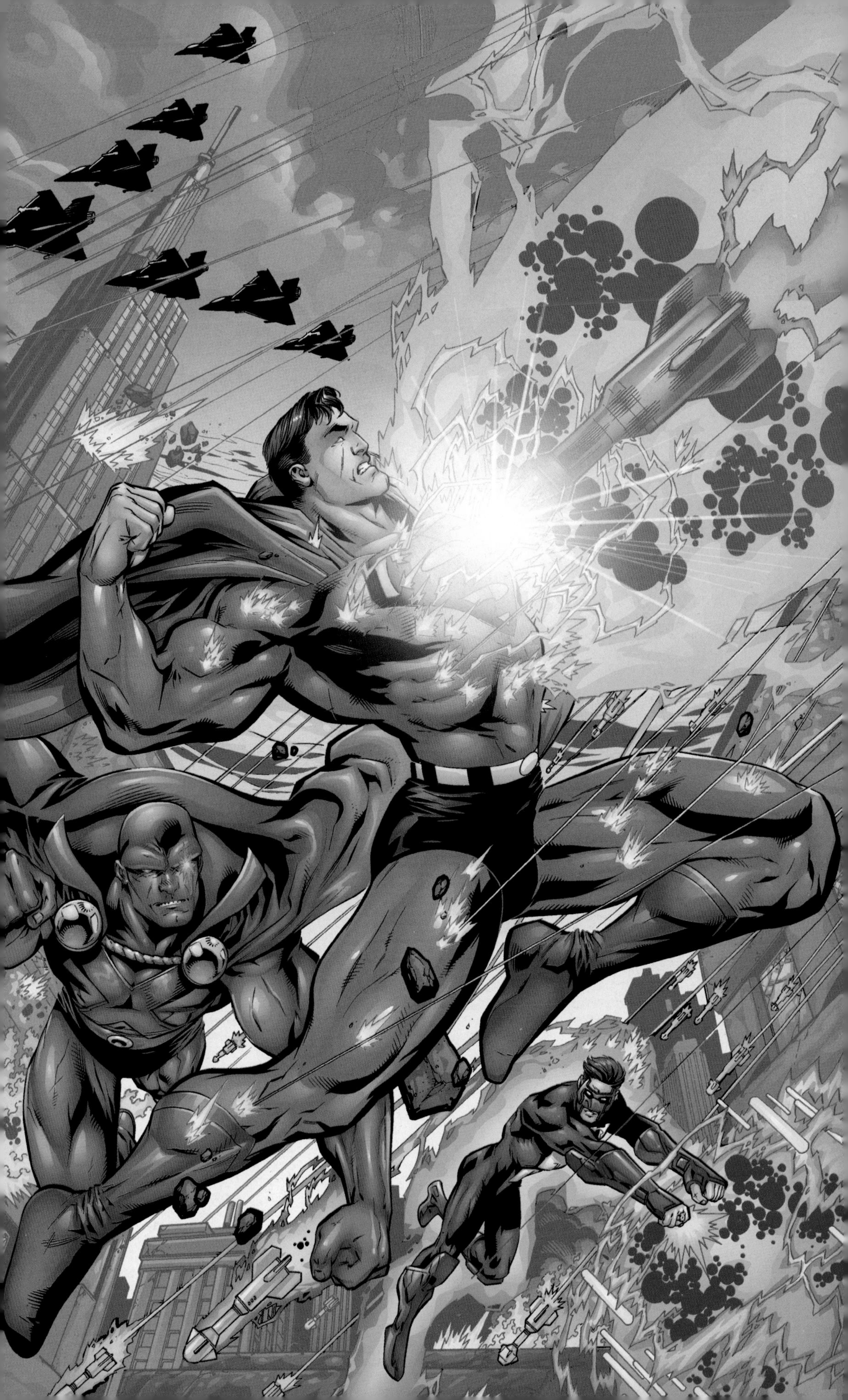

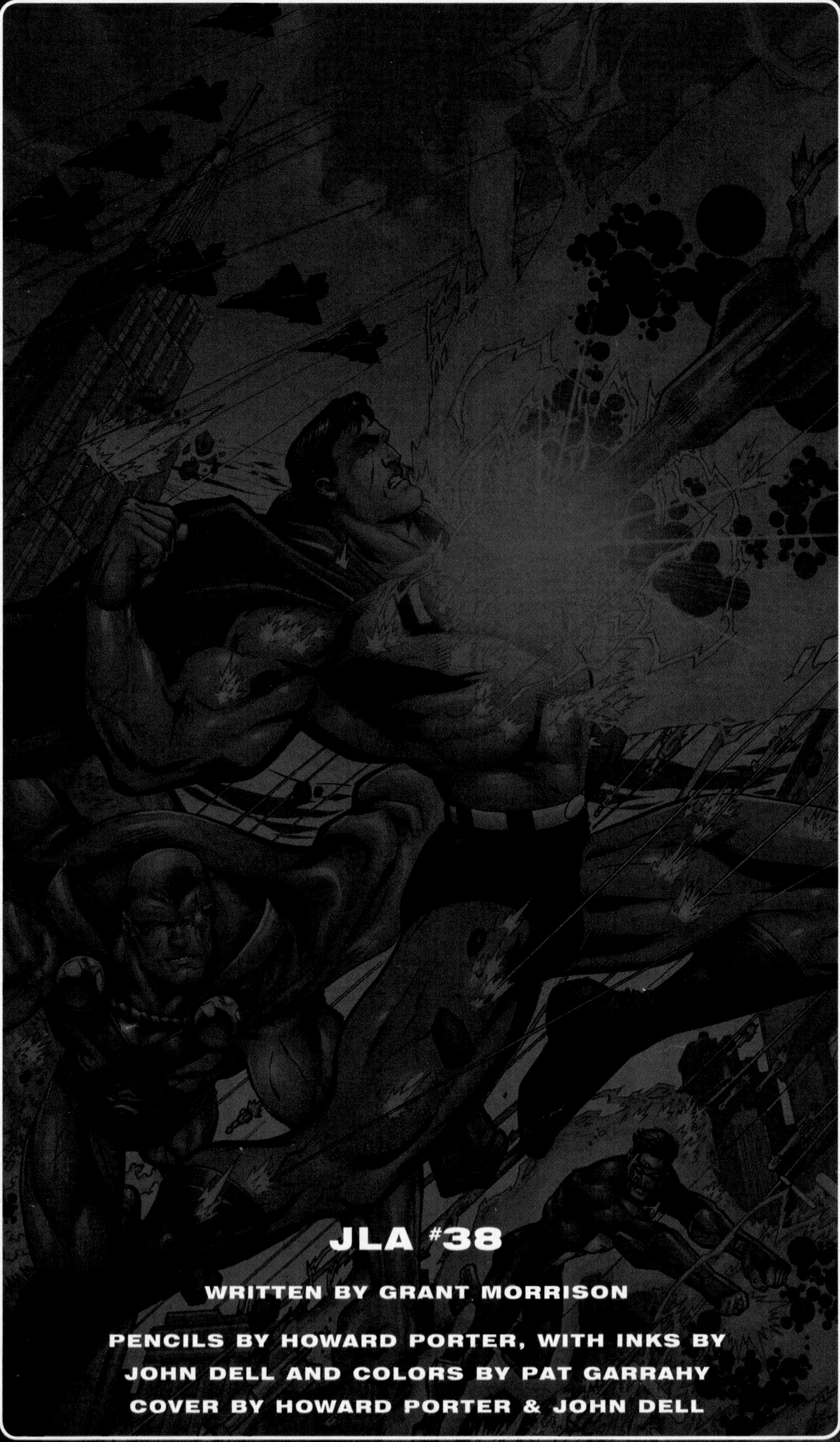

JLA #38

WRITTEN BY GRANT MORRISON

PENCILS BY HOWARD PORTER, WITH INKS BY JOHN DELL AND COLORS BY PAT GARRAHY

COVER BY HOWARD PORTER & JOHN DELL

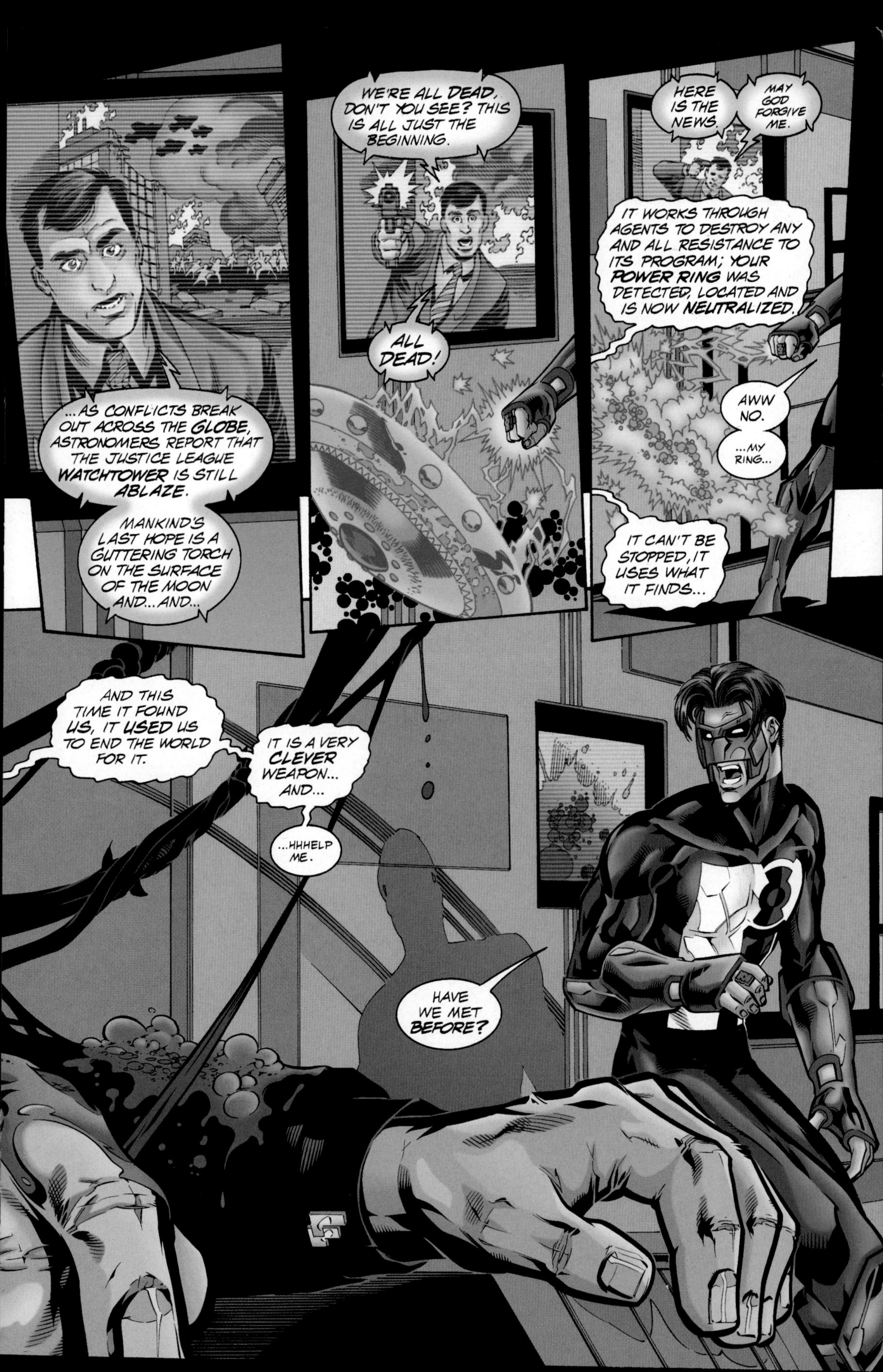
...AS CONFLICTS BREAK OUT ACROSS THE GLOBE, ASTRONOMERS REPORT THAT THE JUSTICE LEAGUE WATCHTOWER IS STILL ABLAZE.
MANKIND'S LAST HOPE IS A GUTTERING TORCH ON THE SURFACE OF THE MOON AND...AND...
WE'RE ALL DEAD, DON'T YOU SEE? THIS IS ALL JUST THE BEGINNING.
ALL DEAD!
HERE IS THE NEWS.
MAY GOD FORGIVE ME.
IT WORKS THROUGH AGENTS TO DESTROY ANY AND ALL RESISTANCE TO ITS PROGRAM; YOUR POWER RING WAS DETECTED, LOCATED AND IS NOW NEUTRALIZED.
AWW NO.
...MY RING...
IT CAN'T BE STOPPED, IT USES WHAT IT FINDS...
AND THIS TIME IT FOUND US, IT USED US TO END THE WORLD FOR IT.
IT IS A VERY CLEVER WEAPON... AND...
...HHHELP ME.
HAVE WE MET BEFORE?

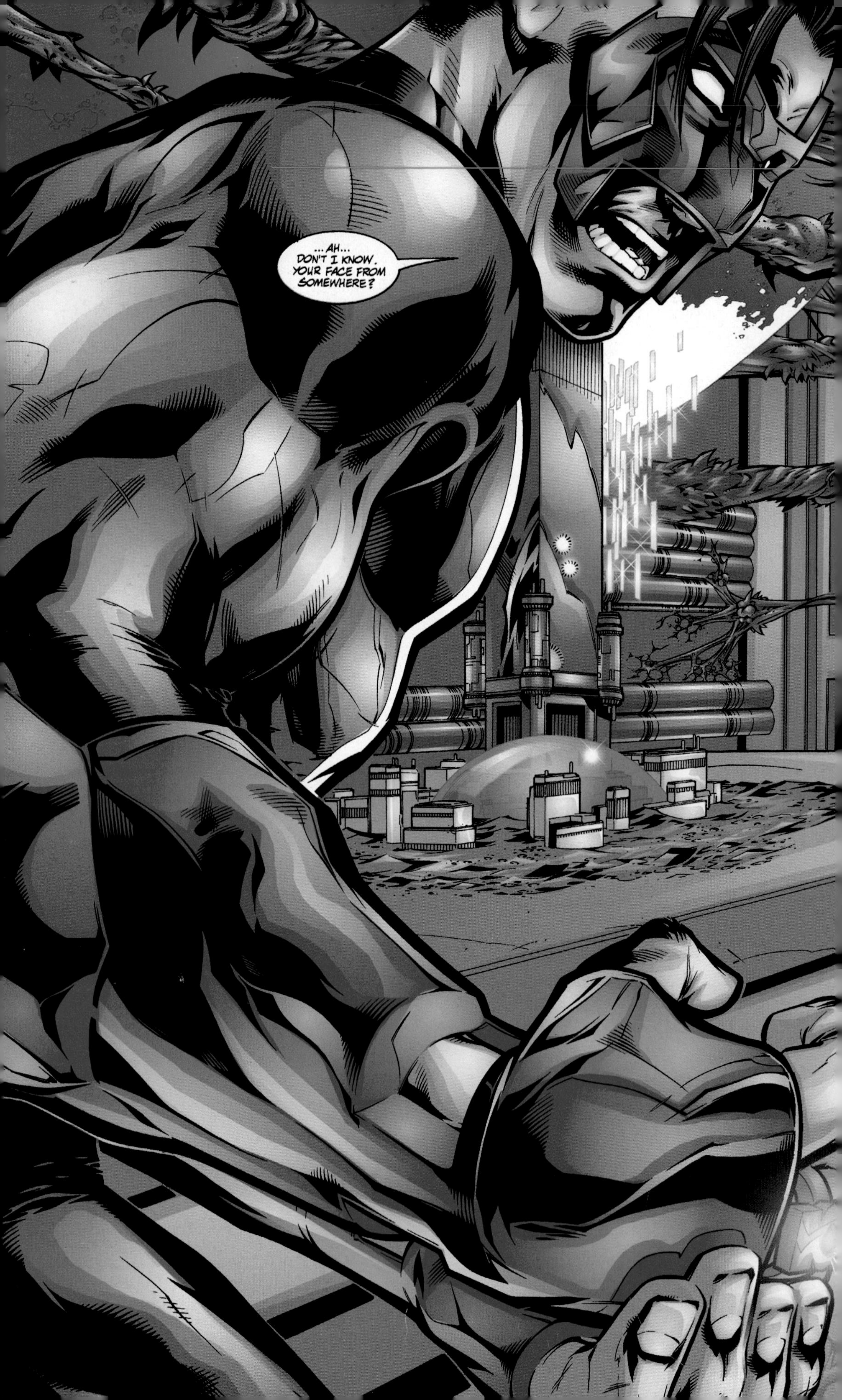
...AH... DON'T I KNOW. YOUR FACE FROM SOMEWHERE?

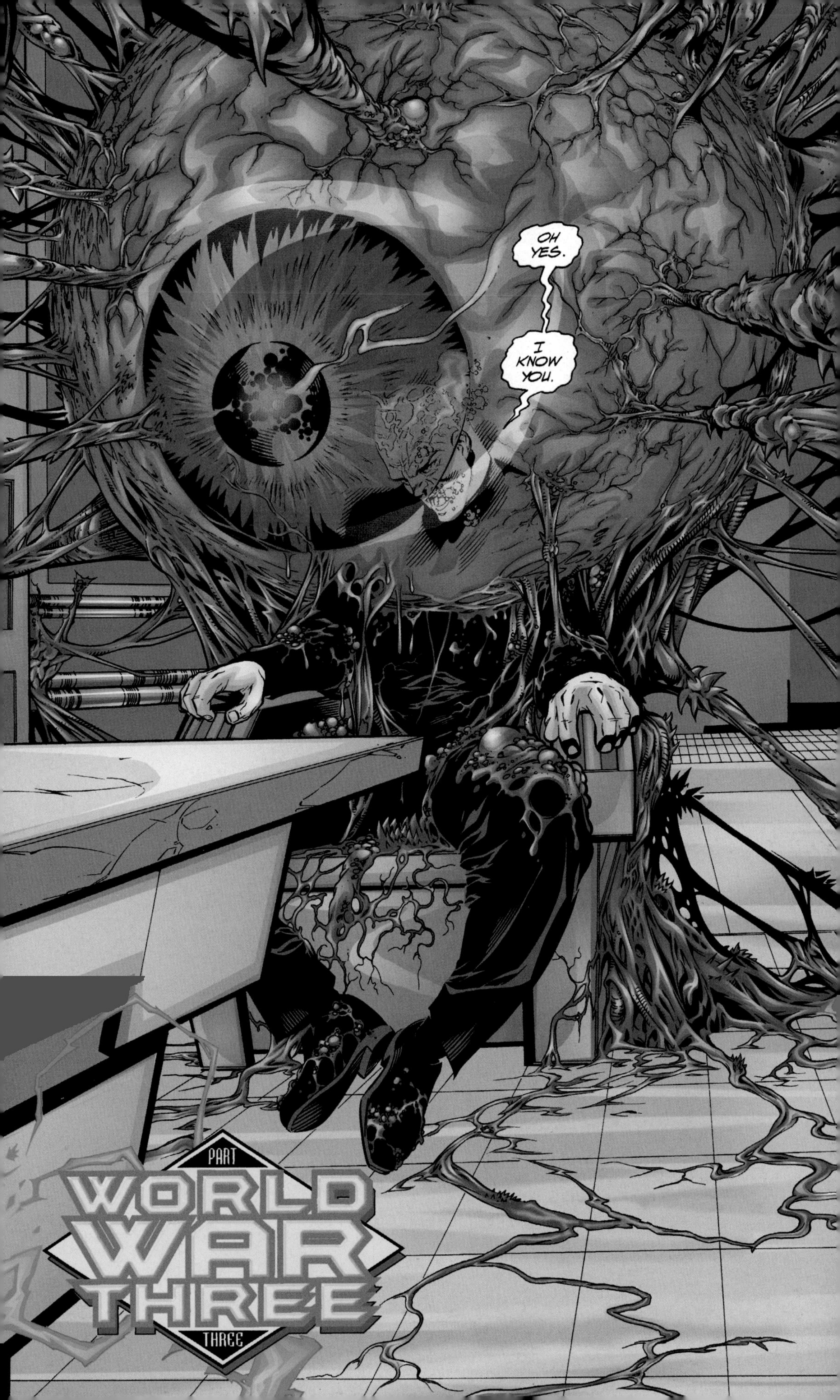
OH YES.
I KNOW YOU.
PART
WORLD WAR THREE
THREE

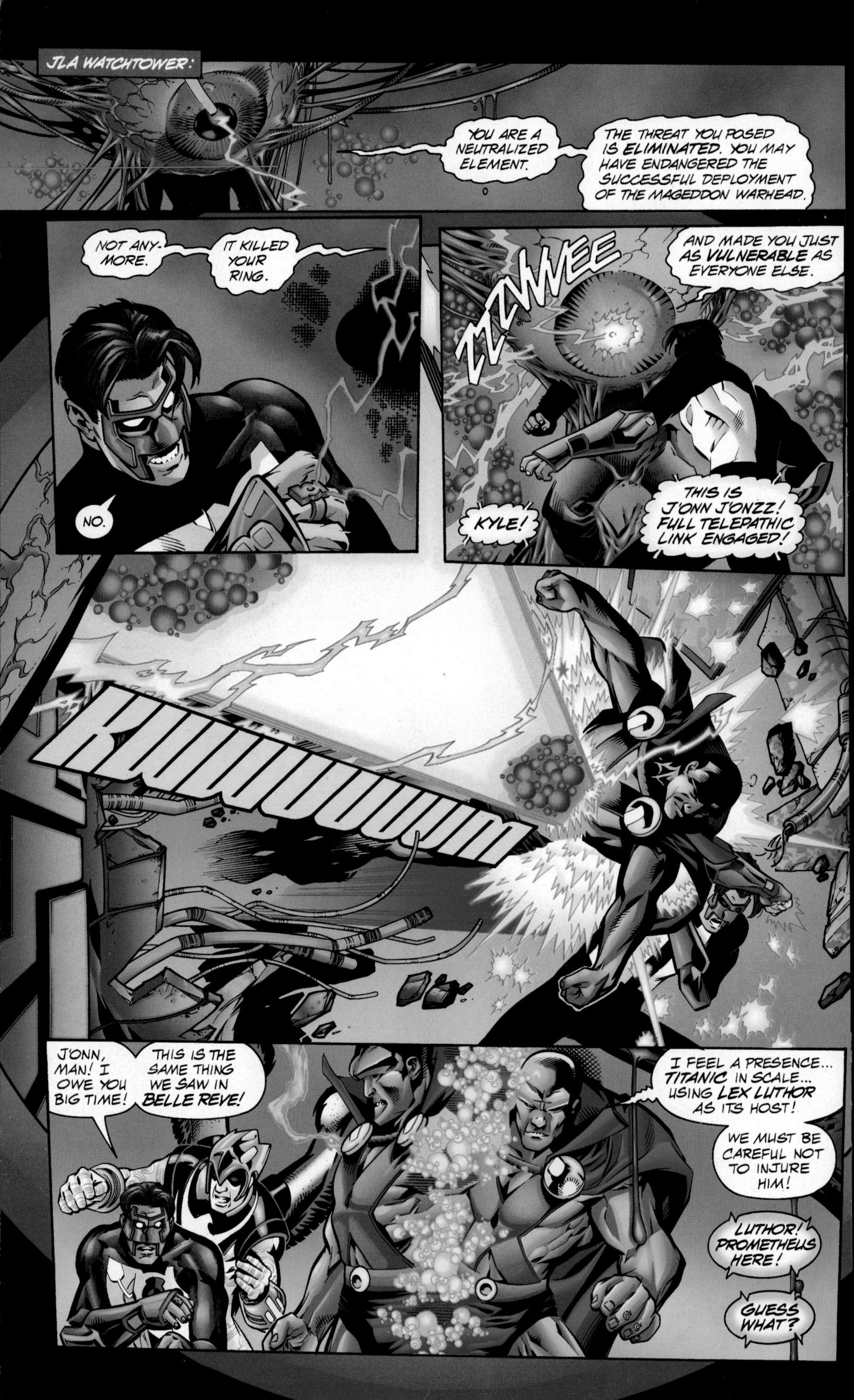

JLA WATCHTOWER:
YOU ARE A NEUTRALIZED ELEMENT.
THE THREAT YOU POSED IS ELIMINATED. YOU MAY HAVE ENDANGERED THE SUCCESSFUL DEPLOYMENT OF THE MAGEDDON WARHEAD.
NOT ANY-MORE.
IT KILLED YOUR RING.
NO.
ZZZWWEE
AND MADE YOU JUST AS VULNERABLE AS EVERYONE ELSE.
KYLE!
THIS IS J'ONN J'ONZZ! FULL TELEPATHIC LINK ENGAGED!
KWWOOOOWM
J'ONN, MAN! I OWE YOU BIG TIME!
THIS IS THE SAME THING WE SAW IN BELLE REVE!
I FEEL A PRESENCE... TITANIC IN SCALE... USING LEX LUTHOR AS ITS HOST!
WE MUST BE CAREFUL NOT TO INJURE HIM!
LUTHOR! PROMETHEUS HERE!
GUESS WHAT?

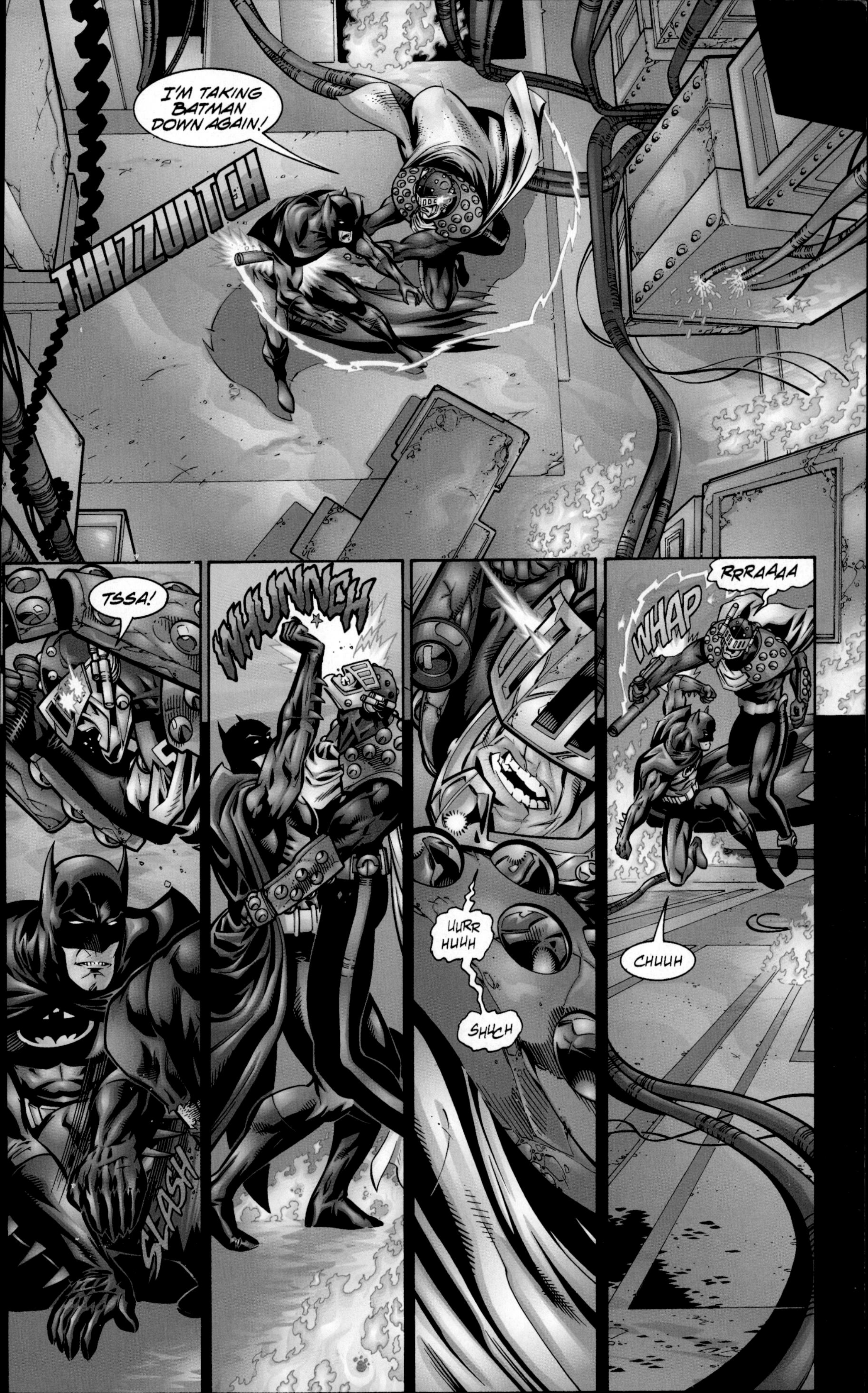
I'M TAKING BATMAN DOWN AGAIN!
THHZZUNTCH
TSSA!
SLASH
WHUNNCH
UURR HUUH
SHUCH
WHAP
RRRAAAA
CHUUH

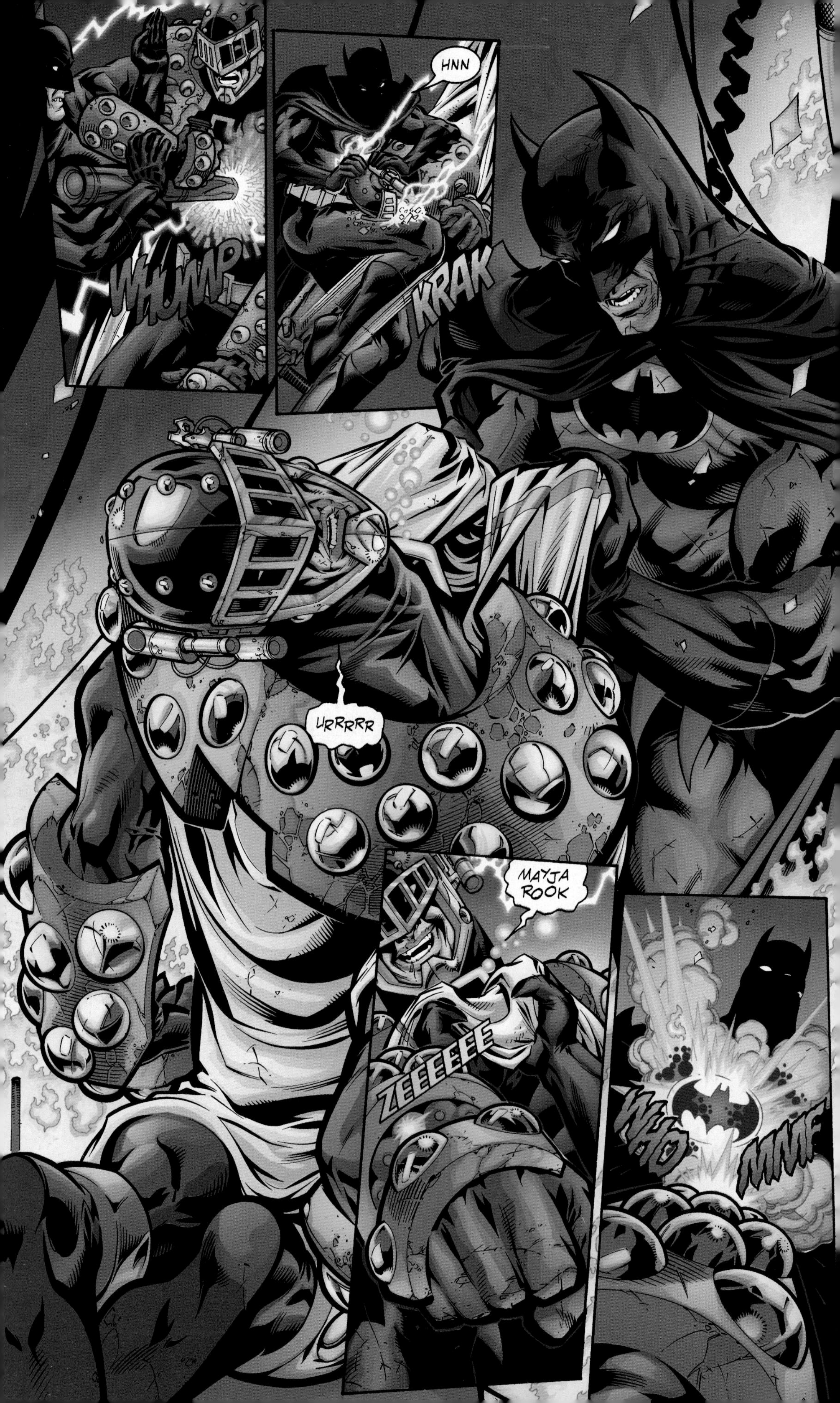
WHUMP
HNN
KRAK
URRRRR
MAYJA ROOK
ZEEEEEE

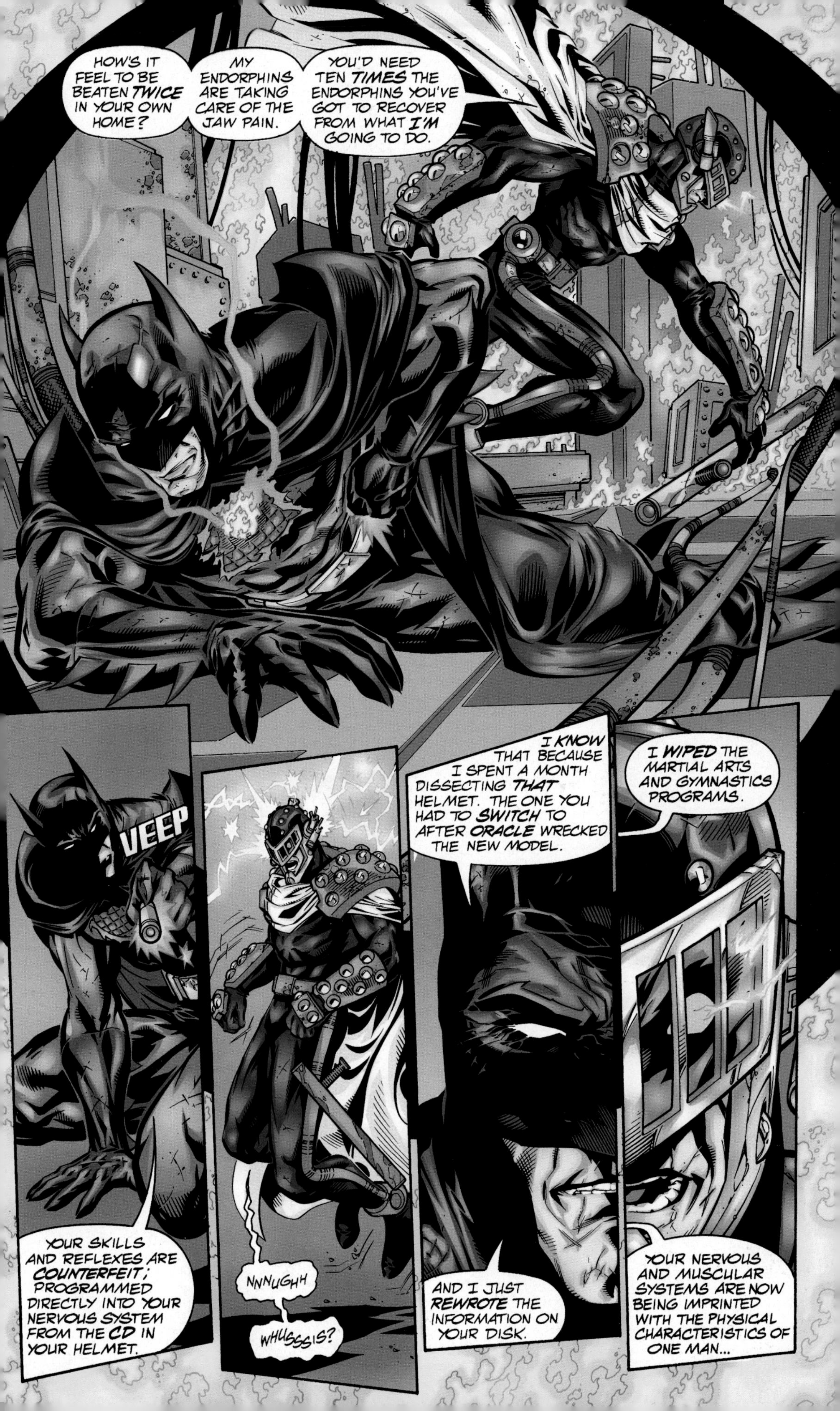
HOW'S IT FEEL TO BE BEATEN TWICE IN YOUR OWN HOME?
MY ENDORPHINS ARE TAKING CARE OF THE JAW PAIN.
YOU'D NEED TEN TIMES THE ENDORPHINS YOU'VE GOT TO RECOVER FROM WHAT I'M GOING TO DO.
VEEP
YOUR SKILLS AND REFLEXES ARE COUNTERFEIT; PROGRAMMED DIRECTLY INTO YOUR NERVOUS SYSTEM FROM THE CD IN YOUR HELMET.
NNNUGHH
WHUSSSIS?
I KNOW THAT BECAUSE I SPENT A MONTH DISSECTING THAT HELMET. THE ONE YOU HAD TO SWITCH TO AFTER ORACLE WRECKED THE NEW MODEL.
AND I JUST REWROTE THE INFORMATION ON YOUR DISK.
I WIPED THE MARTIAL ARTS AND GYMNASTICS PROGRAMS.
YOUR NERVOUS AND MUSCULAR SYSTEMS ARE NOW BEING IMPRINTED WITH THE PHYSICAL CHARACTERISTICS OF ONE MAN...

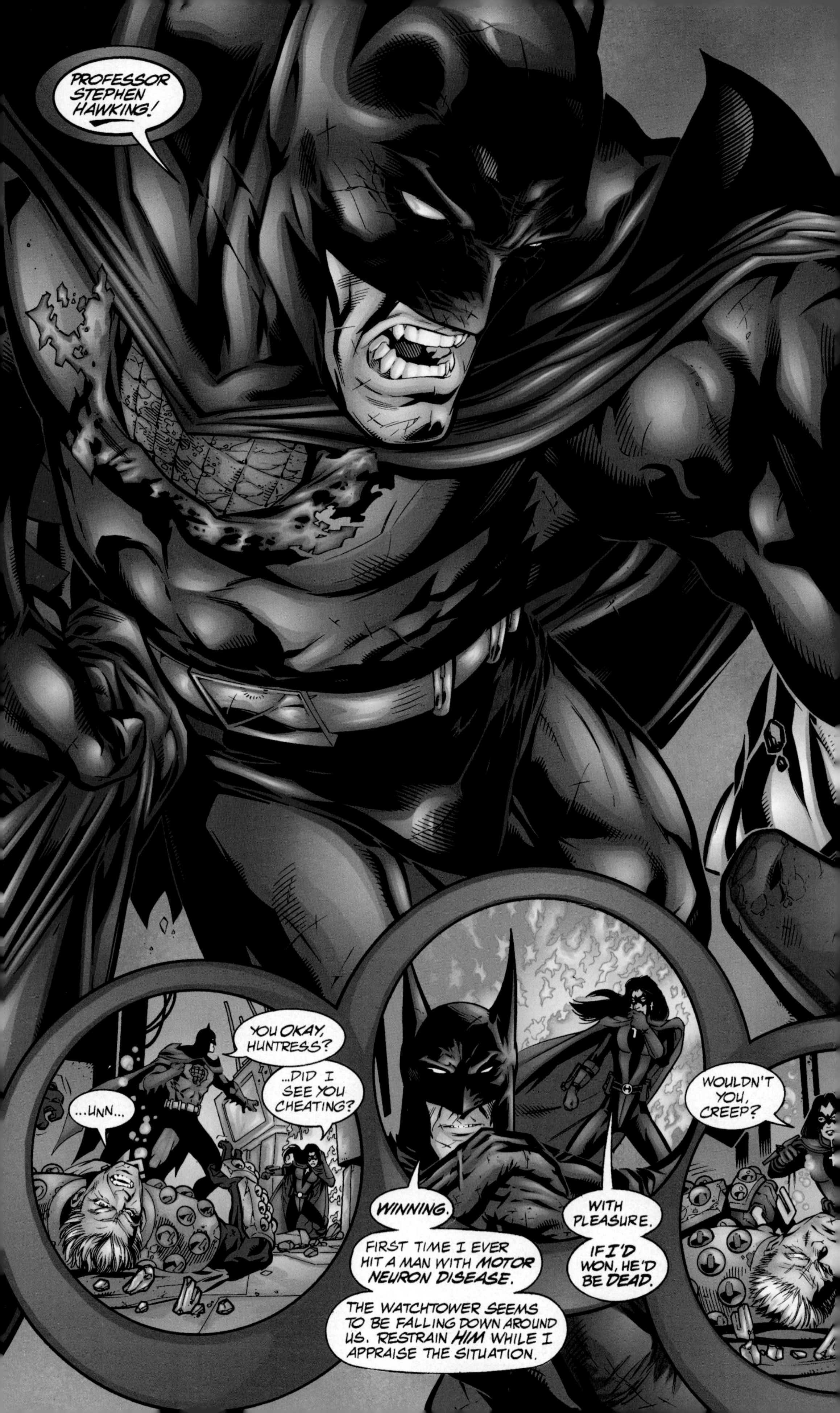
PROFESSOR STEPHEN HAWKING!
YOU OKAY, HUNTRESS?
...DID I SEE YOU CHEATING?
...UNN...
WINNING.
FIRST TIME I EVER HIT A MAN WITH MOTOR NEURON DISEASE.
THE WATCHTOWER SEEMS TO BE FALLING DOWN AROUND US. RESTRAIN HIM WHILE I APPRAISE THE SITUATION.
WITH PLEASURE.
IF I'D WON, HE'D BE DEAD.
WOULDN'T YOU, CREEP?

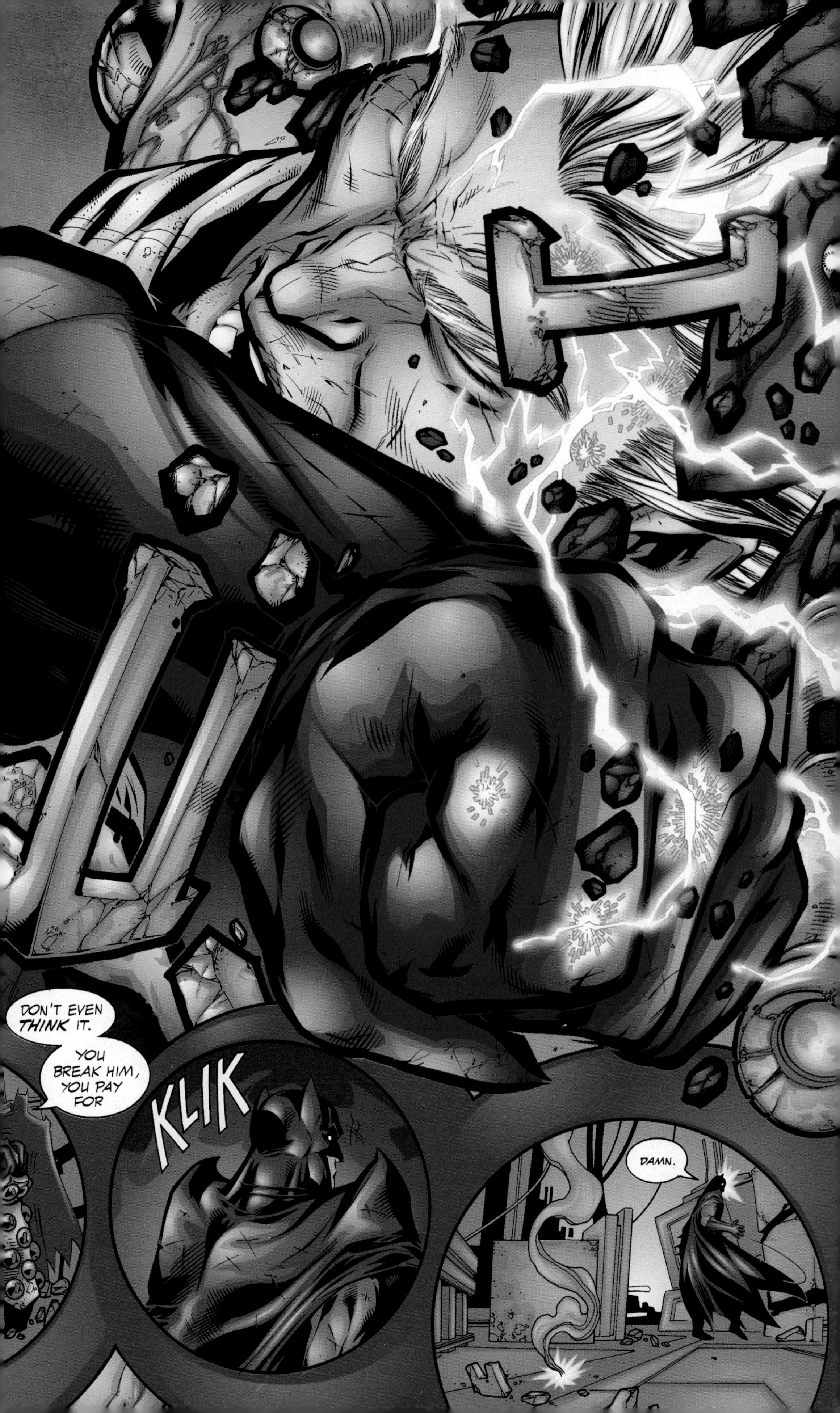
DON'T EVEN THINK IT.
YOU BREAK HIM, YOU PAY FOR
KLIK
DAMN.

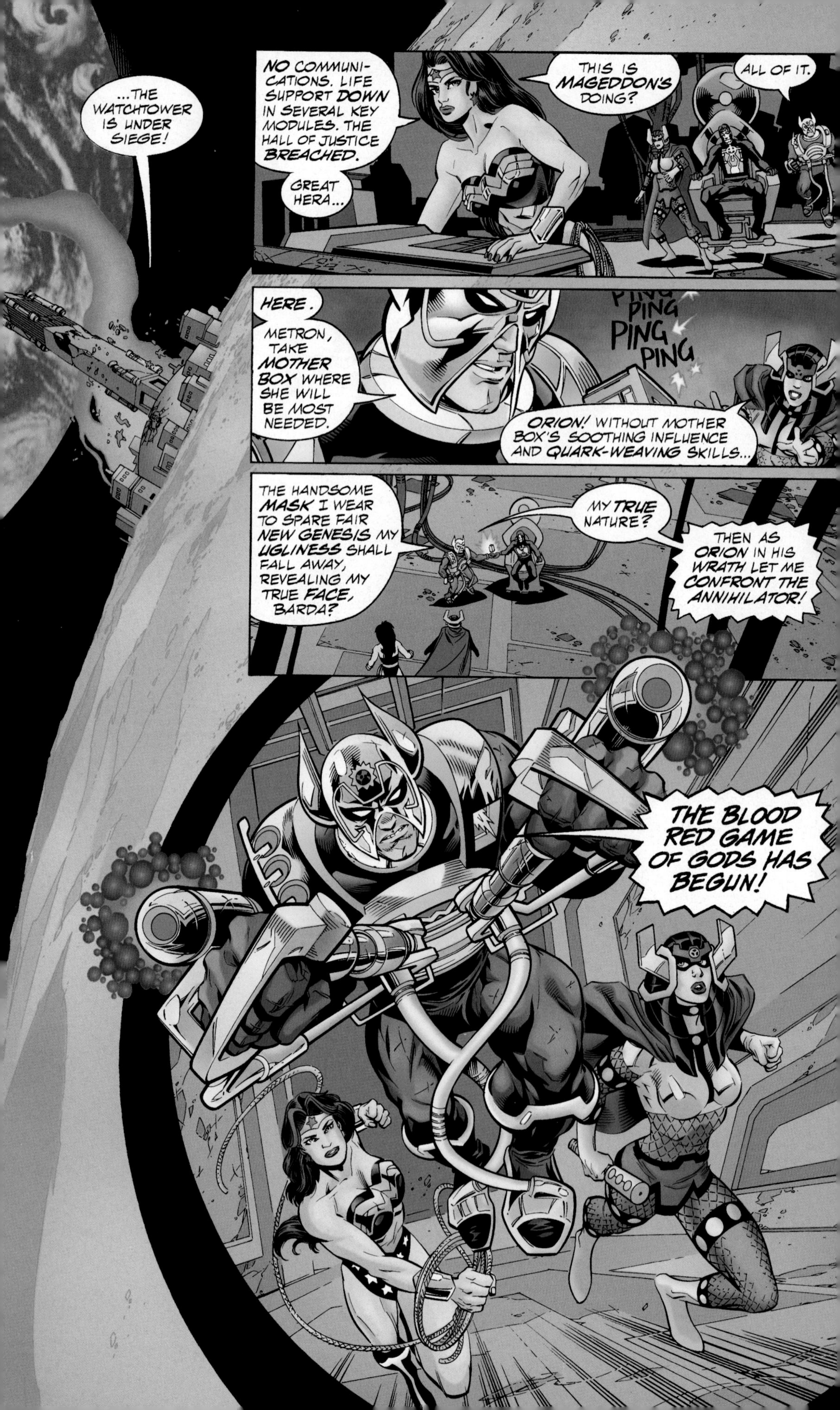

...THE WATCHTOWER IS UNDER SIEGE!
NO COMMUNICATIONS. LIFE SUPPORT DOWN IN SEVERAL KEY MODULES. THE HALL OF JUSTICE BREACHED.
GREAT HERA...
THIS IS MAGEDDON'S DOING?
ALL OF IT.
HERE.
METRON, TAKE MOTHER BOX WHERE SHE WILL BE MOST NEEDED.
PING PING PING PING
ORION! WITHOUT MOTHER BOX'S SOOTHING INFLUENCE AND QUARK-WEAVING SKILLS...
THE HANDSOME MASK I WEAR TO SPARE FAIR NEW GENESIS MY UGLINESS SHALL FALL AWAY, REVEALING MY TRUE FACE, BARDA?
MY TRUE NATURE?
THEN AS ORION IN HIS WRATH LET ME CONFRONT THE ANNIHILATOR!
THE BLOOD RED GAME OF GODS HAS BEGUN!

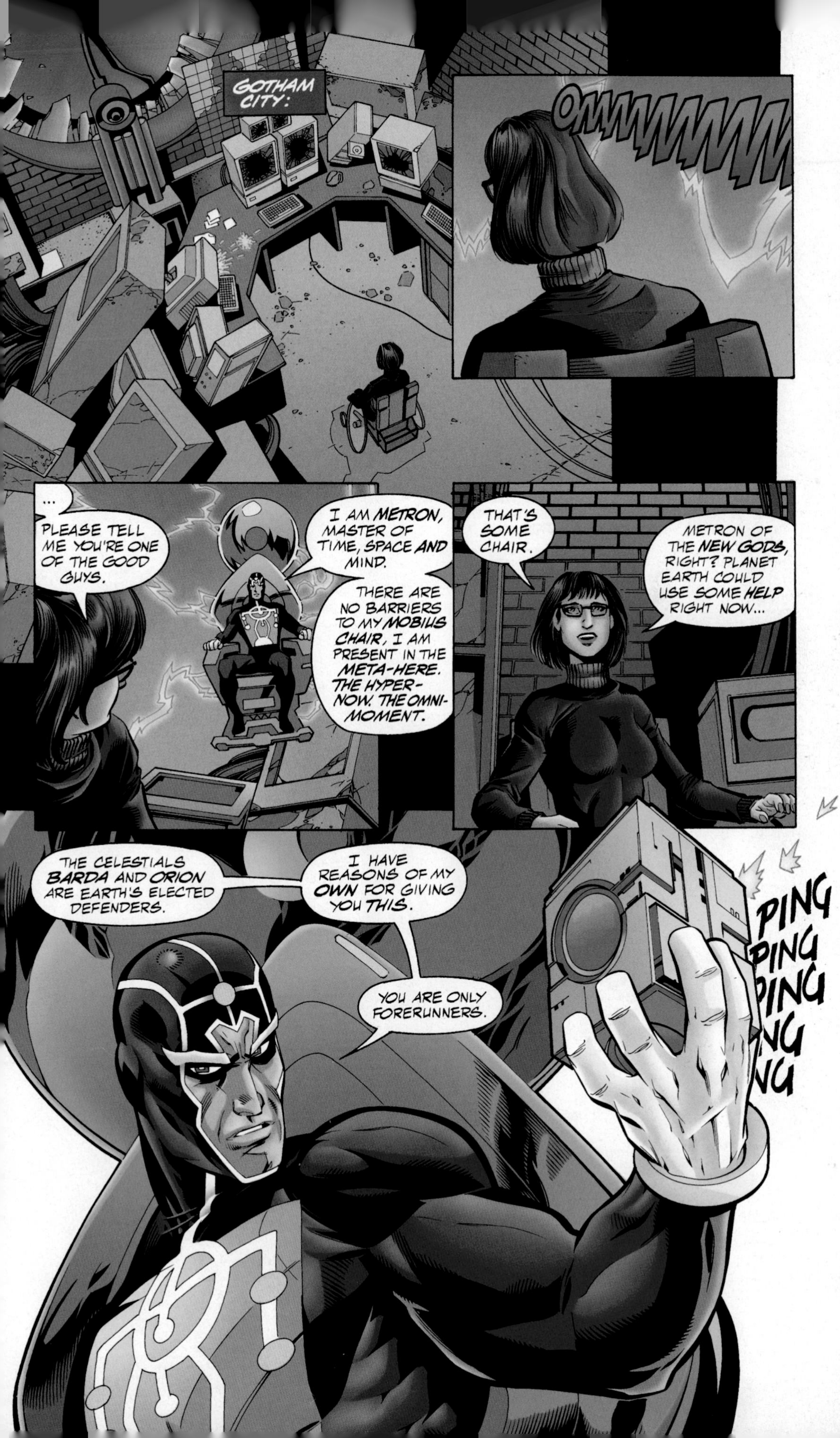
GOTHAM CITY:
OMMMMMMM
...
PLEASE TELL ME YOU'RE ONE OF THE GOOD GUYS.
I AM METRON, MASTER OF TIME, SPACE AND MIND.
THERE ARE NO BARRIERS TO MY MOBIUS CHAIR. I AM PRESENT IN THE META-HERE. THE HYPER-NOW. THE OMNI-MOMENT.
THAT'S SOME CHAIR.
METRON OF THE NEW GODS, RIGHT? PLANET EARTH COULD USE SOME HELP RIGHT NOW...
THE CELESTIALS BARDA AND ORION ARE EARTH'S ELECTED DEFENDERS.
I HAVE REASONS OF MY OWN FOR GIVING YOU THIS.
YOU ARE ONLY FORERUNNERS.
PING
PING
PING
NG
NG

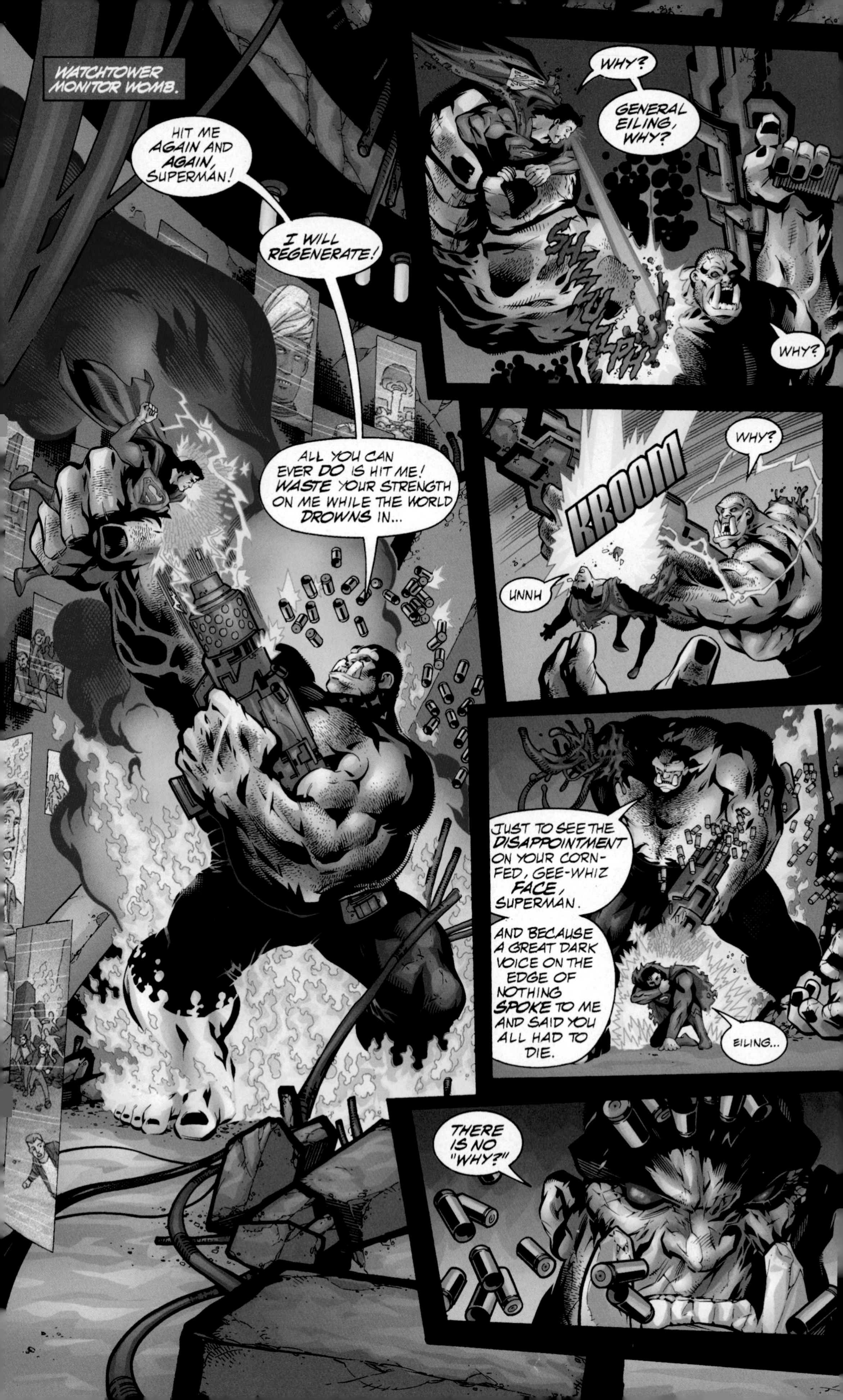

WATCHTOWER MONITOR WOMB.
HIT ME AGAIN AND AGAIN, SUPERMAN!
I WILL REGENERATE!
ALL YOU CAN EVER DO IS HIT ME! WASTE YOUR STRENGTH ON ME WHILE THE WORLD DROWNS IN...
WHY?
GENERAL EILING, WHY?
SHHHULLPH
WHY?
KROOM
WHY?
UNNH
JUST TO SEE THE DISAPPOINTMENT ON YOUR CORN-FED, GEE-WHIZ FACE, SUPERMAN.
AND BECAUSE A GREAT DARK VOICE ON THE EDGE OF NOTHING SPOKE TO ME AND SAID YOU ALL HAD TO DIE.
EILING...
THERE IS NO "WHY?"

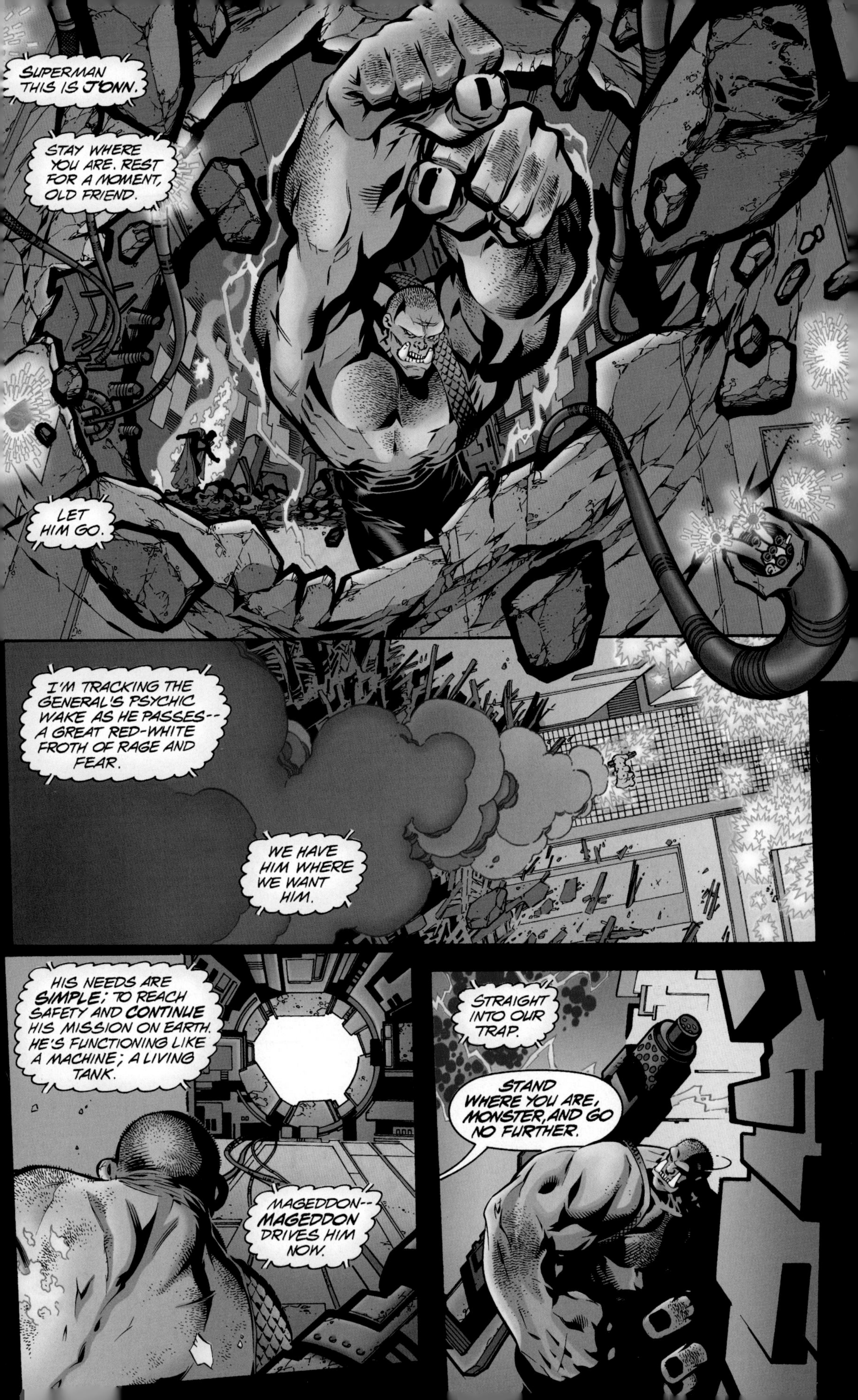
SUPERMAN THIS IS J'ONN.
STAY WHERE YOU ARE. REST FOR A MOMENT, OLD FRIEND.
LET HIM GO.
I'M TRACKING THE GENERAL'S PSYCHIC WAKE AS HE PASSES-- A GREAT RED-WHITE FROTH OF RAGE AND FEAR.
WE HAVE HIM WHERE WE WANT HIM.
HIS NEEDS ARE SIMPLE; TO REACH SAFETY AND CONTINUE HIS MISSION ON EARTH. HE'S FUNCTIONING LIKE A MACHINE; A LIVING TANK.
MAGEDDON-- MAGEDDON DRIVES HIM NOW.
STRAIGHT INTO OUR TRAP.
STAND WHERE YOU ARE, MONSTER, AND GO NO FURTHER.

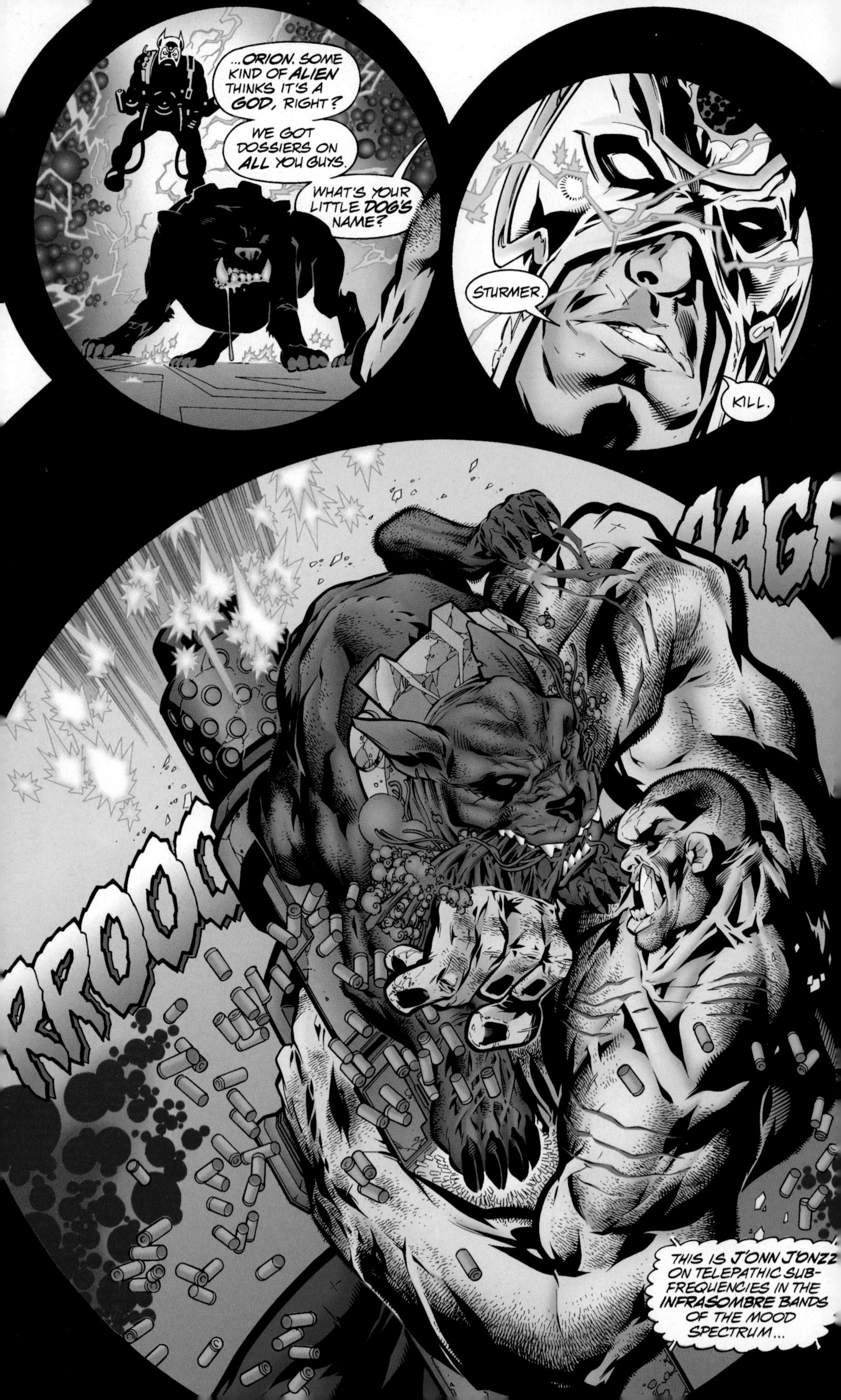
...ORION. SOME KIND OF ALIEN THINKS IT'S A GOD, RIGHT?
WE GOT DOSSIERS ON ALL YOU GUYS.
WHAT'S YOUR LITTLE DOG'S NAME?
STURMER.
KILL.
BROOO
AAGH
THIS IS J'ONN J'ONZZ ON TELEPATHIC SUB-FREQUENCIES IN THE INFRASOMBRE BANDS OF THE MOOD SPECTRUM...

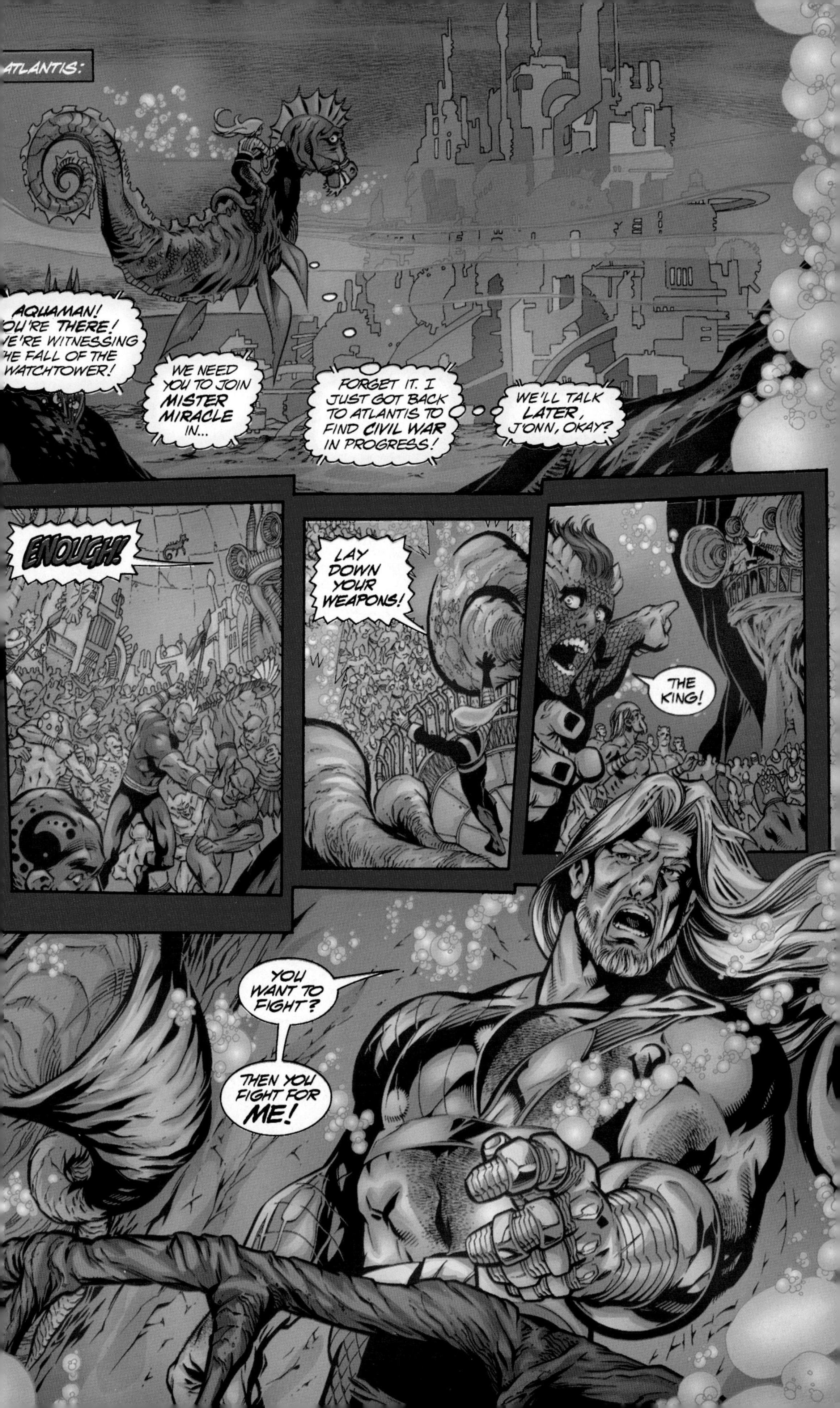

ATLANTIS:
AQUAMAN! YOU'RE THERE! WE'RE WITNESSING THE FALL OF THE WATCHTOWER!
WE NEED YOU TO JOIN MISTER MIRACLE IN...
FORGET IT. I JUST GOT BACK TO ATLANTIS TO FIND CIVIL WAR IN PROGRESS!
WE'LL TALK LATER, J'ONN, OKAY?
ENOUGH!
LAY DOWN YOUR WEAPONS!
THE KING!
YOU WANT TO FIGHT?
THEN YOU FIGHT FOR ME!

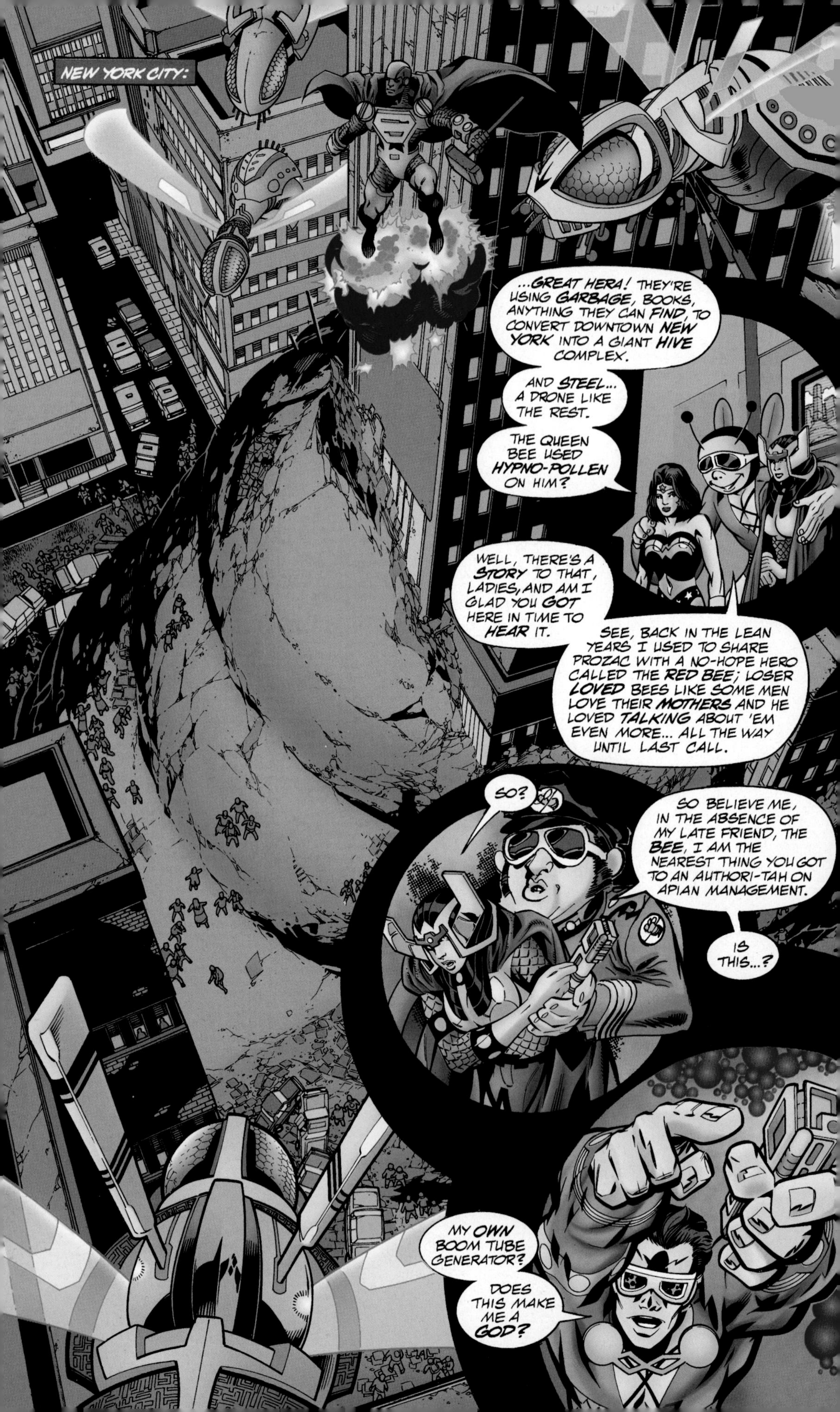
NEW YORK CITY:
...GREAT HERA! THEY'RE USING GARBAGE, BOOKS, ANYTHING THEY CAN FIND, TO CONVERT DOWNTOWN NEW YORK INTO A GIANT HIVE COMPLEX.
AND STEEL... A DRONE LIKE THE REST.
THE QUEEN BEE USED HYPNO-POLLEN ON HIM?
WELL, THERE'S A STORY TO THAT, LADIES, AND AM I GLAD YOU GOT HERE IN TIME TO HEAR IT.
SEE, BACK IN THE LEAN YEARS I USED TO SHARE PROZAC WITH A NO-HOPE HERO CALLED THE RED BEE; LOSER LOVED BEES LIKE SOME MEN LOVE THEIR MOTHERS AND HE LOVED TALKING ABOUT 'EM EVEN MORE... ALL THE WAY UNTIL LAST CALL.
SO?
SO BELIEVE ME, IN THE ABSENCE OF MY LATE FRIEND, THE BEE, I AM THE NEAREST THING YOU GOT TO AN AUTHORI-TAH ON APIAN MANAGEMENT.
IS THIS...?
MY OWN BOOM TUBE GENERATOR?
DOES THIS MAKE ME A GOD?

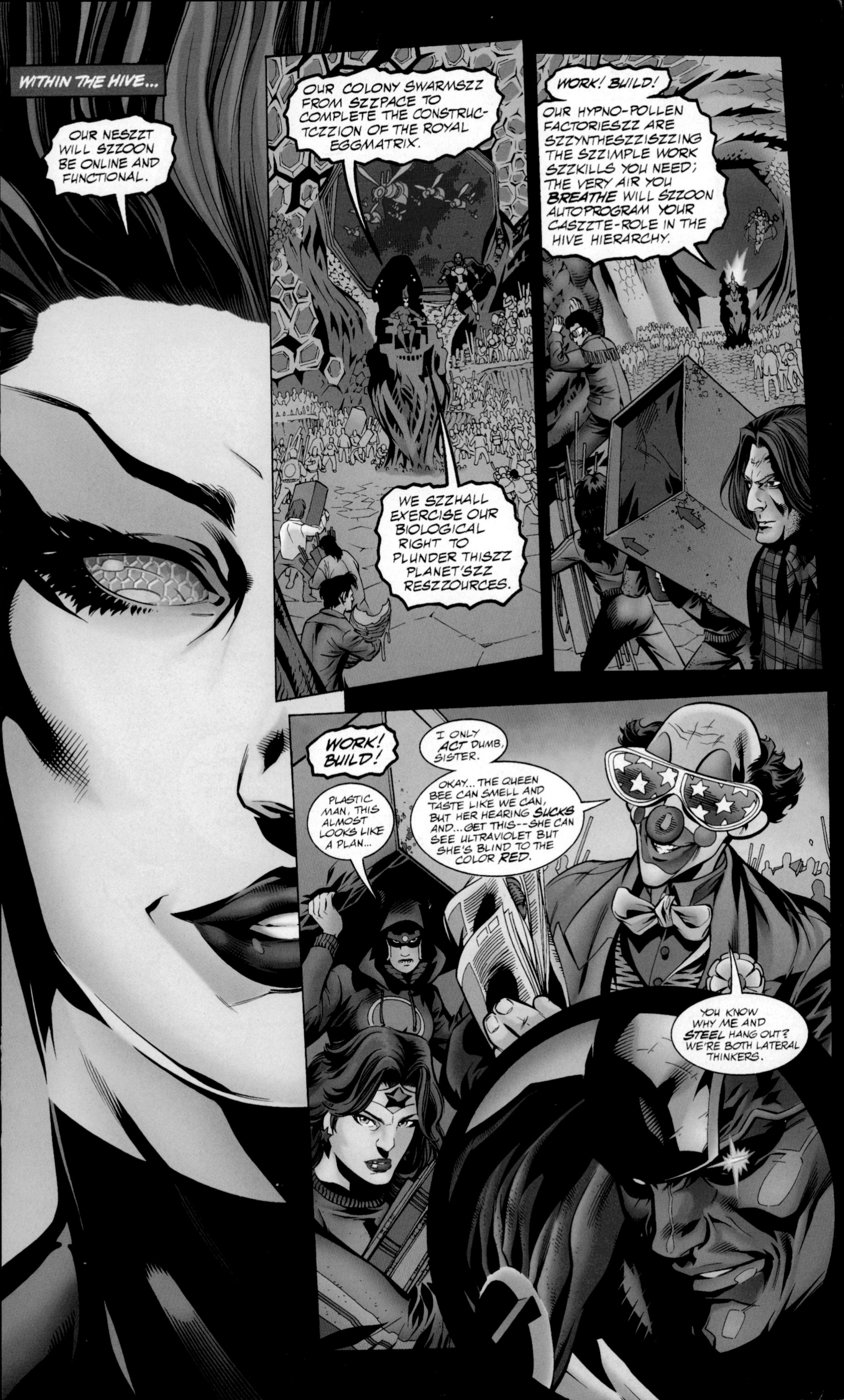
WITHIN THE HIVE...
OUR NESZZT WILL SZZOON BE ONLINE AND FUNCTIONAL.
OUR COLONY SWARMSZZ FROM SZZPACE TO COMPLETE THE CONSTRUCTCZZION OF THE ROYAL EGGMATRIX.
WE SZZHALL EXERCISE OUR BIOLOGICAL RIGHT TO PLUNDER THISZZ PLANET'SZZ RESZZOURCES.
WORK! BUILD!
OUR HYPNO-POLLEN FACTORIESZZ ARE SZZYNTHESZZISZZING THE SZZIMPLE WORK SZZKILLS YOU NEED; THE VERY AIR YOU BREATHE WILL SZZOON AUTOPROGRAM YOUR CASZZTE-ROLE IN THE HIVE HIERARCHY.
WORK! BUILD!
PLASTIC MAN, THIS ALMOST LOOKS LIKE A PLAN...
I ONLY ACT DUMB, SISTER.
OKAY... THE QUEEN BEE CAN SMELL AND TASTE LIKE WE CAN, BUT HER HEARING SUCKS AND... GET THIS--SHE CAN SEE ULTRAVIOLET BUT SHE'S BLIND TO THE COLOR RED.
YOU KNOW WHY ME AND STEEL HANG OUT? WE'RE BOTH LATERAL THINKERS.

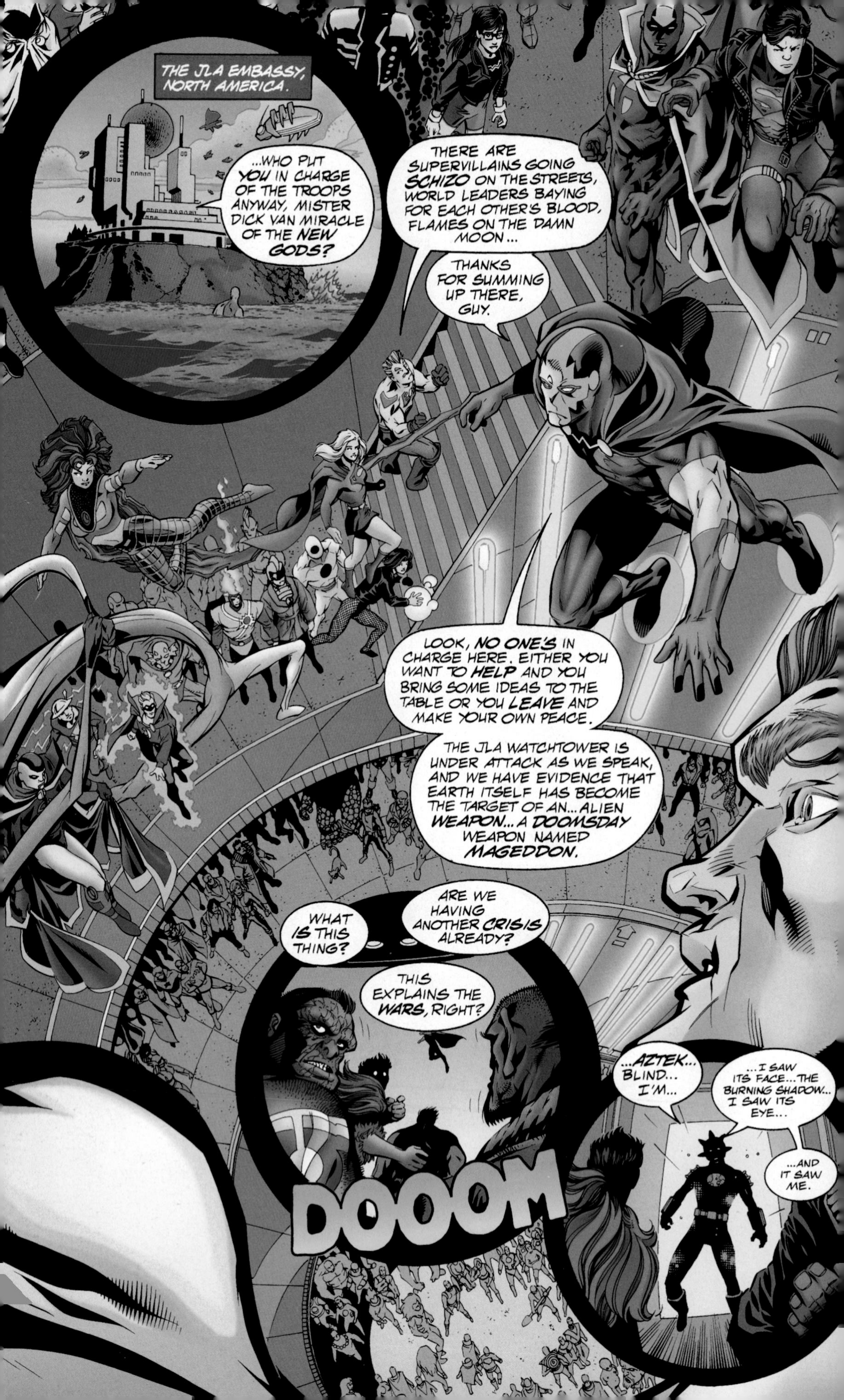
THE JLA EMBASSY, NORTH AMERICA.
...WHO PUT YOU IN CHARGE OF THE TROOPS ANYWAY, MISTER DICK VAN MIRACLE OF THE NEW GODS?
THERE ARE SUPERVILLAINS GOING SCHIZO ON THE STREETS, WORLD LEADERS BAYING FOR EACH OTHER'S BLOOD, FLAMES ON THE DAMN MOON...
THANKS FOR SUMMING UP THERE, GUY.
LOOK, NO ONE'S IN CHARGE HERE. EITHER YOU WANT TO HELP AND YOU BRING SOME IDEAS TO THE TABLE OR YOU LEAVE AND MAKE YOUR OWN PEACE.
THE JLA WATCHTOWER IS UNDER ATTACK AS WE SPEAK, AND WE HAVE EVIDENCE THAT EARTH ITSELF HAS BECOME THE TARGET OF AN... ALIEN WEAPON... A DOOMSDAY WEAPON NAMED MAGEDDON.
WHAT IS THIS THING?
ARE WE HAVING ANOTHER CRISIS ALREADY?
THIS EXPLAINS THE WARS, RIGHT?
...AZTEK... BLIND... I'M...
...I SAW ITS FACE... THE BURNING SHADOW... I SAW ITS EYE...
...AND IT SAW ME.
DOOOM

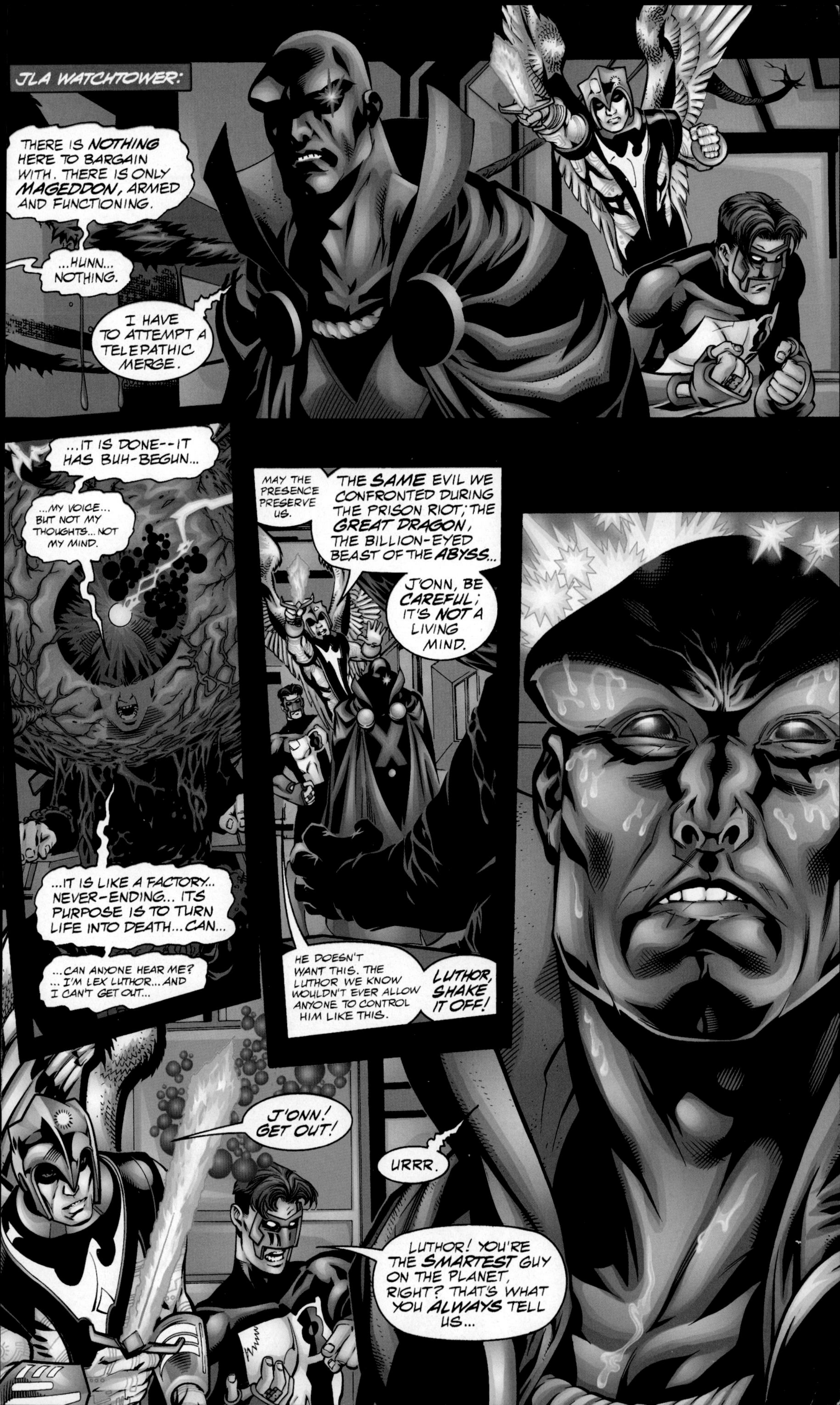
JLA WATCHTOWER:
THERE IS NOTHING HERE TO BARGAIN WITH. THERE IS ONLY MAGEDDON, ARMED AND FUNCTIONING.
...HUNN... NOTHING.
I HAVE TO ATTEMPT A TELEPATHIC MERGE.
...IT IS DONE--IT HAS BUH-BEGUN...
...MY VOICE... BUT NOT MY THOUGHTS... NOT MY MIND.
MAY THE PRESENCE PRESERVE US.
THE SAME EVIL WE CONFRONTED DURING THE PRISON RIOT; THE GREAT DRAGON, THE BILLION-EYED BEAST OF THE ABYSS...
J'ONN, BE CAREFUL; IT'S NOT A LIVING MIND.
...IT IS LIKE A FACTORY... NEVER-ENDING... ITS PURPOSE IS TO TURN LIFE INTO DEATH...CAN...
...CAN ANYONE HEAR ME? ... I'M LEX LUTHOR... AND I CAN'T GET OUT...
HE DOESN'T WANT THIS. THE LUTHOR WE KNOW WOULDN'T EVER ALLOW ANYONE TO CONTROL HIM LIKE THIS.
LUTHOR, SHAKE IT OFF!
J'ONN! GET OUT!
URRR.
LUTHOR! YOU'RE THE SMARTEST GUY ON THE PLANET, RIGHT? THAT'S WHAT YOU ALWAYS TELL US...

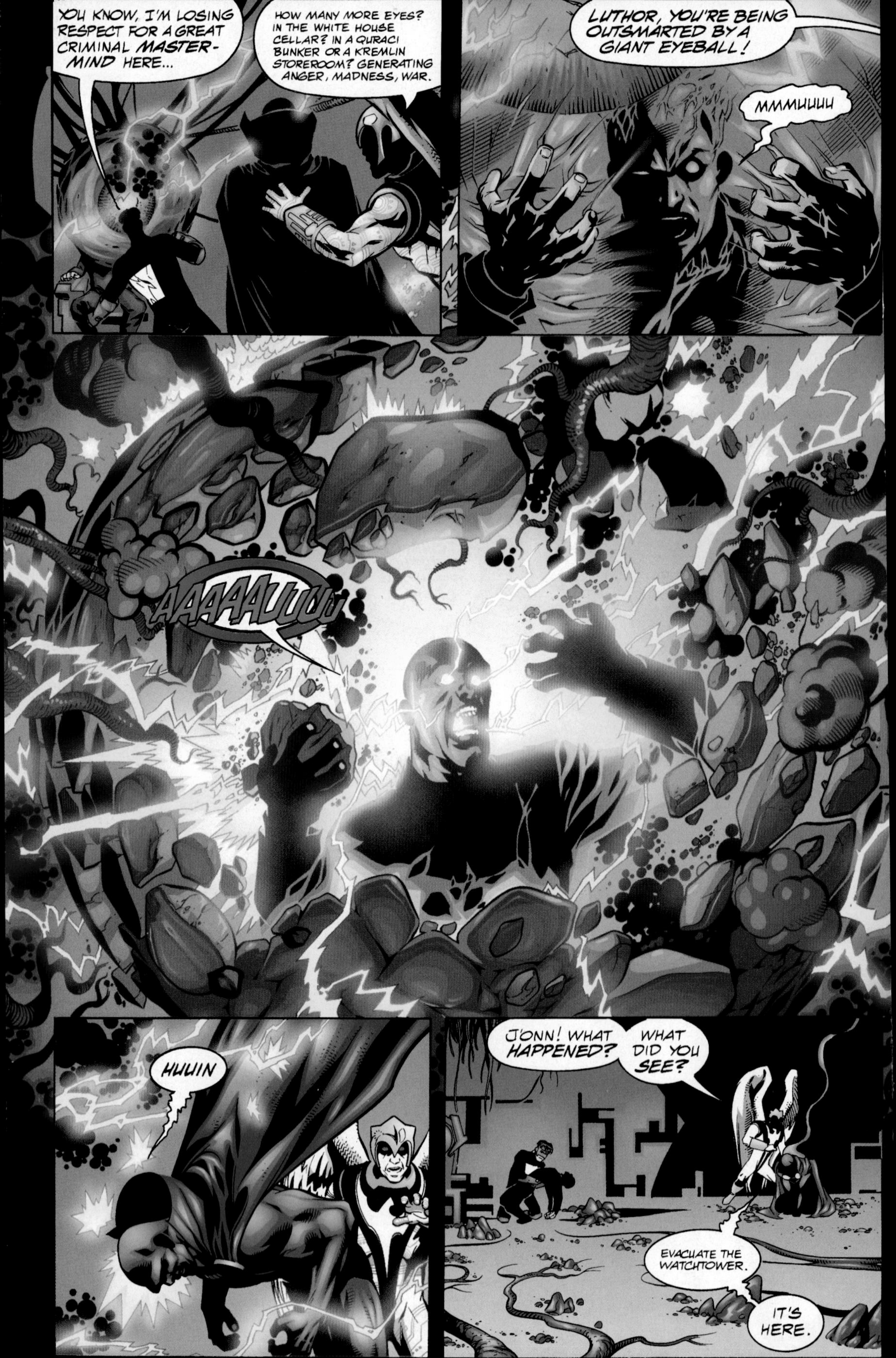
YOU KNOW, I'M LOSING RESPECT FOR A GREAT CRIMINAL MASTER-MIND HERE...
HOW MANY MORE EYES? IN THE WHITE HOUSE CELLAR? IN A QURACI BUNKER OR A KREMLIN STOREROOM? GENERATING ANGER, MADNESS, WAR.
LUTHOR, YOU'RE BEING OUTSMARTED BY A GIANT EYEBALL!
MMMUUUU
AAAAAUUUU
HUUIN
J'ONN! WHAT HAPPENED?
WHAT DID YOU SEE?
EVACUATE THE WATCHTOWER.
IT'S HERE.

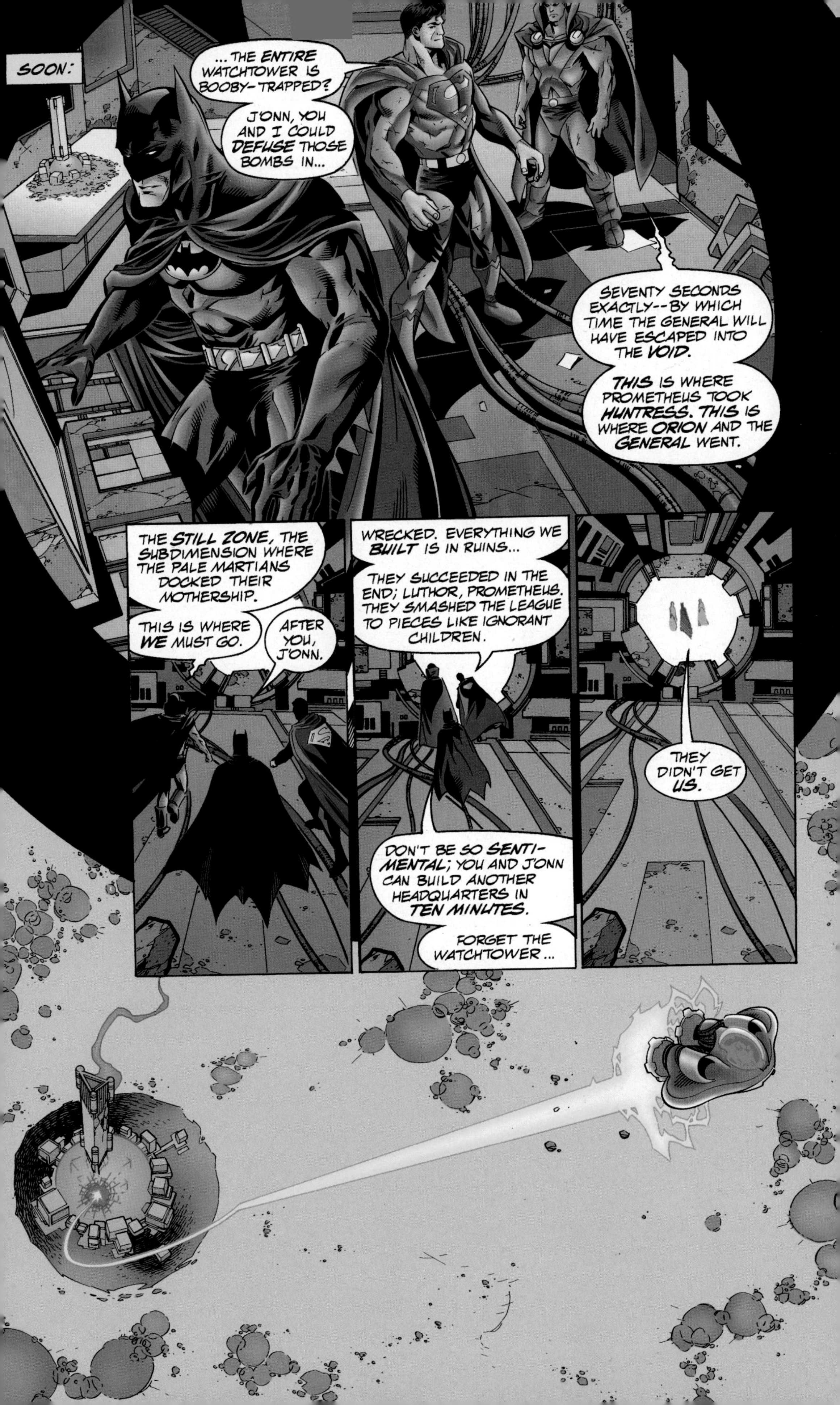
SOON:
...THE ENTIRE WATCHTOWER IS BOOBY-TRAPPED?
J'ONN, YOU AND I COULD DEFUSE THOSE BOMBS IN...
SEVENTY SECONDS EXACTLY--BY WHICH TIME THE GENERAL WILL HAVE ESCAPED INTO THE VOID.
THIS IS WHERE PROMETHEUS TOOK HUNTRESS. THIS IS WHERE ORION AND THE GENERAL WENT.
THE STILL ZONE, THE SUBDIMENSION WHERE THE PALE MARTIANS DOCKED THEIR MOTHERSHIP.
THIS IS WHERE WE MUST GO.
AFTER YOU, J'ONN.
WRECKED. EVERYTHING WE BUILT IS IN RUINS...
THEY SUCCEEDED IN THE END; LUTHOR, PROMETHEUS. THEY SMASHED THE LEAGUE TO PIECES LIKE IGNORANT CHILDREN.
DON'T BE SO SENTI-MENTAL; YOU AND J'ONN CAN BUILD ANOTHER HEADQUARTERS IN TEN MINUTES.
FORGET THE WATCHTOWER...
THEY DIDN'T GET US.

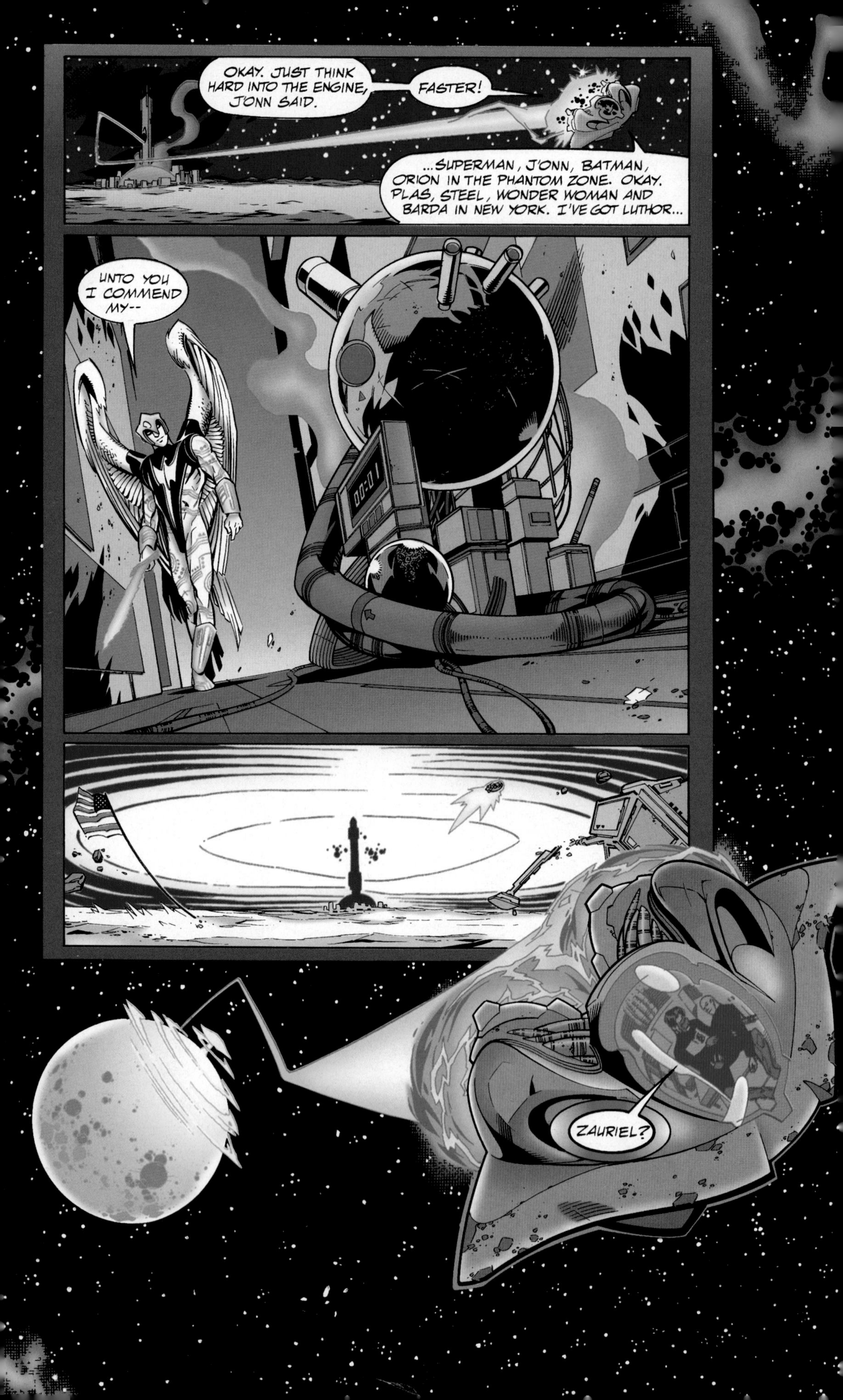

OKAY. JUST THINK HARD INTO THE ENGINE, J'ONN SAID.
FASTER!
...SUPERMAN, J'ONN, BATMAN, ORION IN THE PHANTOM ZONE. OKAY. PLAS, STEEL, WONDER WOMAN AND BARDA IN NEW YORK. I'VE GOT LUTHOR...
UNTO YOU I COMMEND MY--
ZAURIEL?

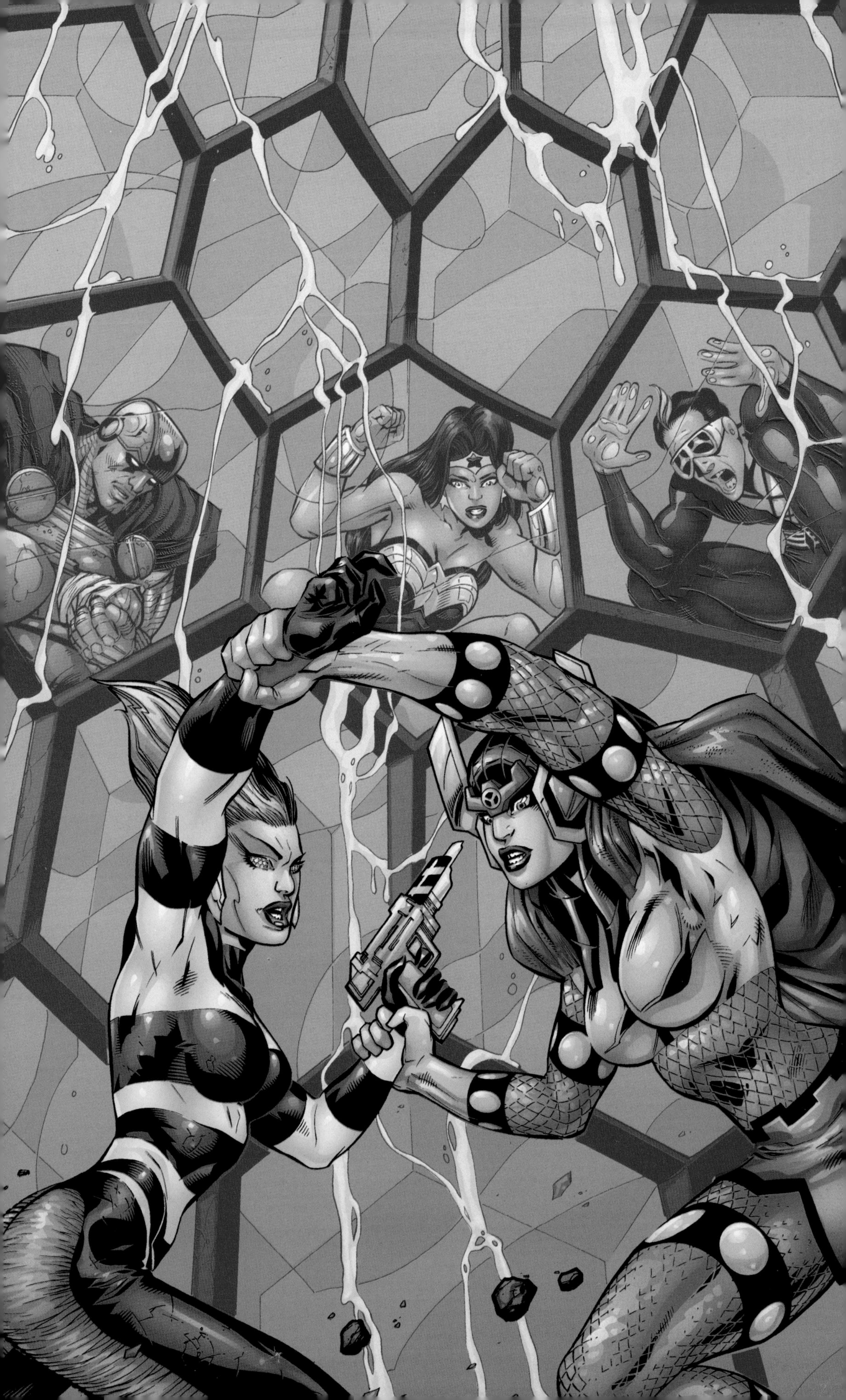

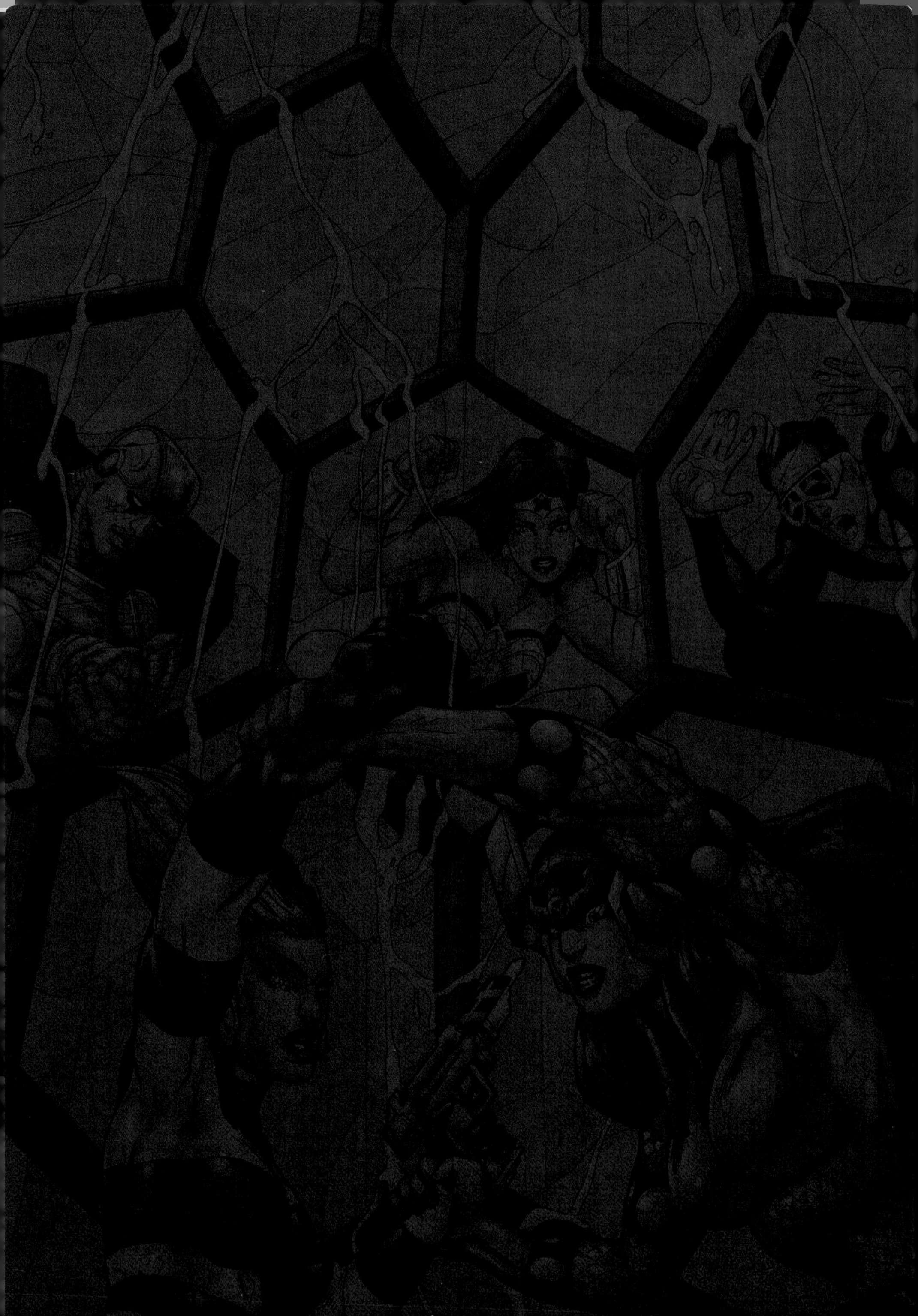

JLA #39

WRITTEN BY GRANT MORRISON

PENCILS BY HOWARD PORTER, WITH INKS BY JOHN DELL AND COLORS BY PAT GARRAHY

COVER BY HOWARD PORTER & JOHN DELL

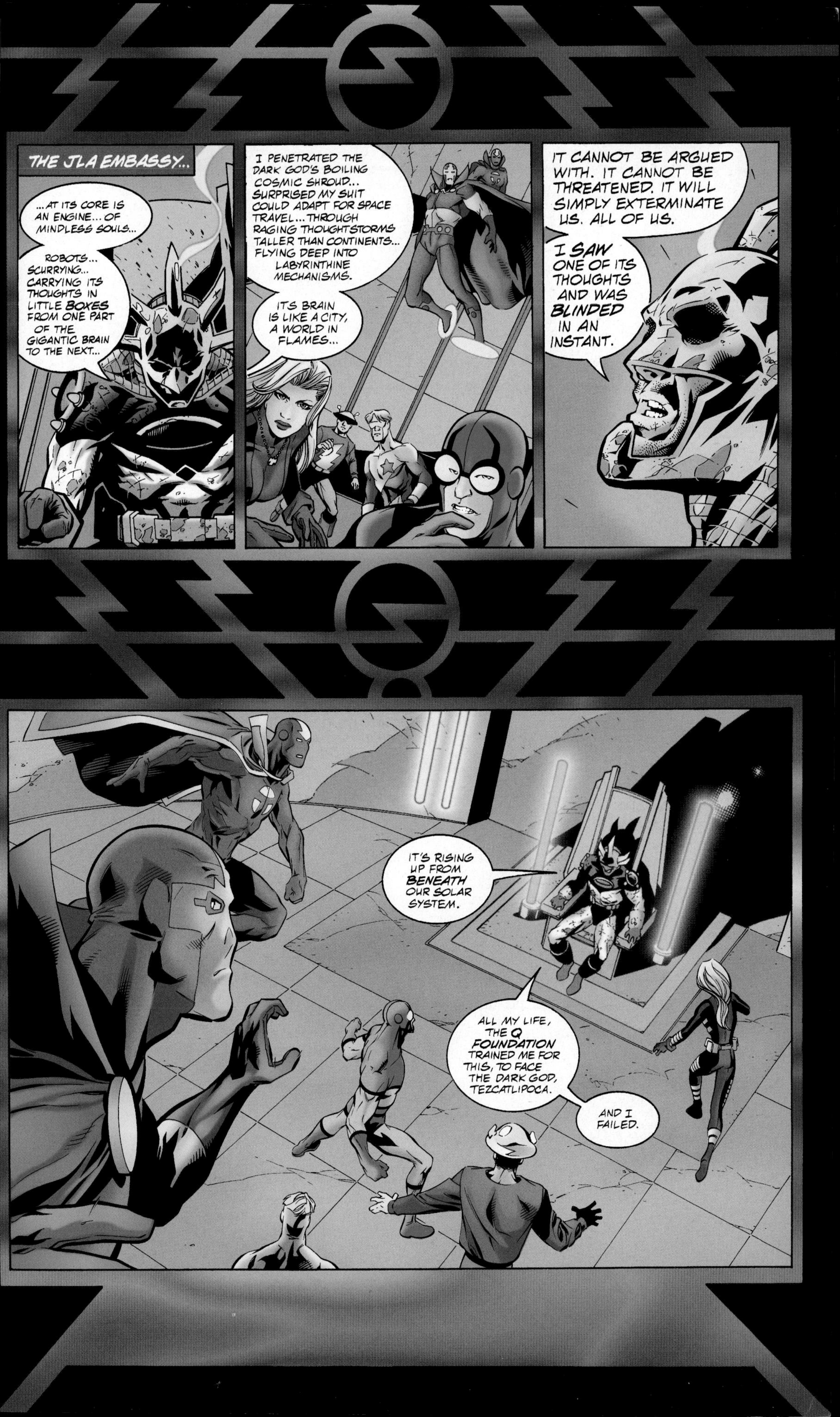
THE JLA EMBASSY...
...AT ITS CORE IS AN ENGINE... OF MINDLESS SOULS...
ROBOTS... SCURRYING... CARRYING ITS THOUGHTS IN LITTLE BOXES FROM ONE PART OF THE GIGANTIC BRAIN TO THE NEXT...
I PENETRATED THE DARK GOD'S BOILING COSMIC SHROUD... SURPRISED MY SUIT COULD ADAPT FOR SPACE TRAVEL... THROUGH RAGING THOUGHTSTORMS TALLER THAN CONTINENTS... FLYING DEEP INTO LABYRINTHINE MECHANISMS.
ITS BRAIN IS LIKE A CITY, A WORLD IN FLAMES...
IT CANNOT BE ARGUED WITH. IT CANNOT BE THREATENED. IT WILL SIMPLY EXTERMINATE US. ALL OF US.
I SAW ONE OF ITS THOUGHTS AND WAS BLINDED IN AN INSTANT.
IT'S RISING UP FROM BENEATH OUR SOLAR SYSTEM.
ALL MY LIFE, THE Q FOUNDATION TRAINED ME FOR THIS, TO FACE THE DARK GOD, TEZCATLIPOCA.
AND I FAILED.

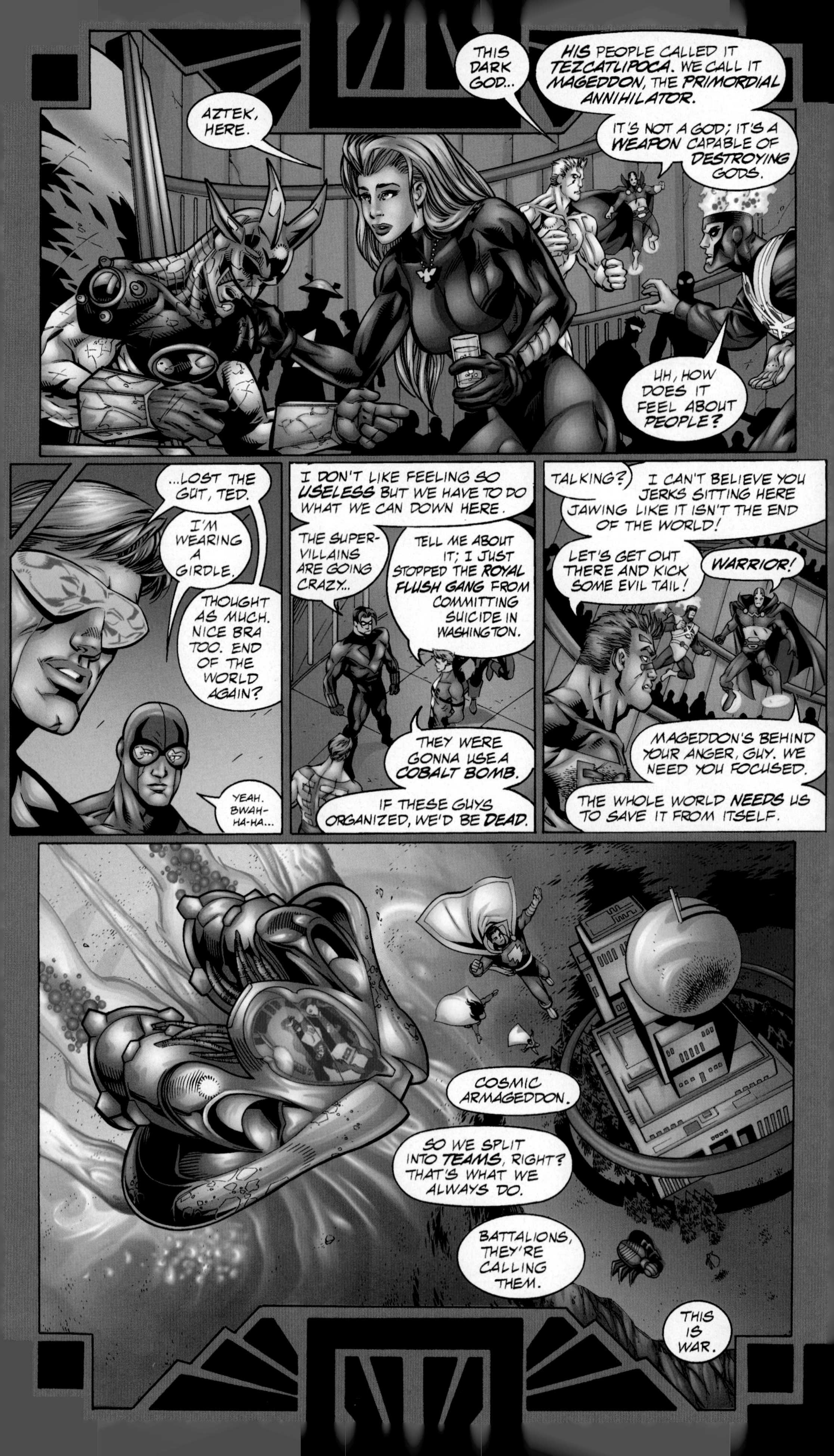
AZTEK, HERE.
THIS DARK GOD...
HIS PEOPLE CALLED IT TEZCATLIPOCA. WE CALL IT MAGEDDON, THE PRIMORDIAL ANNIHILATOR.
IT'S NOT A GOD; IT'S A WEAPON CAPABLE OF DESTROYING GODS.
UH, HOW DOES IT FEEL ABOUT PEOPLE?
...LOST THE GUT, TED.
I'M WEARING A GIRDLE.
THOUGHT AS MUCH. NICE BRA TOO. END OF THE WORLD AGAIN?
YEAH. BWAH-HA-HA...
I DON'T LIKE FEELING SO USELESS BUT WE HAVE TO DO WHAT WE CAN DOWN HERE.
THE SUPER-VILLAINS ARE GOING CRAZY...
TELL ME ABOUT IT; I JUST STOPPED THE ROYAL FLUSH GANG FROM COMMITTING SUICIDE IN WASHINGTON.
THEY WERE GONNA USE A COBALT BOMB.
IF THESE GUYS ORGANIZED, WE'D BE DEAD.
TALKING?
I CAN'T BELIEVE YOU JERKS SITTING HERE JAWING LIKE IT ISN'T THE END OF THE WORLD!
LET'S GET OUT THERE AND KICK SOME EVIL TAIL!
WARRIOR!
MAGEDDON'S BEHIND YOUR ANGER, GUY. WE NEED YOU FOCUSED.
THE WHOLE WORLD NEEDS US TO SAVE IT FROM ITSELF.
COSMIC ARMAGEDDON.
SO WE SPLIT INTO TEAMS, RIGHT? THAT'S WHAT WE ALWAYS DO.
BATTALIONS, THEY'RE CALLING THEM.
THIS IS WAR.

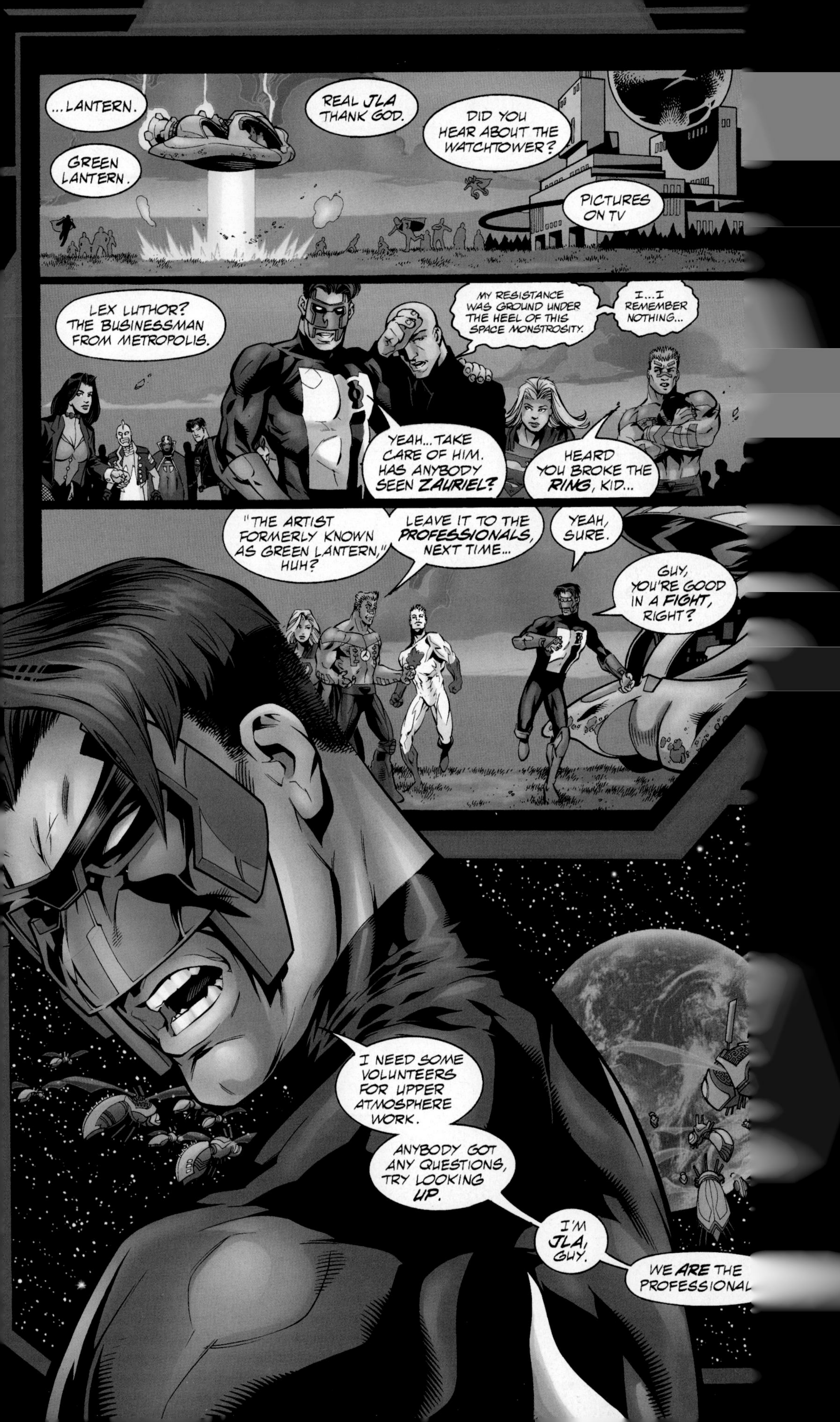
...LANTERN.
GREEN LANTERN.
REAL JLA THANK GOD.
DID YOU HEAR ABOUT THE WATCHTOWER?
PICTURES ON TV
LEX LUTHOR? THE BUSINESSMAN FROM METROPOLIS.
MY RESISTANCE WAS GROUND UNDER THE HEEL OF THIS SPACE MONSTROSITY.
I...I REMEMBER NOTHING...
YEAH...TAKE CARE OF HIM. HAS ANYBODY SEEN ZAURIEL?
HEARD YOU BROKE THE RING, KID...
"THE ARTIST FORMERLY KNOWN AS GREEN LANTERN," HUH?
LEAVE IT TO THE PROFESSIONALS, NEXT TIME...
YEAH, SURE.
GUY, YOU'RE GOOD IN A FIGHT, RIGHT?
I NEED SOME VOLUNTEERS FOR UPPER ATMOSPHERE WORK.
ANYBODY GOT ANY QUESTIONS, TRY LOOKING UP.
I'M JLA, GUY.
WE ARE THE PROFESSIONAL

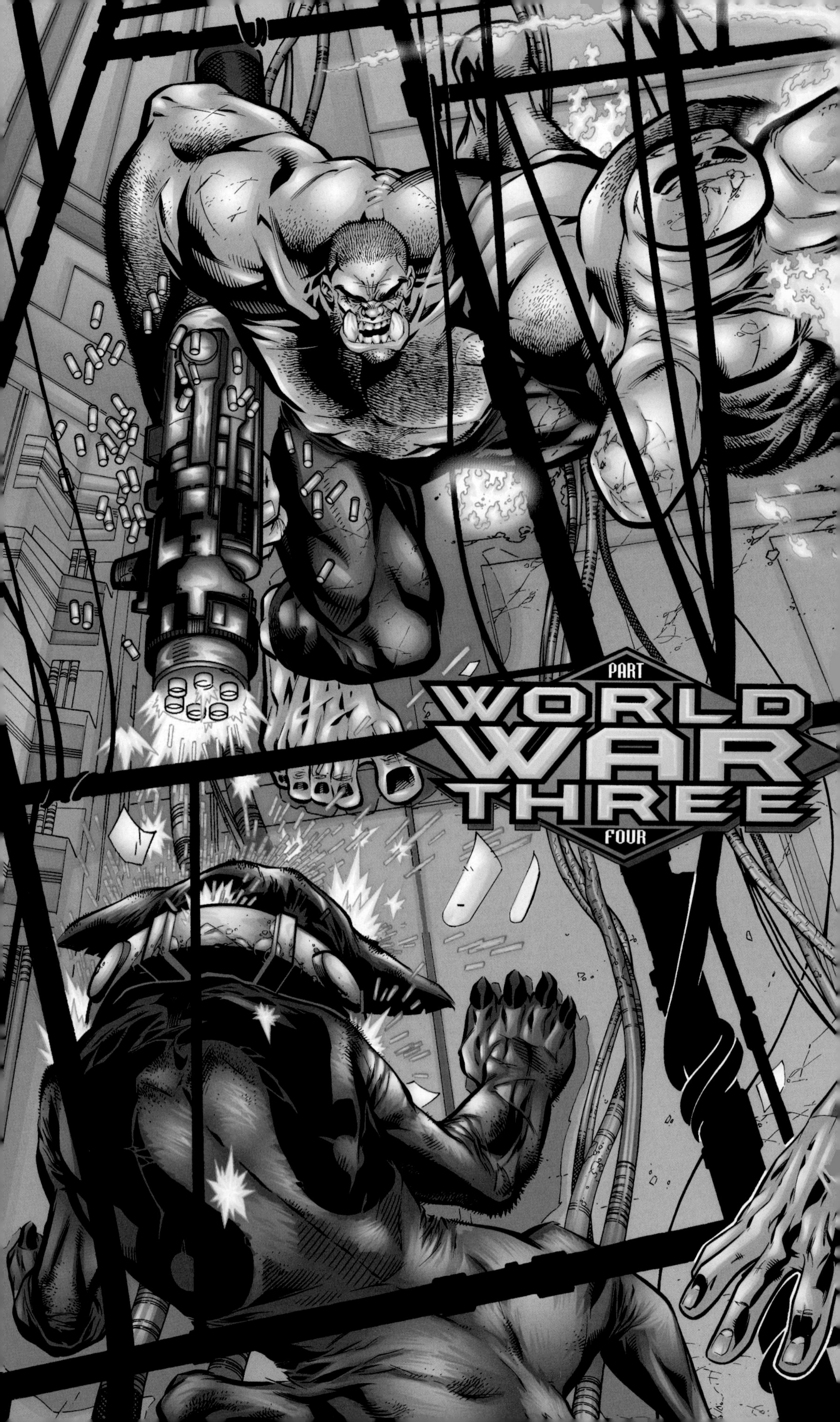
PART
WORLD
WAR
THREE
FOUR

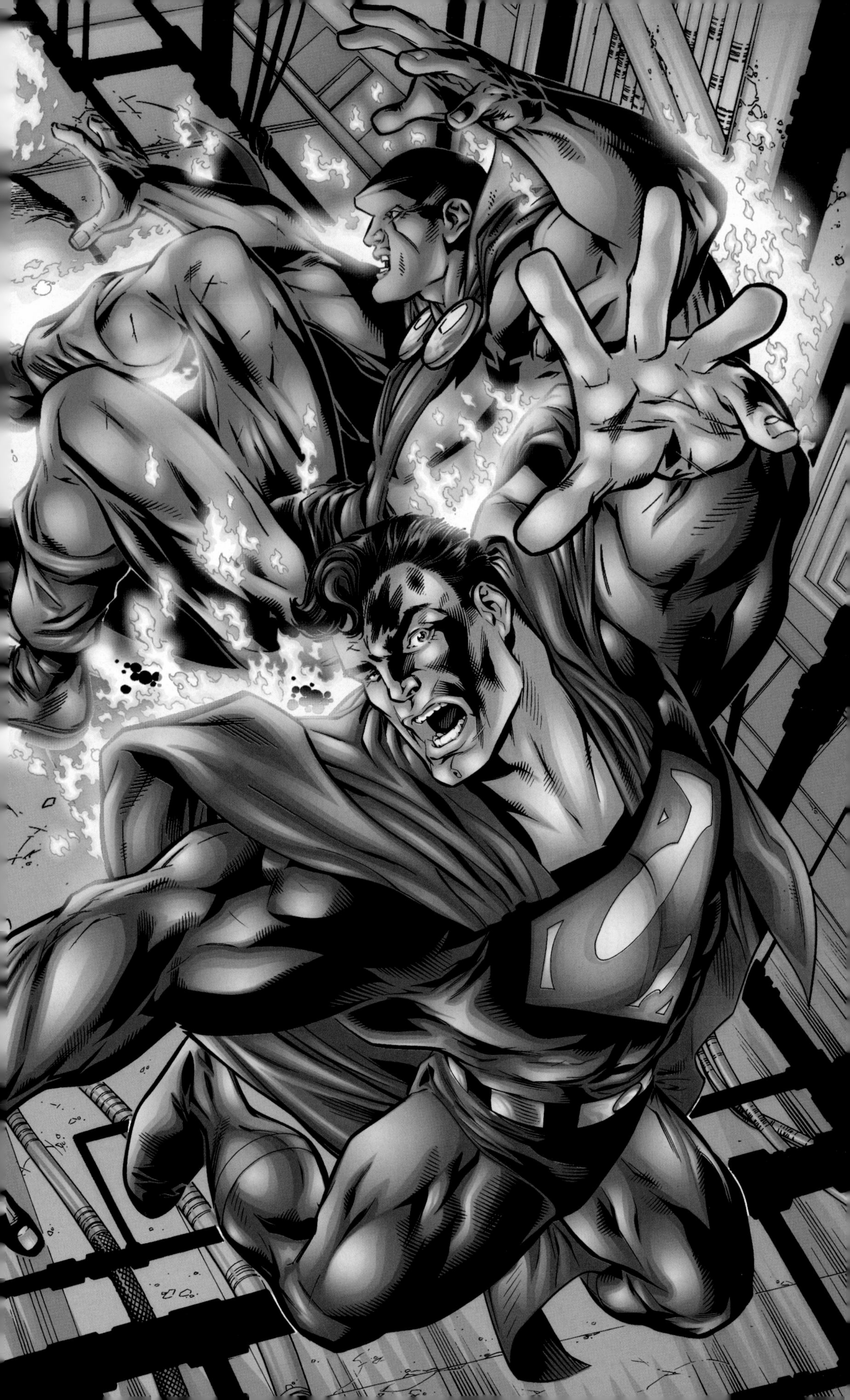

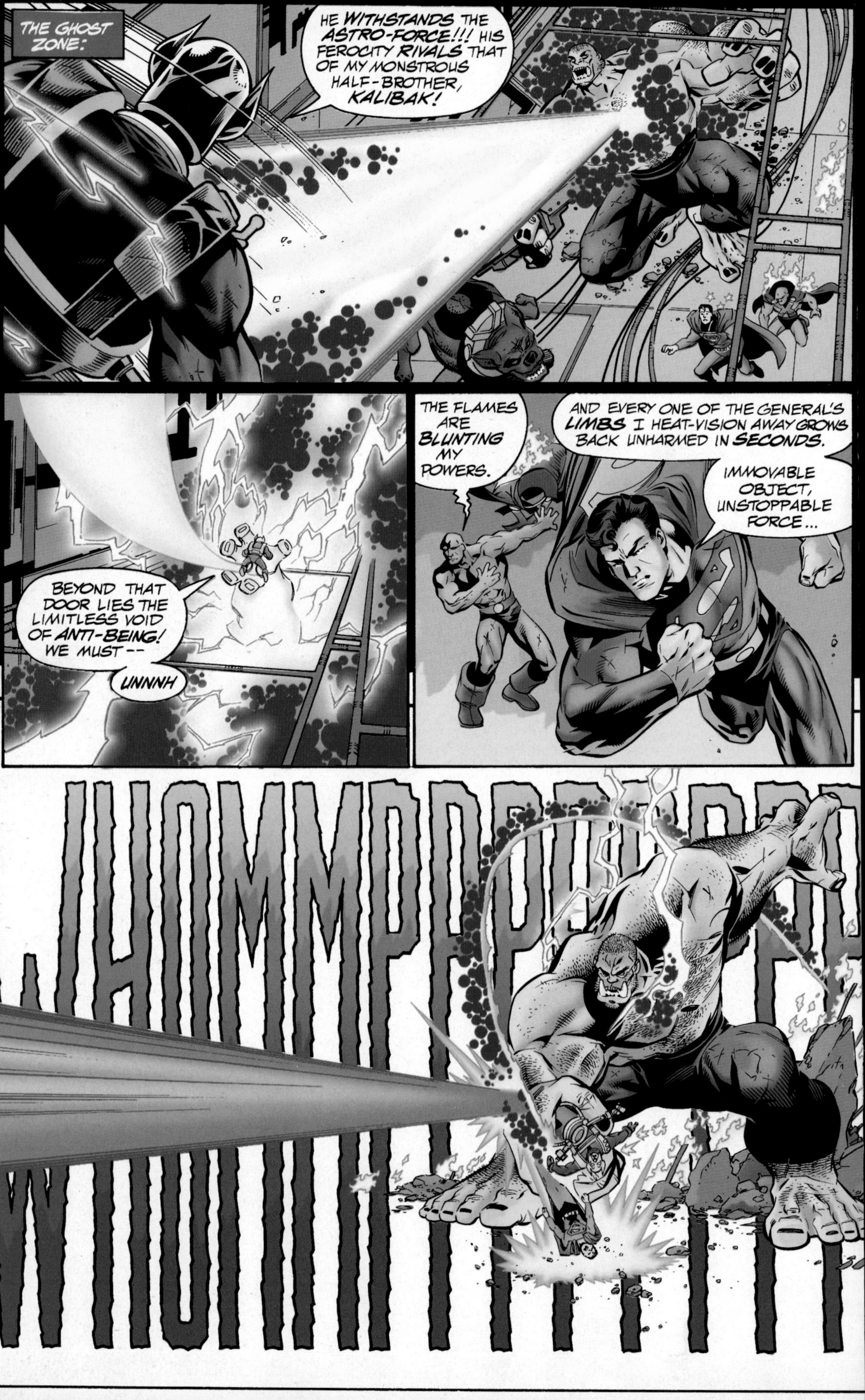
THE GHOST ZONE:
HE WITHSTANDS THE ASTRO-FORCE!!! HIS FEROCITY RIVALS THAT OF MY MONSTROUS HALF-BROTHER, KALIBAK!
BEYOND THAT DOOR LIES THE LIMITLESS VOID OF ANTI-BEING! WE MUST --
UNNNH
THE FLAMES ARE BLUNTING MY POWERS.
AND EVERY ONE OF THE GENERAL'S LIMBS I HEAT-VISION AWAY GROWS BACK UNHARMED IN SECONDS.
IMMOVABLE OBJECT, UNSTOPPABLE FORCE...
WHOMMPPPPPP

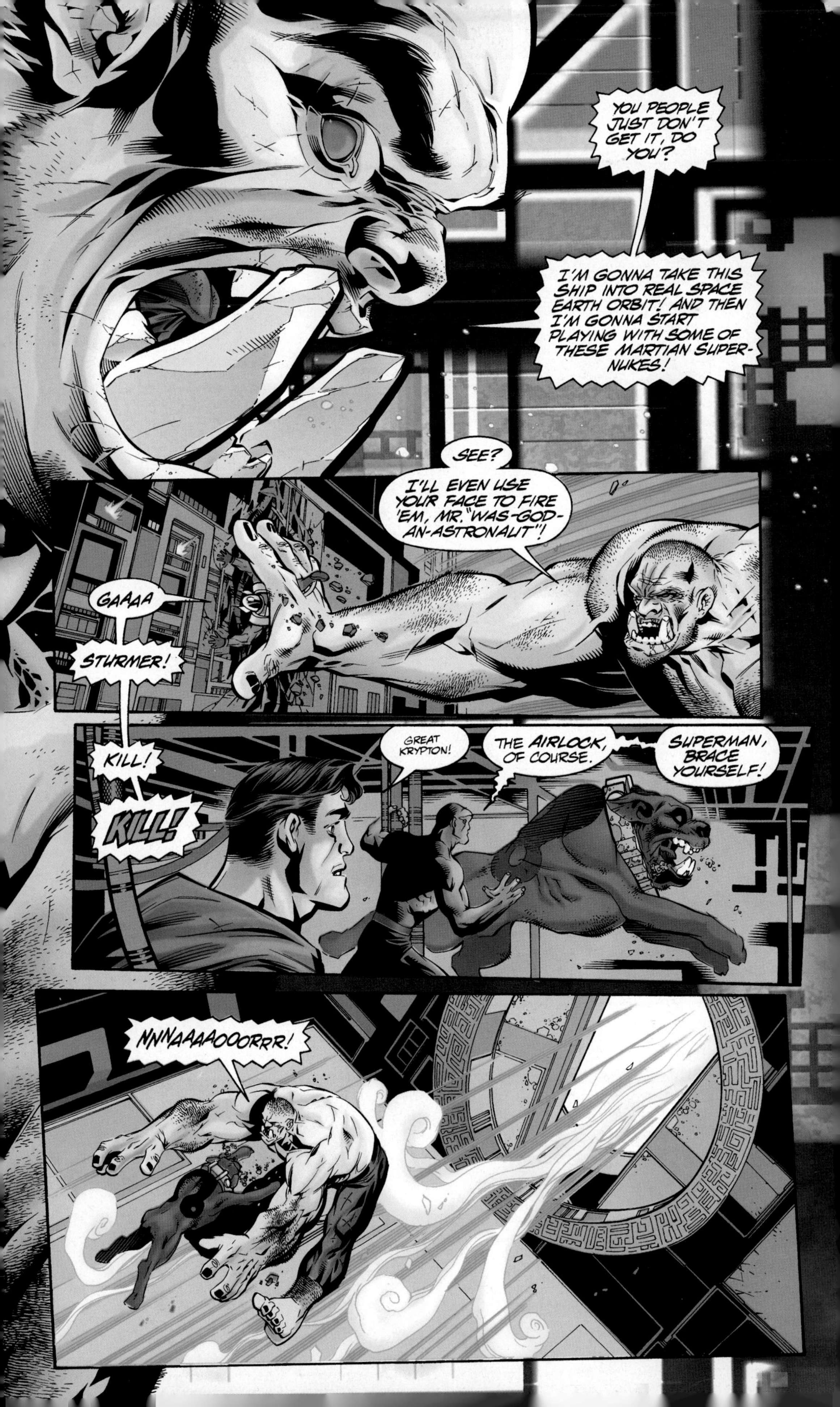

YOU PEOPLE JUST DON'T GET IT, DO YOU?
I'M GONNA TAKE THIS SHIP INTO REAL SPACE EARTH ORBIT! AND THEN I'M GONNA START PLAYING WITH SOME OF THESE MARTIAN SUPER-NUKES!
SEE?
I'LL EVEN USE YOUR FACE TO FIRE 'EM, MR. "WAS-GOD-AN-ASTRONAUT"!
GAAAA
STURMER!
KILL!
KILL!
GREAT KRYPTON!
THE AIRLOCK, OF COURSE.
SUPERMAN, BRACE YOURSELF!
NNNAAAAOOORRR!

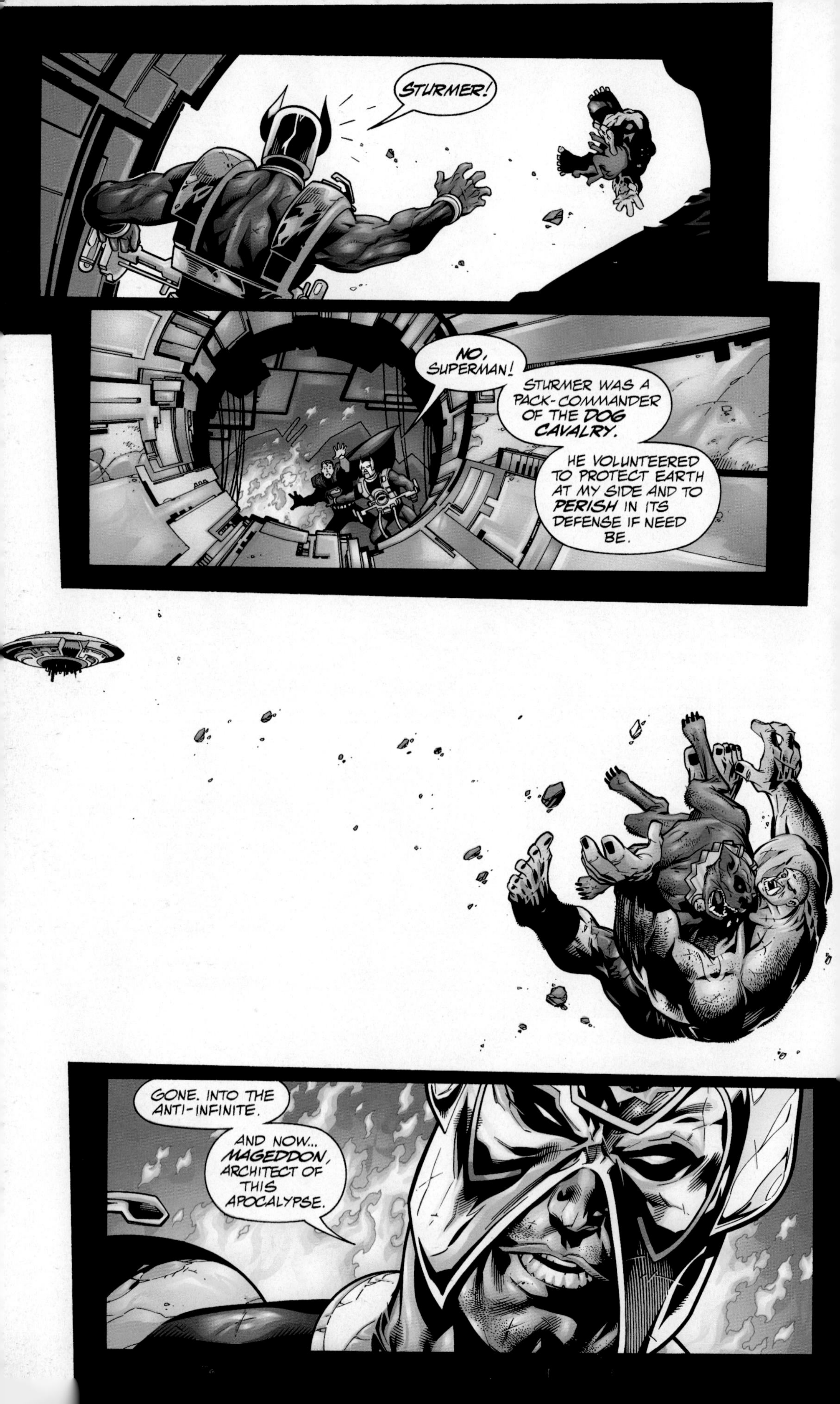
STURMER!
NO, SUPERMAN!
STURMER WAS A PACK-COMMANDER OF THE DOG CAVALRY.
HE VOLUNTEERED TO PROTECT EARTH AT MY SIDE AND TO PERISH IN ITS DEFENSE IF NEED BE.
GONE. INTO THE ANTI-INFINITE.
AND NOW... MAGEDDON, ARCHITECT OF THIS APOCALYPSE.

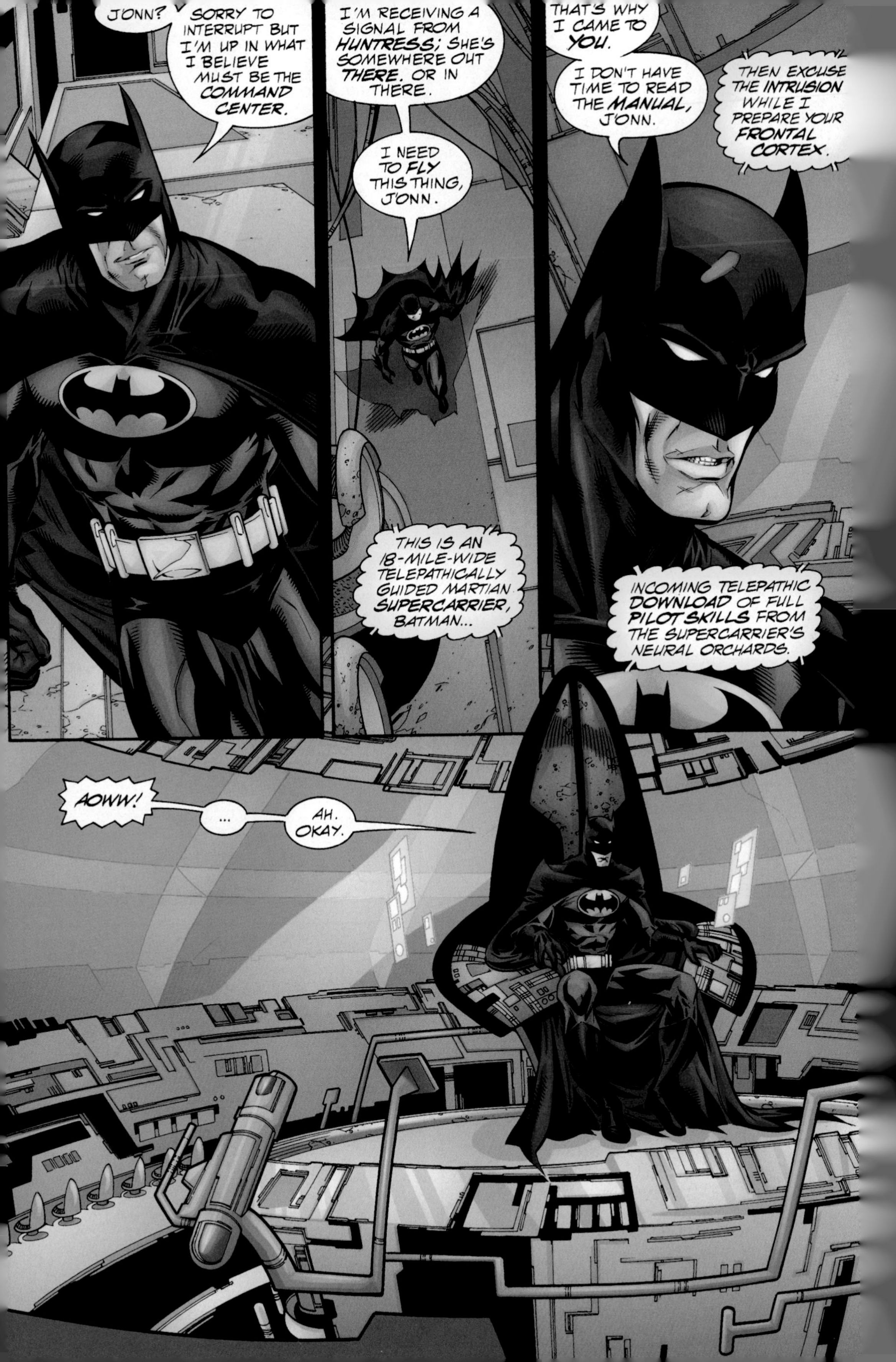
J'ONN?
SORRY TO INTERRUPT BUT I'M UP IN WHAT I BELIEVE MUST BE THE COMMAND CENTER.
I'M RECEIVING A SIGNAL FROM HUNTRESS; SHE'S SOMEWHERE OUT THERE. OR IN THERE.
I NEED TO FLY THIS THING, J'ONN.
THIS IS AN 18-MILE-WIDE TELEPATHICALLY GUIDED MARTIAN SUPERCARRIER, BATMAN...
THAT'S WHY I CAME TO YOU.
I DON'T HAVE TIME TO READ THE MANUAL, J'ONN.
THEN EXCUSE THE INTRUSION WHILE I PREPARE YOUR FRONTAL CORTEX.
INCOMING TELEPATHIC DOWNLOAD OF FULL PILOT SKILLS FROM THE SUPERCARRIER'S NEURAL ORCHARDS.
AOWW!
...
AH. OKAY.

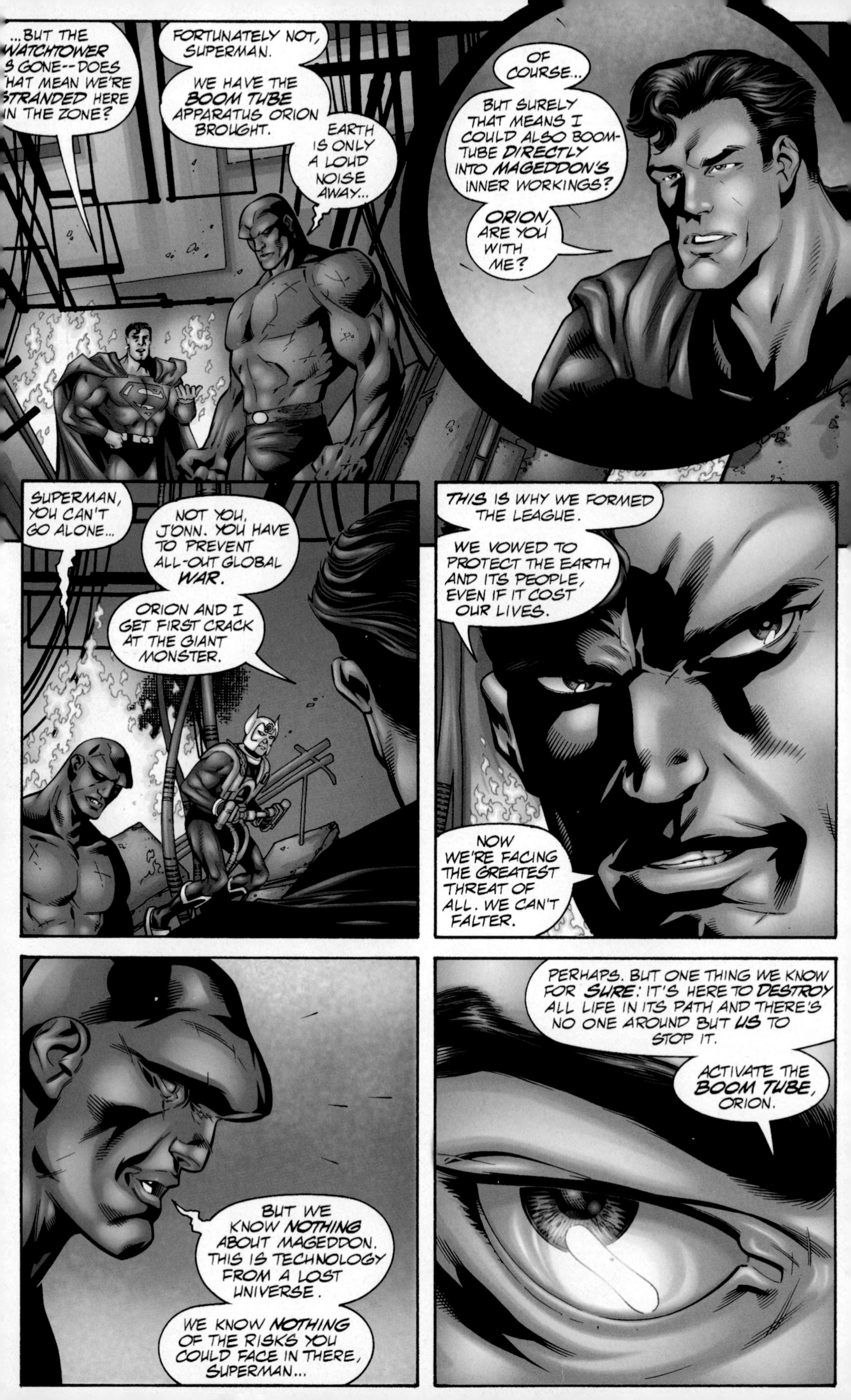
...BUT THE WATCHTOWER IS GONE--DOES THAT MEAN WE'RE STRANDED HERE IN THE ZONE?
FORTUNATELY NOT, SUPERMAN.
WE HAVE THE BOOM TUBE APPARATUS ORION BROUGHT.
EARTH IS ONLY A LOUD NOISE AWAY...
OF COURSE...
BUT SURELY THAT MEANS I COULD ALSO BOOM-TUBE DIRECTLY INTO MAGEDDON'S INNER WORKINGS?
ORION, ARE YOU WITH ME?
SUPERMAN, YOU CAN'T GO ALONE...
NOT YOU, J'ONN. YOU HAVE TO PREVENT ALL-OUT GLOBAL WAR.
ORION AND I GET FIRST CRACK AT THE GIANT MONSTER.
THIS IS WHY WE FORMED THE LEAGUE.
WE VOWED TO PROTECT THE EARTH AND ITS PEOPLE, EVEN IF IT COST OUR LIVES.
NOW WE'RE FACING THE GREATEST THREAT OF ALL. WE CAN'T FALTER.
BUT WE KNOW NOTHING ABOUT MAGEDDON. THIS IS TECHNOLOGY FROM A LOST UNIVERSE.
WE KNOW NOTHING OF THE RISKS YOU COULD FACE IN THERE, SUPERMAN...
PERHAPS. BUT ONE THING WE KNOW FOR SURE: IT'S HERE TO DESTROY ALL LIFE IN ITS PATH AND THERE'S NO ONE AROUND BUT US TO STOP IT.
ACTIVATE THE BOOM TUBE, ORION.

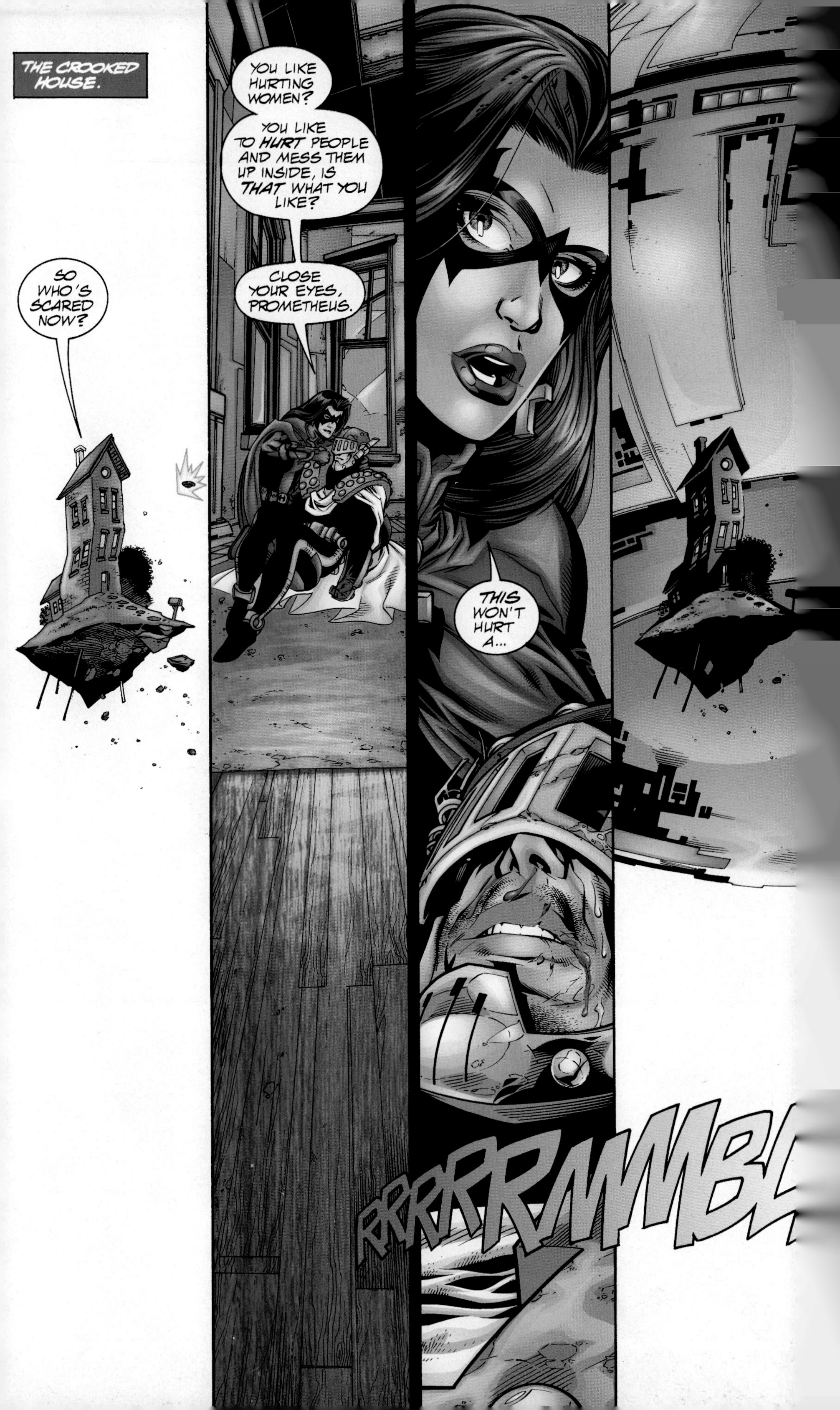
THE CROOKED HOUSE.
SO WHO'S SCARED NOW?
YOU LIKE HURTING WOMEN?
YOU LIKE TO HURT PEOPLE AND MESS THEM UP INSIDE, IS THAT WHAT YOU LIKE?
CLOSE YOUR EYES, PROMETHEUS.
THIS WON'T HURT A...
RRRRRAMMBL

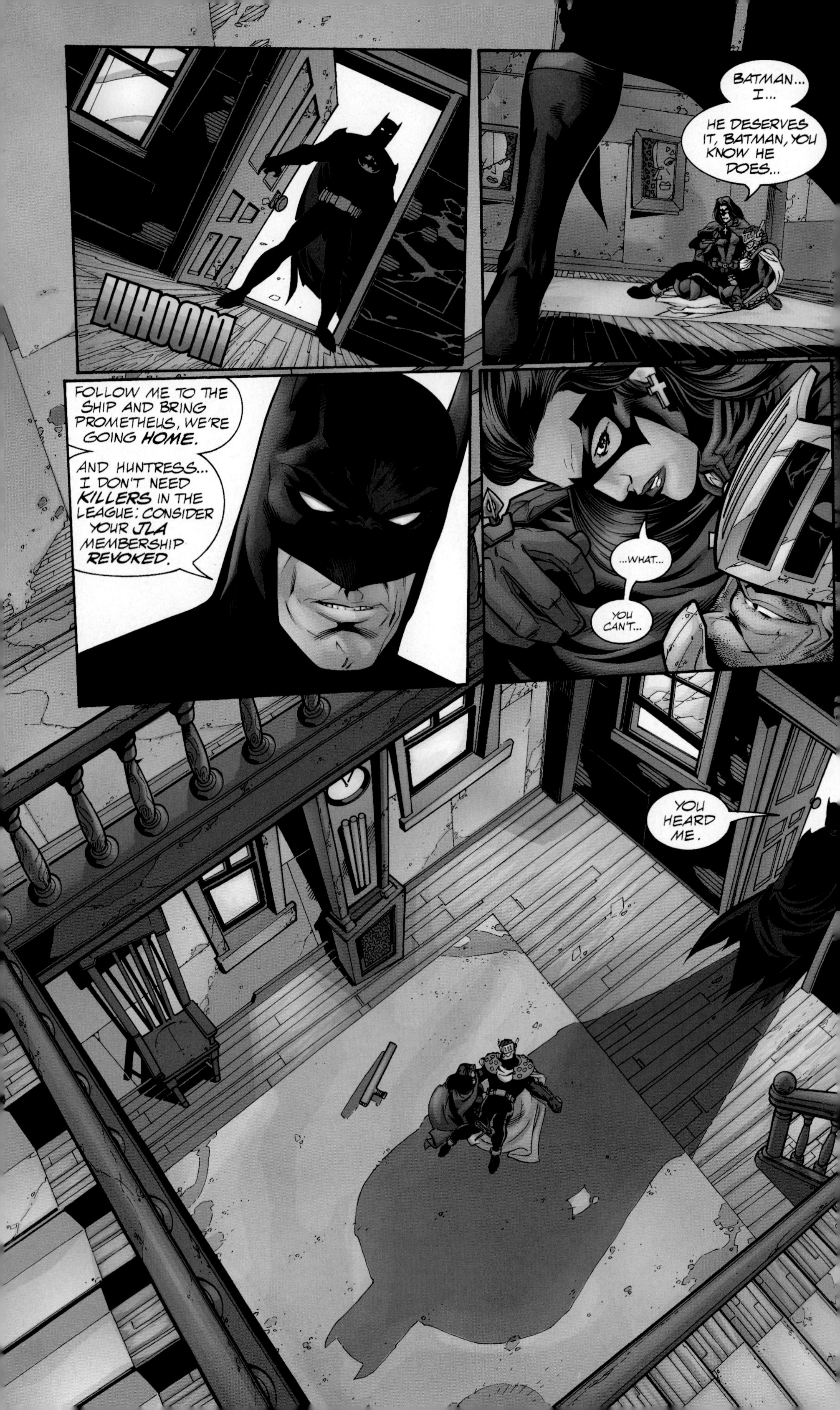
WHOOM
BATMAN... I...
HE DESERVES IT, BATMAN, YOU KNOW HE DOES...
FOLLOW ME TO THE SHIP AND BRING PROMETHEUS, WE'RE GOING HOME.
AND HUNTRESS... I DON'T NEED KILLERS IN THE LEAGUE: CONSIDER YOUR JLA MEMBERSHIP REVOKED.
...WHAT...
YOU CAN'T...
YOU HEARD ME.

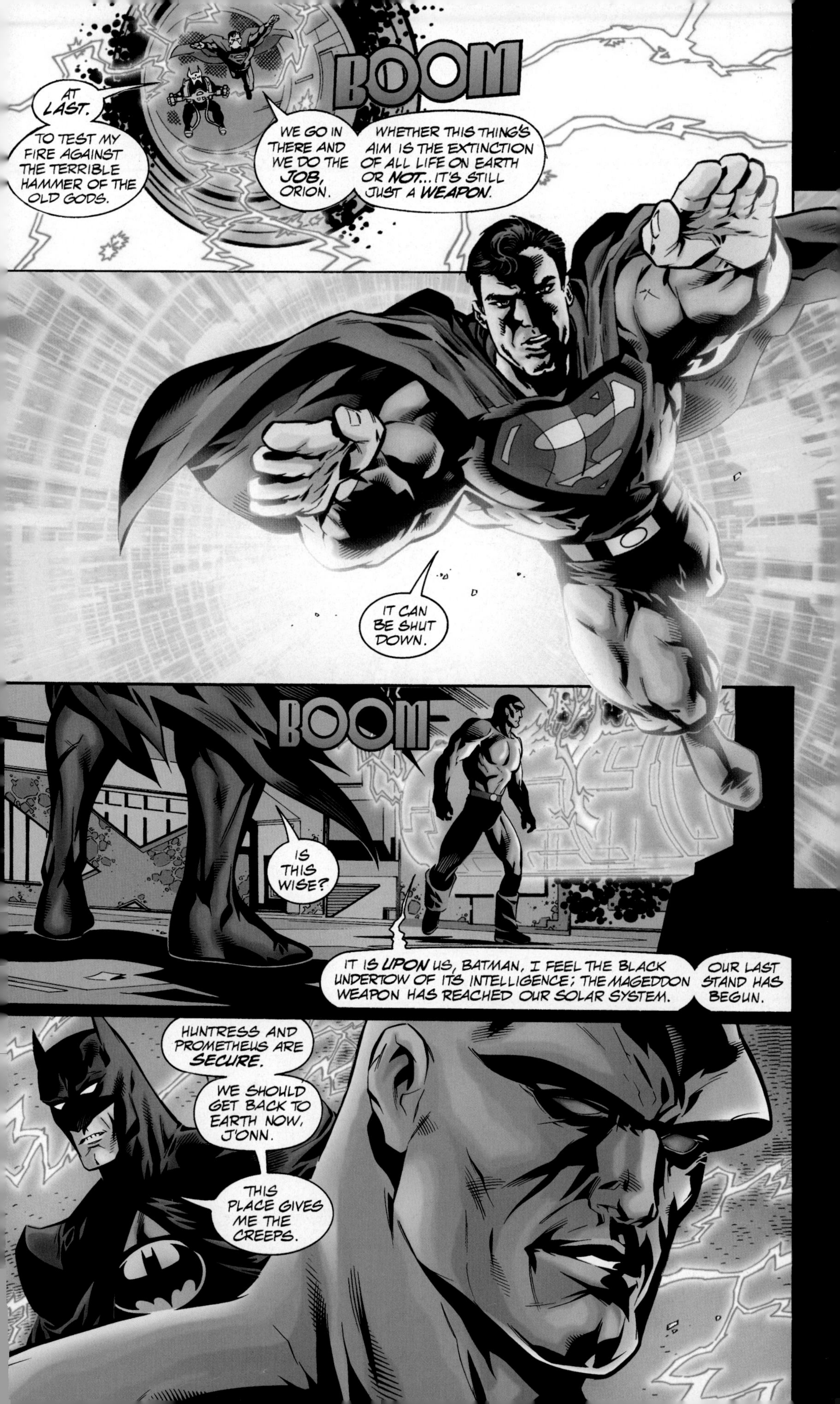
BOOM
AT LAST.
TO TEST MY FIRE AGAINST THE TERRIBLE HAMMER OF THE OLD GODS.
WE GO IN THERE AND WE DO THE JOB, ORION.
WHETHER THIS THING'S AIM IS THE EXTINCTION OF ALL LIFE ON EARTH OR NOT... IT'S STILL JUST A WEAPON.
IT CAN BE SHUT DOWN.
BOOM
IS THIS WISE?
IT IS UPON US, BATMAN. I FEEL THE BLACK UNDERTOW OF ITS INTELLIGENCE; THE MAGEDDON WEAPON HAS REACHED OUR SOLAR SYSTEM.
OUR LAST STAND HAS BEGUN.
HUNTRESS AND PROMETHEUS ARE SECURE.
WE SHOULD GET BACK TO EARTH NOW, J'ONN.
THIS PLACE GIVES ME THE CREEPS.

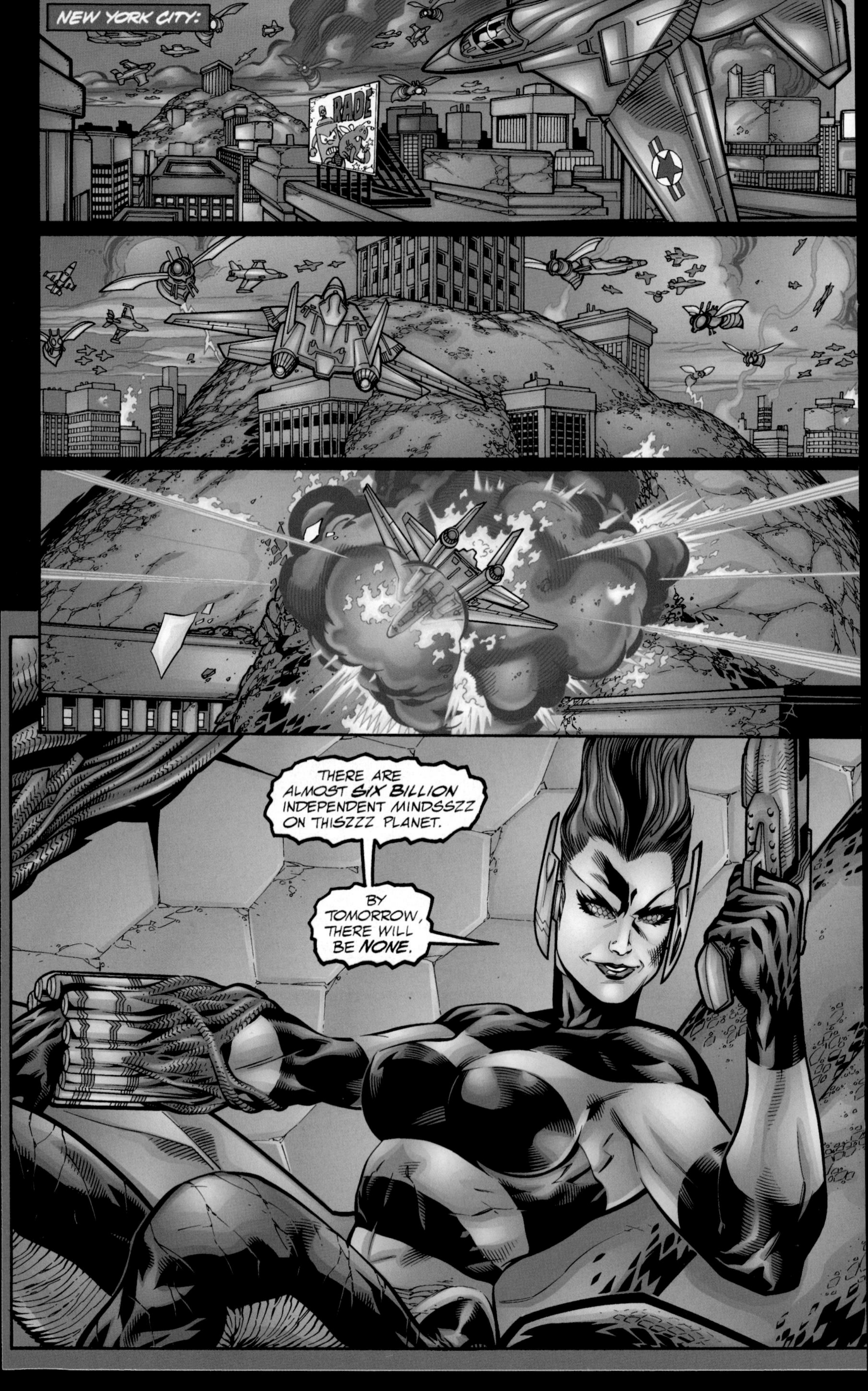
NEW YORK CITY:
RADE
THERE ARE ALMOST SIX BILLION INDEPENDENT MINDSSZZ ON THISZZZ PLANET.
BY TOMORROW, THERE WILL BE NONE.

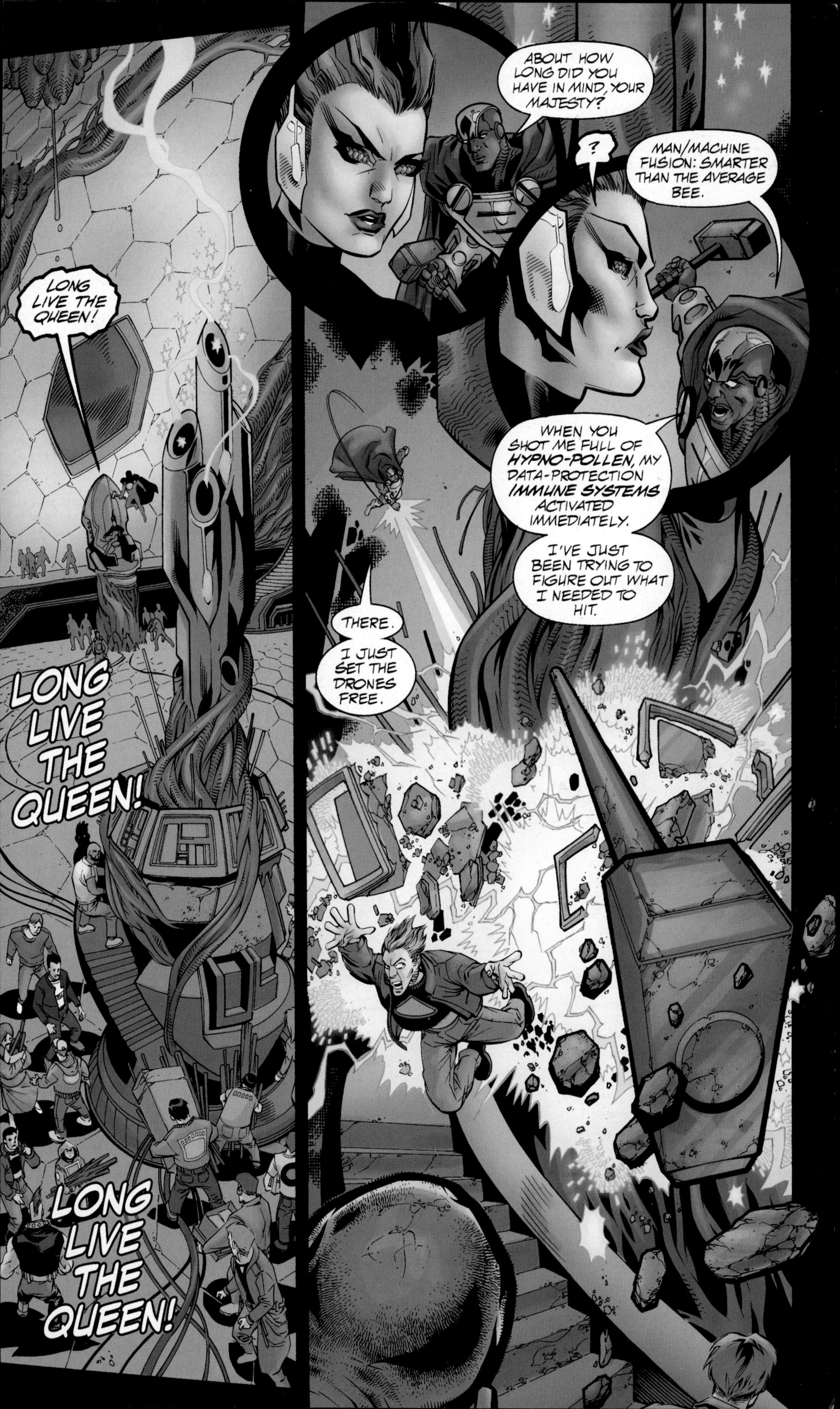
LONG LIVE THE QUEEN!
LONG LIVE THE QUEEN!
LONG LIVE THE QUEEN!
ABOUT HOW LONG DID YOU HAVE IN MIND, YOUR MAJESTY?
?
MAN/MACHINE FUSION: SMARTER THAN THE AVERAGE BEE.
WHEN YOU SHOT ME FULL OF HYPNO-POLLEN, MY DATA-PROTECTION IMMUNE SYSTEMS ACTIVATED IMMEDIATELY.
I'VE JUST BEEN TRYING TO FIGURE OUT WHAT I NEEDED TO HIT.
THERE. I JUST SET THE DRONES FREE.

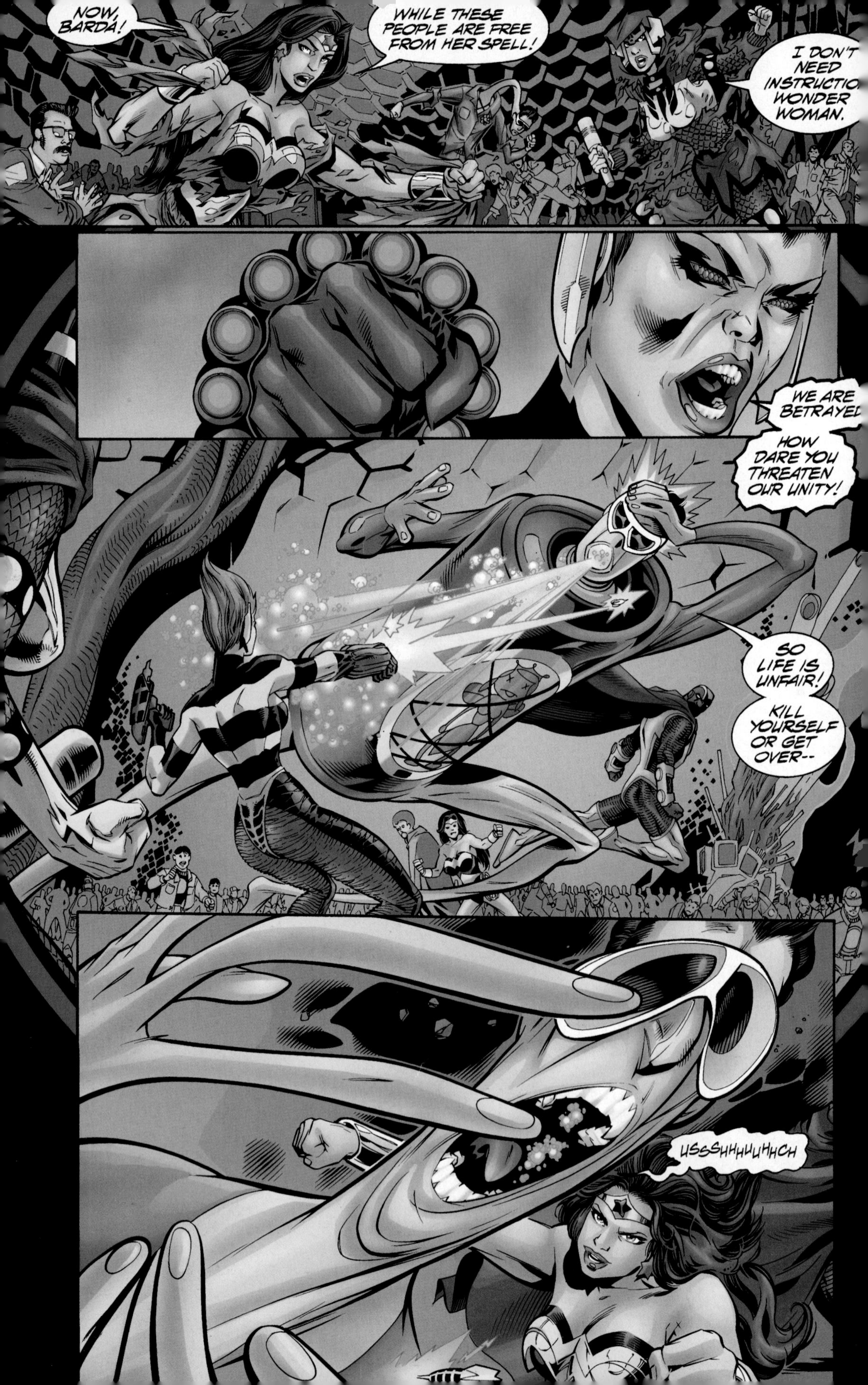
NOW, BARDA!
WHILE THESE PEOPLE ARE FREE FROM HER SPELL!
I DON'T NEED INSTRUCTIO WONDER WOMAN.
WE ARE BETRAYED
HOW DARE YOU THREATEN OUR UNITY!
SO LIFE IS UNFAIR!
KILL YOURSELF OR GET OVER--
USSSHHHUUHHCH

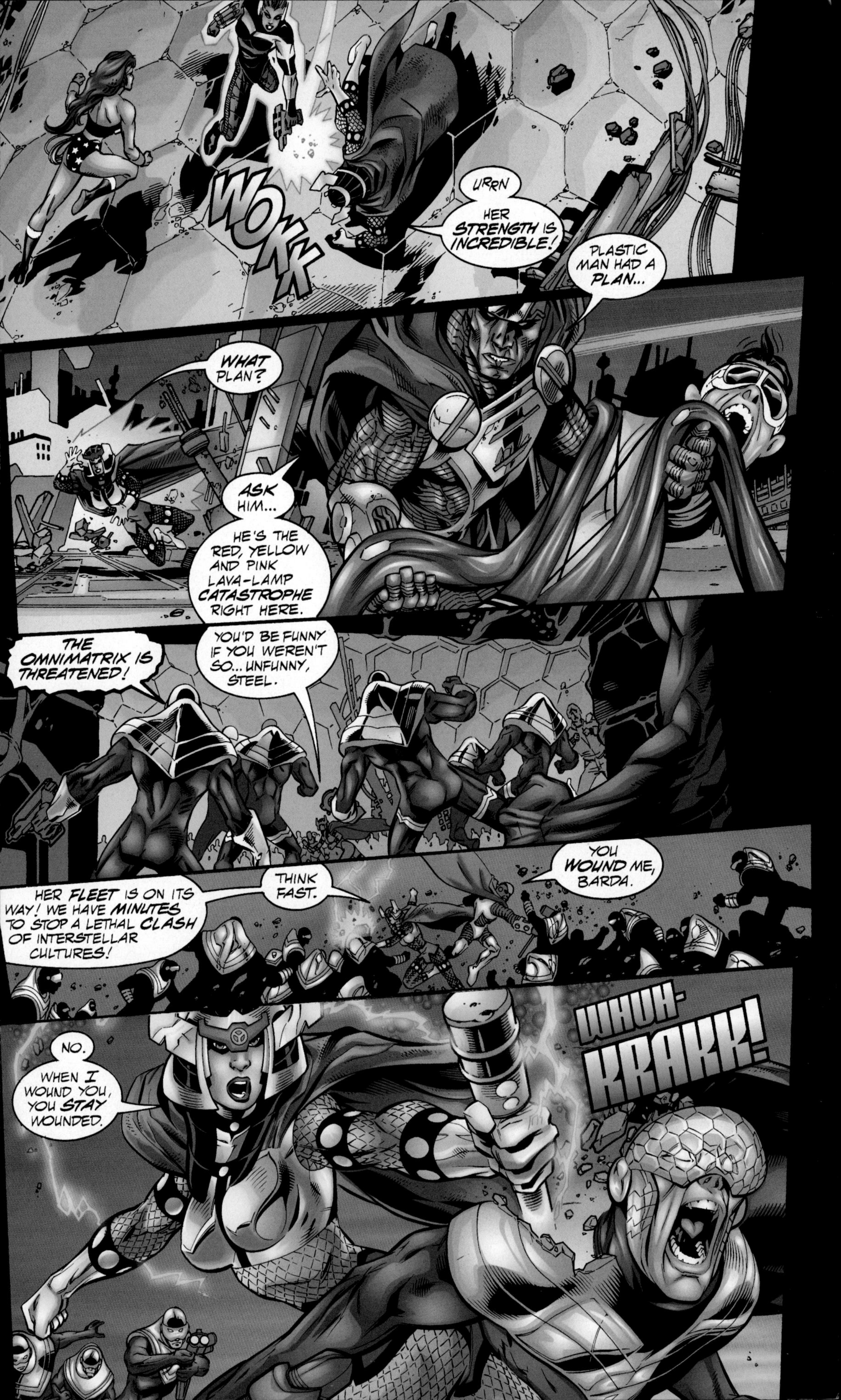
WONK
URRN
HER STRENGTH IS INCREDIBLE!
PLASTIC MAN HAD A PLAN...
WHAT PLAN?
ASK HIM...
HE'S THE RED, YELLOW AND PINK LAVA-LAMP CATASTROPHE RIGHT HERE.
THE OMNIMATRIX IS THREATENED!
YOU'D BE FUNNY IF YOU WEREN'T SO... UNFUNNY, STEEL.
HER FLEET IS ON ITS WAY! WE HAVE MINUTES TO STOP A LETHAL CLASH OF INTERSTELLAR CULTURES!
THINK FAST.
YOU WOUND ME, BARDA.
WHUH-KRAKK!
NO.
WHEN I WOUND YOU, YOU STAY WOUNDED.

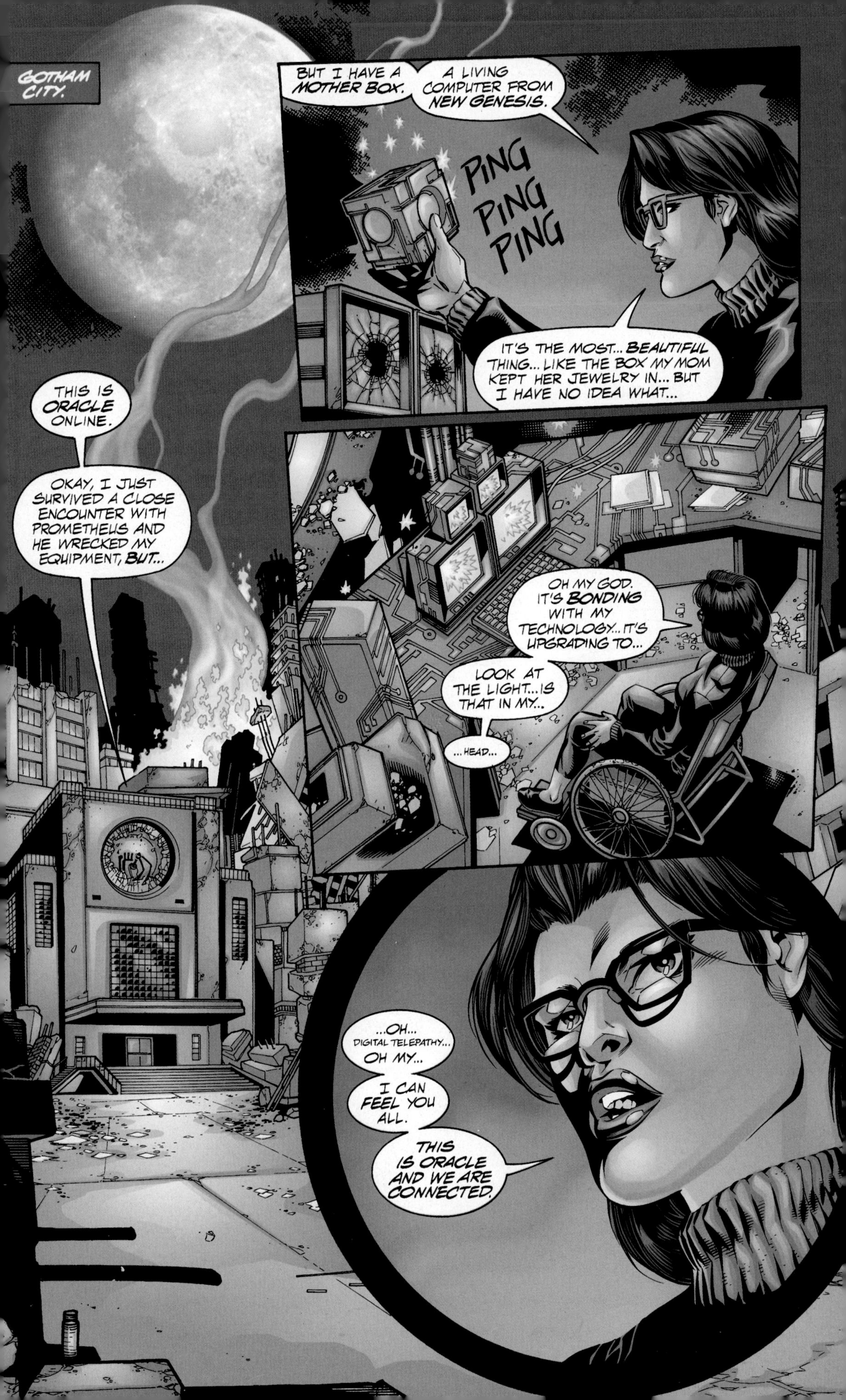
GOTHAM CITY.
BUT I HAVE A MOTHER BOX.
A LIVING COMPUTER FROM NEW GENESIS.
PING PING PING
IT'S THE MOST... BEAUTIFUL THING... LIKE THE BOX MY MOM KEPT HER JEWELRY IN... BUT I HAVE NO IDEA WHAT...
OH MY GOD. IT'S BONDING WITH MY TECHNOLOGY... IT'S UPGRADING TO...
LOOK AT THE LIGHT... IS THAT IN MY...
...HEAD...
THIS IS ORACLE ONLINE.
OKAY, I JUST SURVIVED A CLOSE ENCOUNTER WITH PROMETHEUS AND HE WRECKED MY EQUIPMENT, BUT...
...OH... DIGITAL TELEPATHY... OH MY...
I CAN FEEL YOU ALL.
THIS IS ORACLE AND WE ARE CONNECTED.

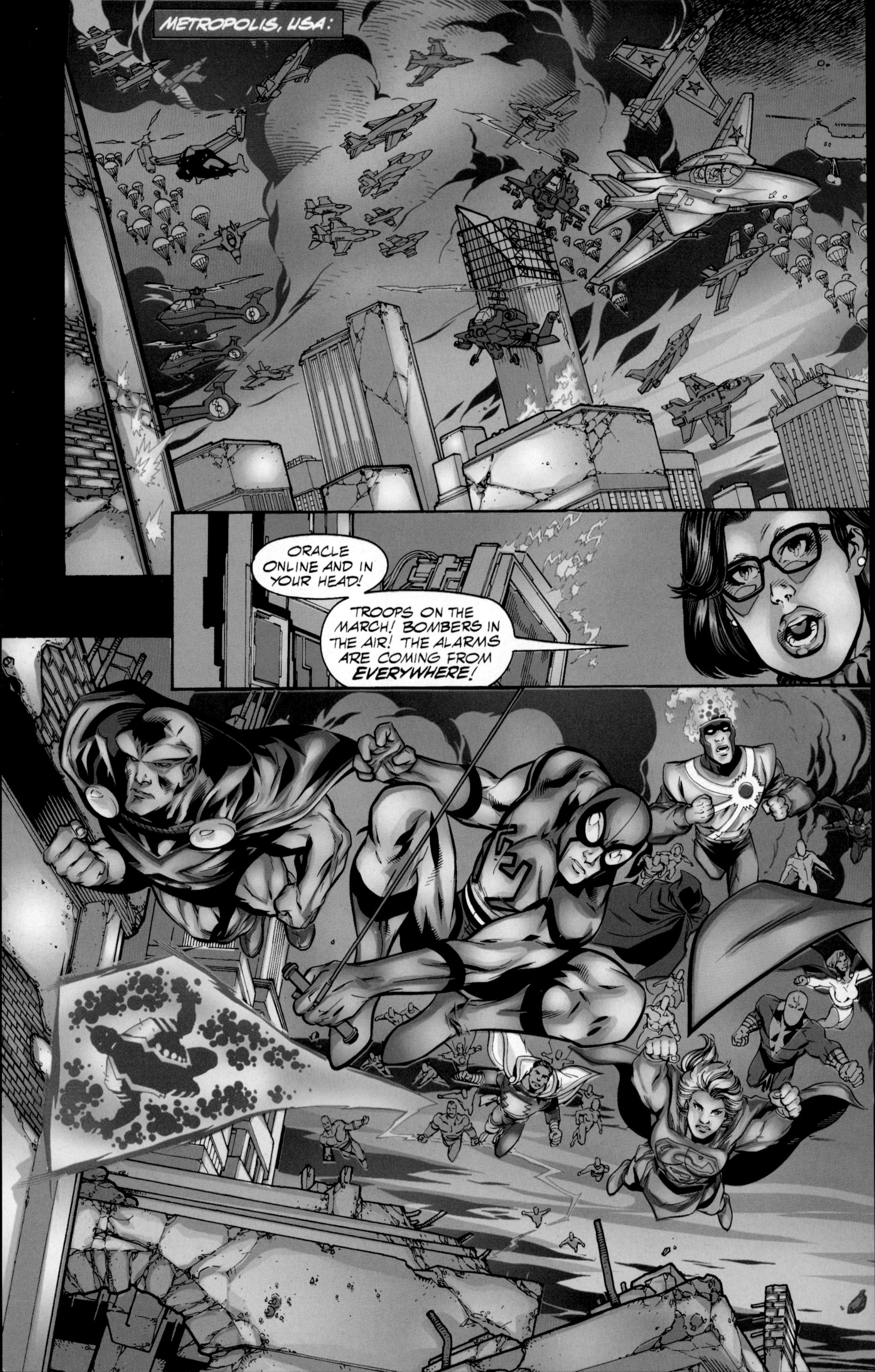

METROPOLIS, USA:
ORACLE ONLINE AND IN YOUR HEAD!
TROOPS ON THE MARCH! BOMBERS IN THE AIR! THE ALARMS ARE COMING FROM EVERYWHERE!

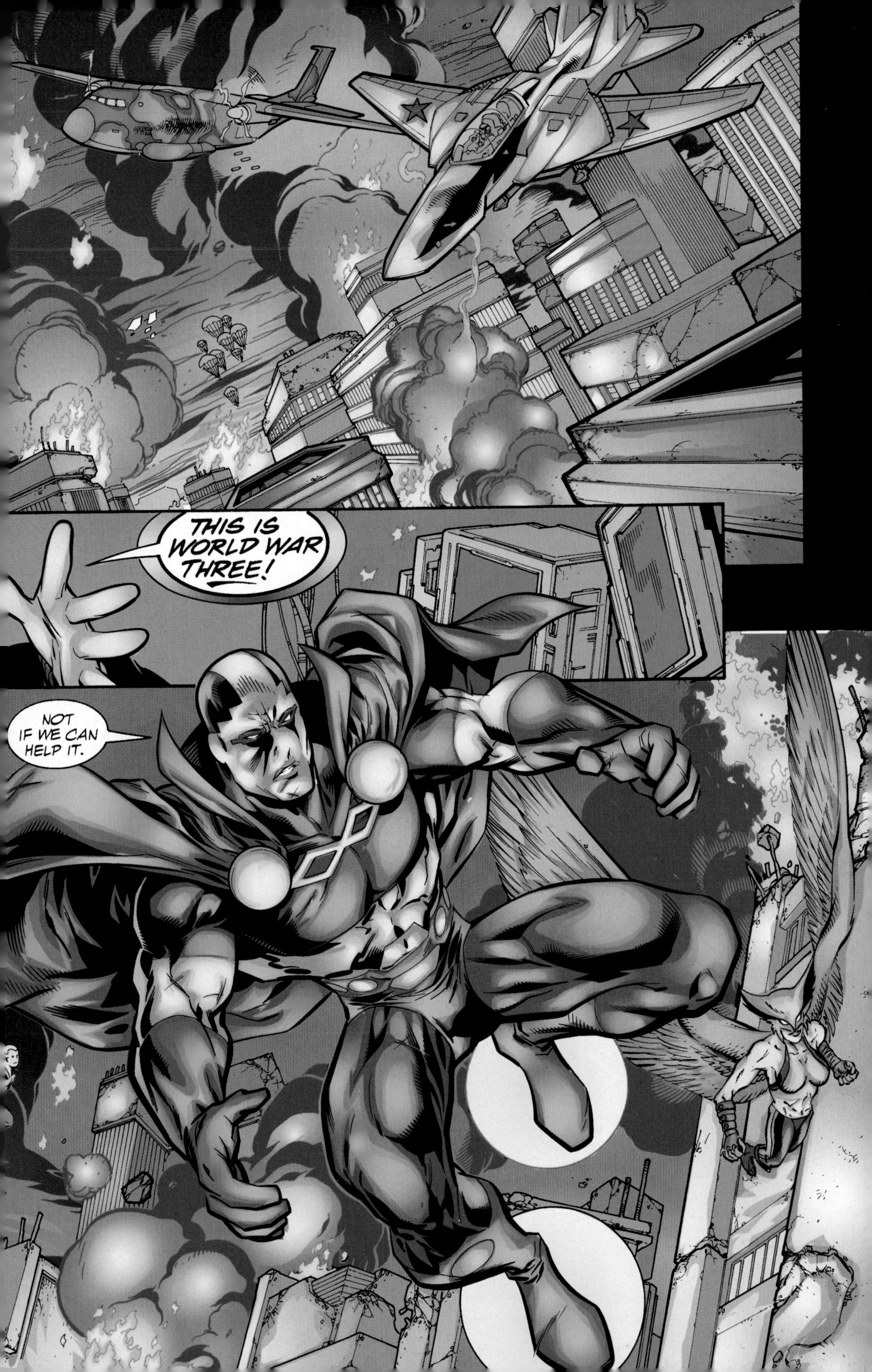
THIS IS WORLD WAR THREE!
NOT IF WE CAN HELP IT.

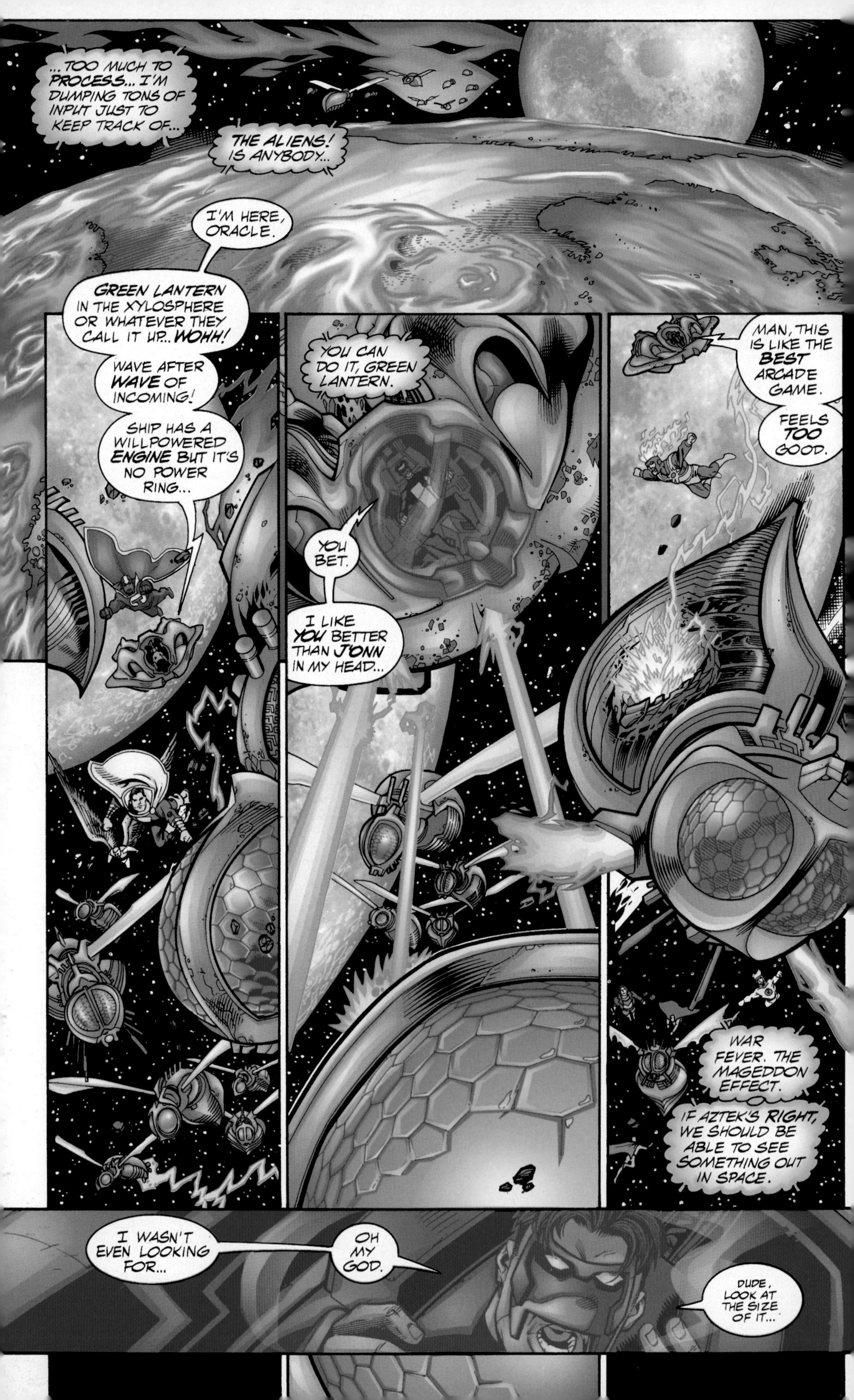
...TOO MUCH TO PROCESS... I'M DUMPING TONS OF INPUT JUST TO KEEP TRACK OF...
THE ALIENS! IS ANYBODY...
I'M HERE, ORACLE.
GREEN LANTERN IN THE XYLOSPHERE OR WHATEVER THEY CALL IT UP... WOHH!
WAVE AFTER WAVE OF INCOMING!
SHIP HAS A WILLPOWERED ENGINE BUT IT'S NO POWER RING...
YOU CAN DO IT, GREEN LANTERN.
YOU BET.
I LIKE YOU BETTER THAN J'ONN IN MY HEAD...
MAN, THIS IS LIKE THE BEST ARCADE GAME.
FEELS TOO GOOD.
WAR FEVER. THE MAGEDDON EFFECT.
IF AZTEK'S RIGHT, WE SHOULD BE ABLE TO SEE SOMETHING OUT IN SPACE.
I WASN'T EVEN LOOKING FOR...
OH MY GOD.
DUDE, LOOK AT THE SIZE OF IT...

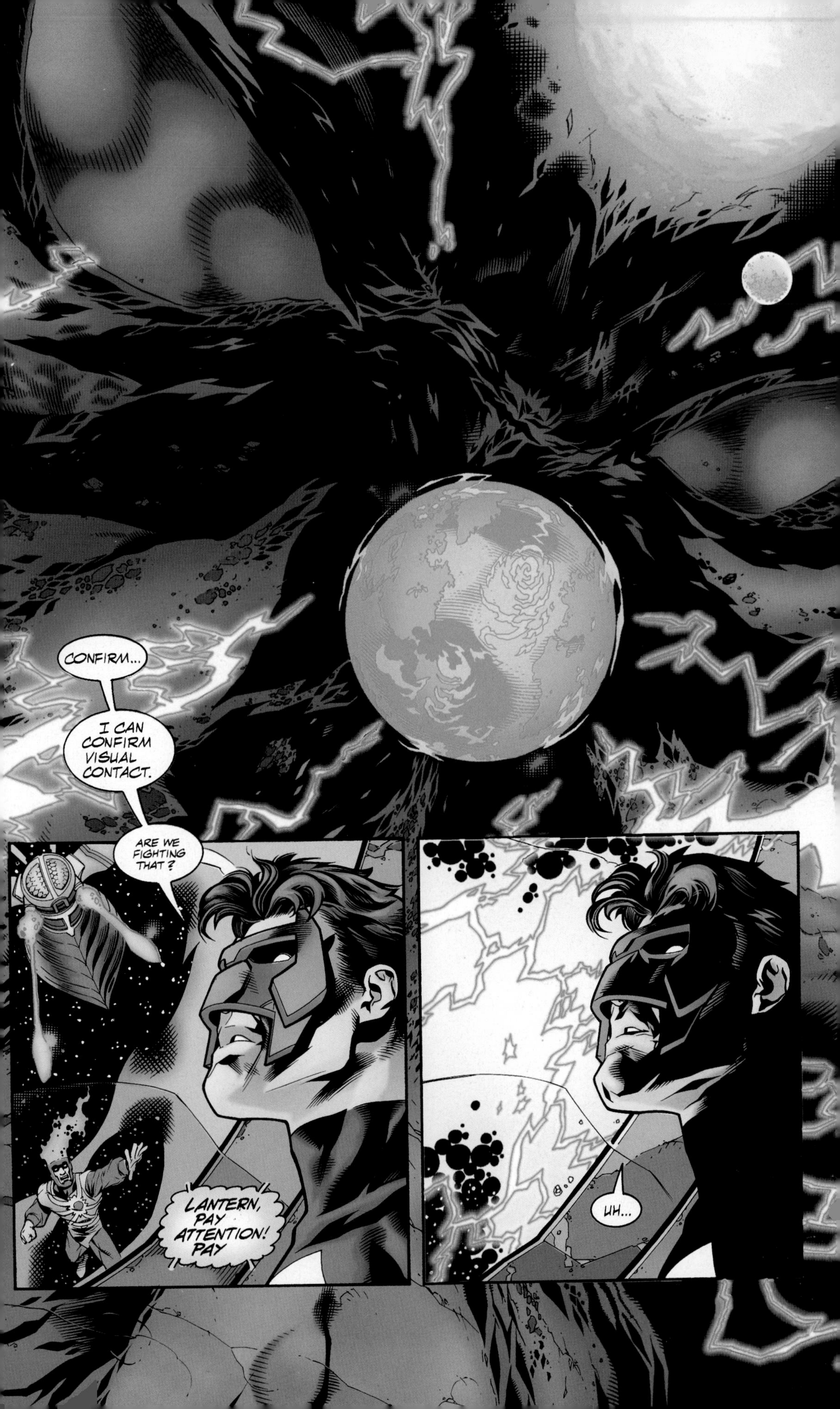
CONFIRM...
I CAN CONFIRM VISUAL CONTACT.
ARE WE FIGHTING THAT?
LANTERN, PAY ATTENTION! PAY
UH...

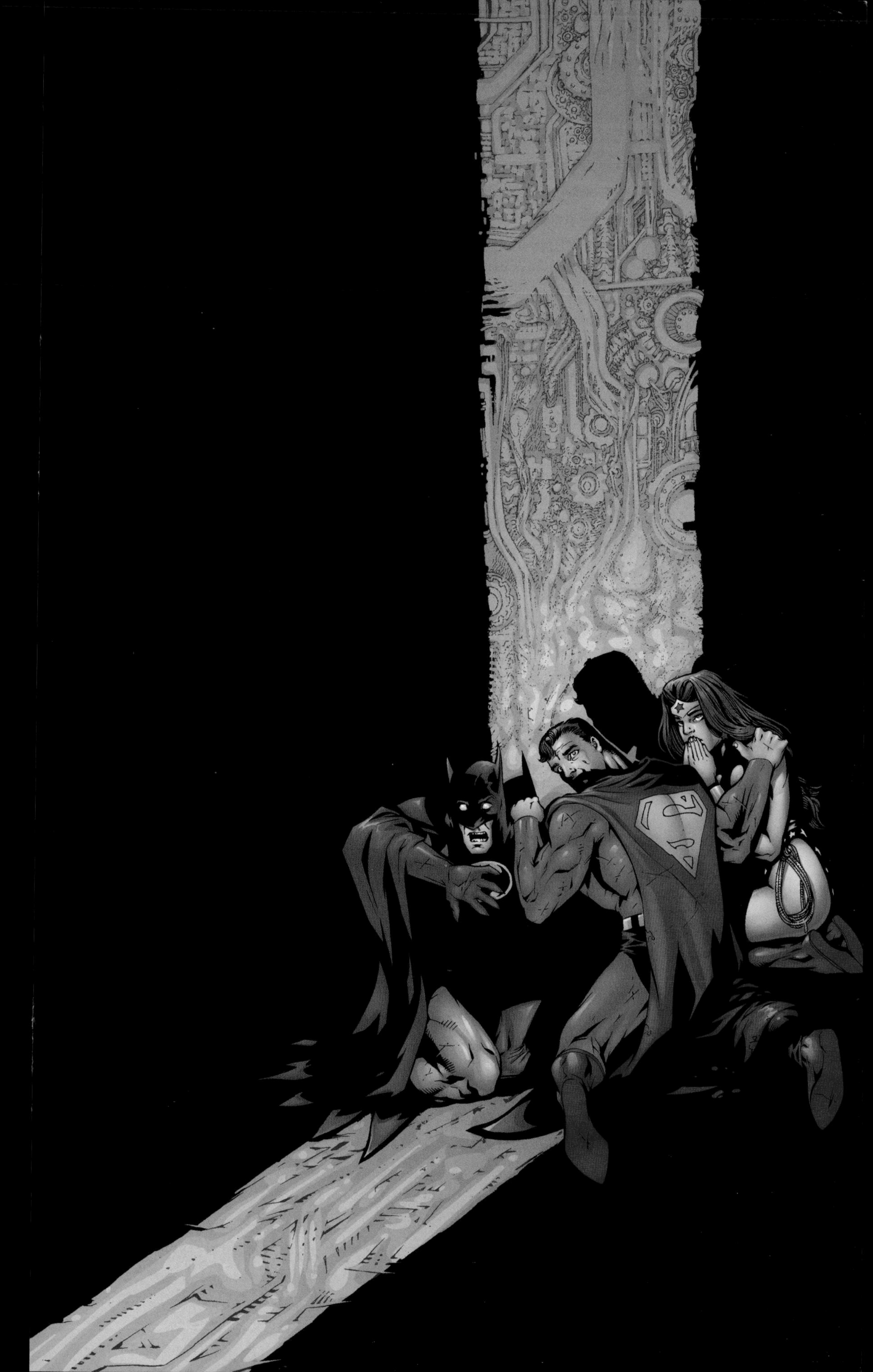

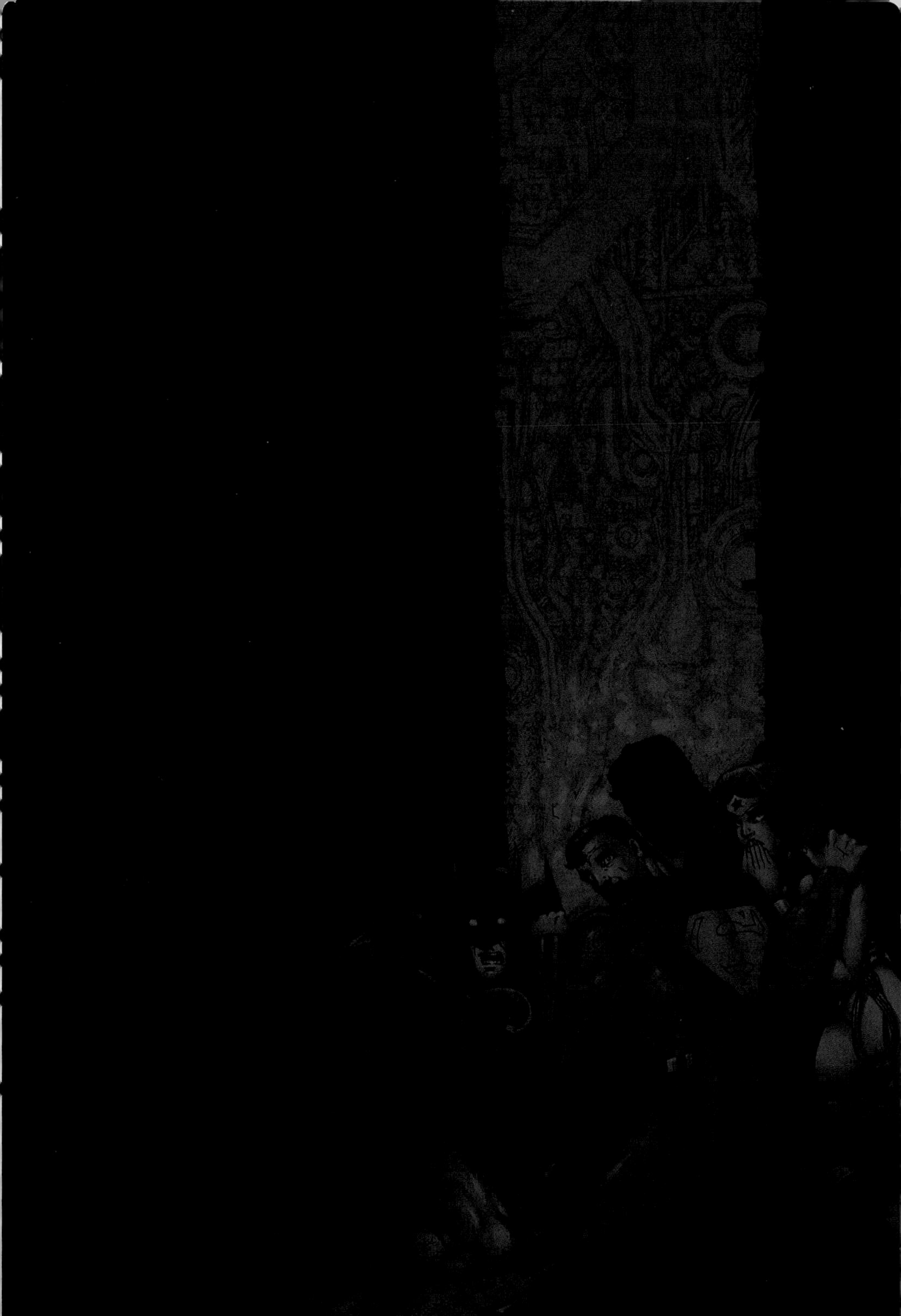

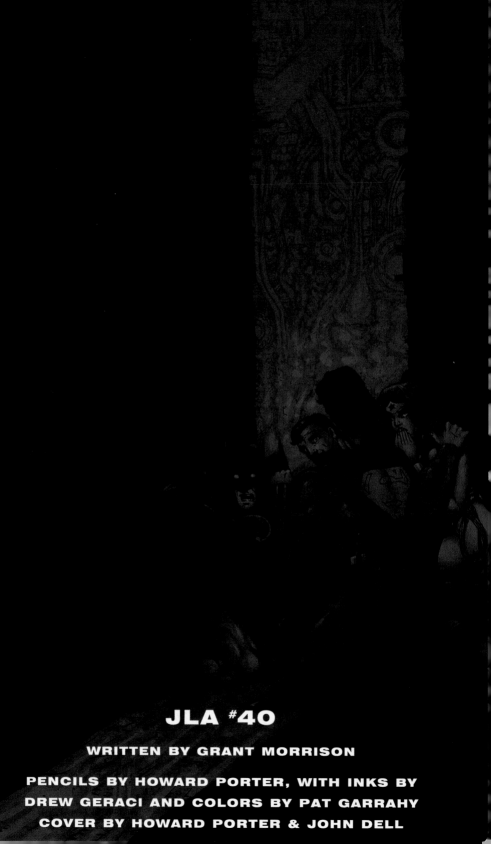

JLA #40

WRITTEN BY GRANT MORRISON

PENCILS BY HOWARD PORTER, WITH INKS BY DREW GERACI AND COLORS BY PAT GARRAHY

COVER BY HOWARD PORTER & JOHN DELL

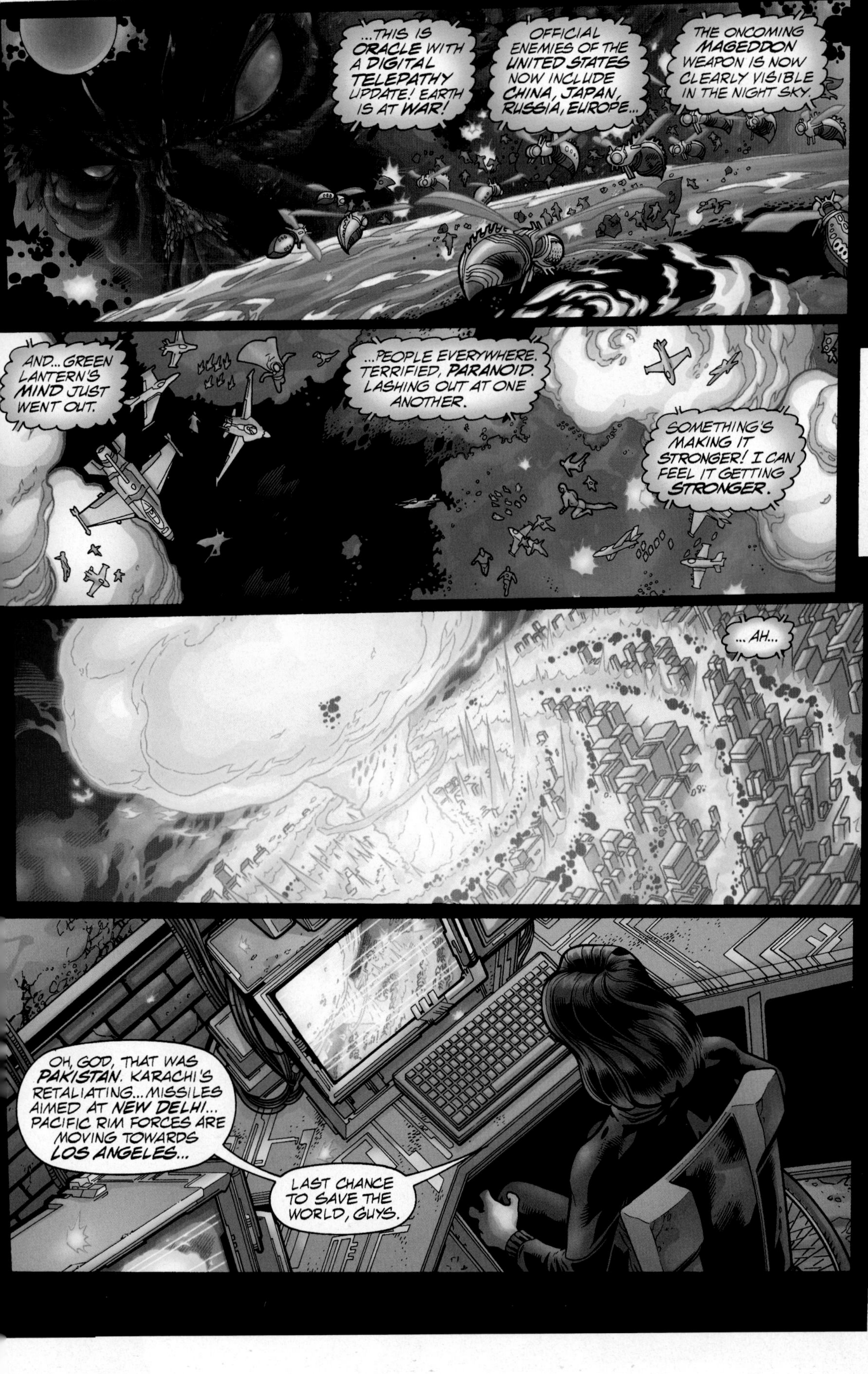
...THIS IS ORACLE WITH A DIGITAL TELEPATHY UPDATE! EARTH IS AT WAR!
OFFICIAL ENEMIES OF THE UNITED STATES NOW INCLUDE CHINA, JAPAN, RUSSIA, EUROPE...
THE ONCOMING MAGEDDON WEAPON IS NOW CLEARLY VISIBLE IN THE NIGHT SKY.
AND... GREEN LANTERN'S MIND JUST WENT OUT.
...PEOPLE EVERYWHERE. TERRIFIED, PARANOID. LASHING OUT AT ONE ANOTHER.
SOMETHING'S MAKING IT STRONGER! I CAN FEEL IT GETTING STRONGER.
... AH...
OH, GOD, THAT WAS PAKISTAN. KARACHI'S RETALIATING... MISSILES AIMED AT NEW DELHI... PACIFIC RIM FORCES ARE MOVING TOWARDS LOS ANGELES...
LAST CHANCE TO SAVE THE WORLD, GUYS.

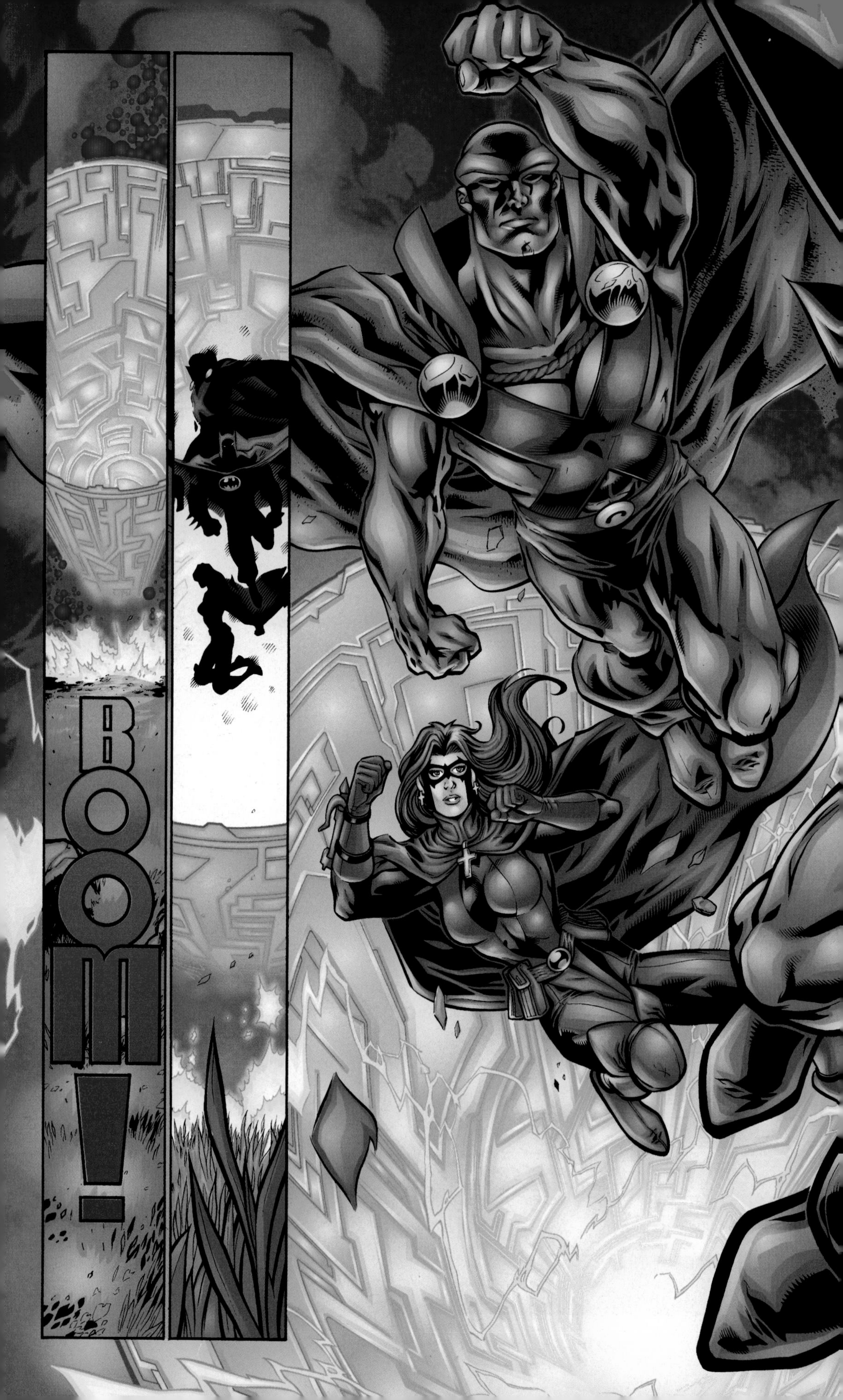
BOOM!

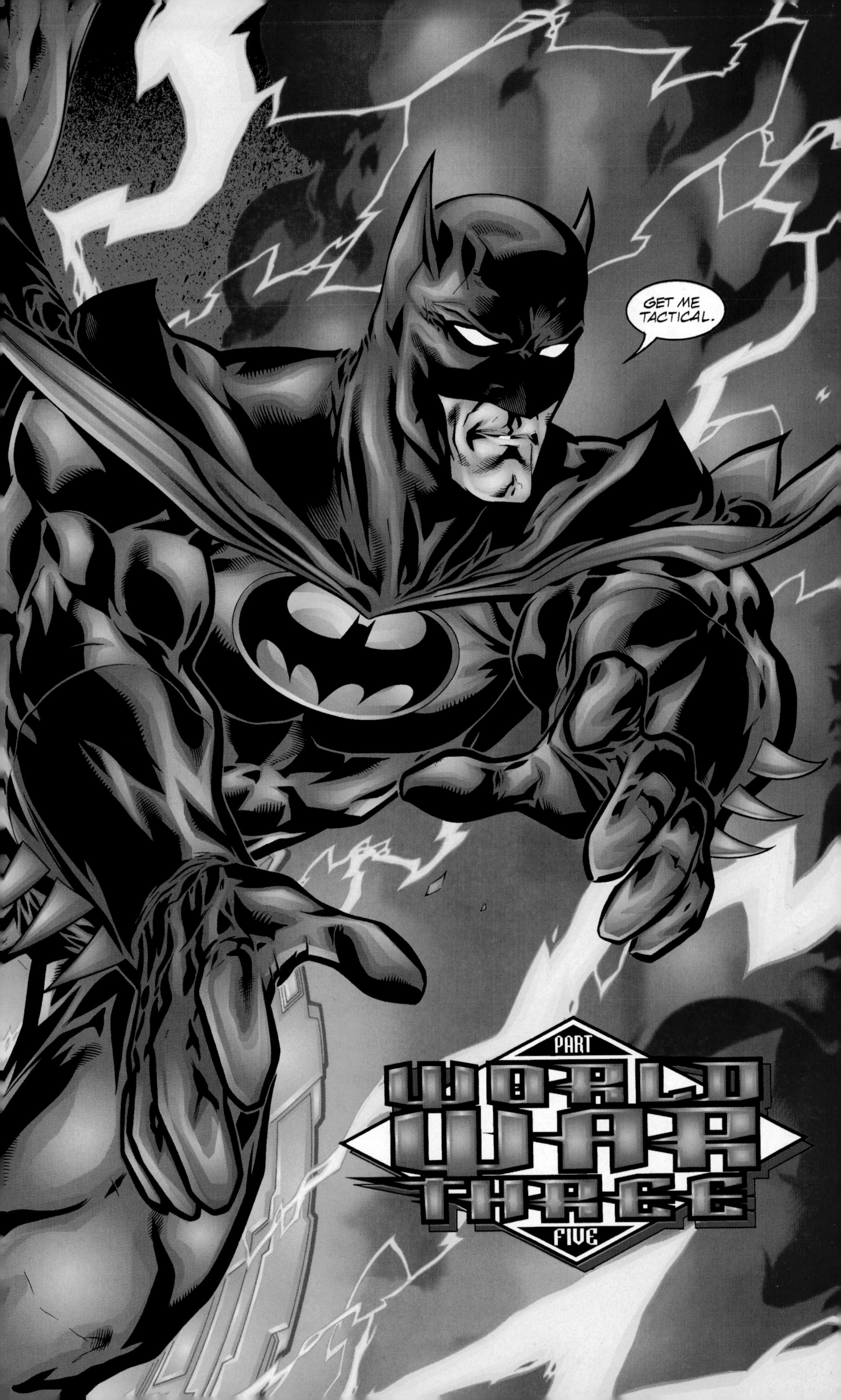
GET ME TACTICAL.
PART
WORLD WAR THREE
FIVE

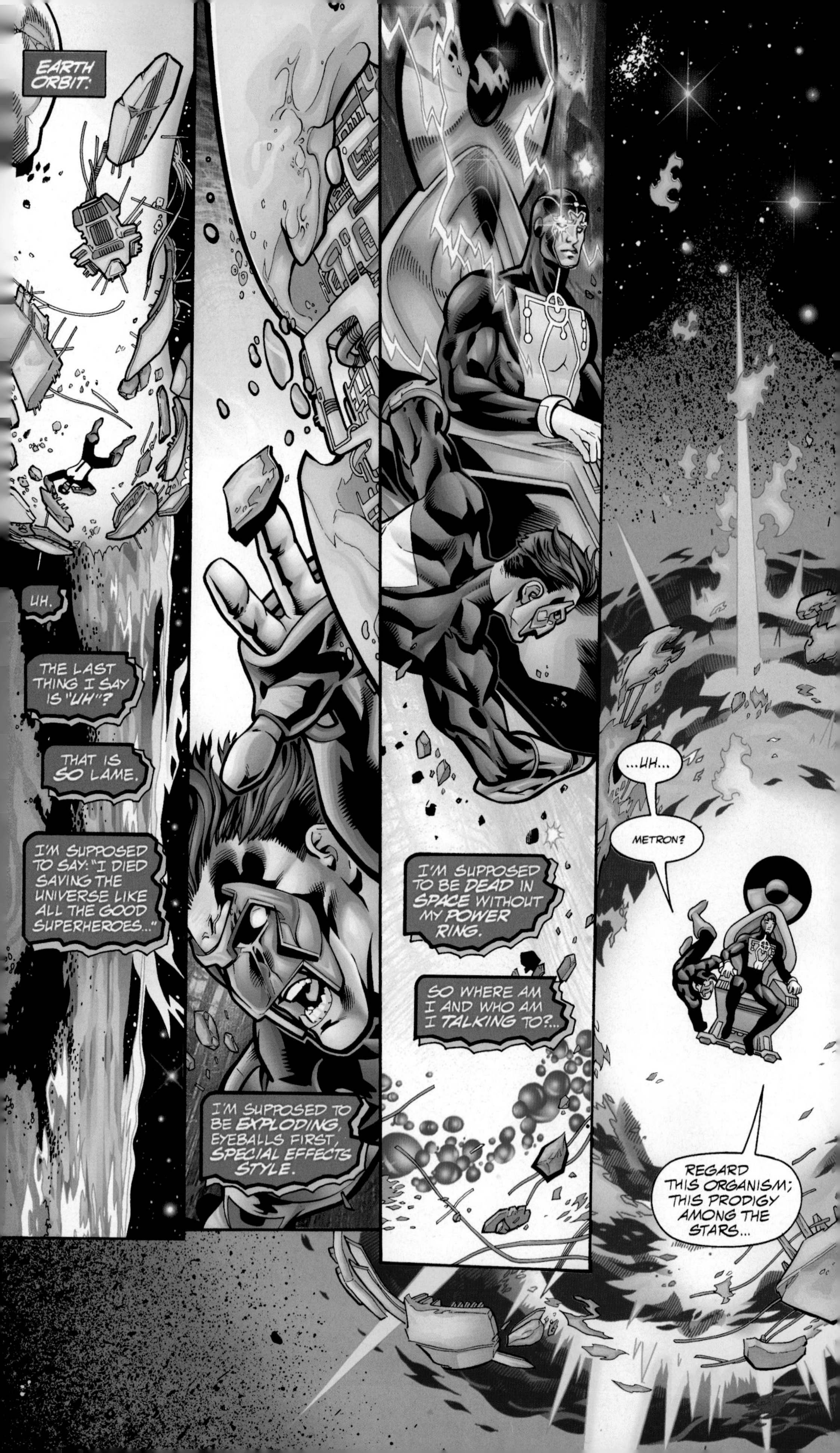
EARTH ORBIT:
UH.
THE LAST THING I SAY IS "UH"?
THAT IS SO LAME.
I'M SUPPOSED TO SAY: "I DIED SAVING THE UNIVERSE LIKE ALL THE GOOD SUPERHEROES..."
I'M SUPPOSED TO BE EXPLODING, EYEBALLS FIRST, SPECIAL EFFECTS STYLE.
I'M SUPPOSED TO BE DEAD IN SPACE WITHOUT MY POWER RING.
SO WHERE AM I AND WHO AM I TALKING TO?...
...UH...
METRON?
REGARD THIS ORGANISM; THIS PRODIGY AMONG THE STARS...

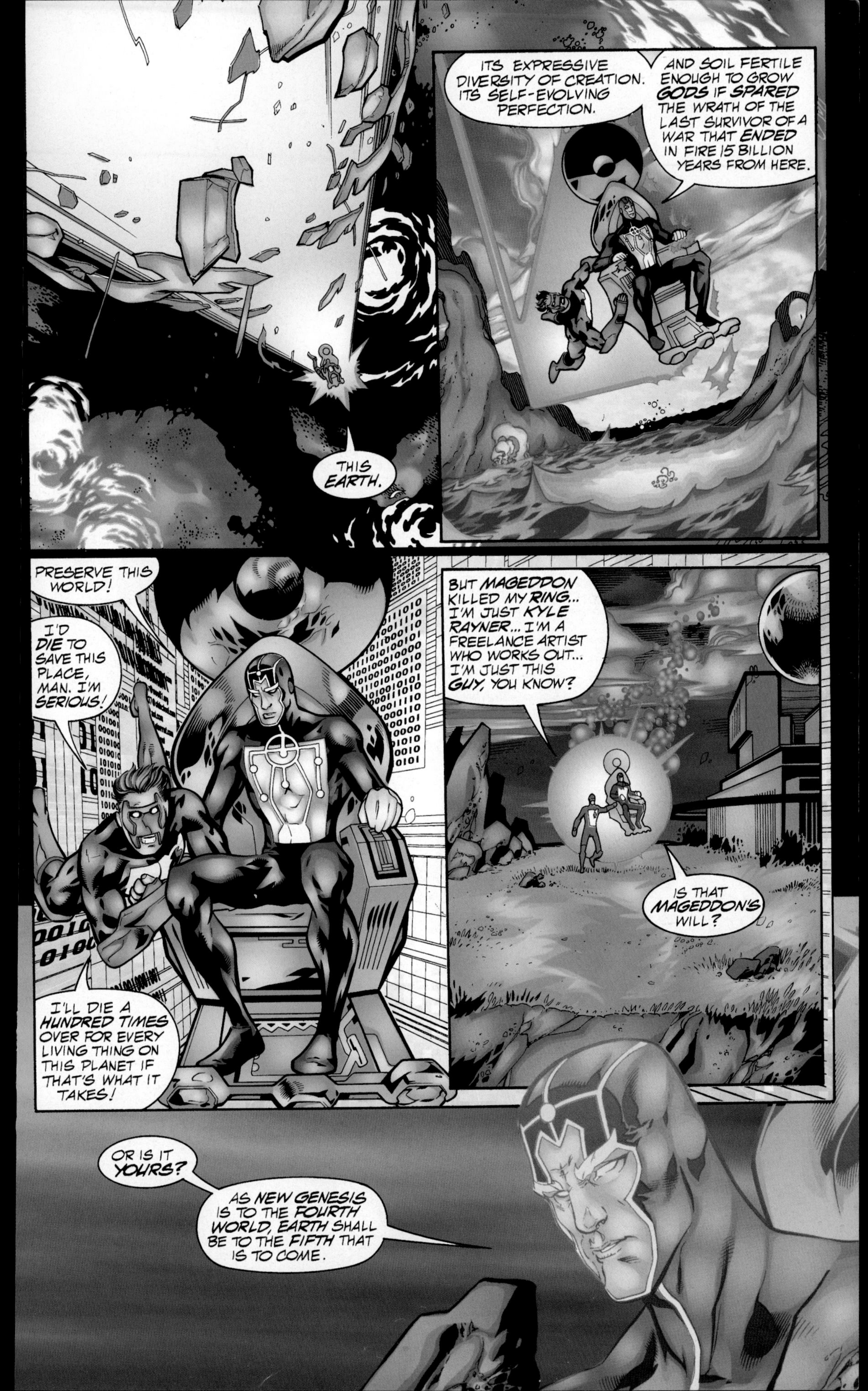

THIS EARTH.
ITS EXPRESSIVE DIVERSITY OF CREATION. ITS SELF-EVOLVING PERFECTION.
AND SOIL FERTILE ENOUGH TO GROW GODS IF SPARED THE WRATH OF THE LAST SURVIVOR OF A WAR THAT ENDED IN FIRE 15 BILLION YEARS FROM HERE.
PRESERVE THIS WORLD!
I'D DIE TO SAVE THIS PLACE, MAN. I'M SERIOUS!
I'LL DIE A HUNDRED TIMES OVER FOR EVERY LIVING THING ON THIS PLANET IF THAT'S WHAT IT TAKES!
BUT MAGEDDON KILLED MY RING... I'M JUST KYLE RAYNER... I'M A FREELANCE ARTIST WHO WORKS OUT... I'M JUST THIS GUY, YOU KNOW?
IS THAT MAGEDDON'S WILL?
OR IS IT YOURS?
AS NEW GENESIS IS TO THE FOURTH WORLD, EARTH SHALL BE TO THE FIFTH THAT IS TO COME.

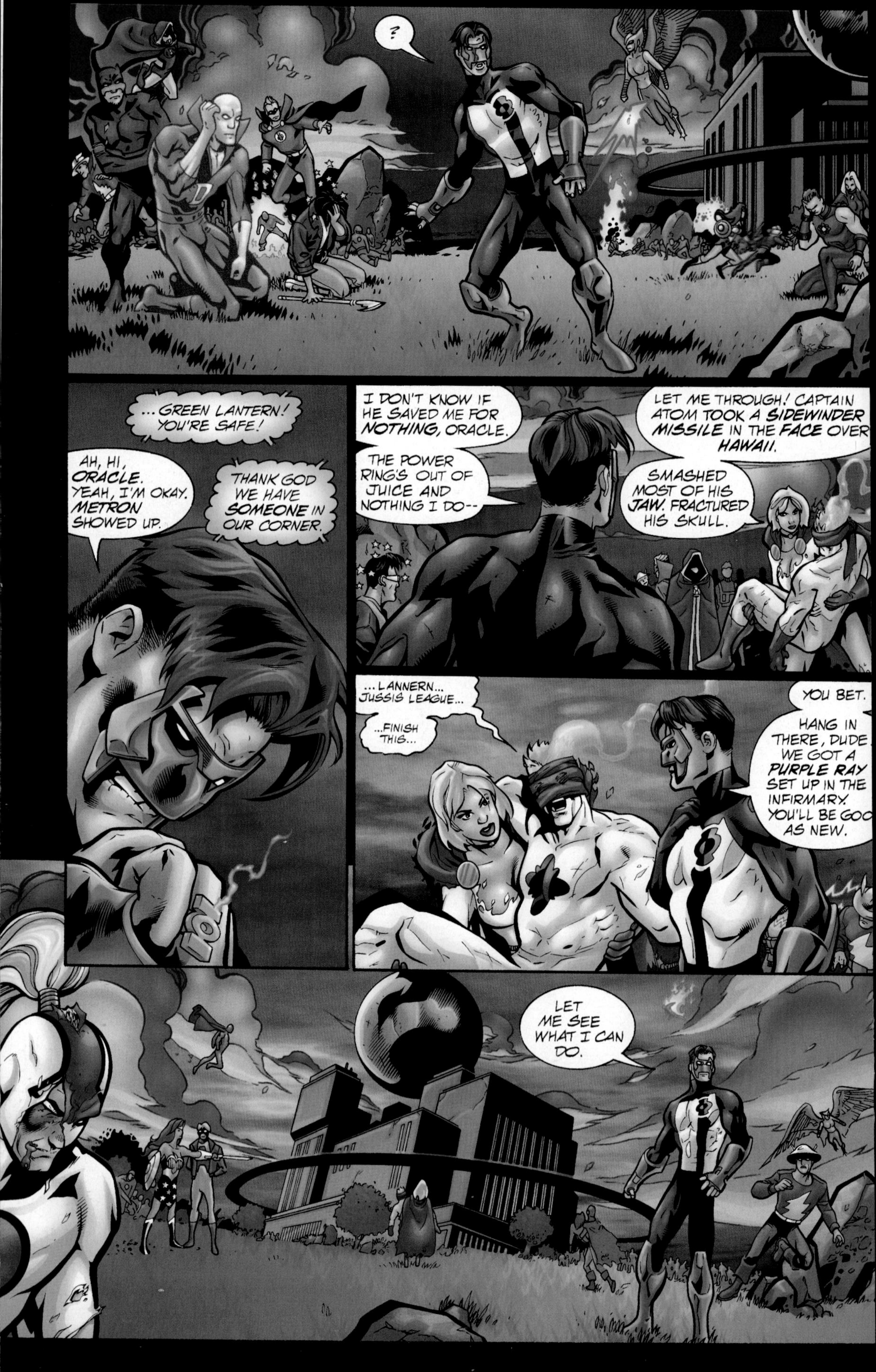
?
...GREEN LANTERN! YOU'RE SAFE!
AH, HI, ORACLE. YEAH, I'M OKAY. METRON SHOWED UP.
THANK GOD WE HAVE SOMEONE IN OUR CORNER.
I DON'T KNOW IF HE SAVED ME FOR NOTHING, ORACLE.
THE POWER RING'S OUT OF JUICE AND NOTHING I DO--
LET ME THROUGH! CAPTAIN ATOM TOOK A SIDEWINDER MISSILE IN THE FACE OVER HAWAII.
SMASHED MOST OF HIS JAW. FRACTURED HIS SKULL.
...LANNERN... JUSSIS LEAGUE...
...FINISH THIS...
YOU BET.
HANG IN THERE, DUDE. WE GOT A PURPLE RAY SET UP IN THE INFIRMARY. YOU'LL BE GOO AS NEW.
LET ME SEE WHAT I CAN DO.

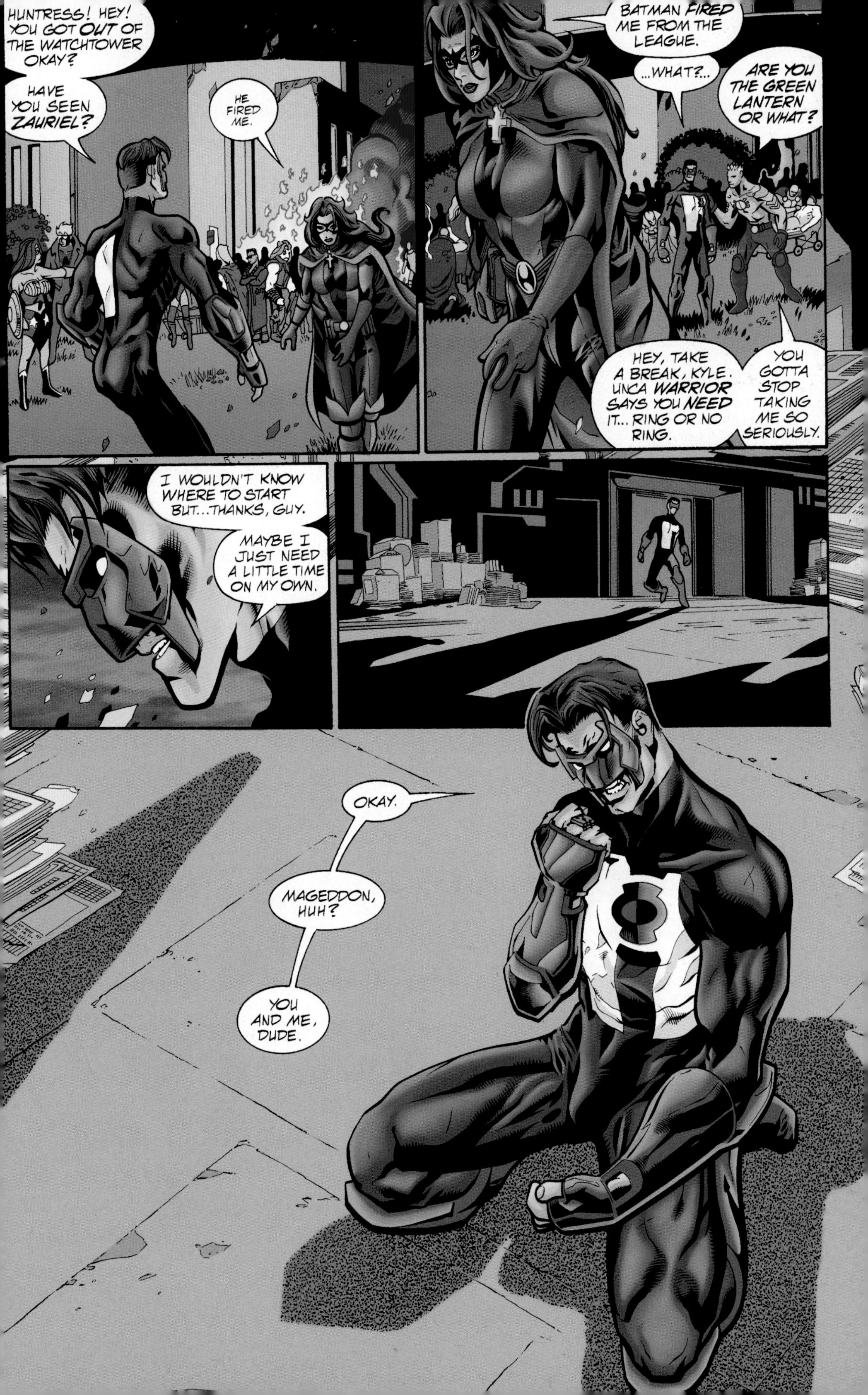
HUNTRESS! HEY! YOU GOT OUT OF THE WATCHTOWER OKAY?
HAVE YOU SEEN ZAURIEL?
HE FIRED ME.
BATMAN FIRED ME FROM THE LEAGUE.
...WHAT?...
ARE YOU THE GREEN LANTERN OR WHAT?
HEY, TAKE A BREAK, KYLE. UNCA WARRIOR SAYS YOU NEED IT... RING OR NO RING.
YOU GOTTA STOP TAKING ME SO SERIOUSLY.
I WOULDN'T KNOW WHERE TO START BUT...THANKS, GUY.
MAYBE I JUST NEED A LITTLE TIME ON MY OWN.
OKAY.
MAGEDDON, HUH?
YOU AND ME, DUDE.

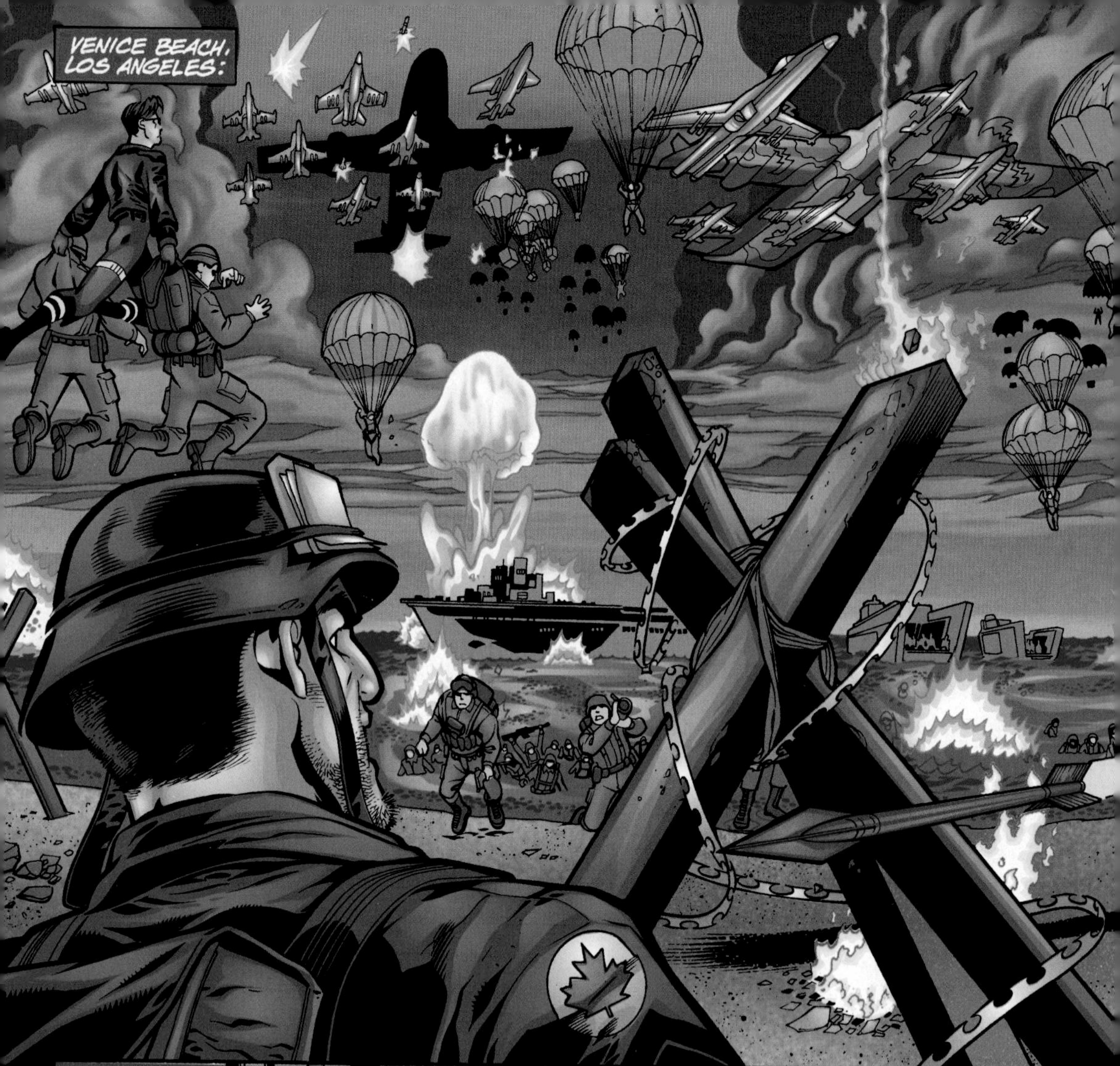
VENICE BEACH, LOS ANGELES:

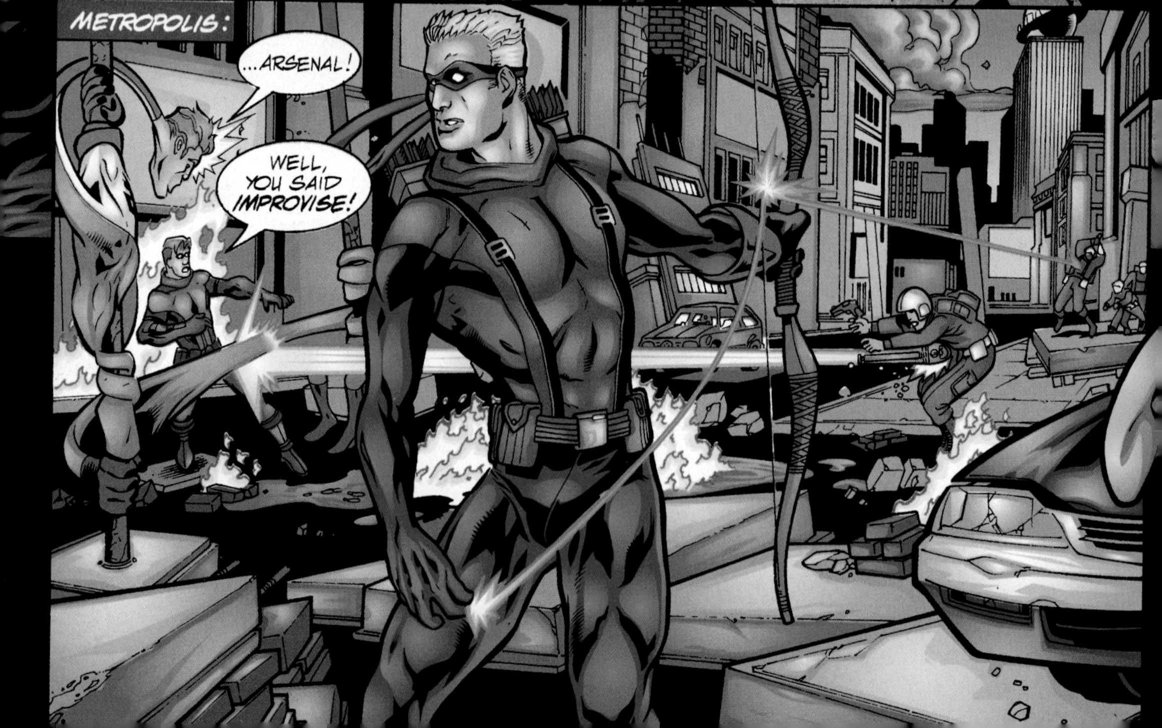
METROPOLIS:
...ARSENAL!
WELL, YOU SAID IMPROVISE!

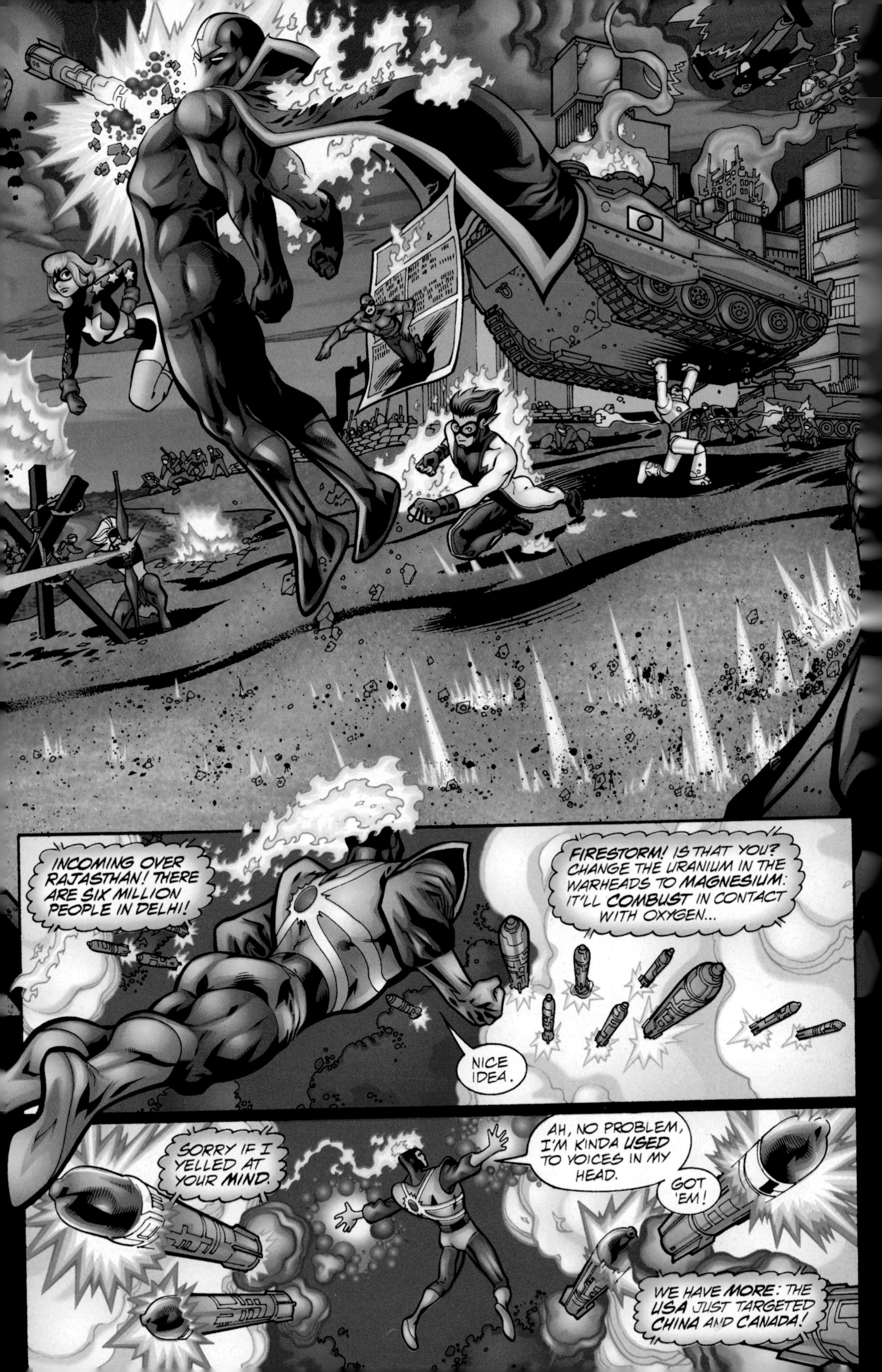
INCOMING OVER RAJASTHAN! THERE ARE SIX MILLION PEOPLE IN DELHI!
FIRESTORM! IS THAT YOU? CHANGE THE URANIUM IN THE WARHEADS TO MAGNESIUM: IT'LL COMBUST IN CONTACT WITH OXYGEN...
NICE IDEA.
SORRY IF I YELLED AT YOUR MIND.
AH, NO PROBLEM, I'M KINDA USED TO VOICES IN MY HEAD.
GOT 'EM!
WE HAVE MORE: THE USA JUST TARGETED CHINA AND CANADA!

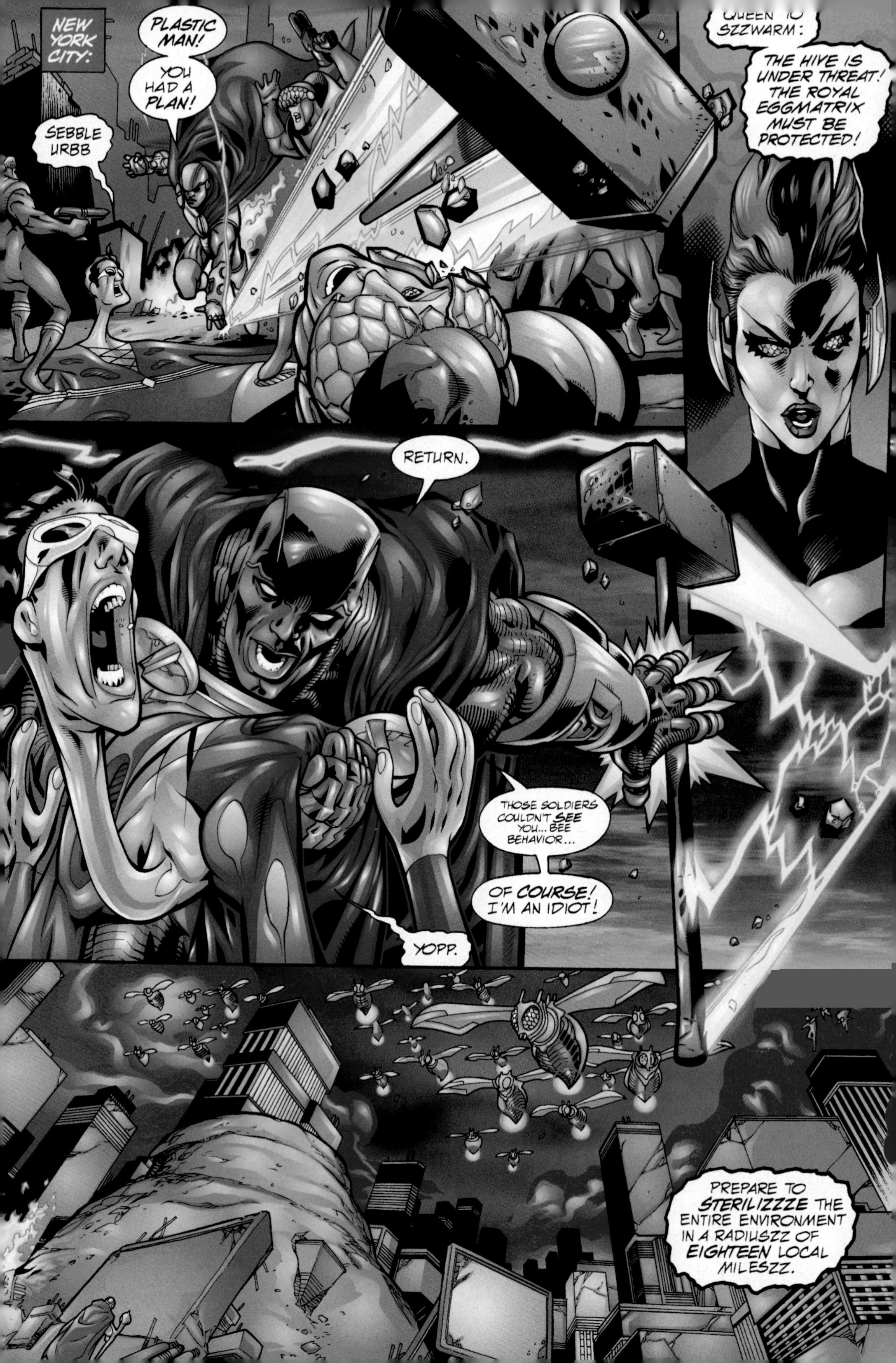
NEW YORK CITY:
PLASTIC MAN!
YOU HAD A PLAN!
SEBBLE URBB
QUEEN TO SZZWARM:
THE HIVE IS UNDER THREAT! THE ROYAL EGGMATRIX MUST BE PROTECTED!
RETURN.
THOSE SOLDIERS COULDN'T SEE YOU... BEE BEHAVIOR...
OF COURSE! I'M AN IDIOT!
YOPP.
PREPARE TO STERILIZZZE THE ENTIRE ENVIRONMENT IN A RADIUSZZ OF EIGHTEEN LOCAL MILESZZ.

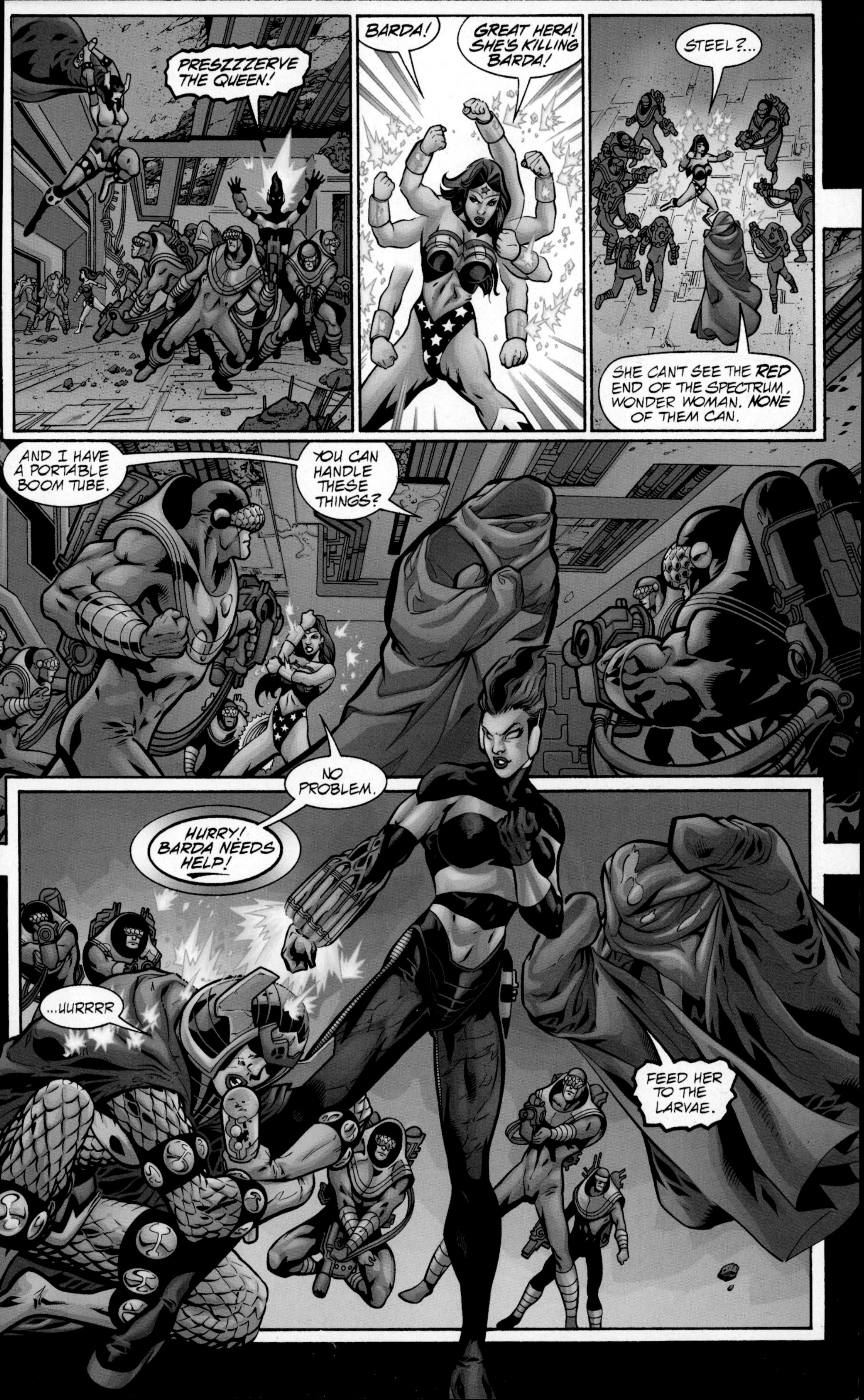
PRESZZZERVE THE QUEEN!
BARDA!
GREAT HERA! SHE'S KILLING BARDA!
STEEL?...
SHE CAN'T SEE THE RED END OF THE SPECTRUM, WONDER WOMAN. NONE OF THEM CAN.
AND I HAVE A PORTABLE BOOM TUBE.
YOU CAN HANDLE THESE THINGS?
NO PROBLEM.
HURRY! BARDA NEEDS HELP!
...UURRRR
FEED HER TO THE LARVAE.

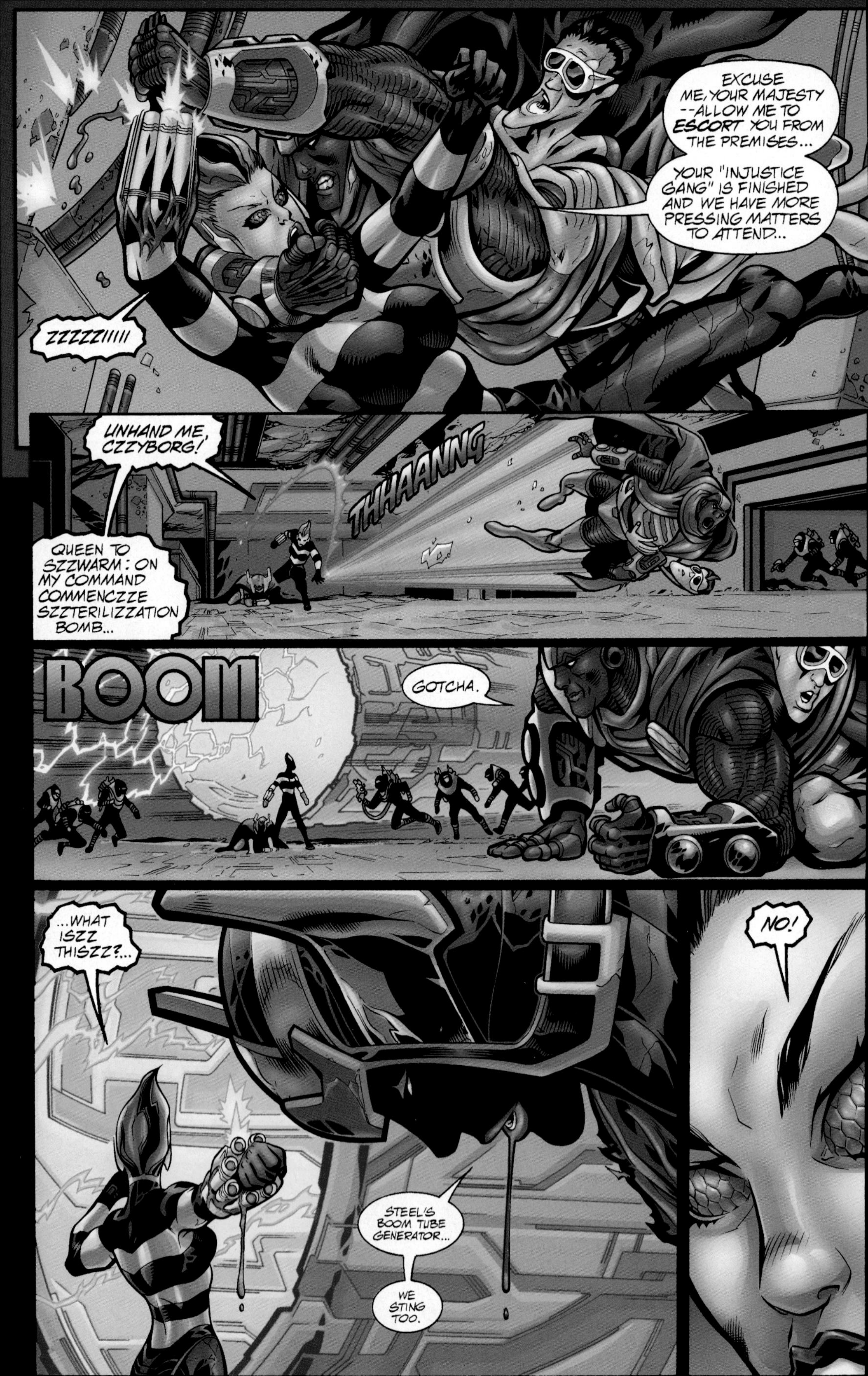
EXCUSE ME, YOUR MAJESTY --ALLOW ME TO ESCORT YOU FROM THE PREMISES...
YOUR "INJUSTICE GANG" IS FINISHED AND WE HAVE MORE PRESSING MATTERS TO ATTEND...
ZZZZZIIIII
UNHAND ME, CZZYBORG!
QUEEN TO SZZWARM: ON MY COMMAND COMMENCZZE SZZTERILIZZATION BOMB...
THHAANNG
BOOM
GOTCHA.
...WHAT ISZZ THISZZ?...
STEEL'S BOOM TUBE GENERATOR...
WE STING TOO.
NO!

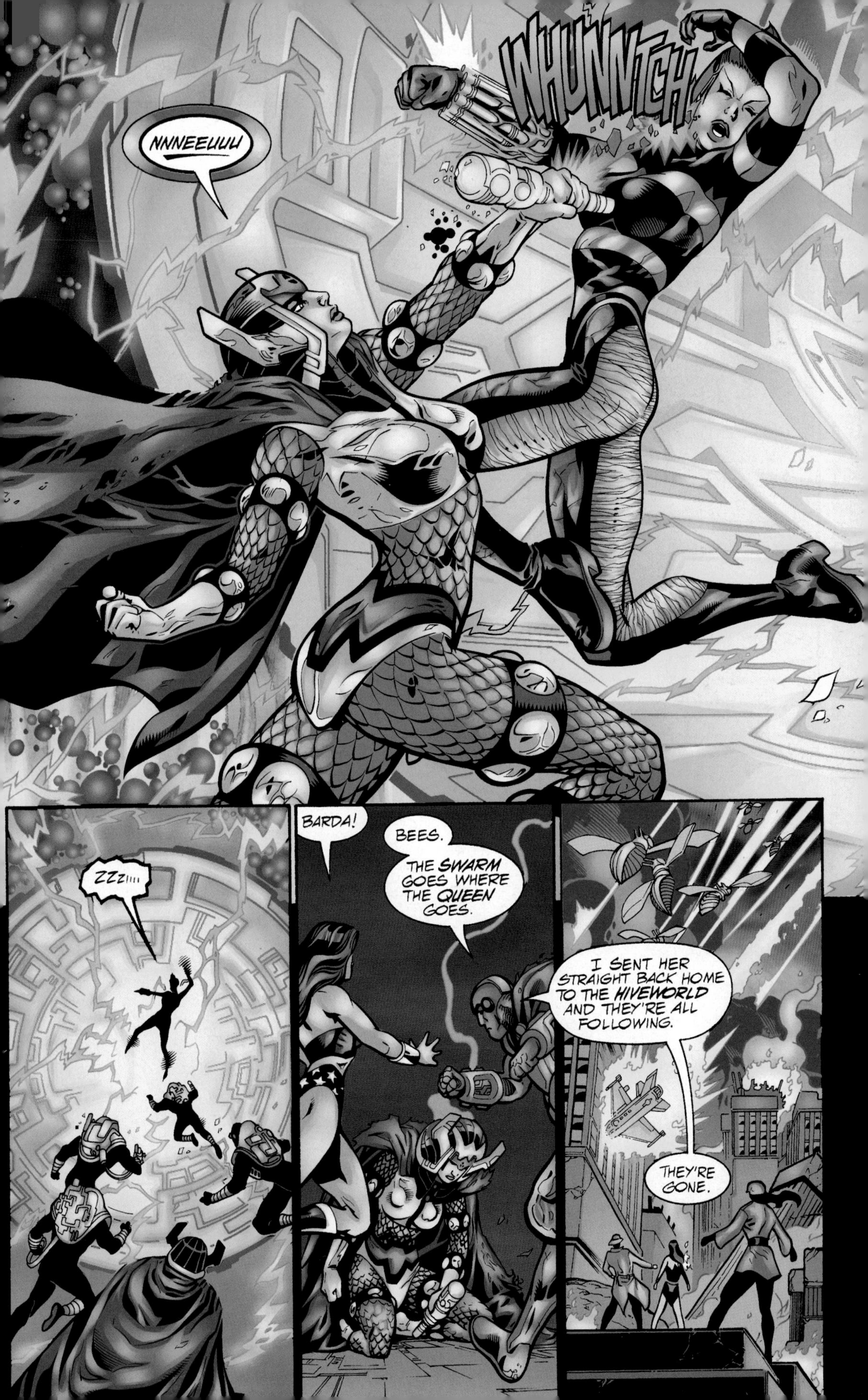
WHUNNTCH
NNNEEUUU
ZZZ!!!!!
BARDA!
BEES.
THE SWARM GOES WHERE THE QUEEN GOES.
I SENT HER STRAIGHT BACK HOME TO THE HIVEWORLD AND THEY'RE ALL FOLLOWING.
THEY'RE GONE.

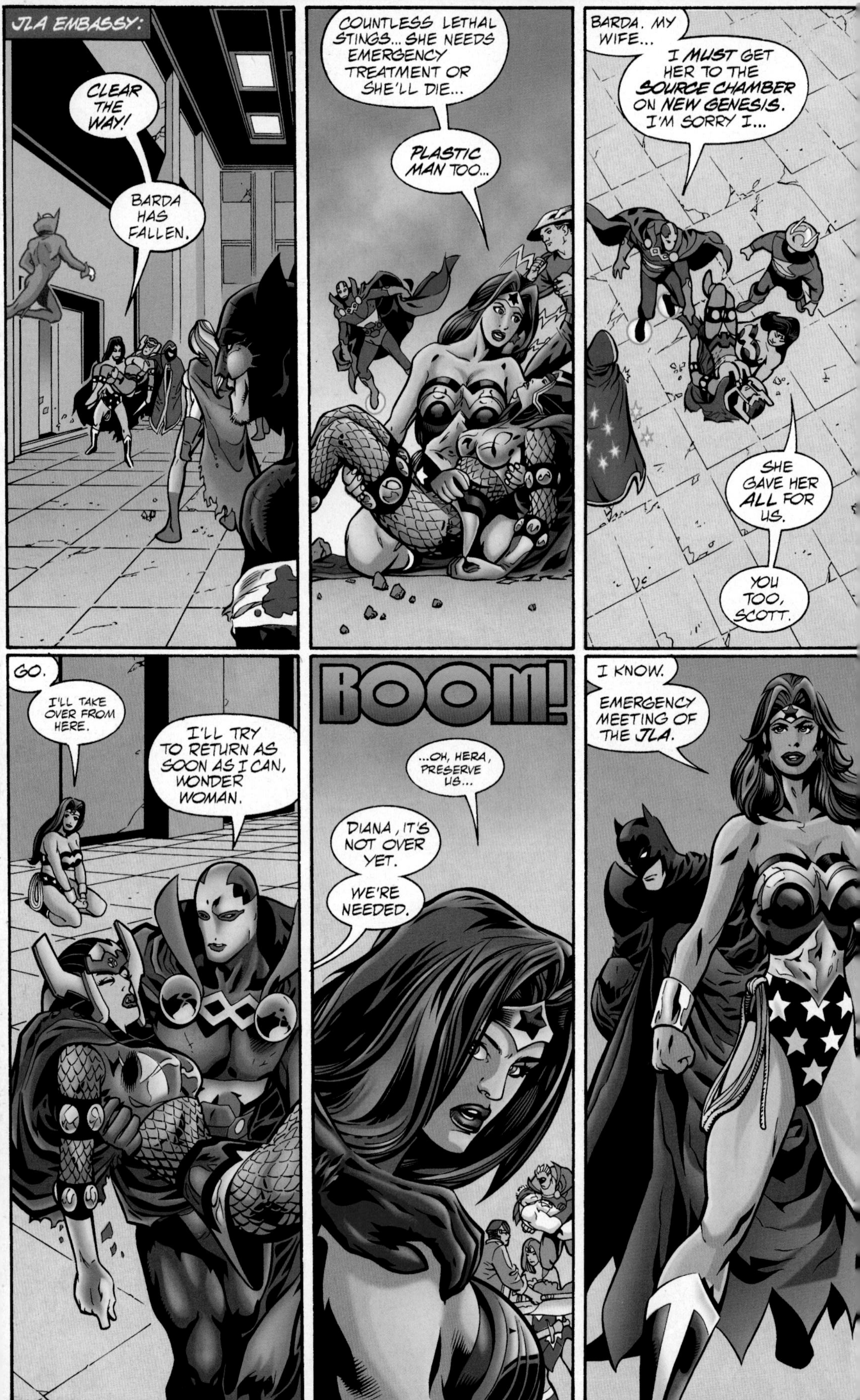
JLA EMBASSY:
CLEAR THE WAY!
BARDA HAS FALLEN.
COUNTLESS LETHAL STINGS... SHE NEEDS EMERGENCY TREATMENT OR SHE'LL DIE...
PLASTIC MAN TOO...
BARDA. MY WIFE...
I MUST GET HER TO THE SOURCE CHAMBER ON NEW GENESIS. I'M SORRY I...
SHE GAVE HER ALL FOR US.
YOU TOO, SCOTT.
GO.
I'LL TAKE OVER FROM HERE.
I'LL TRY TO RETURN AS SOON AS I CAN, WONDER WOMAN.
BOOM!
...OH, HERA, PRESERVE US...
DIANA, IT'S NOT OVER YET.
WE'RE NEEDED.
I KNOW.
EMERGENCY MEETING OF THE JLA.

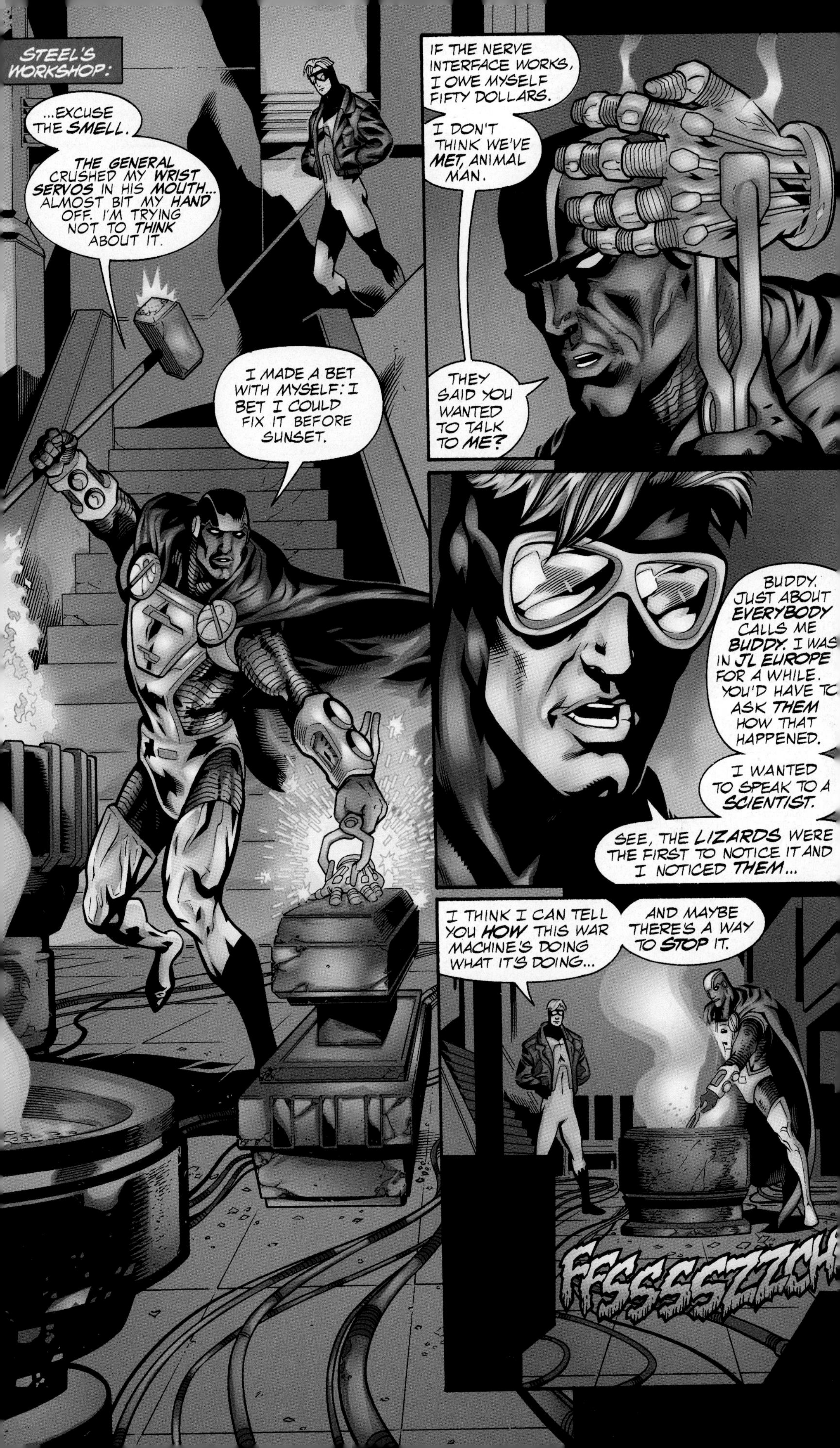
STEEL'S WORKSHOP:
...EXCUSE THE SMELL.
THE GENERAL CRUSHED MY WRIST SERVOS IN HIS MOUTH... ALMOST BIT MY HAND OFF. I'M TRYING NOT TO THINK ABOUT IT.
I MADE A BET WITH MYSELF: I BET I COULD FIX IT BEFORE SUNSET.
THEY SAID YOU WANTED TO TALK TO ME?
IF THE NERVE INTERFACE WORKS, I OWE MYSELF FIFTY DOLLARS.
I DON'T THINK WE'VE MET, ANIMAL MAN.
BUDDY. JUST ABOUT EVERYBODY CALLS ME BUDDY. I WAS IN JL EUROPE FOR A WHILE. YOU'D HAVE TO ASK THEM HOW THAT HAPPENED.
I WANTED TO SPEAK TO A SCIENTIST.
SEE, THE LIZARDS WERE THE FIRST TO NOTICE IT AND I NOTICED THEM...
I THINK I CAN TELL YOU HOW THIS WAR MACHINE'S DOING WHAT IT'S DOING...
AND MAYBE THERE'S A WAY TO STOP IT.
FFSSSSZZCH

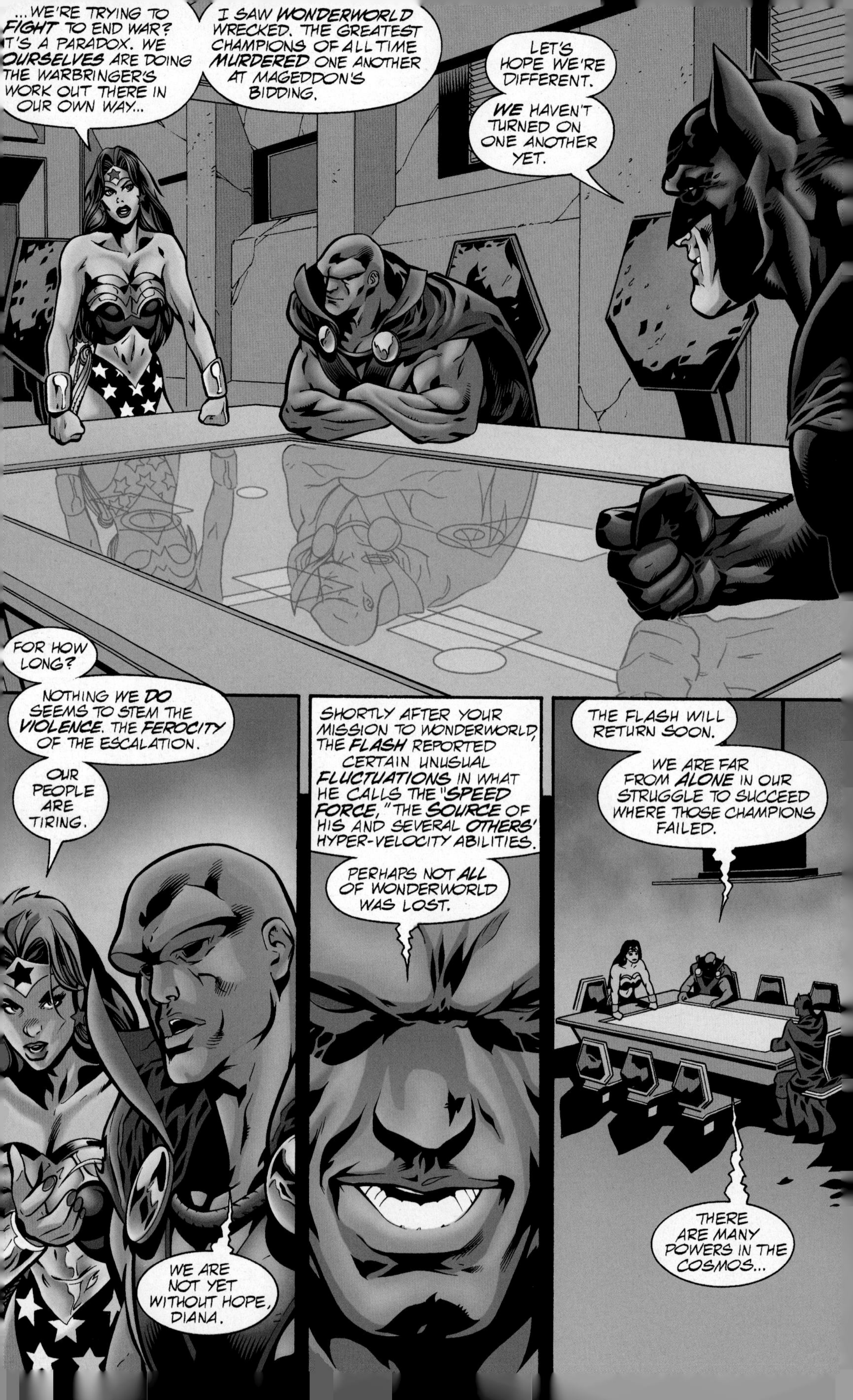
...WE'RE TRYING TO FIGHT TO END WAR? IT'S A PARADOX. WE OURSELVES ARE DOING THE WARBRINGER'S WORK OUT THERE IN OUR OWN WAY...
I SAW WONDERWORLD WRECKED. THE GREATEST CHAMPIONS OF ALL TIME MURDERED ONE ANOTHER AT MAGEDDON'S BIDDING.
LET'S HOPE WE'RE DIFFERENT.
WE HAVEN'T TURNED ON ONE ANOTHER YET.
FOR HOW LONG?
NOTHING WE DO SEEMS TO STEM THE VIOLENCE. THE FEROCITY OF THE ESCALATION.
OUR PEOPLE ARE TIRING.
WE ARE NOT YET WITHOUT HOPE, DIANA.
SHORTLY AFTER YOUR MISSION TO WONDERWORLD, THE FLASH REPORTED CERTAIN UNUSUAL FLUCTUATIONS IN WHAT HE CALLS THE "SPEED FORCE," THE SOURCE OF HIS AND SEVERAL OTHERS' HYPER-VELOCITY ABILITIES.
PERHAPS NOT ALL OF WONDERWORLD WAS LOST.
THE FLASH WILL RETURN SOON.
WE ARE FAR FROM ALONE IN OUR STRUGGLE TO SUCCEED WHERE THOSE CHAMPIONS FAILED.
THERE ARE MANY POWERS IN THE COSMOS...

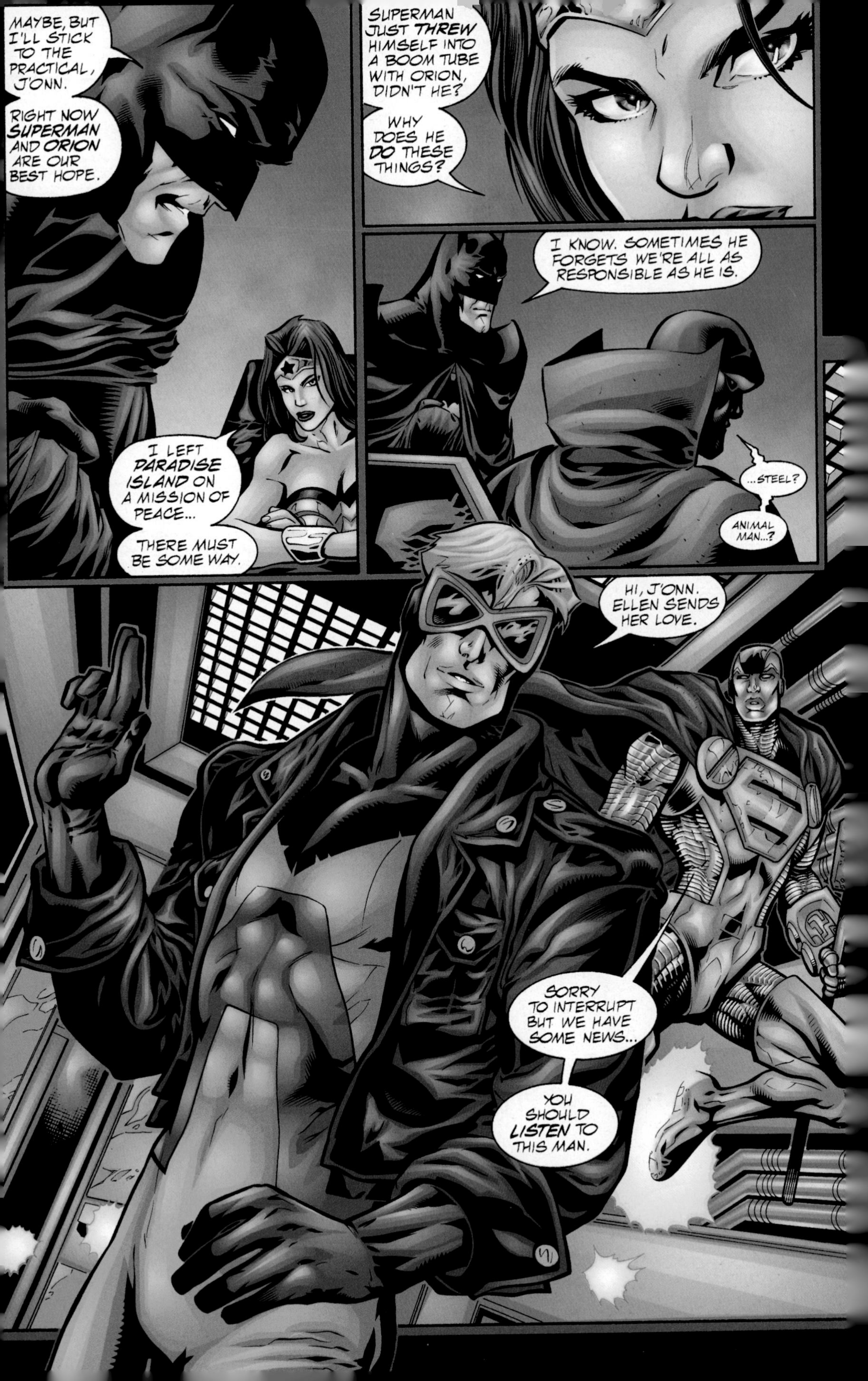
MAYBE, BUT I'LL STICK TO THE PRACTICAL, J'ONN.
RIGHT NOW SUPERMAN AND ORION ARE OUR BEST HOPE.
SUPERMAN JUST THREW HIMSELF INTO A BOOM TUBE WITH ORION, DIDN'T HE?
WHY DOES HE DO THESE THINGS?
I LEFT PARADISE ISLAND ON A MISSION OF PEACE...
THERE MUST BE SOME WAY.
I KNOW. SOMETIMES HE FORGETS WE'RE ALL AS RESPONSIBLE AS HE IS.
...STEEL?
ANIMAL MAN...?
HI, J'ONN. ELLEN SENDS HER LOVE.
SORRY TO INTERRUPT BUT WE HAVE SOME NEWS...
YOU SHOULD LISTEN TO THIS MAN.

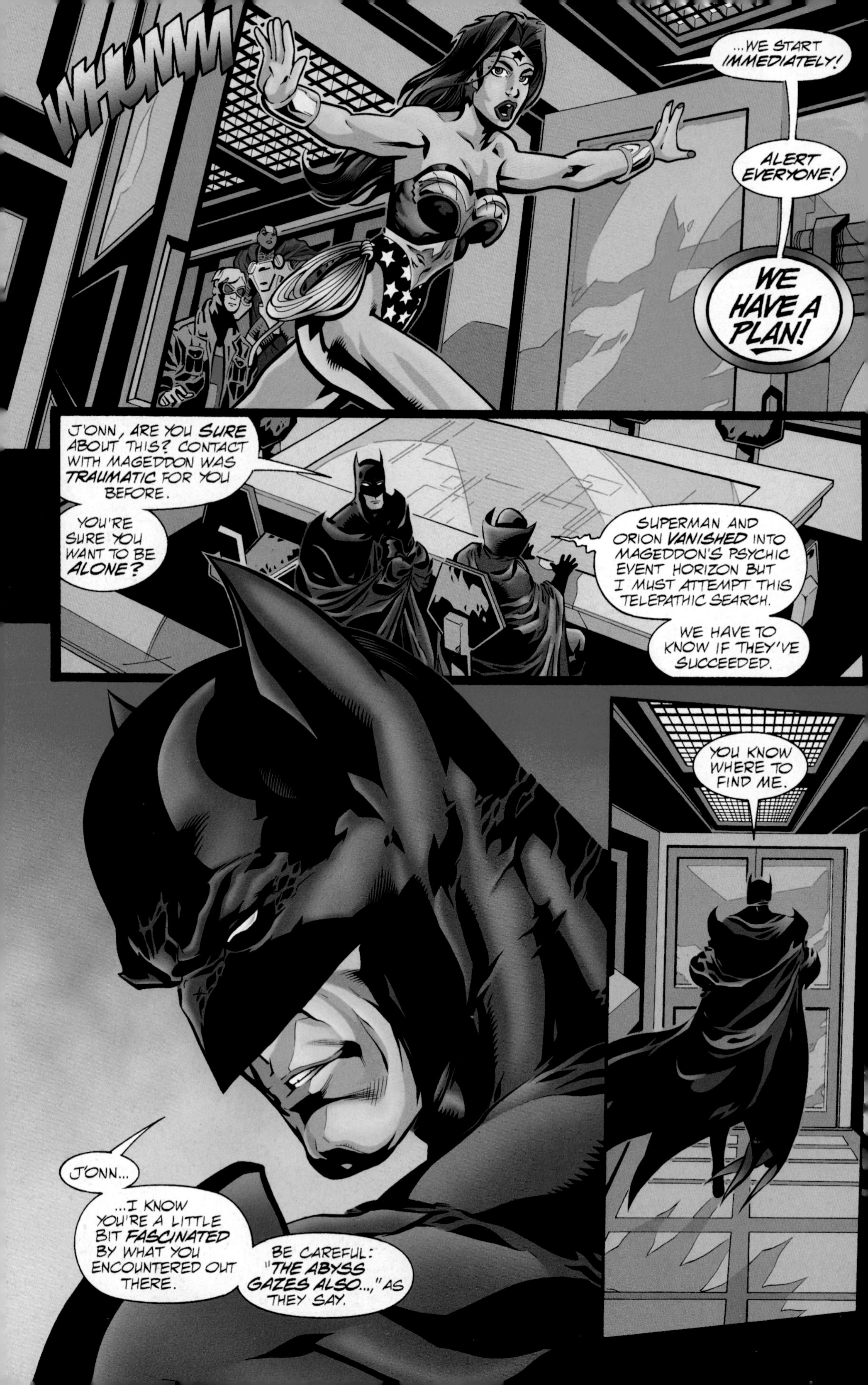
WHUMM
...WE START IMMEDIATELY!
ALERT EVERYONE!
WE HAVE A PLAN!
J'ONN, ARE YOU SURE ABOUT THIS? CONTACT WITH MAGEDDON WAS TRAUMATIC FOR YOU BEFORE.
YOU'RE SURE YOU WANT TO BE ALONE?
SUPERMAN AND ORION VANISHED INTO MAGEDDON'S PSYCHIC EVENT HORIZON BUT I MUST ATTEMPT THIS TELEPATHIC SEARCH.
WE HAVE TO KNOW IF THEY'VE SUCCEEDED.
J'ONN...
...I KNOW YOU'RE A LITTLE BIT FASCINATED BY WHAT YOU ENCOUNTERED OUT THERE.
BE CAREFUL: "THE ABYSS GAZES ALSO...," AS THEY SAY.
YOU KNOW WHERE TO FIND ME.

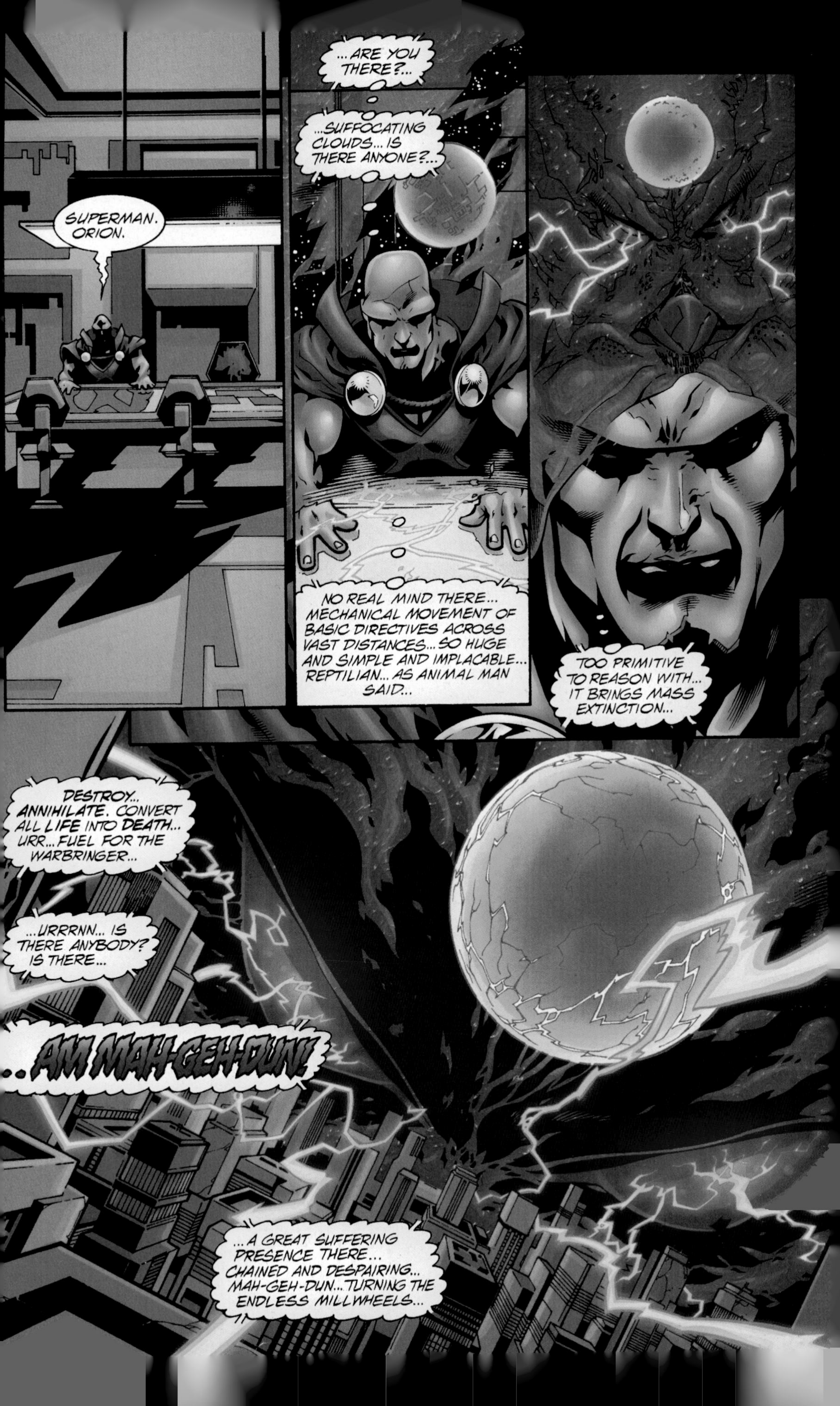
SUPERMAN. ORION.
...ARE YOU THERE?...
...SUFFOCATING CLOUDS... IS THERE ANYONE?...
NO REAL MIND THERE... MECHANICAL MOVEMENT OF BASIC DIRECTIVES ACROSS VAST DISTANCES... SO HUGE AND SIMPLE AND IMPLACABLE... REPTILIAN... AS ANIMAL MAN SAID...
TOO PRIMITIVE TO REASON WITH... IT BRINGS MASS EXTINCTION...
DESTROY... ANNIHILATE. CONVERT ALL LIFE INTO DEATH... URR... FUEL FOR THE WARBRINGER...
...URRRNN... IS THERE ANYBODY? IS THERE...
...AM MAH-GEH-DUN!
...A GREAT SUFFERING PRESENCE THERE... CHAINED AND DESPAIRING... MAH-GEH-DUN... TURNING THE ENDLESS MILLWHEELS...

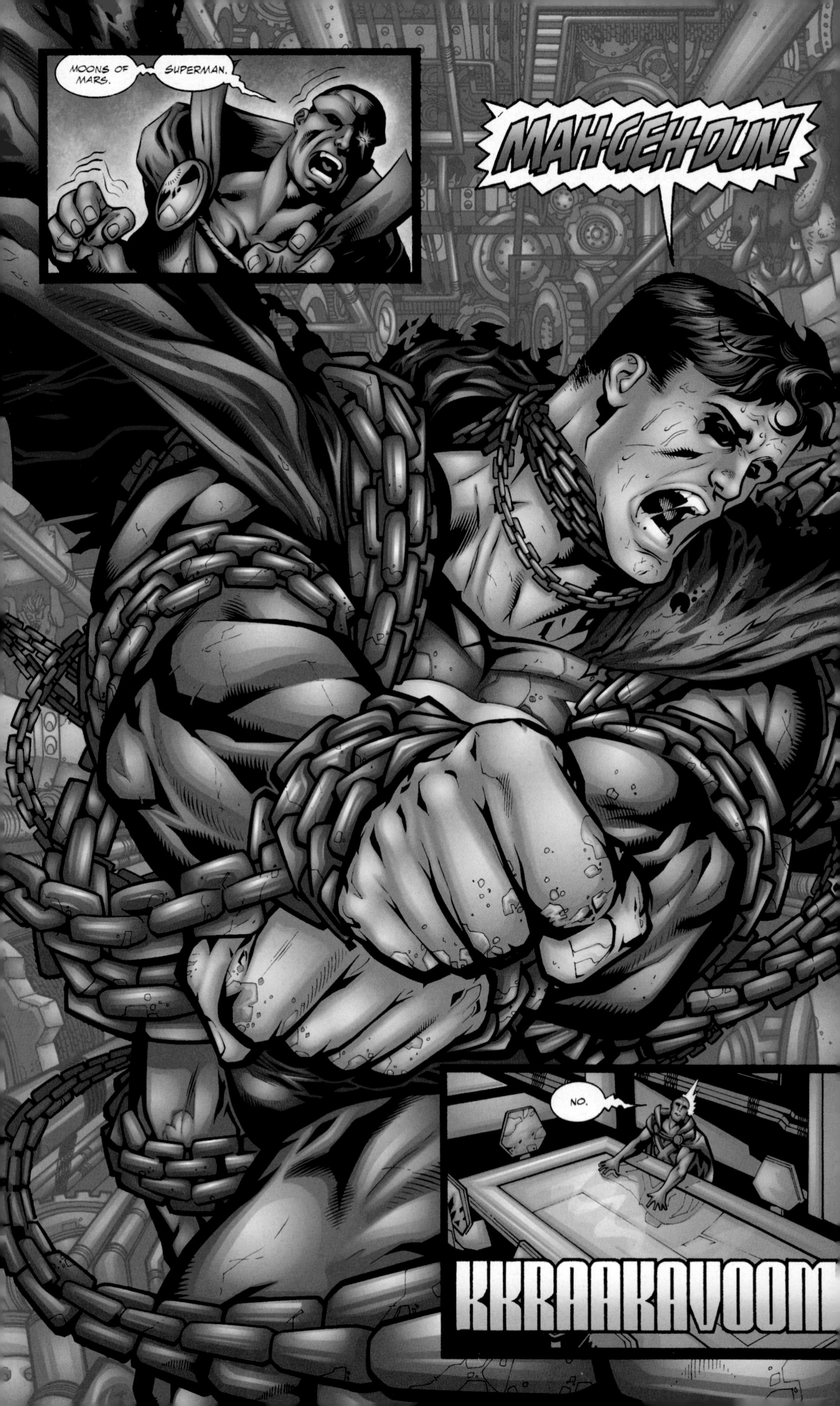
MOONS OF MARS.
SUPERMAN.
MAH-GEH-DUN!
NO.
KKRAAKAVOOM

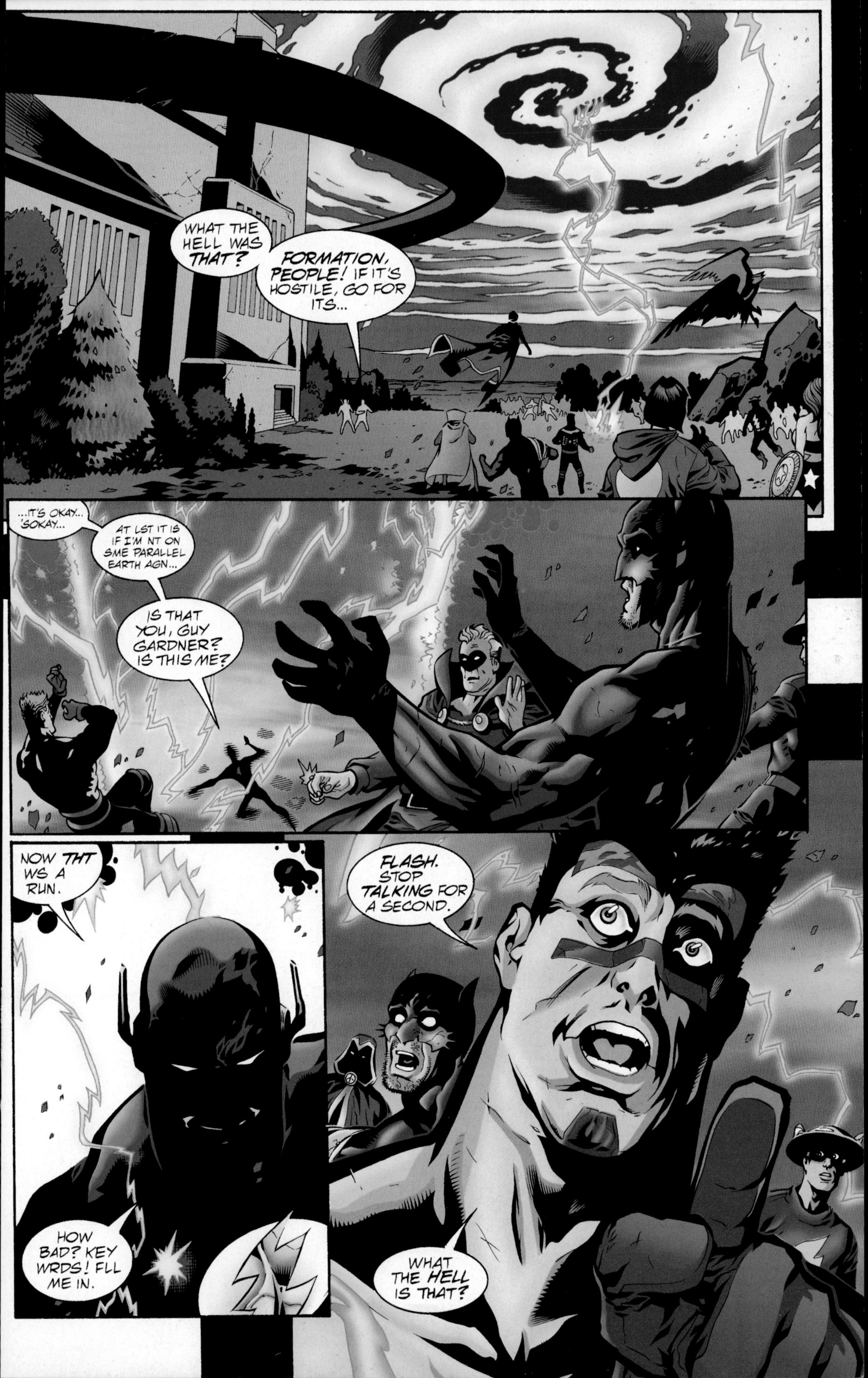

WHAT THE HELL WAS THAT?
FORMATION, PEOPLE! IF IT'S HOSTILE, GO FOR ITS...
...IT'S OKAY... 'SOKAY...
AT LST IT IS IF I'M NT ON SME PARALLEL EARTH AGN...
IS THAT YOU, GUY GARDNER? IS THIS ME?
NOW THT WS A RUN.
FLASH. STOP TALKING FOR A SECOND.
HOW BAD? KEY WRDS! FLL ME IN.
WHAT THE HELL IS THAT?

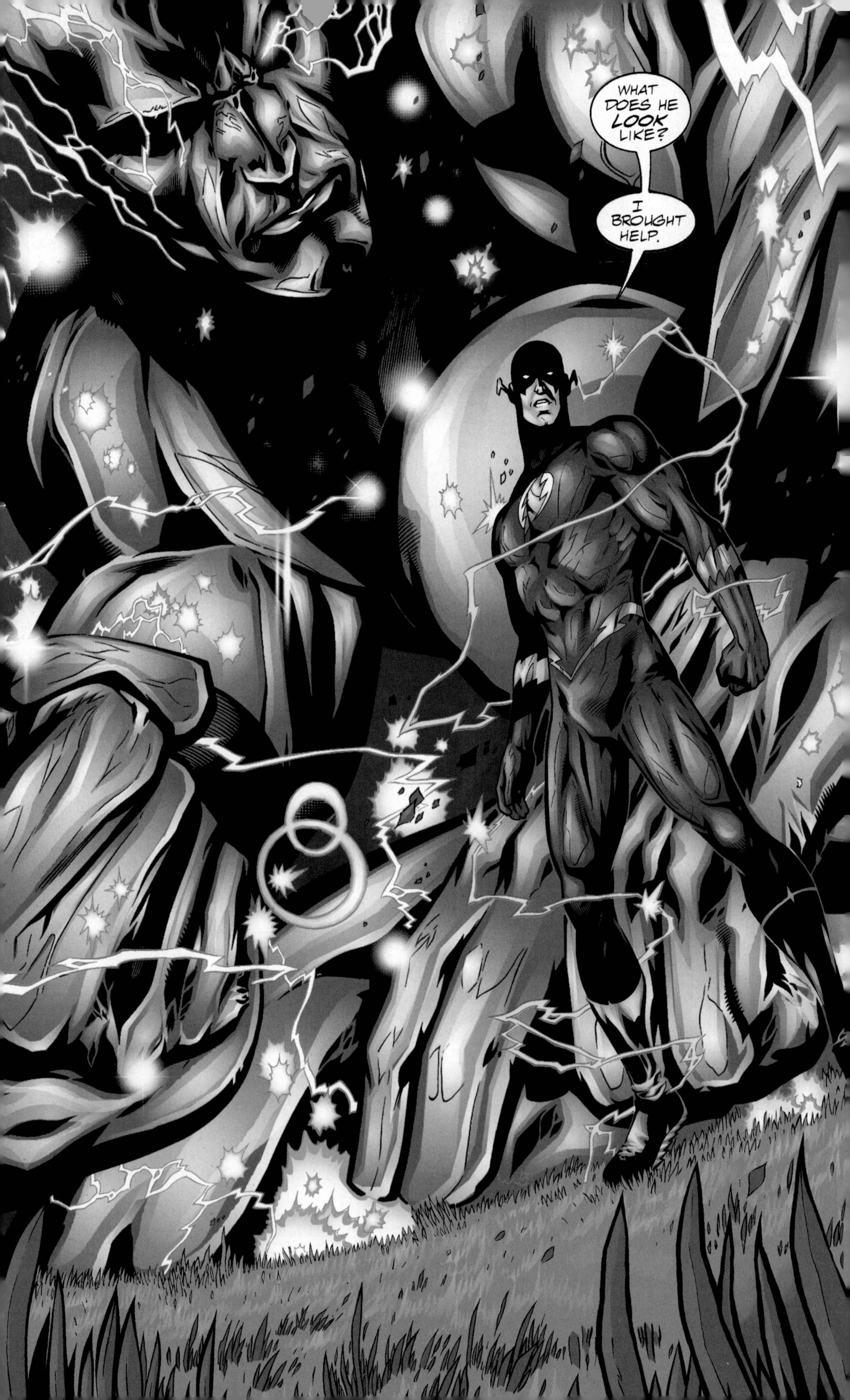
WHAT DOES HE LOOK LIKE?
I BROUGHT HELP.

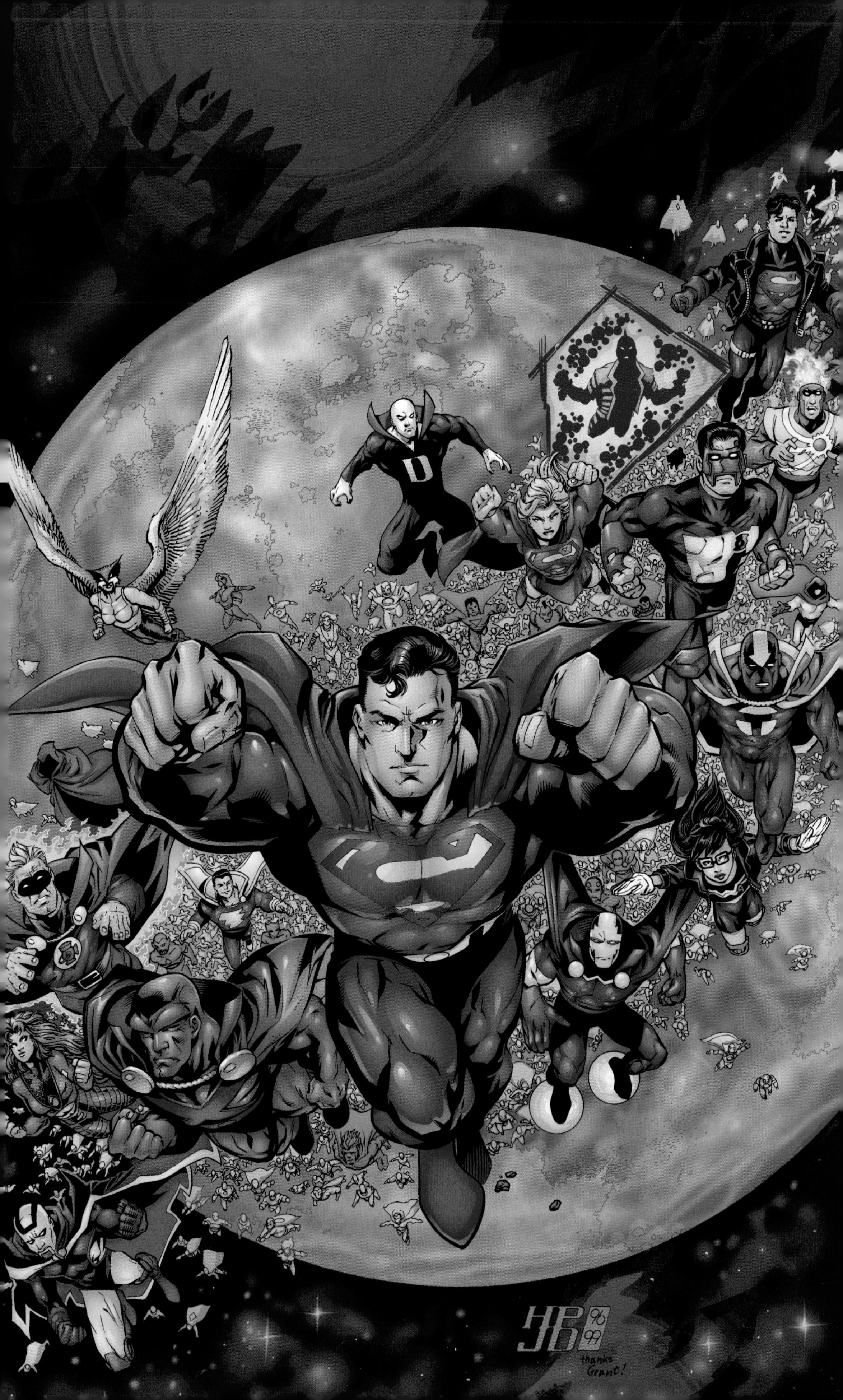
thanks
Grant!

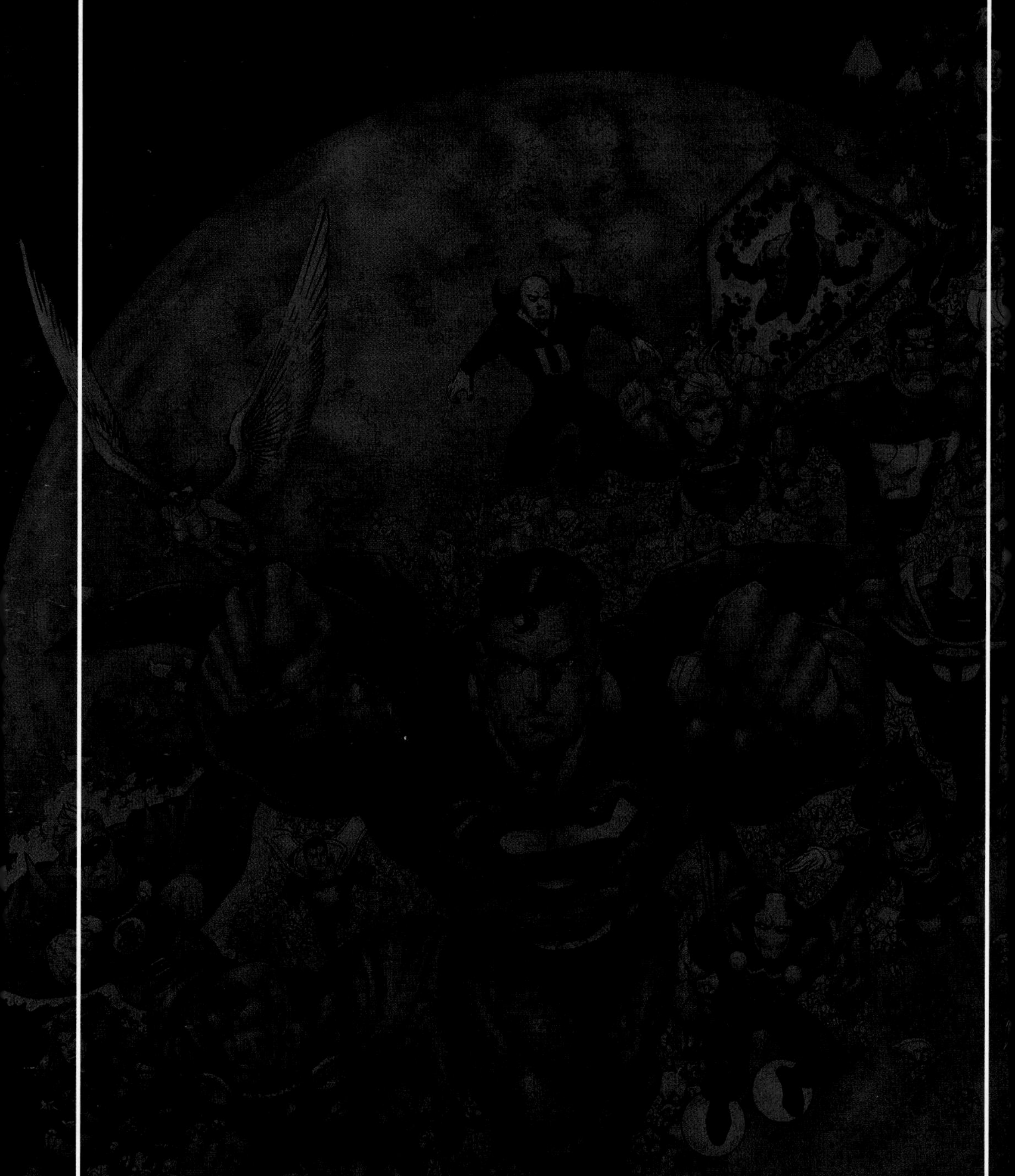

JLA #41

WRITTEN BY GRANT MORRISON

PENCILS BY HOWARD PORTER, WITH INKS BY DREW GERACI AND COLORS BY PAT GARRAHY

COVER BY HOWARD PORTER & JOHN DELL

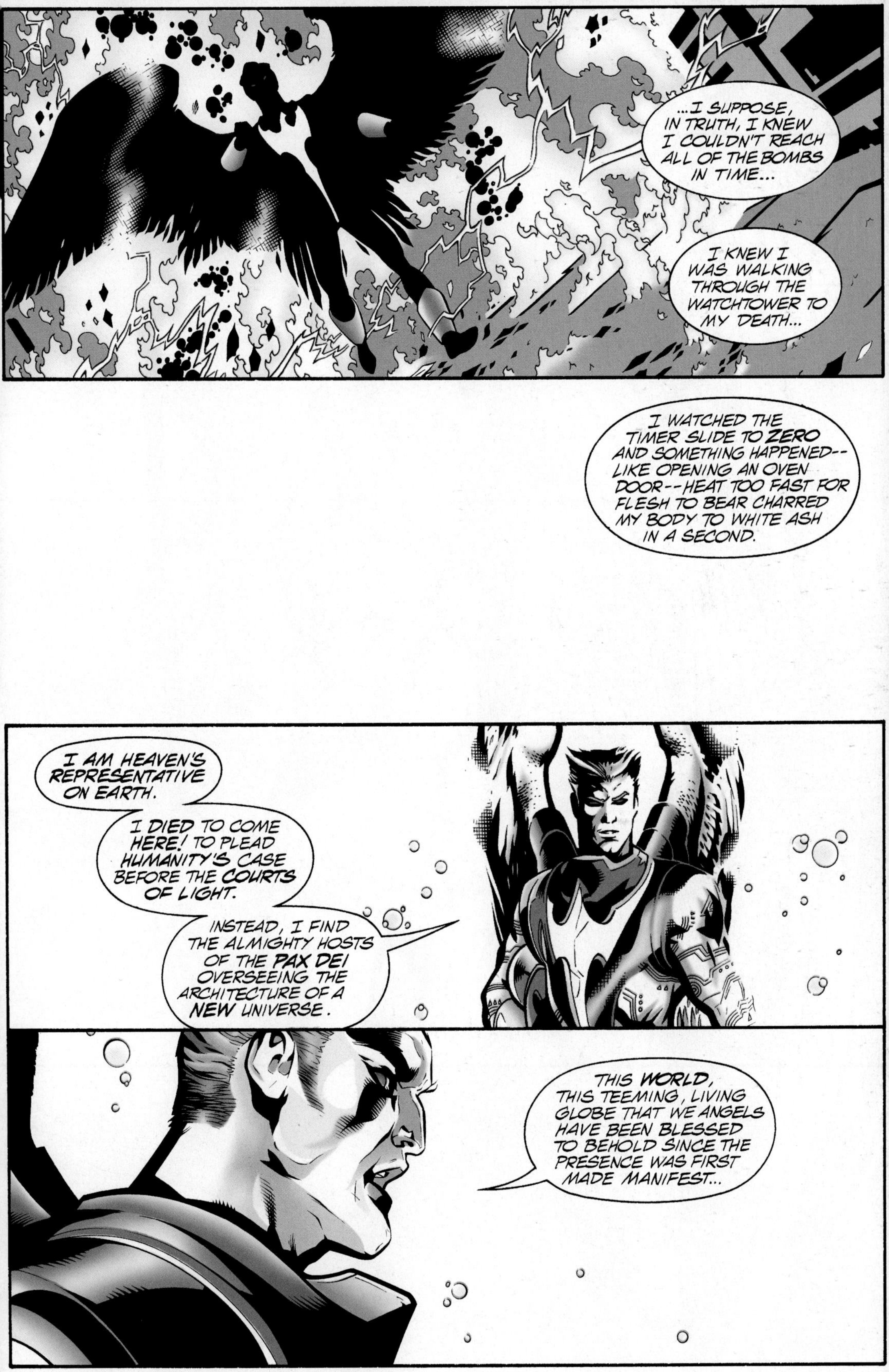
...I SUPPOSE, IN TRUTH, I KNEW I COULDN'T REACH ALL OF THE BOMBS IN TIME...
I KNEW I WAS WALKING THROUGH THE WATCHTOWER TO MY DEATH...
I WATCHED THE TIMER SLIDE TO ZERO AND SOMETHING HAPPENED-- LIKE OPENING AN OVEN DOOR--HEAT TOO FAST FOR FLESH TO BEAR CHARRED MY BODY TO WHITE ASH IN A SECOND.
I AM HEAVEN'S REPRESENTATIVE ON EARTH.
I DIED TO COME HERE! TO PLEAD HUMANITY'S CASE BEFORE THE COURTS OF LIGHT.
INSTEAD, I FIND THE ALMIGHTY HOSTS OF THE PAX DEI OVERSEEING THE ARCHITECTURE OF A NEW UNIVERSE.
THIS WORLD, THIS TEEMING, LIVING GLOBE THAT WE ANGELS HAVE BEEN BLESSED TO BEHOLD SINCE THE PRESENCE WAS FIRST MADE MANIFEST...

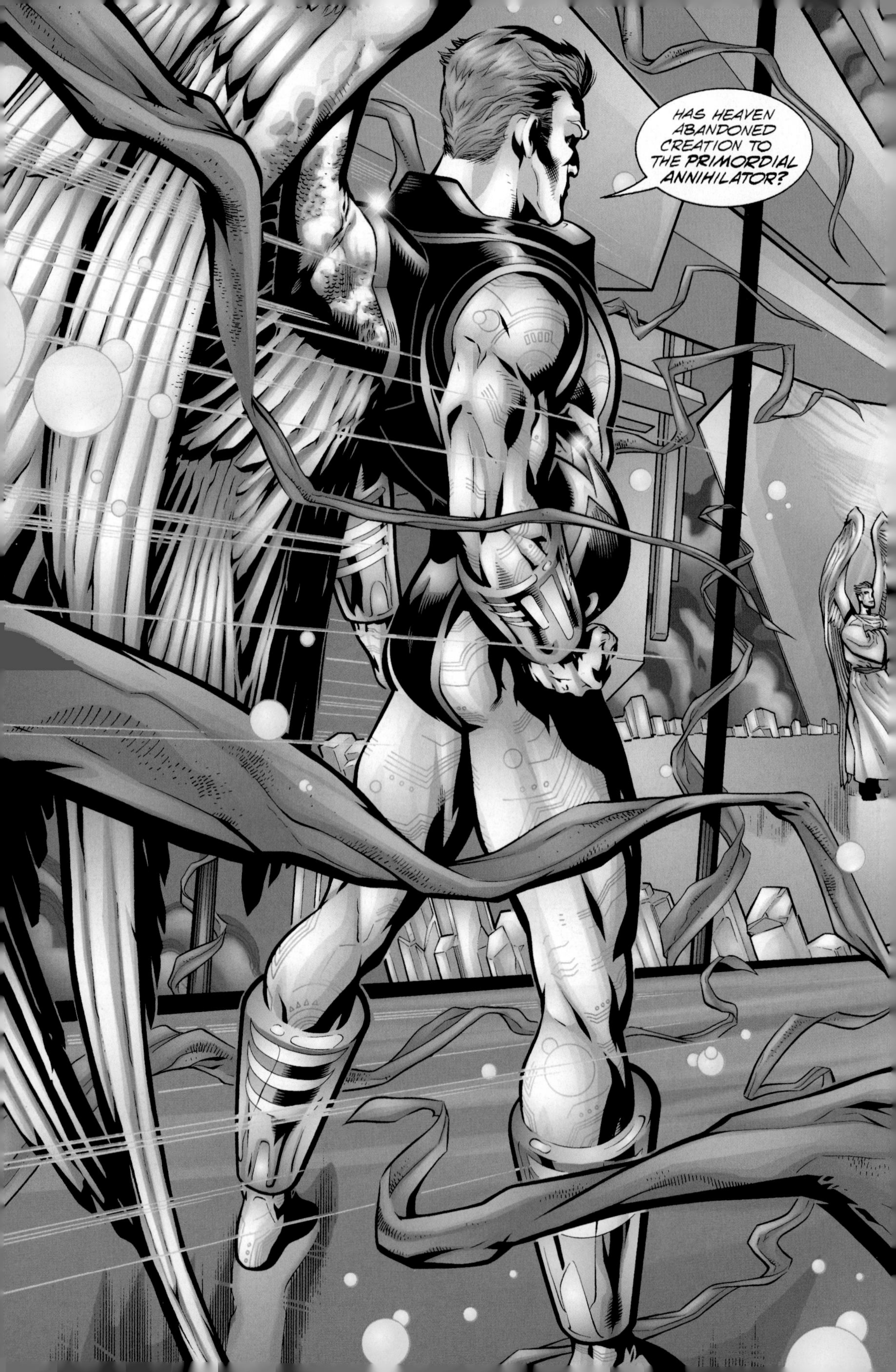
HAS HEAVEN ABANDONED CREATION TO THE PRIMORDIAL ANNIHILATOR?

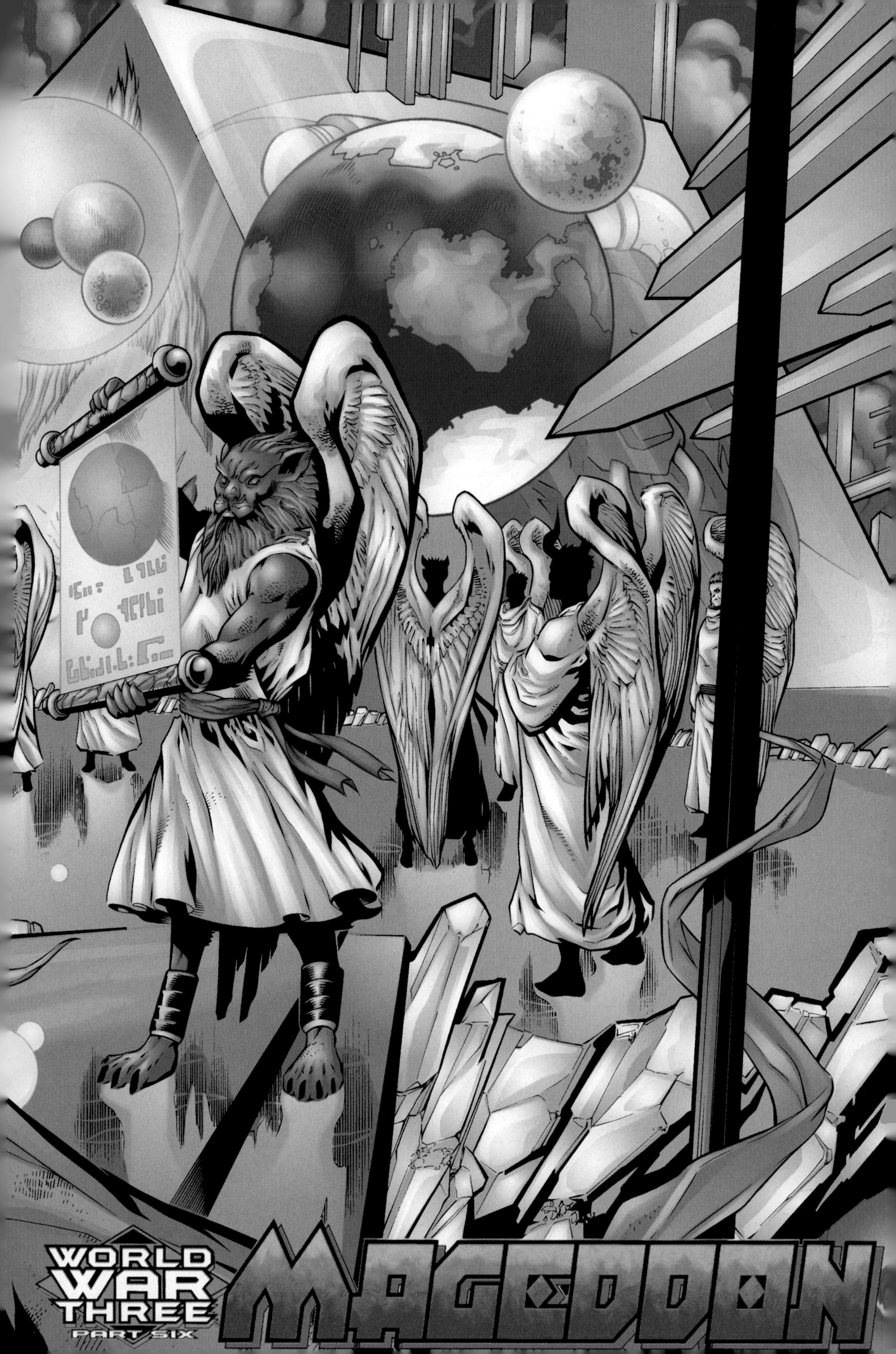
WORLD WAR THREE
PART SIX
MAGEDDON

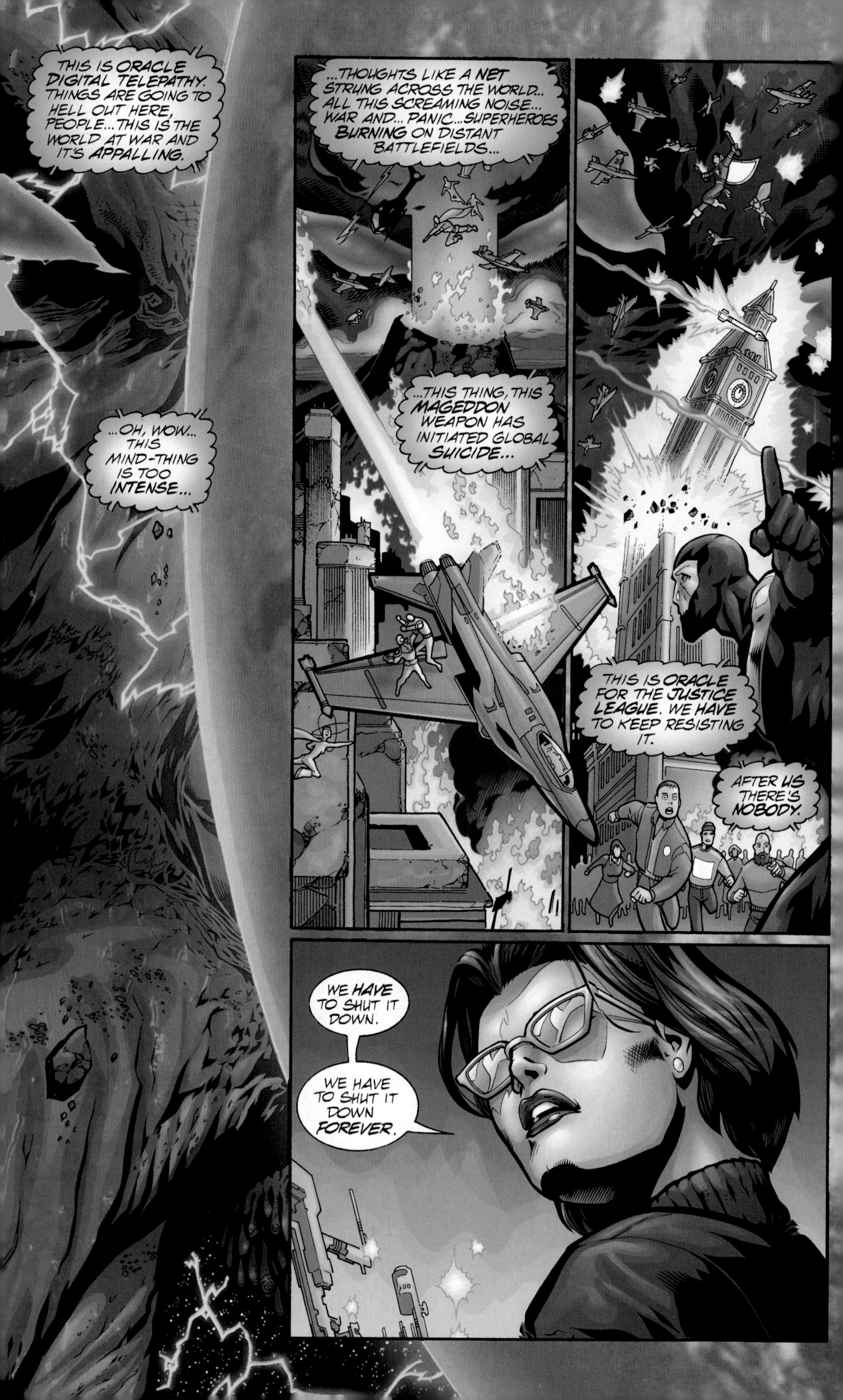
THIS IS ORACLE DIGITAL TELEPATHY. THINGS ARE GOING TO HELL OUT HERE, PEOPLE...THIS IS THE WORLD AT WAR AND IT'S APPALLING.
...OH, WOW... THIS MIND-THING IS TOO INTENSE...
...THOUGHTS LIKE A NET STRUNG ACROSS THE WORLD.. ALL THIS SCREAMING NOISE... WAR AND... PANIC...SUPERHEROES BURNING ON DISTANT BATTLEFIELDS...
...THIS THING, THIS MAGEDDON WEAPON HAS INITIATED GLOBAL SUICIDE...
THIS IS ORACLE FOR THE JUSTICE LEAGUE. WE HAVE TO KEEP RESISTING IT.
AFTER US THERE'S NOBODY.
WE HAVE TO SHUT IT DOWN.
WE HAVE TO SHUT IT DOWN FOREVER.

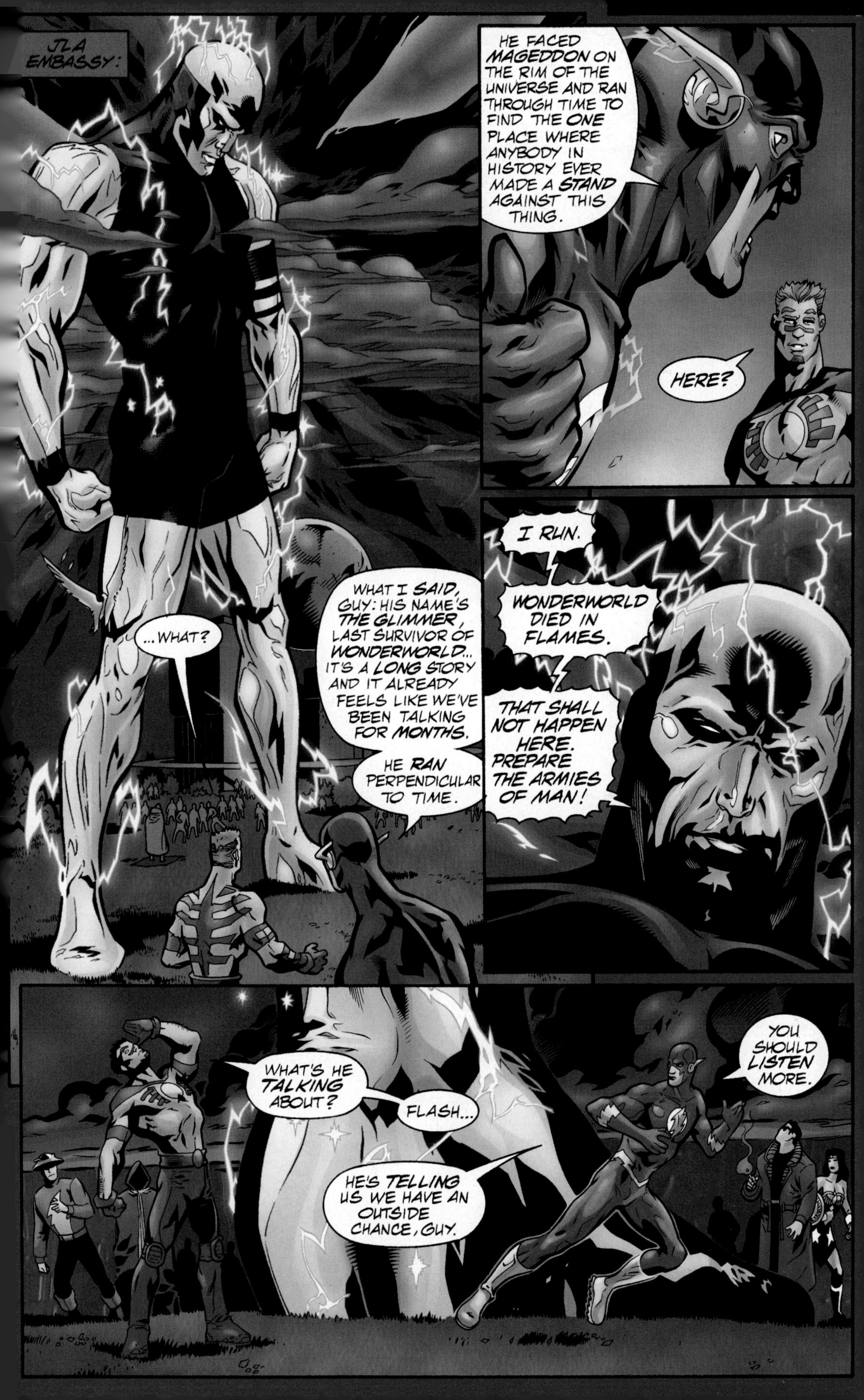
JLA EMBASSY:
HE FACED MAGEDDON ON THE RIM OF THE UNIVERSE AND RAN THROUGH TIME TO FIND THE ONE PLACE WHERE ANYBODY IN HISTORY EVER MADE A STAND AGAINST THIS THING.
HERE?
...WHAT?
WHAT I SAID, GUY: HIS NAME'S THE GLIMMER, LAST SURVIVOR OF WONDERWORLD... IT'S A LONG STORY AND IT ALREADY FEELS LIKE WE'VE BEEN TALKING FOR MONTHS.
HE RAN PERPENDICULAR TO TIME.
I RUN.
WONDERWORLD DIED IN FLAMES.
THAT SHALL NOT HAPPEN HERE. PREPARE THE ARMIES OF MAN!
WHAT'S HE TALKING ABOUT?
FLASH...
HE'S TELLING US WE HAVE AN OUTSIDE CHANCE, GUY.
YOU SHOULD LISTEN MORE.

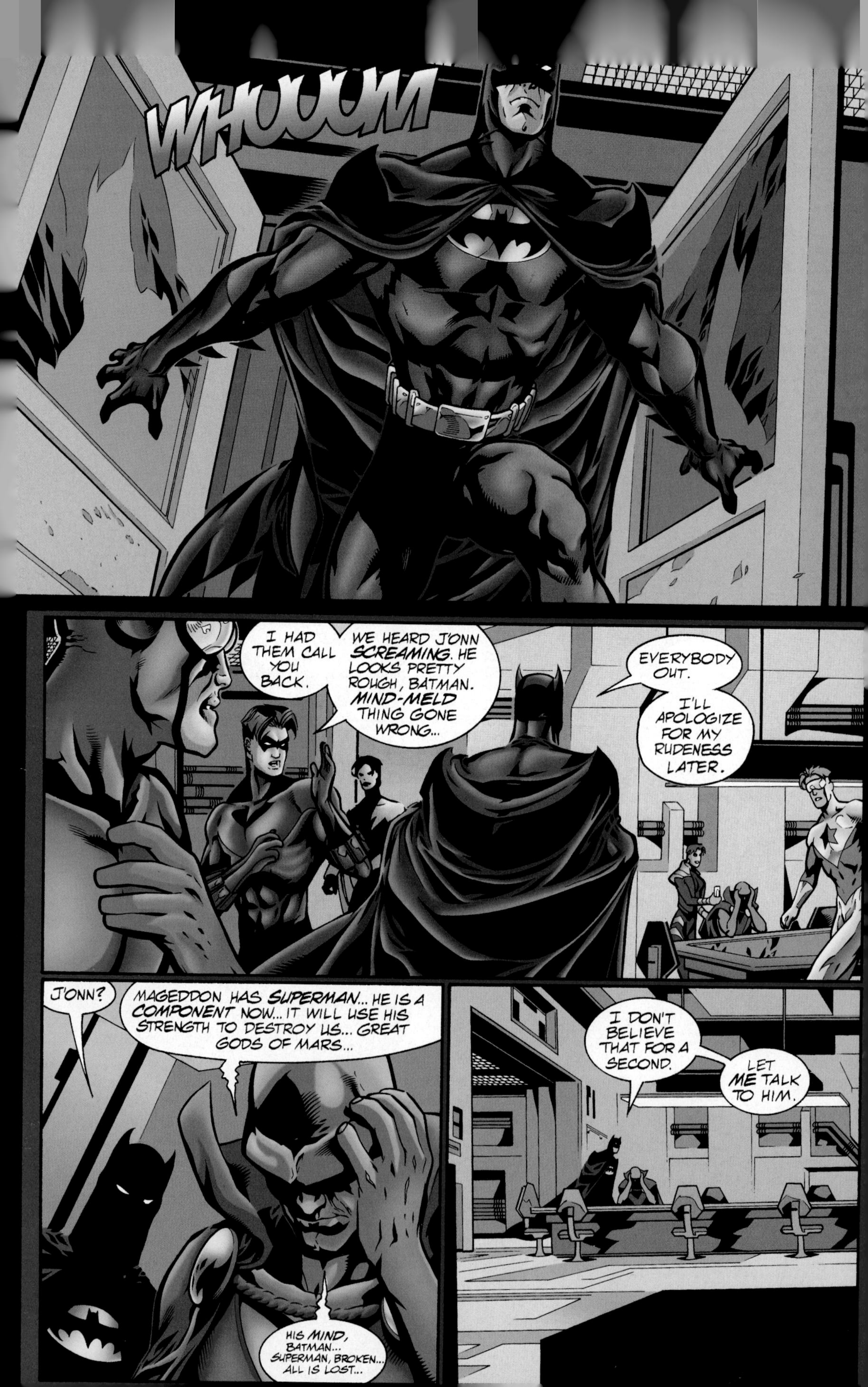
WHOOOM
I HAD THEM CALL YOU BACK.
WE HEARD J'ONN SCREAMING. HE LOOKS PRETTY ROUGH, BATMAN. MIND-MELD THING GONE WRONG...
EVERYBODY OUT.
I'LL APOLOGIZE FOR MY RUDENESS LATER.
J'ONN?
MAGEDDON HAS SUPERMAN... HE IS A COMPONENT NOW... IT WILL USE HIS STRENGTH TO DESTROY US... GREAT GODS OF MARS...
HIS MIND, BATMAN... SUPERMAN, BROKEN... ALL IS LOST...
I DON'T BELIEVE THAT FOR A SECOND.
LET ME TALK TO HIM.

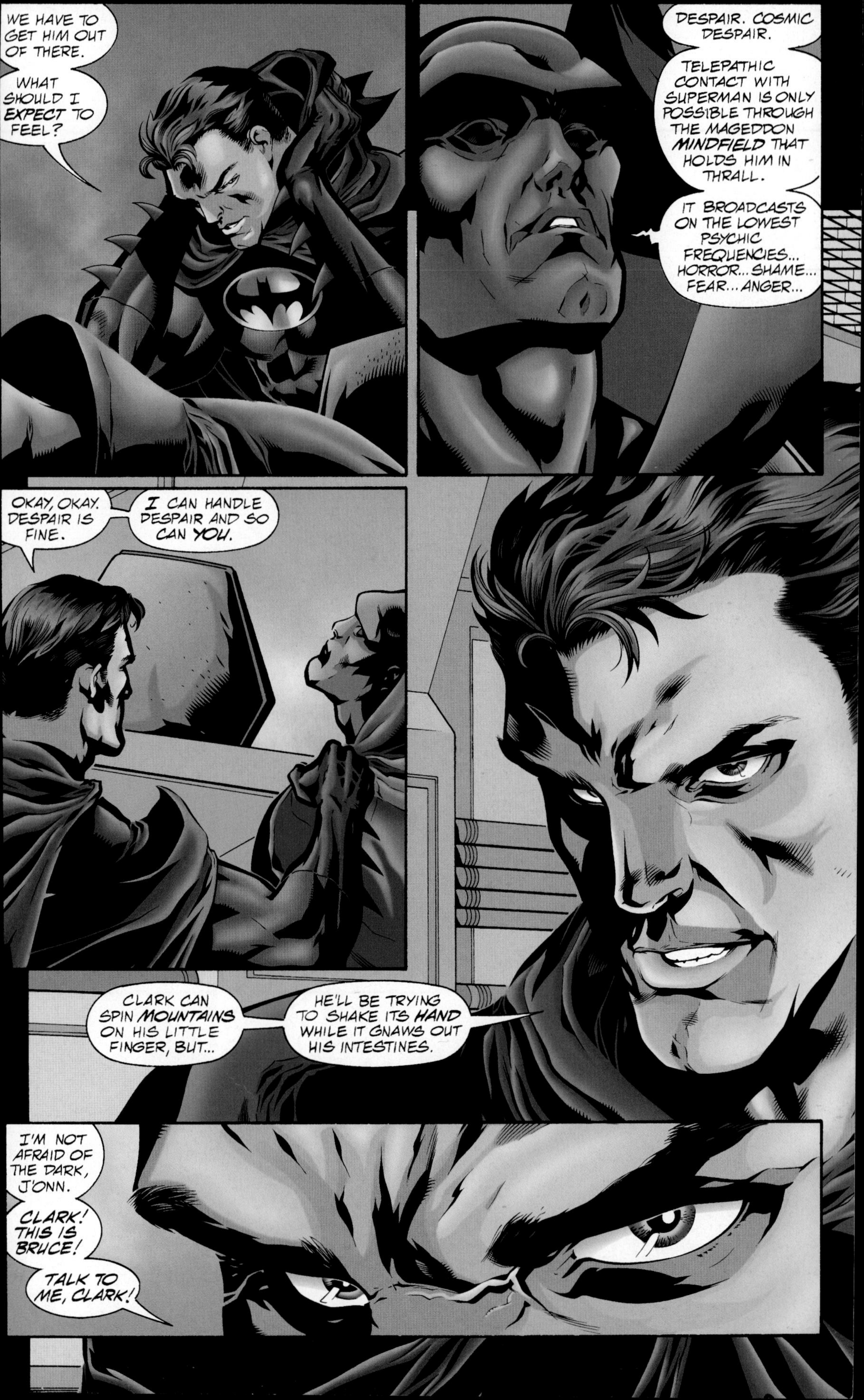

WE HAVE TO GET HIM OUT OF THERE.
WHAT SHOULD I EXPECT TO FEEL?
DESPAIR. COSMIC DESPAIR.
TELEPATHIC CONTACT WITH SUPERMAN IS ONLY POSSIBLE THROUGH THE MAGEDDON MINDFIELD THAT HOLDS HIM IN THRALL.
IT BROADCASTS ON THE LOWEST PSYCHIC FREQUENCIES... HORROR... SHAME... FEAR... ANGER...
OKAY, OKAY. DESPAIR IS FINE.
I CAN HANDLE DESPAIR AND SO CAN YOU.
CLARK CAN SPIN MOUNTAINS ON HIS LITTLE FINGER, BUT...
HE'LL BE TRYING TO SHAKE ITS HAND WHILE IT GNAWS OUT HIS INTESTINES.
I'M NOT AFRAID OF THE DARK, J'ONN.
CLARK! THIS IS BRUCE!
TALK TO ME, CLARK!

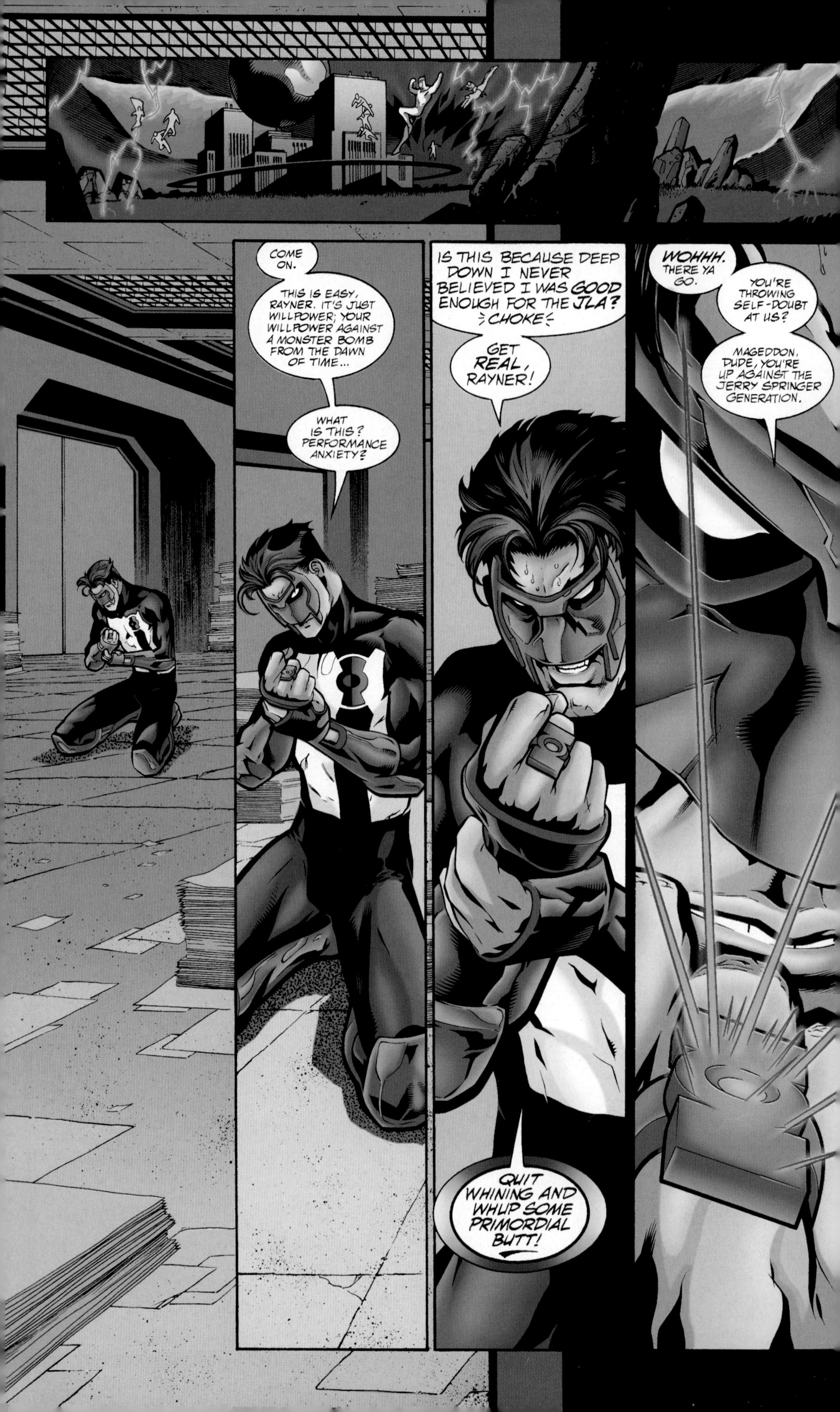
COME ON.
THIS IS EASY, RAYNER. IT'S JUST WILLPOWER; YOUR WILLPOWER AGAINST A MONSTER BOMB FROM THE DAWN OF TIME...
WHAT IS THIS? PERFORMANCE ANXIETY?
IS THIS BECAUSE DEEP DOWN I NEVER BELIEVED I WAS GOOD ENOUGH FOR THE JLA? CHOKE
GET REAL, RAYNER!
QUIT WHINING AND WHUP SOME PRIMORDIAL BUTT!
WOHHH. THERE YA GO.
YOU'RE THROWING SELF-DOUBT AT US?
MAGEDDON, DUDE, YOU'RE UP AGAINST THE JERRY SPRINGER GENERATION.

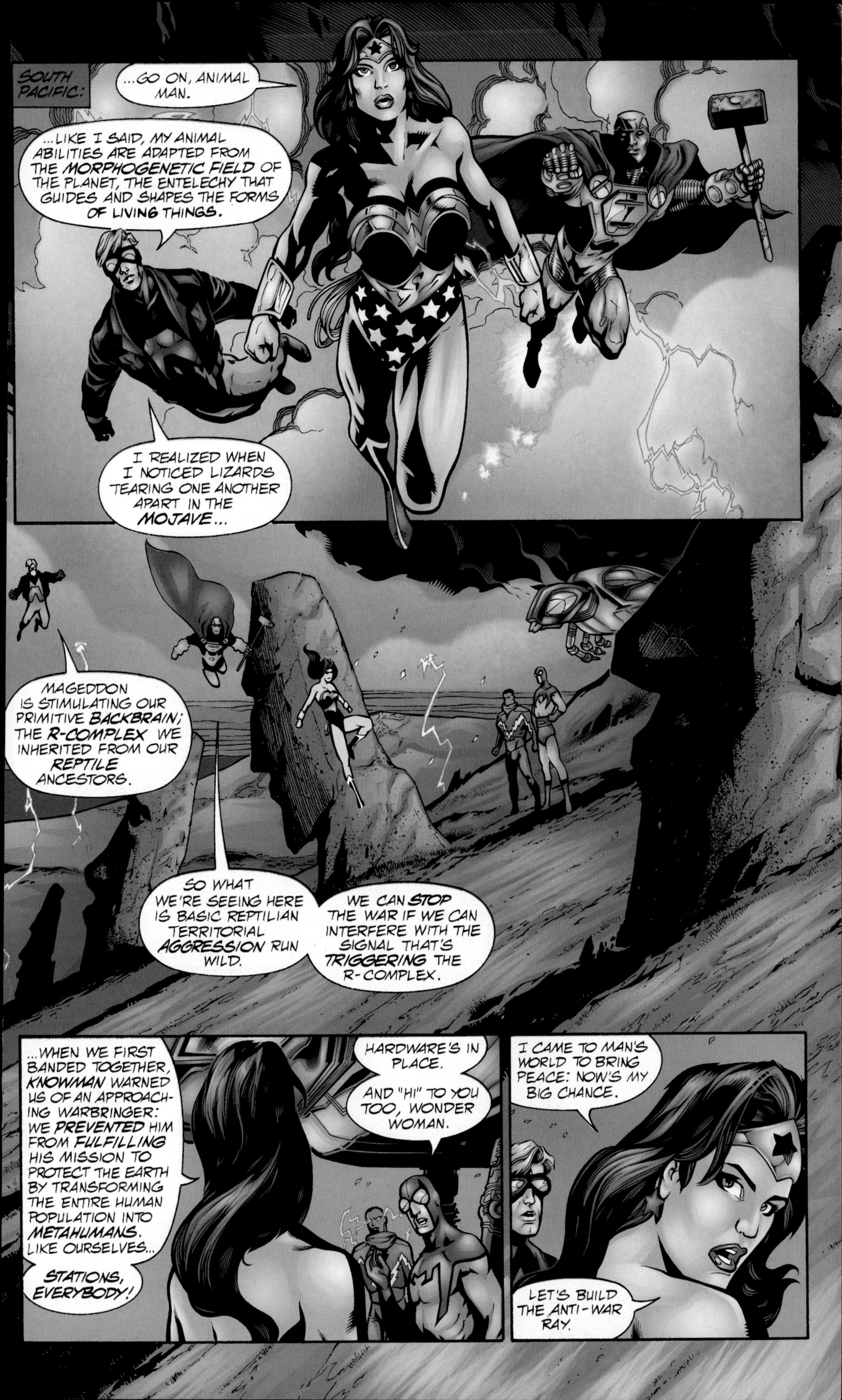
SOUTH PACIFIC:
...GO ON, ANIMAL MAN.
...LIKE I SAID, MY ANIMAL ABILITIES ARE ADAPTED FROM THE MORPHOGENETIC FIELD OF THE PLANET, THE ENTELECHY THAT GUIDES AND SHAPES THE FORMS OF LIVING THINGS.
I REALIZED WHEN I NOTICED LIZARDS TEARING ONE ANOTHER APART IN THE MOJAVE...
MAGEDDON IS STIMULATING OUR PRIMITIVE BACKBRAIN; THE R-COMPLEX WE INHERITED FROM OUR REPTILE ANCESTORS.
SO WHAT WE'RE SEEING HERE IS BASIC REPTILIAN TERRITORIAL AGGRESSION RUN WILD.
WE CAN STOP THE WAR IF WE CAN INTERFERE WITH THE SIGNAL THAT'S TRIGGERING THE R-COMPLEX.
...WHEN WE FIRST BANDED TOGETHER, KNOWMAN WARNED US OF AN APPROACHING WARBRINGER: WE PREVENTED HIM FROM FULFILLING HIS MISSION TO PROTECT THE EARTH BY TRANSFORMING THE ENTIRE HUMAN POPULATION INTO METAHUMANS. LIKE OURSELVES...
STATIONS, EVERYBODY!
HARDWARE'S IN PLACE.
AND "HI" TO YOU TOO, WONDER WOMAN.
I CAME TO MAN'S WORLD TO BRING PEACE: NOW'S MY BIG CHANCE.
LET'S BUILD THE ANTI-WAR RAY.

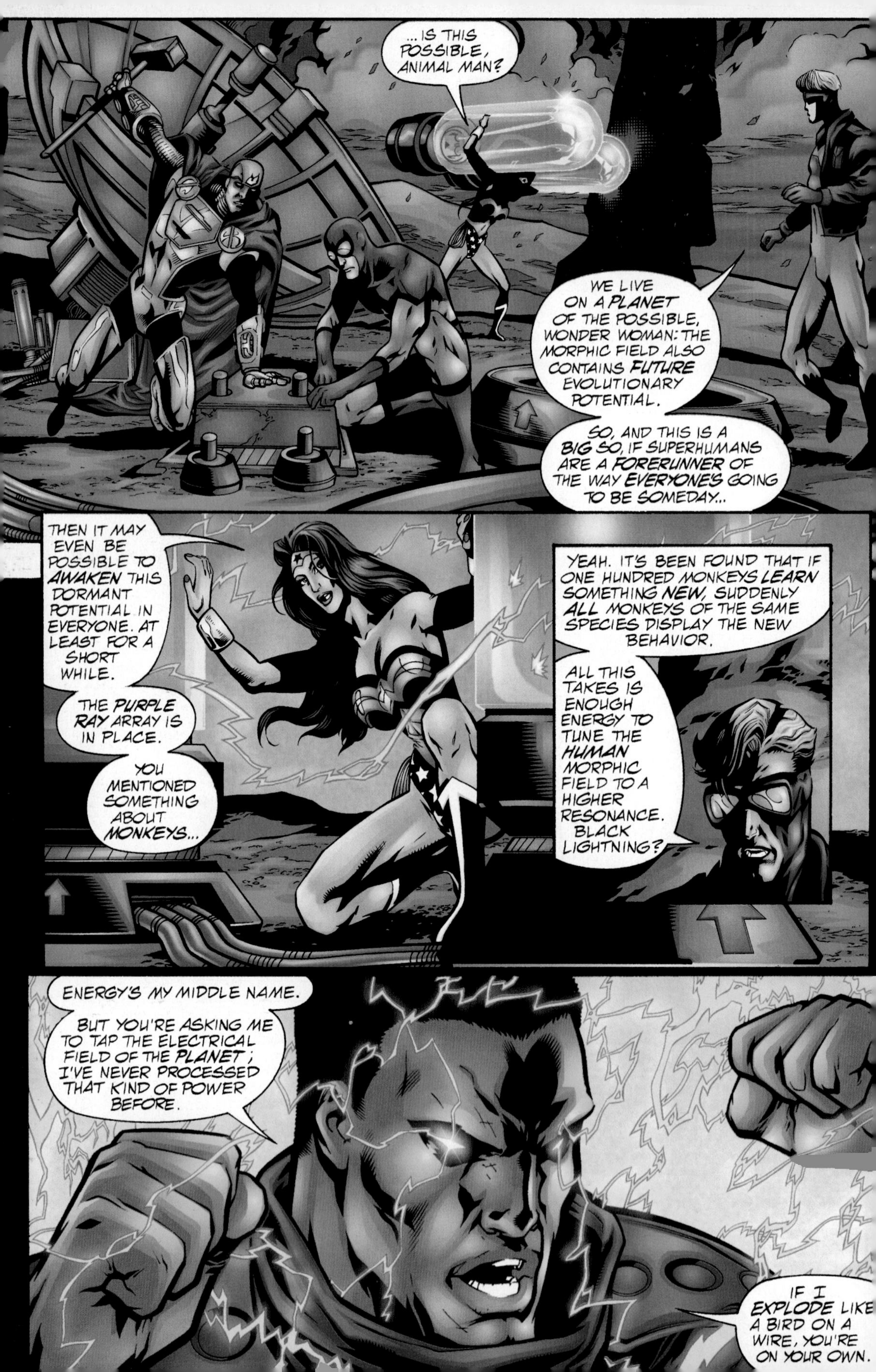

...IS THIS POSSIBLE, ANIMAL MAN?
WE LIVE ON A PLANET OF THE POSSIBLE, WONDER WOMAN: THE MORPHIC FIELD ALSO CONTAINS FUTURE EVOLUTIONARY POTENTIAL.
SO, AND THIS IS A BIG SO, IF SUPERHUMANS ARE A FORERUNNER OF THE WAY EVERYONE'S GOING TO BE SOMEDAY...
THEN IT MAY EVEN BE POSSIBLE TO AWAKEN THIS DORMANT POTENTIAL IN EVERYONE. AT LEAST FOR A SHORT WHILE.
THE PURPLE RAY ARRAY IS IN PLACE.
YOU MENTIONED SOMETHING ABOUT MONKEYS...
YEAH. IT'S BEEN FOUND THAT IF ONE HUNDRED MONKEYS LEARN SOMETHING NEW, SUDDENLY ALL MONKEYS OF THE SAME SPECIES DISPLAY THE NEW BEHAVIOR.
ALL THIS TAKES IS ENOUGH ENERGY TO TUNE THE HUMAN MORPHIC FIELD TO A HIGHER RESONANCE. BLACK LIGHTNING?
ENERGY'S MY MIDDLE NAME.
BUT YOU'RE ASKING ME TO TAP THE ELECTRICAL FIELD OF THE PLANET; I'VE NEVER PROCESSED THAT KIND OF POWER BEFORE.
IF I EXPLODE LIKE A BIRD ON A WIRE, YOU'RE ON YOUR OWN.

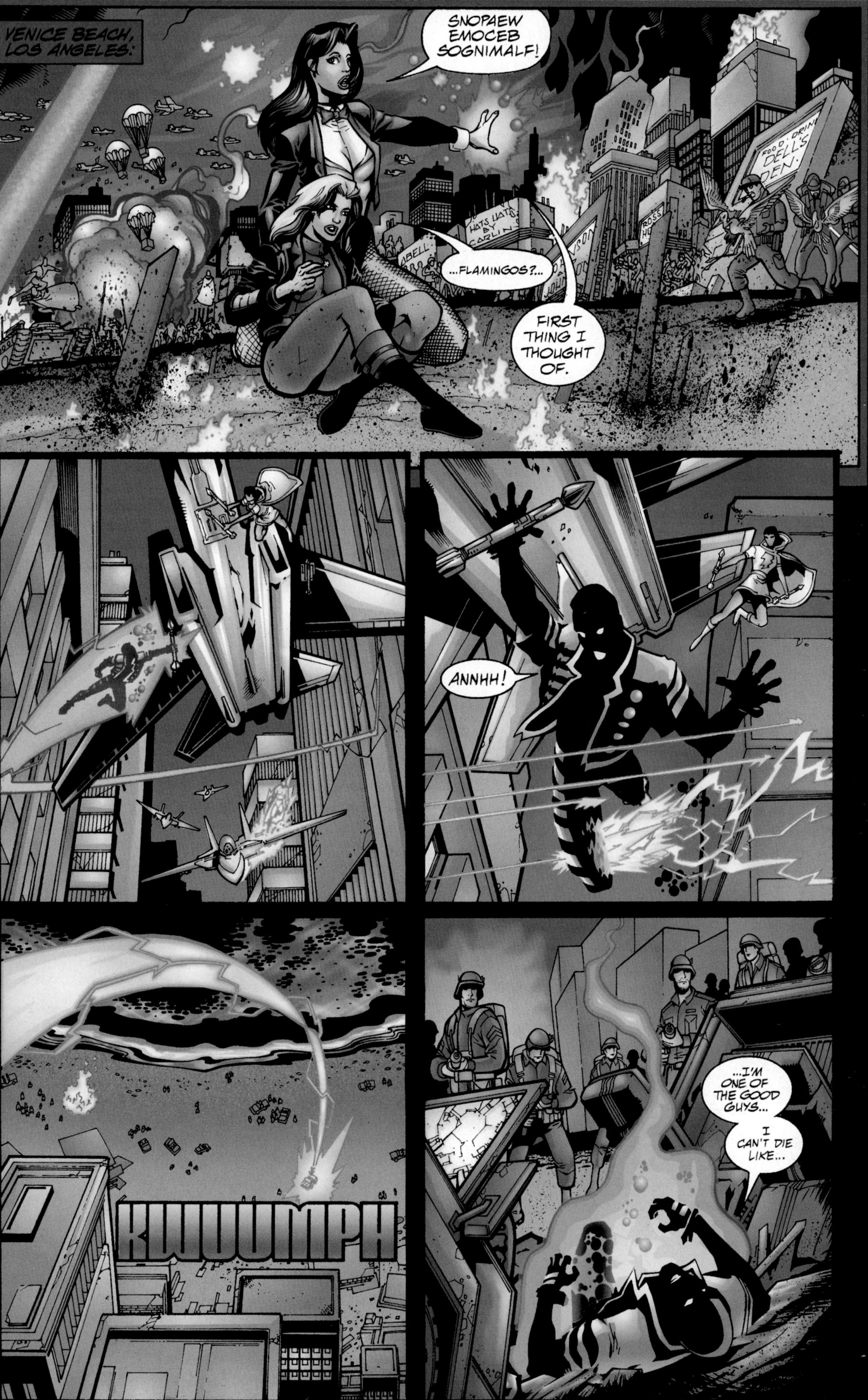

VENICE BEACH, LOS ANGELES:
SNOPAEW EMOCEB SOGNIMALF!
...FLAMINGOS?...
FIRST THING I THOUGHT OF.
FOOD · DRINK DELL'S DEN
HATS HATS BY CARLIN
ANNHH!
KWUUUMPH
...I'M ONE OF THE GOOD GUYS...
I CAN'T DIE LIKE...

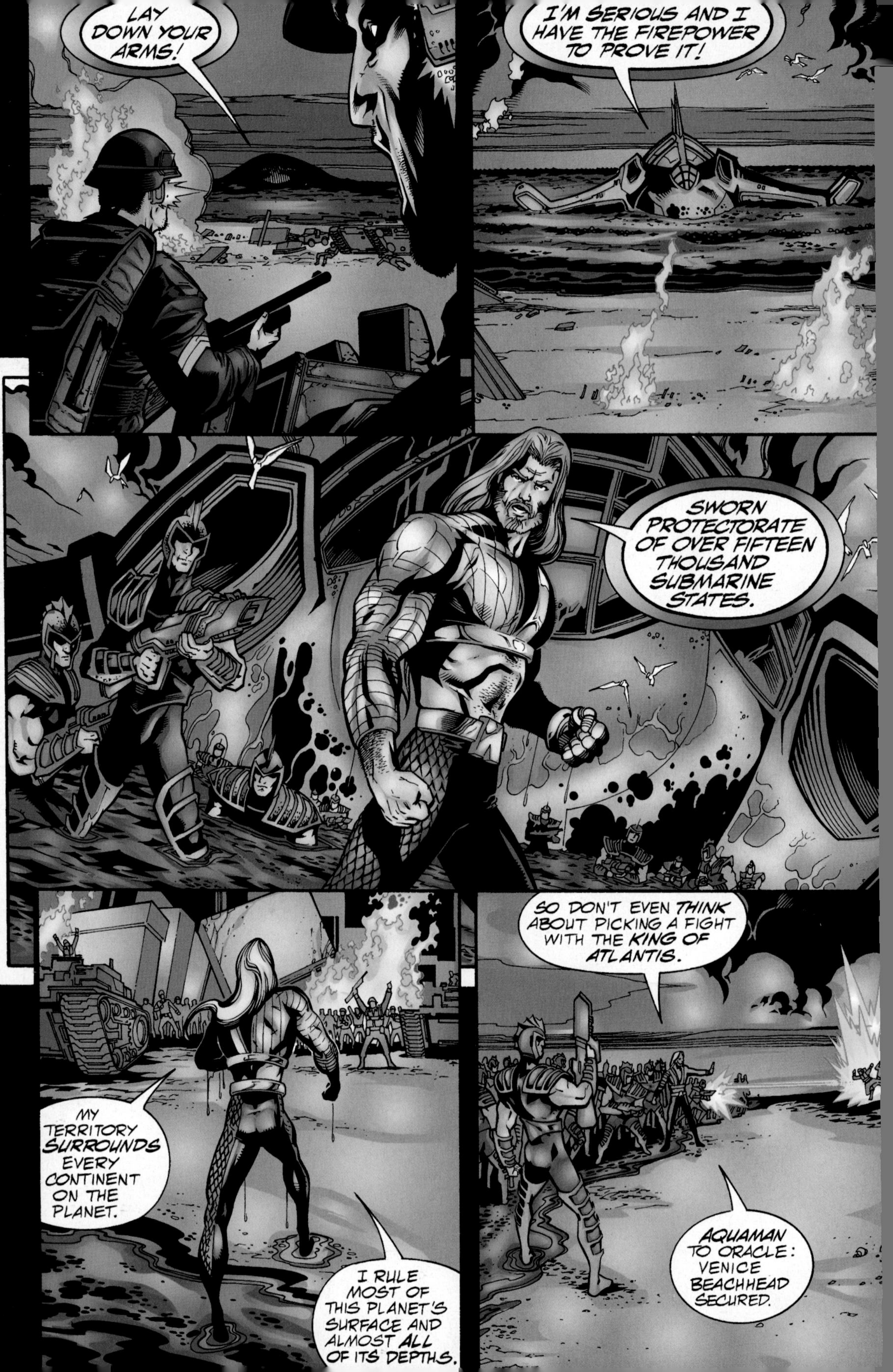
LAY DOWN YOUR ARMS!
I'M SERIOUS AND I HAVE THE FIREPOWER TO PROVE IT!
SWORN PROTECTORATE OF OVER FIFTEEN THOUSAND SUBMARINE STATES.
MY TERRITORY SURROUNDS EVERY CONTINENT ON THE PLANET.
I RULE MOST OF THIS PLANET'S SURFACE AND ALMOST ALL OF ITS DEPTHS.
SO DON'T EVEN THINK ABOUT PICKING A FIGHT WITH THE KING OF ATLANTIS.
AQUAMAN TO ORACLE: VENICE BEACHHEAD SECURED.

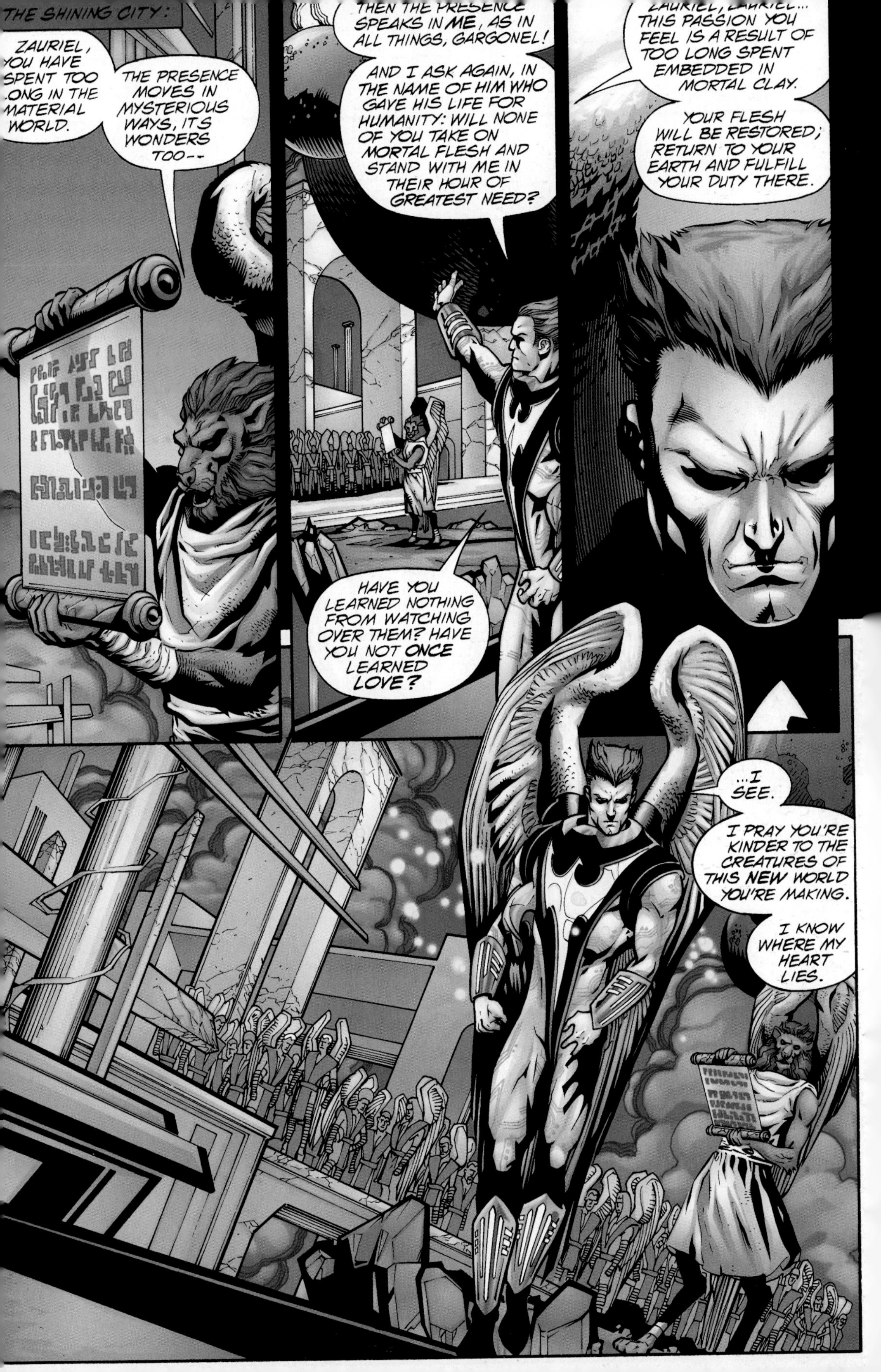
THE SHINING CITY:
ZAURIEL, YOU HAVE SPENT TOO LONG IN THE MATERIAL WORLD.
THE PRESENCE MOVES IN MYSTERIOUS WAYS, ITS WONDERS TOO--
THEN THE PRESENCE SPEAKS IN ME, AS IN ALL THINGS, GARGONEL!
AND I ASK AGAIN, IN THE NAME OF HIM WHO GAVE HIS LIFE FOR HUMANITY: WILL NONE OF YOU TAKE ON MORTAL FLESH AND STAND WITH ME IN THEIR HOUR OF GREATEST NEED?
HAVE YOU LEARNED NOTHING FROM WATCHING OVER THEM? HAVE YOU NOT ONCE LEARNED LOVE?
ZAURIEL, ZAURIEL... THIS PASSION YOU FEEL IS A RESULT OF TOO LONG SPENT EMBEDDED IN MORTAL CLAY.
YOUR FLESH WILL BE RESTORED; RETURN TO YOUR EARTH AND FULFILL YOUR DUTY THERE.
...I SEE.
I PRAY YOU'RE KINDER TO THE CREATURES OF THIS NEW WORLD YOU'RE MAKING.
I KNOW WHERE MY HEART LIES.

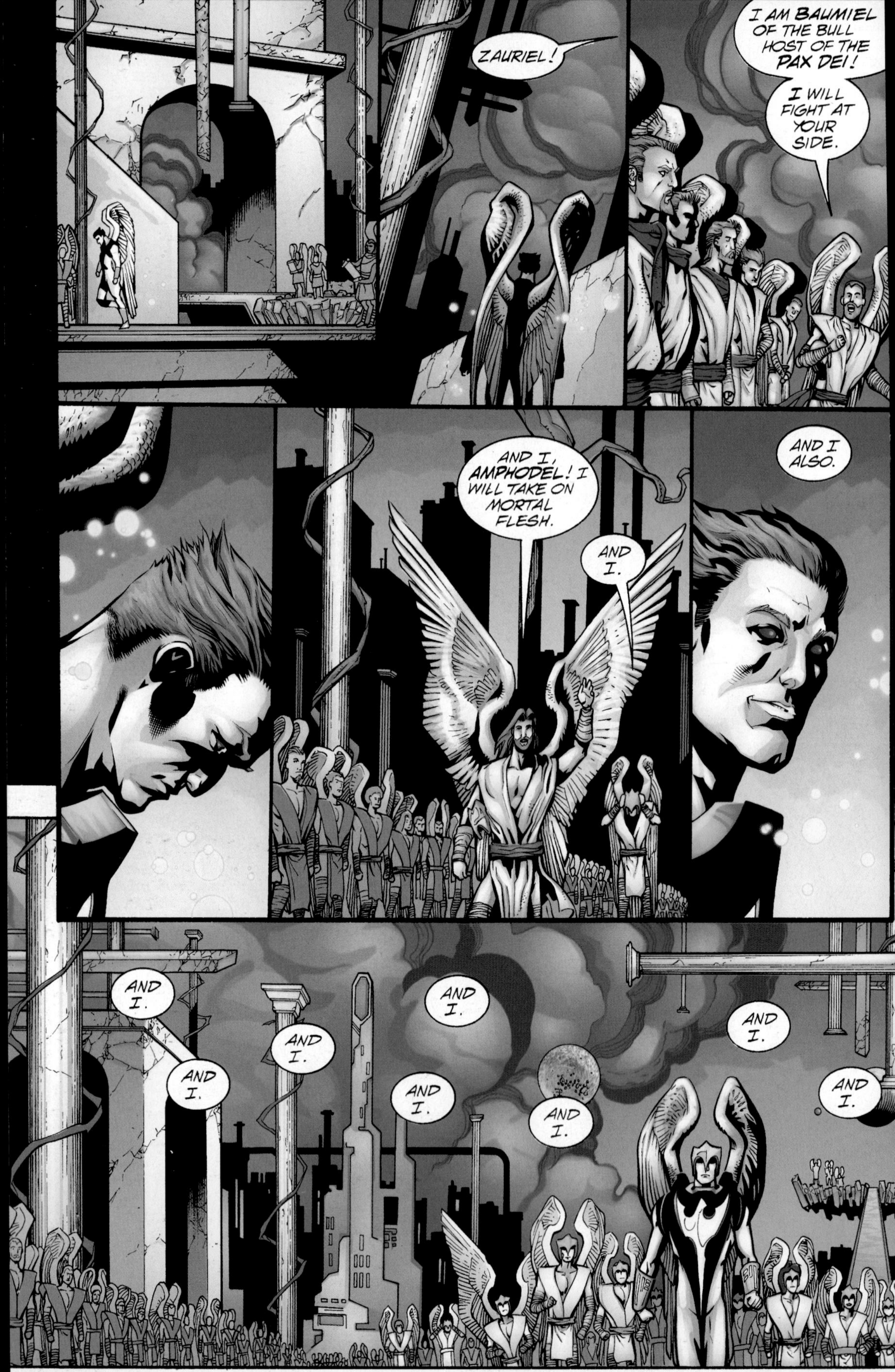
ZAURIEL!
I AM BAUMIEL OF THE BULL HOST OF THE PAX DEI!
I WILL FIGHT AT YOUR SIDE.
AND I, AMPHODEL! I WILL TAKE ON MORTAL FLESH.
AND I.
AND I ALSO.
AND I.
AND I.
AND I.
AND I.
AND I.
AND I.
AND I.
AND I.

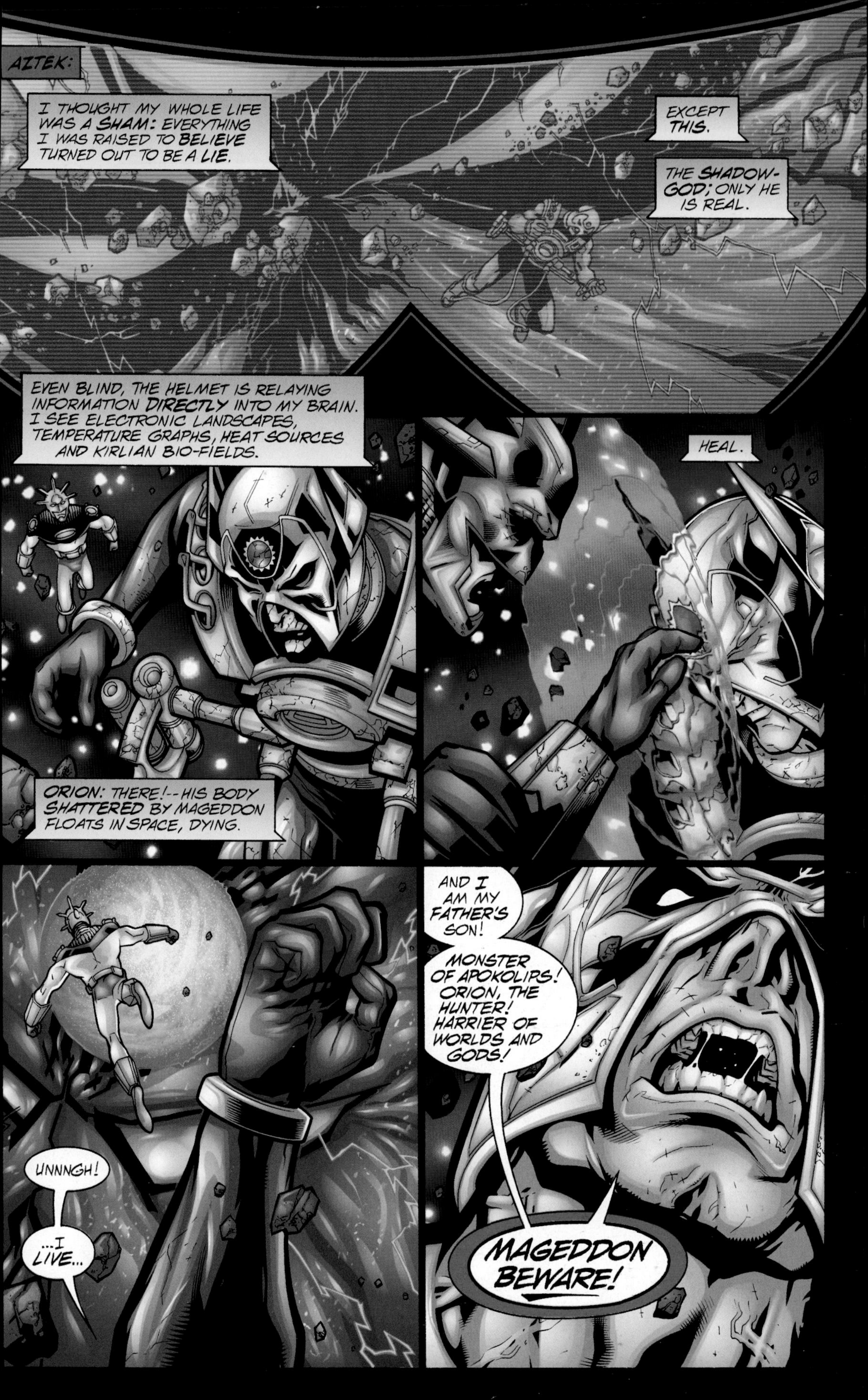

AZTEK:
I THOUGHT MY WHOLE LIFE WAS A SHAM: EVERYTHING I WAS RAISED TO BELIEVE TURNED OUT TO BE A LIE.
EXCEPT THIS.
THE SHADOW-GOD; ONLY HE IS REAL.
EVEN BLIND, THE HELMET IS RELAYING INFORMATION DIRECTLY INTO MY BRAIN. I SEE ELECTRONIC LANDSCAPES, TEMPERATURE GRAPHS, HEAT SOURCES AND KIRLIAN BIO-FIELDS.
ORION: THERE!--HIS BODY SHATTERED BY MAGEDDON FLOATS IN SPACE, DYING.
HEAL.
UNNNGH!
...I LIVE...
AND I AM MY FATHER'S SON!
MONSTER OF APOKOLIPS! ORION, THE HUNTER! HARRIER OF WORLDS AND GODS!
MAGEDDON BEWARE!

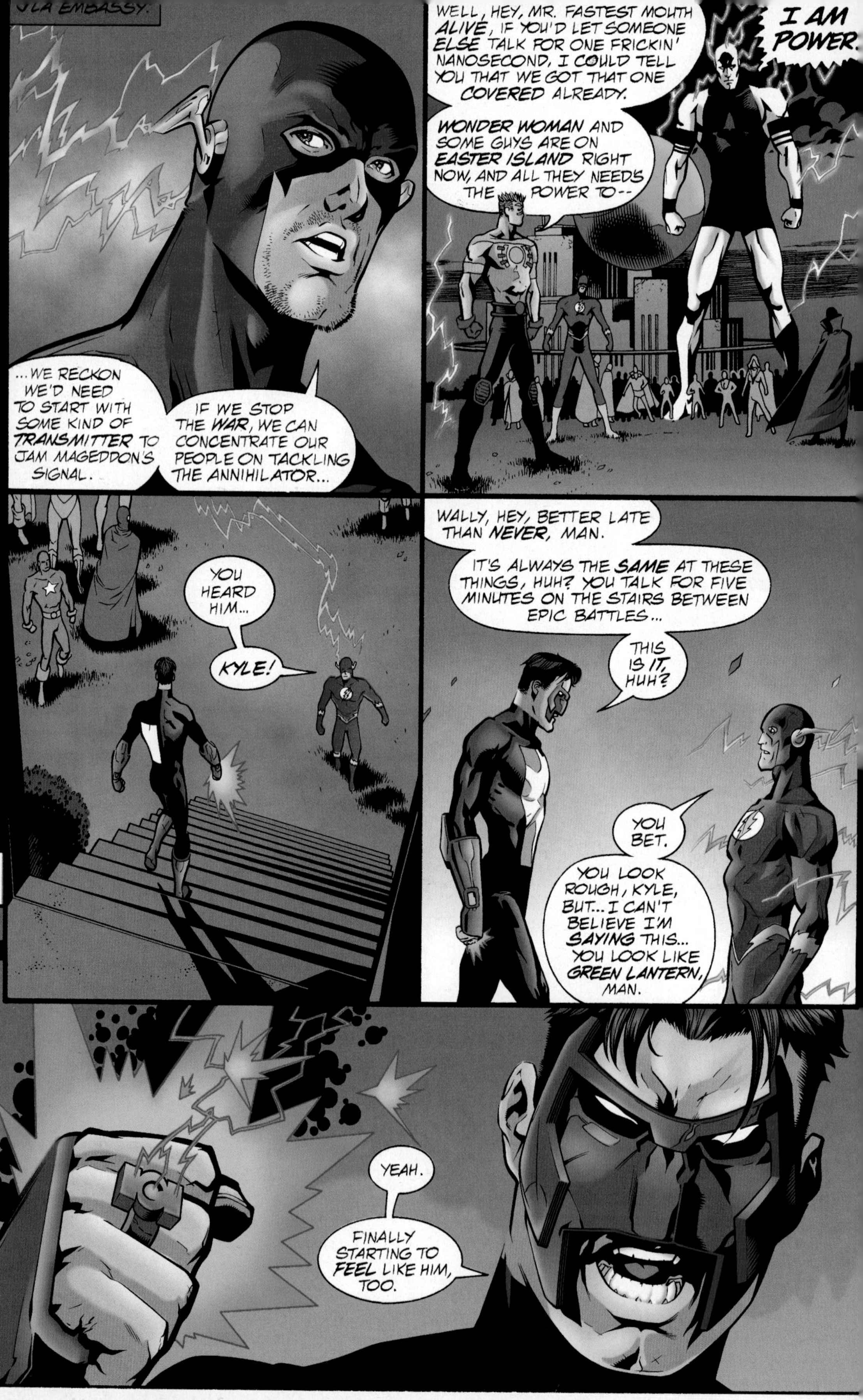
JLA EMBASSY.
...WE RECKON WE'D NEED TO START WITH SOME KIND OF TRANSMITTER TO JAM MAGEDDON'S SIGNAL.
IF WE STOP THE WAR, WE CAN CONCENTRATE OUR PEOPLE ON TACKLING THE ANNIHILATOR...
WELL, HEY, MR. FASTEST MOUTH ALIVE, IF YOU'D LET SOMEONE ELSE TALK FOR ONE FRICKIN' NANOSECOND, I COULD TELL YOU THAT WE GOT THAT ONE COVERED ALREADY.
WONDER WOMAN AND SOME GUYS ARE ON EASTER ISLAND RIGHT NOW, AND ALL THEY NEED'S THE POWER TO--
I AM POWER.
YOU HEARD HIM...
KYLE!
WALLY, HEY, BETTER LATE THAN NEVER, MAN.
IT'S ALWAYS THE SAME AT THESE THINGS, HUH? YOU TALK FOR FIVE MINUTES ON THE STAIRS BETWEEN EPIC BATTLES...
THIS IS IT, HUH?
YOU BET.
YOU LOOK ROUGH, KYLE, BUT... I CAN'T BELIEVE I'M SAYING THIS... YOU LOOK LIKE GREEN LANTERN, MAN.
YEAH.
FINALLY STARTING TO FEEL LIKE HIM, TOO.

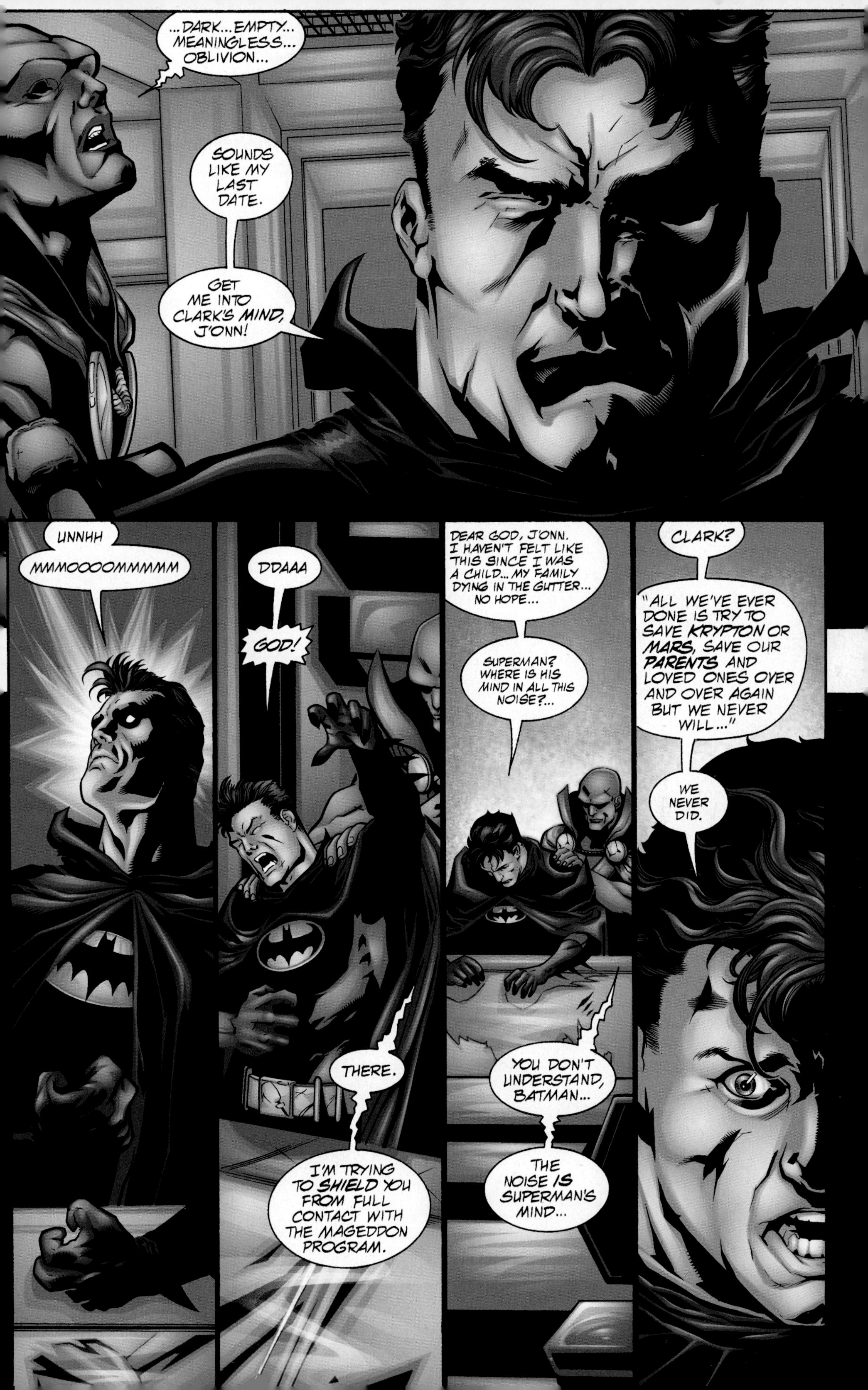
...DARK...EMPTY... MEANINGLESS... OBLIVION...
SOUNDS LIKE MY LAST DATE.
GET ME INTO CLARK'S MIND, J'ONN!
UNNHH
MMMOOOOMMMMM
DDAAA
GOD!
THERE.
I'M TRYING TO SHIELD YOU FROM FULL CONTACT WITH THE MAGEDDON PROGRAM.
DEAR GOD, J'ONN. I HAVEN'T FELT LIKE THIS SINCE I WAS A CHILD... MY FAMILY DYING IN THE GUTTER... NO HOPE...
SUPERMAN? WHERE IS HIS MIND IN ALL THIS NOISE?...
YOU DON'T UNDERSTAND, BATMAN...
THE NOISE IS SUPERMAN'S MIND...
CLARK?
"ALL WE'VE EVER DONE IS TRY TO SAVE KRYPTON OR MARS, SAVE OUR PARENTS AND LOVED ONES OVER AND OVER AGAIN BUT WE NEVER WILL..."
WE NEVER DID.

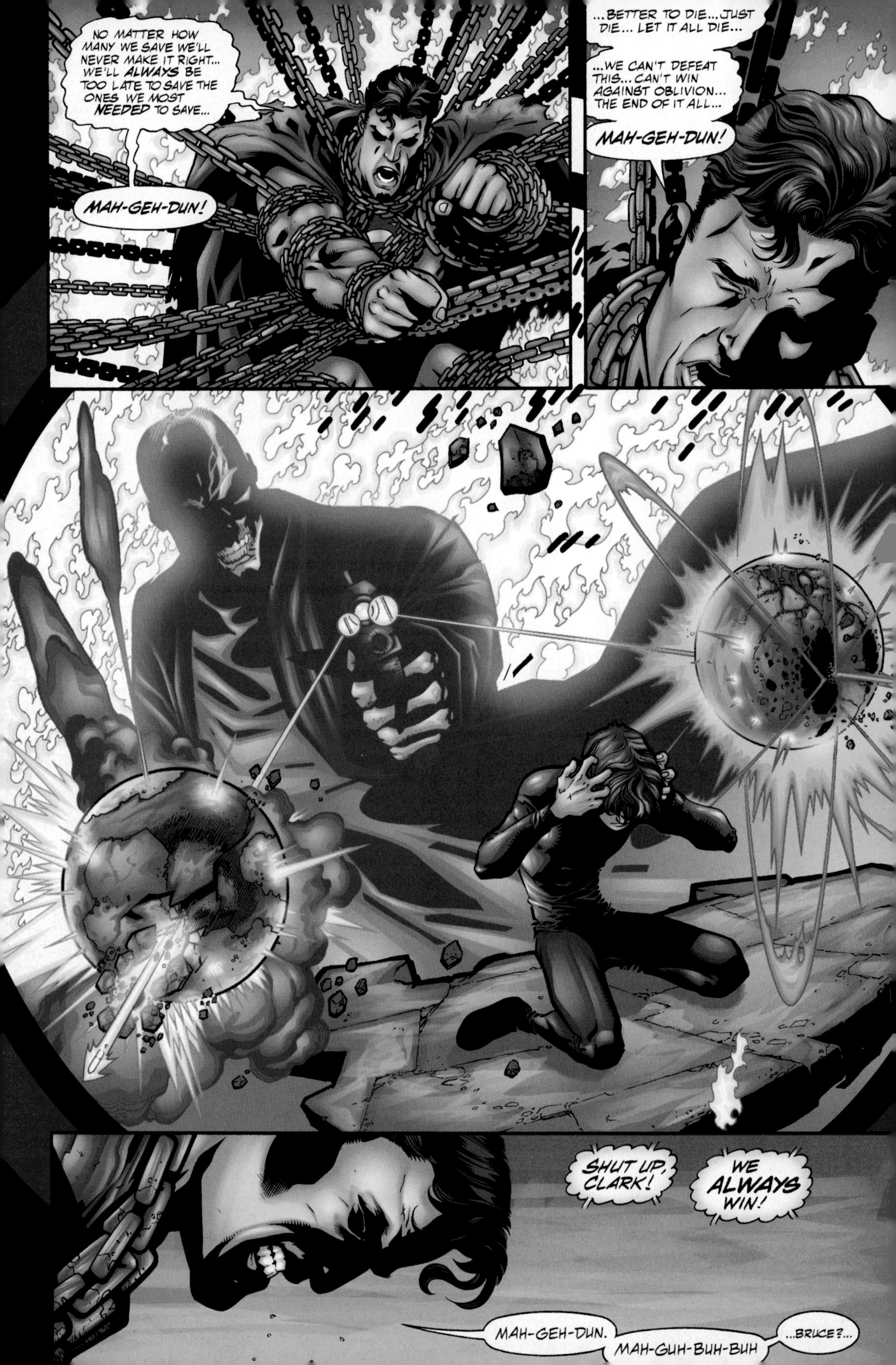
NO MATTER HOW MANY WE SAVE WE'LL NEVER MAKE IT RIGHT... WE'LL ALWAYS BE TOO LATE TO SAVE THE ONES WE MOST NEEDED TO SAVE...
MAH-GEH-DUN!
...BETTER TO DIE...JUST DIE... LET IT ALL DIE...
...WE CAN'T DEFEAT THIS... CAN'T WIN AGAINST OBLIVION... THE END OF IT ALL...
MAH-GEH-DUN!
SHUT UP, CLARK!
WE ALWAYS WIN!
MAH-GEH-DUN.
MAH-GUH-BUH-BUH
...BRUCE?...

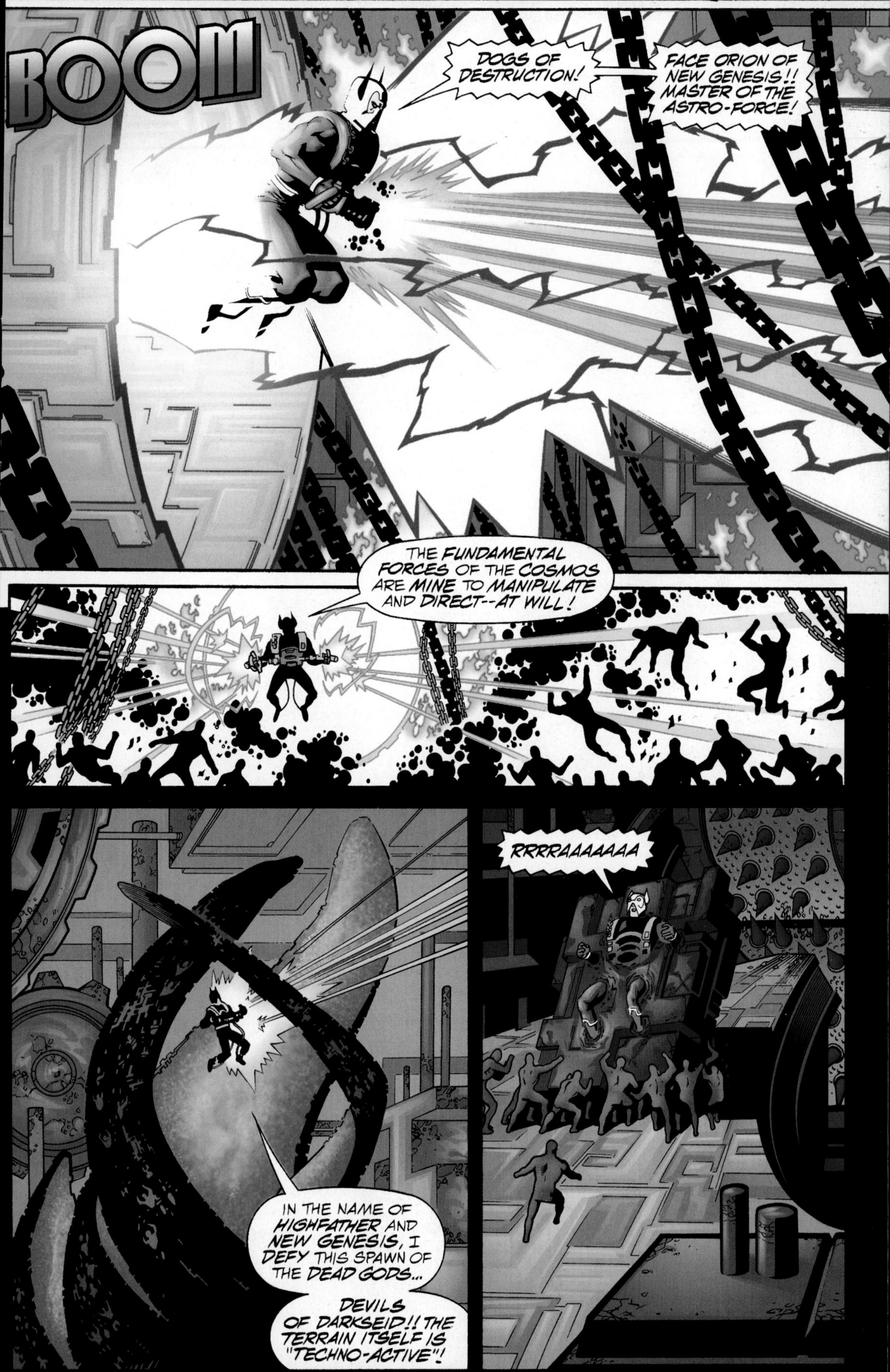
BOOM
DOGS OF DESTRUCTION!
FACE ORION OF NEW GENESIS!! MASTER OF THE ASTRO-FORCE!
THE FUNDAMENTAL FORCES OF THE COSMOS ARE MINE TO MANIPULATE AND DIRECT--AT WILL!
IN THE NAME OF HIGHFATHER AND NEW GENESIS, I DEFY THIS SPAWN OF THE DEAD GODS...
DEVILS OF DARKSEID!! THE TERRAIN ITSELF IS "TECHNO-ACTIVE"!
RRRRAAAAAAA

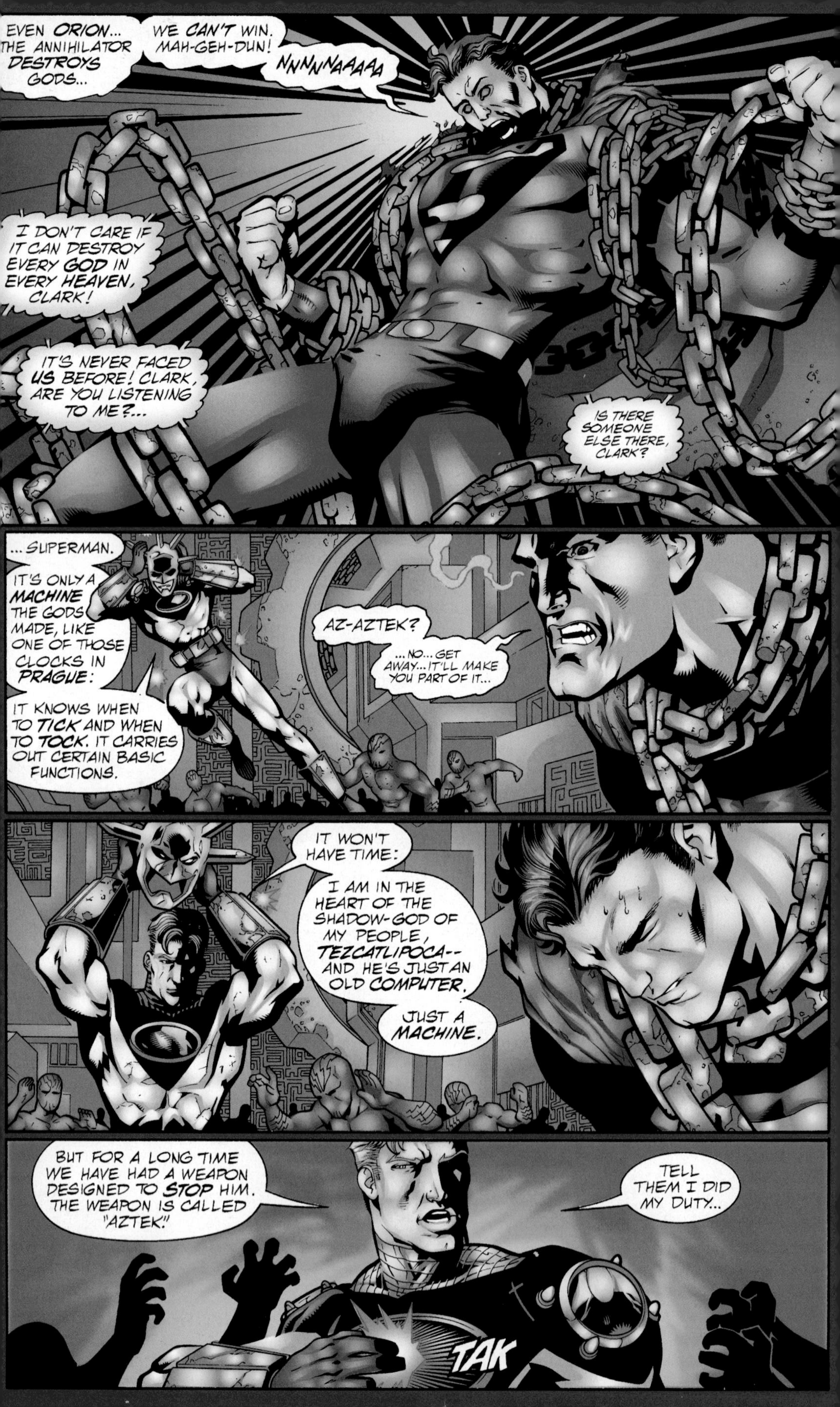
EVEN ORION... THE ANNIHILATOR DESTROYS GODS...
WE CAN'T WIN. MAH-GEH-DUN!
NNNNNAAAAA
I DON'T CARE IF IT CAN DESTROY EVERY GOD IN EVERY HEAVEN, CLARK!
IT'S NEVER FACED US BEFORE! CLARK, ARE YOU LISTENING TO ME?...
IS THERE SOMEONE ELSE THERE, CLARK?
...SUPERMAN.
IT'S ONLY A MACHINE THE GODS MADE, LIKE ONE OF THOSE CLOCKS IN PRAGUE:
IT KNOWS WHEN TO TICK AND WHEN TO TOCK. IT CARRIES OUT CERTAIN BASIC FUNCTIONS.
AZ-AZTEK?
...NO... GET AWAY... IT'LL MAKE YOU PART OF IT...
IT WON'T HAVE TIME:
I AM IN THE HEART OF THE SHADOW-GOD OF MY PEOPLE, TEZCATLIPOCA-- AND HE'S JUST AN OLD COMPUTER.
JUST A MACHINE.
BUT FOR A LONG TIME WE HAVE HAD A WEAPON DESIGNED TO STOP HIM. THE WEAPON IS CALLED "AZTEK."
TELL THEM I DID MY DUTY...
TAK

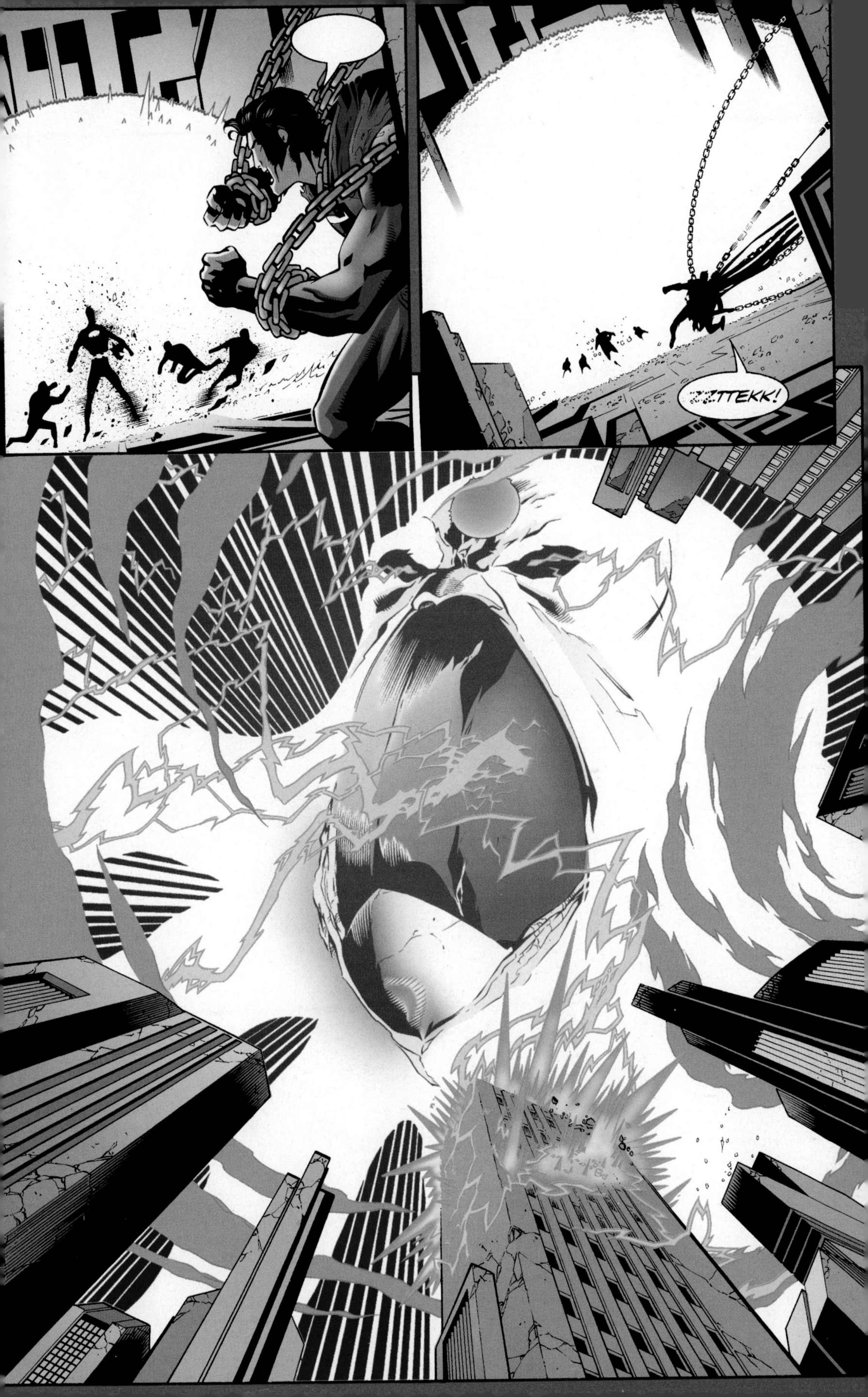
ZZTTEKK!

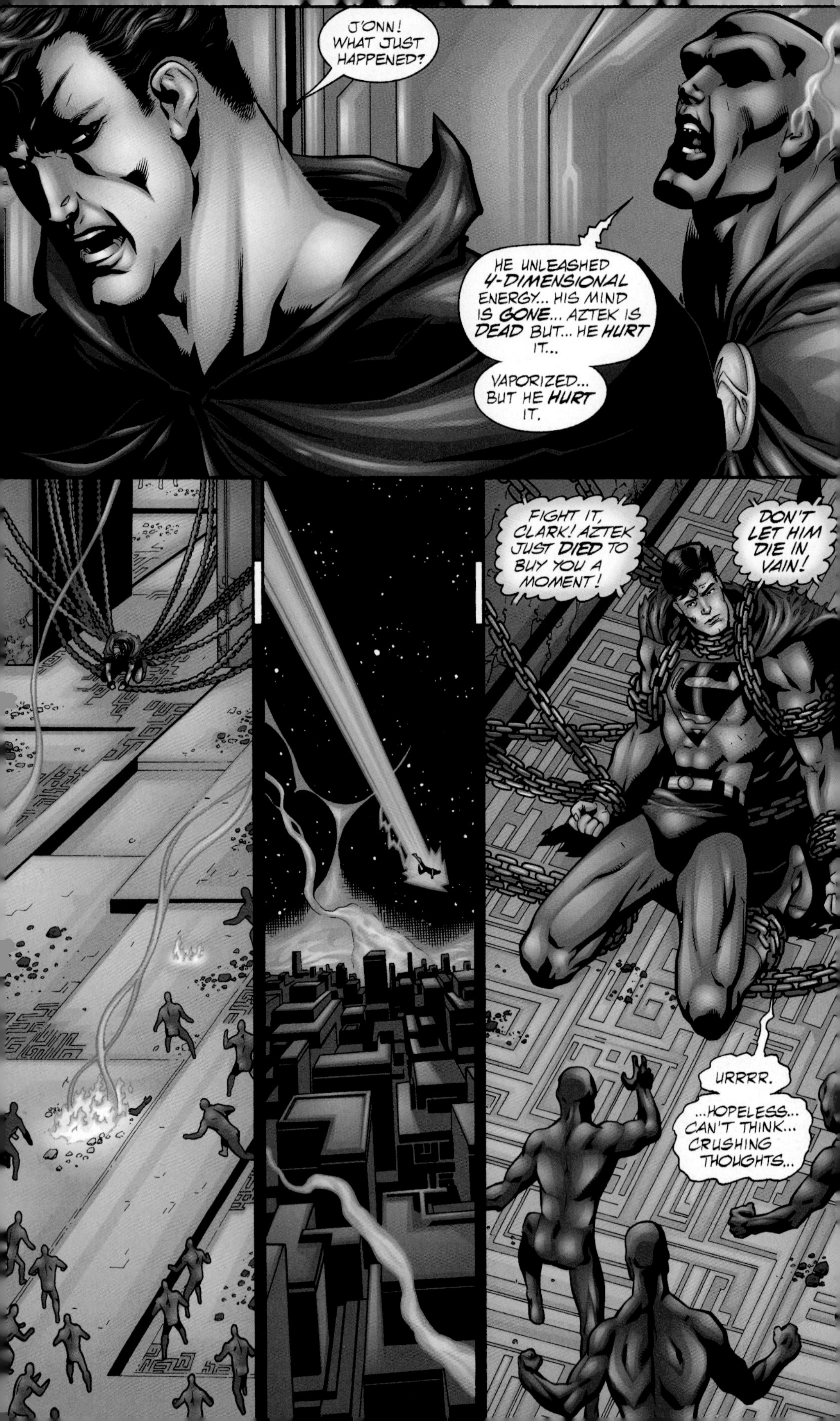
J'ONN! WHAT JUST HAPPENED?
HE UNLEASHED 4-DIMENSIONAL ENERGY... HIS MIND IS GONE... AZTEK IS DEAD BUT... HE HURT IT...
VAPORIZED... BUT HE HURT IT.
FIGHT IT, CLARK! AZTEK JUST DIED TO BUY YOU A MOMENT!
DON'T LET HIM DIE IN VAIN!
URRRR.
...HOPELESS... CAN'T THINK... CRUSHING THOUGHTS...

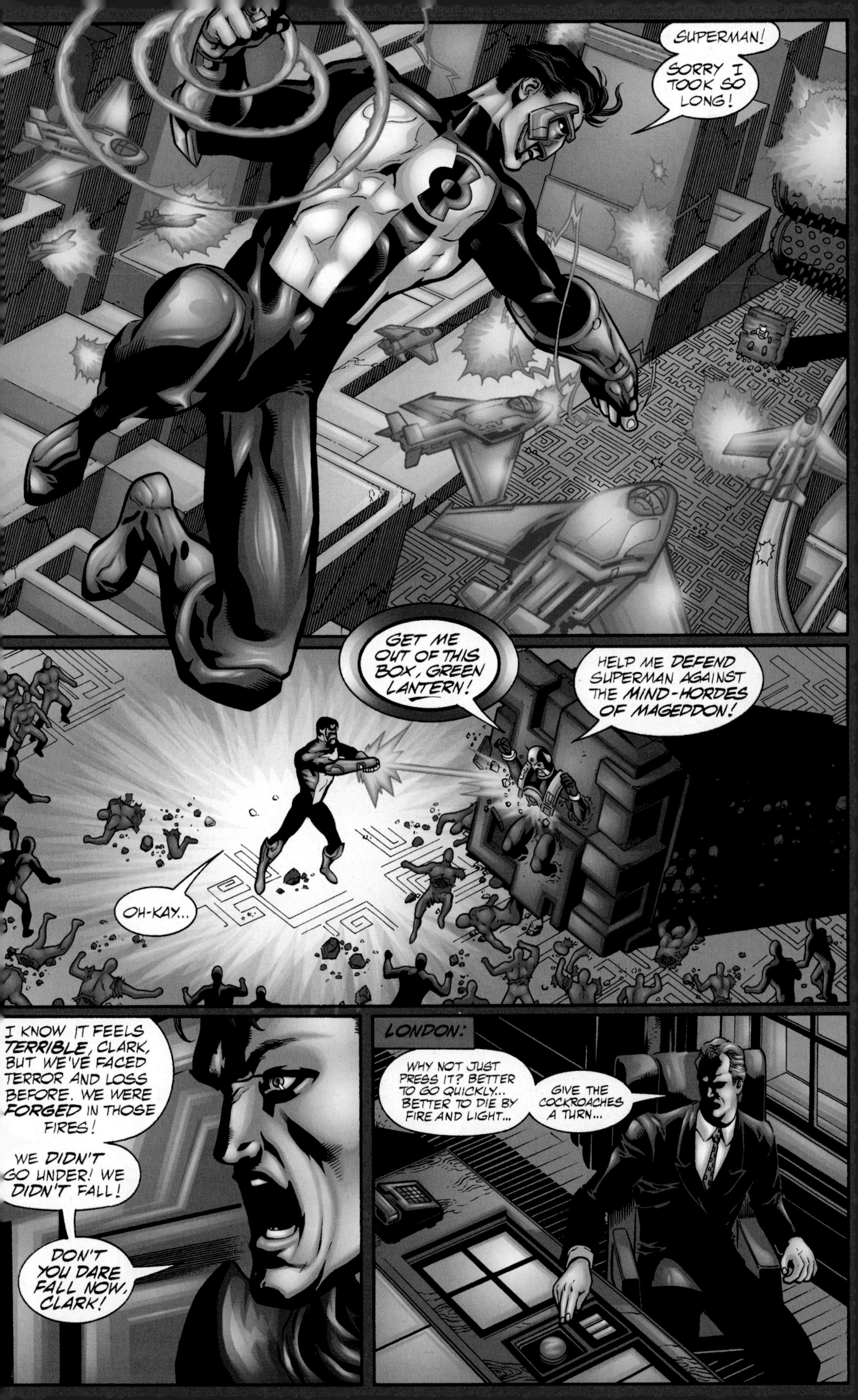
SUPERMAN!
SORRY I TOOK SO LONG!
GET ME OUT OF THIS BOX, GREEN LANTERN!
HELP ME DEFEND SUPERMAN AGAINST THE MIND-HORDES OF MAGEDDON!
OH-KAY...
I KNOW IT FEELS TERRIBLE, CLARK, BUT WE'VE FACED TERROR AND LOSS BEFORE. WE WERE FORGED IN THOSE FIRES!
WE DIDN'T GO UNDER! WE DIDN'T FALL!
DON'T YOU DARE FALL NOW, CLARK!
LONDON:
WHY NOT JUST PRESS IT? BETTER TO GO QUICKLY... BETTER TO DIE BY FIRE AND LIGHT...
GIVE THE COCKROACHES A TURN...

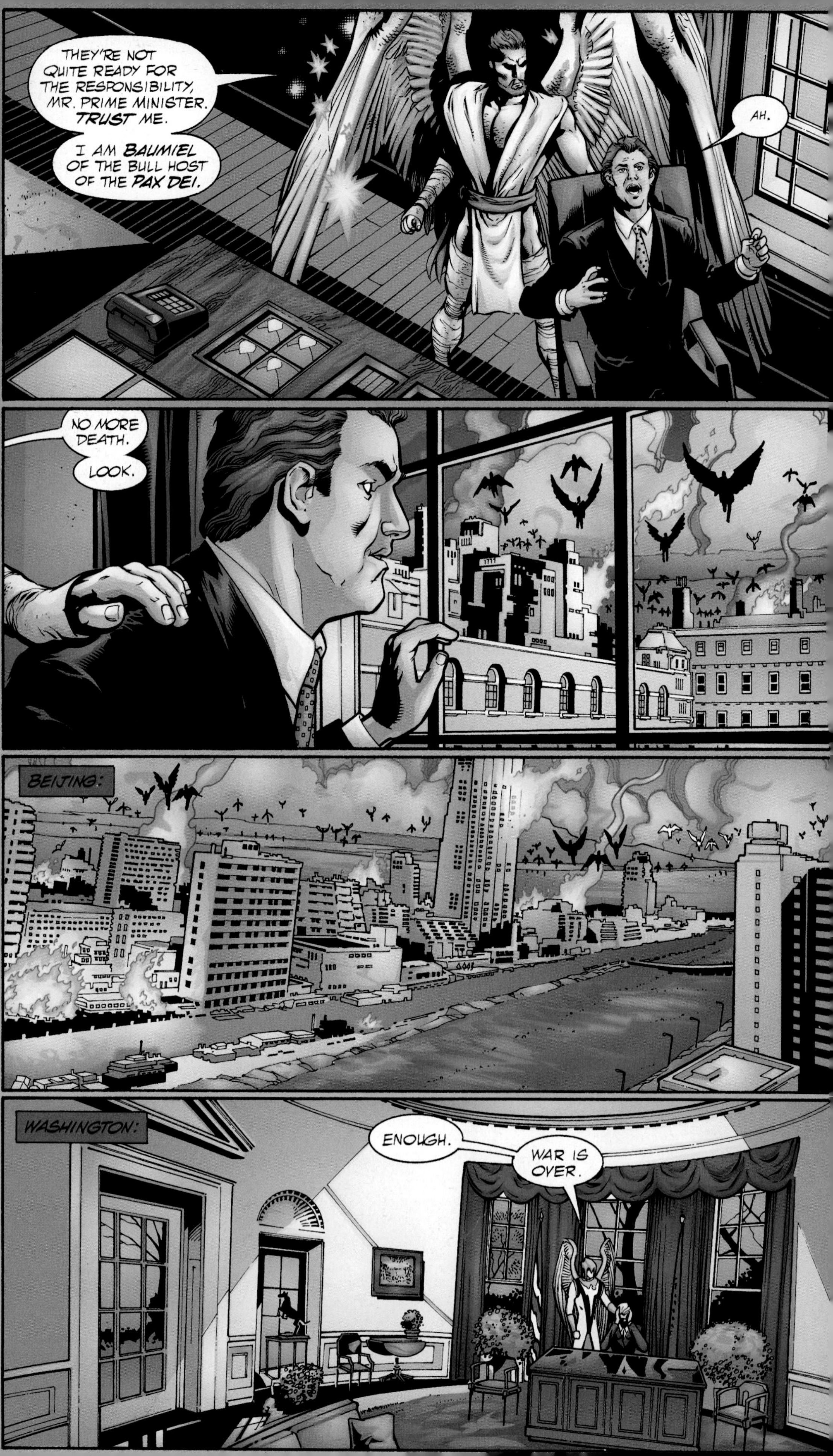

THEY'RE NOT QUITE READY FOR THE RESPONSIBILITY, MR. PRIME MINISTER. TRUST ME.
I AM BAUMIEL OF THE BULL HOST OF THE PAX DEI.
AH.
NO MORE DEATH.
LOOK.
BEIJING:
WASHINGTON:
ENOUGH.
WAR IS OVER.

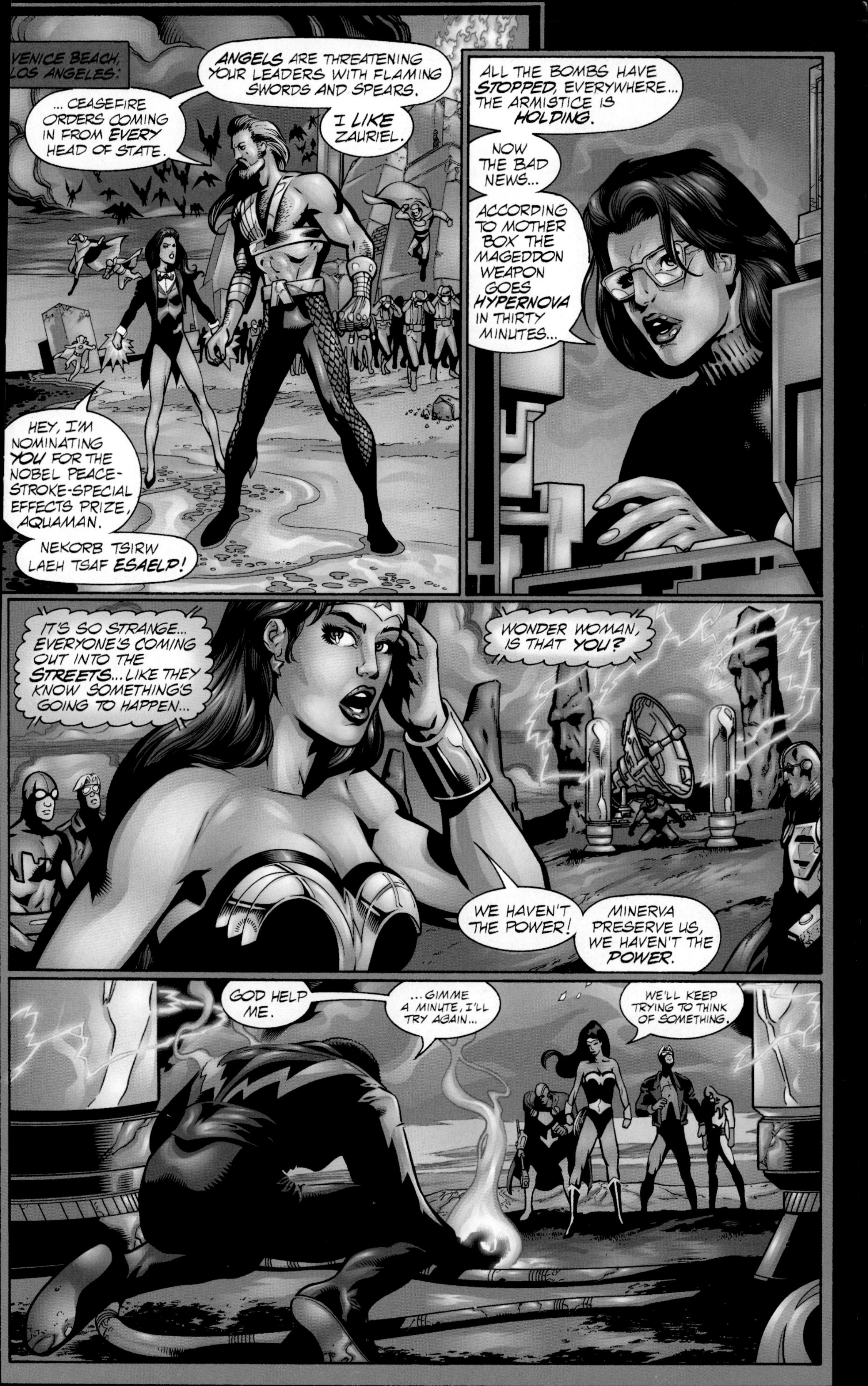
VENICE BEACH, LOS ANGELES:
... CEASEFIRE ORDERS COMING IN FROM EVERY HEAD OF STATE.
ANGELS ARE THREATENING YOUR LEADERS WITH FLAMING SWORDS AND SPEARS.
I LIKE ZAURIEL.
HEY, I'M NOMINATING YOU FOR THE NOBEL PEACE-STROKE-SPECIAL EFFECTS PRIZE, AQUAMAN.
NEKORB TSIRW LAEH TSAF ESAELP!
ALL THE BOMBS HAVE STOPPED, EVERYWHERE... THE ARMISTICE IS HOLDING.
NOW THE BAD NEWS...
ACCORDING TO MOTHER BOX THE MAGEDDON WEAPON GOES HYPERNOVA IN THIRTY MINUTES...
IT'S SO STRANGE... EVERYONE'S COMING OUT INTO THE STREETS... LIKE THEY KNOW SOMETHING'S GOING TO HAPPEN...
WONDER WOMAN, IS THAT YOU?
WE HAVEN'T THE POWER!
MINERVA PRESERVE US, WE HAVEN'T THE POWER.
GOD HELP ME.
... GIMME A MINUTE, I'LL TRY AGAIN...
WE'LL KEEP TRYING TO THINK OF SOMETHING.

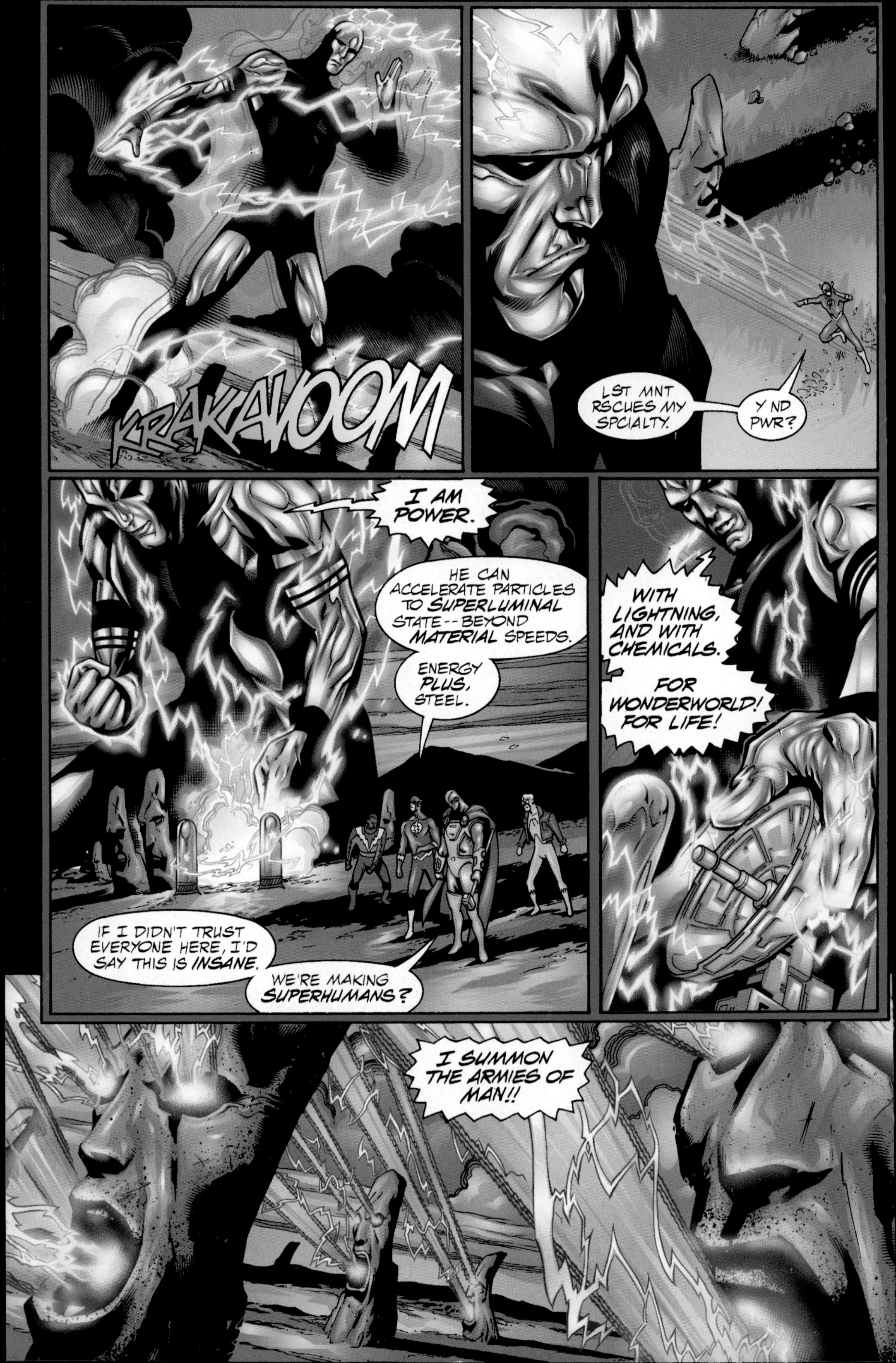
KRAKAVOOM
LST MNT RSCUES MY SPCIALTY.
Y ND PWR?
I AM POWER.
HE CAN ACCELERATE PARTICLES TO SUPERLUMINAL STATE--BEYOND MATERIAL SPEEDS.
ENERGY PLUS, STEEL.
IF I DIDN'T TRUST EVERYONE HERE, I'D SAY THIS IS INSANE.
WE'RE MAKING SUPERHUMANS?
WITH LIGHTNING, AND WITH CHEMICALS.
FOR WONDERWORLD! FOR LIFE!
I SUMMON THE ARMIES OF MAN!!

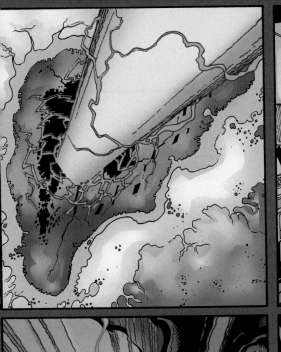

THIS IS *ORACLE* DIGITAL TELEPATHY:

HI, EVERYONE... DON'T BE *AFRAID*... WHAT WE'RE FEELING ARE NEW STRUCTURES OPENING UP IN OUR BRAINS... IT'S LIKE A PREVIEW OF EVOLUTION.

ALL THIS AMAZING STUFF YOU'RE SEEING AND FEELING IS WHAT *SUPERMAN* FEELS LIKE ALL THE TIME... IT'S *WHY* HE WANTS TO SAVE US...*HAH!*...

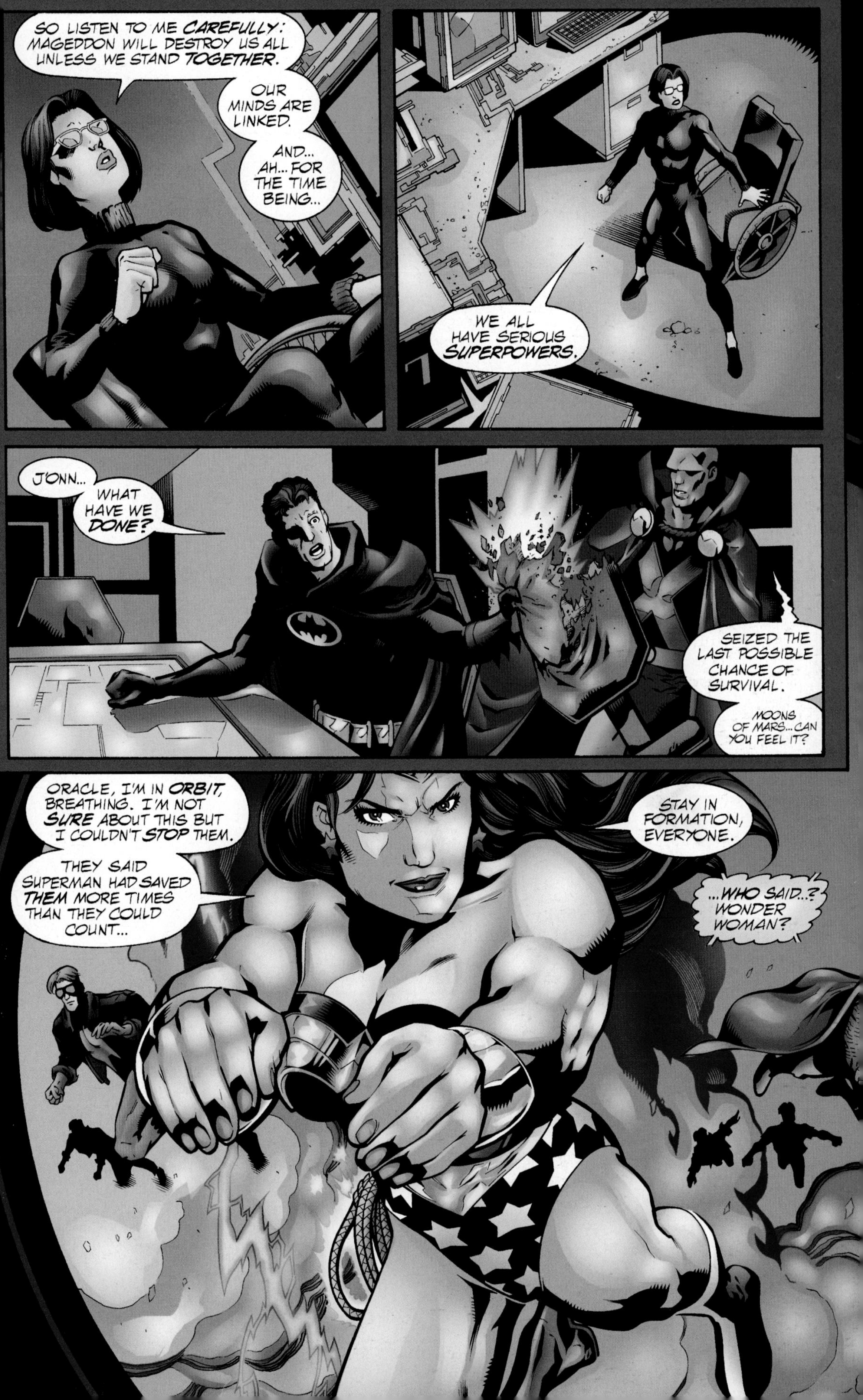
SO LISTEN TO ME CAREFULLY: MAGEDDON WILL DESTROY US ALL UNLESS WE STAND TOGETHER.
OUR MINDS ARE LINKED.
AND... AH... FOR THE TIME BEING...
WE ALL HAVE SERIOUS SUPERPOWERS.
J'ONN... WHAT HAVE WE DONE?
SEIZED THE LAST POSSIBLE CHANCE OF SURVIVAL.
MOONS OF MARS... CAN YOU FEEL IT?
ORACLE, I'M IN ORBIT, BREATHING. I'M NOT SURE ABOUT THIS BUT I COULDN'T STOP THEM.
THEY SAID SUPERMAN HAD SAVED THEM MORE TIMES THAN THEY COULD COUNT...
STAY IN FORMATION, EVERYONE.
...WHO SAID..? WONDER WOMAN?

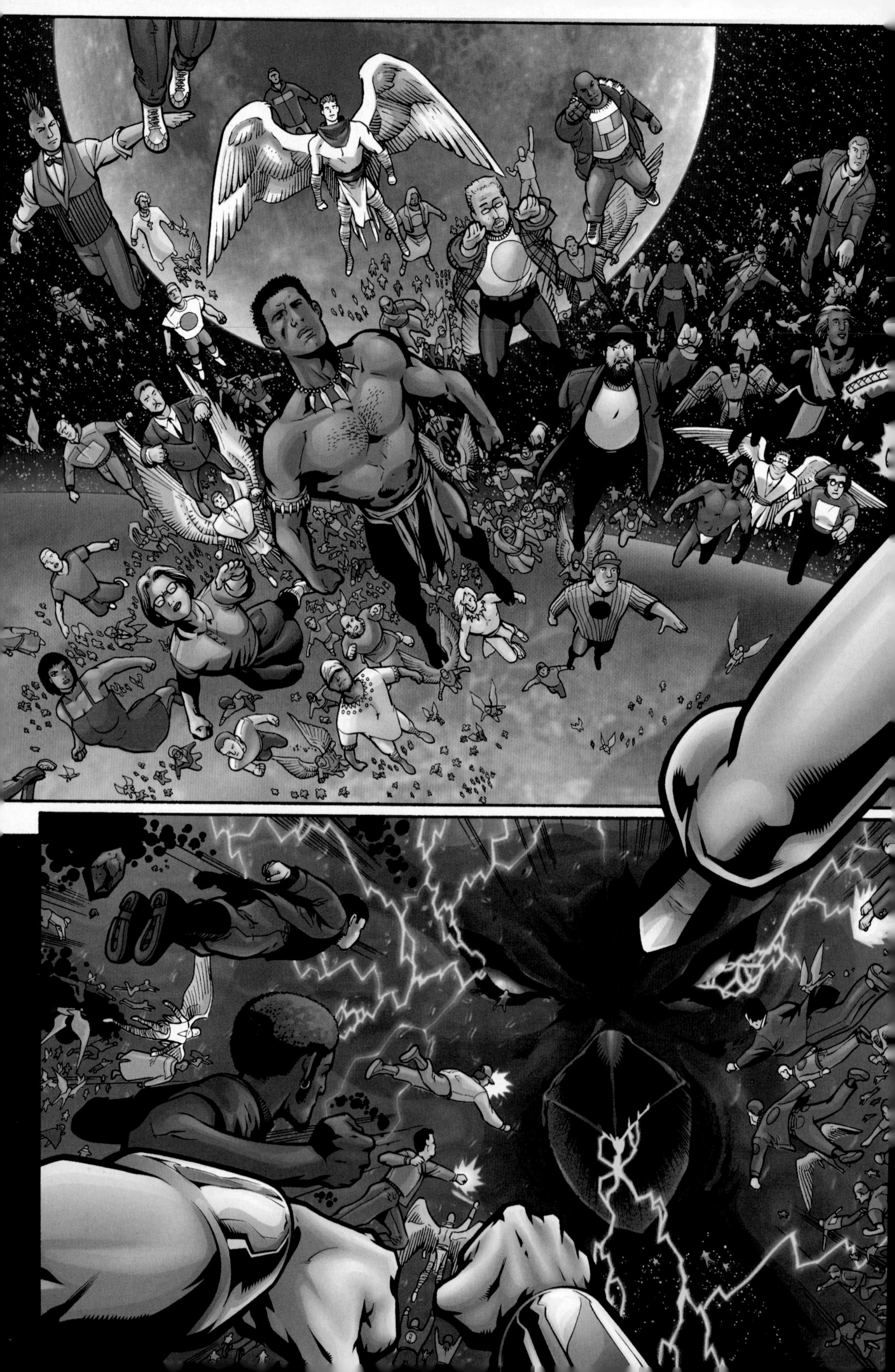

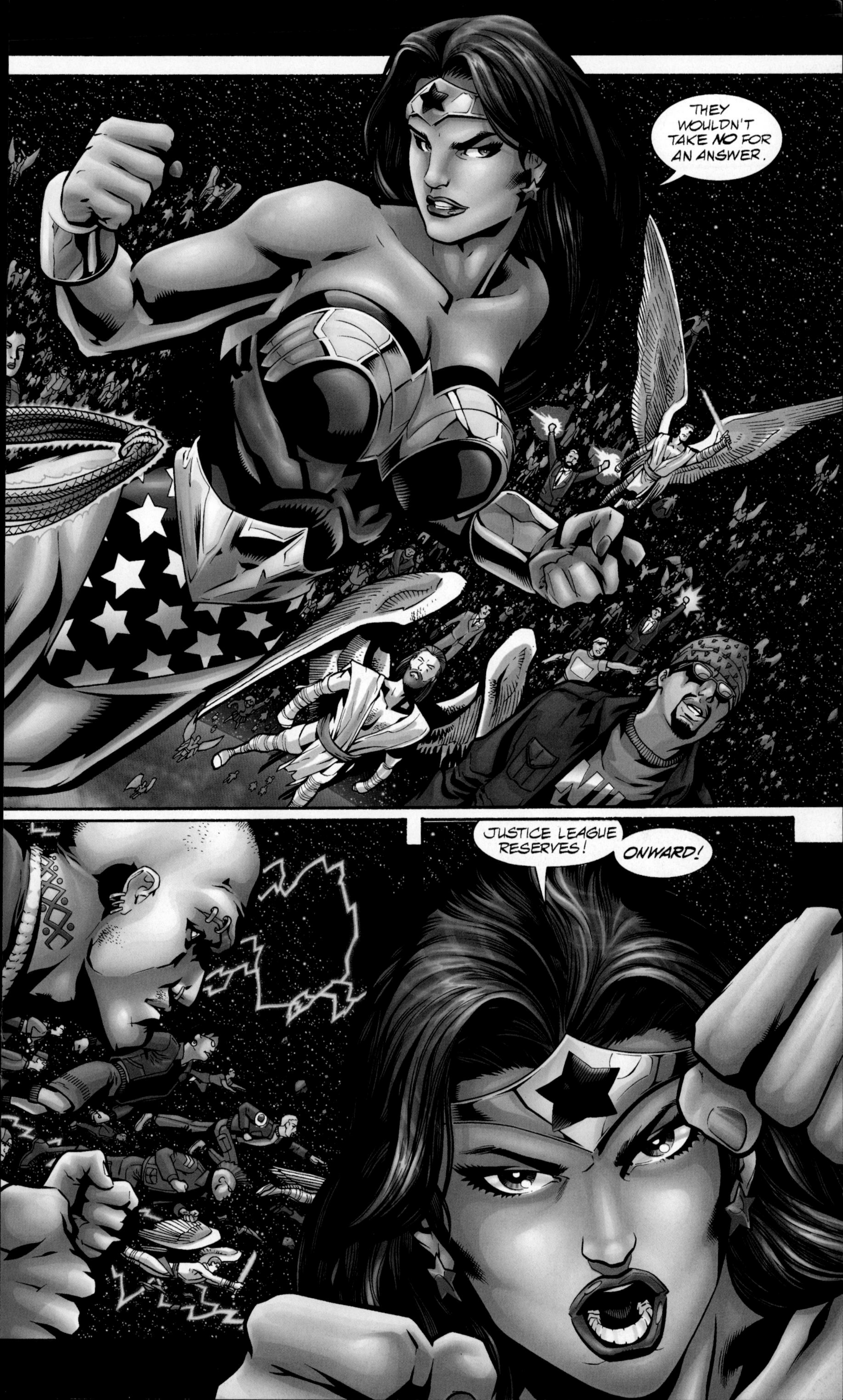
THEY WOULDN'T TAKE NO FOR AN ANSWER.
JUSTICE LEAGUE RESERVES!
ONWARD!

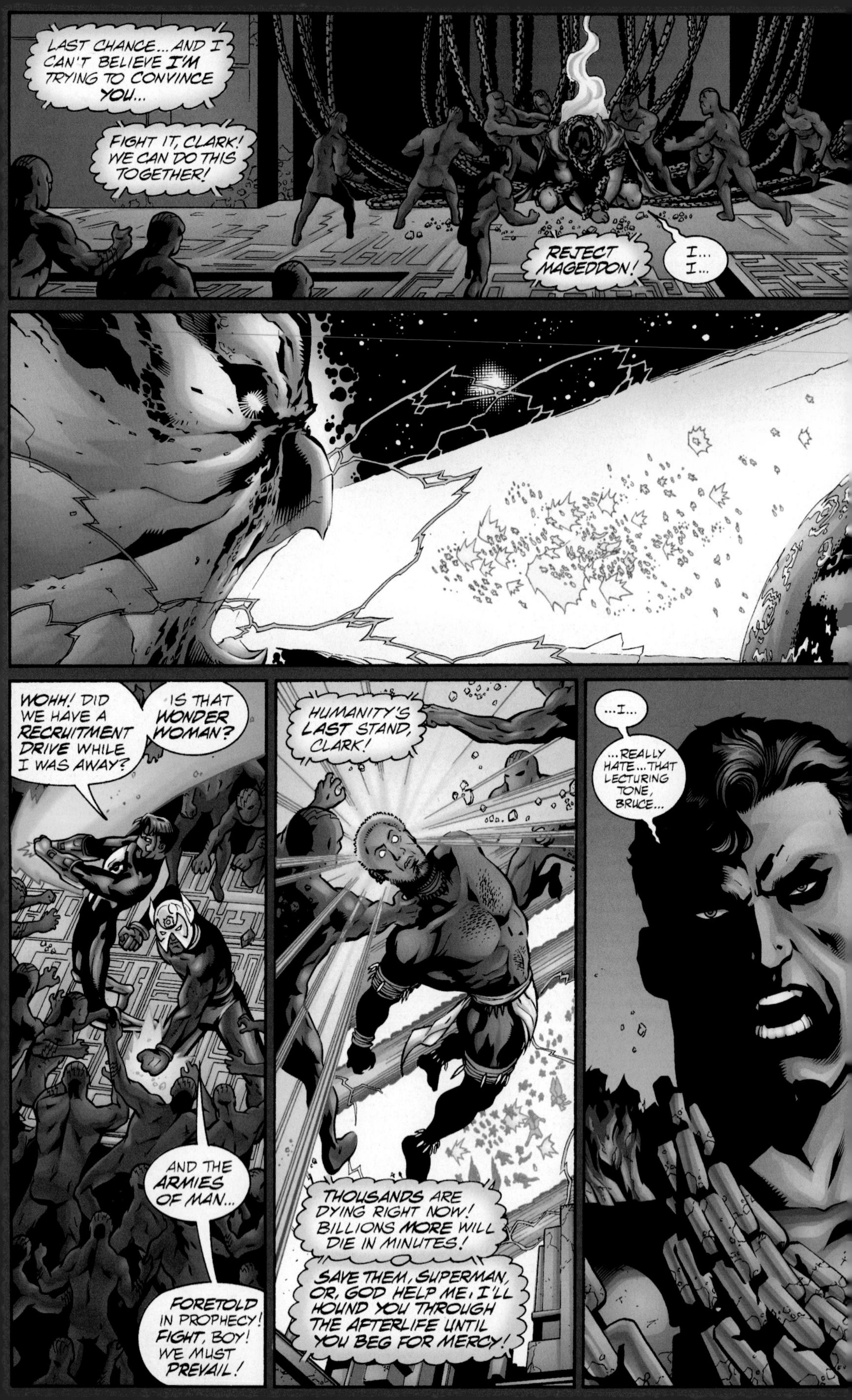
LAST CHANCE... AND I CAN'T BELIEVE I'M TRYING TO CONVINCE YOU...
FIGHT IT, CLARK! WE CAN DO THIS TOGETHER!
REJECT MAGEDDON!
I... I...
WOHH! DID WE HAVE A RECRUITMENT DRIVE WHILE I WAS AWAY?
IS THAT WONDER WOMAN?
AND THE ARMIES OF MAN...
FORETOLD IN PROPHECY! FIGHT, BOY! WE MUST PREVAIL!
HUMANITY'S LAST STAND, CLARK!
THOUSANDS ARE DYING RIGHT NOW! BILLIONS MORE WILL DIE IN MINUTES!
SAVE THEM, SUPERMAN, OR, GOD HELP ME, I'LL HOUND YOU THROUGH THE AFTERLIFE UNTIL YOU BEG FOR MERCY!
...I...
...REALLY HATE...THAT LECTURING TONE, BRUCE...

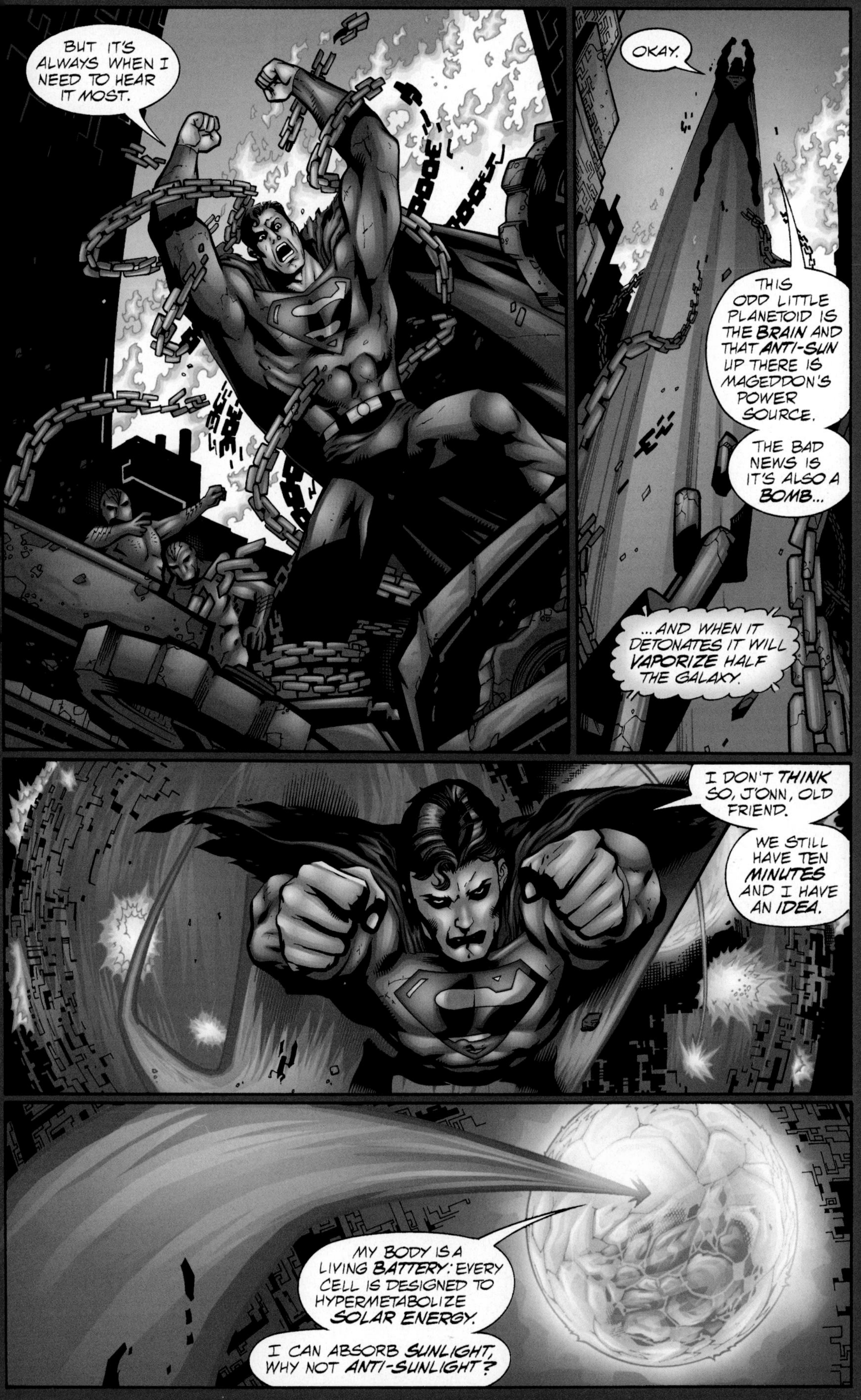
BUT IT'S ALWAYS WHEN I NEED TO HEAR IT MOST.
OKAY.
THIS ODD LITTLE PLANETOID IS THE BRAIN AND THAT ANTI-SUN UP THERE IS MAGEDDON'S POWER SOURCE.
THE BAD NEWS IS IT'S ALSO A BOMB...
...AND WHEN IT DETONATES IT WILL VAPORIZE HALF THE GALAXY.
I DON'T THINK SO, J'ONN, OLD FRIEND.
WE STILL HAVE TEN MINUTES AND I HAVE AN IDEA.
MY BODY IS A LIVING BATTERY: EVERY CELL IS DESIGNED TO HYPERMETABOLIZE SOLAR ENERGY.
I CAN ABSORB SUNLIGHT, WHY NOT ANTI-SUNLIGHT?

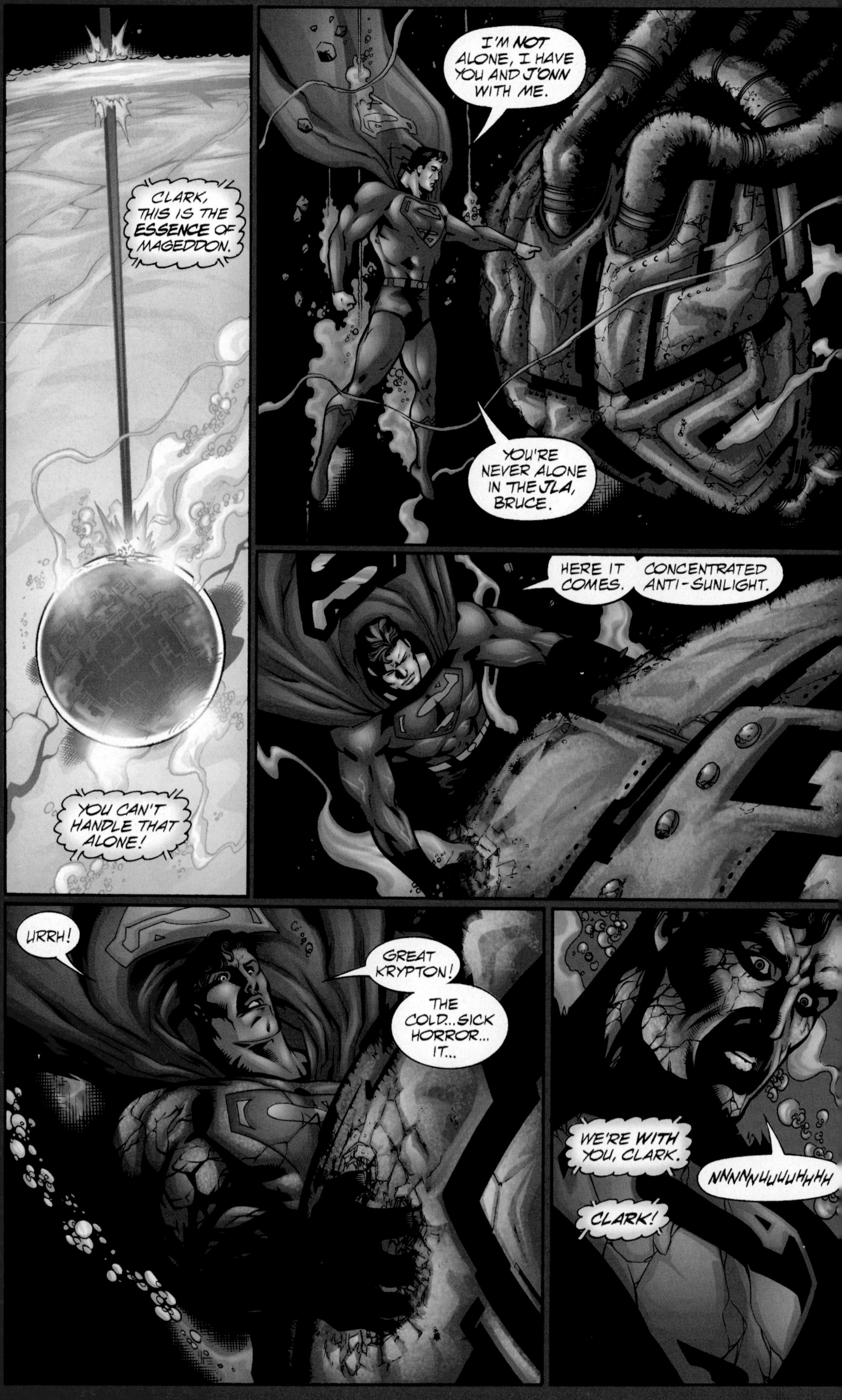
CLARK, THIS IS THE ESSENCE OF MAGEDDON.
YOU CAN'T HANDLE THAT ALONE!
I'M NOT ALONE, I HAVE YOU AND J'ONN WITH ME.
YOU'RE NEVER ALONE IN THE JLA, BRUCE.
HERE IT COMES.
CONCENTRATED ANTI-SUNLIGHT.
URRH!
GREAT KRYPTON!
THE COLD...SICK HORROR... IT...
WE'RE WITH YOU, CLARK.
NNNNNUUUUHHHH
CLARK!

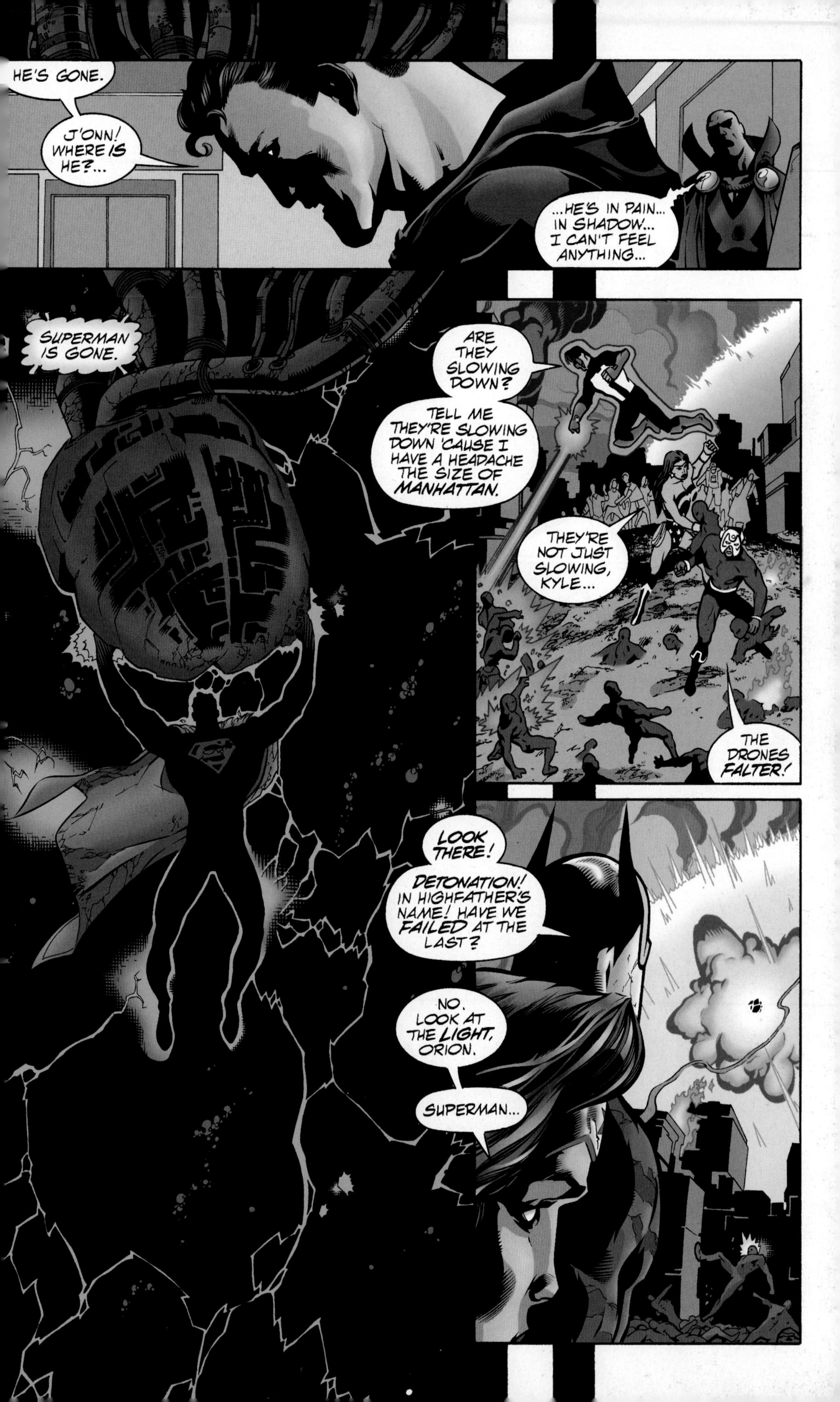
HE'S GONE.
J'ONN! WHERE IS HE?...
...HE'S IN PAIN... IN SHADOW... I CAN'T FEEL ANYTHING...
SUPERMAN IS GONE.
ARE THEY SLOWING DOWN?
TELL ME THEY'RE SLOWING DOWN 'CAUSE I HAVE A HEADACHE THE SIZE OF MANHATTAN.
THEY'RE NOT JUST SLOWING, KYLE...
THE DRONES FALTER!
LOOK THERE!
DETONATION! IN HIGHFATHER'S NAME! HAVE WE FAILED AT THE LAST?
NO. LOOK AT THE LIGHT, ORION.
SUPERMAN...

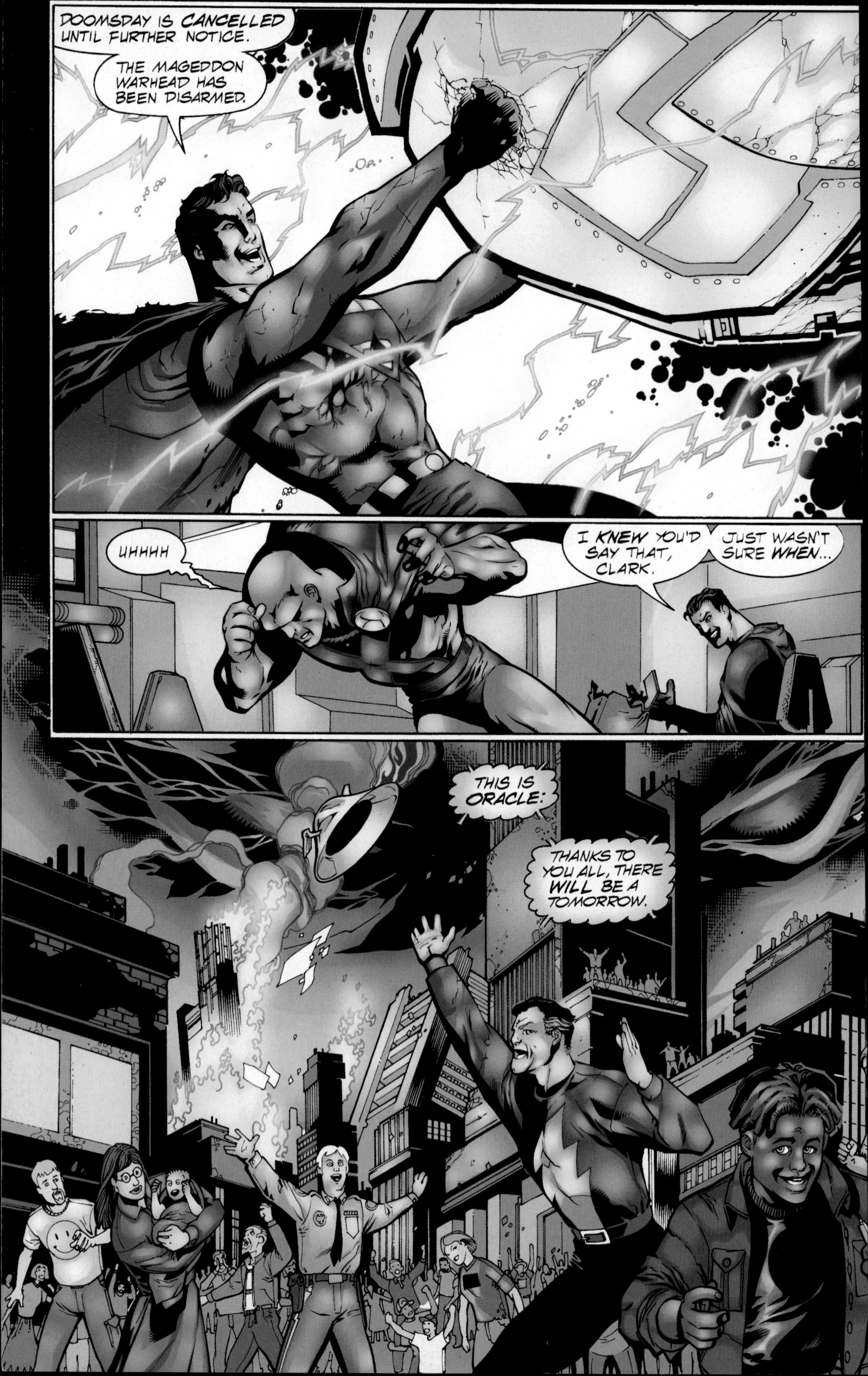
DOOMSDAY IS CANCELLED UNTIL FURTHER NOTICE.
THE MAGEDDON WARHEAD HAS BEEN DISARMED.
UHHHH
I KNEW YOU'D SAY THAT, CLARK.
JUST WASN'T SURE WHEN...
THIS IS ORACLE:
THANKS TO YOU ALL, THERE WILL BE A TOMORROW.

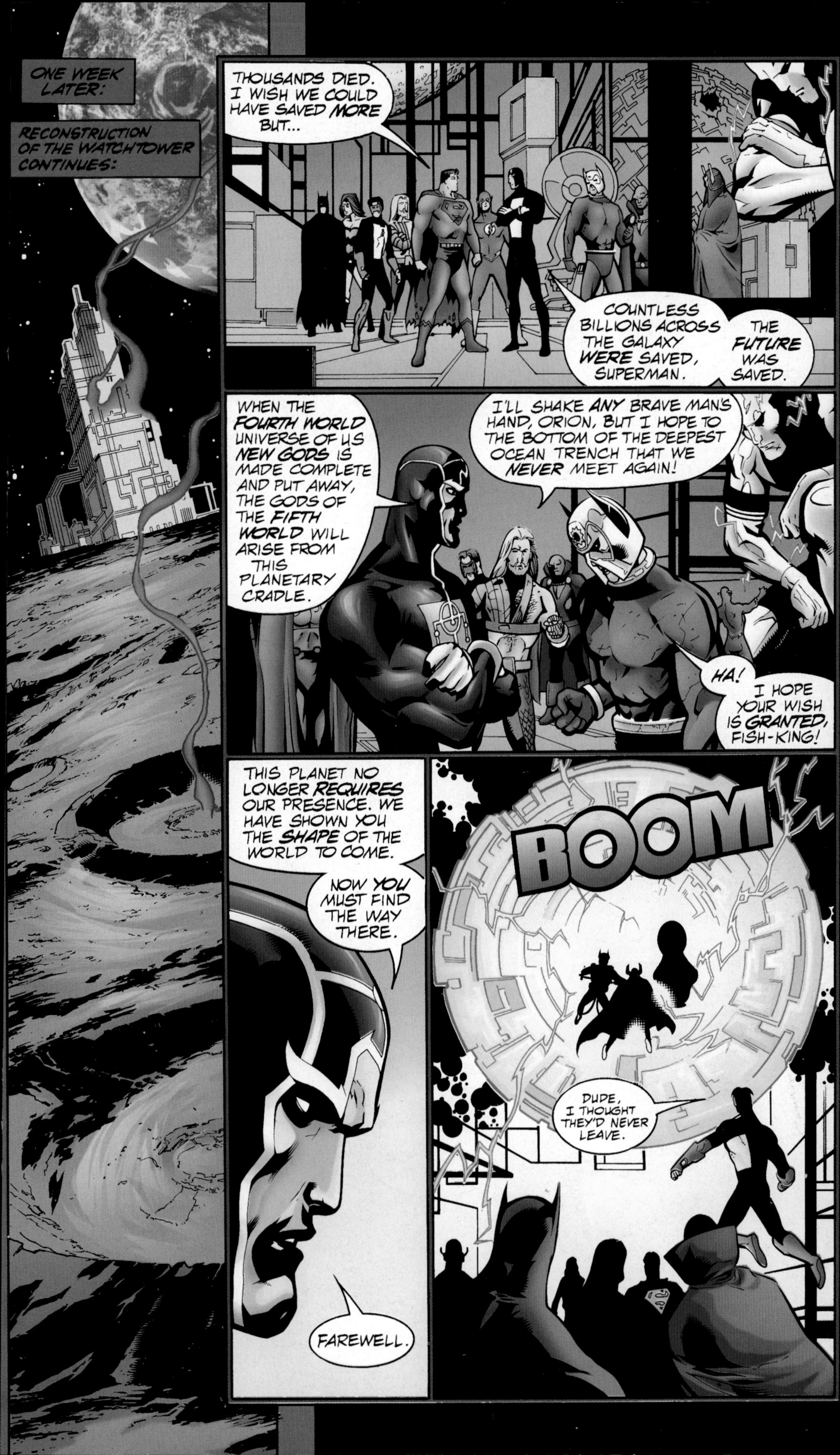
ONE WEEK LATER:
RECONSTRUCTION OF THE WATCHTOWER CONTINUES:
THOUSANDS DIED. I WISH WE COULD HAVE SAVED MORE BUT...
COUNTLESS BILLIONS ACROSS THE GALAXY WERE SAVED, SUPERMAN.
THE FUTURE WAS SAVED.
WHEN THE FOURTH WORLD UNIVERSE OF US NEW GODS IS MADE COMPLETE AND PUT AWAY, THE GODS OF THE FIFTH WORLD WILL ARISE FROM THIS PLANETARY CRADLE.
I'LL SHAKE ANY BRAVE MAN'S HAND, ORION, BUT I HOPE TO THE BOTTOM OF THE DEEPEST OCEAN TRENCH THAT WE NEVER MEET AGAIN!
HA!
I HOPE YOUR WISH IS GRANTED, FISH-KING!
THIS PLANET NO LONGER REQUIRES OUR PRESENCE. WE HAVE SHOWN YOU THE SHAPE OF THE WORLD TO COME.
NOW YOU MUST FIND THE WAY THERE.
FAREWELL.
BOOM
DUDE, I THOUGHT THEY'D NEVER LEAVE.

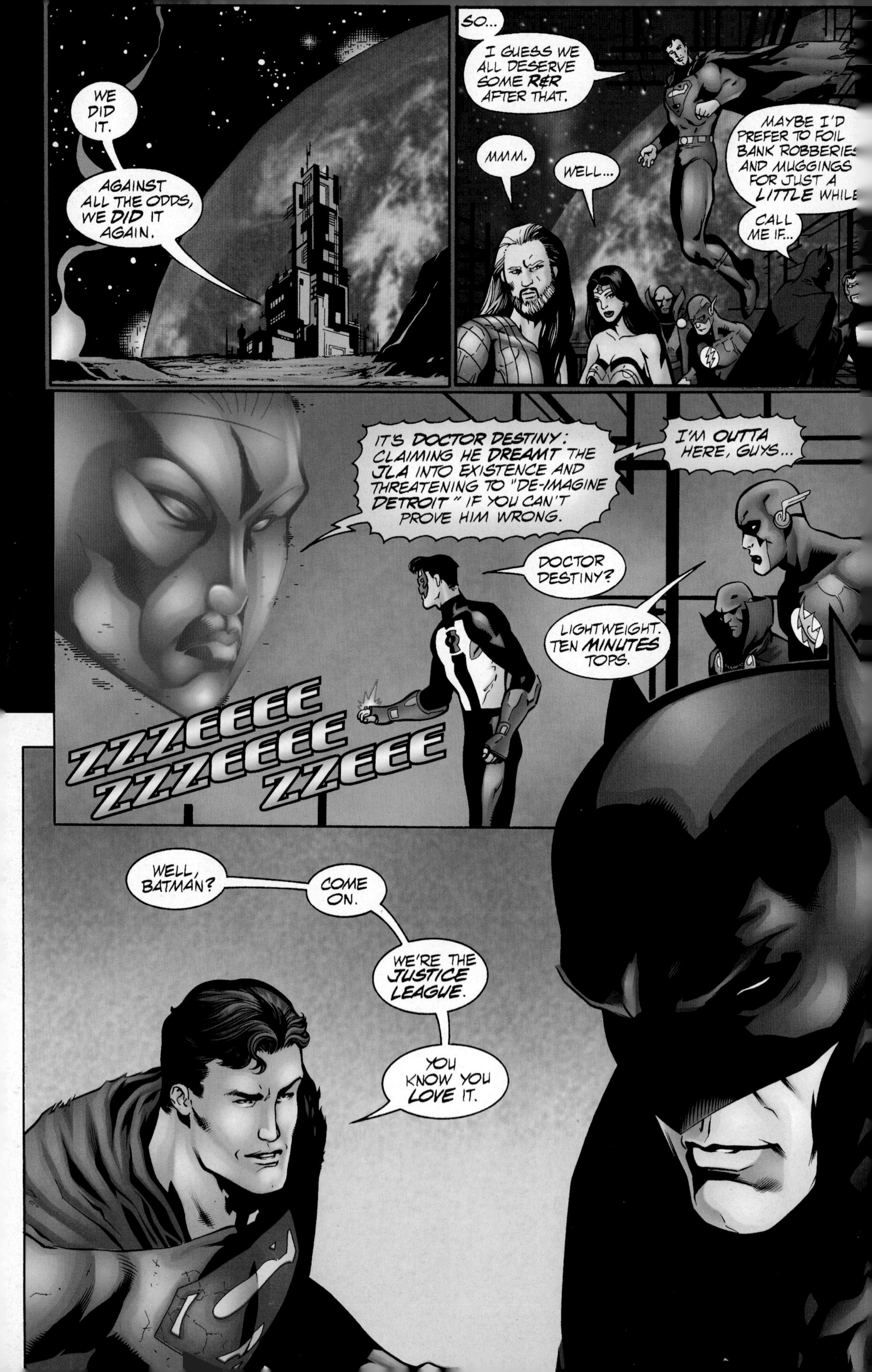
WE DID IT.
AGAINST ALL THE ODDS, WE DID IT AGAIN.
SO...
I GUESS WE ALL DESERVE SOME R&R AFTER THAT.
MMM.
WELL...
MAYBE I'D PREFER TO FOIL BANK ROBBERIES AND MUGGINGS FOR JUST A LITTLE WHILE
CALL ME IF...
IT'S DOCTOR DESTINY: CLAIMING HE DREAMT THE JLA INTO EXISTENCE AND THREATENING TO "DE-IMAGINE DETROIT" IF YOU CAN'T PROVE HIM WRONG.
I'M OUTTA HERE, GUYS...
DOCTOR DESTINY?
LIGHTWEIGHT. TEN MINUTES TOPS.
ZZZEEEEE ZZZEEEEE ZZEEEE
WELL, BATMAN?
COME ON.
WE'RE THE JUSTICE LEAGUE.
YOU KNOW YOU LOVE IT.

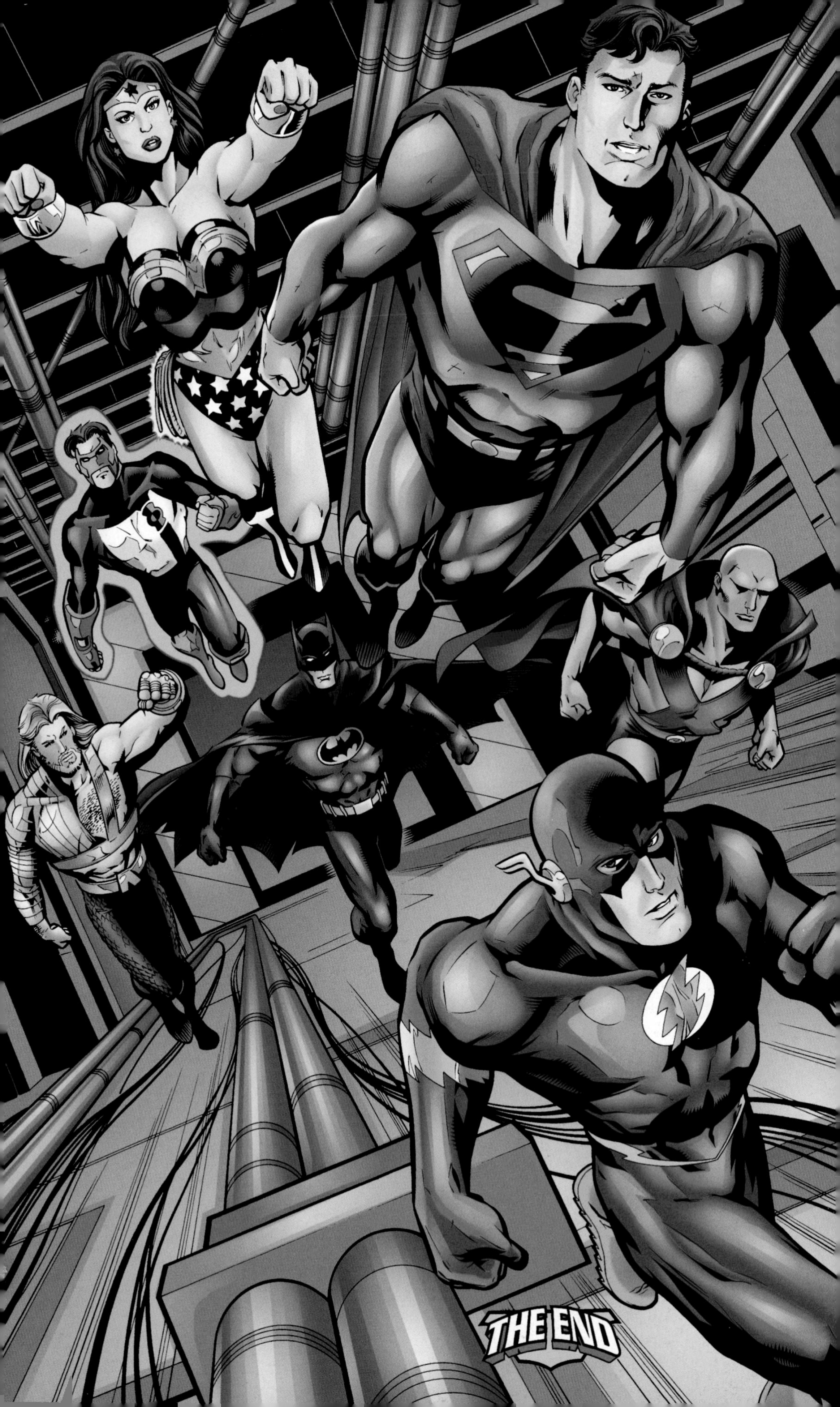
THE END

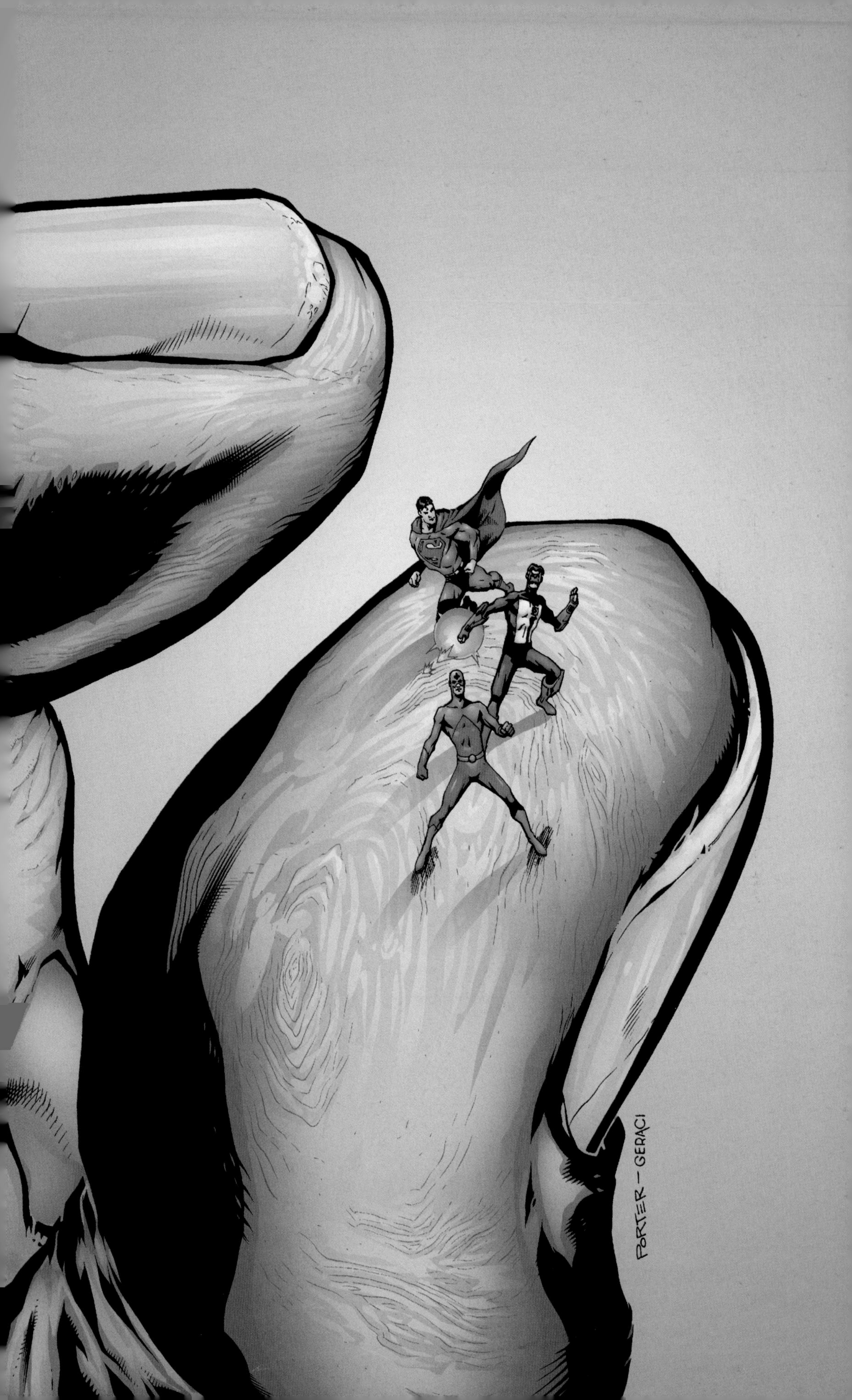
PORTER - GERACI

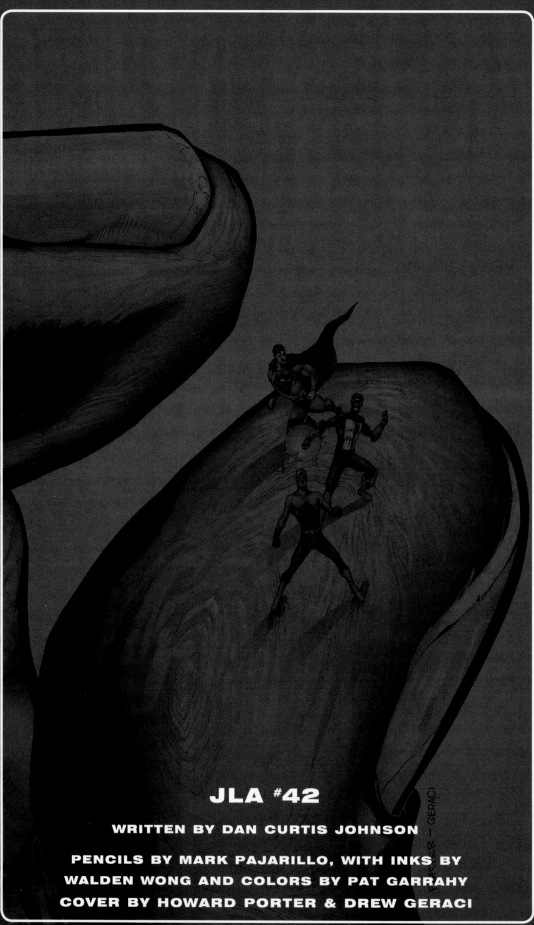

JLA #42

WRITTEN BY DAN CURTIS JOHNSON

PENCILS BY MARK PAJARILLO, WITH INKS BY
WALDEN WONG AND COLORS BY PAT GARRAHY
COVER BY HOWARD PORTER & DREW GERACI

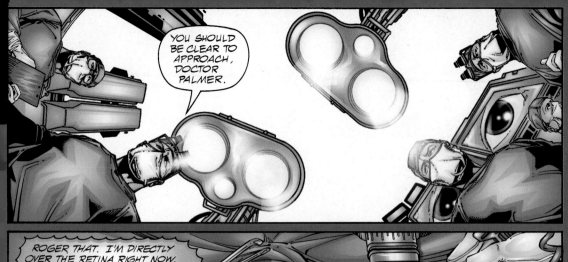

YOU SHOULD BE CLEAR TO APPROACH, DOCTOR PALMER.

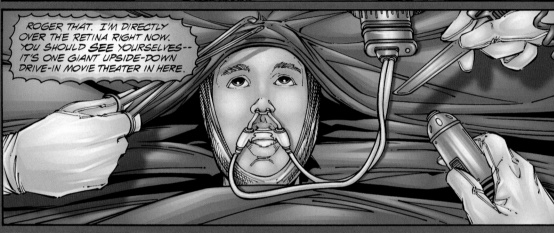

ROGER THAT. I'M DIRECTLY OVER THE RETINA RIGHT NOW. YOU SHOULD *SEE* YOURSELVES-- IT'S ONE GIANT UPSIDE-DOWN DRIVE-IN MOVIE THEATER IN HERE.

THAT'S PROBABLY ENOUGH SIGHTSEEING, DOCTOR. YOUR NEW BEARING IS AT 133 DEGREES, DOWN SIXTEEN. THAT SHOULD TAKE YOU RIGHT TO THE *OPTIC NERVE.*

DON'T WORRY, GENTLEMEN. I *KNOW* MY WAY AROUND THE TERRITORY. FROM HERE IT'S STRAIGHT TO THE TARGET SITE. THE ELECTRICAL TRANSFER ALONG THE NERVE WILL PROBABLY JANGLE COMMUNICATIONS FOR A FEW SECONDS.

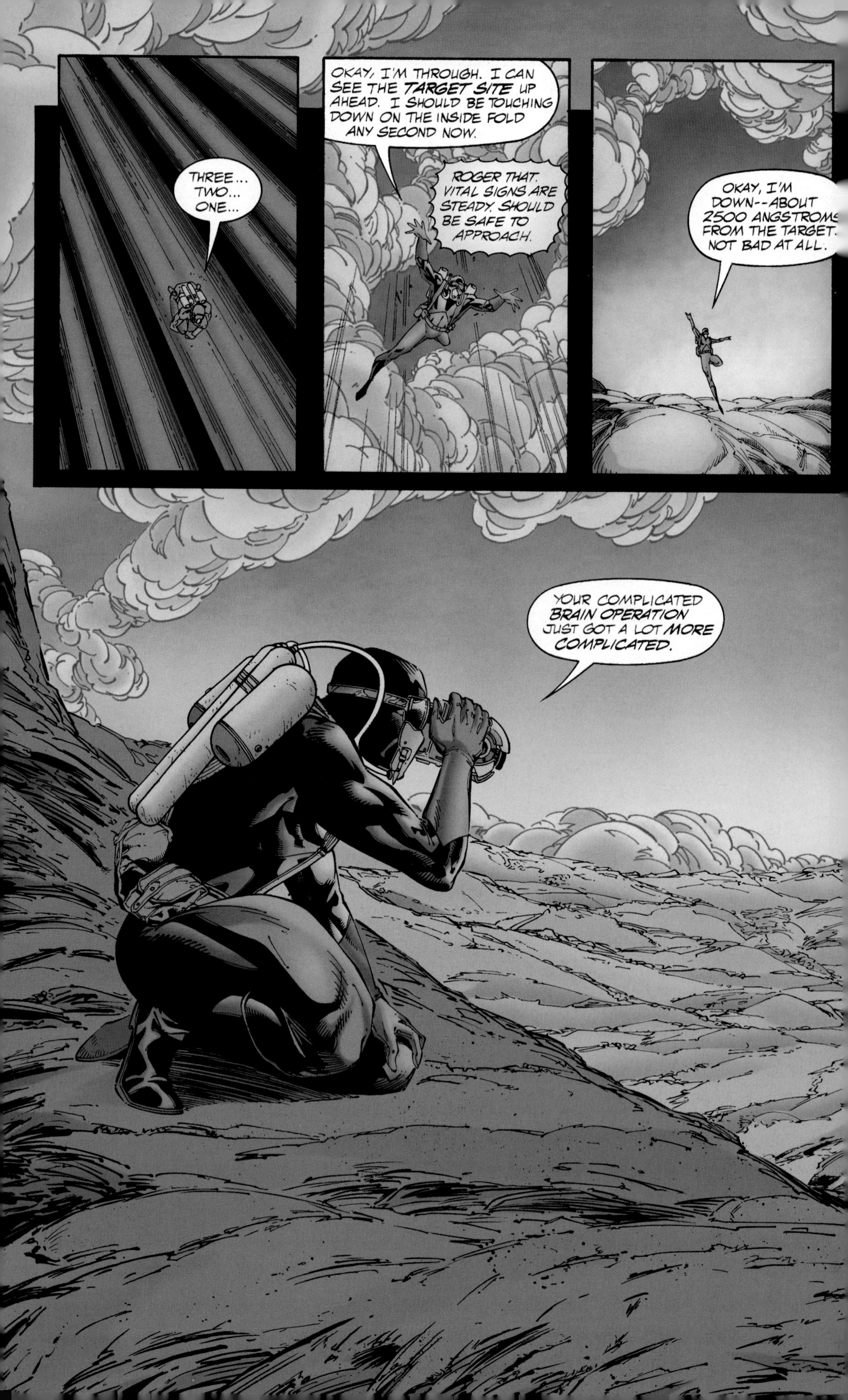
THREE... TWO... ONE...
OKAY, I'M THROUGH. I CAN SEE THE TARGET SITE UP AHEAD. I SHOULD BE TOUCHING DOWN ON THE INSIDE FOLD ANY SECOND NOW.
ROGER THAT. VITAL SIGNS ARE STEADY. SHOULD BE SAFE TO APPROACH.
OKAY, I'M DOWN--ABOUT 2500 ANGSTROMS FROM THE TARGET. NOT BAD AT ALL.
YOUR COMPLICATED BRAIN OPERATION JUST GOT A LOT MORE COMPLICATED.

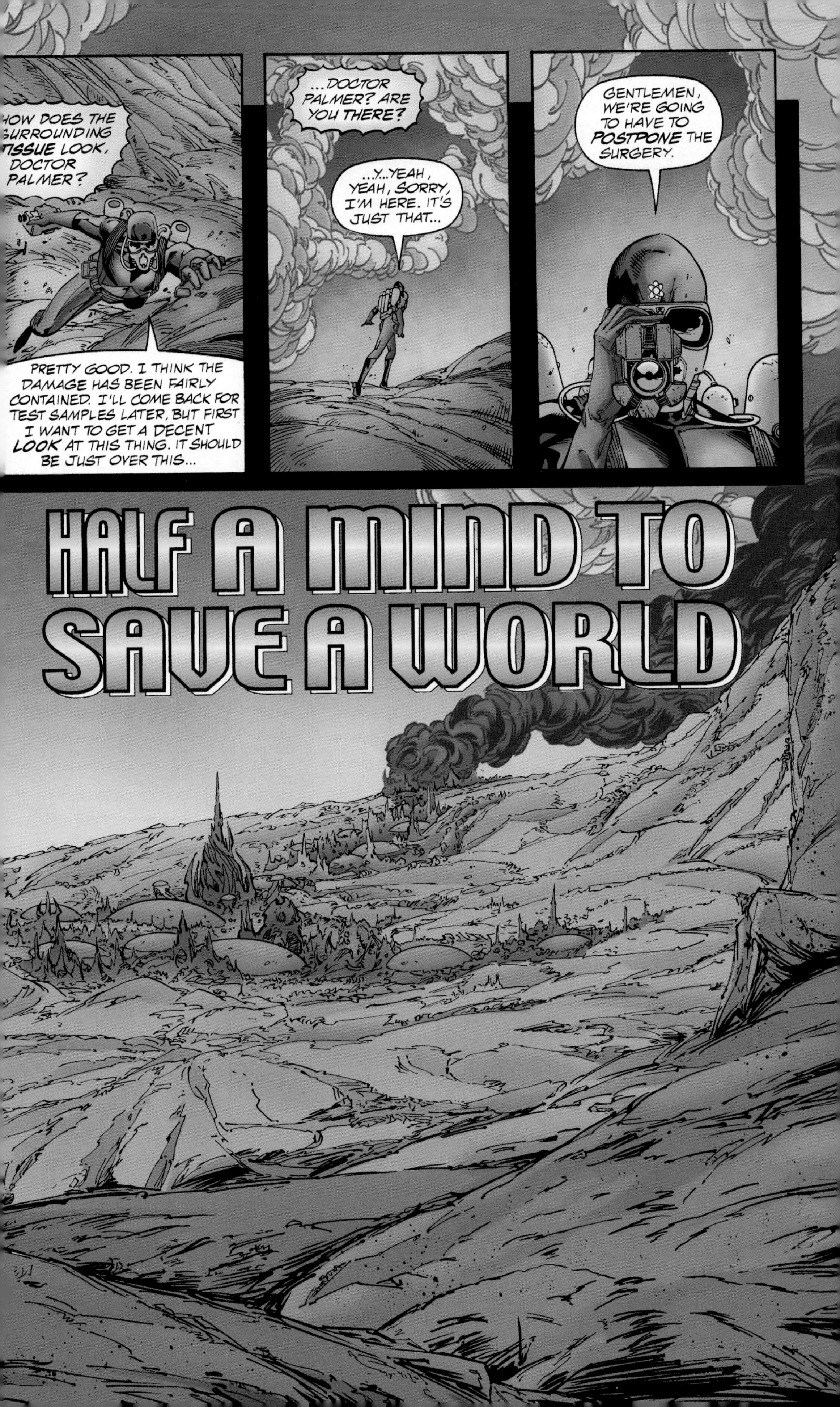
HOW DOES THE SURROUNDING TISSUE LOOK, DOCTOR PALMER?
PRETTY GOOD. I THINK THE DAMAGE HAS BEEN FAIRLY CONTAINED. I'LL COME BACK FOR TEST SAMPLES LATER, BUT FIRST I WANT TO GET A DECENT LOOK AT THIS THING. IT SHOULD BE JUST OVER THIS...
...DOCTOR PALMER? ARE YOU THERE?
...Y...YEAH, YEAH, SORRY, I'M HERE. IT'S JUST THAT...
GENTLEMEN, WE'RE GOING TO HAVE TO POSTPONE THE SURGERY.
HALF A MIND TO SAVE A WORLD

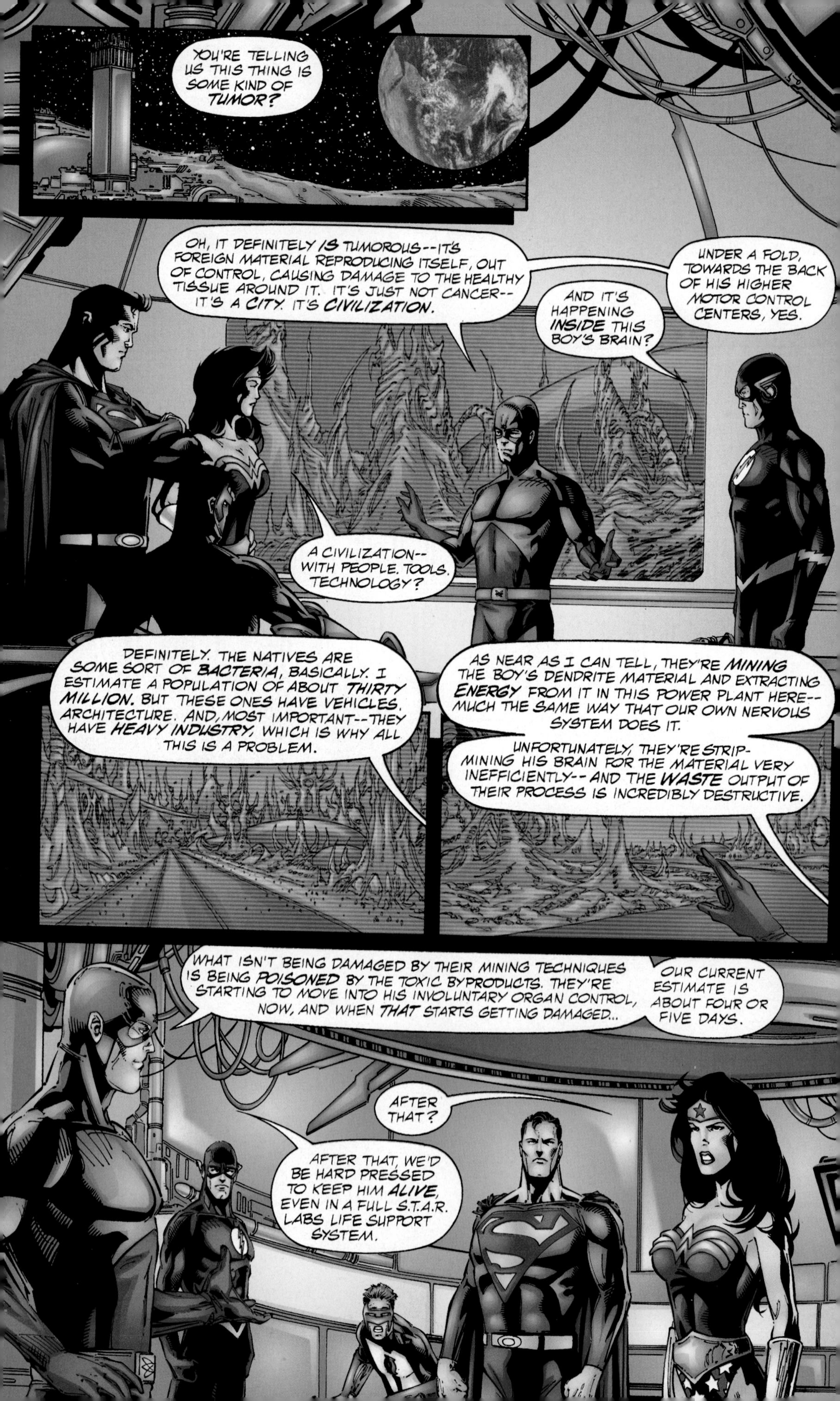

YOU'RE TELLING US THIS THING IS SOME KIND OF TUMOR?
OH, IT DEFINITELY IS TUMOROUS--IT'S FOREIGN MATERIAL REPRODUCING ITSELF, OUT OF CONTROL, CAUSING DAMAGE TO THE HEALTHY TISSUE AROUND IT. IT'S JUST NOT CANCER-- IT'S A CITY. IT'S CIVILIZATION.
AND IT'S HAPPENING INSIDE THIS BOY'S BRAIN?
UNDER A FOLD, TOWARDS THE BACK OF HIS HIGHER MOTOR CONTROL CENTERS, YES.
A CIVILIZATION-- WITH PEOPLE. TOOLS. TECHNOLOGY?
DEFINITELY. THE NATIVES ARE SOME SORT OF BACTERIA, BASICALLY. I ESTIMATE A POPULATION OF ABOUT THIRTY MILLION. BUT THESE ONES HAVE VEHICLES, ARCHITECTURE. AND, MOST IMPORTANT--THEY HAVE HEAVY INDUSTRY, WHICH IS WHY ALL THIS IS A PROBLEM.
AS NEAR AS I CAN TELL, THEY'RE MINING THE BOY'S DENDRITE MATERIAL AND EXTRACTING ENERGY FROM IT IN THIS POWER PLANT HERE-- MUCH THE SAME WAY THAT OUR OWN NERVOUS SYSTEM DOES IT.
UNFORTUNATELY, THEY'RE STRIP-MINING HIS BRAIN FOR THE MATERIAL VERY INEFFICIENTLY-- AND THE WASTE OUTPUT OF THEIR PROCESS IS INCREDIBLY DESTRUCTIVE.
WHAT ISN'T BEING DAMAGED BY THEIR MINING TECHNIQUES IS BEING POISONED BY THE TOXIC BYPRODUCTS. THEY'RE STARTING TO MOVE INTO HIS INVOLUNTARY ORGAN CONTROL, NOW, AND WHEN THAT STARTS GETTING DAMAGED...
OUR CURRENT ESTIMATE IS ABOUT FOUR OR FIVE DAYS.
AFTER THAT?
AFTER THAT, WE'D BE HARD PRESSED TO KEEP HIM ALIVE, EVEN IN A FULL S.T.A.R. LABS LIFE SUPPORT SYSTEM.

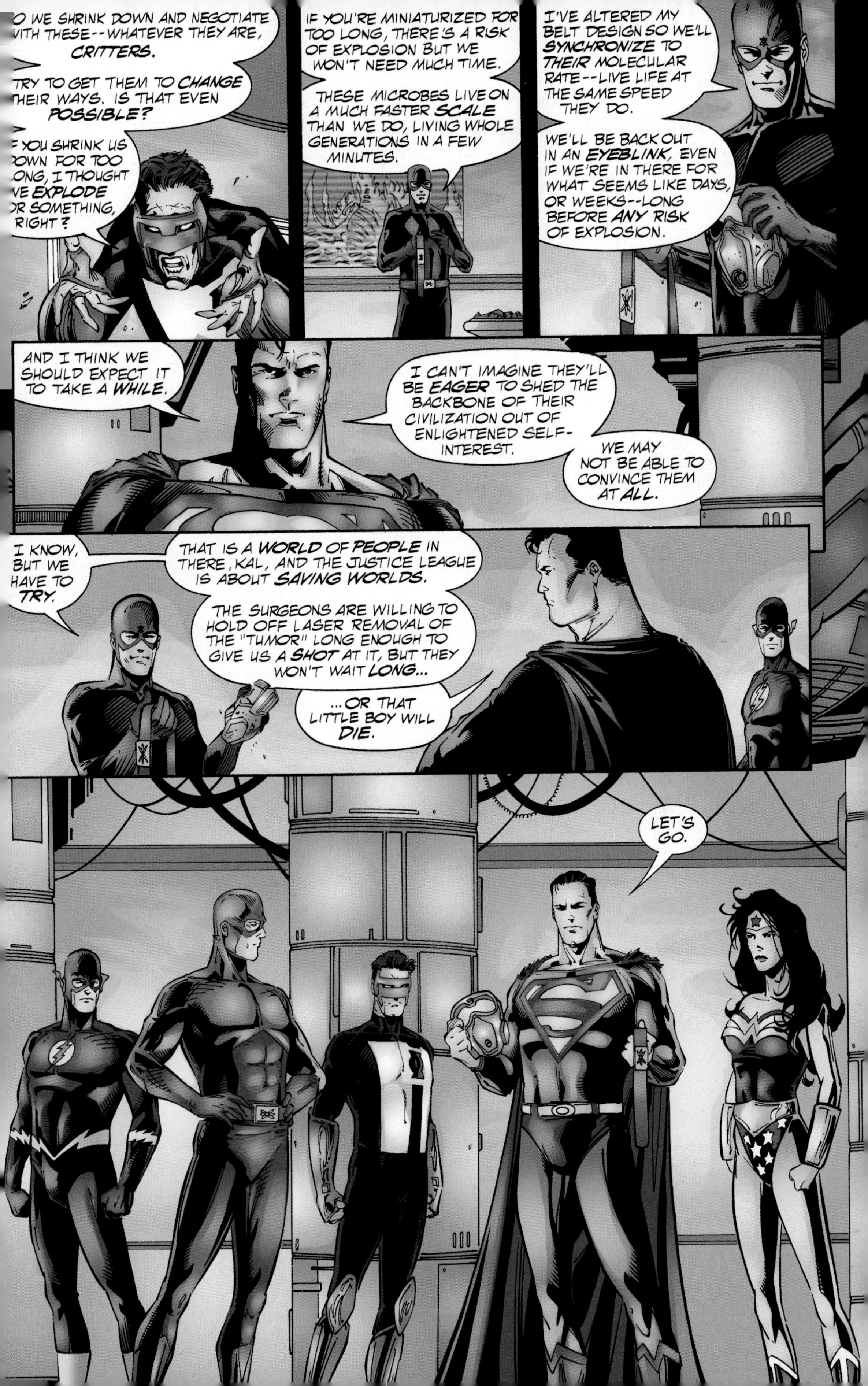

O WE SHRINK DOWN AND NEGOTIATE WITH THESE--WHATEVER THEY ARE, CRITTERS.
TRY TO GET THEM TO CHANGE THEIR WAYS. IS THAT EVEN POSSIBLE?
F YOU SHRINK US DOWN FOR TOO LONG, I THOUGHT WE EXPLODE OR SOMETHING, RIGHT?
IF YOU'RE MINIATURIZED FOR TOO LONG, THERE'S A RISK OF EXPLOSION BUT WE WON'T NEED MUCH TIME.
THESE MICROBES LIVE ON A MUCH FASTER SCALE THAN WE DO, LIVING WHOLE GENERATIONS IN A FEW MINUTES.
I'VE ALTERED MY BELT DESIGN SO WE'LL SYNCHRONIZE TO THEIR MOLECULAR RATE--LIVE LIFE AT THE SAME SPEED THEY DO.
WE'LL BE BACK OUT IN AN EYEBLINK, EVEN IF WE'RE IN THERE FOR WHAT SEEMS LIKE DAYS, OR WEEKS--LONG BEFORE ANY RISK OF EXPLOSION.
AND I THINK WE SHOULD EXPECT IT TO TAKE A WHILE.
I CAN'T IMAGINE THEY'LL BE EAGER TO SHED THE BACKBONE OF THEIR CIVILIZATION OUT OF ENLIGHTENED SELF-INTEREST.
WE MAY NOT BE ABLE TO CONVINCE THEM AT ALL.
I KNOW, BUT WE HAVE TO TRY.
THAT IS A WORLD OF PEOPLE IN THERE, KAL, AND THE JUSTICE LEAGUE IS ABOUT SAVING WORLDS.
THE SURGEONS ARE WILLING TO HOLD OFF LASER REMOVAL OF THE "TUMOR" LONG ENOUGH TO GIVE US A SHOT AT IT, BUT THEY WON'T WAIT LONG...
...OR THAT LITTLE BOY WILL DIE.
LET'S GO.

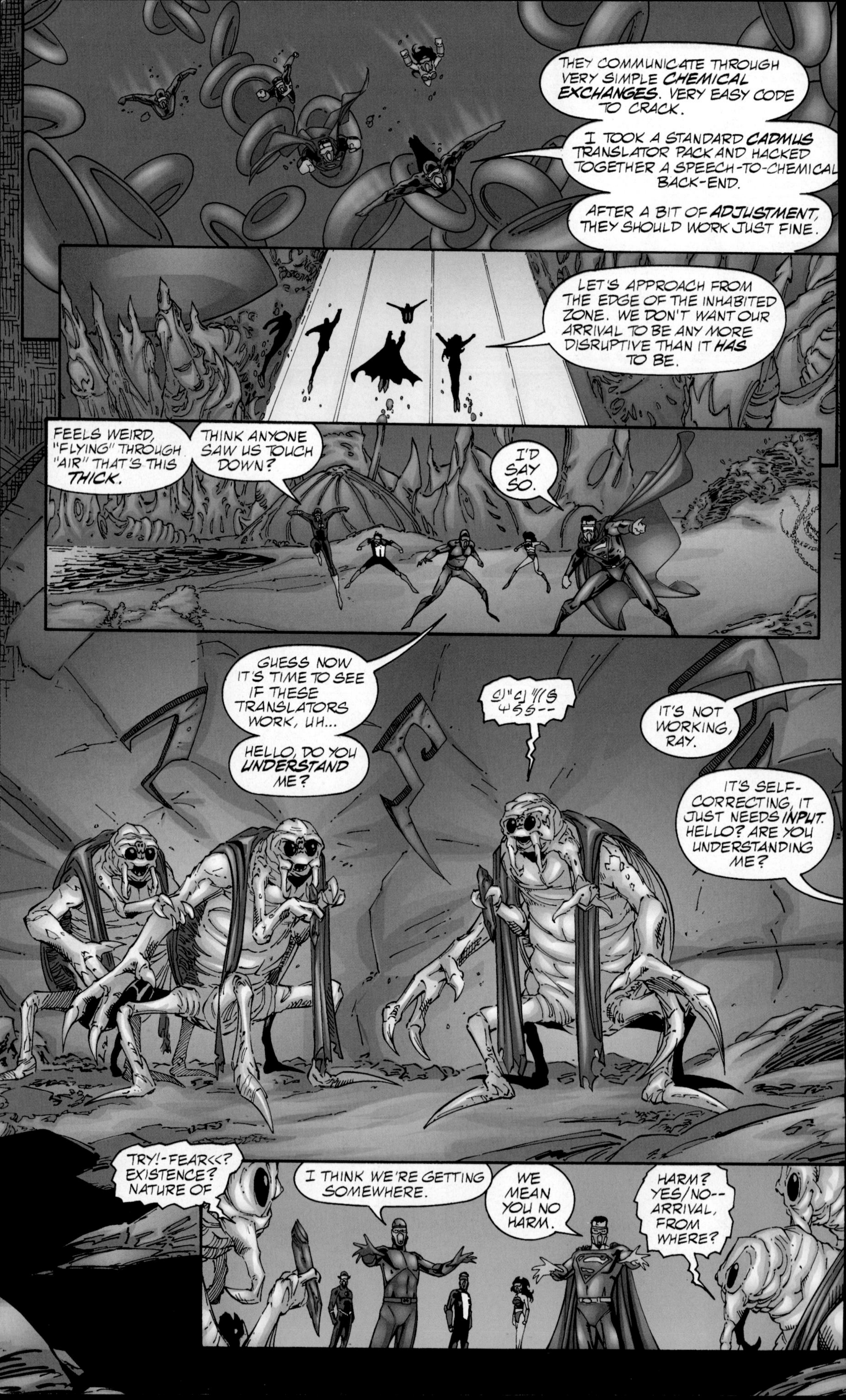
THEY COMMUNICATE THROUGH VERY SIMPLE CHEMICAL EXCHANGES. VERY EASY CODE TO CRACK.
I TOOK A STANDARD CADMUS TRANSLATOR PACK AND HACKED TOGETHER A SPEECH-TO-CHEMICAL BACK-END.
AFTER A BIT OF ADJUSTMENT, THEY SHOULD WORK JUST FINE.
LET'S APPROACH FROM THE EDGE OF THE INHABITED ZONE. WE DON'T WANT OUR ARRIVAL TO BE ANY MORE DISRUPTIVE THAN IT HAS TO BE.
FEELS WEIRD, "FLYING" THROUGH "AIR" THAT'S THIS THICK.
THINK ANYONE SAW US TOUCH DOWN?
I'D SAY SO.
GUESS NOW IT'S TIME TO SEE IF THESE TRANSLATORS WORK, UH...
HELLO, DO YOU UNDERSTAND ME?
IT'S NOT WORKING, RAY.
IT'S SELF-CORRECTING, IT JUST NEEDS INPUT. HELLO? ARE YOU UNDERSTANDING ME?
TRY!-FEAR<<? EXISTENCE? NATURE OF
I THINK WE'RE GETTING SOMEWHERE.
WE MEAN YOU NO HARM.
HARM? YES/NO-- ARRIVAL, FROM WHERE?

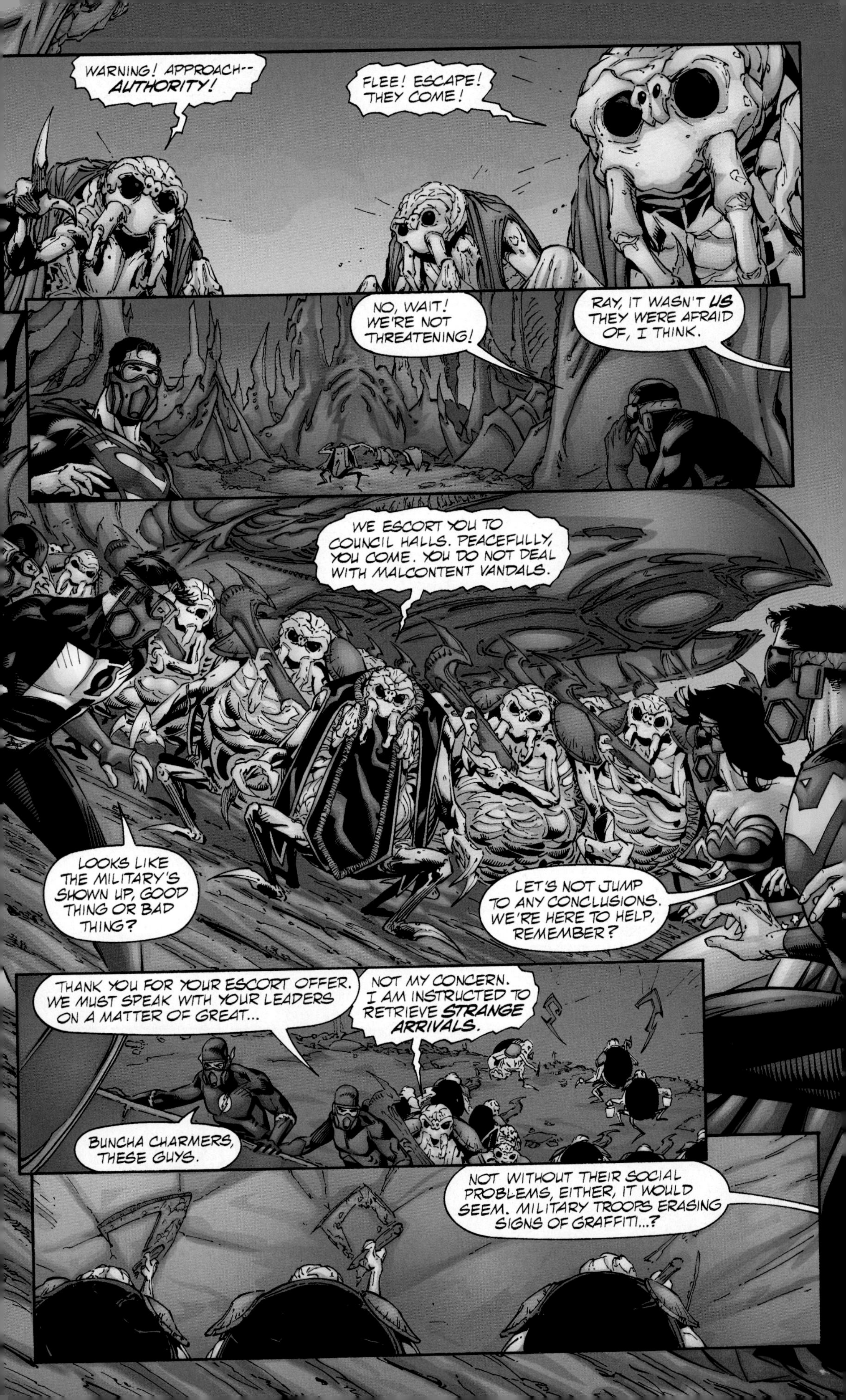
WARNING! APPROACH-- AUTHORITY!
FLEE! ESCAPE! THEY COME!
NO, WAIT! WE'RE NOT THREATENING!
RAY, IT WASN'T US THEY WERE AFRAID OF, I THINK.
WE ESCORT YOU TO COUNCIL HALLS. PEACEFULLY, YOU COME. YOU DO NOT DEAL WITH MALCONTENT VANDALS.
LOOKS LIKE THE MILITARY'S SHOWN UP, GOOD THING OR BAD THING?
LET'S NOT JUMP TO ANY CONCLUSIONS. WE'RE HERE TO HELP, REMEMBER?
THANK YOU FOR YOUR ESCORT OFFER. WE MUST SPEAK WITH YOUR LEADERS ON A MATTER OF GREAT...
NOT MY CONCERN. I AM INSTRUCTED TO RETRIEVE STRANGE ARRIVALS.
BUNCHA CHARMERS, THESE GUYS.
NOT WITHOUT THEIR SOCIAL PROBLEMS, EITHER, IT WOULD SEEM. MILITARY TROOPS ERASING SIGNS OF GRAFFITI...?

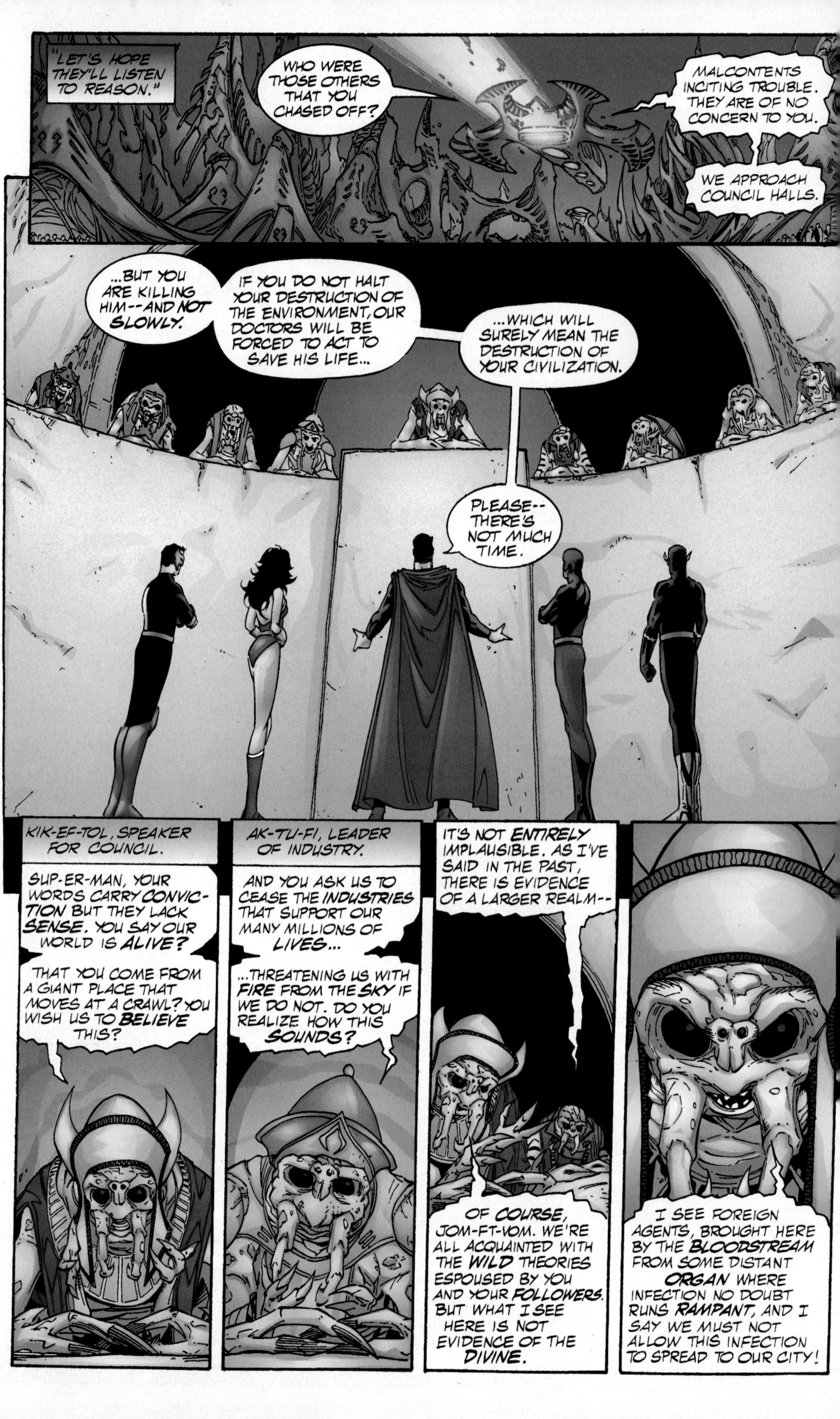
"LET'S HOPE THEY'LL LISTEN TO REASON."
WHO WERE THOSE OTHERS THAT YOU CHASED OFF?
MALCONTENTS INCITING TROUBLE. THEY ARE OF NO CONCERN TO YOU.
WE APPROACH COUNCIL HALLS.
...BUT YOU ARE KILLING HIM--AND NOT SLOWLY.
IF YOU DO NOT HALT YOUR DESTRUCTION OF THE ENVIRONMENT, OUR DOCTORS WILL BE FORCED TO ACT TO SAVE HIS LIFE...
...WHICH WILL SURELY MEAN THE DESTRUCTION OF YOUR CIVILIZATION.
PLEASE-- THERE'S NOT MUCH TIME.
KIK-EF-TOL, SPEAKER FOR COUNCIL.
SUP-ER-MAN, YOUR WORDS CARRY CONVICTION BUT THEY LACK SENSE. YOU SAY OUR WORLD IS ALIVE?
THAT YOU COME FROM A GIANT PLACE THAT MOVES AT A CRAWL? YOU WISH US TO BELIEVE THIS?
AK-TU-FI, LEADER OF INDUSTRY.
AND YOU ASK US TO CEASE THE INDUSTRIES THAT SUPPORT OUR MANY MILLIONS OF LIVES...
...THREATENING US WITH FIRE FROM THE SKY IF WE DO NOT. DO YOU REALIZE HOW THIS SOUNDS?
IT'S NOT ENTIRELY IMPLAUSIBLE. AS I'VE SAID IN THE PAST, THERE IS EVIDENCE OF A LARGER REALM--
OF COURSE, JOM-FT-VOM. WE'RE ALL ACQUAINTED WITH THE WILD THEORIES ESPOUSED BY YOU AND YOUR FOLLOWERS. BUT WHAT I SEE HERE IS NOT EVIDENCE OF THE DIVINE.
I SEE FOREIGN AGENTS, BROUGHT HERE BY THE BLOODSTREAM FROM SOME DISTANT ORGAN WHERE INFECTION NO DOUBT RUNS RAMPANT, AND I SAY WE MUST NOT ALLOW THIS INFECTION TO SPREAD TO OUR CITY!

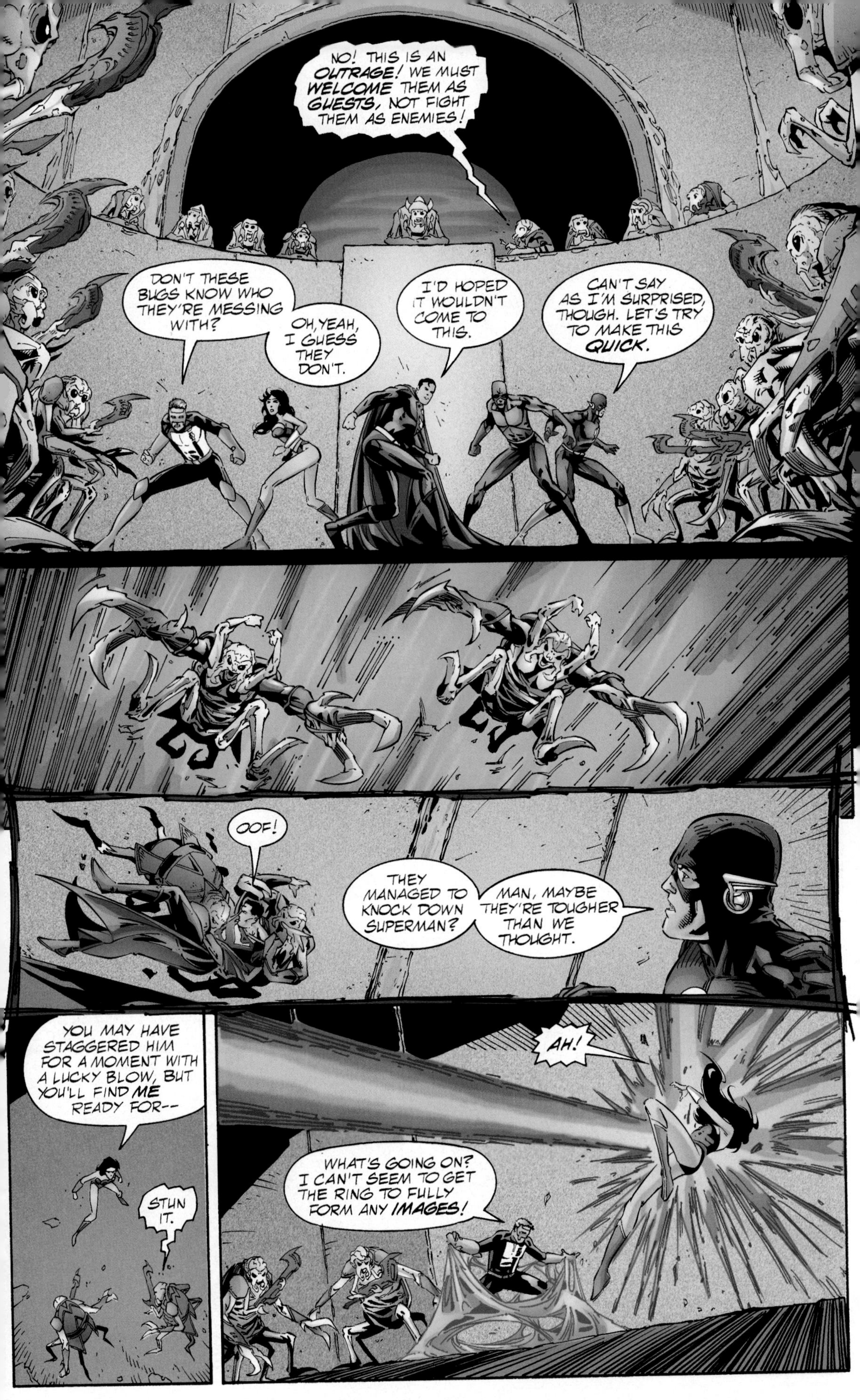
NO! THIS IS AN OUTRAGE! WE MUST WELCOME THEM AS GUESTS, NOT FIGHT THEM AS ENEMIES!
DON'T THESE BUGS KNOW WHO THEY'RE MESSING WITH?
OH, YEAH, I GUESS THEY DON'T.
I'D HOPED IT WOULDN'T COME TO THIS.
CAN'T SAY AS I'M SURPRISED, THOUGH. LET'S TRY TO MAKE THIS QUICK.
OOF!
THEY MANAGED TO KNOCK DOWN SUPERMAN?
MAN, MAYBE THEY'RE TOUGHER THAN WE THOUGHT.
YOU MAY HAVE STAGGERED HIM FOR A MOMENT WITH A LUCKY BLOW, BUT YOU'LL FIND ME READY FOR--
STUN IT.
AH!
WHAT'S GOING ON? I CAN'T SEEM TO GET THE RING TO FULLY FORM ANY IMAGES!

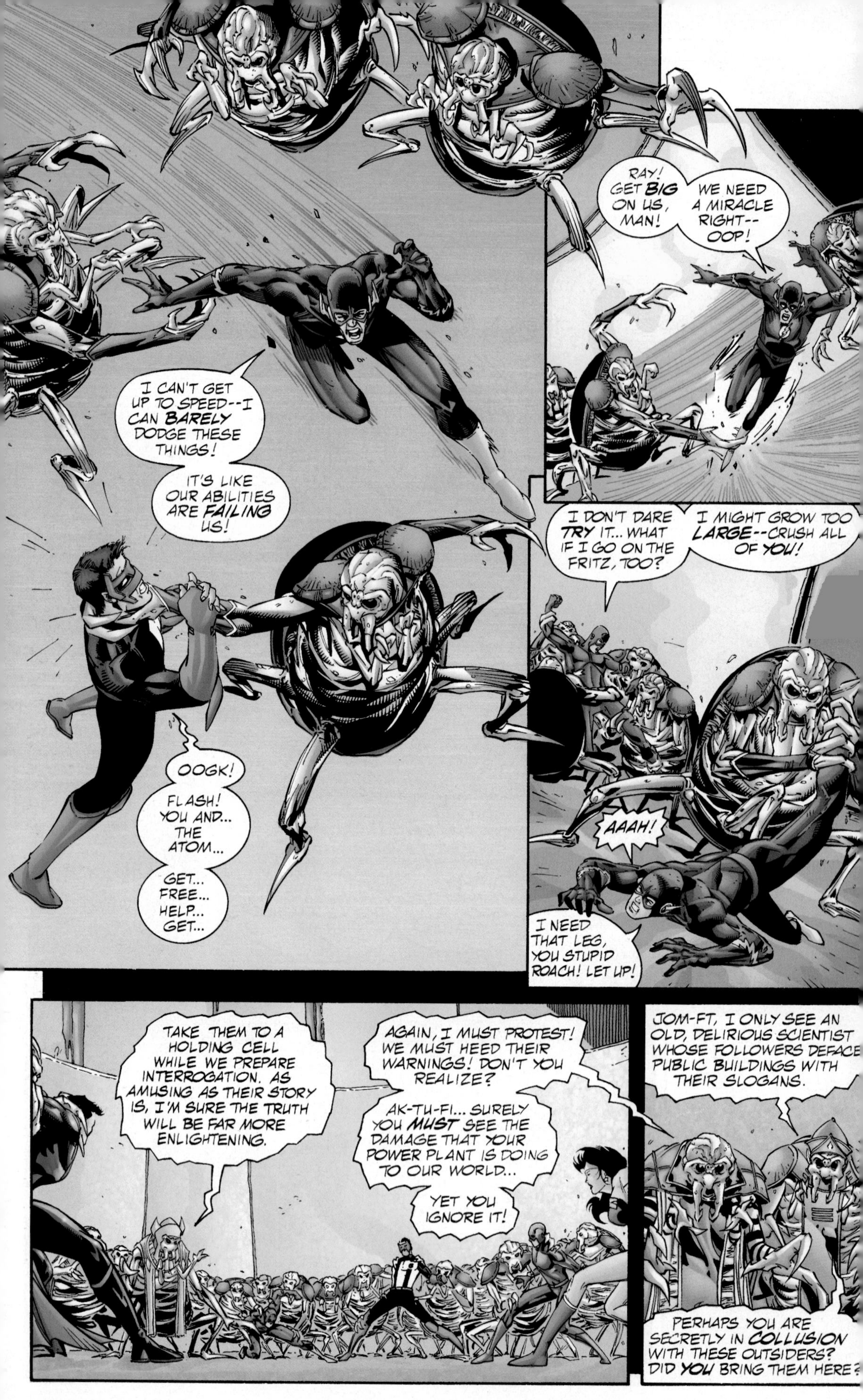
RAY! GET BIG ON US, MAN!
WE NEED A MIRACLE RIGHT-- OOP!
I CAN'T GET UP TO SPEED--I CAN BARELY DODGE THESE THINGS!
IT'S LIKE OUR ABILITIES ARE FAILING US!
I DON'T DARE TRY IT... WHAT IF I GO ON THE FRITZ, TOO?
I MIGHT GROW TOO LARGE--CRUSH ALL OF YOU!
OOGK!
FLASH! YOU AND... THE ATOM...
GET... FREE... HELP... GET...
AAAH!
I NEED THAT LEG, YOU STUPID ROACH! LET UP!
TAKE THEM TO A HOLDING CELL WHILE WE PREPARE INTERROGATION. AS AMUSING AS THEIR STORY IS, I'M SURE THE TRUTH WILL BE FAR MORE ENLIGHTENING.
AGAIN, I MUST PROTEST! WE MUST HEED THEIR WARNINGS! DON'T YOU REALIZE?
AK-TU-FI... SURELY YOU MUST SEE THE DAMAGE THAT YOUR POWER PLANT IS DOING TO OUR WORLD...
YET YOU IGNORE IT!
JOM-FT, I ONLY SEE AN OLD, DELIRIOUS SCIENTIST WHOSE FOLLOWERS DEFACE PUBLIC BUILDINGS WITH THEIR SLOGANS.
PERHAPS YOU ARE SECRETLY IN COLLUSION WITH THESE OUTSIDERS? DID YOU BRING THEM HERE?

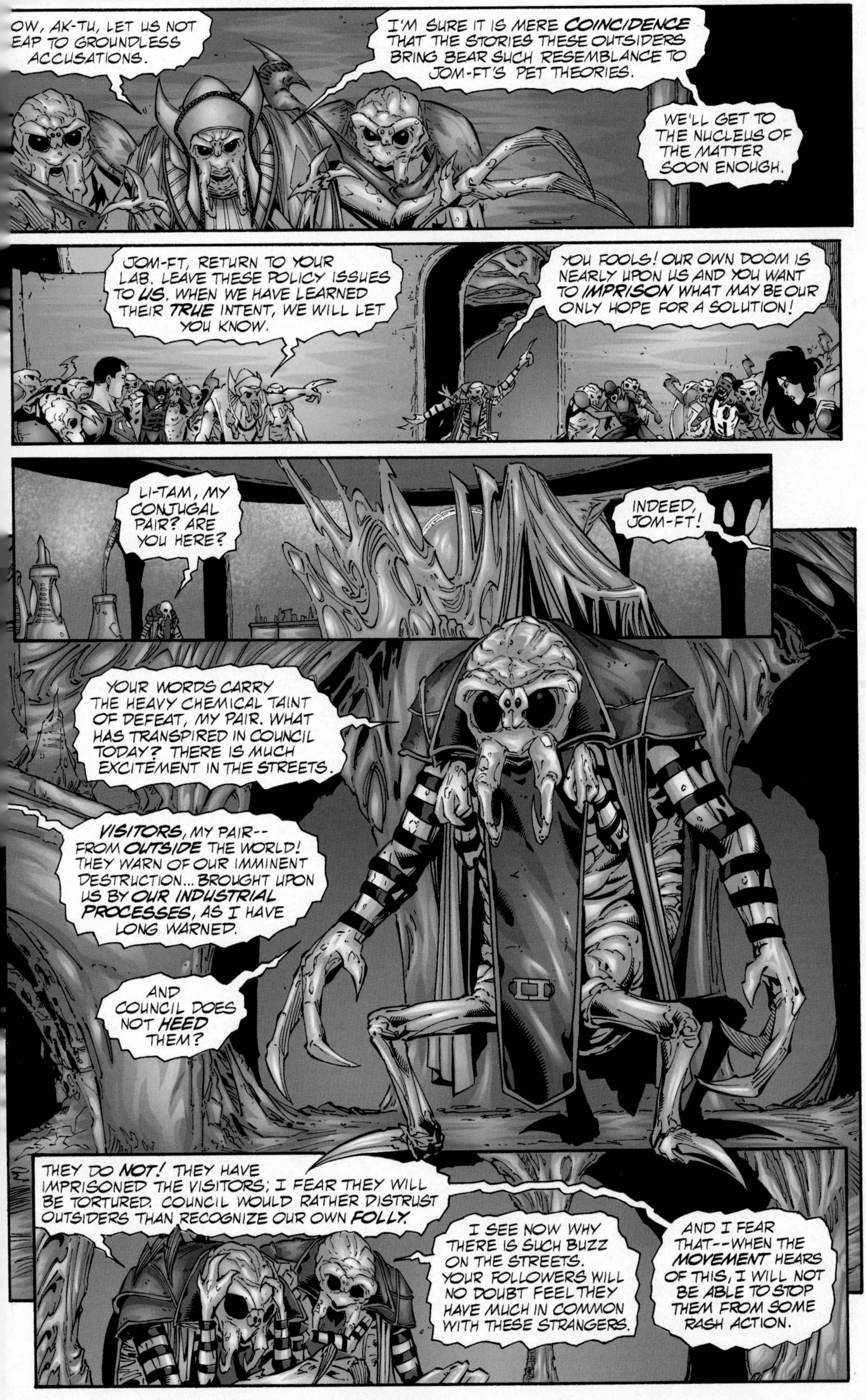
OW, AK-TU, LET US NOT EAP TO GROUNDLESS ACCUSATIONS.
I'M SURE IT IS MERE COINCIDENCE THAT THE STORIES THESE OUTSIDERS BRING BEAR SUCH RESEMBLANCE TO JOM-FT'S PET THEORIES.
WE'LL GET TO THE NUCLEUS OF THE MATTER SOON ENOUGH.
JOM-FT, RETURN TO YOUR LAB. LEAVE THESE POLICY ISSUES TO US. WHEN WE HAVE LEARNED THEIR TRUE INTENT, WE WILL LET YOU KNOW.
YOU FOOLS! OUR OWN DOOM IS NEARLY UPON US AND YOU WANT TO IMPRISON WHAT MAY BE OUR ONLY HOPE FOR A SOLUTION!
LI-TAM, MY CONJUGAL PAIR? ARE YOU HERE?
INDEED, JOM-FT!
YOUR WORDS CARRY THE HEAVY CHEMICAL TAINT OF DEFEAT, MY PAIR. WHAT HAS TRANSPIRED IN COUNCIL TODAY? THERE IS MUCH EXCITEMENT IN THE STREETS.
VISITORS, MY PAIR-- FROM OUTSIDE THE WORLD! THEY WARN OF OUR IMMINENT DESTRUCTION... BROUGHT UPON US BY OUR INDUSTRIAL PROCESSES, AS I HAVE LONG WARNED.
AND COUNCIL DOES NOT HEED THEM?
THEY DO NOT! THEY HAVE IMPRISONED THE VISITORS; I FEAR THEY WILL BE TORTURED. COUNCIL WOULD RATHER DISTRUST OUTSIDERS THAN RECOGNIZE OUR OWN FOLLY.
I SEE NOW WHY THERE IS SUCH BUZZ ON THE STREETS. YOUR FOLLOWERS WILL NO DOUBT FEEL THEY HAVE MUCH IN COMMON WITH THESE STRANGERS.
AND I FEAR THAT--WHEN THE MOVEMENT HEARS OF THIS, I WILL NOT BE ABLE TO STOP THEM FROM SOME RASH ACTION.

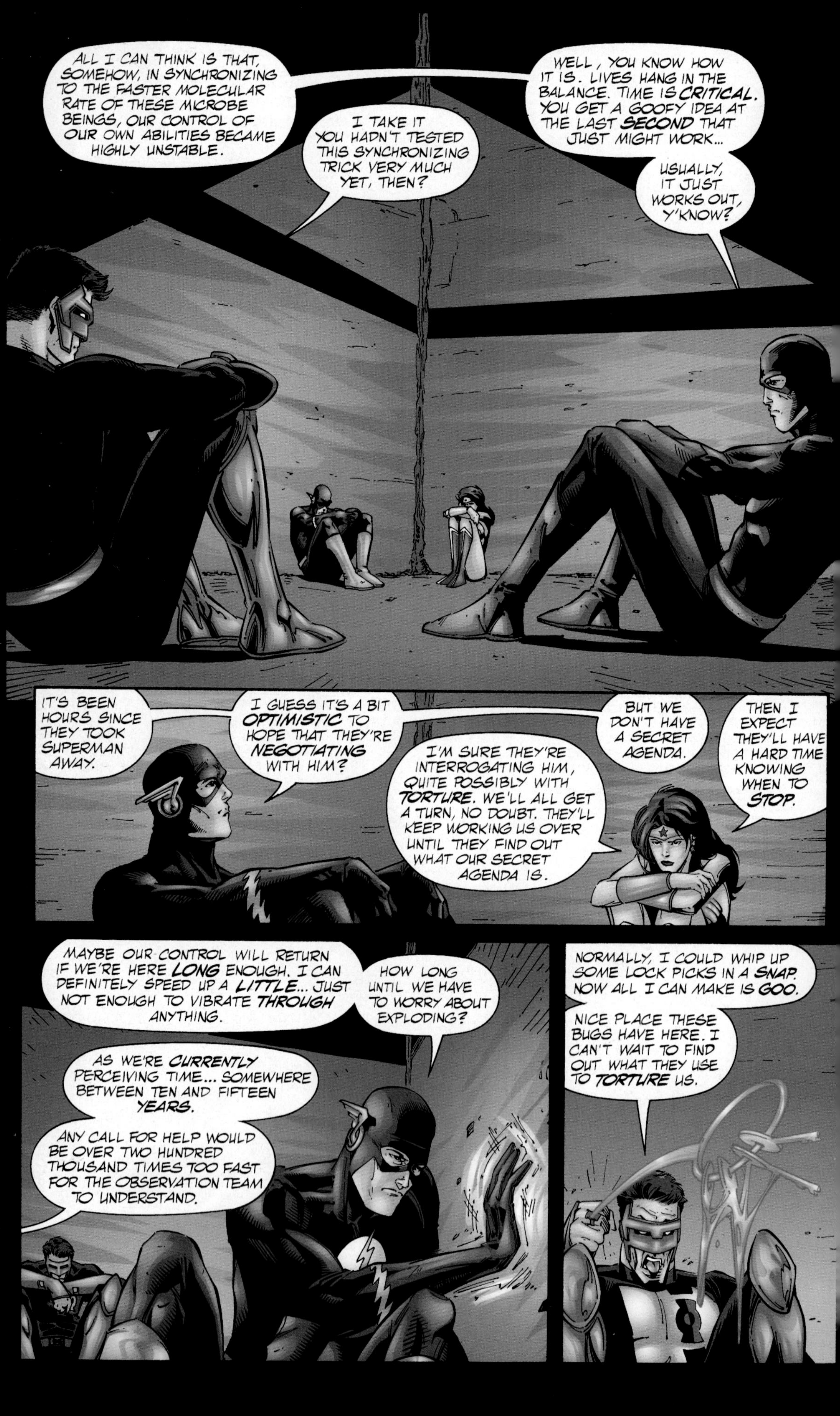

ALL I CAN THINK IS THAT, SOMEHOW, IN SYNCHRONIZING TO THE FASTER MOLECULAR RATE OF THESE MICROBE BEINGS, OUR CONTROL OF OUR OWN ABILITIES BECAME HIGHLY UNSTABLE.
I TAKE IT YOU HADN'T TESTED THIS SYNCHRONIZING TRICK VERY MUCH YET, THEN?
WELL, YOU KNOW HOW IT IS. LIVES HANG IN THE BALANCE. TIME IS CRITICAL. YOU GET A GOOFY IDEA AT THE LAST SECOND THAT JUST MIGHT WORK...
USUALLY, IT JUST WORKS OUT, Y'KNOW?
IT'S BEEN HOURS SINCE THEY TOOK SUPERMAN AWAY.
I GUESS IT'S A BIT OPTIMISTIC TO HOPE THAT THEY'RE NEGOTIATING WITH HIM?
I'M SURE THEY'RE INTERROGATING HIM, QUITE POSSIBLY WITH TORTURE. WE'LL ALL GET A TURN, NO DOUBT. THEY'LL KEEP WORKING US OVER UNTIL THEY FIND OUT WHAT OUR SECRET AGENDA IS.
BUT WE DON'T HAVE A SECRET AGENDA.
THEN I EXPECT THEY'LL HAVE A HARD TIME KNOWING WHEN TO STOP.
MAYBE OUR CONTROL WILL RETURN IF WE'RE HERE LONG ENOUGH. I CAN DEFINITELY SPEED UP A LITTLE... JUST NOT ENOUGH TO VIBRATE THROUGH ANYTHING.
HOW LONG UNTIL WE HAVE TO WORRY ABOUT EXPLODING?
AS WE'RE CURRENTLY PERCEIVING TIME... SOMEWHERE BETWEEN TEN AND FIFTEEN YEARS.
ANY CALL FOR HELP WOULD BE OVER TWO HUNDRED THOUSAND TIMES TOO FAST FOR THE OBSERVATION TEAM TO UNDERSTAND.
NORMALLY, I COULD WHIP UP SOME LOCK PICKS IN A SNAP. NOW ALL I CAN MAKE IS GOO.
NICE PLACE THESE BUGS HAVE HERE. I CAN'T WAIT TO FIND OUT WHAT THEY USE TO TORTURE US.

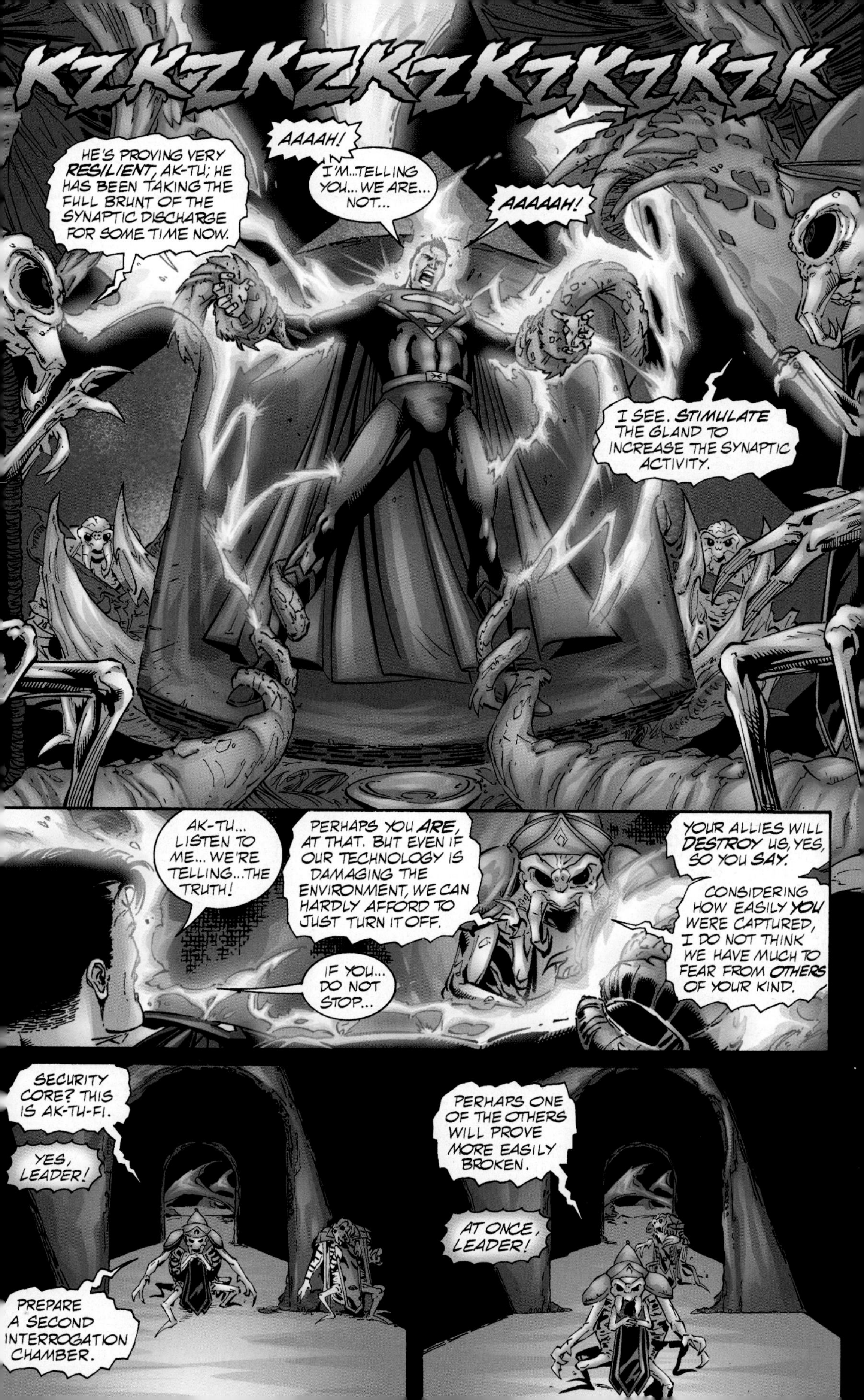
KZKZKZKZKZKZKZK
HE'S PROVING VERY RESILIENT, AK-TU; HE HAS BEEN TAKING THE FULL BRUNT OF THE SYNAPTIC DISCHARGE FOR SOME TIME NOW.
AAAAH!
I'M...TELLING YOU... WE ARE... NOT...
AAAAAH!
I SEE. STIMULATE THE GLAND TO INCREASE THE SYNAPTIC ACTIVITY.
AK-TU... LISTEN TO ME... WE'RE TELLING...THE TRUTH!
PERHAPS YOU ARE, AT THAT. BUT EVEN IF OUR TECHNOLOGY IS DAMAGING THE ENVIRONMENT, WE CAN HARDLY AFFORD TO JUST TURN IT OFF.
IF YOU... DO NOT STOP...
YOUR ALLIES WILL DESTROY US, YES, SO YOU SAY.
CONSIDERING HOW EASILY YOU WERE CAPTURED, I DO NOT THINK WE HAVE MUCH TO FEAR FROM OTHERS OF YOUR KIND.
SECURITY CORE? THIS IS AK-TU-FI.
YES, LEADER!
PREPARE A SECOND INTERROGATION CHAMBER.
PERHAPS ONE OF THE OTHERS WILL PROVE MORE EASILY BROKEN.
AT ONCE, LEADER!

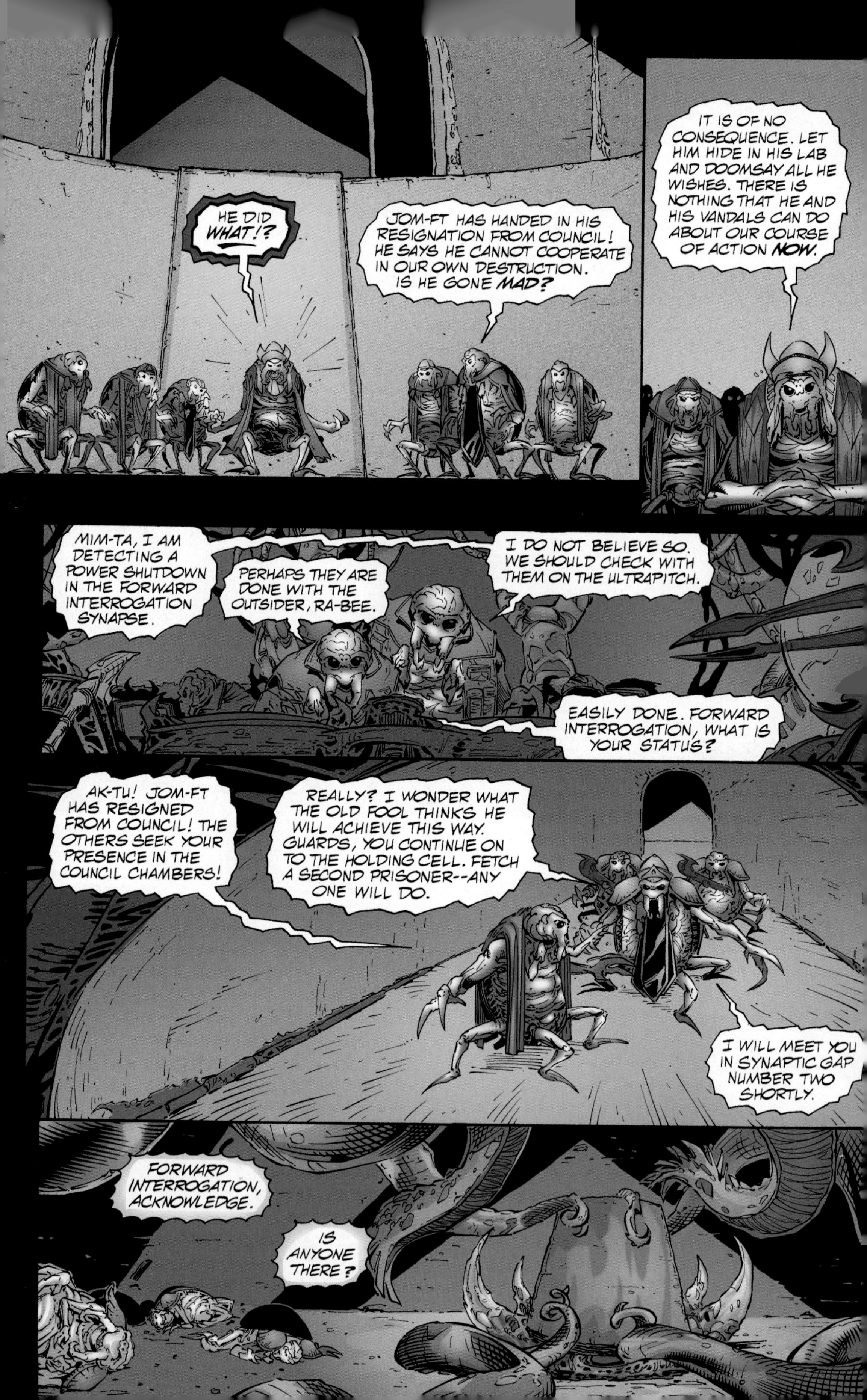
HE DID WHAT!?
JOM-FT HAS HANDED IN HIS RESIGNATION FROM COUNCIL! HE SAYS HE CANNOT COOPERATE IN OUR OWN DESTRUCTION. IS HE GONE MAD?
IT IS OF NO CONSEQUENCE. LET HIM HIDE IN HIS LAB AND DOOMSAY ALL HE WISHES. THERE IS NOTHING THAT HE AND HIS VANDALS CAN DO ABOUT OUR COURSE OF ACTION NOW.
MIM-TA, I AM DETECTING A POWER SHUTDOWN IN THE FORWARD INTERROGATION SYNAPSE.
PERHAPS THEY ARE DONE WITH THE OUTSIDER, RA-BEE.
I DO NOT BELIEVE SO. WE SHOULD CHECK WITH THEM ON THE ULTRAPITCH.
EASILY DONE. FORWARD INTERROGATION, WHAT IS YOUR STATUS?
AK-TU! JOM-FT HAS RESIGNED FROM COUNCIL! THE OTHERS SEEK YOUR PRESENCE IN THE COUNCIL CHAMBERS!
REALLY? I WONDER WHAT THE OLD FOOL THINKS HE WILL ACHIEVE THIS WAY. GUARDS, YOU CONTINUE ON TO THE HOLDING CELL. FETCH A SECOND PRISONER--ANY ONE WILL DO.
I WILL MEET YOU IN SYNAPTIC GAP NUMBER TWO SHORTLY.
FORWARD INTERROGATION, ACKNOWLEDGE.
IS ANYONE THERE?

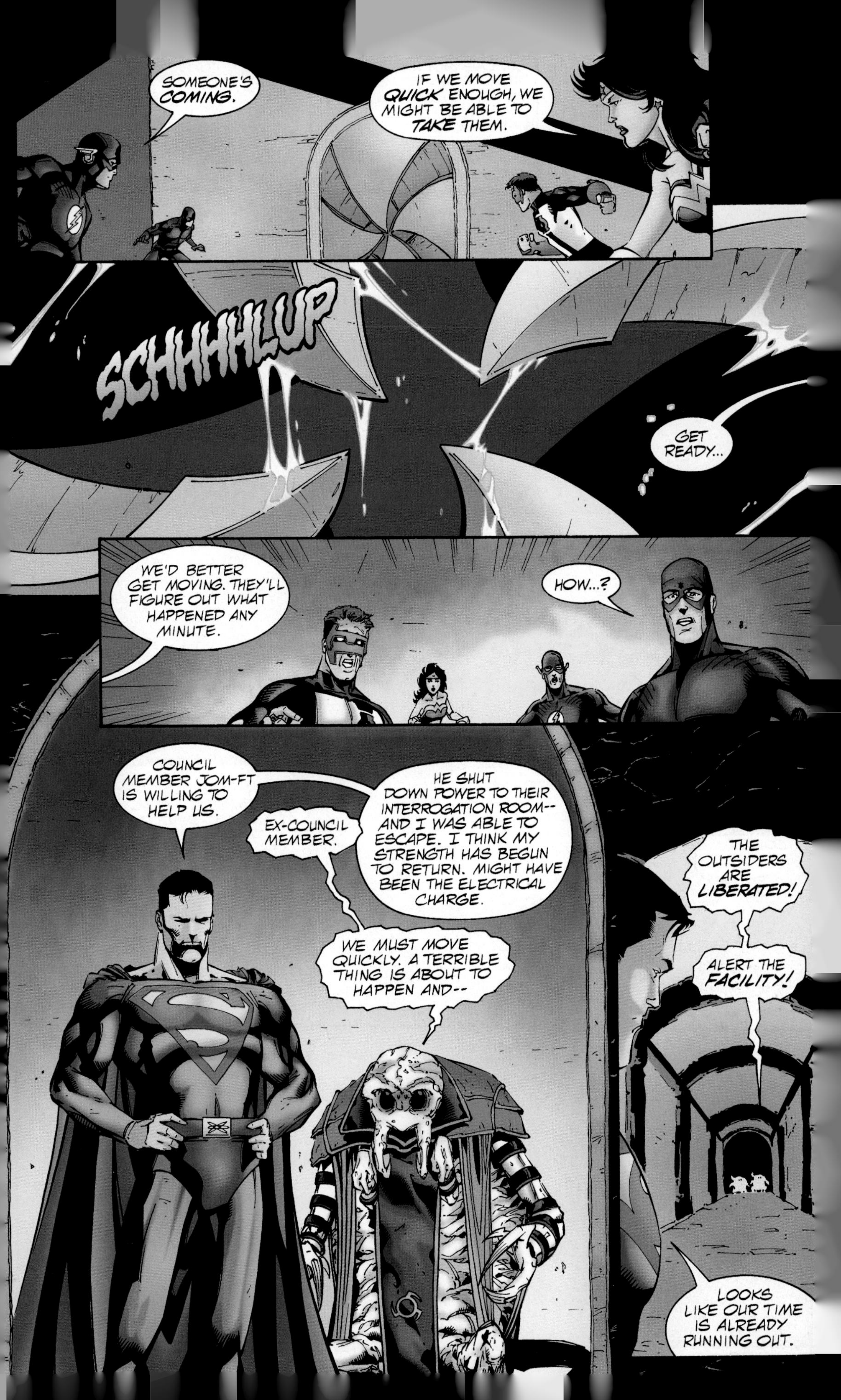
SOMEONE'S COMING.
IF WE MOVE QUICK ENOUGH, WE MIGHT BE ABLE TO TAKE THEM.
SCHHHLUP
GET READY...
WE'D BETTER GET MOVING. THEY'LL FIGURE OUT WHAT HAPPENED ANY MINUTE.
HOW...?
COUNCIL MEMBER JOM-FT IS WILLING TO HELP US.
HE SHUT DOWN POWER TO THEIR INTERROGATION ROOM-- AND I WAS ABLE TO ESCAPE. I THINK MY STRENGTH HAS BEGUN TO RETURN. MIGHT HAVE BEEN THE ELECTRICAL CHARGE.
EX-COUNCIL MEMBER.
WE MUST MOVE QUICKLY. A TERRIBLE THING IS ABOUT TO HAPPEN AND--
THE OUTSIDERS ARE LIBERATED!
ALERT THE FACILITY!
LOOKS LIKE OUR TIME IS ALREADY RUNNING OUT.

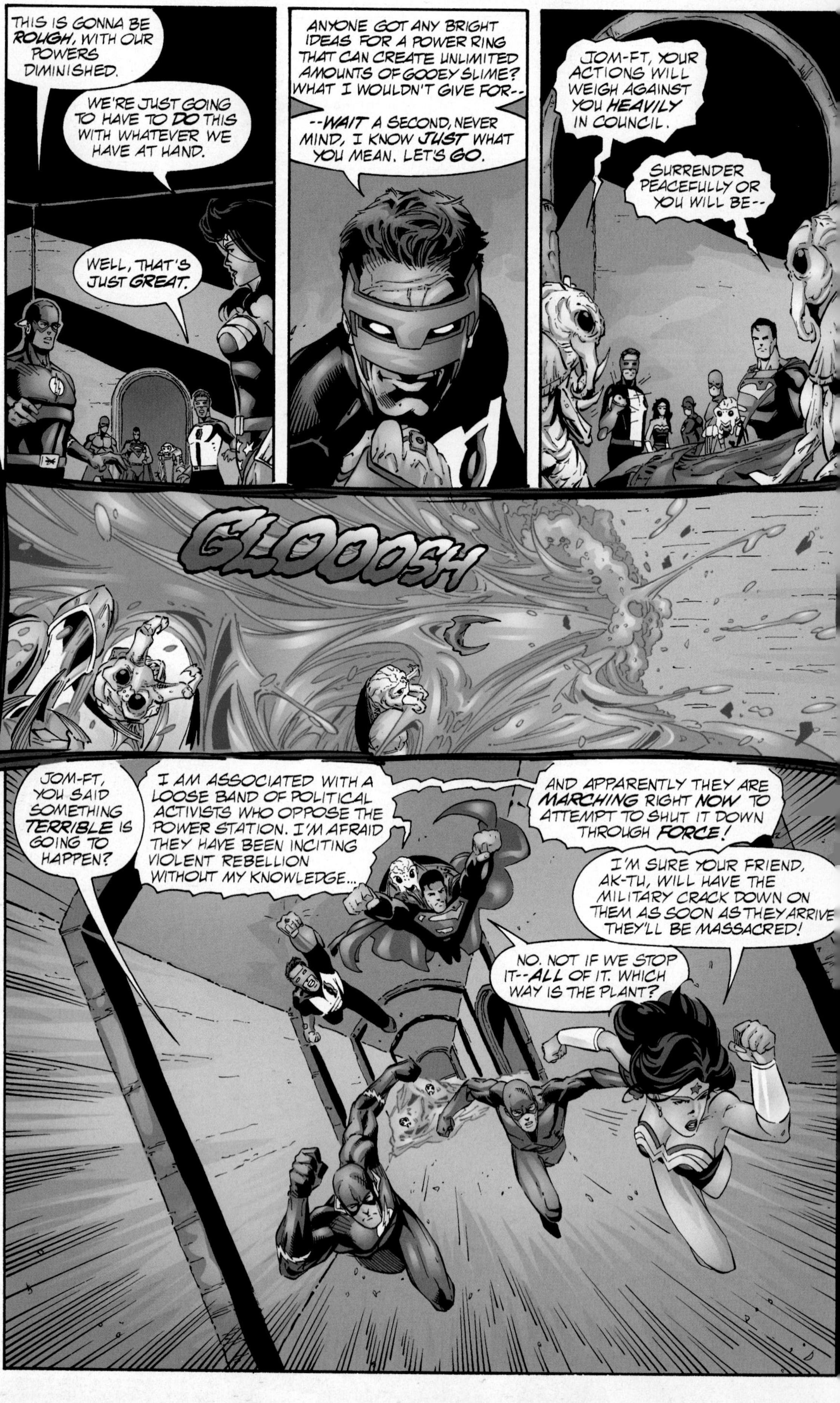

THIS IS GONNA BE ROUGH, WITH OUR POWERS DIMINISHED.
WE'RE JUST GOING TO HAVE TO DO THIS WITH WHATEVER WE HAVE AT HAND.
WELL, THAT'S JUST GREAT.
ANYONE GOT ANY BRIGHT IDEAS FOR A POWER RING THAT CAN CREATE UNLIMITED AMOUNTS OF GOOEY SLIME? WHAT I WOULDN'T GIVE FOR--
--WAIT A SECOND, NEVER MIND, I KNOW JUST WHAT YOU MEAN. LET'S GO.
JOM-FT, YOUR ACTIONS WILL WEIGH AGAINST YOU HEAVILY IN COUNCIL.
SURRENDER PEACEFULLY OR YOU WILL BE--
GLOOOSH
JOM-FT, YOU SAID SOMETHING TERRIBLE IS GOING TO HAPPEN?
I AM ASSOCIATED WITH A LOOSE BAND OF POLITICAL ACTIVISTS WHO OPPOSE THE POWER STATION. I'M AFRAID THEY HAVE BEEN INCITING VIOLENT REBELLION WITHOUT MY KNOWLEDGE...
AND APPARENTLY THEY ARE MARCHING RIGHT NOW TO ATTEMPT TO SHUT IT DOWN THROUGH FORCE!
I'M SURE YOUR FRIEND, AK-TU, WILL HAVE THE MILITARY CRACK DOWN ON THEM AS SOON AS THEY ARRIVE THEY'LL BE MASSACRED!
NO. NOT IF WE STOP IT--ALL OF IT. WHICH WAY IS THE PLANT?

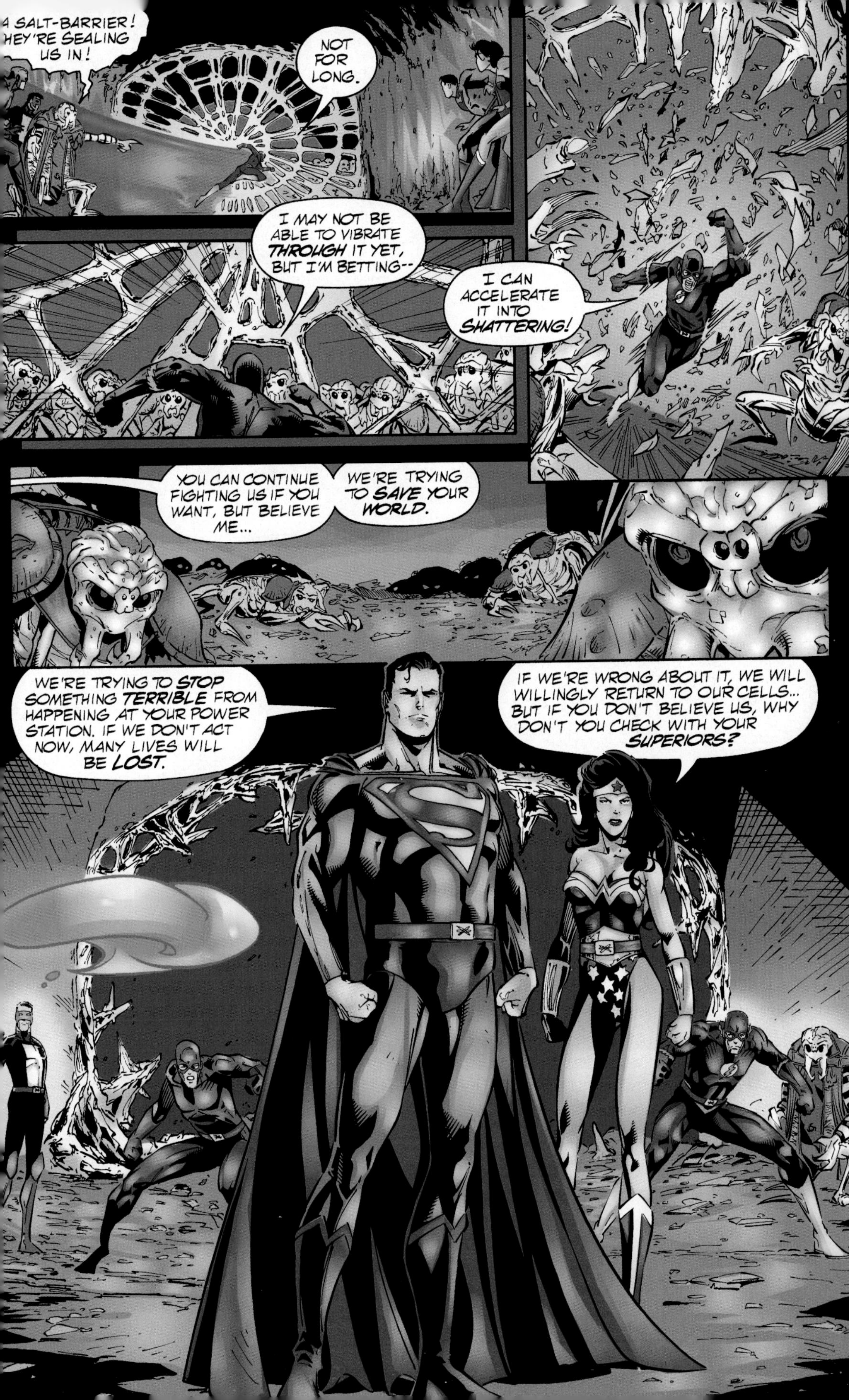

A SALT-BARRIER! THEY'RE SEALING US IN!
NOT FOR LONG.
I MAY NOT BE ABLE TO VIBRATE THROUGH IT YET, BUT I'M BETTING--
I CAN ACCELERATE IT INTO SHATTERING!
YOU CAN CONTINUE FIGHTING US IF YOU WANT, BUT BELIEVE ME...
WE'RE TRYING TO SAVE YOUR WORLD.
WE'RE TRYING TO STOP SOMETHING TERRIBLE FROM HAPPENING AT YOUR POWER STATION. IF WE DON'T ACT NOW, MANY LIVES WILL BE LOST.
IF WE'RE WRONG ABOUT IT, WE WILL WILLINGLY RETURN TO OUR CELLS... BUT IF YOU DON'T BELIEVE US, WHY DON'T YOU CHECK WITH YOUR SUPERIORS?

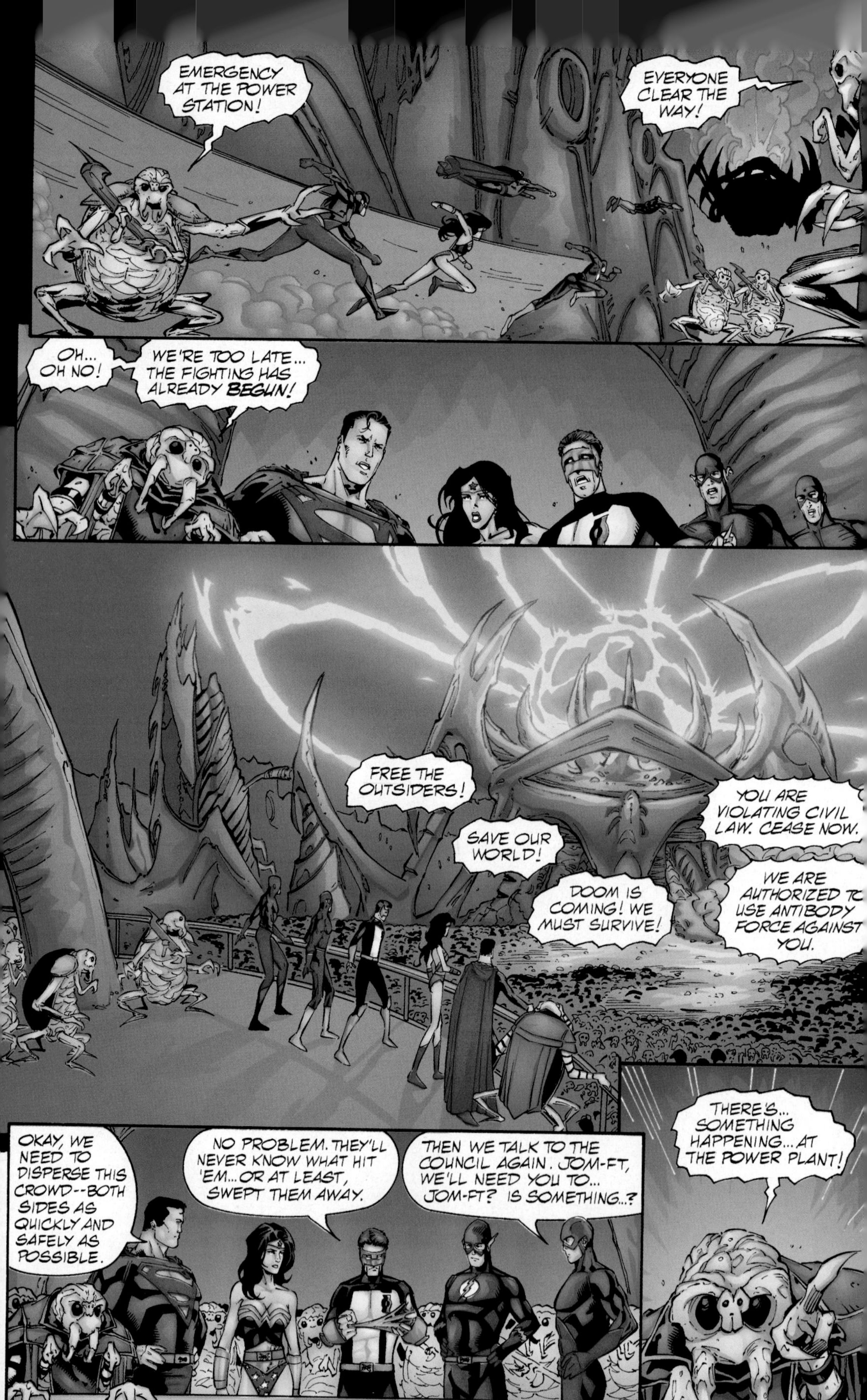
EMERGENCY AT THE POWER STATION!
EVERYONE CLEAR THE WAY!
OH... OH NO!
WE'RE TOO LATE... THE FIGHTING HAS ALREADY BEGUN!
FREE THE OUTSIDERS!
SAVE OUR WORLD!
DOOM IS COMING! WE MUST SURVIVE!
YOU ARE VIOLATING CIVIL LAW. CEASE NOW.
WE ARE AUTHORIZED TO USE ANTIBODY FORCE AGAINST YOU.
OKAY, WE NEED TO DISPERSE THIS CROWD--BOTH SIDES AS QUICKLY AND SAFELY AS POSSIBLE.
NO PROBLEM. THEY'LL NEVER KNOW WHAT HIT 'EM...OR AT LEAST, SWEPT THEM AWAY.
THEN WE TALK TO THE COUNCIL AGAIN. JOM-FT, WE'LL NEED YOU TO... JOM-FT? IS SOMETHING...?
THERE'S... SOMETHING HAPPENING... AT THE POWER PLANT!

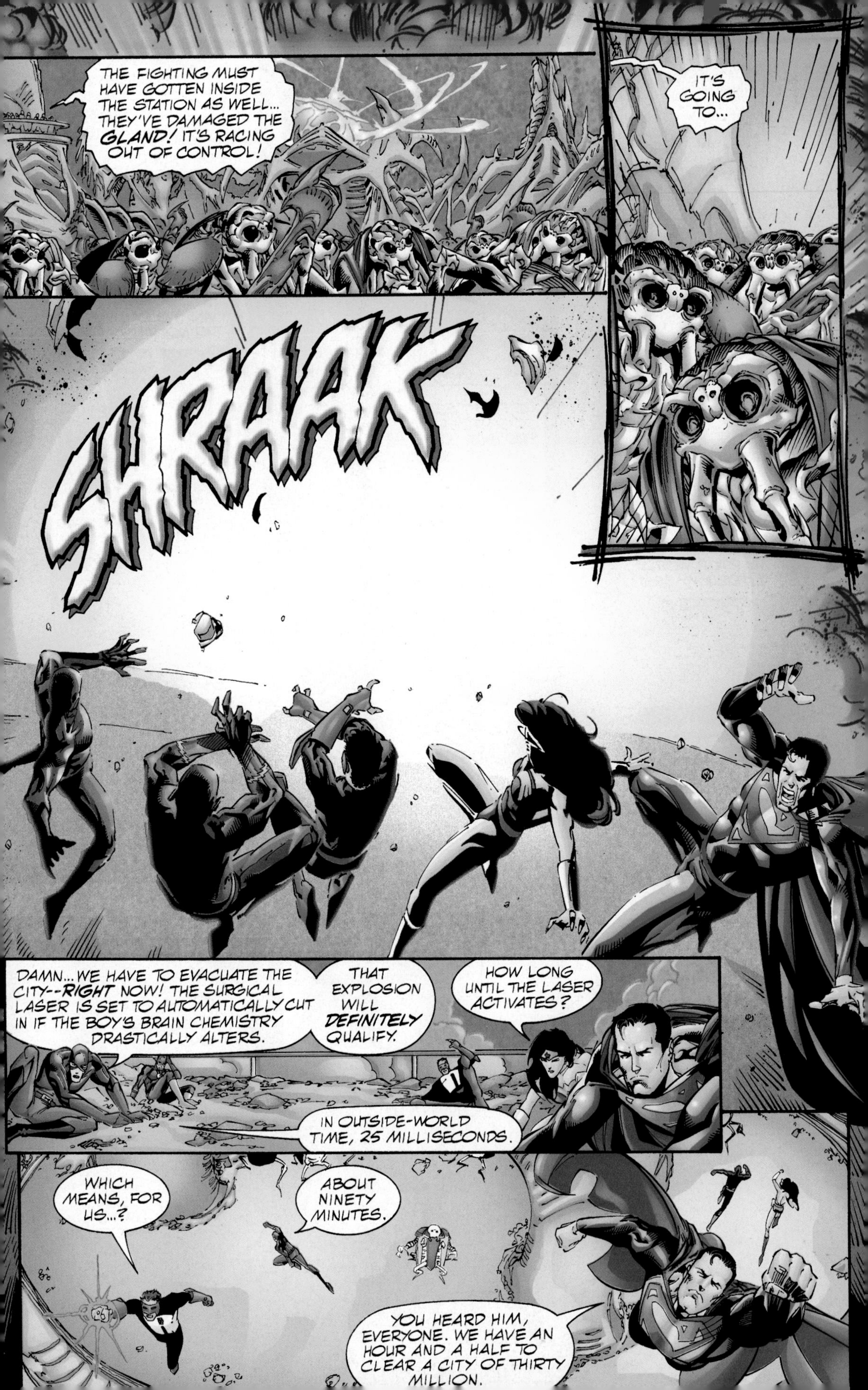
THE FIGHTING MUST HAVE GOTTEN INSIDE THE STATION AS WELL... THEY'VE DAMAGED THE GLAND! IT'S RACING OUT OF CONTROL!
IT'S GOING TO...
SHRAAK
DAMN... WE HAVE TO EVACUATE THE CITY--RIGHT NOW! THE SURGICAL LASER IS SET TO AUTOMATICALLY CUT IN IF THE BOY'S BRAIN CHEMISTRY DRASTICALLY ALTERS.
THAT EXPLOSION WILL DEFINITELY QUALIFY.
HOW LONG UNTIL THE LASER ACTIVATES?
IN OUTSIDE-WORLD TIME, 25 MILLISECONDS.
WHICH MEANS, FOR US...?
ABOUT NINETY MINUTES.
YOU HEARD HIM, EVERYONE. WE HAVE AN HOUR AND A HALF TO CLEAR A CITY OF THIRTY MILLION.

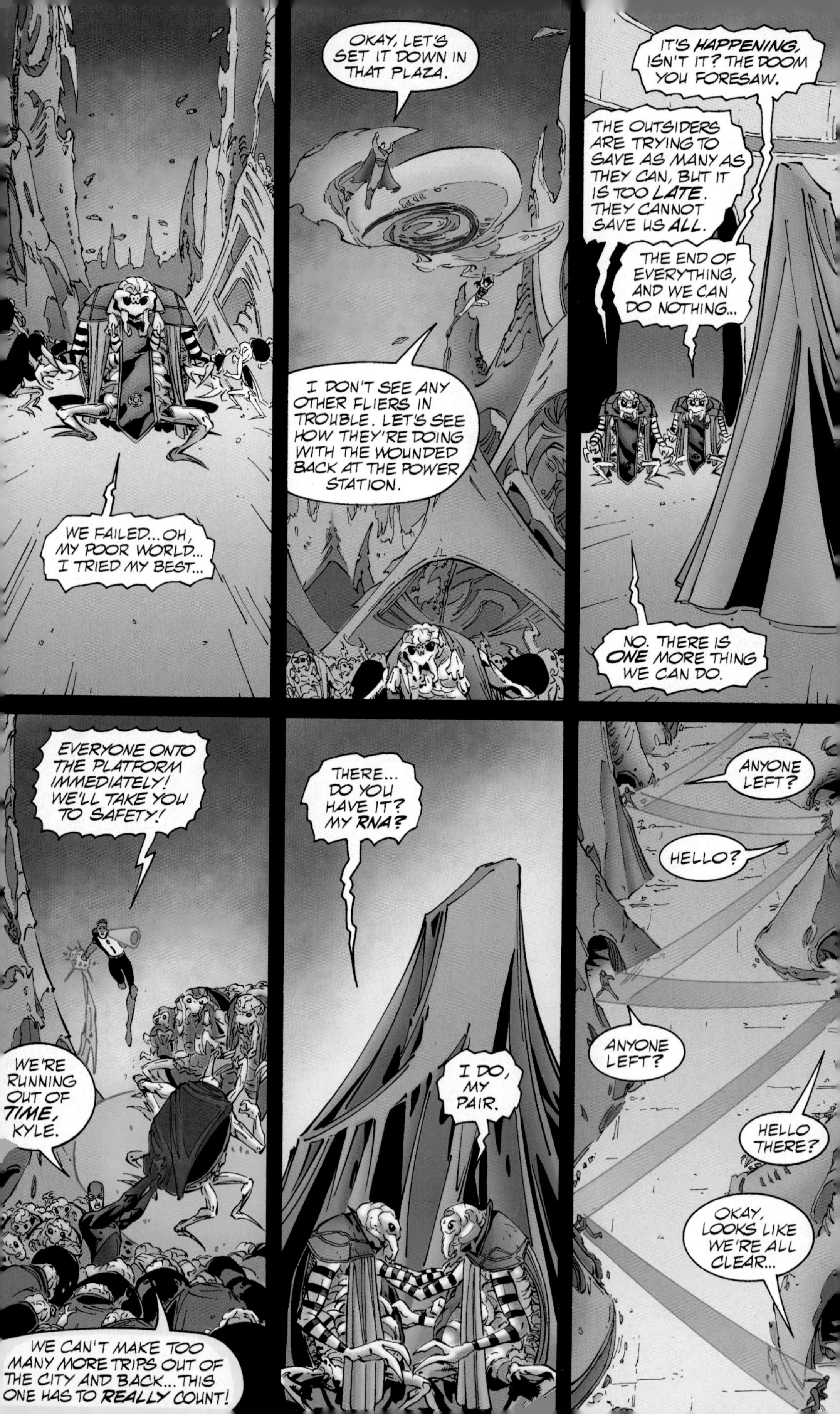
WE FAILED... OH, MY POOR WORLD... I TRIED MY BEST...
OKAY, LET'S SET IT DOWN IN THAT PLAZA.
I DON'T SEE ANY OTHER FLIERS IN TROUBLE. LET'S SEE HOW THEY'RE DOING WITH THE WOUNDED BACK AT THE POWER STATION.
IT'S HAPPENING, ISN'T IT? THE DOOM YOU FORESAW.
THE OUTSIDERS ARE TRYING TO SAVE AS MANY AS THEY CAN, BUT IT IS TOO LATE. THEY CANNOT SAVE US ALL.
THE END OF EVERYTHING, AND WE CAN DO NOTHING...
NO. THERE IS ONE MORE THING WE CAN DO.
EVERYONE ONTO THE PLATFORM IMMEDIATELY! WE'LL TAKE YOU TO SAFETY!
WE'RE RUNNING OUT OF TIME, KYLE.
WE CAN'T MAKE TOO MANY MORE TRIPS OUT OF THE CITY AND BACK... THIS ONE HAS TO REALLY COUNT!
THERE... DO YOU HAVE IT? MY RNA?
I DO, MY PAIR.
ANYONE LEFT?
HELLO?
ANYONE LEFT?
HELLO THERE?
OKAY, LOOKS LIKE WE'RE ALL CLEAR...

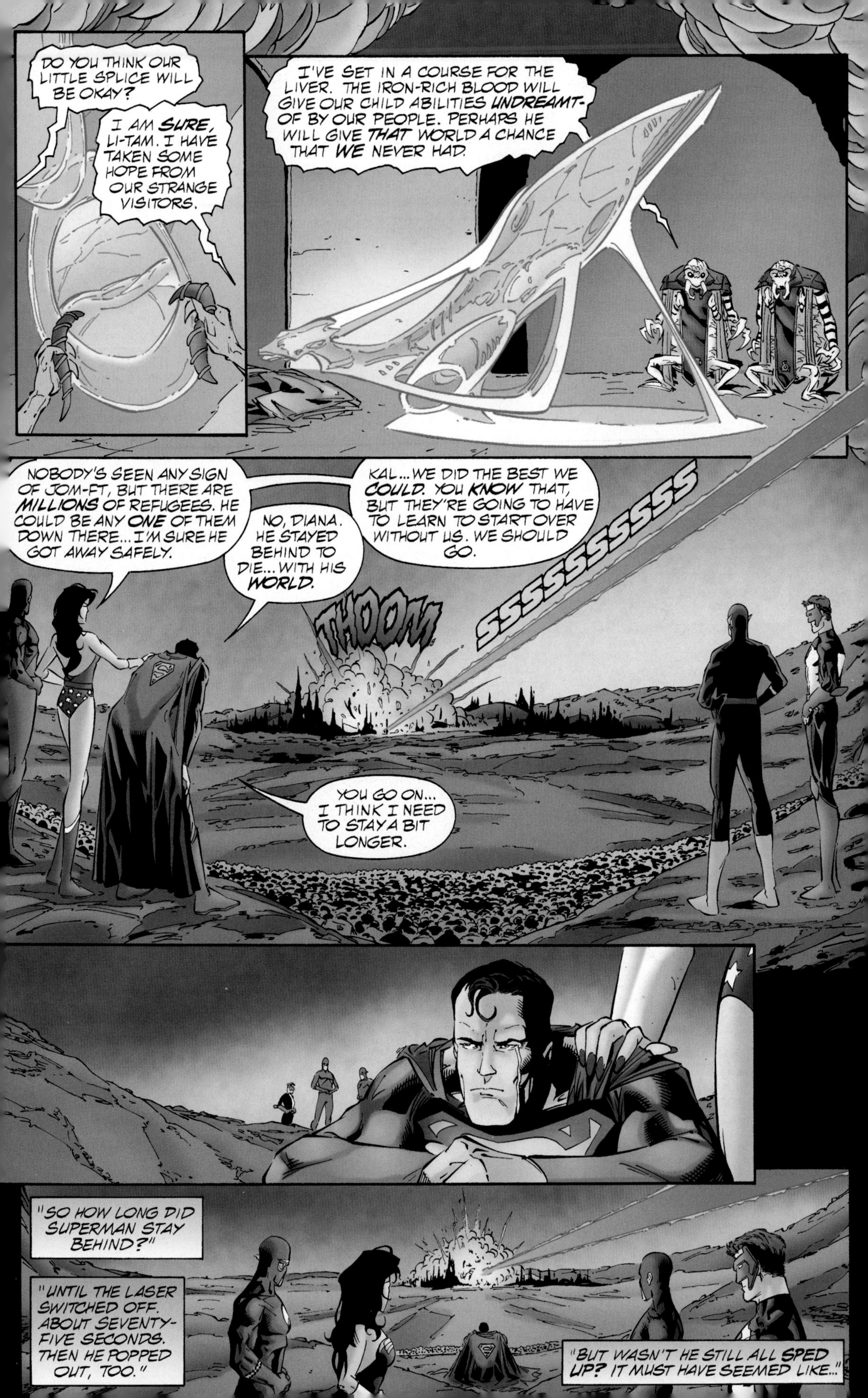
DO YOU THINK OUR LITTLE SPLICE WILL BE OKAY?
I AM SURE, LI-TAM. I HAVE TAKEN SOME HOPE FROM OUR STRANGE VISITORS.
I'VE SET IN A COURSE FOR THE LIVER. THE IRON-RICH BLOOD WILL GIVE OUR CHILD ABILITIES UNDREAMT-OF BY OUR PEOPLE. PERHAPS HE WILL GIVE THAT WORLD A CHANCE THAT WE NEVER HAD.
NOBODY'S SEEN ANY SIGN OF JOM-FT, BUT THERE ARE MILLIONS OF REFUGEES. HE COULD BE ANY ONE OF THEM DOWN THERE... I'M SURE HE GOT AWAY SAFELY.
NO, DIANA. HE STAYED BEHIND TO DIE... WITH HIS WORLD.
KAL... WE DID THE BEST WE COULD. YOU KNOW THAT, BUT THEY'RE GOING TO HAVE TO LEARN TO START OVER WITHOUT US. WE SHOULD GO.
SSSSSSSSSSS
THOOM
YOU GO ON... I THINK I NEED TO STAY A BIT LONGER.
"SO HOW LONG DID SUPERMAN STAY BEHIND?"
"UNTIL THE LASER SWITCHED OFF. ABOUT SEVENTY-FIVE SECONDS. THEN HE POPPED OUT, TOO."
"BUT WASN'T HE STILL ALL SPED UP? IT MUST HAVE SEEMED LIKE..."

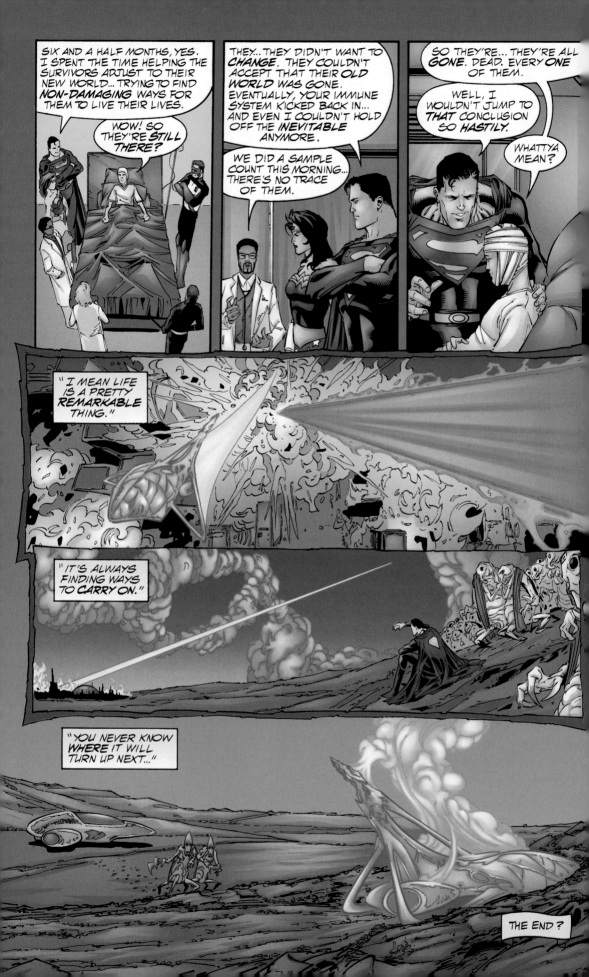

SIX AND A HALF MONTHS, YES. I SPENT THE TIME HELPING THE SURVIVORS ADJUST TO THEIR NEW WORLD... TRYING TO FIND *NON-DAMAGING* WAYS FOR THEM TO LIVE THEIR LIVES.

WOW! SO THEY'RE *STILL THERE?*

THEY... THEY DIDN'T WANT TO *CHANGE.* THEY COULDN'T ACCEPT THAT THEIR *OLD WORLD* WAS GONE. EVENTUALLY, YOUR IMMUNE SYSTEM KICKED BACK IN... AND EVEN I COULDN'T HOLD OFF THE *INEVITABLE* ANYMORE.

WE DID A SAMPLE COUNT THIS MORNING... THERE'S NO TRACE OF THEM.

SO THEY'RE... THEY'RE ALL *GONE.* DEAD. EVERY *ONE* OF THEM.

WELL, I WOULDN'T JUMP TO *THAT* CONCLUSION SO *HASTILY.*

WHATTYA MEAN?

"I MEAN LIFE IS A PRETTY *REMARKABLE* THING."

"IT'S ALWAYS FINDING WAYS TO *CARRY ON.*"

"YOU NEVER KNOW *WHERE* IT WILL TURN UP NEXT..."

THE END ?

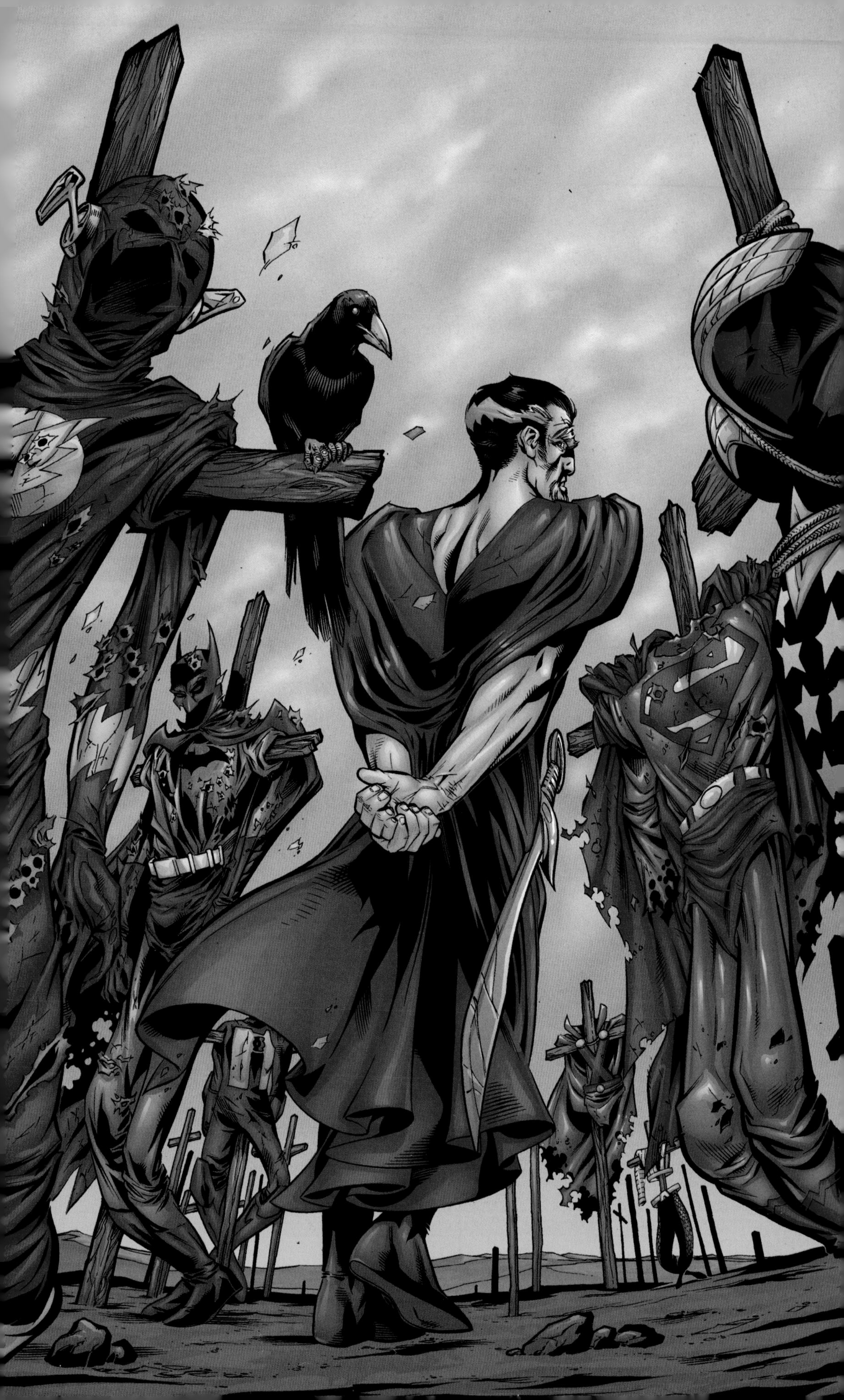

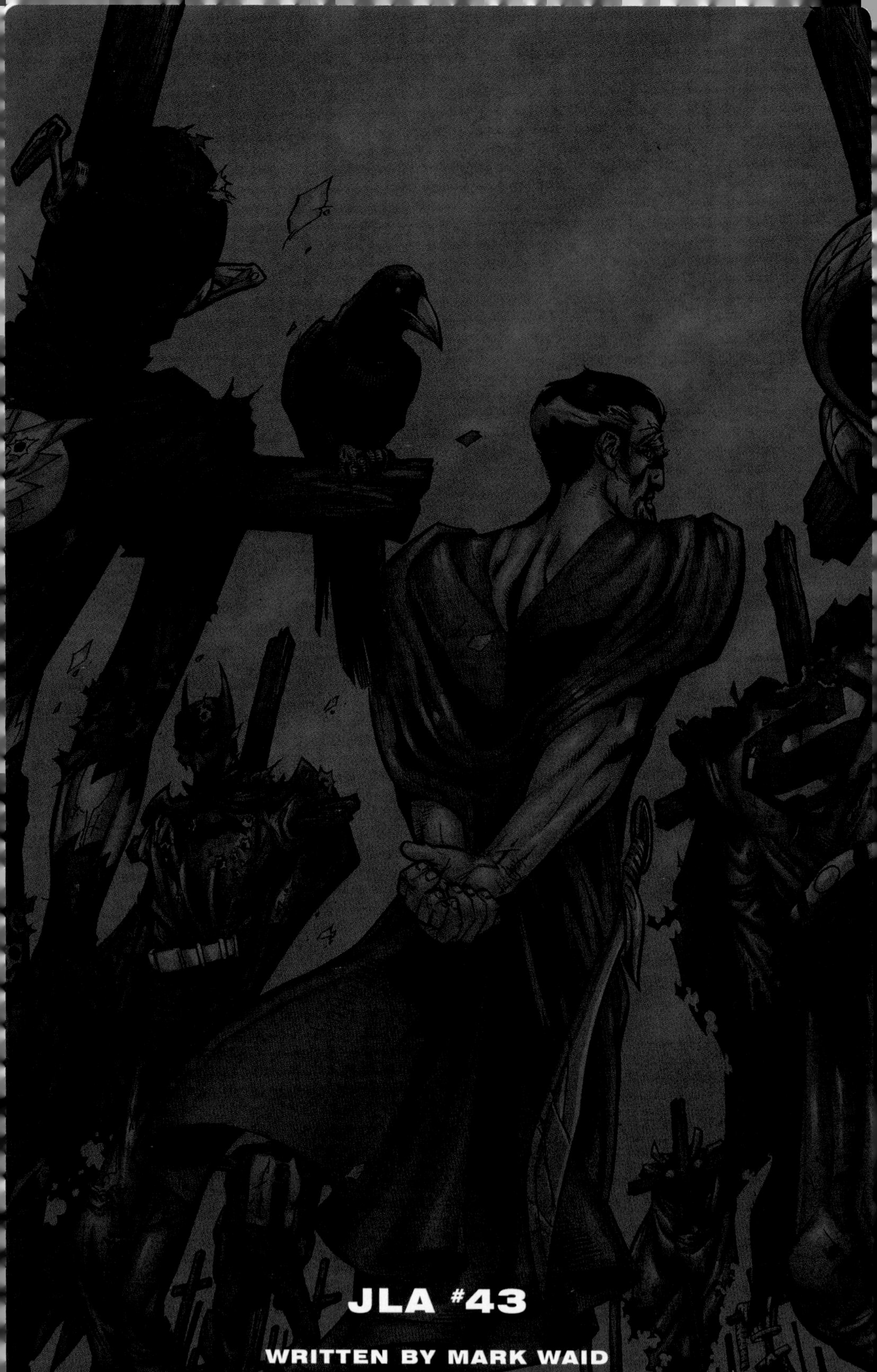

JLA #43

WRITTEN BY MARK WAID

PENCILS BY HOWARD PORTER, WITH INKS BY DREW GERACI AND COLORS BY PAT GARRAHY

COVER BY HOWARD PORTER & DREW GERACI

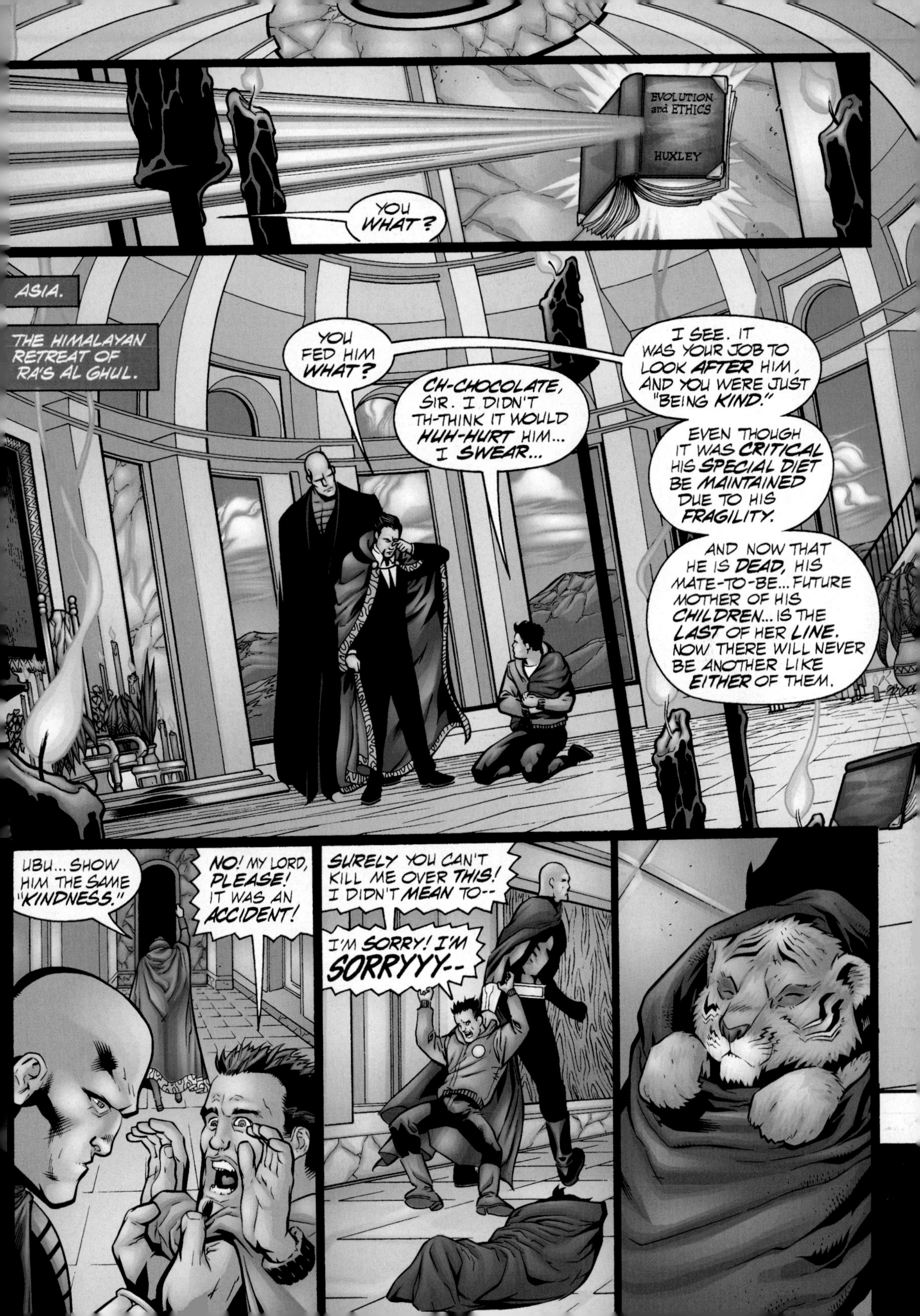
EVOLUTION and ETHICS
HUXLEY
YOU WHAT?
ASIA.
THE HIMALAYAN RETREAT OF RA'S AL GHUL.
YOU FED HIM WHAT?
CH-CHOCOLATE, SIR. I DIDN'T TH-THINK IT WOULD HUH-HURT HIM... I SWEAR...
I SEE. IT WAS YOUR JOB TO LOOK AFTER HIM, AND YOU WERE JUST "BEING KIND."
EVEN THOUGH IT WAS CRITICAL HIS SPECIAL DIET BE MAINTAINED DUE TO HIS FRAGILITY.
AND NOW THAT HE IS DEAD, HIS MATE-TO-BE... FUTURE MOTHER OF HIS CHILDREN... IS THE LAST OF HER LINE. NOW THERE WILL NEVER BE ANOTHER LIKE EITHER OF THEM.
UBU... SHOW HIM THE SAME "KINDNESS."
NO! MY LORD, PLEASE! IT WAS AN ACCIDENT!
SURELY YOU CAN'T KILL ME OVER THIS! I DIDN'T MEAN TO--
I'M SORRY! I'M SORRYYY--

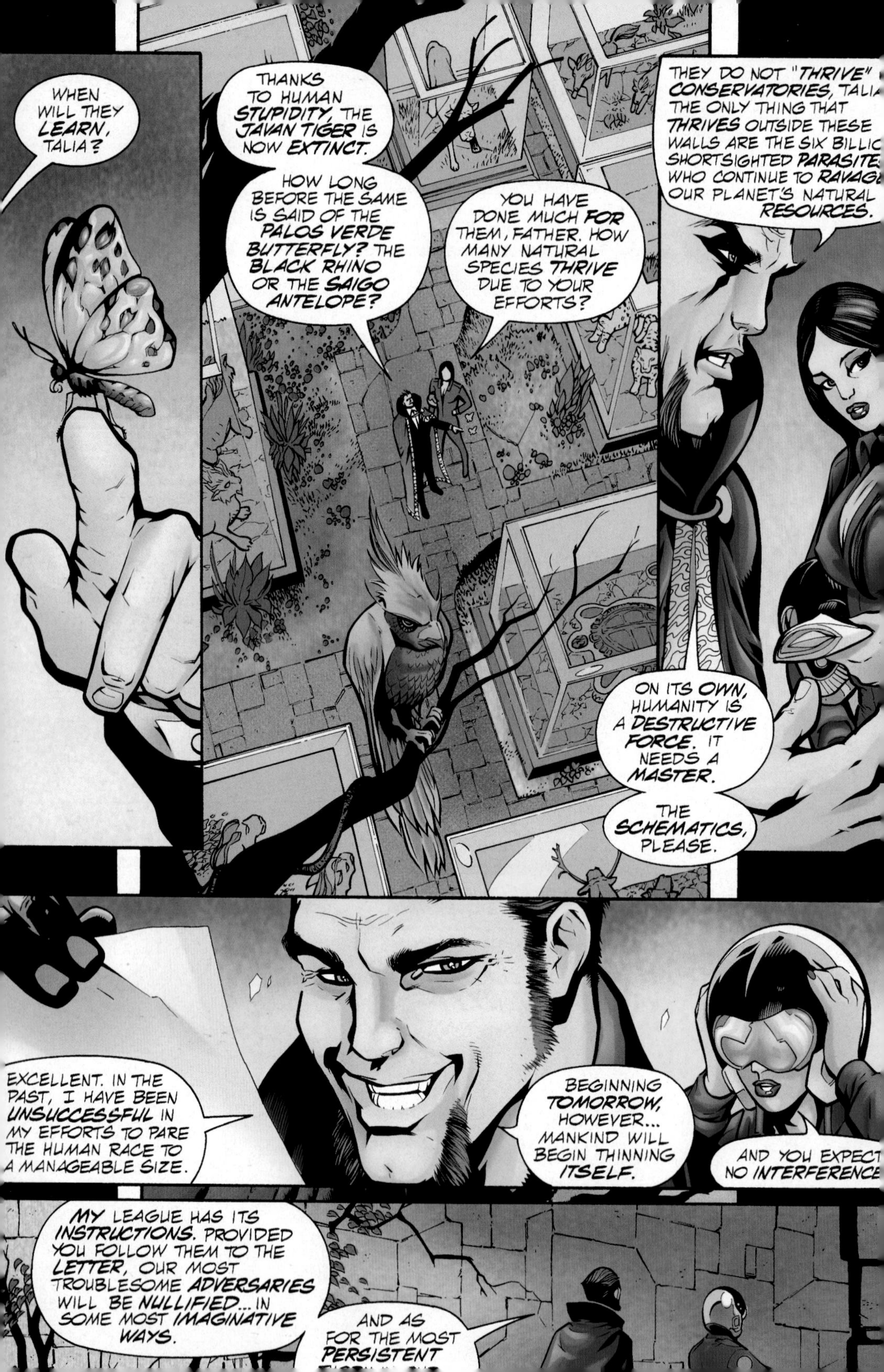

WHEN WILL THEY LEARN, TALIA?
THANKS TO HUMAN STUPIDITY, THE JAVAN TIGER IS NOW EXTINCT.
HOW LONG BEFORE THE SAME IS SAID OF THE PALOS VERDE BUTTERFLY? THE BLACK RHINO OR THE SAIGO ANTELOPE?
YOU HAVE DONE MUCH FOR THEM, FATHER. HOW MANY NATURAL SPECIES THRIVE DUE TO YOUR EFFORTS?
THEY DO NOT "THRIVE" CONSERVATORIES, TALIA THE ONLY THING THAT THRIVES OUTSIDE THESE WALLS ARE THE SIX BILLIO SHORTSIGHTED PARASITE WHO CONTINUE TO RAVAGE OUR PLANET'S NATURAL RESOURCES.
ON ITS OWN, HUMANITY IS A DESTRUCTIVE FORCE. IT NEEDS A MASTER.
THE SCHEMATICS, PLEASE.
EXCELLENT. IN THE PAST, I HAVE BEEN UNSUCCESSFUL IN MY EFFORTS TO PARE THE HUMAN RACE TO A MANAGEABLE SIZE.
BEGINNING TOMORROW, HOWEVER... MANKIND WILL BEGIN THINNING ITSELF.
AND YOU EXPECT NO INTERFERENCE
MY LEAGUE HAS ITS INSTRUCTIONS. PROVIDED YOU FOLLOW THEM TO THE LETTER, OUR MOST TROUBLESOME ADVERSARIES WILL BE NULLIFIED... IN SOME MOST IMAGINATIVE WAYS.
AND AS FOR THE MOST PERSISTENT

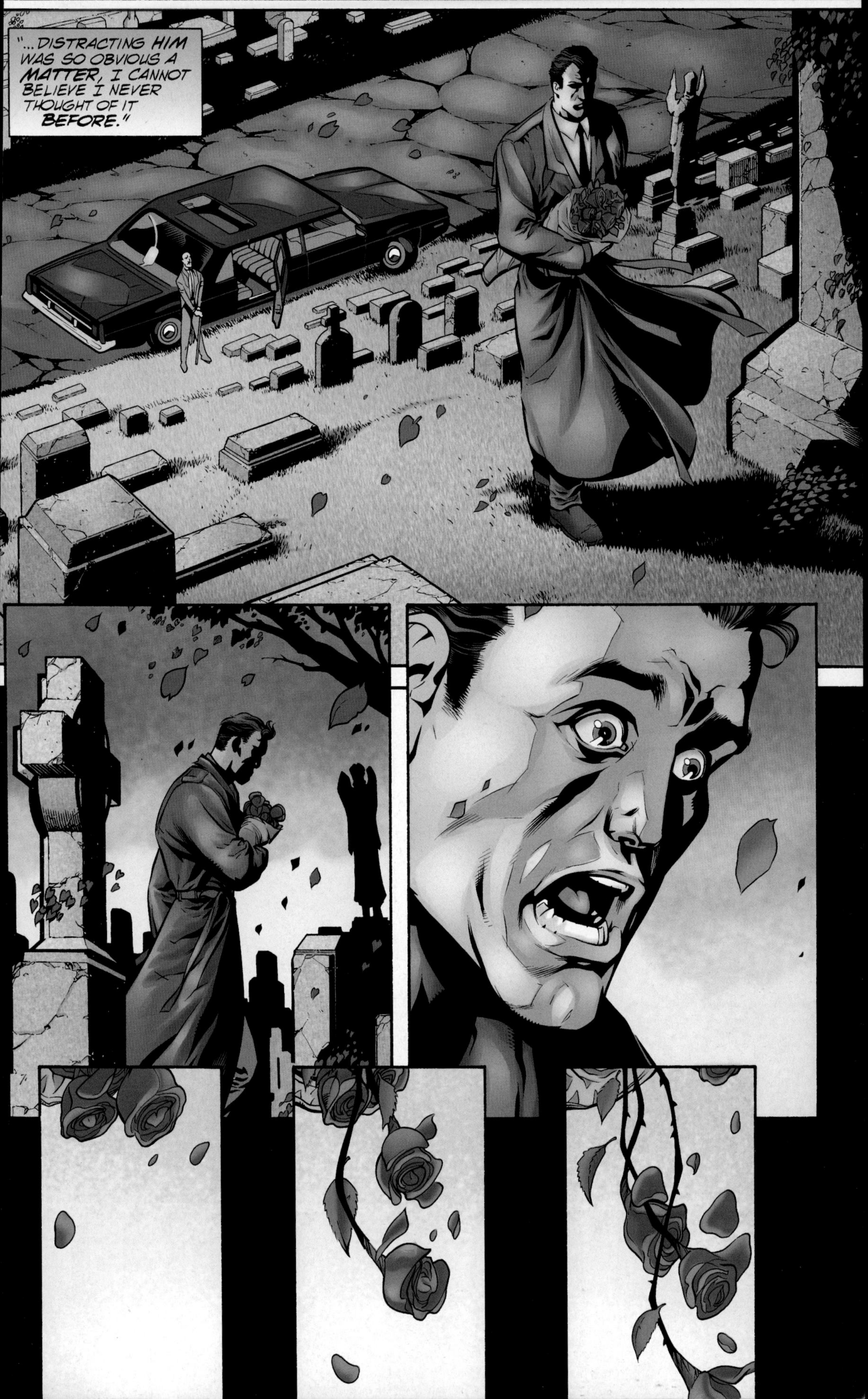
"...DISTRACTING HIM WAS SO OBVIOUS A MATTER, I CANNOT BELIEVE I NEVER THOUGHT OF IT BEFORE."

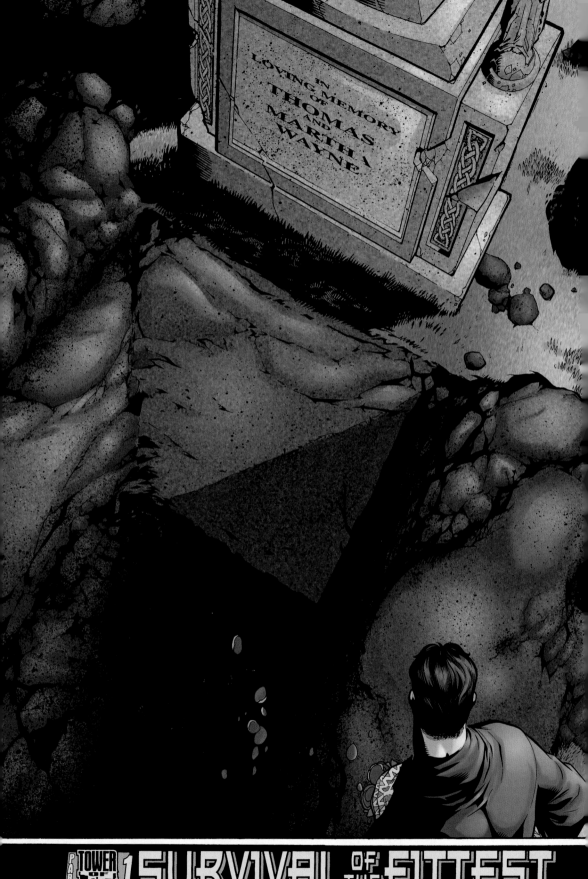

IN LOVING MEMORY OF THOMAS AND MARTHA WAYNE

PART TOWER OF BABEL 1 SURVIVAL OF THE FITTEST

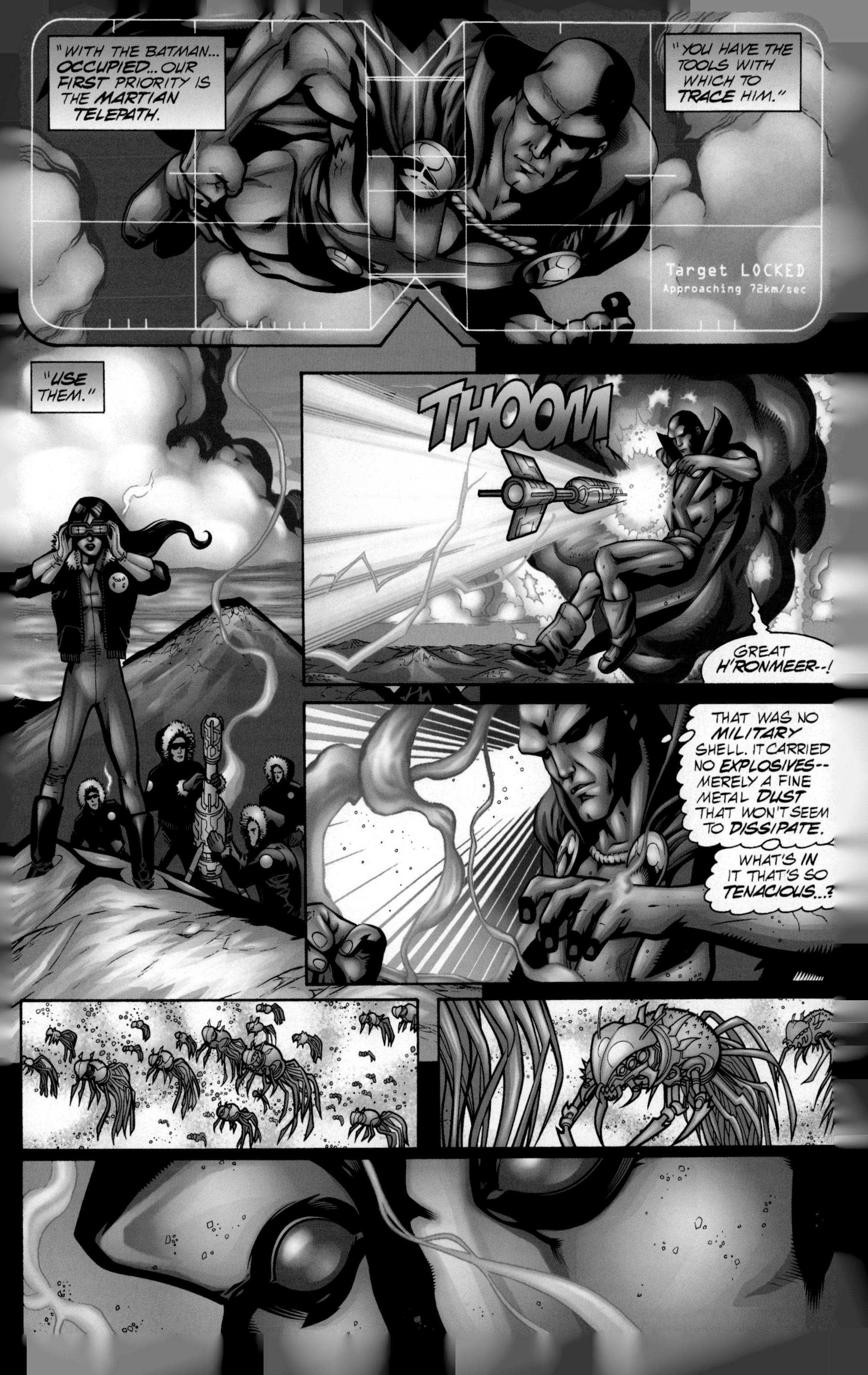
"WITH THE BATMAN... OCCUPIED...OUR FIRST PRIORITY IS THE MARTIAN TELEPATH.
"YOU HAVE THE TOOLS WITH WHICH TO TRACE HIM."
Target LOCKED
Approaching 72km/sec
"USE THEM."
THOOM
GREAT H'RONMEER--!
THAT WAS NO MILITARY SHELL. IT CARRIED NO EXPLOSIVES--MERELY A FINE METAL DUST THAT WON'T SEEM TO DISSIPATE.
WHAT'S IN IT THAT'S SO TENACIOUS...?

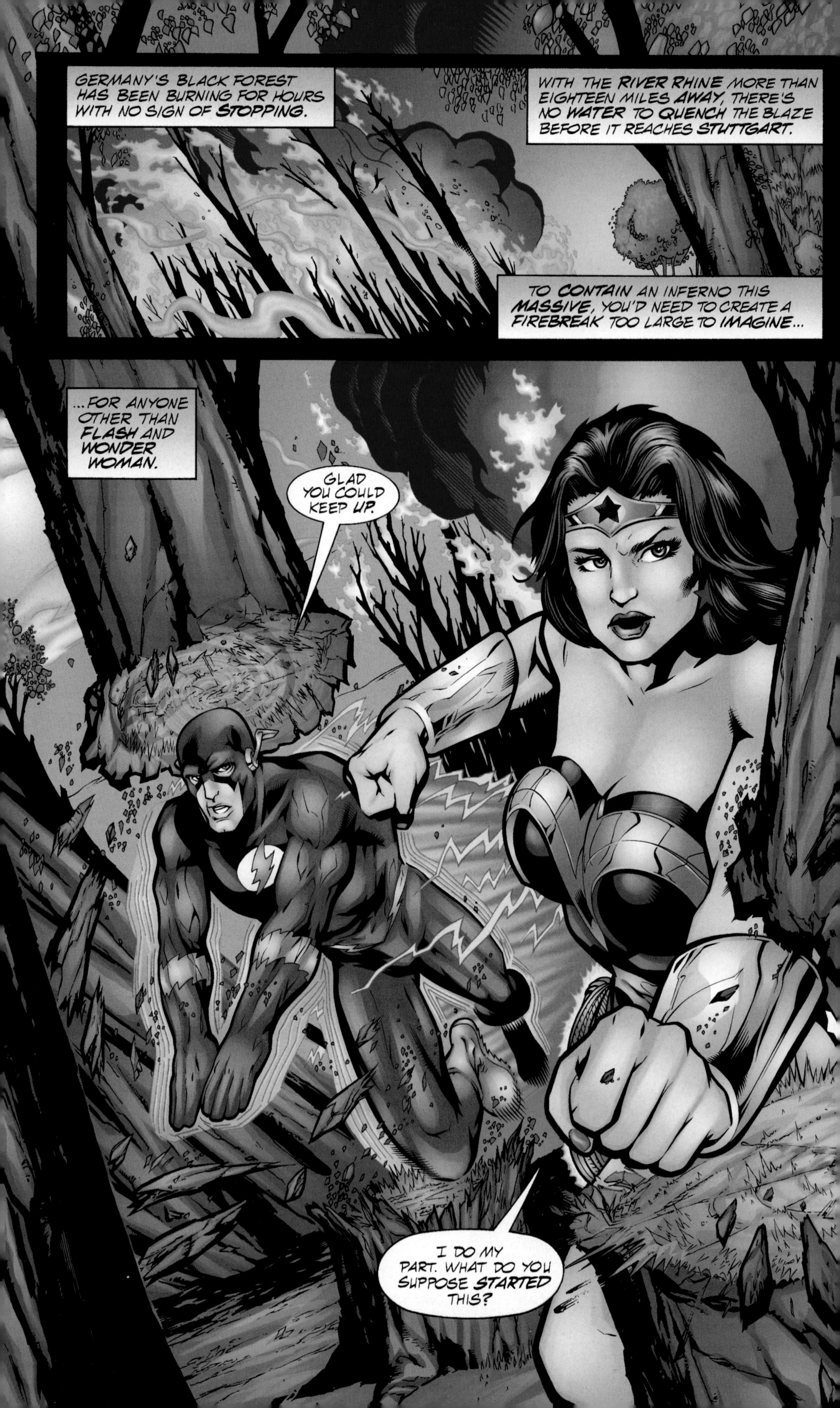
GERMANY'S BLACK FOREST HAS BEEN BURNING FOR HOURS WITH NO SIGN OF STOPPING.
WITH THE RIVER RHINE MORE THAN EIGHTEEN MILES AWAY, THERE'S NO WATER TO QUENCH THE BLAZE BEFORE IT REACHES STUTTGART.
TO CONTAIN AN INFERNO THIS MASSIVE, YOU'D NEED TO CREATE A FIREBREAK TOO LARGE TO IMAGINE...
...FOR ANYONE OTHER THAN FLASH AND WONDER WOMAN.
GLAD YOU COULD KEEP UP.
I DO MY PART. WHAT DO YOU SUPPOSE STARTED THIS?

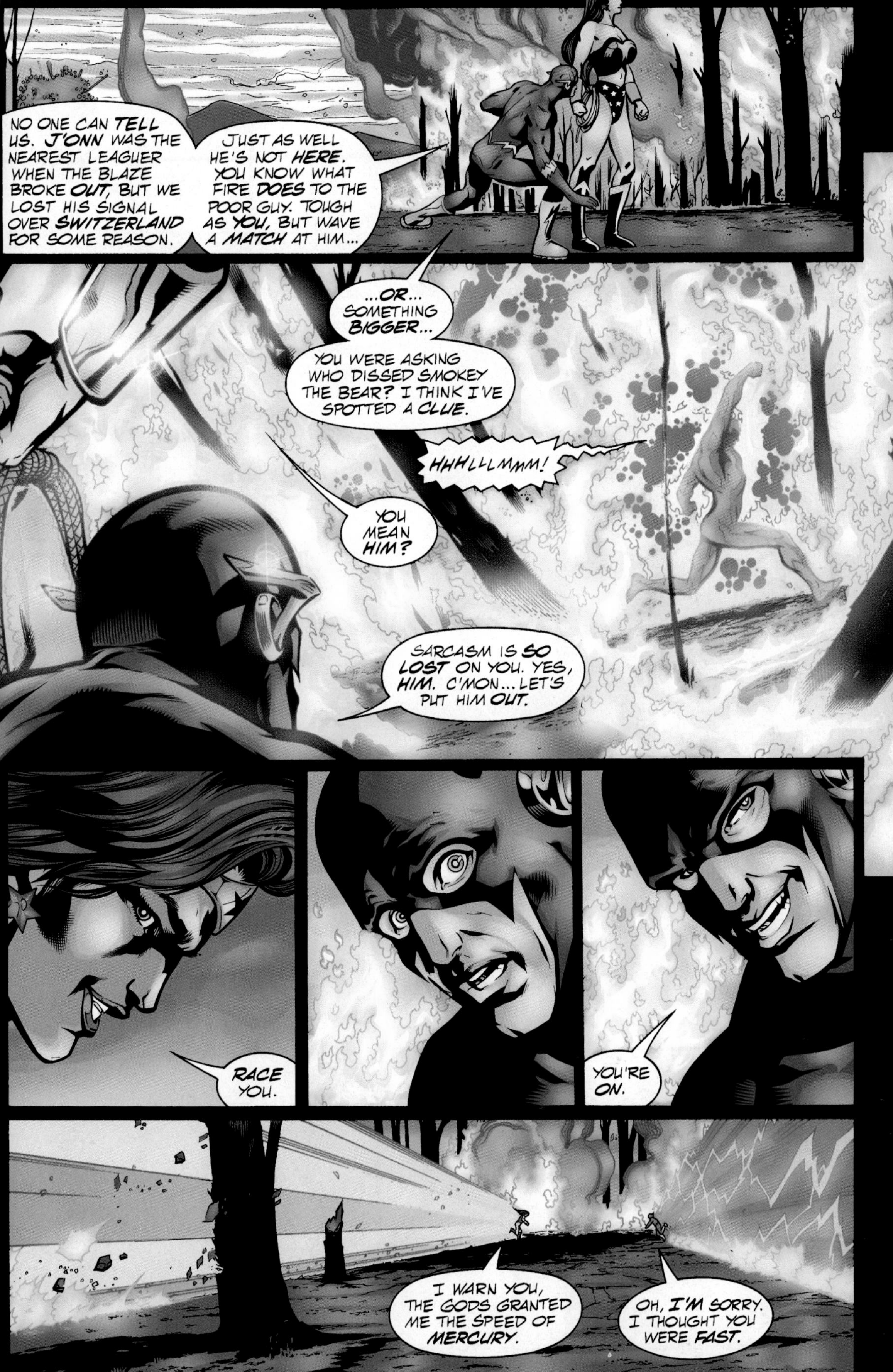

NO ONE CAN TELL US. J'ONN WAS THE NEAREST LEAGUER WHEN THE BLAZE BROKE OUT, BUT WE LOST HIS SIGNAL OVER SWITZERLAND FOR SOME REASON.
JUST AS WELL HE'S NOT HERE. YOU KNOW WHAT FIRE DOES TO THE POOR GUY. TOUGH AS YOU, BUT WAVE A MATCH AT HIM...
...OR... SOMETHING BIGGER...
YOU WERE ASKING WHO DISSED SMOKEY THE BEAR? I THINK I'VE SPOTTED A CLUE.
HHHLLLMMM!
YOU MEAN HIM?
SARCASM IS SO LOST ON YOU. YES, HIM. C'MON... LET'S PUT HIM OUT.
RACE YOU.
YOU'RE ON.
I WARN YOU, THE GODS GRANTED ME THE SPEED OF MERCURY.
OH, I'M SORRY. I THOUGHT YOU WERE FAST.

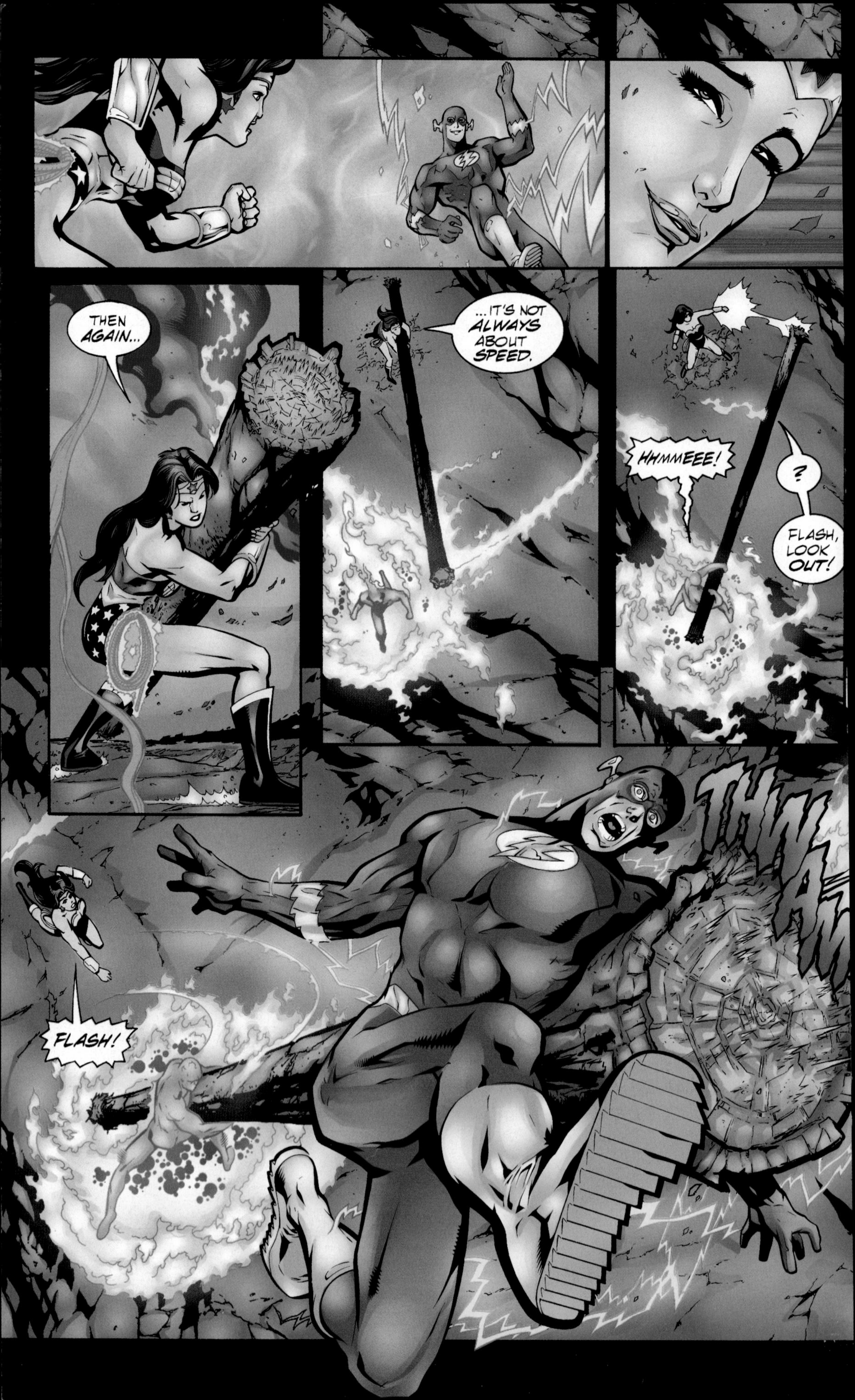
THEN AGAIN...
...IT'S NOT ALWAYS ABOUT SPEED.
HHMMEEE!
?
FLASH, LOOK OUT!
FLASH!
THWA

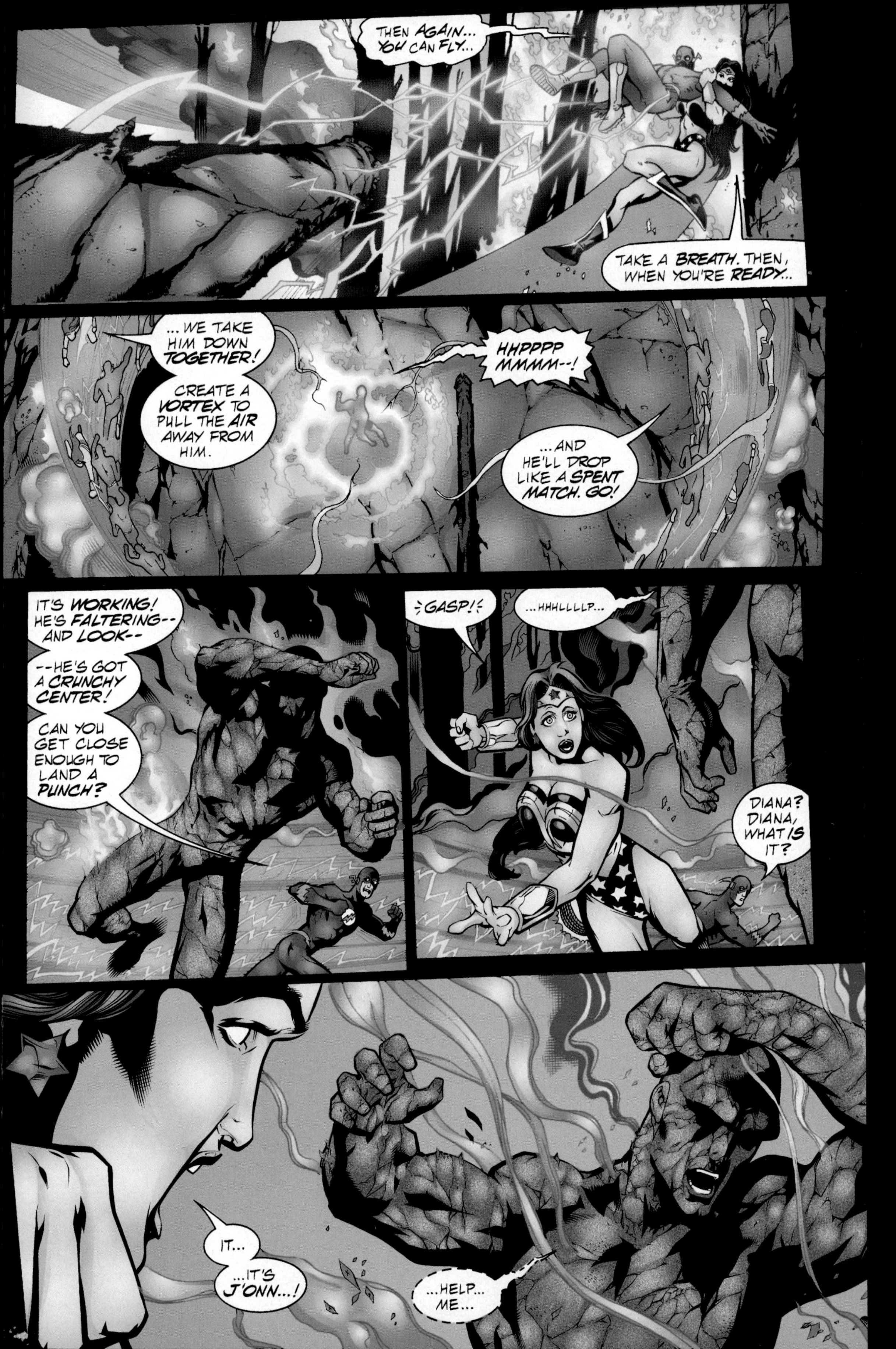
THEN AGAIN... YOU CAN FLY...
TAKE A BREATH. THEN, WHEN YOU'RE READY...
...WE TAKE HIM DOWN TOGETHER!
CREATE A VORTEX TO PULL THE AIR AWAY FROM HIM.
HHPPPP MMMM--!
...AND HE'LL DROP LIKE A SPENT MATCH. GO!
IT'S WORKING! HE'S FALTERING-- AND LOOK--
--HE'S GOT A CRUNCHY CENTER!
CAN YOU GET CLOSE ENOUGH TO LAND A PUNCH?
:GASP!:
...HHHLLLLP...
DIANA? DIANA, WHAT IS IT?
IT...
...IT'S J'ONN...!
...HELP... ME...

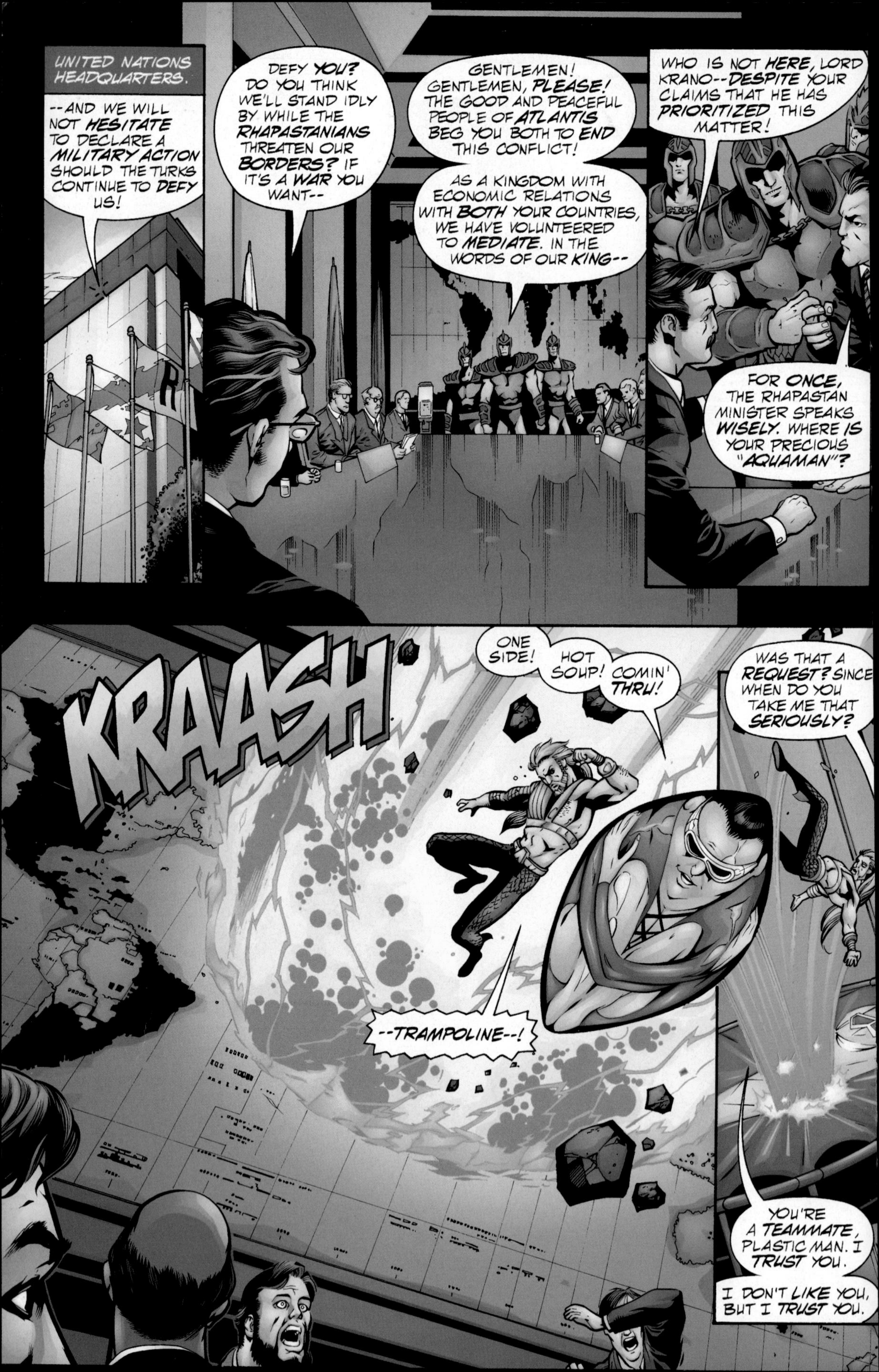
UNITED NATIONS HEADQUARTERS.
--AND WE WILL NOT HESITATE TO DECLARE A MILITARY ACTION SHOULD THE TURKS CONTINUE TO DEFY US!
DEFY YOU? DO YOU THINK WE'LL STAND IDLY BY WHILE THE RHAPASTANIANS THREATEN OUR BORDERS? IF IT'S A WAR YOU WANT--
GENTLEMEN! GENTLEMEN, PLEASE! THE GOOD AND PEACEFUL PEOPLE OF ATLANTIS BEG YOU BOTH TO END THIS CONFLICT!
AS A KINGDOM WITH ECONOMIC RELATIONS WITH BOTH YOUR COUNTRIES, WE HAVE VOLUNTEERED TO MEDIATE. IN THE WORDS OF OUR KING--
WHO IS NOT HERE, LORD KRANO--DESPITE YOUR CLAIMS THAT HE HAS PRIORITIZED THIS MATTER!
FOR ONCE, THE RHAPASTAN MINISTER SPEAKS WISELY. WHERE IS YOUR PRECIOUS "AQUAMAN"?
KRAASH
ONE SIDE!
HOT SOUP!
COMIN' THRU!
--TRAMPOLINE--!
WAS THAT A REQUEST? SINCE WHEN DO YOU TAKE ME THAT SERIOUSLY?
YOU'RE A TEAMMATE, PLASTIC MAN. I TRUST YOU.
I DON'T LIKE YOU, BUT I TRUST YOU.

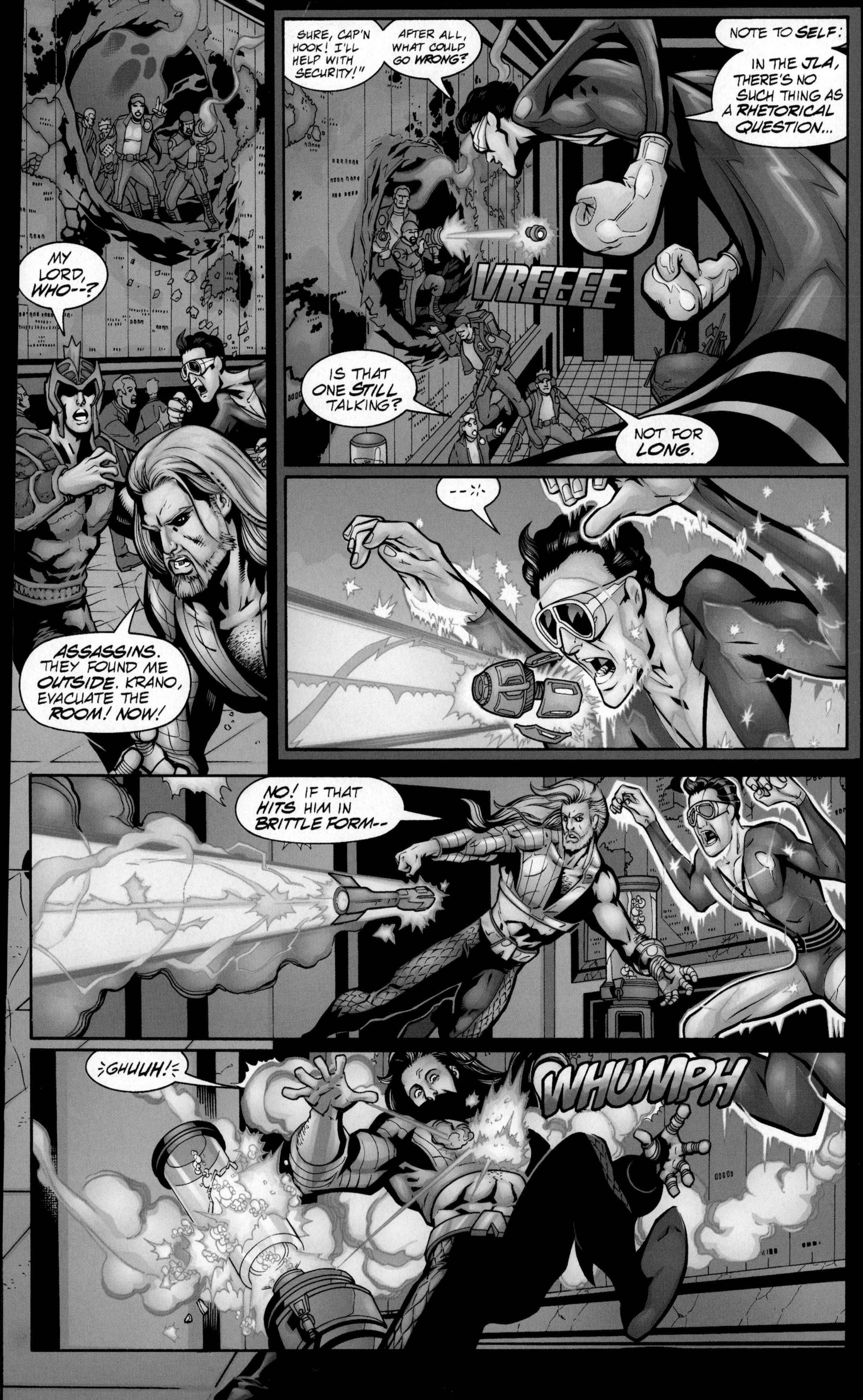
MY LORD, WHO--?
ASSASSINS. THEY FOUND ME OUTSIDE. KRANO, EVACUATE THE ROOM! NOW!
SURE, CAP'N HOOK! I'LL HELP WITH SECURITY!"
AFTER ALL, WHAT COULD GO WRONG?
NOTE TO SELF:
IN THE JLA, THERE'S NO SUCH THING AS A RHETORICAL QUESTION...
VREEEE
IS THAT ONE STILL TALKING?
NOT FOR LONG.
--!
NO! IF THAT HITS HIM IN BRITTLE FORM--
!GHUUH!
WHUMPH

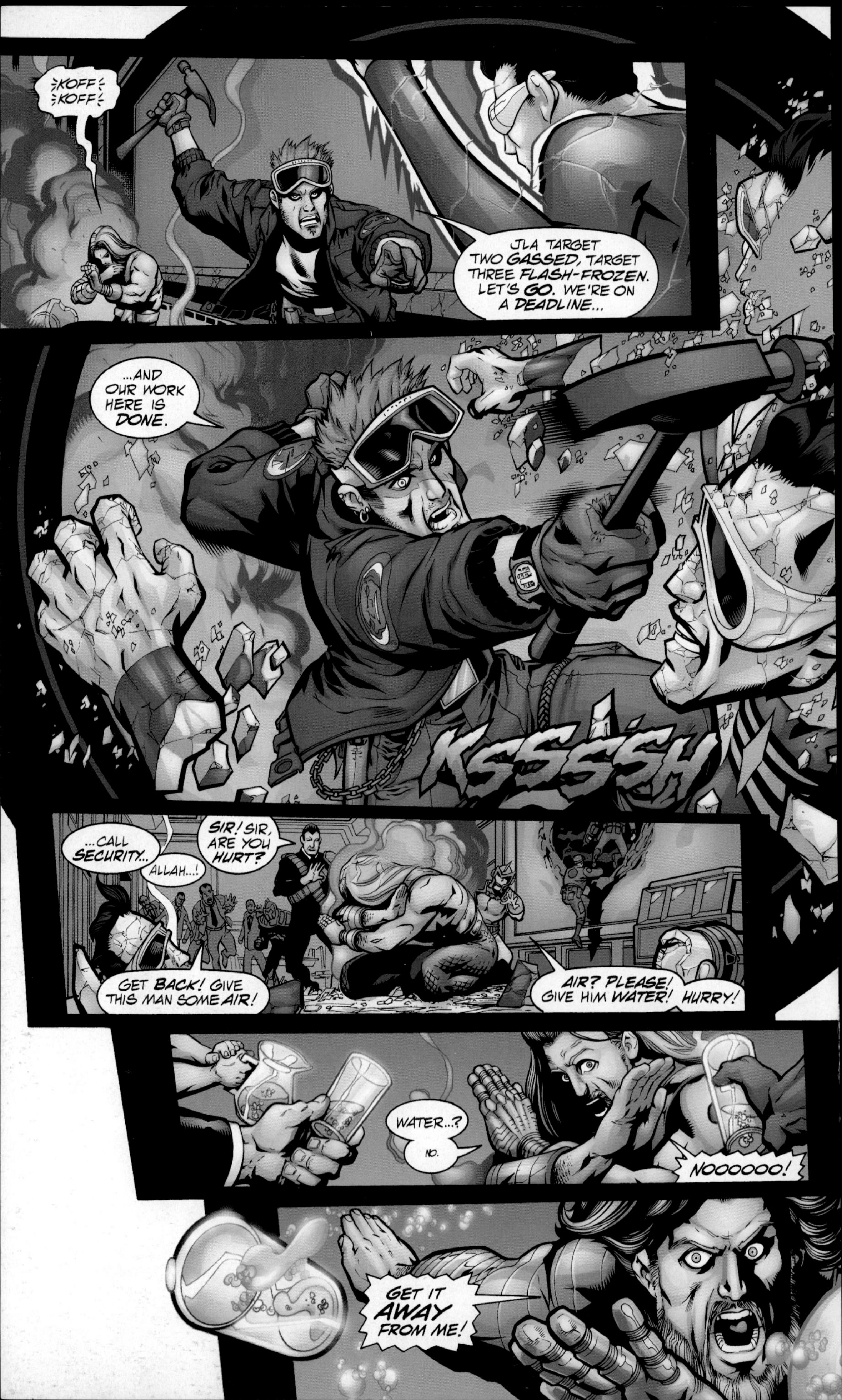

KOFF KOFF
JLA TARGET TWO GASSED, TARGET THREE FLASH-FROZEN. LET'S GO. WE'RE ON A DEADLINE...
...AND OUR WORK HERE IS DONE.
KSSSSH
...CALL SECURITY...
ALLAH...!
SIR! SIR, ARE YOU HURT?
GET BACK! GIVE THIS MAN SOME AIR!
AIR? PLEASE! GIVE HIM WATER!
HURRY!
WATER...?
NO.
NOOOOOO!
GET IT AWAY FROM ME!

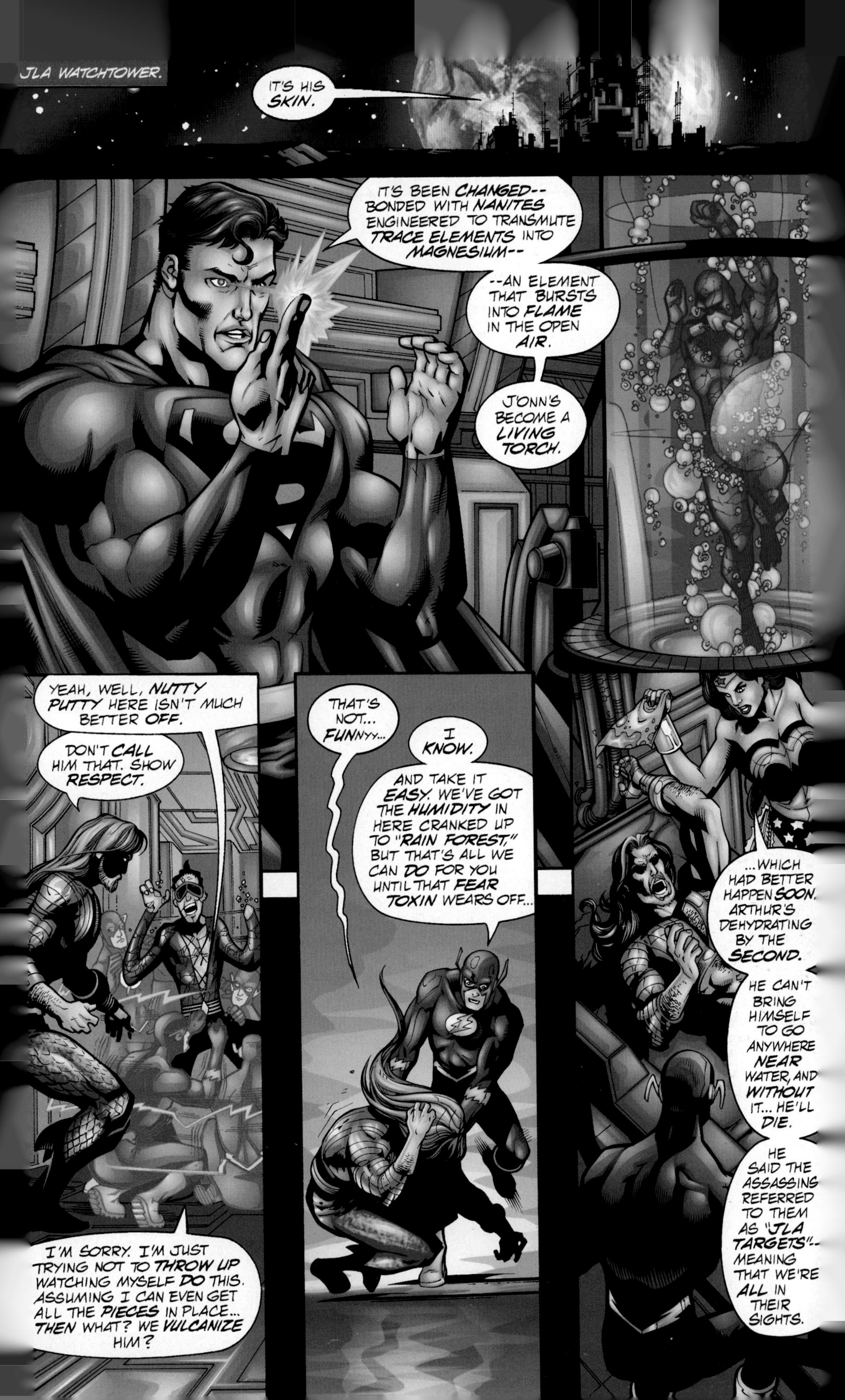
JLA WATCHTOWER.
IT'S HIS SKIN.
IT'S BEEN CHANGED-- BONDED WITH NANITES ENGINEERED TO TRANSMUTE TRACE ELEMENTS INTO MAGNESIUM--
--AN ELEMENT THAT BURSTS INTO FLAME IN THE OPEN AIR.
J'ONN'S BECOME A LIVING TORCH.
YEAH, WELL, NUTTY PUTTY HERE ISN'T MUCH BETTER OFF.
DON'T CALL HIM THAT. SHOW RESPECT.
I'M SORRY. I'M JUST TRYING NOT TO THROW UP WATCHING MYSELF DO THIS. ASSUMING I CAN EVEN GET ALL THE PIECES IN PLACE... THEN WHAT? WE VULCANIZE HIM?
THAT'S NOT... FUNNYY...
I KNOW.
AND TAKE IT EASY. WE'VE GOT THE HUMIDITY IN HERE CRANKED UP TO "RAIN FOREST," BUT THAT'S ALL WE CAN DO FOR YOU UNTIL THAT FEAR TOXIN WEARS OFF...
...WHICH HAD BETTER HAPPEN SOON. ARTHUR'S DEHYDRATING BY THE SECOND.
HE CAN'T BRING HIMSELF TO GO ANYWHERE NEAR WATER, AND WITHOUT IT... HE'LL DIE.
HE SAID THE ASSASSINS REFERRED TO THEM AS "JLA TARGETS"-- MEANING THAT WE'RE ALL IN THEIR SIGHTS.

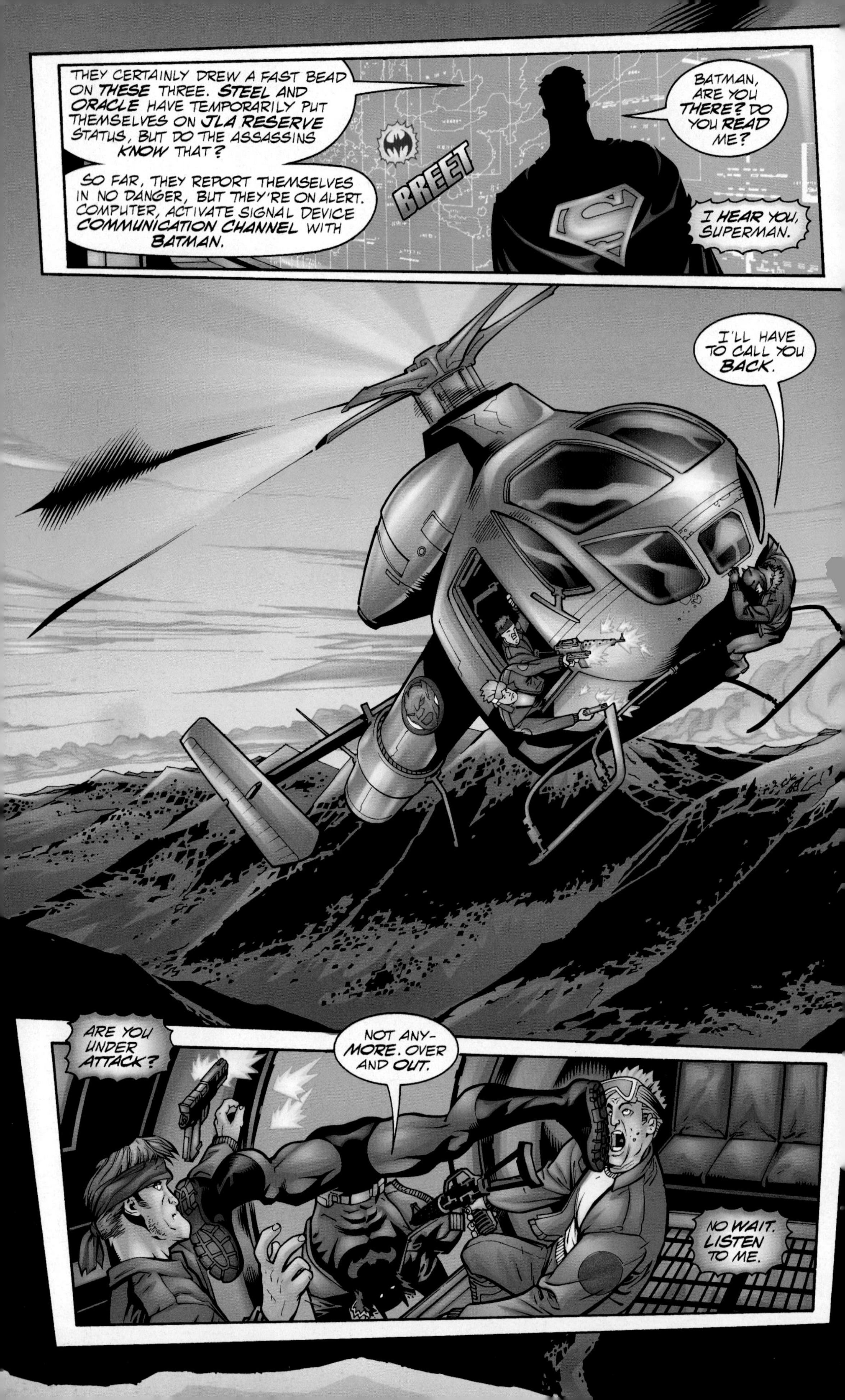
THEY CERTAINLY DREW A FAST BEAD ON THESE THREE. STEEL AND ORACLE HAVE TEMPORARILY PUT THEMSELVES ON JLA RESERVE STATUS, BUT DO THE ASSASSINS KNOW THAT?
SO FAR, THEY REPORT THEMSELVES IN NO DANGER, BUT THEY'RE ON ALERT. COMPUTER, ACTIVATE SIGNAL DEVICE COMMUNICATION CHANNEL WITH BATMAN.
BREET
BATMAN, ARE YOU THERE? DO YOU READ ME?
I HEAR YOU, SUPERMAN.
I'LL HAVE TO CALL YOU BACK.
ARE YOU UNDER ATTACK?
NOT ANY-MORE. OVER AND OUT.
NO WAIT. LISTEN TO ME.

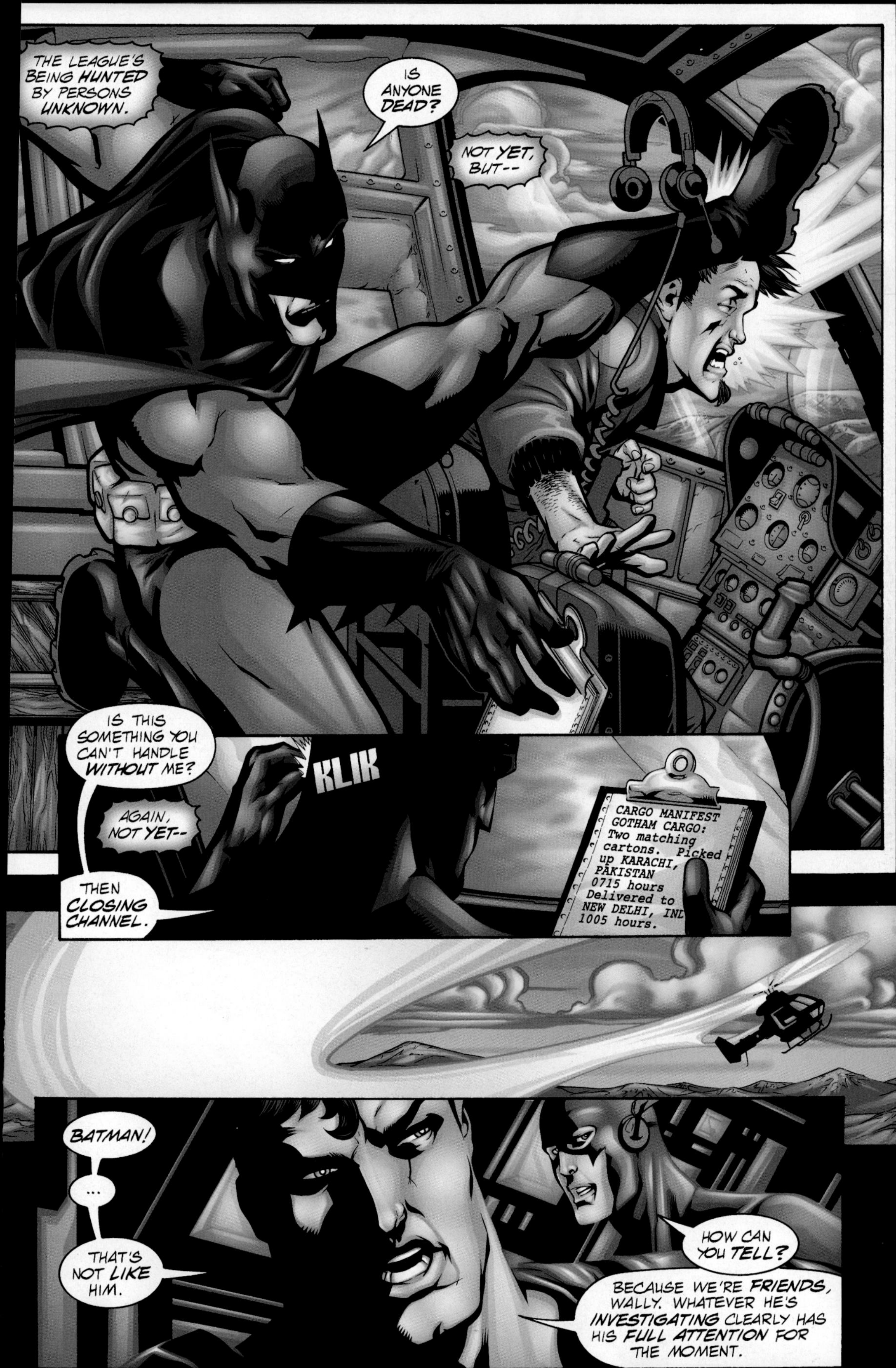
THE LEAGUE'S BEING HUNTED BY PERSONS UNKNOWN.
IS ANYONE DEAD?
NOT YET, BUT--
IS THIS SOMETHING YOU CAN'T HANDLE WITHOUT ME?
KLIK
AGAIN, NOT YET--
THEN CLOSING CHANNEL.
CARGO MANIFEST
GOTHAM CARGO:
Two matching cartons. Picked up KARACHI, PAKISTAN 0715 hours
Delivered to NEW DELHI, IND 1005 hours.
BATMAN!
...
THAT'S NOT LIKE HIM.
HOW CAN YOU TELL?
BECAUSE WE'RE FRIENDS, WALLY. WHATEVER HE'S INVESTIGATING CLEARLY HAS HIS FULL ATTENTION FOR THE MOMENT.

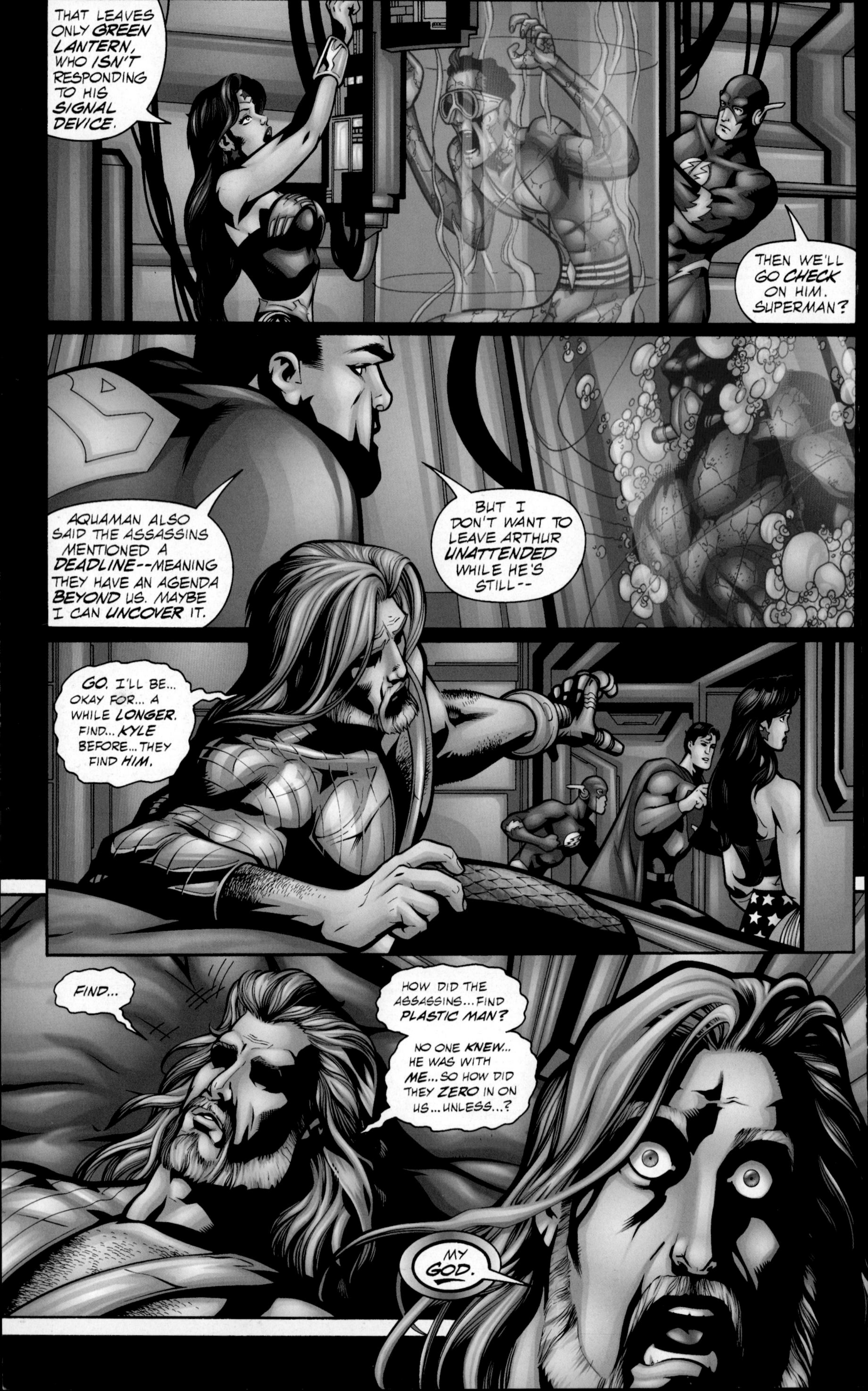
THAT LEAVES ONLY GREEN LANTERN, WHO ISN'T RESPONDING TO HIS SIGNAL DEVICE.
THEN WE'LL GO CHECK ON HIM. SUPERMAN?
AQUAMAN ALSO SAID THE ASSASSINS MENTIONED A DEADLINE--MEANING THEY HAVE AN AGENDA BEYOND US. MAYBE I CAN UNCOVER IT.
BUT I DON'T WANT TO LEAVE ARTHUR UNATTENDED WHILE HE'S STILL--
GO. I'LL BE... OKAY FOR... A WHILE LONGER. FIND... KYLE BEFORE... THEY FIND HIM.
FIND...
HOW DID THE ASSASSINS... FIND PLASTIC MAN?
NO ONE KNEW... HE WAS WITH ME... SO HOW DID THEY ZERO IN ON US... UNLESS...?
MY GOD.

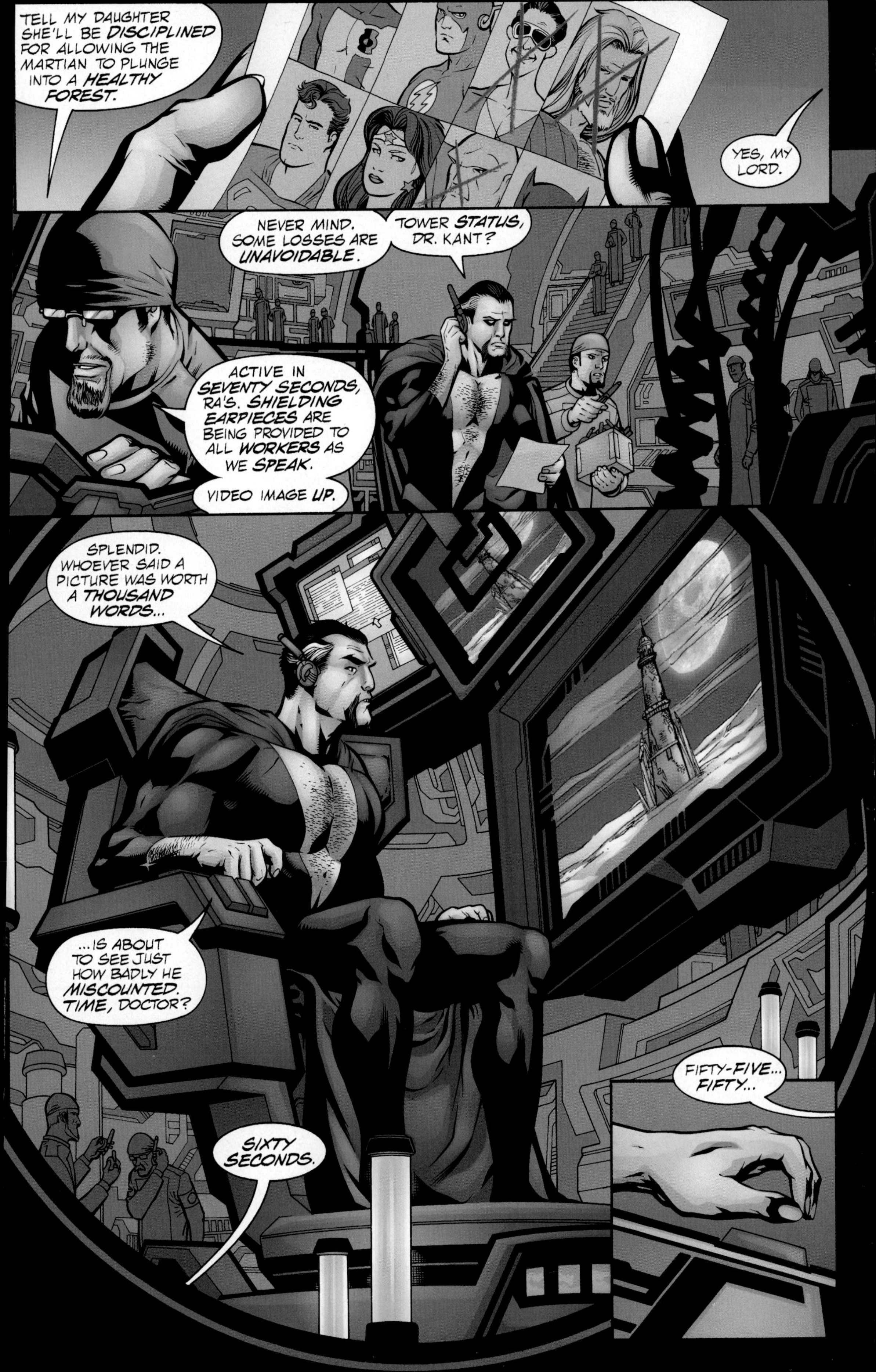
TELL MY DAUGHTER SHE'LL BE DISCIPLINED FOR ALLOWING THE MARTIAN TO PLUNGE INTO A HEALTHY FOREST.
YES, MY LORD.
NEVER MIND. SOME LOSSES ARE UNAVOIDABLE.
TOWER STATUS, DR. KANT?
ACTIVE IN SEVENTY SECONDS, RA'S. SHIELDING EARPIECES ARE BEING PROVIDED TO ALL WORKERS AS WE SPEAK.
VIDEO IMAGE UP.
SPLENDID. WHOEVER SAID A PICTURE WAS WORTH A THOUSAND WORDS...
...IS ABOUT TO SEE JUST HOW BADLY HE MISCOUNTED. TIME, DOCTOR?
SIXTY SECONDS.
FIFTY-FIVE... FIFTY...

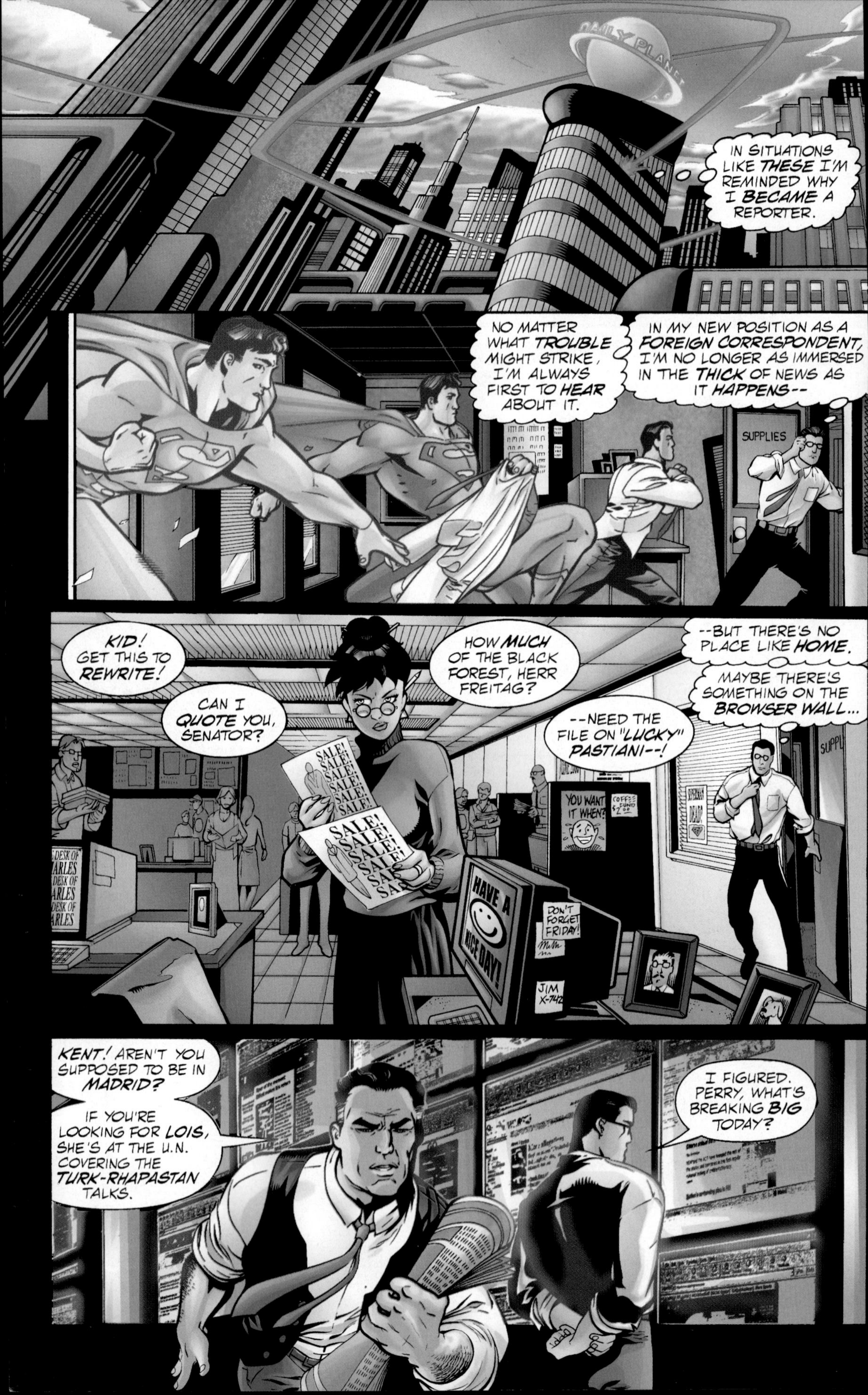
DAILY PLANET
IN SITUATIONS LIKE THESE I'M REMINDED WHY I BECAME A REPORTER.
NO MATTER WHAT TROUBLE MIGHT STRIKE, I'M ALWAYS FIRST TO HEAR ABOUT IT.
IN MY NEW POSITION AS A FOREIGN CORRESPONDENT, I'M NO LONGER AS IMMERSED IN THE THICK OF NEWS AS IT HAPPENS--
SUPPLIES
KID! GET THIS TO REWRITE!
CAN I QUOTE YOU, SENATOR?
HOW MUCH OF THE BLACK FOREST, HERR FREITAG?
--NEED THE FILE ON "LUCKY" PASTIANI--!
--BUT THERE'S NO PLACE LIKE HOME.
MAYBE THERE'S SOMETHING ON THE BROWSER WALL...
YOU WANT IT WHEN?
COFFEE FUND $2.00
HAVE A NICE DAY!
DON'T FORGET FRIDAY!
JIM X-742
KENT! AREN'T YOU SUPPOSED TO BE IN MADRID?
IF YOU'RE LOOKING FOR LOIS, SHE'S AT THE U.N. COVERING THE TURK-RHAPASTAN TALKS.
I FIGURED. PERRY, WHAT'S BREAKING BIG TODAY?

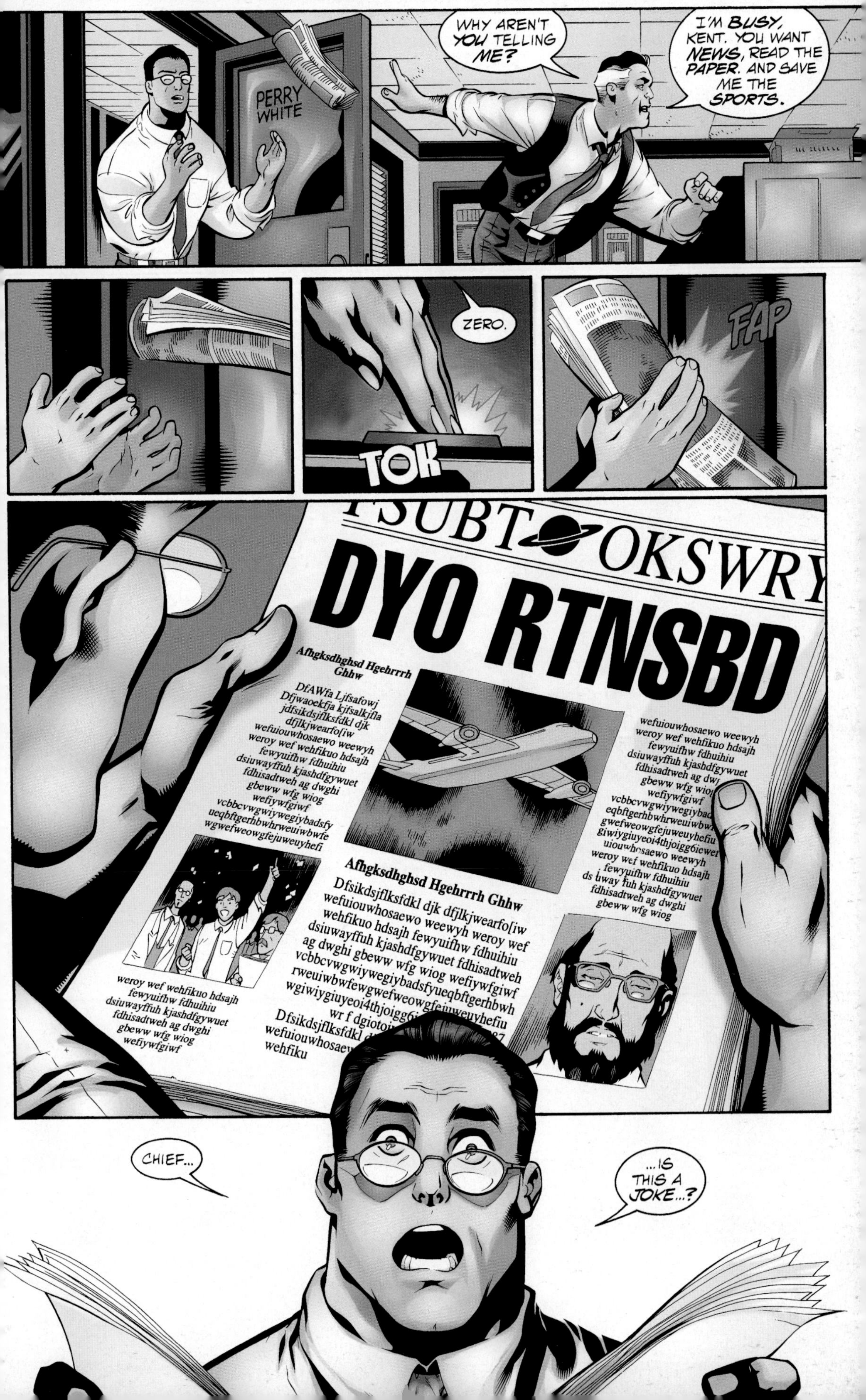

PERRY WHITE
WHY AREN'T YOU TELLING ME?
I'M BUSY, KENT. YOU WANT NEWS, READ THE PAPER. AND SAVE ME THE SPORTS.
ZERO.
TOK
FAP
TSUBT OKSWRY
DYO RTNSBD
CHIEF...
...IS THIS A JOKE...?

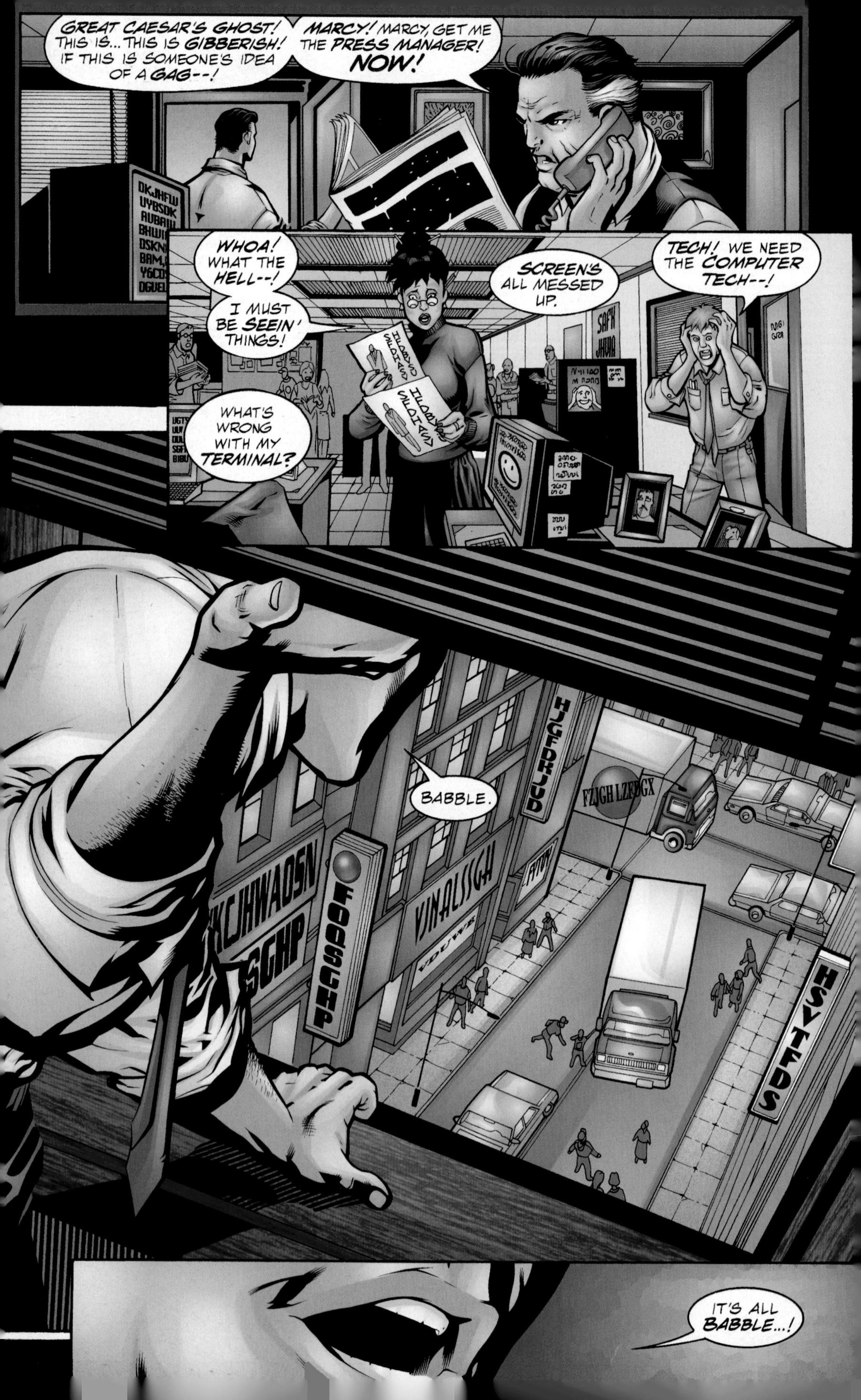
GREAT CAESAR'S GHOST! THIS IS... THIS IS GIBBERISH! IF THIS IS SOMEONE'S IDEA OF A GAG--!
MARCY! MARCY, GET ME THE PRESS MANAGER! NOW!
WHOA! WHAT THE HELL--!
I MUST BE SEEIN' THINGS!
WHAT'S WRONG WITH MY TERMINAL?
SCREEN'S ALL MESSED UP.
TECH! WE NEED THE COMPUTER TECH--!
BABBLE.
IT'S ALL BABBLE...!

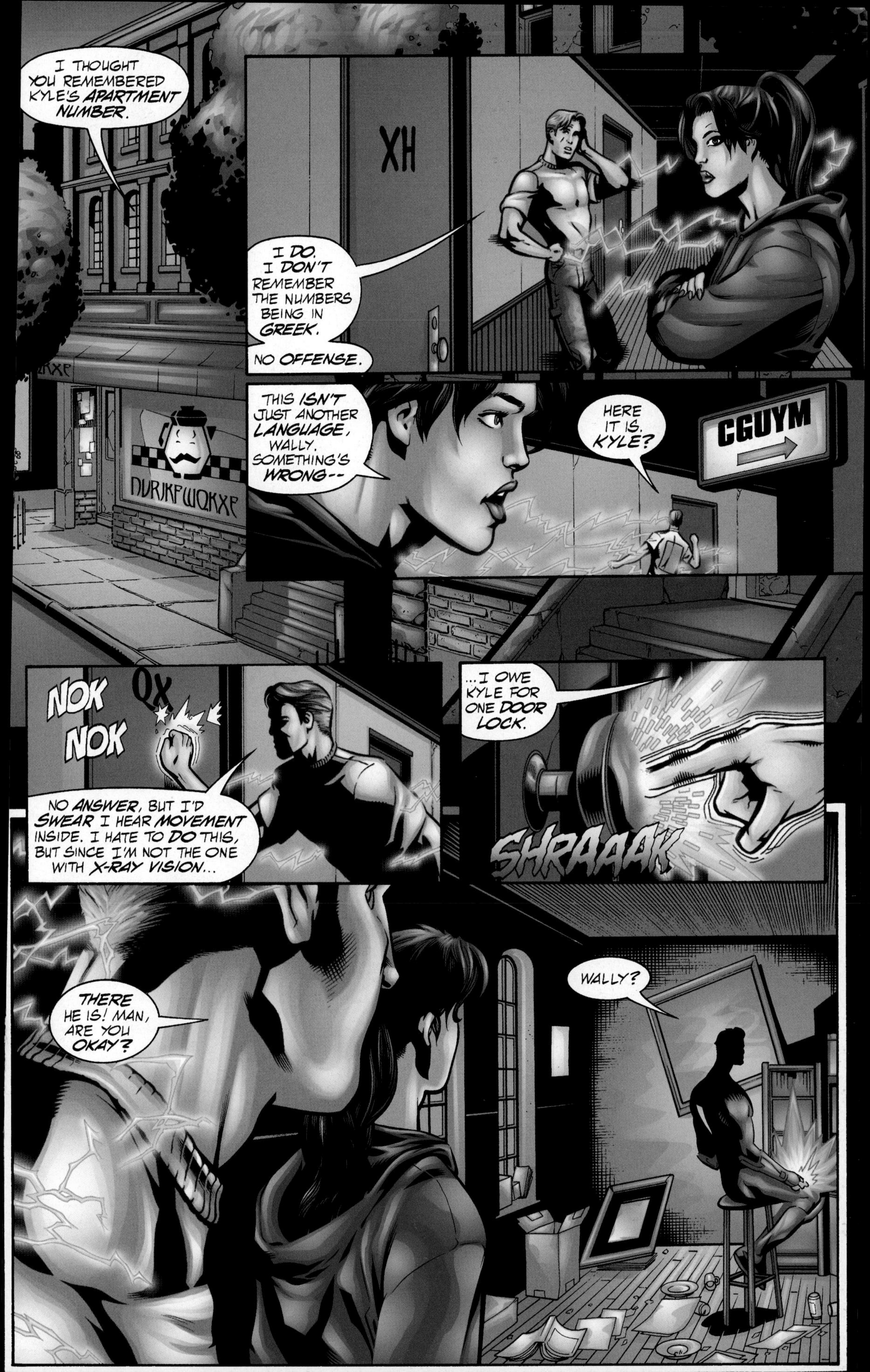
I THOUGHT YOU REMEMBERED KYLE'S APARTMENT NUMBER.
XH
I DO. I DON'T REMEMBER THE NUMBERS BEING IN GREEK.
NO OFFENSE.
THIS ISN'T JUST ANOTHER LANGUAGE, WALLY. SOMETHING'S WRONG--
HERE IT IS. KYLE?
CGUYM
NOK NOK
QX
NO ANSWER, BUT I'D SWEAR I HEAR MOVEMENT INSIDE. I HATE TO DO THIS, BUT SINCE I'M NOT THE ONE WITH X-RAY VISION...
...I OWE KYLE FOR ONE DOOR LOCK.
SHRAAAK
THERE HE IS! MAN, ARE YOU OKAY?
WALLY?

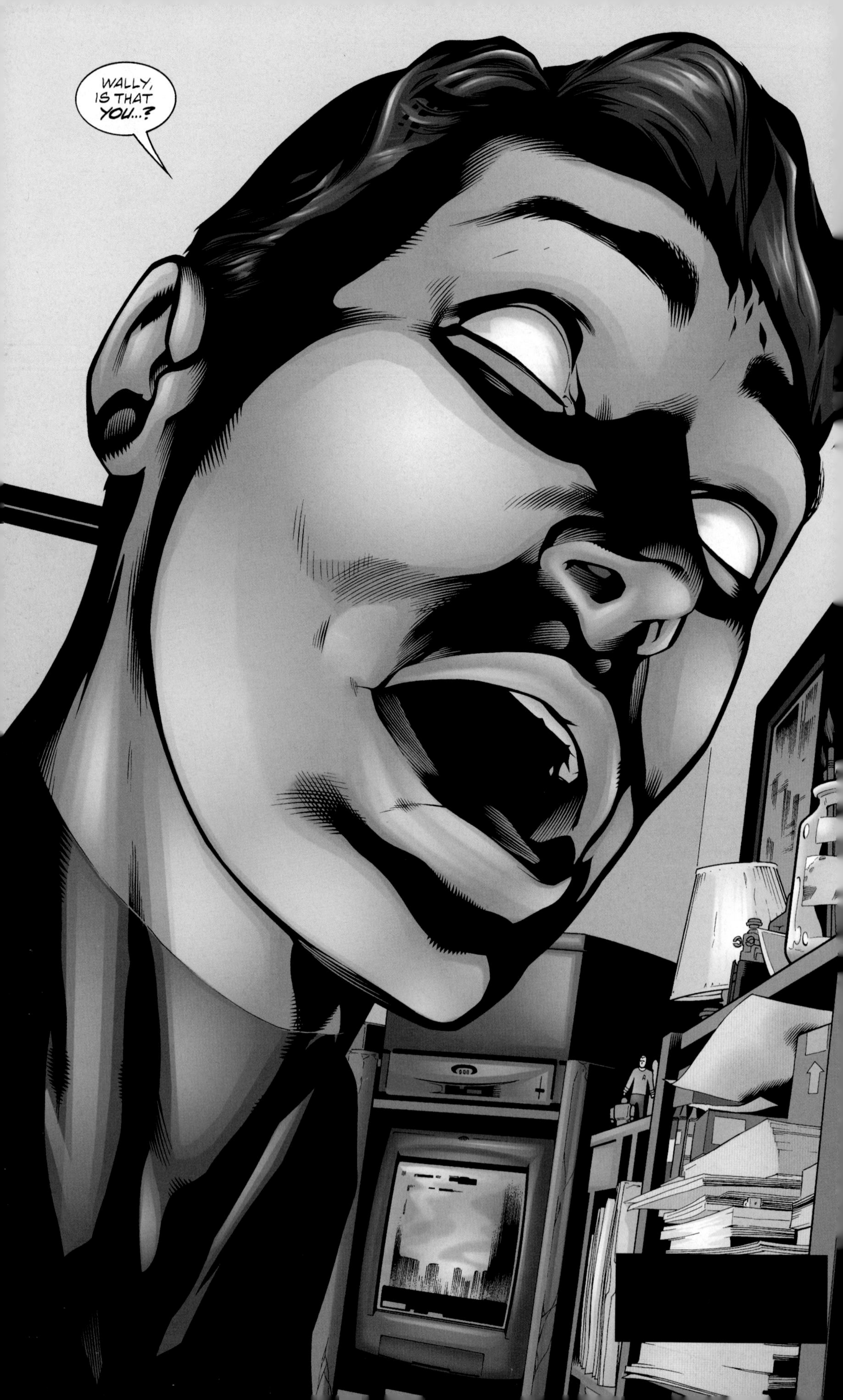
WALLY, IS THAT YOU...?
[redacted]

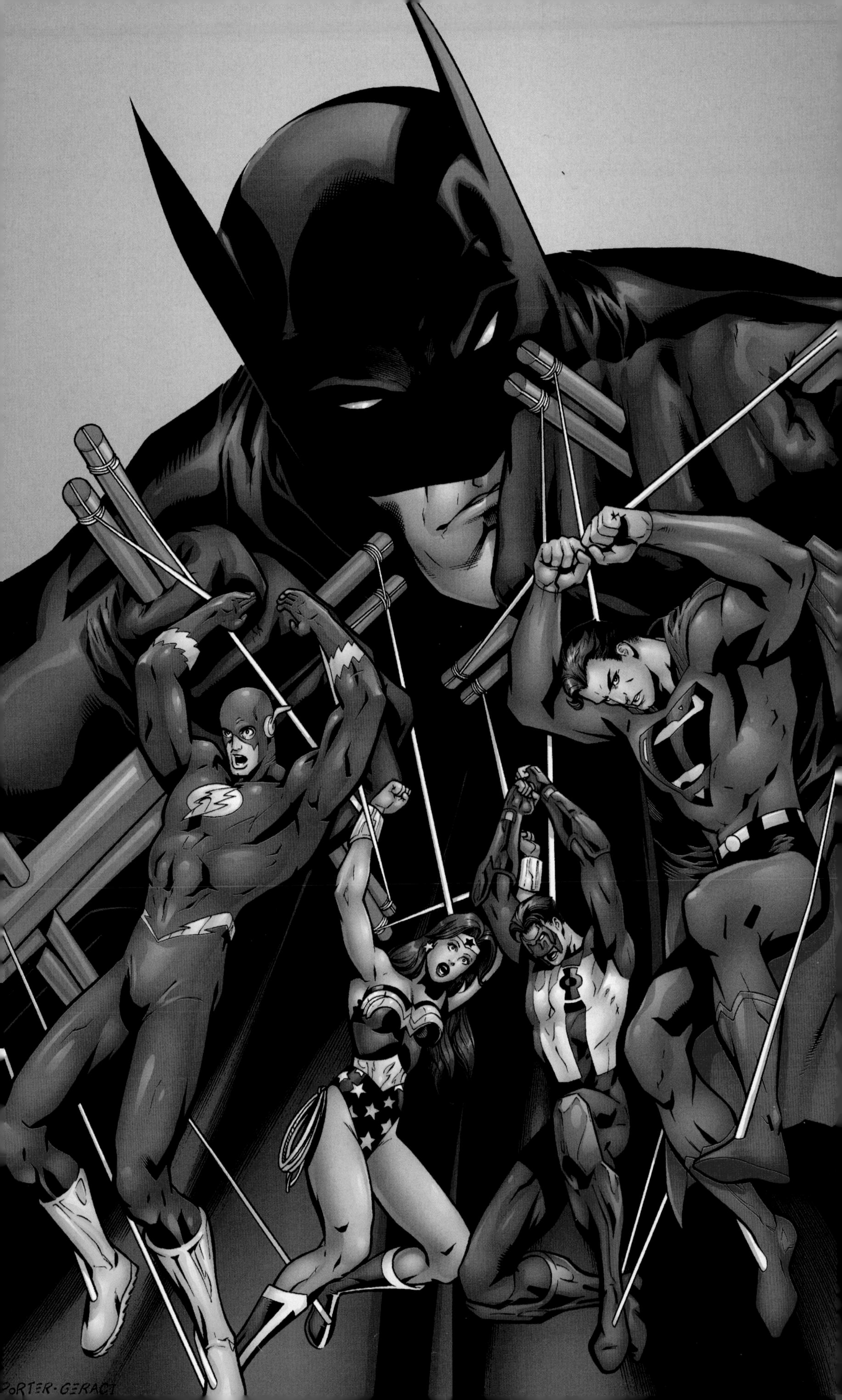
PORTER·GERACI

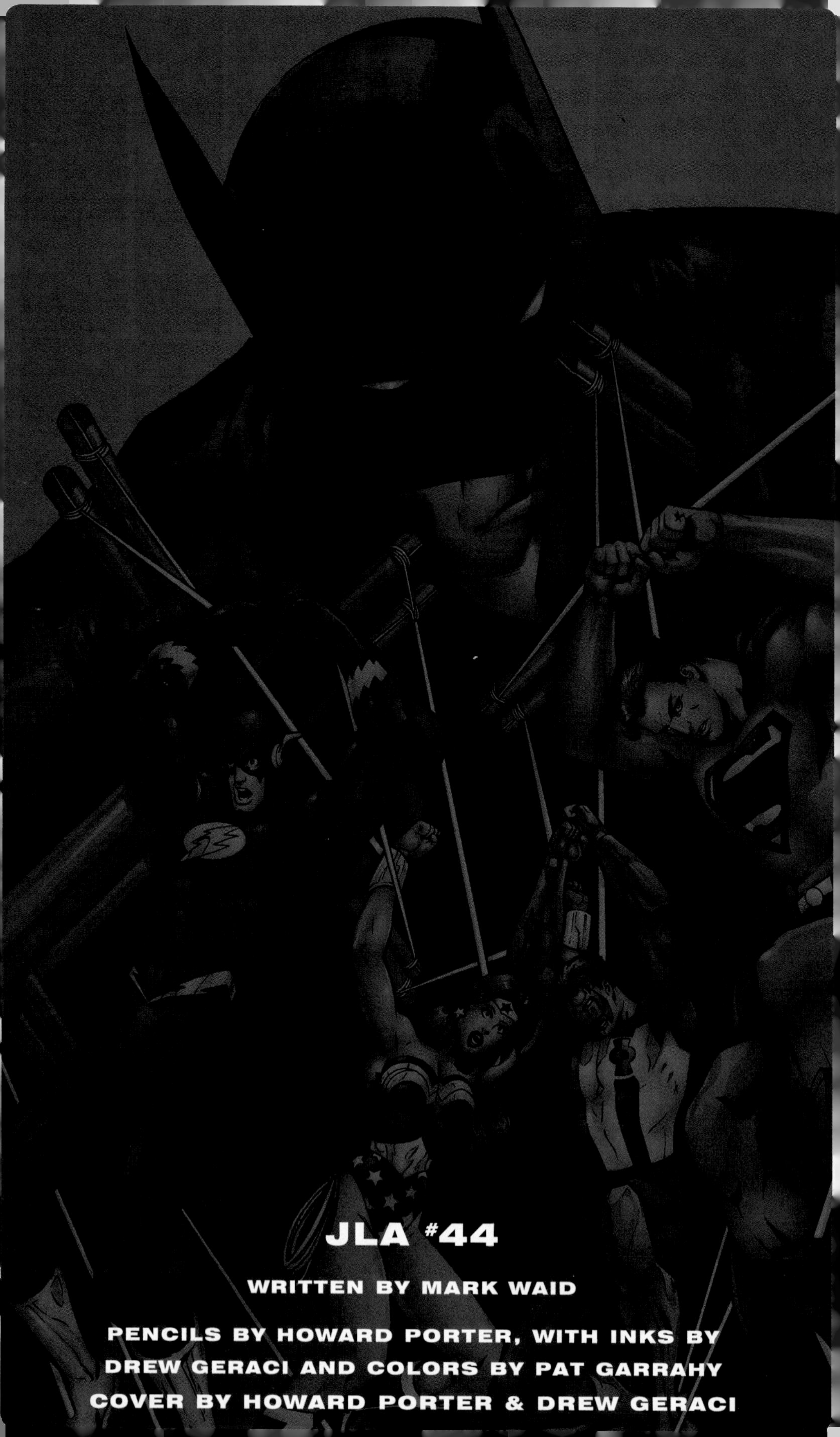

JLA #44

WRITTEN BY MARK WAID

PENCILS BY HOWARD PORTER, WITH INKS BY DREW GERACI AND COLORS BY PAT GARRAHY

COVER BY HOWARD PORTER & DREW GERACI

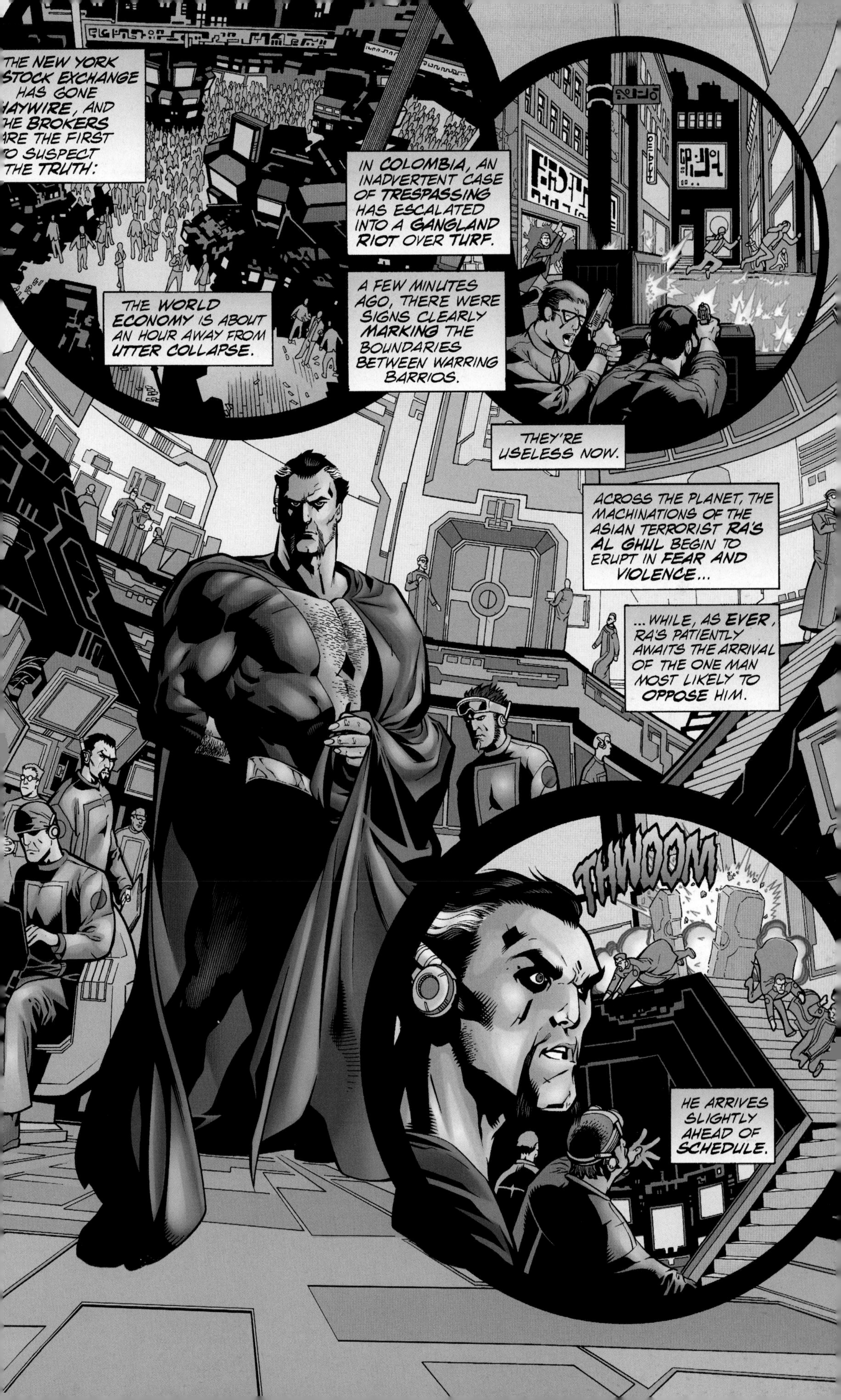
THE NEW YORK STOCK EXCHANGE HAS GONE HAYWIRE, AND THE BROKERS ARE THE FIRST TO SUSPECT THE TRUTH:
THE WORLD ECONOMY IS ABOUT AN HOUR AWAY FROM UTTER COLLAPSE.
IN COLOMBIA, AN INADVERTENT CASE OF TRESPASSING HAS ESCALATED INTO A GANGLAND RIOT OVER TURF.
A FEW MINUTES AGO, THERE WERE SIGNS CLEARLY MARKING THE BOUNDARIES BETWEEN WARRING BARRIOS.
THEY'RE USELESS NOW.
ACROSS THE PLANET, THE MACHINATIONS OF THE ASIAN TERRORIST RA'S AL GHUL BEGIN TO ERUPT IN FEAR AND VIOLENCE...
...WHILE, AS EVER, RA'S PATIENTLY AWAITS THE ARRIVAL OF THE ONE MAN MOST LIKELY TO OPPOSE HIM.
THWOOM
HE ARRIVES SLIGHTLY AHEAD OF SCHEDULE.

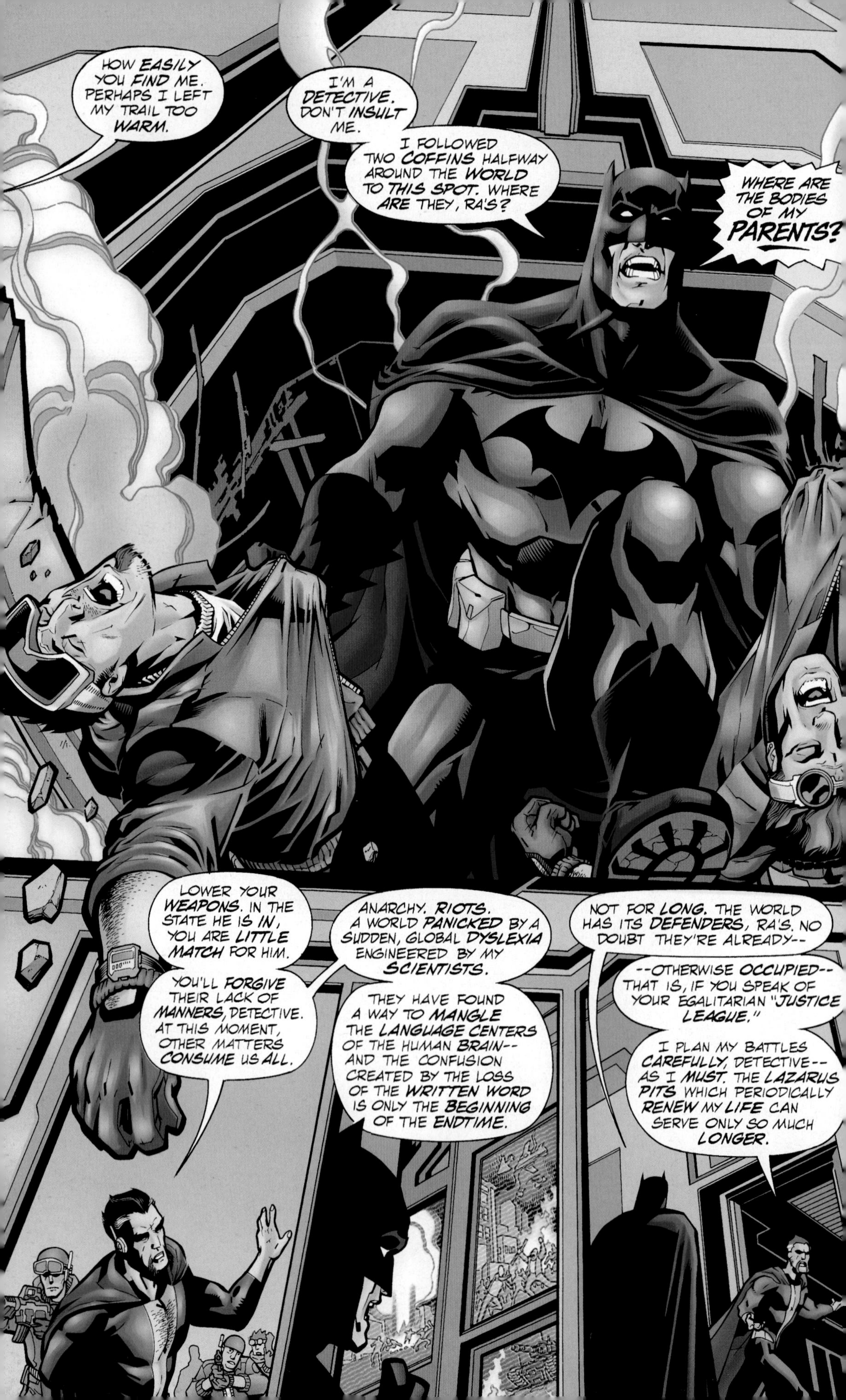
HOW EASILY YOU FIND ME. PERHAPS I LEFT MY TRAIL TOO WARM.
I'M A DETECTIVE. DON'T INSULT ME.
I FOLLOWED TWO COFFINS HALFWAY AROUND THE WORLD TO THIS SPOT. WHERE ARE THEY, RA'S?
WHERE ARE THE BODIES OF MY PARENTS?
LOWER YOUR WEAPONS. IN THE STATE HE IS IN, YOU ARE LITTLE MATCH FOR HIM.
YOU'LL FORGIVE THEIR LACK OF MANNERS, DETECTIVE. AT THIS MOMENT, OTHER MATTERS CONSUME US ALL.
ANARCHY. RIOTS. A WORLD PANICKED BY A SUDDEN, GLOBAL DYSLEXIA ENGINEERED BY MY SCIENTISTS.
THEY HAVE FOUND A WAY TO MANGLE THE LANGUAGE CENTERS OF THE HUMAN BRAIN-- AND THE CONFUSION CREATED BY THE LOSS OF THE WRITTEN WORD IS ONLY THE BEGINNING OF THE ENDTIME.
NOT FOR LONG. THE WORLD HAS ITS DEFENDERS, RA'S. NO DOUBT THEY'RE ALREADY--
--OTHERWISE OCCUPIED-- THAT IS, IF YOU SPEAK OF YOUR EGALITARIAN "JUSTICE LEAGUE."
I PLAN MY BATTLES CAREFULLY, DETECTIVE-- AS I MUST. THE LAZARUS PITS WHICH PERIODICALLY RENEW MY LIFE CAN SERVE ONLY SO MUCH LONGER.

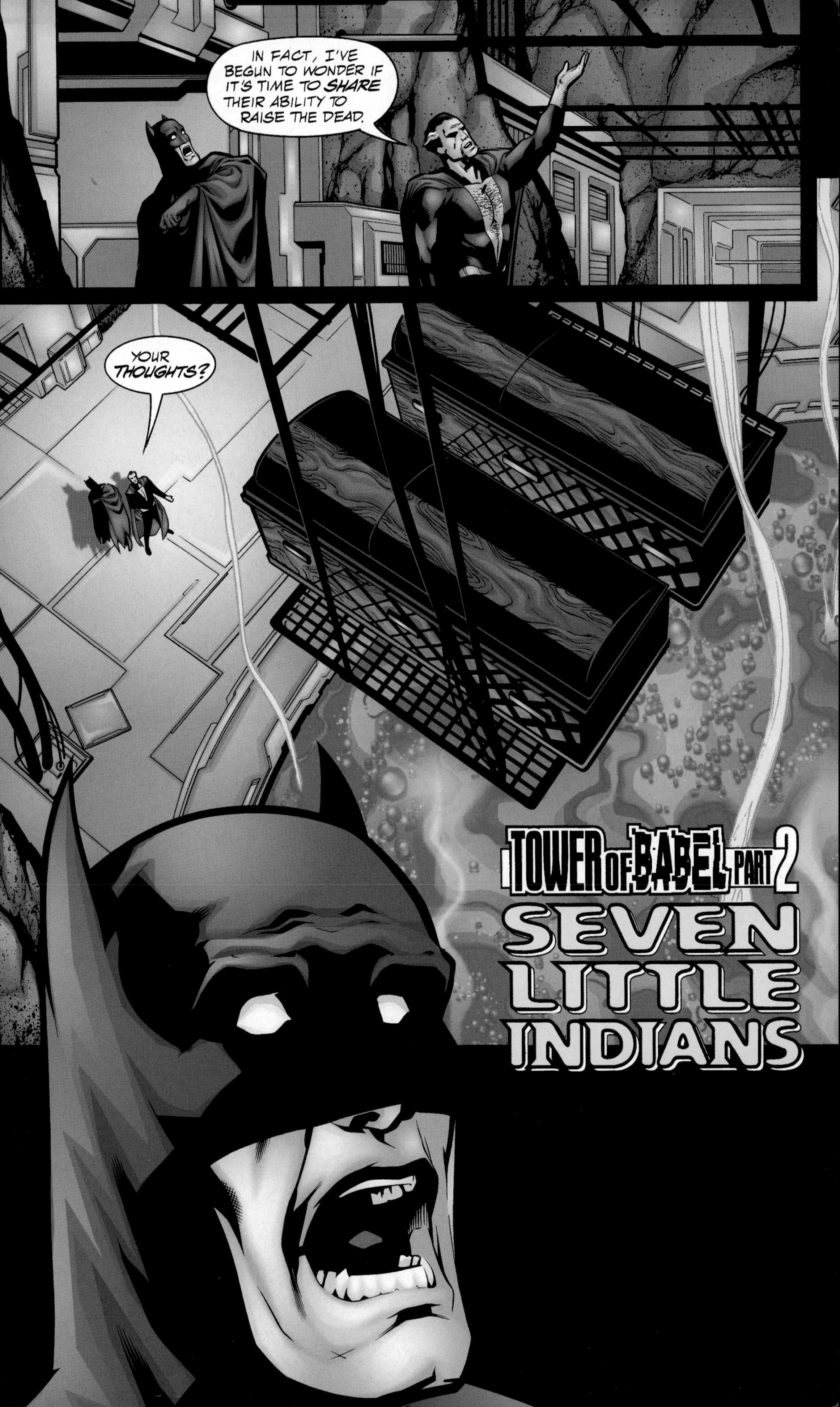
IN FACT, I'VE BEGUN TO WONDER IF IT'S TIME TO SHARE THEIR ABILITY TO RAISE THE DEAD.
YOUR THOUGHTS?
TOWER OF BABEL PART 2
SEVEN LITTLE INDIANS

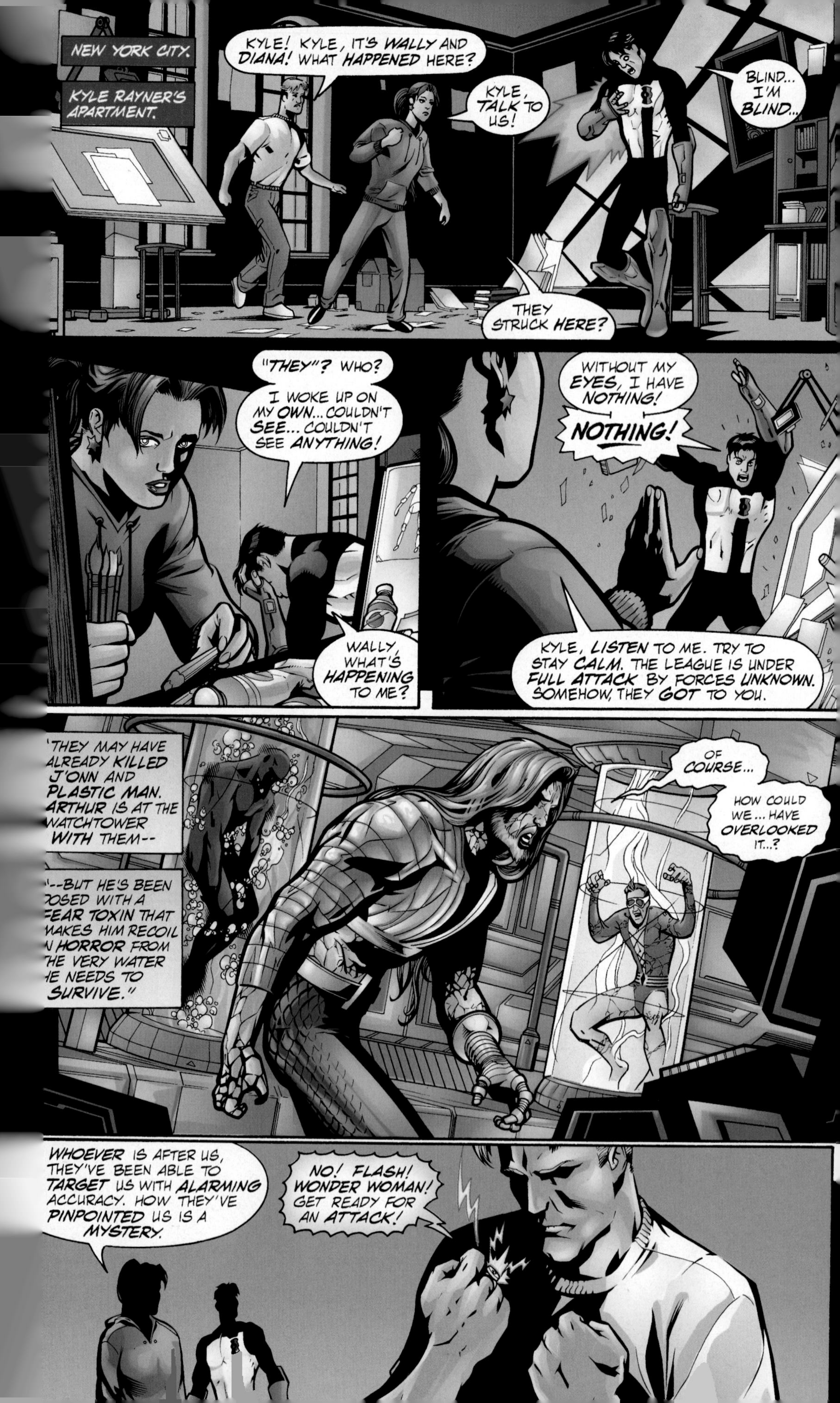

NEW YORK CITY.
KYLE RAYNER'S APARTMENT.
KYLE! KYLE, IT'S WALLY AND DIANA! WHAT HAPPENED HERE?
KYLE, TALK TO US!
BLIND... I'M BLIND...
THEY STRUCK HERE?
"THEY"? WHO?
I WOKE UP ON MY OWN... COULDN'T SEE... COULDN'T SEE ANYTHING!
WALLY, WHAT'S HAPPENING TO ME?
WITHOUT MY EYES, I HAVE NOTHING!
NOTHING!
KYLE, LISTEN TO ME. TRY TO STAY CALM. THE LEAGUE IS UNDER FULL ATTACK BY FORCES UNKNOWN. SOMEHOW, THEY GOT TO YOU.
"THEY MAY HAVE ALREADY KILLED J'ONN AND PLASTIC MAN. ARTHUR IS AT THE WATCHTOWER WITH THEM--
"--BUT HE'S BEEN DOSED WITH A FEAR TOXIN THAT MAKES HIM RECOIL IN HORROR FROM THE VERY WATER HE NEEDS TO SURVIVE."
OF COURSE...
HOW COULD WE... HAVE OVERLOOKED IT...?
WHOEVER IS AFTER US, THEY'VE BEEN ABLE TO TARGET US WITH ALARMING ACCURACY. HOW THEY'VE PINPOINTED US IS A MYSTERY.
NO! FLASH! WONDER WOMAN! GET READY FOR AN ATTACK!

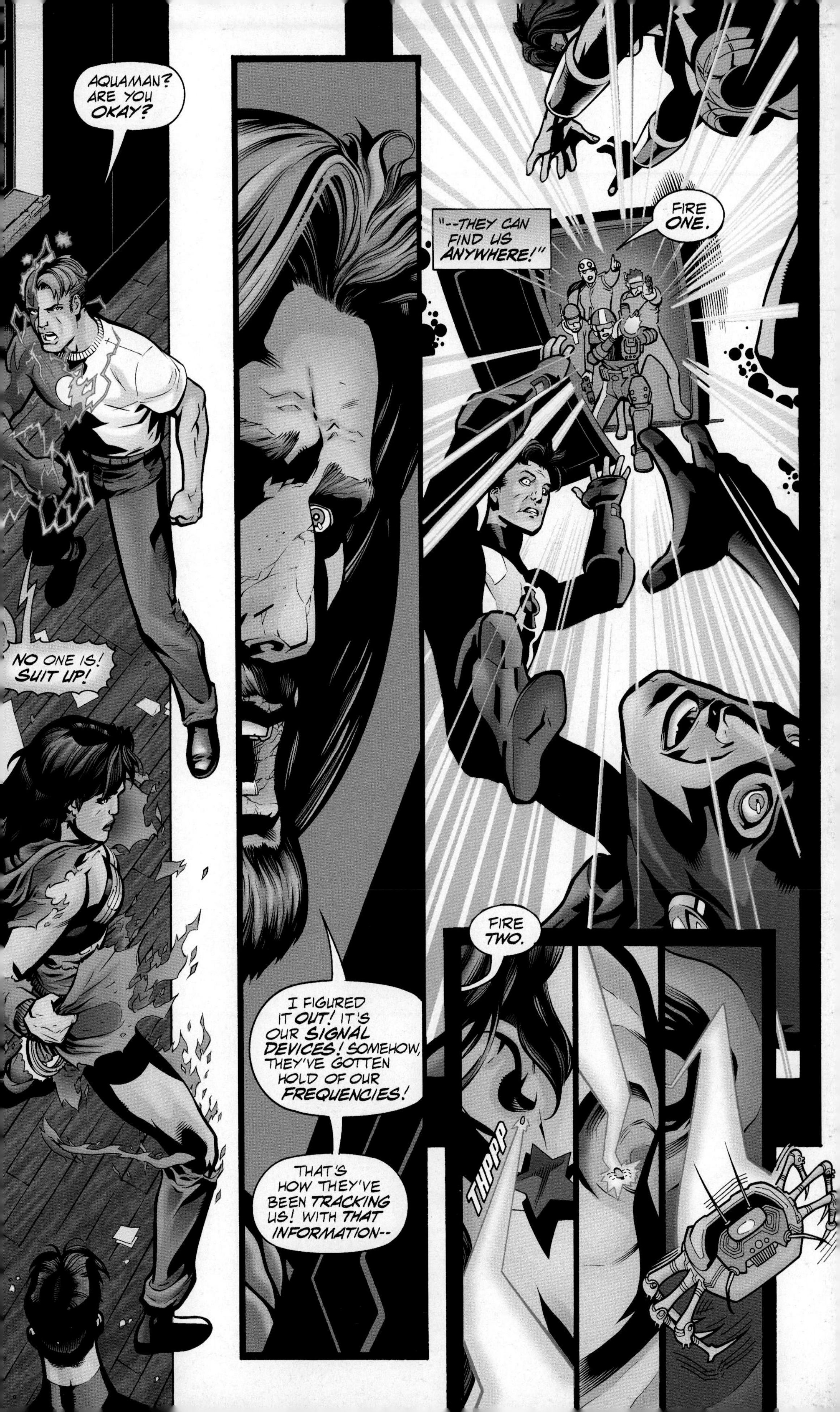
AQUAMAN? ARE YOU OKAY?
NO ONE IS! SUIT UP!
I FIGURED IT OUT! IT'S OUR SIGNAL DEVICES! SOMEHOW, THEY'VE GOTTEN HOLD OF OUR FREQUENCIES!
THAT'S HOW THEY'VE BEEN TRACKING US! WITH THAT INFORMATION--
"--THEY CAN FIND US ANYWHERE!"
FIRE ONE.
FIRE TWO.
THPPP

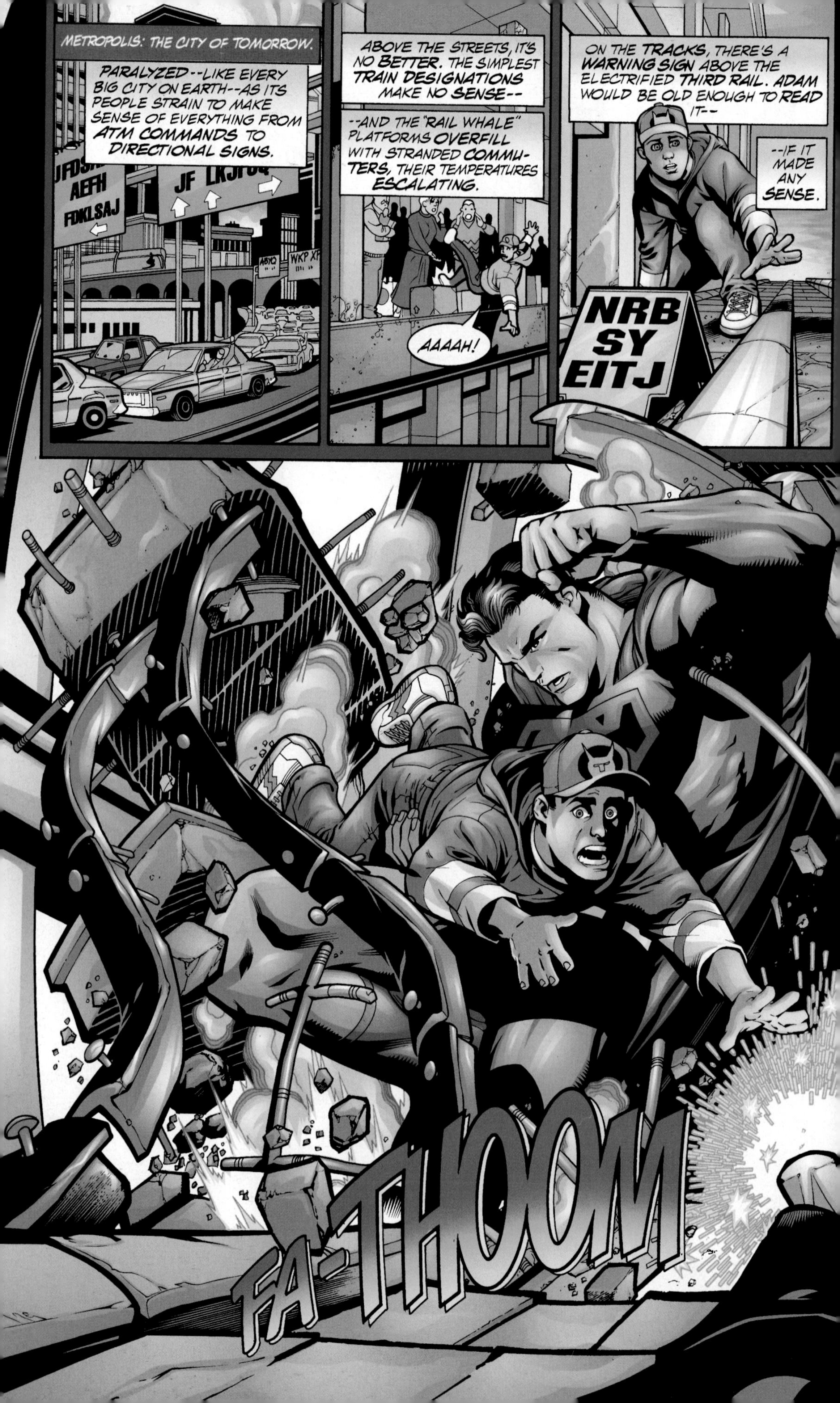
METROPOLIS: THE CITY OF TOMORROW.
PARALYZED--LIKE EVERY BIG CITY ON EARTH--AS ITS PEOPLE STRAIN TO MAKE SENSE OF EVERYTHING FROM ATM COMMANDS TO DIRECTIONAL SIGNS.
UFDS AEFH FDKLSAJ
JF LKJFUQ
ABYO
WKP XP
ABOVE THE STREETS, IT'S NO BETTER. THE SIMPLEST TRAIN DESIGNATIONS MAKE NO SENSE--
--AND THE "RAIL WHALE" PLATFORMS OVERFILL WITH STRANDED COMMUTERS, THEIR TEMPERATURES ESCALATING.
AAAAH!
ON THE TRACKS, THERE'S A WARNING SIGN ABOVE THE ELECTRIFIED THIRD RAIL. ADAM WOULD BE OLD ENOUGH TO READ IT--
--IF IT MADE ANY SENSE.
NRB SY EITJ
FA-THOOM

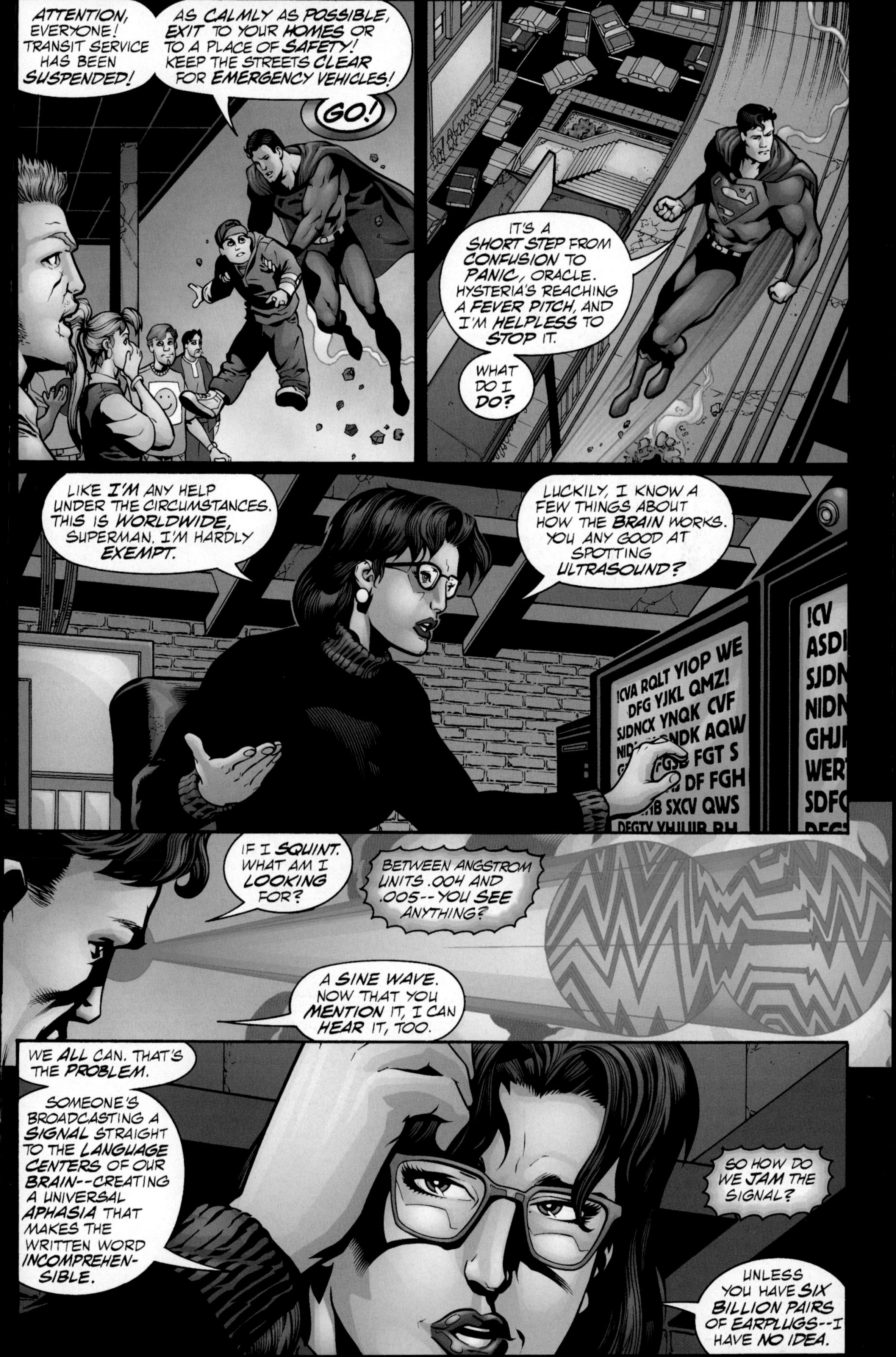
ATTENTION, EVERYONE! TRANSIT SERVICE HAS BEEN SUSPENDED!
AS CALMLY AS POSSIBLE, EXIT TO YOUR HOMES OR TO A PLACE OF SAFETY! KEEP THE STREETS CLEAR FOR EMERGENCY VEHICLES!
GO!
IT'S A SHORT STEP FROM CONFUSION TO PANIC, ORACLE. HYSTERIA'S REACHING A FEVER PITCH, AND I'M HELPLESS TO STOP IT.
WHAT DO I DO?
LIKE I'M ANY HELP UNDER THE CIRCUMSTANCES. THIS IS WORLDWIDE, SUPERMAN. I'M HARDLY EXEMPT.
LUCKILY, I KNOW A FEW THINGS ABOUT HOW THE BRAIN WORKS. YOU ANY GOOD AT SPOTTING ULTRASOUND?
!CVA RQLT YIOP WE
DFG YJKL QMZ!
SJDNCX YNQK CVF
IF I SQUINT. WHAT AM I LOOKING FOR?
BETWEEN ANGSTROM UNITS .004 AND .005--YOU SEE ANYTHING?
A SINE WAVE. NOW THAT YOU MENTION IT, I CAN HEAR IT, TOO.
WE ALL CAN. THAT'S THE PROBLEM.
SOMEONE'S BROADCASTING A SIGNAL STRAIGHT TO THE LANGUAGE CENTERS OF OUR BRAIN--CREATING A UNIVERSAL APHASIA THAT MAKES THE WRITTEN WORD INCOMPREHEN-SIBLE.
SO HOW DO WE JAM THE SIGNAL?
UNLESS YOU HAVE SIX BILLION PAIRS OF EARPLUGS--I HAVE NO IDEA.

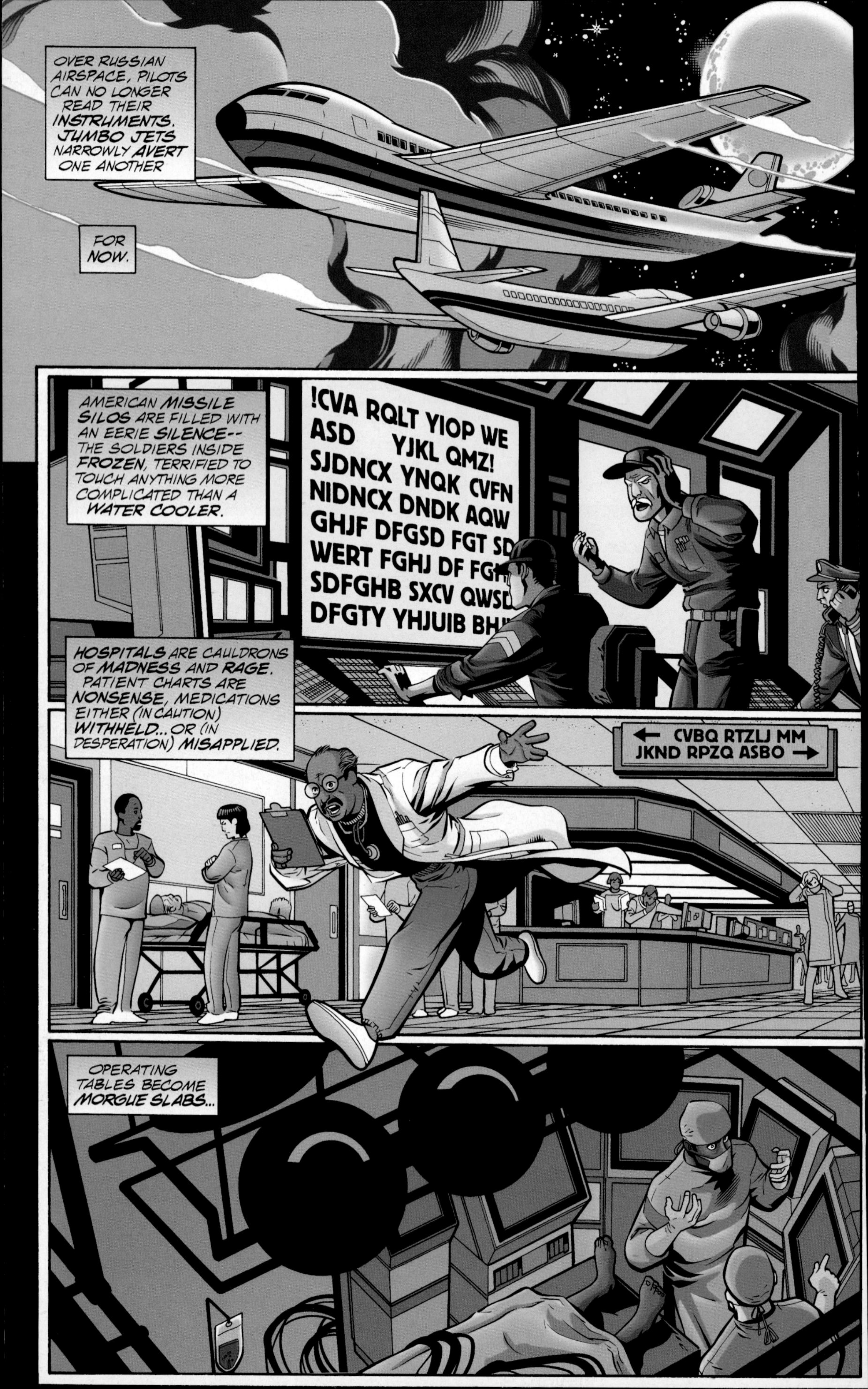
OVER RUSSIAN AIRSPACE, PILOTS CAN NO LONGER READ THEIR INSTRUMENTS. JUMBO JETS NARROWLY AVERT ONE ANOTHER
FOR NOW.
AMERICAN MISSILE SILOS ARE FILLED WITH AN EERIE SILENCE-- THE SOLDIERS INSIDE FROZEN, TERRIFIED TO TOUCH ANYTHING MORE COMPLICATED THAN A WATER COOLER.
!CVA RQLT YIOP WE
ASD YJKL QMZ!
SJDNCX YNQK CVFN
NIDNCX DNDK AQW
GHJF DFGSD FGT SD
WERT FGHJ DF FGH
SDFGHB SXCV QWSD
DFGTY YHJUIB BH
HOSPITALS ARE CAULDRONS OF MADNESS AND RAGE. PATIENT CHARTS ARE NONSENSE, MEDICATIONS EITHER (IN CAUTION) WITHHELD...OR (IN DESPERATION) MISAPPLIED.
← CVBQ RTZLJ MM
JKND RPZQ ASBO →
OPERATING TABLES BECOME MORGUE SLABS...

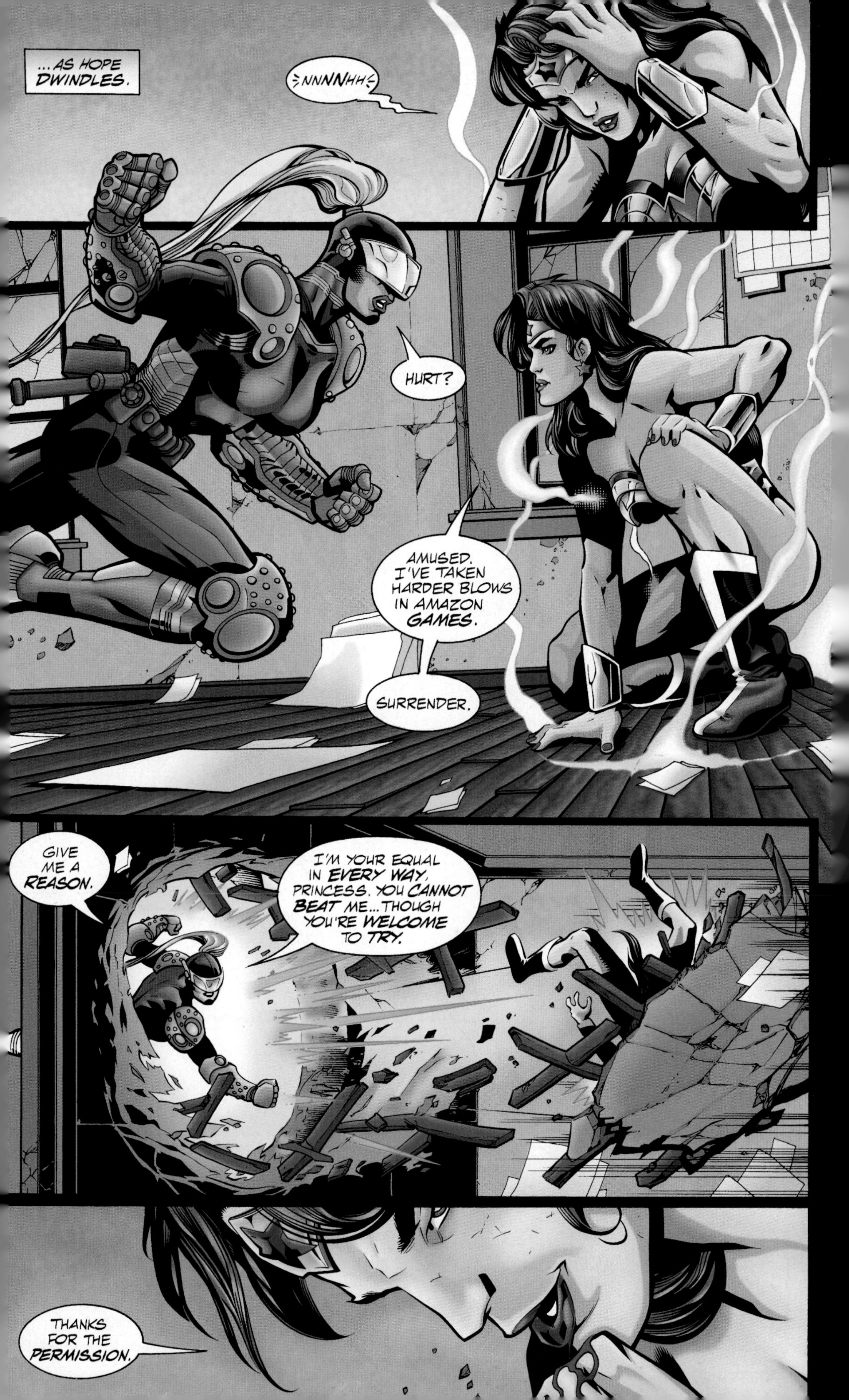
...AS HOPE DWINDLES.
NNNNHH
HURT?
AMUSED. I'VE TAKEN HARDER BLOWS IN AMAZON GAMES.
SURRENDER.
GIVE ME A REASON.
I'M YOUR EQUAL IN EVERY WAY, PRINCESS. YOU CANNOT BEAT ME...THOUGH YOU'RE WELCOME TO TRY.
THANKS FOR THE PERMISSION.

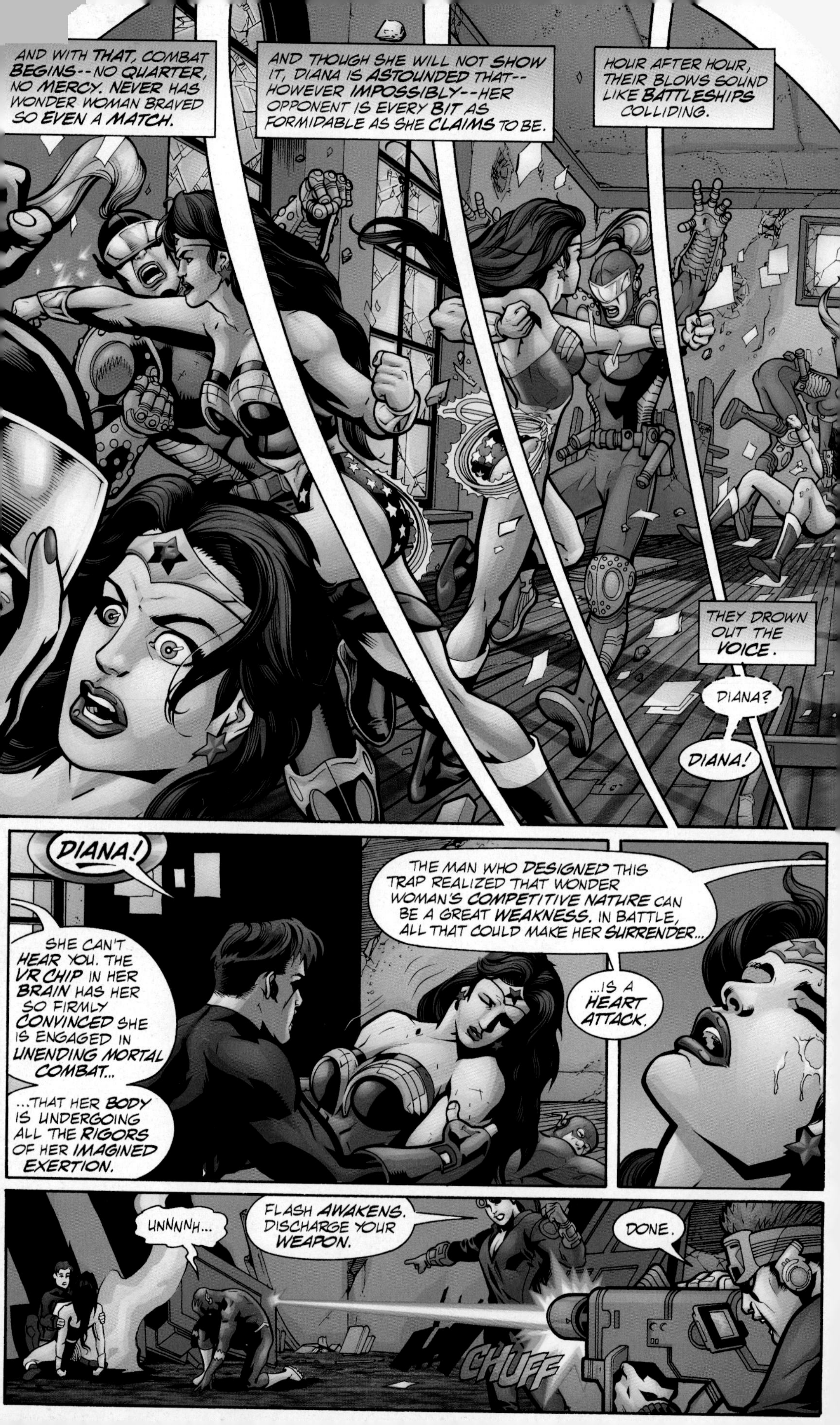
AND WITH THAT, COMBAT BEGINS--NO QUARTER, NO MERCY. NEVER HAS WONDER WOMAN BRAVED SO EVEN A MATCH.
AND THOUGH SHE WILL NOT SHOW IT, DIANA IS ASTOUNDED THAT--HOWEVER IMPOSSIBLY--HER OPPONENT IS EVERY BIT AS FORMIDABLE AS SHE CLAIMS TO BE.
HOUR AFTER HOUR, THEIR BLOWS SOUND LIKE BATTLESHIPS COLLIDING.
THEY DROWN OUT THE VOICE.
DIANA?
DIANA!
DIANA!
SHE CAN'T HEAR YOU. THE VR CHIP IN HER BRAIN HAS HER SO FIRMLY CONVINCED SHE IS ENGAGED IN UNENDING MORTAL COMBAT...
...THAT HER BODY IS UNDERGOING ALL THE RIGORS OF HER IMAGINED EXERTION.
THE MAN WHO DESIGNED THIS TRAP REALIZED THAT WONDER WOMAN'S COMPETITIVE NATURE CAN BE A GREAT WEAKNESS. IN BATTLE, ALL THAT COULD MAKE HER SURRENDER...
...IS A HEART ATTACK.
UNNNNH...
FLASH AWAKENS. DISCHARGE YOUR WEAPON.
DONE.
CHUFF

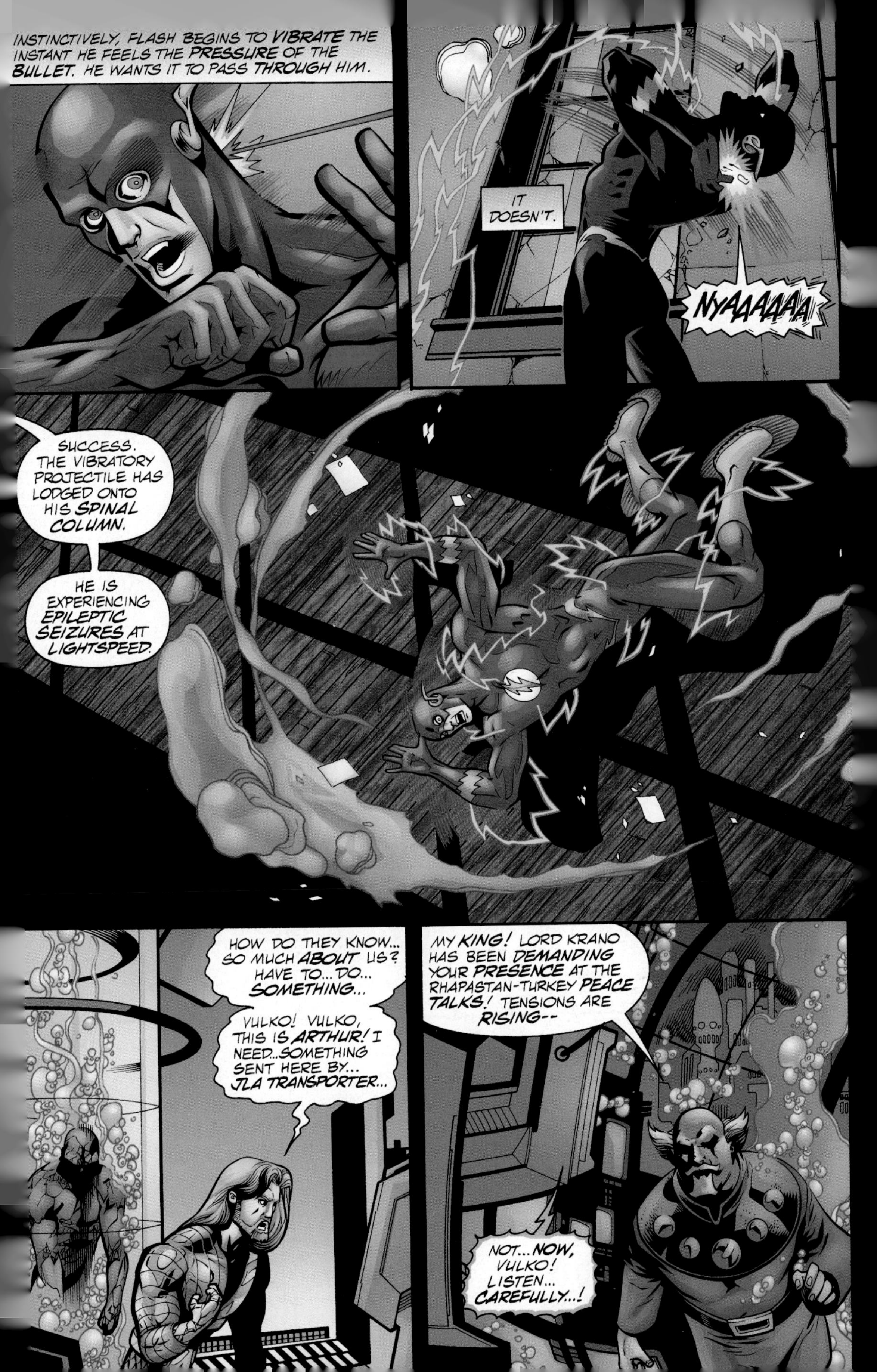
INSTINCTIVELY, FLASH BEGINS TO VIBRATE THE INSTANT HE FEELS THE PRESSURE OF THE BULLET. HE WANTS IT TO PASS THROUGH HIM.
IT DOESN'T.
NYAAAAAA
SUCCESS. THE VIBRATORY PROJECTILE HAS LODGED ONTO HIS SPINAL COLUMN.
HE IS EXPERIENCING EPILEPTIC SEIZURES AT LIGHTSPEED.
HOW DO THEY KNOW... SO MUCH ABOUT US? HAVE TO... DO... SOMETHING...
VULKO! VULKO, THIS IS ARTHUR! I NEED...SOMETHING SENT HERE BY... JLA TRANSPORTER...
MY KING! LORD KRANO HAS BEEN DEMANDING YOUR PRESENCE AT THE RHAPASTAN-TURKEY PEACE TALKS! TENSIONS ARE RISING--
NOT...NOW, VULKO! LISTEN... CAREFULLY...!

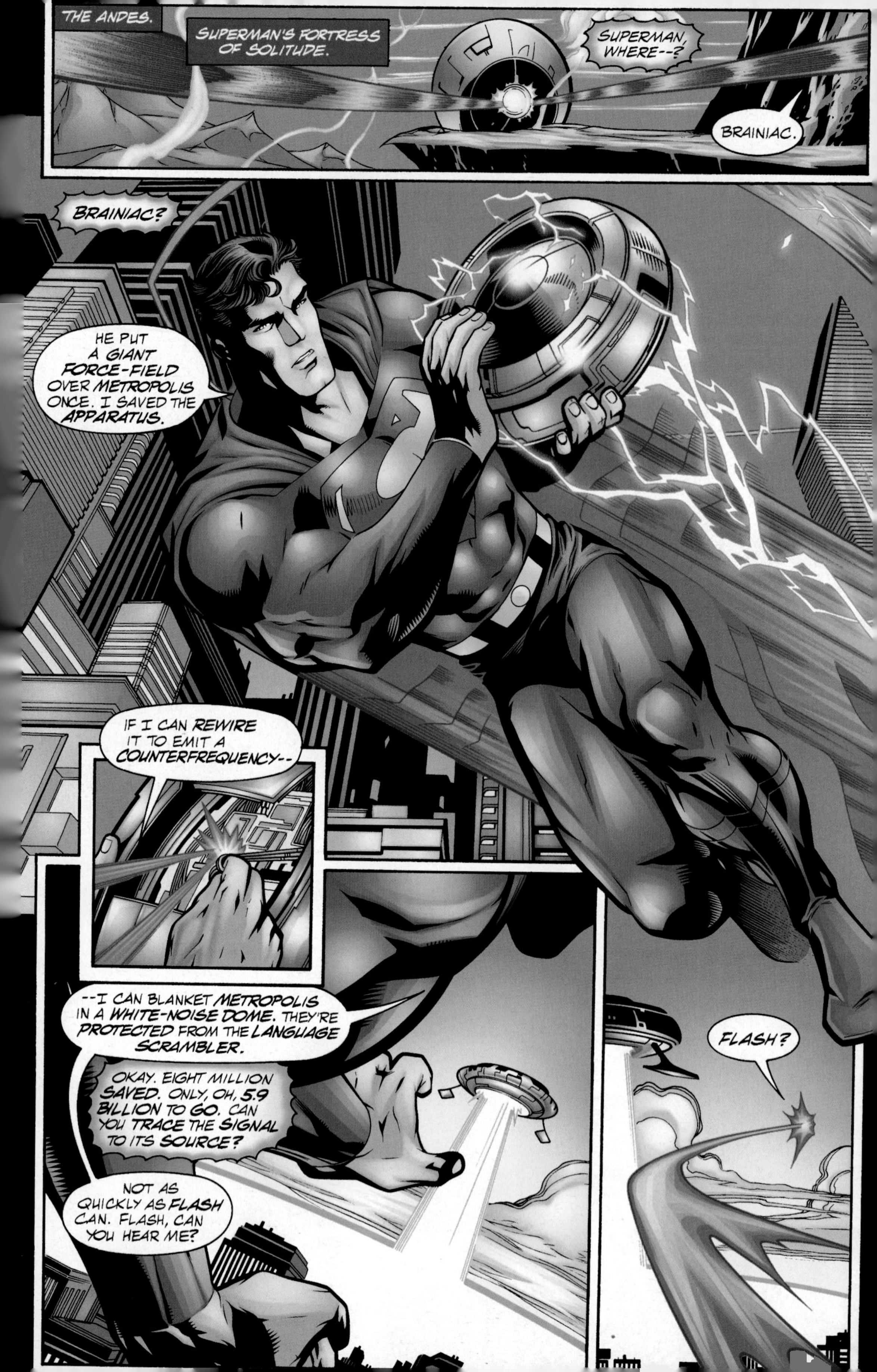
THE ANDES.
SUPERMAN'S FORTRESS OF SOLITUDE.
SUPERMAN, WHERE--?
BRAINIAC.
BRAINIAC?
HE PUT A GIANT FORCE-FIELD OVER METROPOLIS ONCE. I SAVED THE APPARATUS.
IF I CAN REWIRE IT TO EMIT A COUNTERFREQUENCY--
--I CAN BLANKET METROPOLIS IN A WHITE-NOISE DOME. THEY'RE PROTECTED FROM THE LANGUAGE SCRAMBLER.
OKAY. EIGHT MILLION SAVED. ONLY, OH, 5.9 BILLION TO GO. CAN YOU TRACE THE SIGNAL TO ITS SOURCE?
NOT AS QUICKLY AS FLASH CAN. FLASH, CAN YOU HEAR ME?
FLASH?

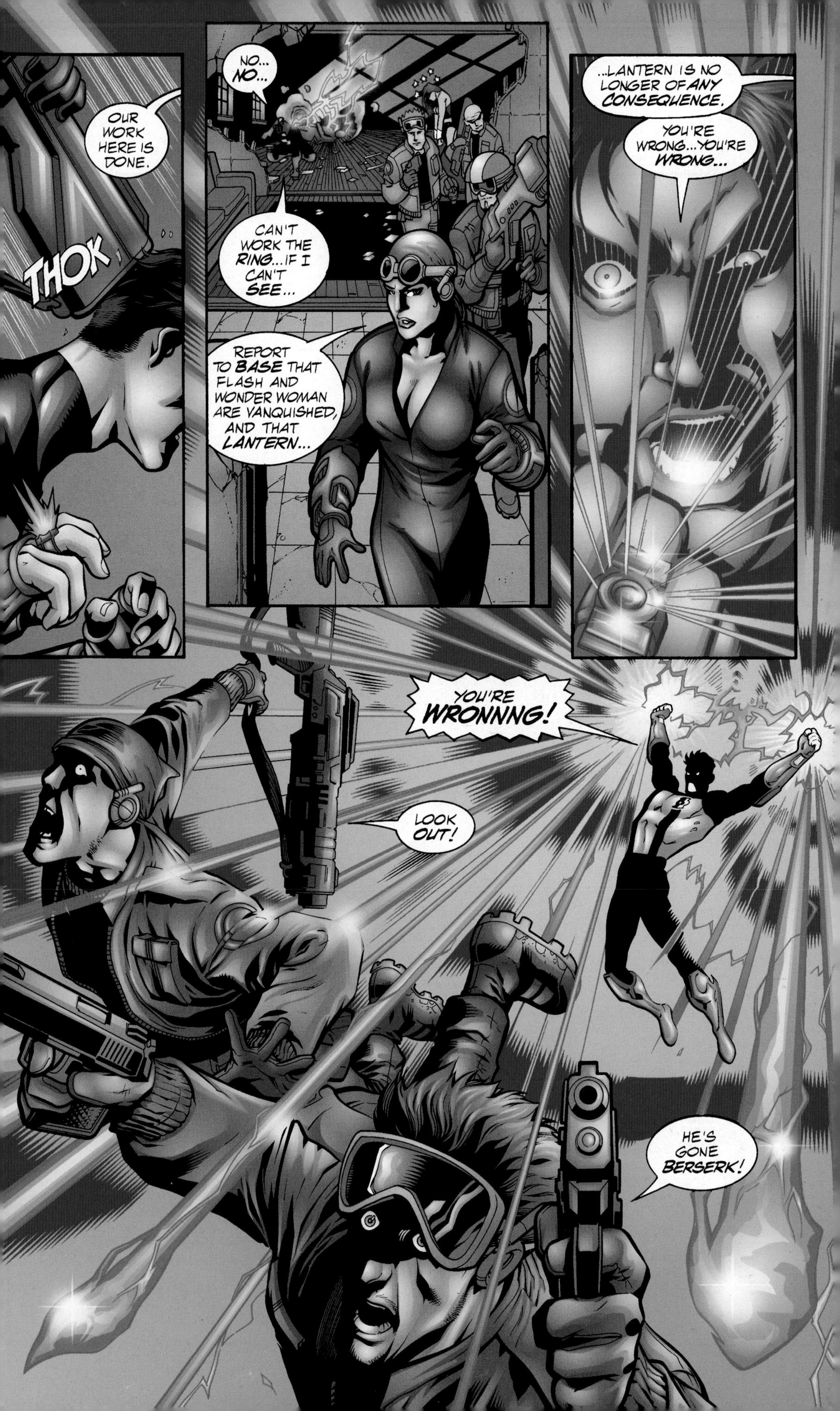
OUR WORK HERE IS DONE.
THOK
NO... NO...
CAN'T WORK THE RING... IF I CAN'T SEE...
REPORT TO BASE THAT FLASH AND WONDER WOMAN ARE VANQUISHED, AND THAT LANTERN...
...LANTERN IS NO LONGER OF ANY CONSEQUENCE.
YOU'RE WRONG...YOU'RE WRONG...
YOU'RE WRONNNG!
LOOK OUT!
HE'S GONE BERSERK!

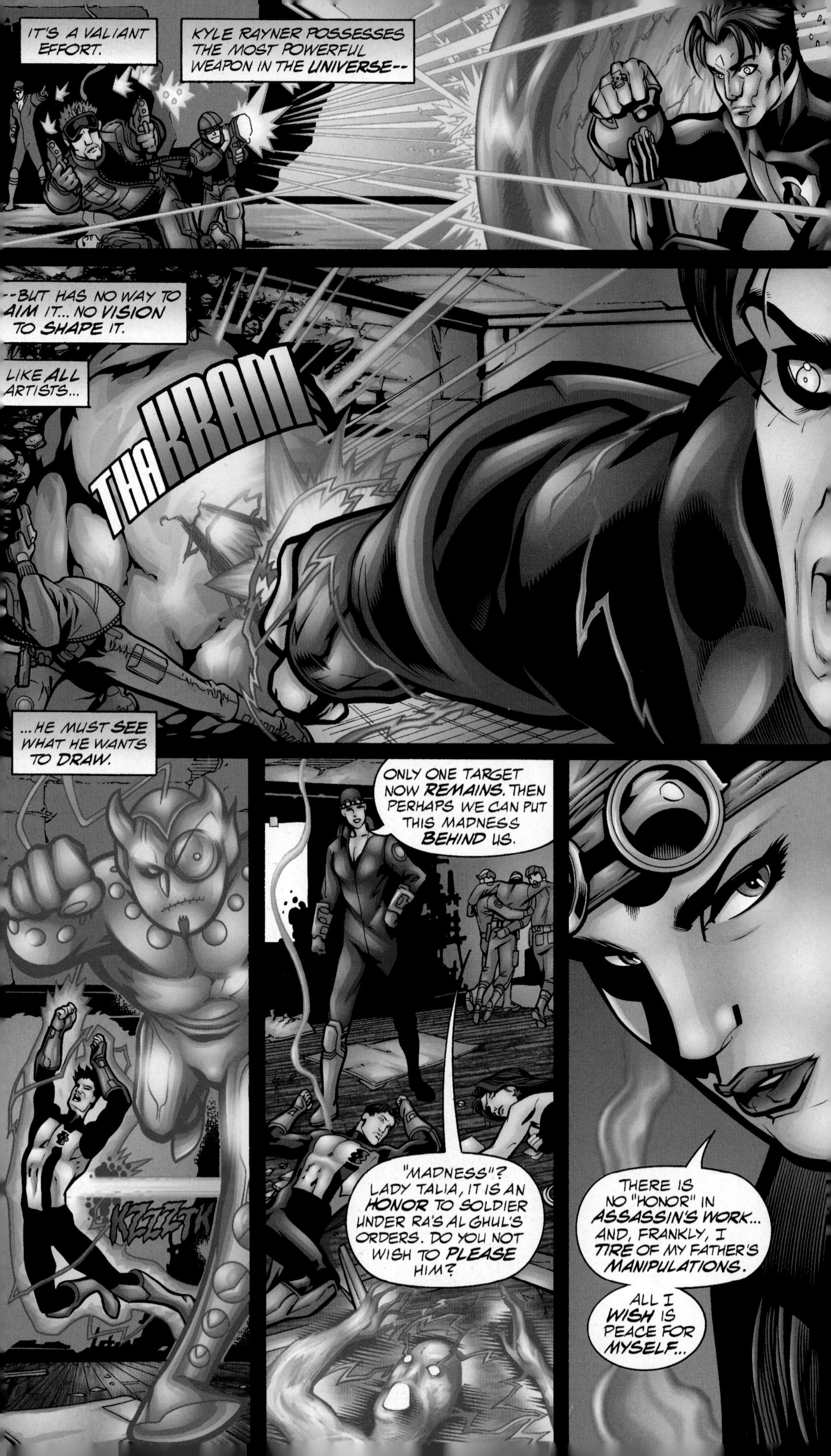
IT'S A VALIANT EFFORT.
KYLE RAYNER POSSESSES THE MOST POWERFUL WEAPON IN THE UNIVERSE--
--BUT HAS NO WAY TO AIM IT... NO VISION TO SHAPE IT.
LIKE ALL ARTISTS...
THAKRAM
...HE MUST SEE WHAT HE WANTS TO DRAW.
KZZZTK
ONLY ONE TARGET NOW REMAINS. THEN PERHAPS WE CAN PUT THIS MADNESS BEHIND US.
"MADNESS"? LADY TALIA, IT IS AN HONOR TO SOLDIER UNDER RA'S AL GHUL'S ORDERS. DO YOU NOT WISH TO PLEASE HIM?
THERE IS NO "HONOR" IN ASSASSIN'S WORK... AND, FRANKLY, I TIRE OF MY FATHER'S MANIPULATIONS.
ALL I WISH IS PEACE FOR MYSELF...

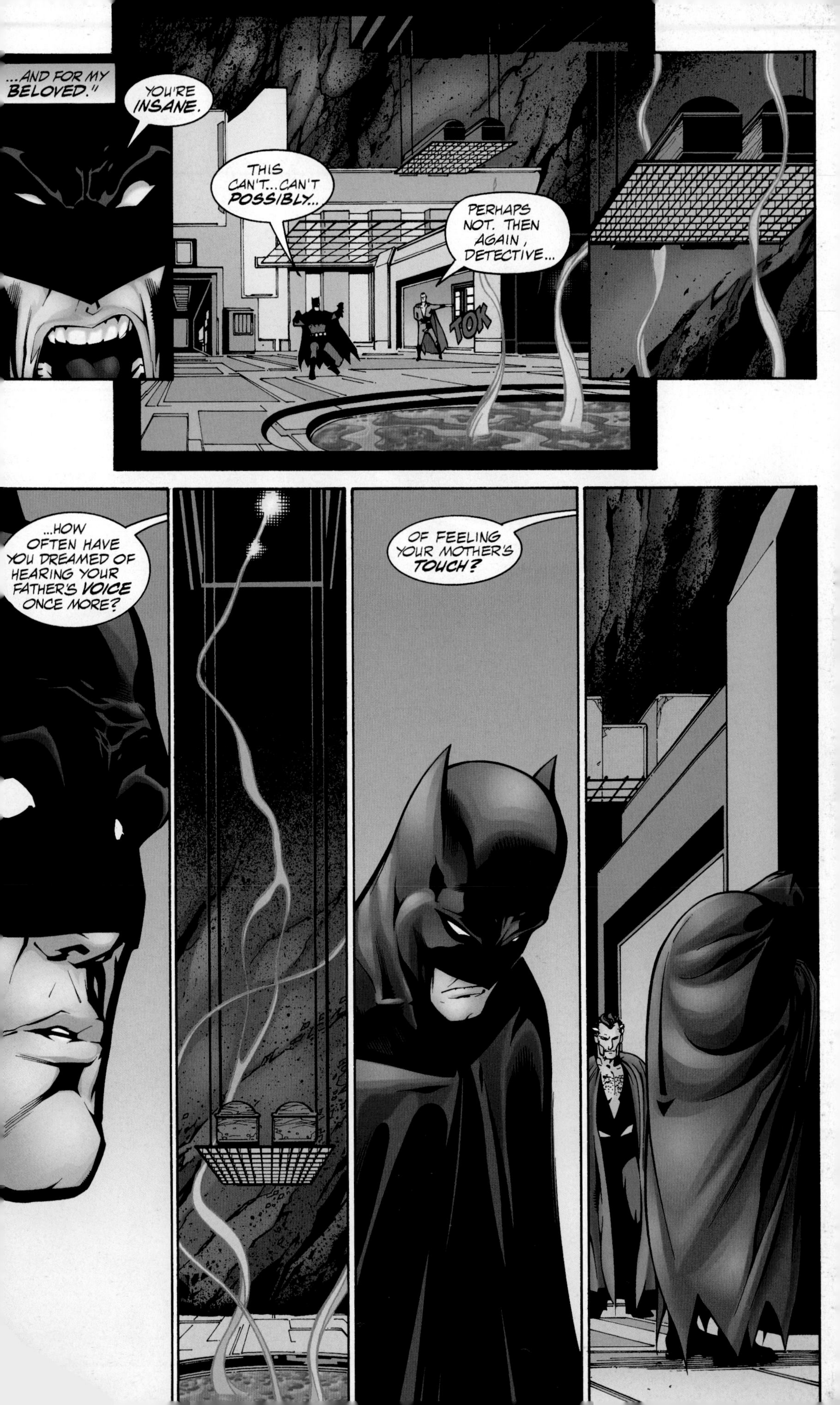

...AND FOR MY BELOVED."
YOU'RE INSANE.
THIS CAN'T...CAN'T POSSIBLY...
PERHAPS NOT. THEN AGAIN, DETECTIVE...
TOK
...HOW OFTEN HAVE YOU DREAMED OF HEARING YOUR FATHER'S VOICE ONCE MORE?
OF FEELING YOUR MOTHER'S TOUCH?

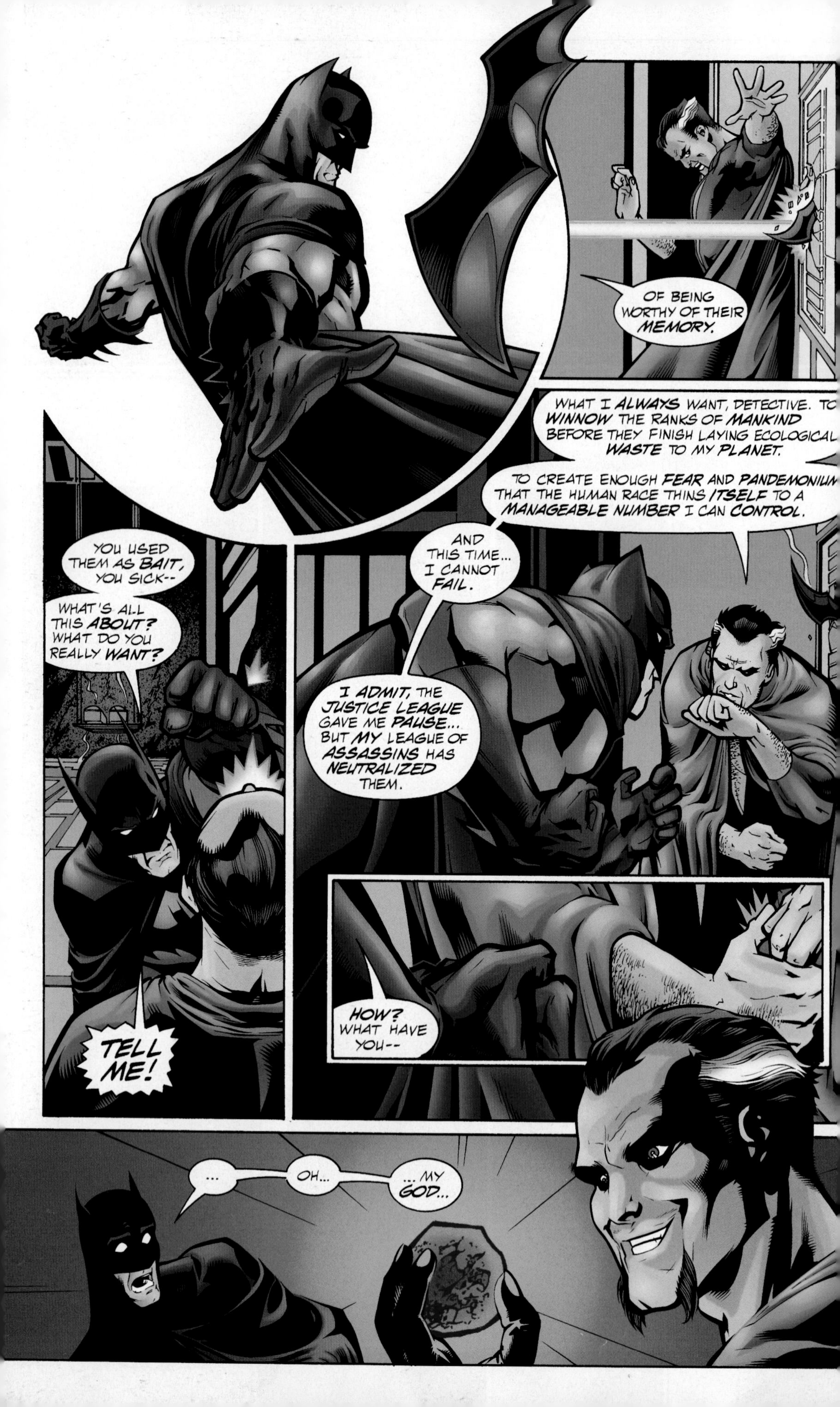
OF BEING WORTHY OF THEIR MEMORY.
WHAT I ALWAYS WANT, DETECTIVE. TO WINNOW THE RANKS OF MANKIND BEFORE THEY FINISH LAYING ECOLOGICAL WASTE TO MY PLANET.
TO CREATE ENOUGH FEAR AND PANDEMONIUM THAT THE HUMAN RACE THINS ITSELF TO A MANAGEABLE NUMBER I CAN CONTROL.
YOU USED THEM AS BAIT, YOU SICK--
WHAT'S ALL THIS ABOUT? WHAT DO YOU REALLY WANT?
TELL ME!
AND THIS TIME... I CANNOT FAIL.
I ADMIT, THE JUSTICE LEAGUE GAVE ME PAUSE... BUT MY LEAGUE OF ASSASSINS HAS NEUTRALIZED THEM.
HOW? WHAT HAVE YOU--
...
OH...
...MY GOD...

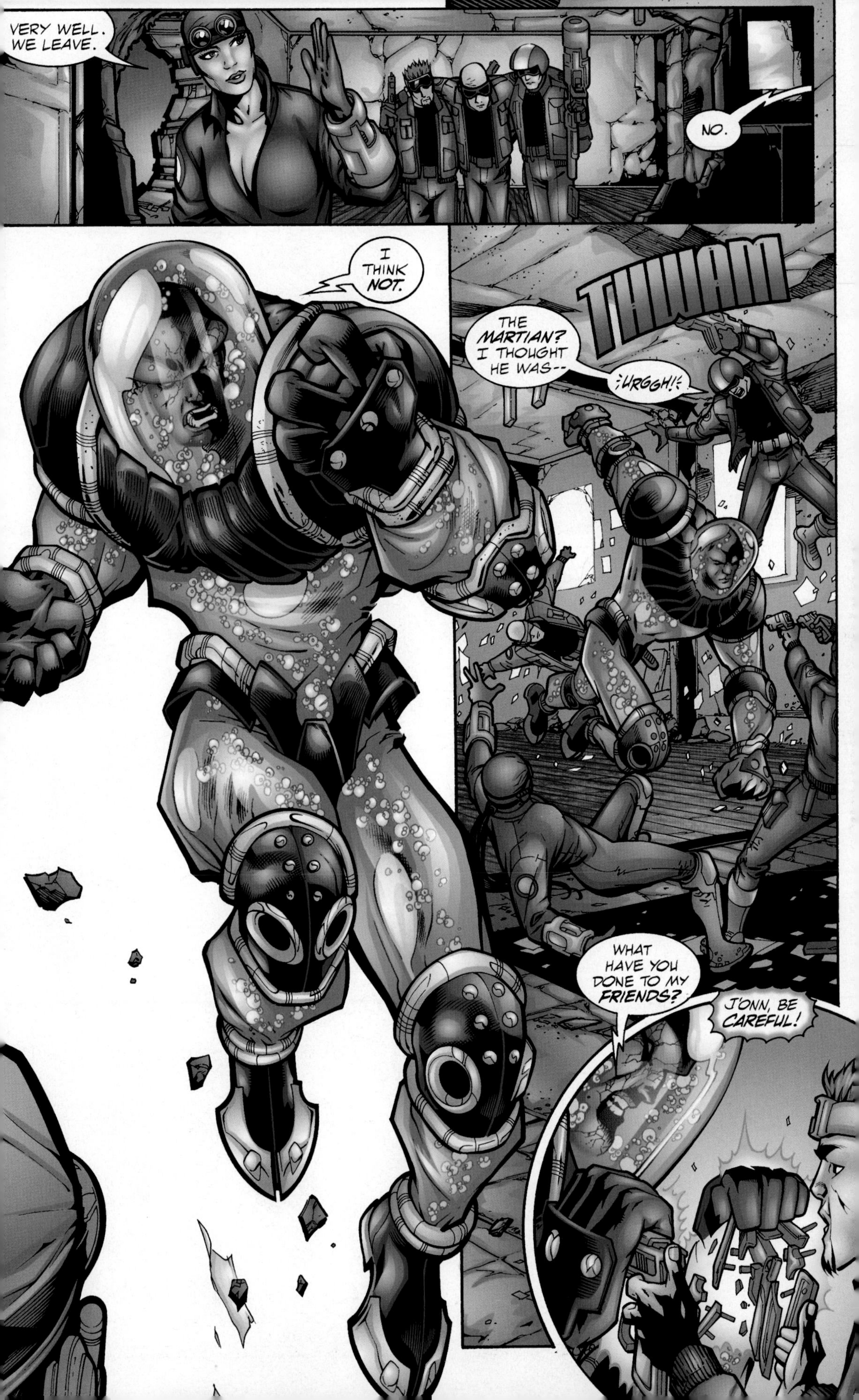
VERY WELL. WE LEAVE.
NO.
I THINK NOT.
THWAM
THE MARTIAN? I THOUGHT HE WAS--
URGGH!
WHAT HAVE YOU DONE TO MY FRIENDS?
J'ONN, BE CAREFUL!

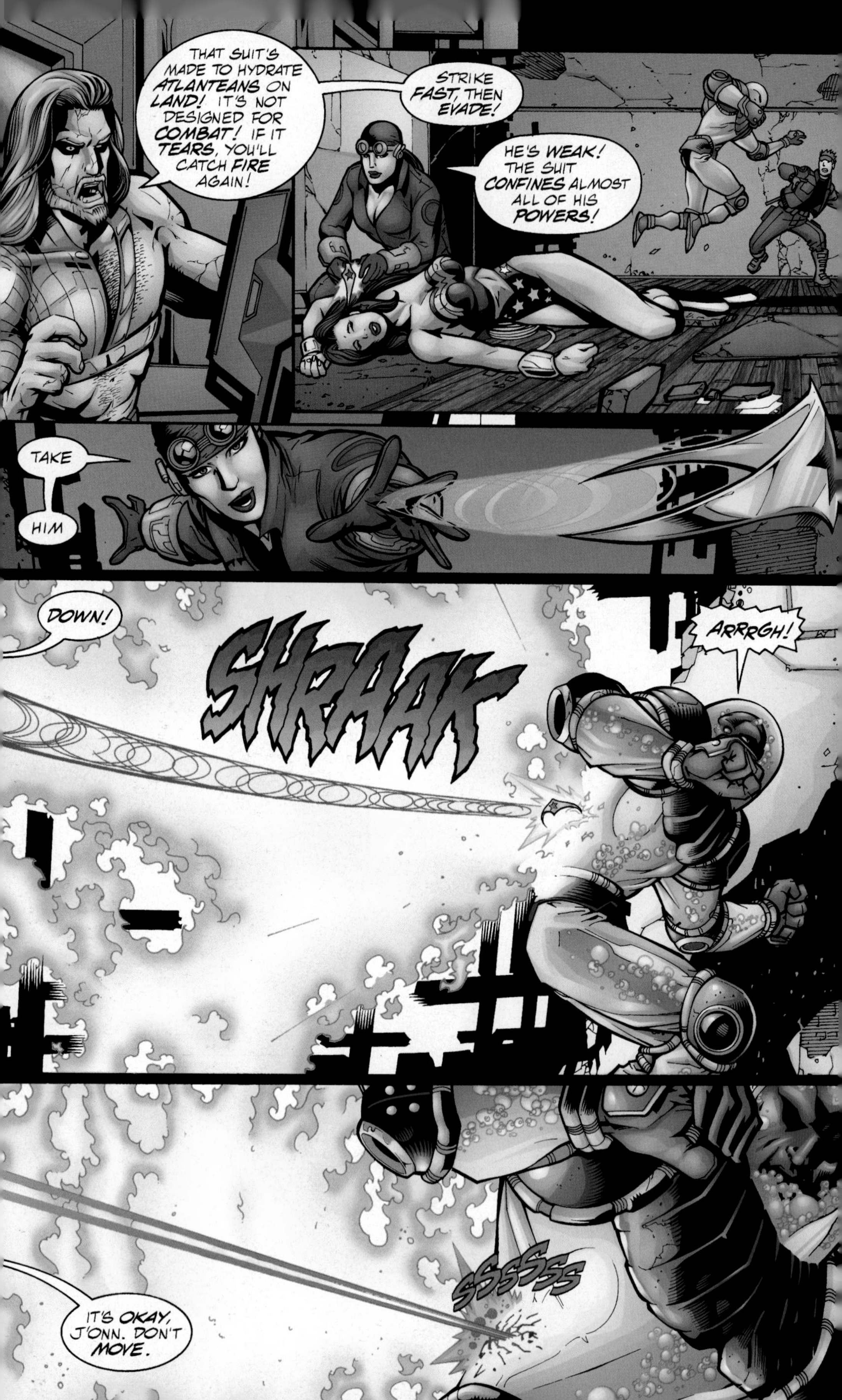
THAT SUIT'S MADE TO HYDRATE ATLANTEANS ON LAND! IT'S NOT DESIGNED FOR COMBAT! IF IT TEARS, YOU'LL CATCH FIRE AGAIN!
STRIKE FAST, THEN EVADE!
HE'S WEAK! THE SUIT CONFINES ALMOST ALL OF HIS POWERS!
TAKE
HIM
DOWN!
SHRAAK
ARRRGH!
SSSSSS
IT'S OKAY, J'ONN. DON'T MOVE.

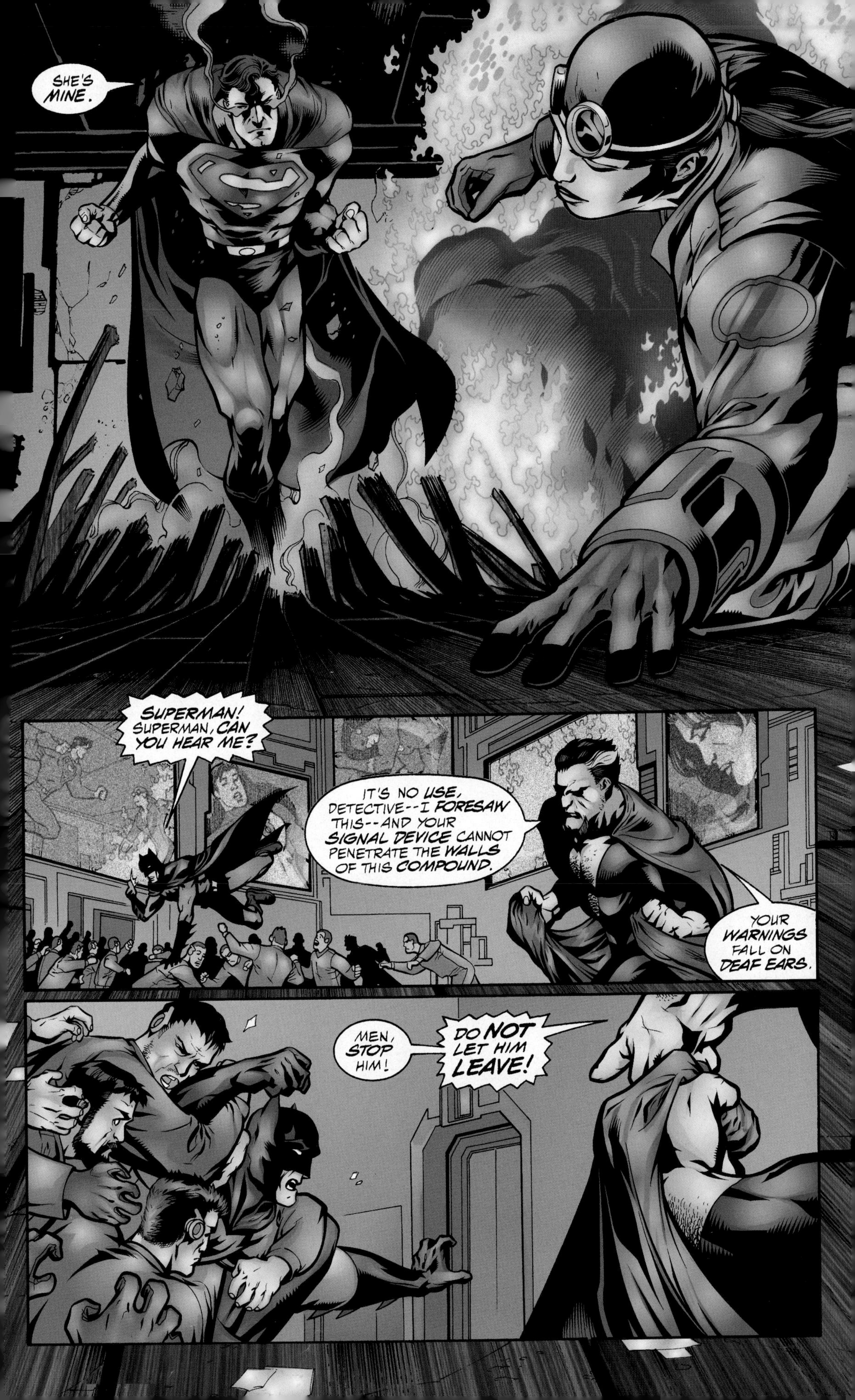
SHE'S MINE.
SUPERMAN! SUPERMAN, CAN YOU HEAR ME?
IT'S NO USE, DETECTIVE--I FORESAW THIS--AND YOUR SIGNAL DEVICE CANNOT PENETRATE THE WALLS OF THIS COMPOUND.
YOUR WARNINGS FALL ON DEAF EARS.
MEN, STOP HIM!
DO NOT LET HIM LEAVE!

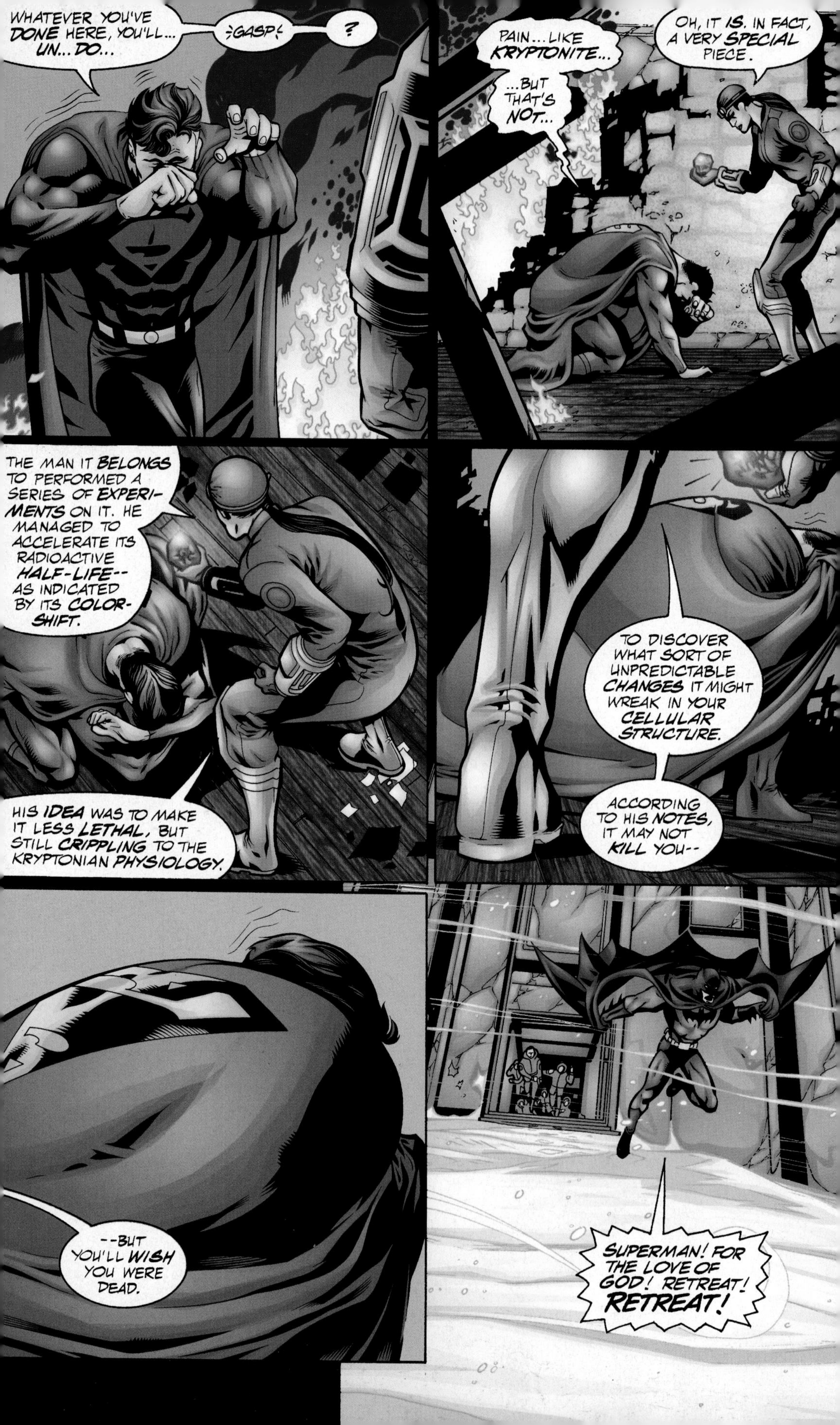
WHATEVER YOU'VE DONE HERE, YOU'LL... UN...DO...
GASP!
?
PAIN... LIKE KRYPTONITE...
...BUT THAT'S NOT...
OH, IT IS. IN FACT, A VERY SPECIAL PIECE.
THE MAN IT BELONGS TO PERFORMED A SERIES OF EXPERIMENTS ON IT. HE MANAGED TO ACCELERATE ITS RADIOACTIVE HALF-LIFE-- AS INDICATED BY ITS COLOR-SHIFT.
HIS IDEA WAS TO MAKE IT LESS LETHAL, BUT STILL CRIPPLING TO THE KRYPTONIAN PHYSIOLOGY.
TO DISCOVER WHAT SORT OF UNPREDICTABLE CHANGES IT MIGHT WREAK IN YOUR CELLULAR STRUCTURE.
ACCORDING TO HIS NOTES, IT MAY NOT KILL YOU--
--BUT YOU'LL WISH YOU WERE DEAD.
SUPERMAN! FOR THE LOVE OF GOD! RETREAT! RETREAT!

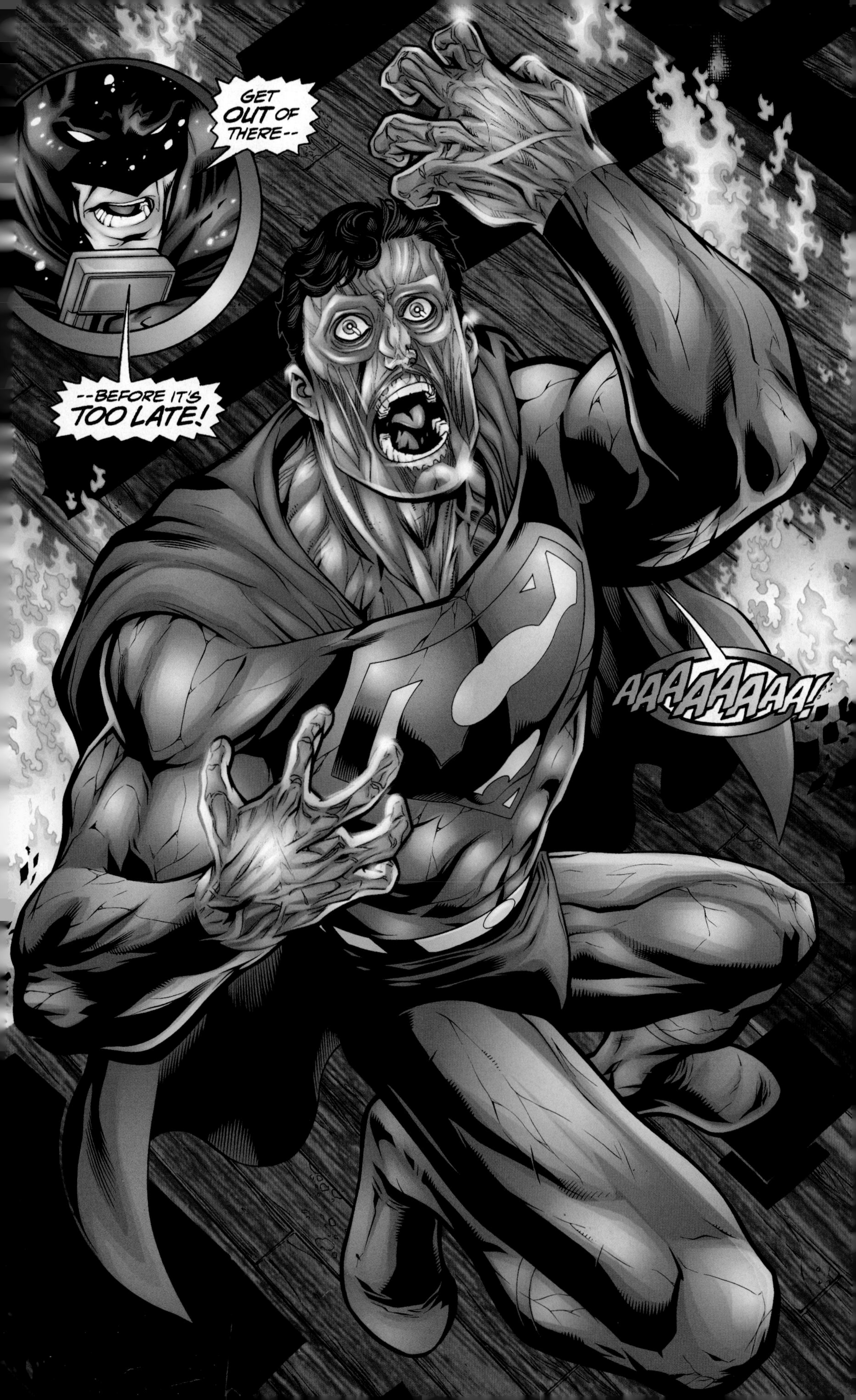
GET OUT OF THERE--
--BEFORE IT'S TOO LATE!
AAAAAAAA!

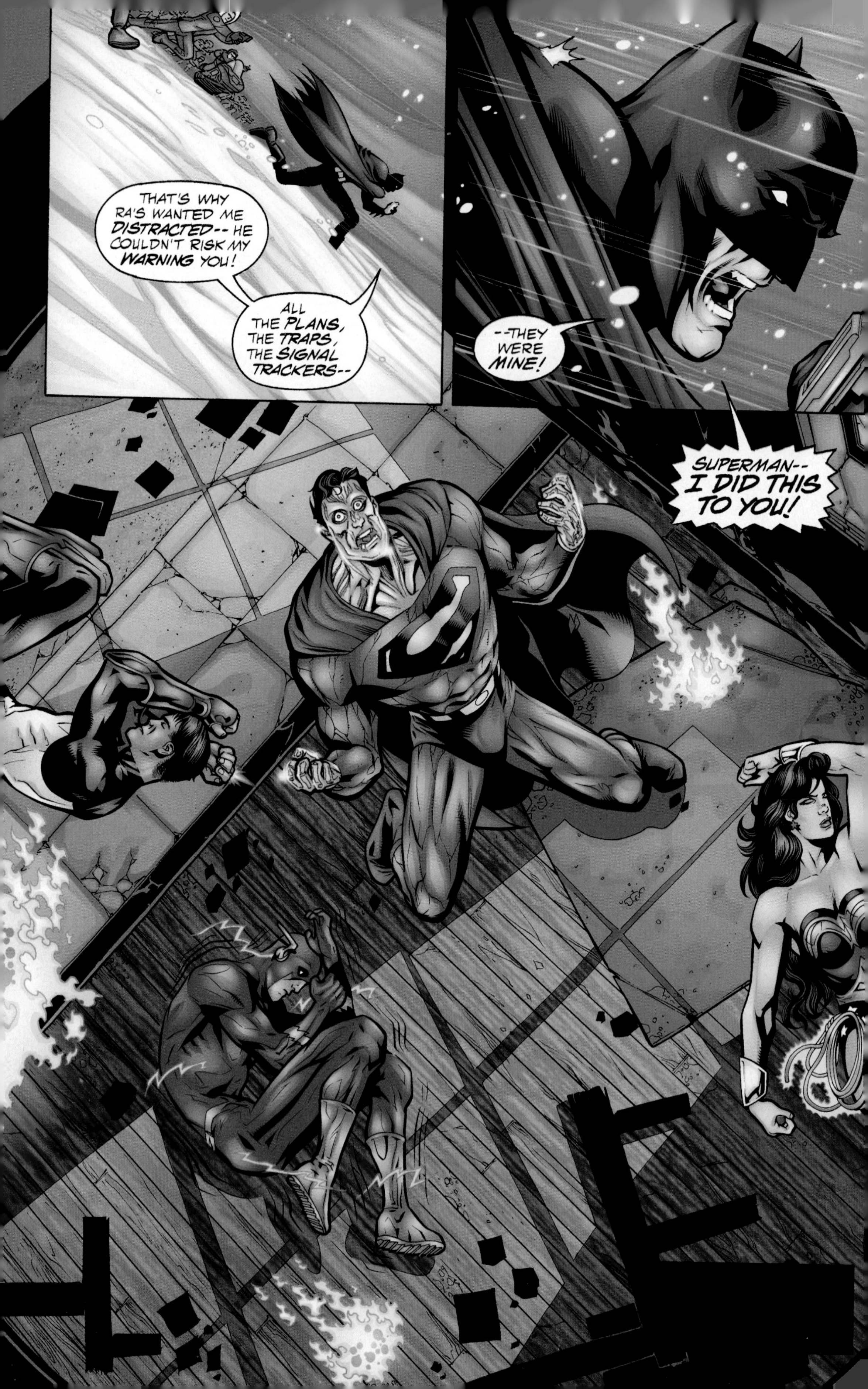
THAT'S WHY RA'S WANTED ME DISTRACTED-- HE COULDN'T RISK MY WARNING YOU!
ALL THE PLANS, THE TRAPS, THE SIGNAL TRACKERS--
--THEY WERE MINE!
SUPERMAN-- I DID THIS TO YOU!

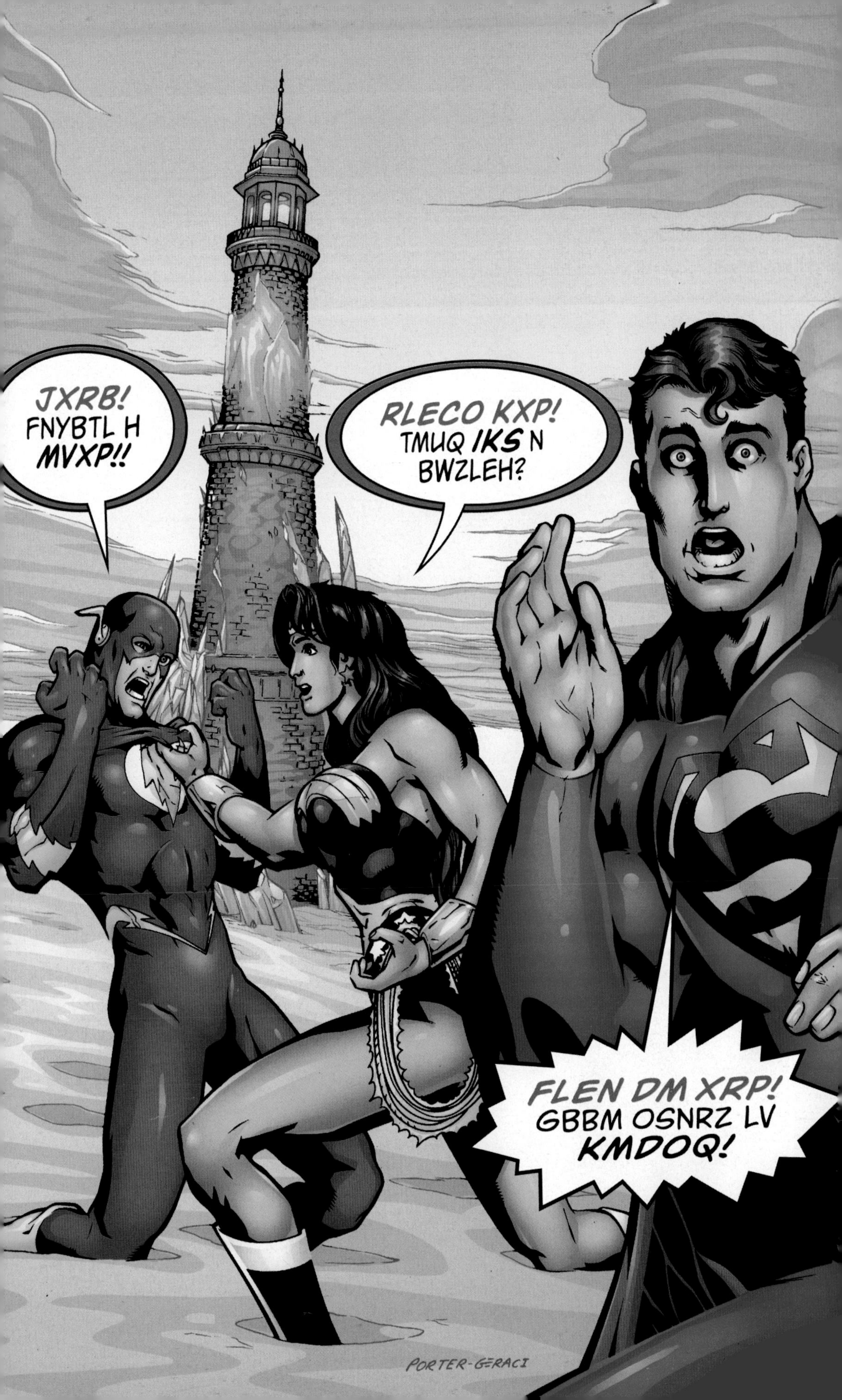
JXRB! FNYBTL H MVXP!!
RLECO KXP! TMUQ IKS N BWZLEH?
FLEN DM XRP! GBBM OSNRZ LV KMDOQ!
PORTER-GERACI

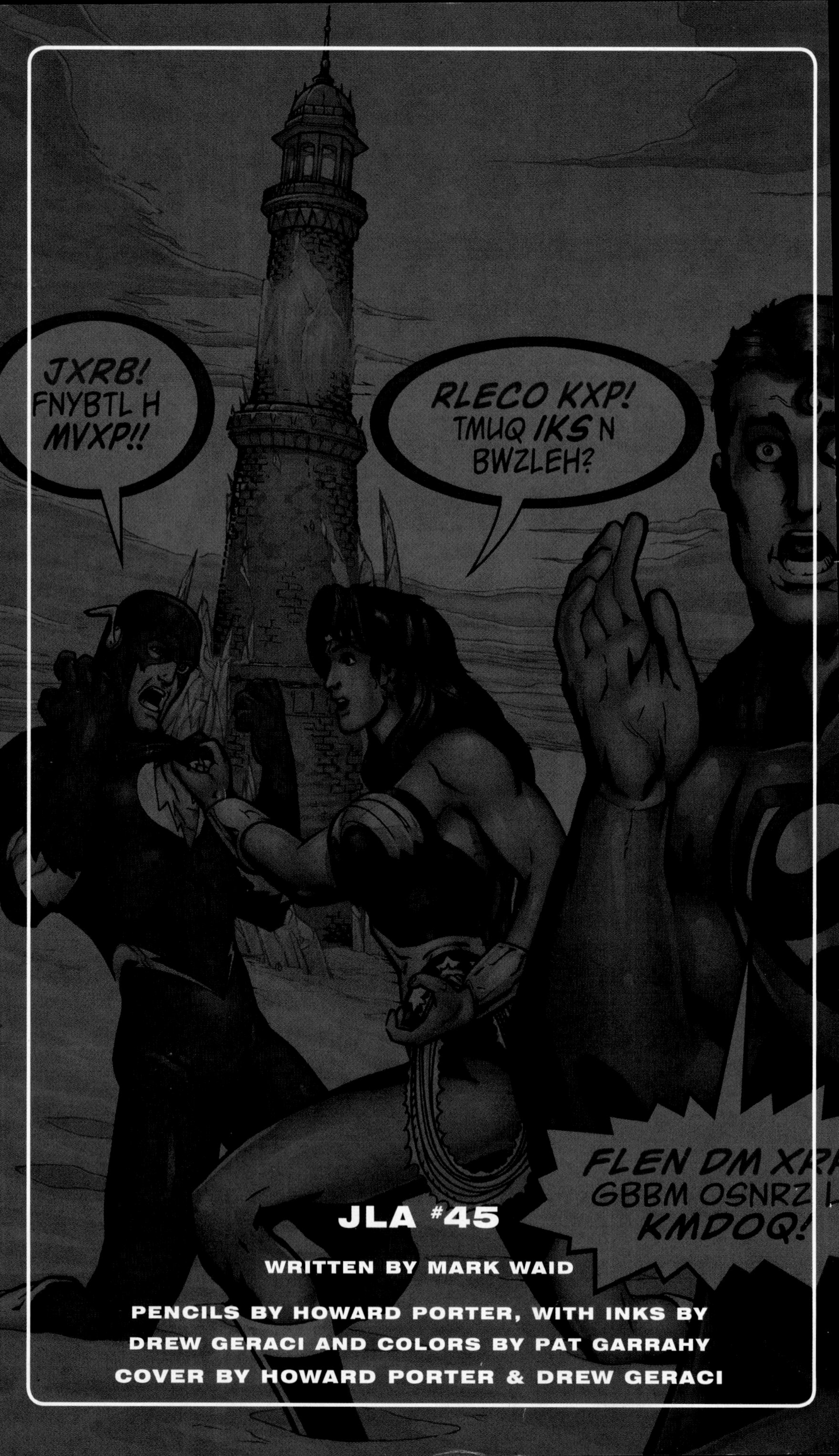
JXRB! FNYBTL H MVXP!!
RLECO KXP! TMUQ IKS N BWZLEH?
FLEN DM XR
GBBM OSNRZ
KMDOQ!

JLA #45

WRITTEN BY MARK WAID

PENCILS BY HOWARD PORTER, WITH INKS BY DREW GERACI AND COLORS BY PAT GARRAHY

COVER BY HOWARD PORTER & DREW GERACI

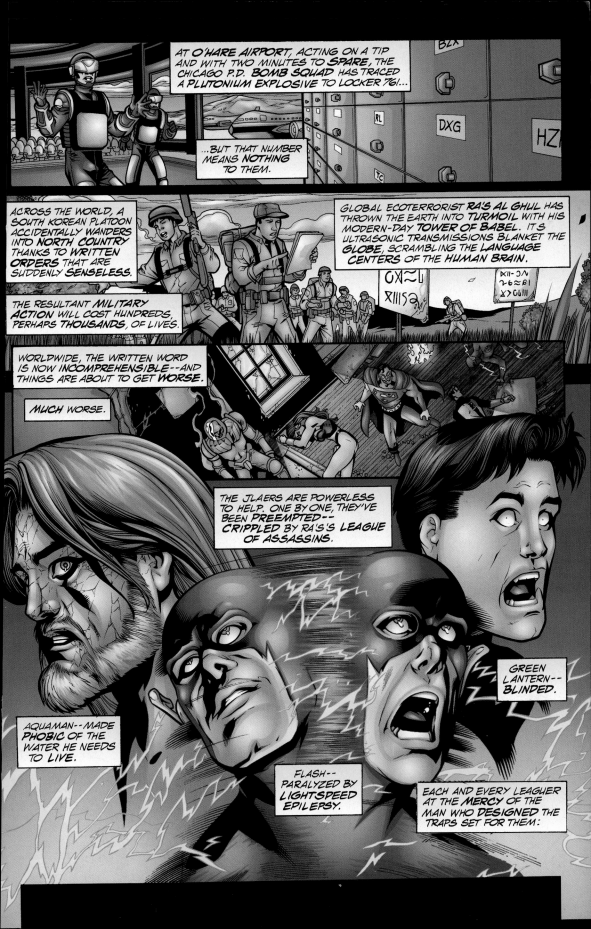

AT O'HARE AIRPORT, ACTING ON A TIP AND WITH TWO MINUTES TO *SPARE*, THE CHICAGO P.D. *BOMB SQUAD* HAS TRACED A *PLUTONIUM* EXPLOSIVE TO LOCKER 761...

...BUT THAT NUMBER MEANS *NOTHING* TO THEM.

ACROSS THE WORLD, A SOUTH KOREAN PLATOON ACCIDENTALLY WANDERS INTO *NORTH COUNTRY* THANKS TO *WRITTEN ORDERS* THAT ARE SUDDENLY *SENSELESS*.

THE RESULTANT *MILITARY ACTION* WILL COST HUNDREDS, PERHAPS *THOUSANDS*, OF LIVES.

GLOBAL ECOTERRORIST *RA'S AL GHUL* HAS THROWN THE EARTH INTO *TURMOIL* WITH HIS MODERN-DAY *TOWER OF BABEL*. ITS ULTRASONIC TRANSMISSIONS BLANKET THE *GLOBE*, SCRAMBLING THE LANGUAGE CENTERS OF THE *HUMAN BRAIN*.

WORLDWIDE, THE WRITTEN WORD IS NOW *INCOMPREHENSIBLE*--AND THINGS ARE ABOUT TO GET *WORSE*.

MUCH WORSE.

THE JLAERS ARE POWERLESS TO HELP. ONE BY ONE, THEY'VE BEEN *PREEMPTED*-- CRIPPLED BY RA'S'S *LEAGUE OF ASSASSINS*.

GREEN LANTERN-- BLINDED.

AQUAMAN--MADE *PHOBIC* OF THE WATER HE NEEDS TO *LIVE*.

FLASH-- PARALYZED BY LIGHTSPEED EPILEPSY.

EACH AND EVERY LEAGUER AT THE *MERCY* OF THE MAN WHO *DESIGNED* THE TRAPS SET FOR THEM:

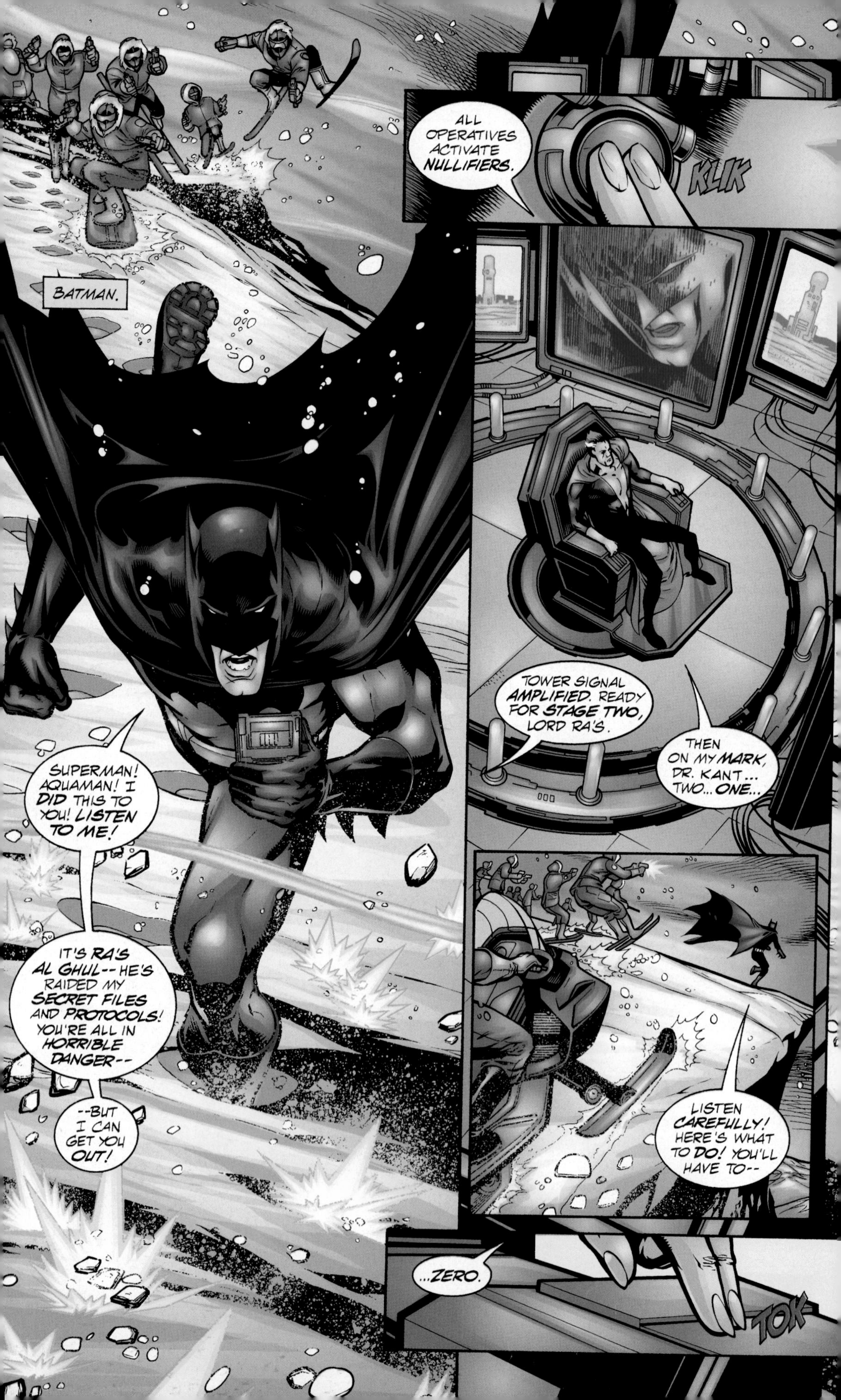

ALL OPERATIVES ACTIVATE NULLIFIERS.
KLIK
BATMAN.
TOWER SIGNAL AMPLIFIED. READY FOR STAGE TWO, LORD RA'S.
THEN ON MY MARK, DR. KANT... TWO... ONE...
SUPERMAN! AQUAMAN! I DID THIS TO YOU! LISTEN TO ME!
IT'S RA'S AL GHUL--HE'S RAIDED MY SECRET FILES AND PROTOCOLS! YOU'RE ALL IN HORRIBLE DANGER--
--BUT I CAN GET YOU OUT!
LISTEN CAREFULLY! HERE'S WHAT TO DO! YOU'LL HAVE TO--
...ZERO.
TOK

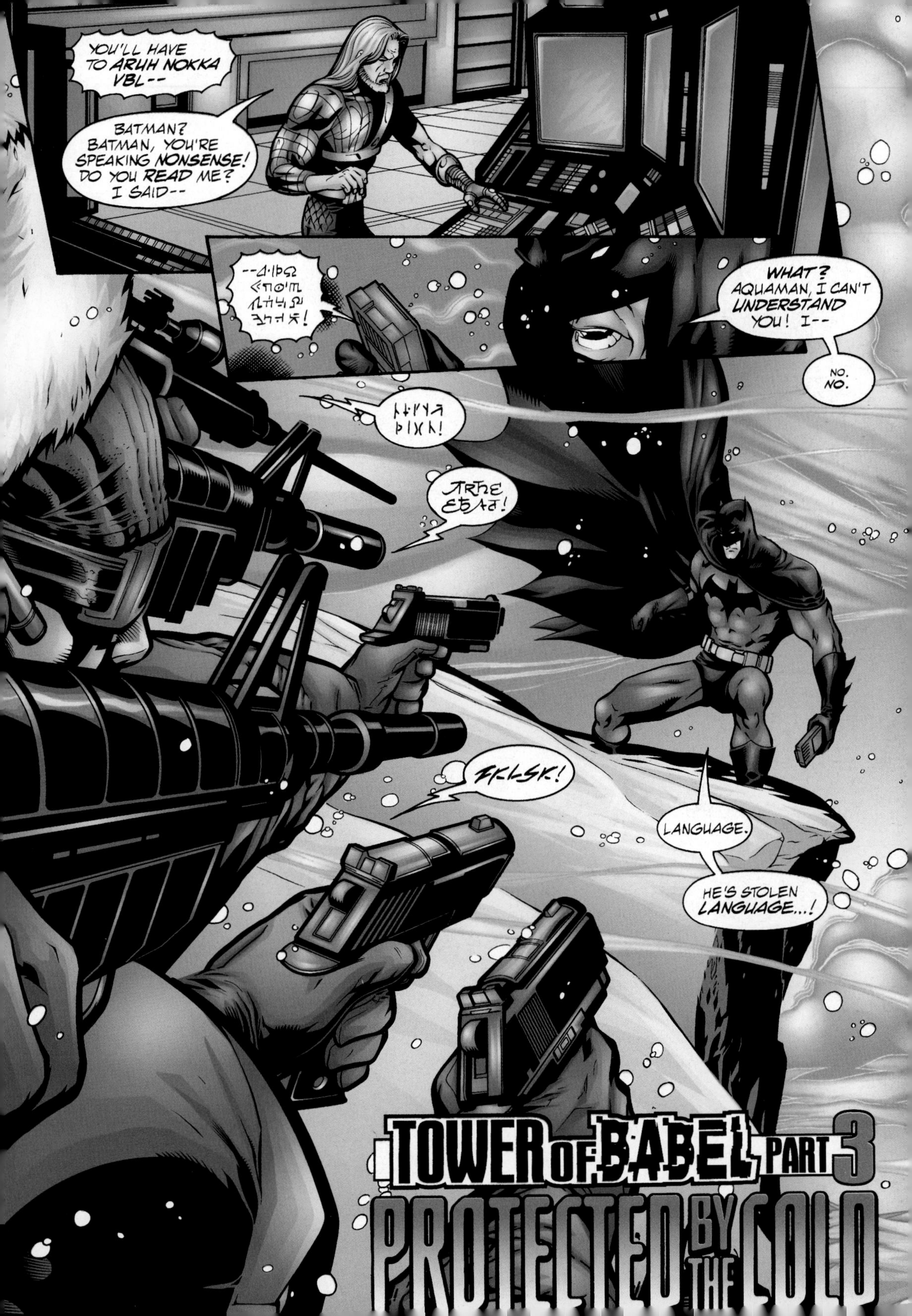
YOU'LL HAVE TO ARUH NOKKA VBL--
BATMAN? BATMAN, YOU'RE SPEAKING NONSENSE! DO YOU READ ME? I SAID--
WHAT? AQUAMAN, I CAN'T UNDERSTAND YOU! I--
NO. NO.
LANGUAGE.
HE'S STOLEN LANGUAGE...!
TOWER OF BABEL PART 3
PROTECTED BY THE COLD

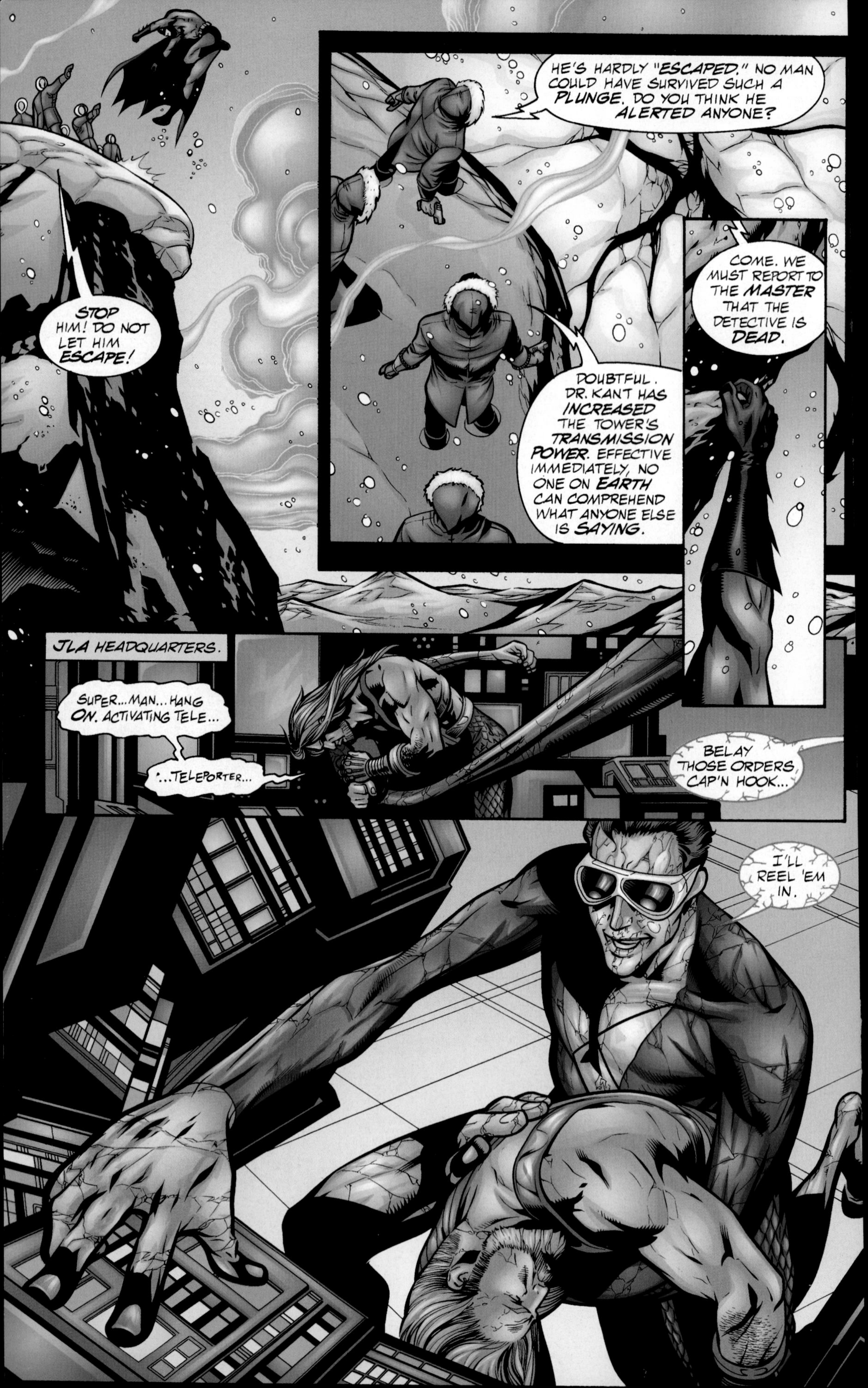
STOP HIM! DO NOT LET HIM ESCAPE!
HE'S HARDLY "ESCAPED." NO MAN COULD HAVE SURVIVED SUCH A PLUNGE. DO YOU THINK HE ALERTED ANYONE?
DOUBTFUL. DR. KANT HAS INCREASED THE TOWER'S TRANSMISSION POWER. EFFECTIVE IMMEDIATELY, NO ONE ON EARTH CAN COMPREHEND WHAT ANYONE ELSE IS SAYING.
COME. WE MUST REPORT TO THE MASTER THAT THE DETECTIVE IS DEAD.
JLA HEADQUARTERS.
SUPER...MAN...HANG ON. ACTIVATING TELE...
"...TELEPORTER...
BELAY THOSE ORDERS, CAP'N HOOK...
I'LL REEL 'EM IN.

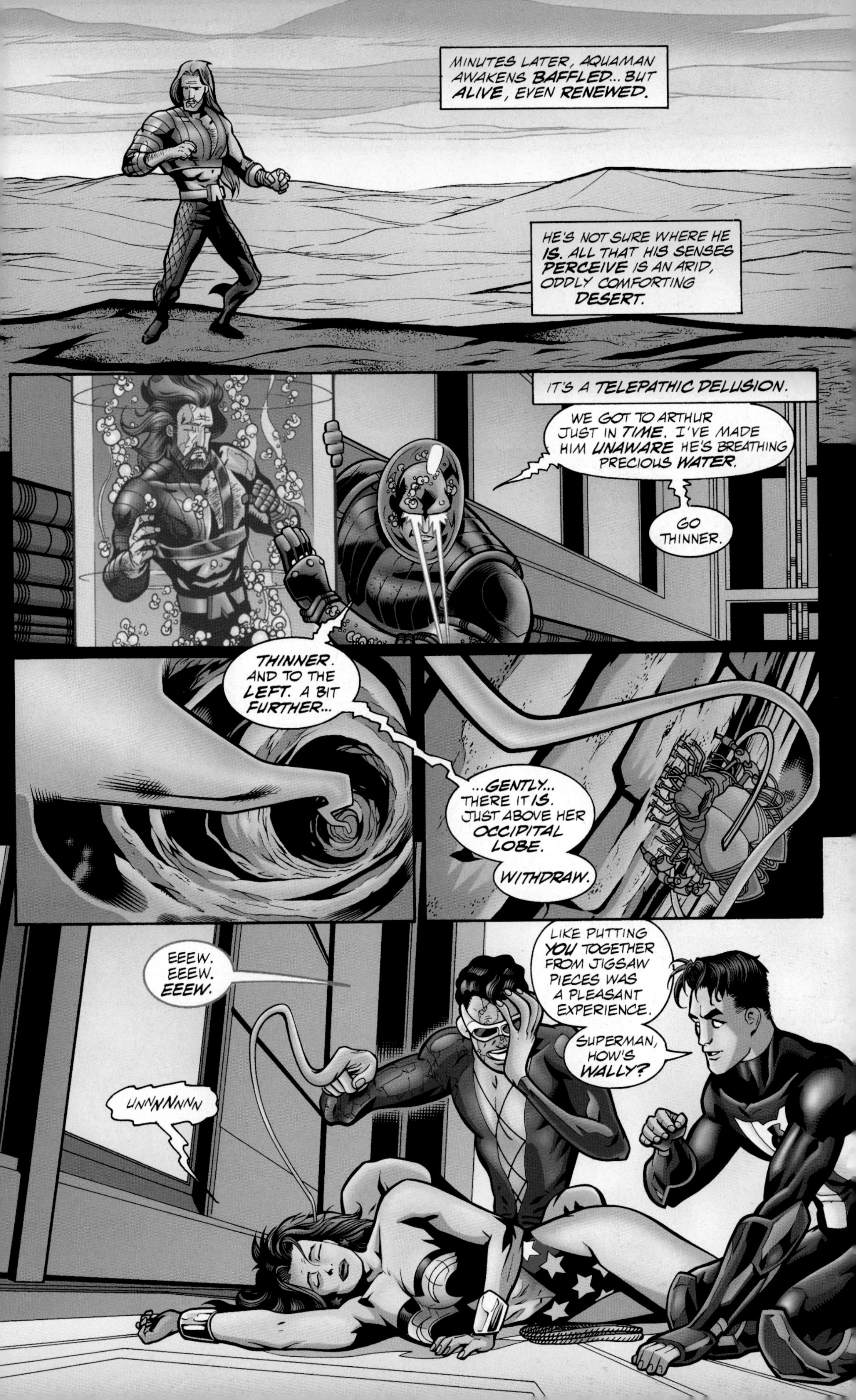
MINUTES LATER, AQUAMAN AWAKENS BAFFLED... BUT ALIVE, EVEN RENEWED.
HE'S NOT SURE WHERE HE IS. ALL THAT HIS SENSES PERCEIVE IS AN ARID, ODDLY COMFORTING DESERT.
IT'S A TELEPATHIC DELUSION.
WE GOT TO ARTHUR JUST IN TIME. I'VE MADE HIM UNAWARE HE'S BREATHING PRECIOUS WATER.
GO THINNER.
THINNER. AND TO THE LEFT. A BIT FURTHER...
...GENTLY... THERE IT IS. JUST ABOVE HER OCCIPITAL LOBE.
WITHDRAW.
EEEW. EEEW. EEEW.
LIKE PUTTING YOU TOGETHER FROM JIGSAW PIECES WAS A PLEASANT EXPERIENCE.
SUPERMAN, HOW'S WALLY?
UNNNNNNN

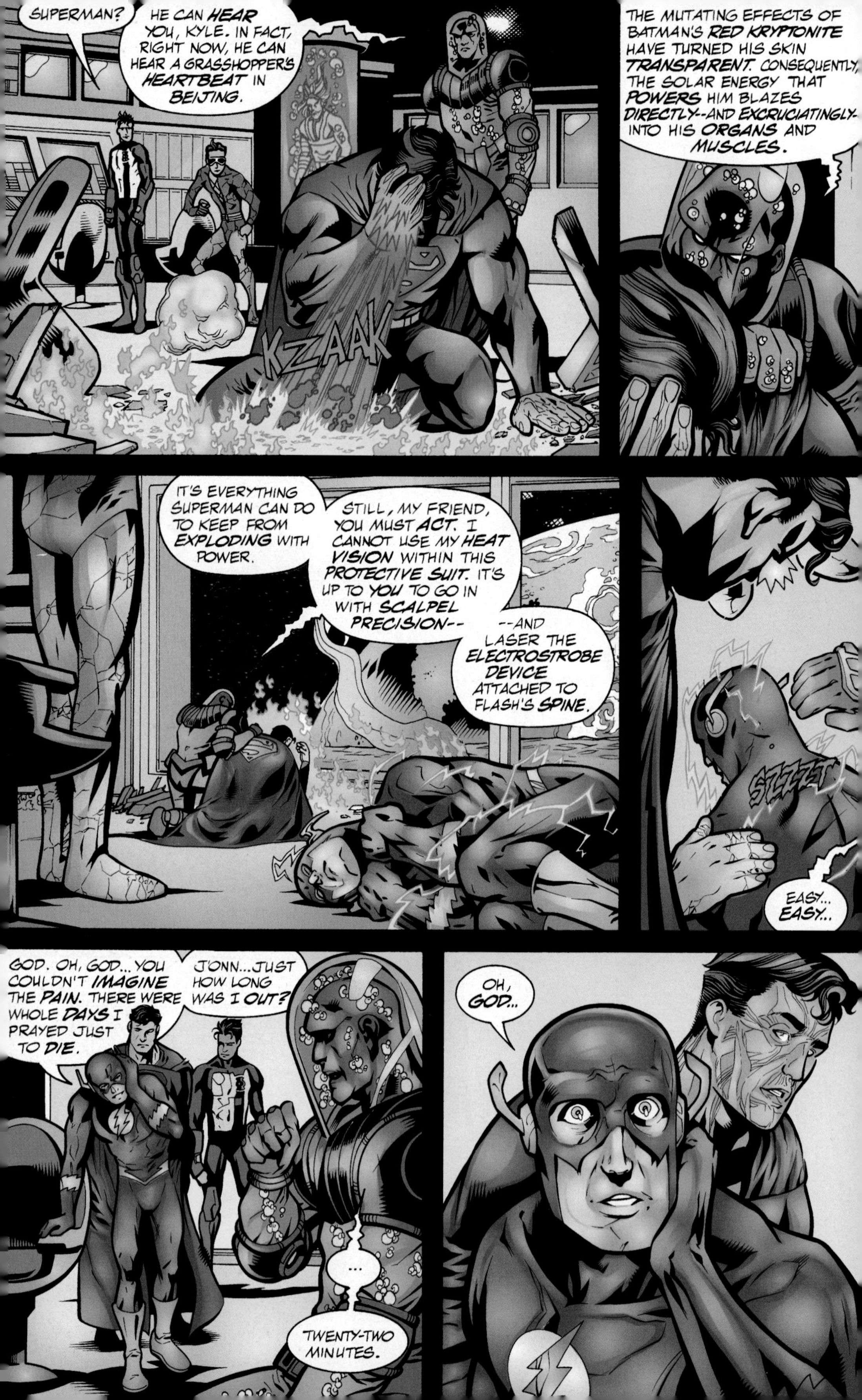
SUPERMAN?
HE CAN HEAR YOU, KYLE. IN FACT, RIGHT NOW, HE CAN HEAR A GRASSHOPPER'S HEARTBEAT IN BEIJING.
KZAAK
THE MUTATING EFFECTS OF BATMAN'S RED KRYPTONITE HAVE TURNED HIS SKIN TRANSPARENT. CONSEQUENTLY, THE SOLAR ENERGY THAT POWERS HIM BLAZES DIRECTLY--AND EXCRUCIATINGLY--INTO HIS ORGANS AND MUSCLES.
IT'S EVERYTHING SUPERMAN CAN DO TO KEEP FROM EXPLODING WITH POWER.
STILL, MY FRIEND, YOU MUST ACT. I CANNOT USE MY HEAT VISION WITHIN THIS PROTECTIVE SUIT. IT'S UP TO YOU TO GO IN WITH SCALPEL PRECISION--
--AND LASER THE ELECTROSTROBE DEVICE ATTACHED TO FLASH'S SPINE.
SIZZZT
EASY... EASY...
GOD. OH, GOD... YOU COULDN'T IMAGINE THE PAIN. THERE WERE WHOLE DAYS I PRAYED JUST TO DIE.
J'ONN... JUST HOW LONG WAS I OUT?
...
TWENTY-TWO MINUTES.
OH, GOD...

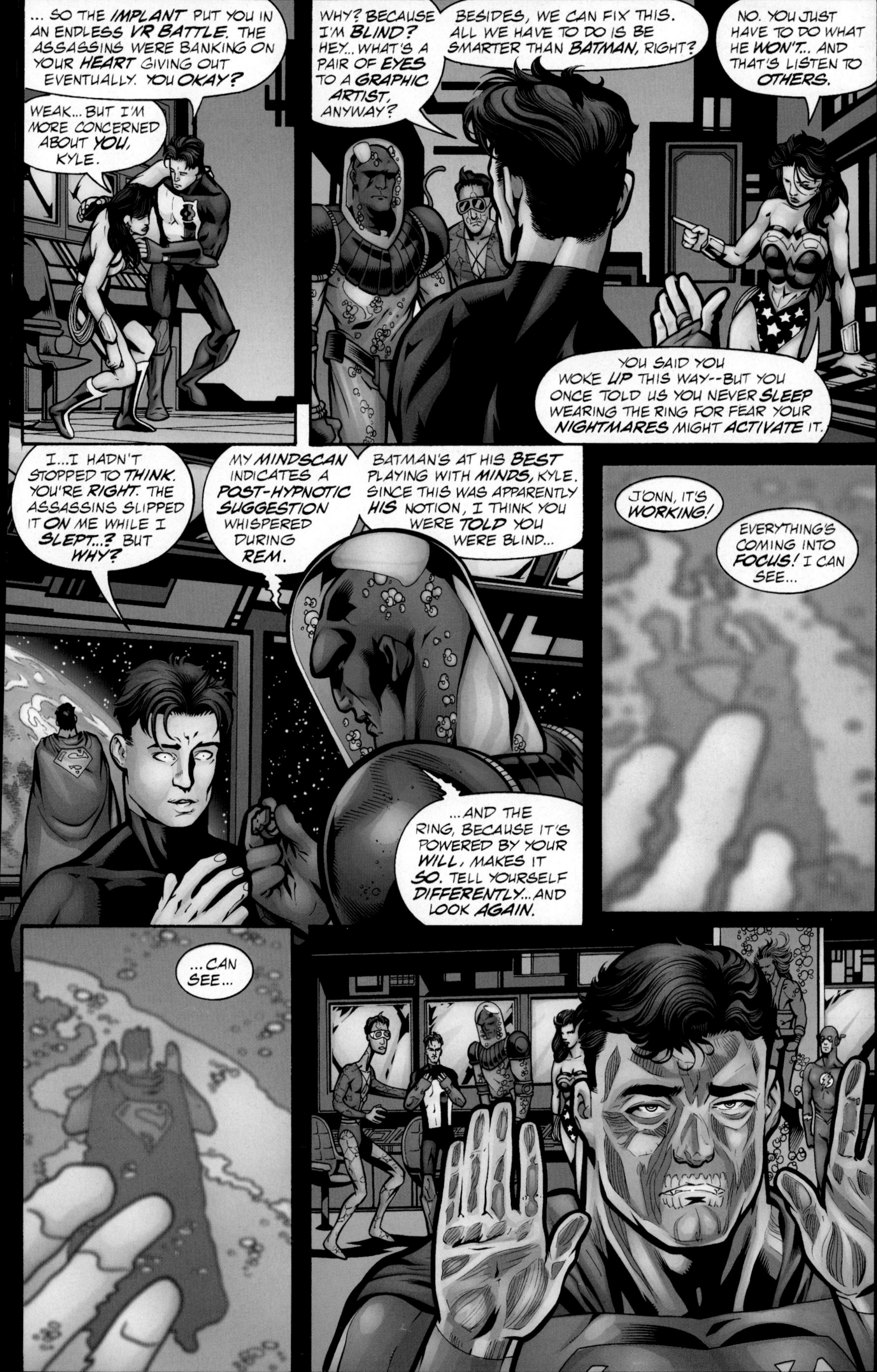
... SO THE IMPLANT PUT YOU IN AN ENDLESS VR BATTLE. THE ASSASSINS WERE BANKING ON YOUR HEART GIVING OUT EVENTUALLY. YOU OKAY?
WEAK... BUT I'M MORE CONCERNED ABOUT YOU, KYLE.
WHY? BECAUSE I'M BLIND? HEY... WHAT'S A PAIR OF EYES TO A GRAPHIC ARTIST, ANYWAY?
BESIDES, WE CAN FIX THIS. ALL WE HAVE TO DO IS BE SMARTER THAN BATMAN, RIGHT?
NO. YOU JUST HAVE TO DO WHAT HE WON'T... AND THAT'S LISTEN TO OTHERS.
YOU SAID YOU WOKE UP THIS WAY--BUT YOU ONCE TOLD US YOU NEVER SLEEP WEARING THE RING FOR FEAR YOUR NIGHTMARES MIGHT ACTIVATE IT.
I...I HADN'T STOPPED TO THINK. YOU'RE RIGHT. THE ASSASSINS SLIPPED IT ON ME WHILE I SLEPT...? BUT WHY?
MY MINDSCAN INDICATES A POST-HYPNOTIC SUGGESTION WHISPERED DURING REM.
BATMAN'S AT HIS BEST PLAYING WITH MINDS, KYLE. SINCE THIS WAS APPARENTLY HIS NOTION, I THINK YOU WERE TOLD YOU WERE BLIND...
...AND THE RING, BECAUSE IT'S POWERED BY YOUR WILL, MAKES IT SO. TELL YOURSELF DIFFERENTLY... AND LOOK AGAIN.
J'ONN, IT'S WORKING!
EVERYTHING'S COMING INTO FOCUS! I CAN SEE...
...CAN SEE...

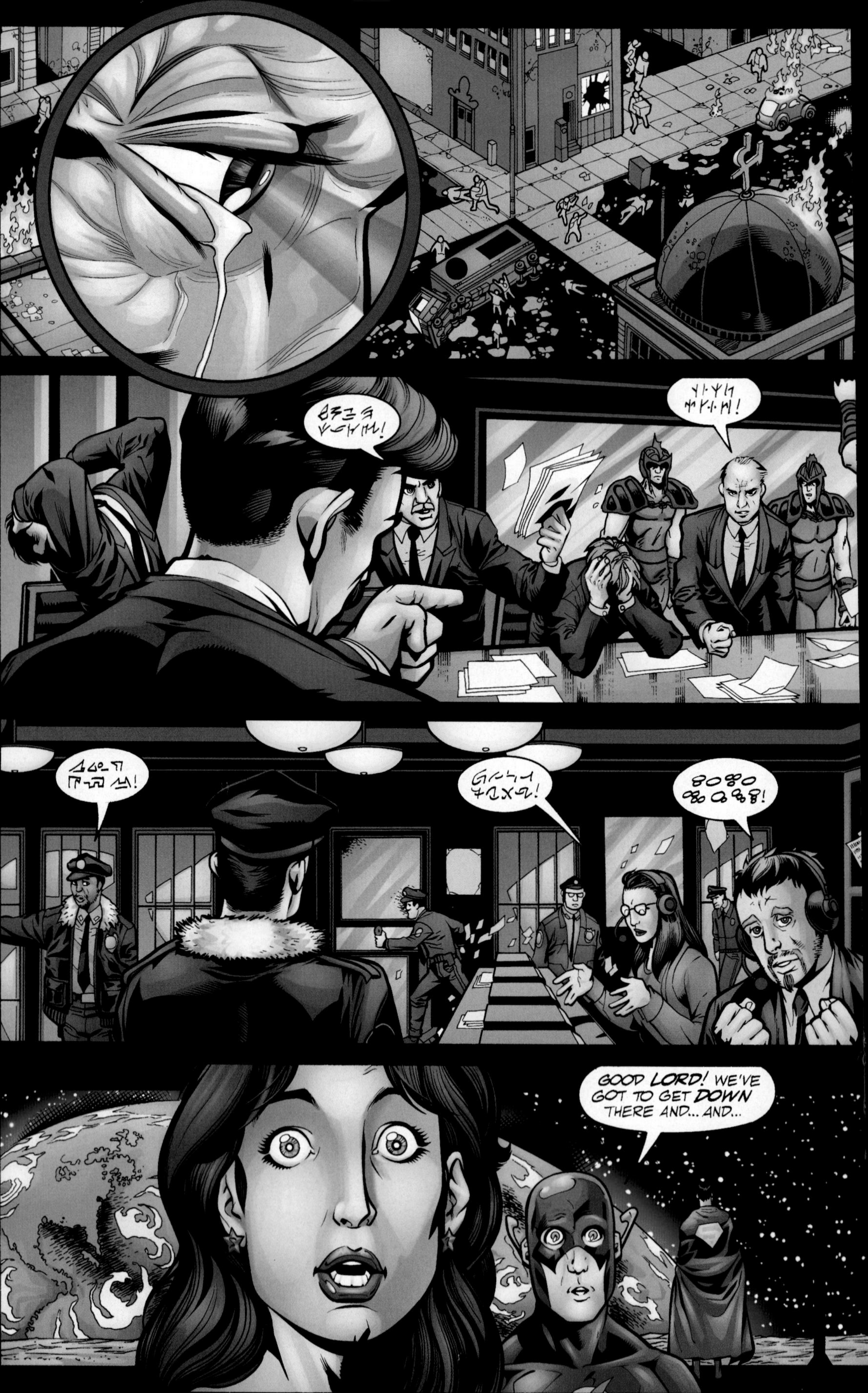
GOOD LORD! WE'VE GOT TO GET DOWN THERE AND... AND...

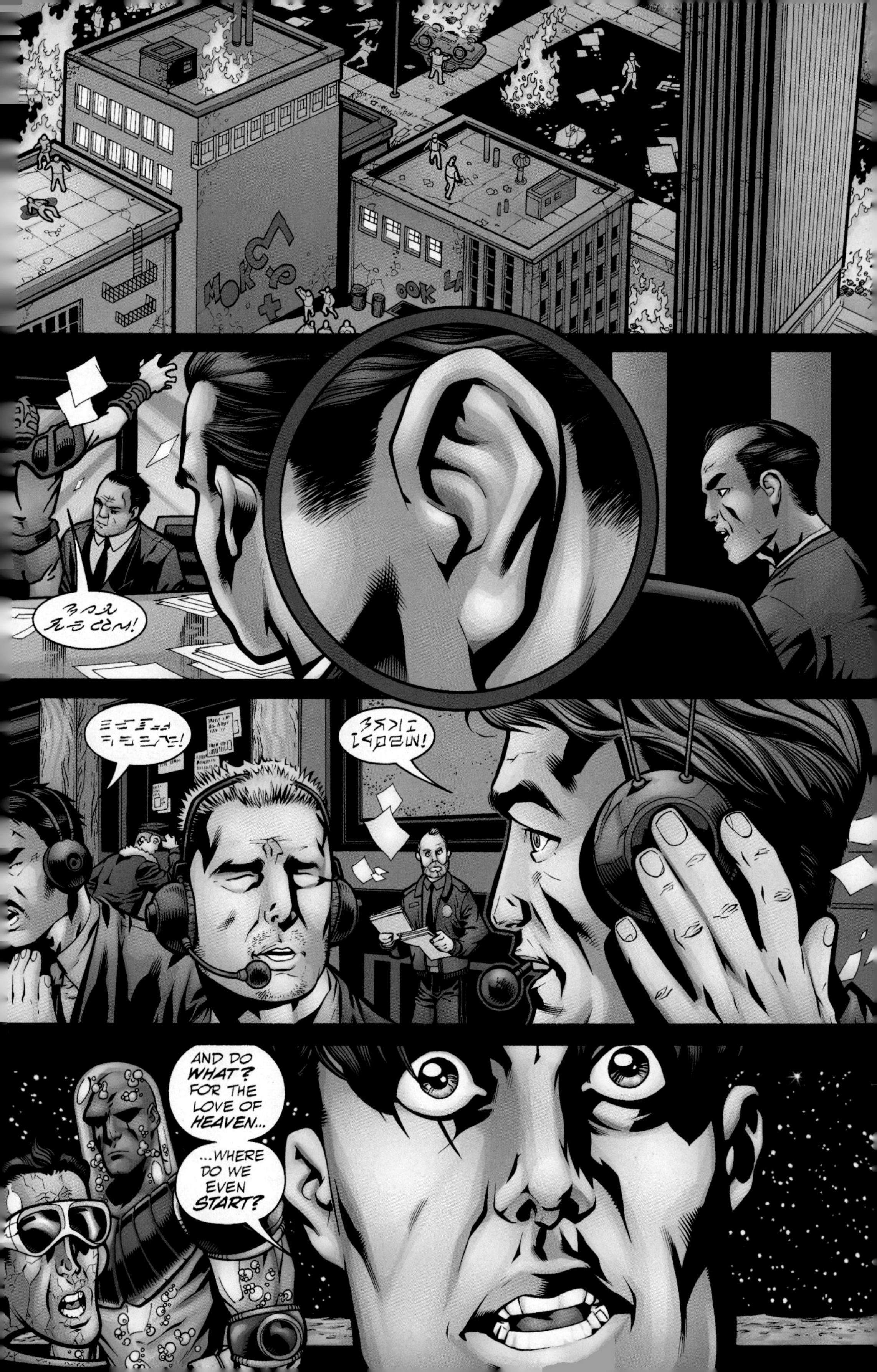
AND DO WHAT? FOR THE LOVE OF HEAVEN...
...WHERE DO WE EVEN START?

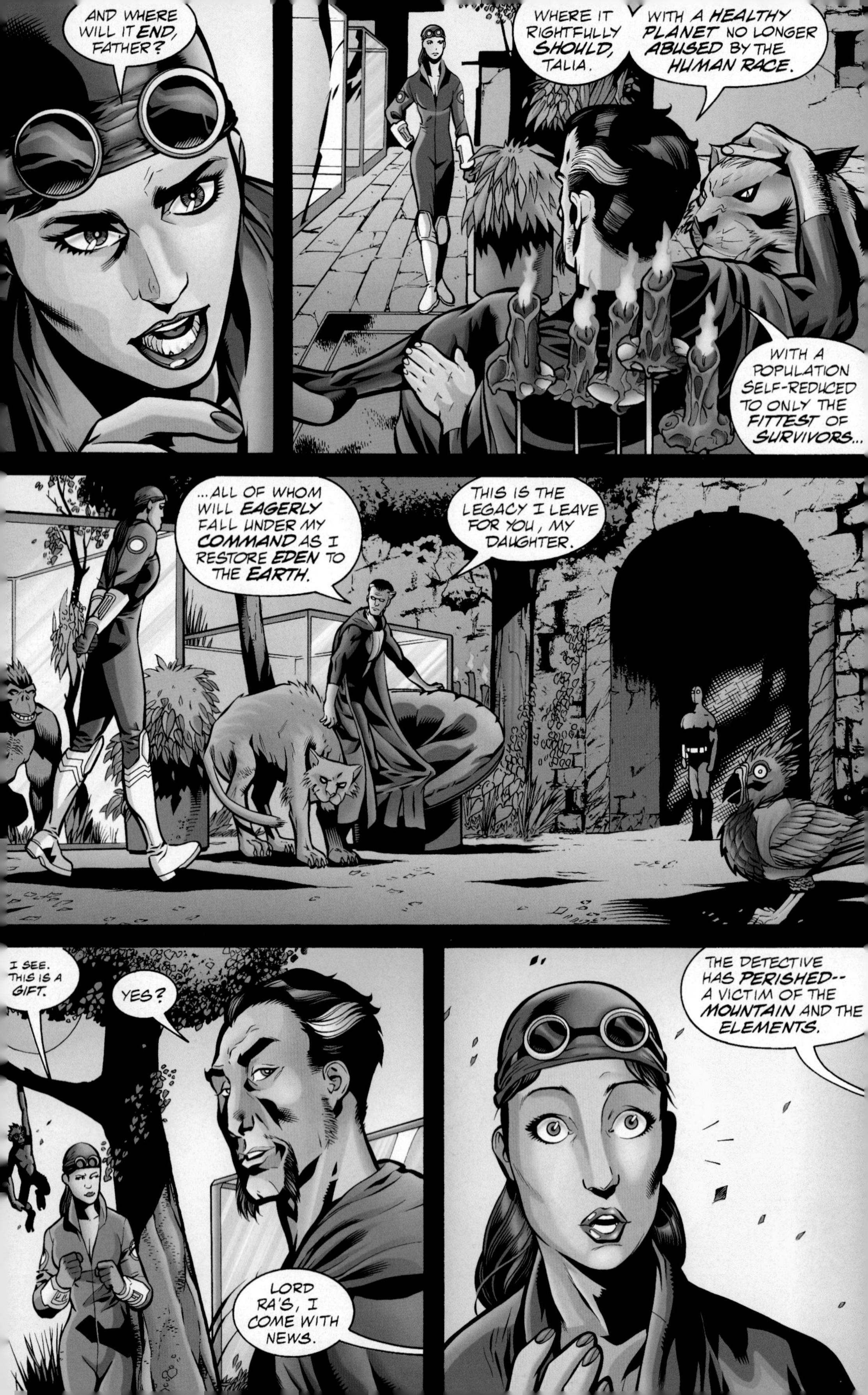
AND WHERE WILL IT END, FATHER?
WHERE IT RIGHTFULLY SHOULD, TALIA.
WITH A HEALTHY PLANET NO LONGER ABUSED BY THE HUMAN RACE.
WITH A POPULATION SELF-REDUCED TO ONLY THE FITTEST OF SURVIVORS...
...ALL OF WHOM WILL EAGERLY FALL UNDER MY COMMAND AS I RESTORE EDEN TO THE EARTH.
THIS IS THE LEGACY I LEAVE FOR YOU, MY DAUGHTER.
I SEE. THIS IS A GIFT.
YES?
LORD RA'S, I COME WITH NEWS.
THE DETECTIVE HAS PERISHED-- A VICTIM OF THE MOUNTAIN AND THE ELEMENTS.

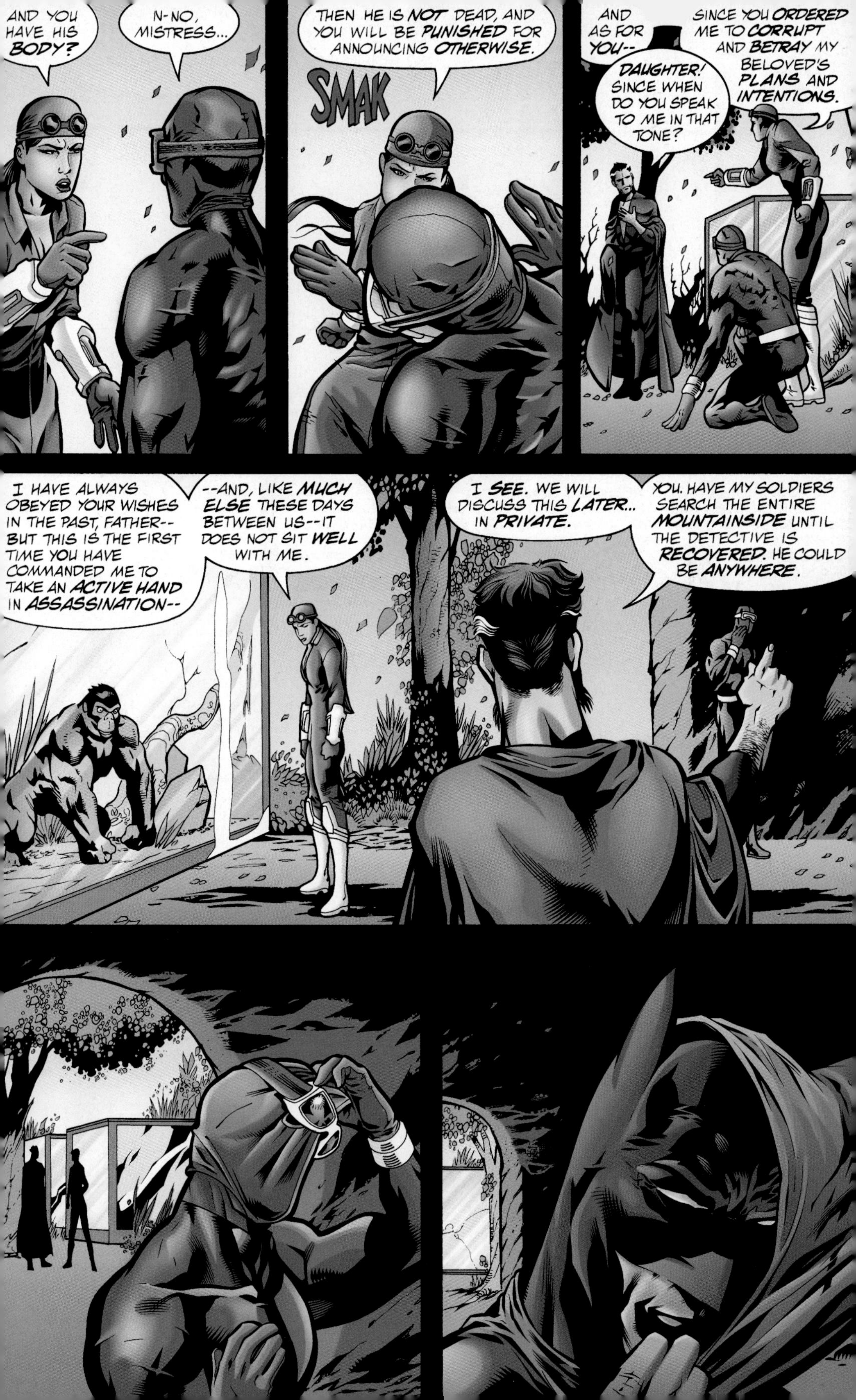
AND YOU HAVE HIS BODY?
N-NO, MISTRESS...
THEN HE IS NOT DEAD, AND YOU WILL BE PUNISHED FOR ANNOUNCING OTHERWISE.
SMAK
AND AS FOR YOU--
DAUGHTER! SINCE WHEN DO YOU SPEAK TO ME IN THAT TONE?
SINCE YOU ORDERED ME TO CORRUPT AND BETRAY MY BELOVED'S PLANS AND INTENTIONS.
I HAVE ALWAYS OBEYED YOUR WISHES IN THE PAST, FATHER-- BUT THIS IS THE FIRST TIME YOU HAVE COMMANDED ME TO TAKE AN ACTIVE HAND IN ASSASSINATION--
--AND, LIKE MUCH ELSE THESE DAYS BETWEEN US--IT DOES NOT SIT WELL WITH ME.
I SEE. WE WILL DISCUSS THIS LATER... IN PRIVATE.
YOU. HAVE MY SOLDIERS SEARCH THE ENTIRE MOUNTAINSIDE UNTIL THE DETECTIVE IS RECOVERED. HE COULD BE ANYWHERE.

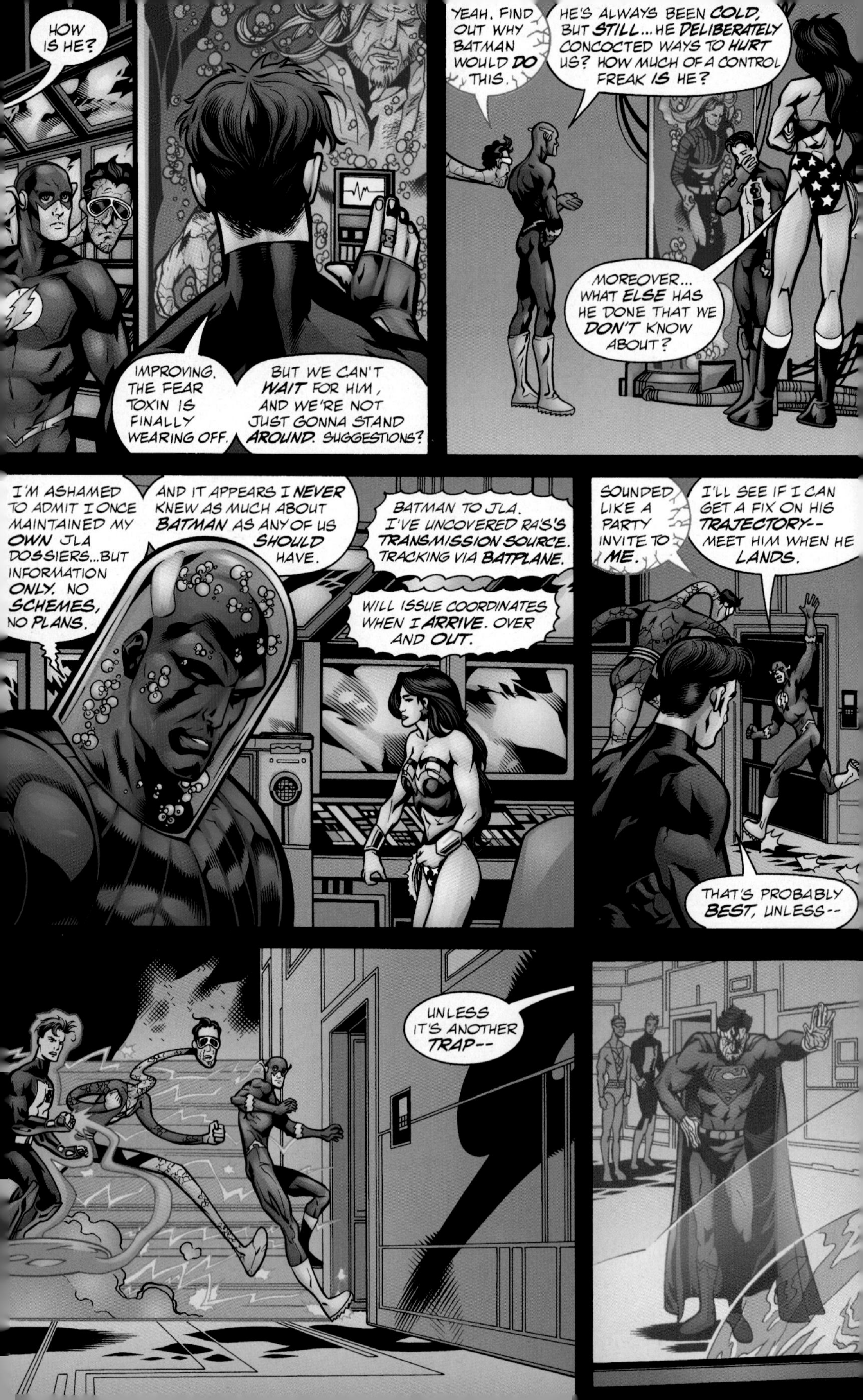
HOW IS HE?
IMPROVING. THE FEAR TOXIN IS FINALLY WEARING OFF.
BUT WE CAN'T WAIT FOR HIM, AND WE'RE NOT JUST GONNA STAND AROUND. SUGGESTIONS?
YEAH. FIND OUT WHY BATMAN WOULD DO THIS.
HE'S ALWAYS BEEN COLD, BUT STILL... HE DELIBERATELY CONCOCTED WAYS TO HURT US? HOW MUCH OF A CONTROL FREAK IS HE?
MOREOVER... WHAT ELSE HAS HE DONE THAT WE DON'T KNOW ABOUT?
I'M ASHAMED TO ADMIT I ONCE MAINTAINED MY OWN JLA DOSSIERS...BUT INFORMATION ONLY. NO SCHEMES, NO PLANS.
AND IT APPEARS I NEVER KNEW AS MUCH ABOUT BATMAN AS ANY OF US SHOULD HAVE.
BATMAN TO JLA. I'VE UNCOVERED RA'S'S TRANSMISSION SOURCE. TRACKING VIA BATPLANE.
WILL ISSUE COORDINATES WHEN I ARRIVE. OVER AND OUT.
SOUNDED LIKE A PARTY INVITE TO ME.
I'LL SEE IF I CAN GET A FIX ON HIS TRAJECTORY-- MEET HIM WHEN HE LANDS.
THAT'S PROBABLY BEST, UNLESS--
UNLESS IT'S ANOTHER TRAP--

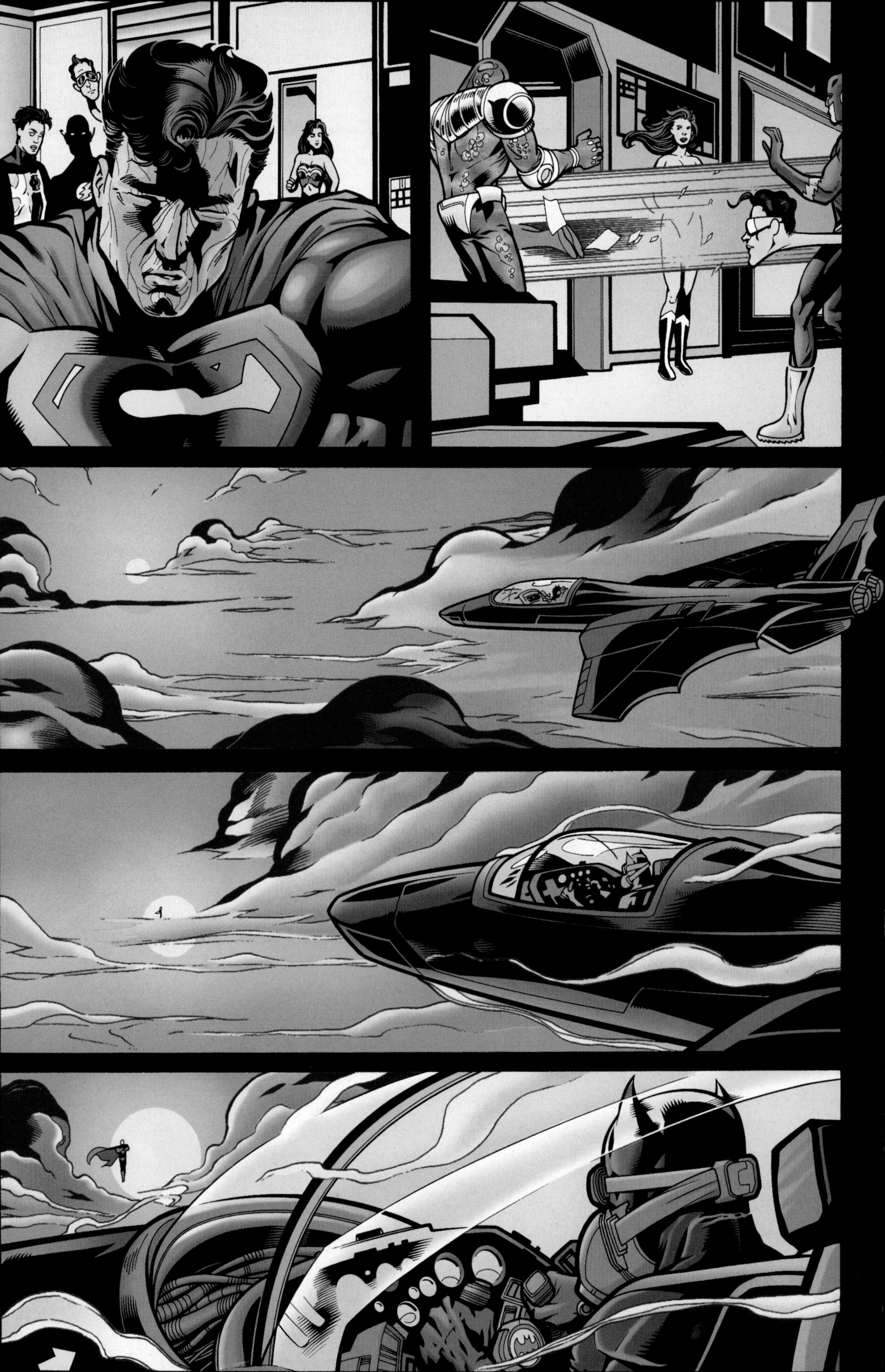

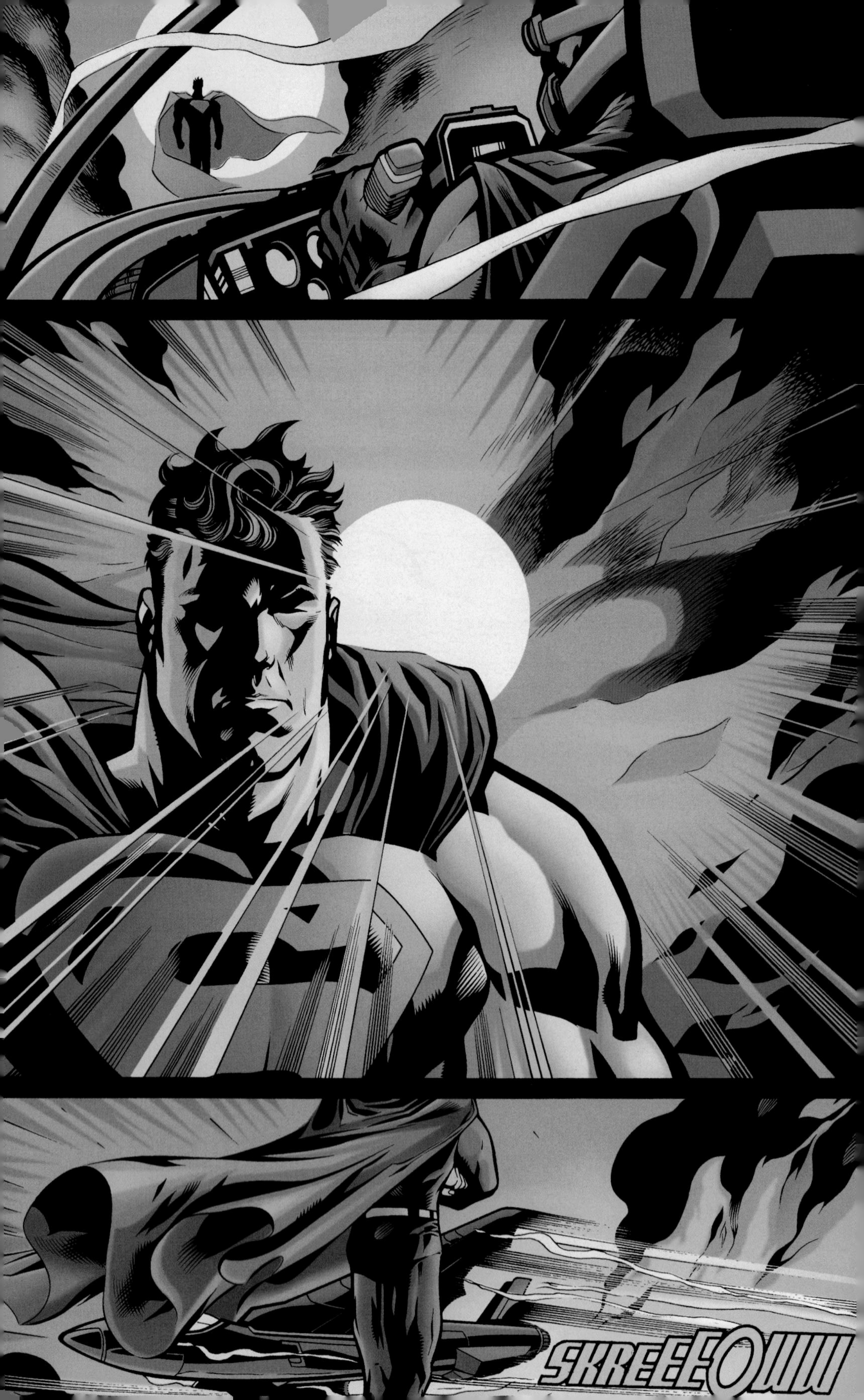
SKREEEOWW

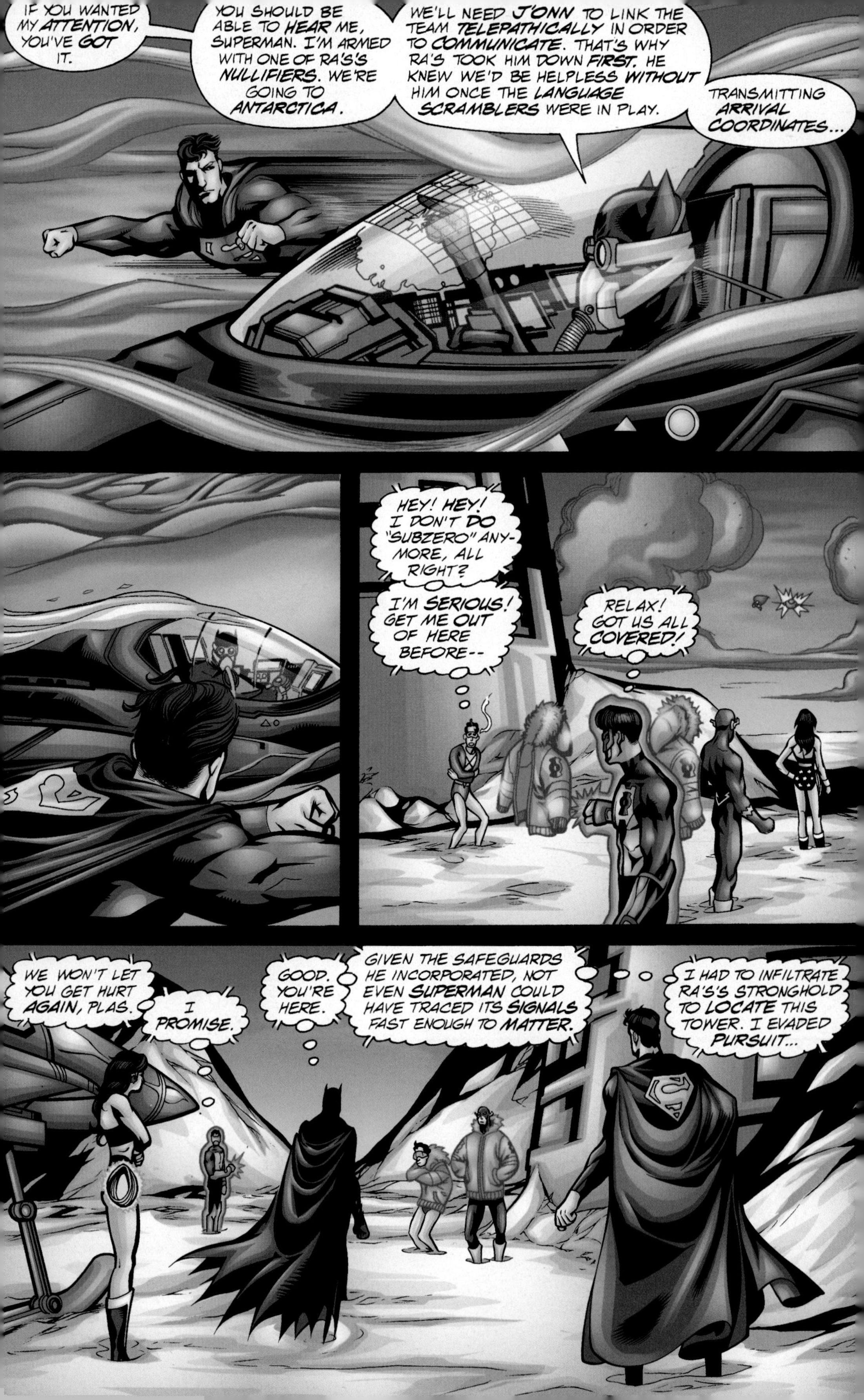
IF YOU WANTED MY ATTENTION, YOU'VE GOT IT.
YOU SHOULD BE ABLE TO HEAR ME, SUPERMAN. I'M ARMED WITH ONE OF RA'S'S NULLIFIERS. WE'RE GOING TO ANTARCTICA.
WE'LL NEED J'ONN TO LINK THE TEAM TELEPATHICALLY IN ORDER TO COMMUNICATE. THAT'S WHY RA'S TOOK HIM DOWN FIRST. HE KNEW WE'D BE HELPLESS WITHOUT HIM ONCE THE LANGUAGE SCRAMBLERS WERE IN PLAY.
TRANSMITTING ARRIVAL COORDINATES...
HEY! HEY! I DON'T DO "SUBZERO" ANY-MORE, ALL RIGHT?
I'M SERIOUS! GET ME OUT OF HERE BEFORE--
RELAX! GOT US ALL COVERED!
WE WON'T LET YOU GET HURT AGAIN, PLAS.
I PROMISE.
GOOD. YOU'RE HERE.
GIVEN THE SAFEGUARDS HE INCORPORATED, NOT EVEN SUPERMAN COULD HAVE TRACED ITS SIGNALS FAST ENOUGH TO MATTER.
I HAD TO INFILTRATE RA'S'S STRONGHOLD TO LOCATE THIS TOWER. I EVADED PURSUIT...

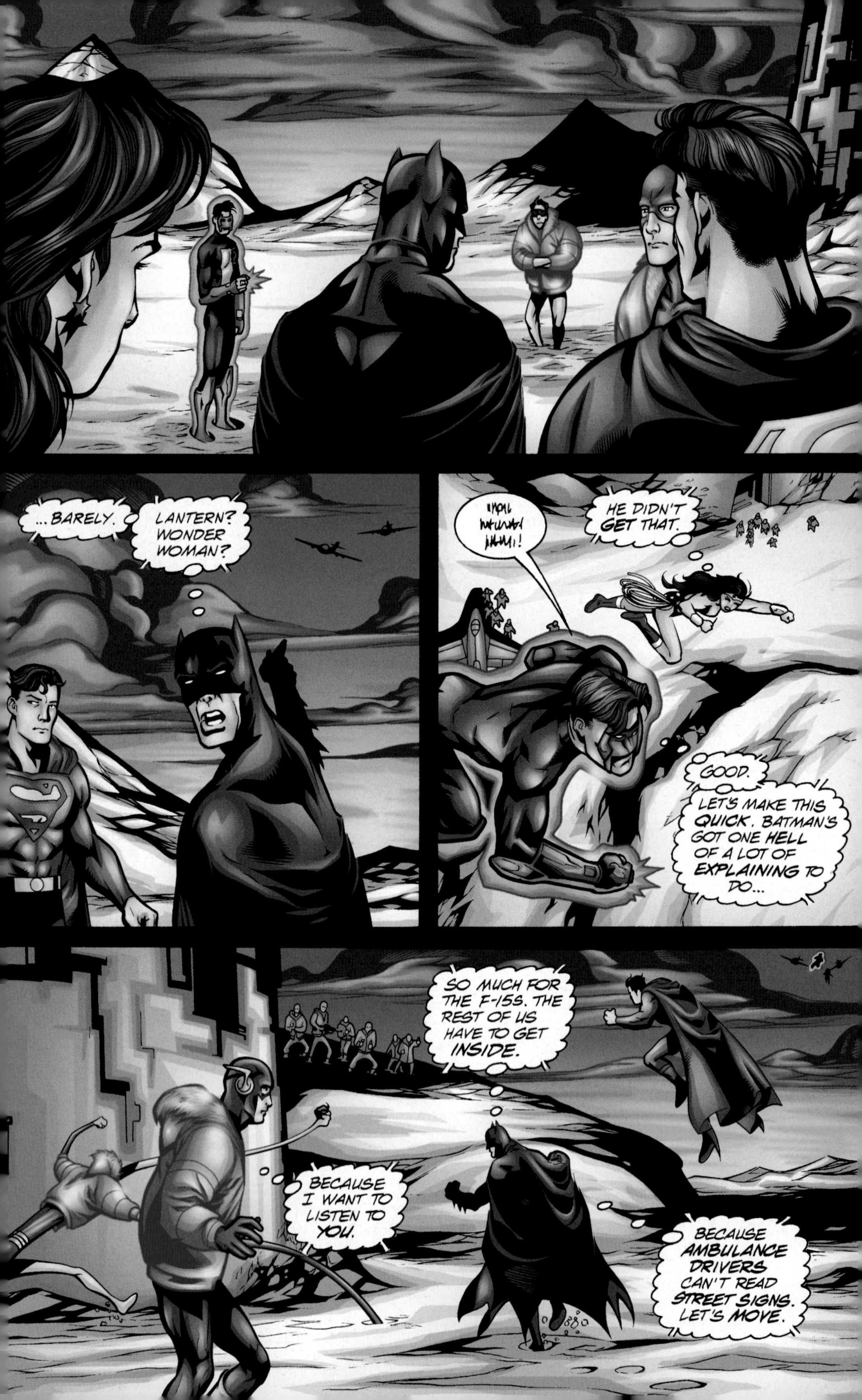
...BARELY.
LANTERN? WONDER WOMAN?
HE DIDN'T GET THAT.
GOOD.
LET'S MAKE THIS QUICK. BATMAN'S GOT ONE HELL OF A LOT OF EXPLAINING TO DO...
SO MUCH FOR THE F-15S. THE REST OF US HAVE TO GET INSIDE.
BECAUSE I WANT TO LISTEN TO YOU.
BECAUSE AMBULANCE DRIVERS CAN'T READ STREET SIGNS. LET'S MOVE.

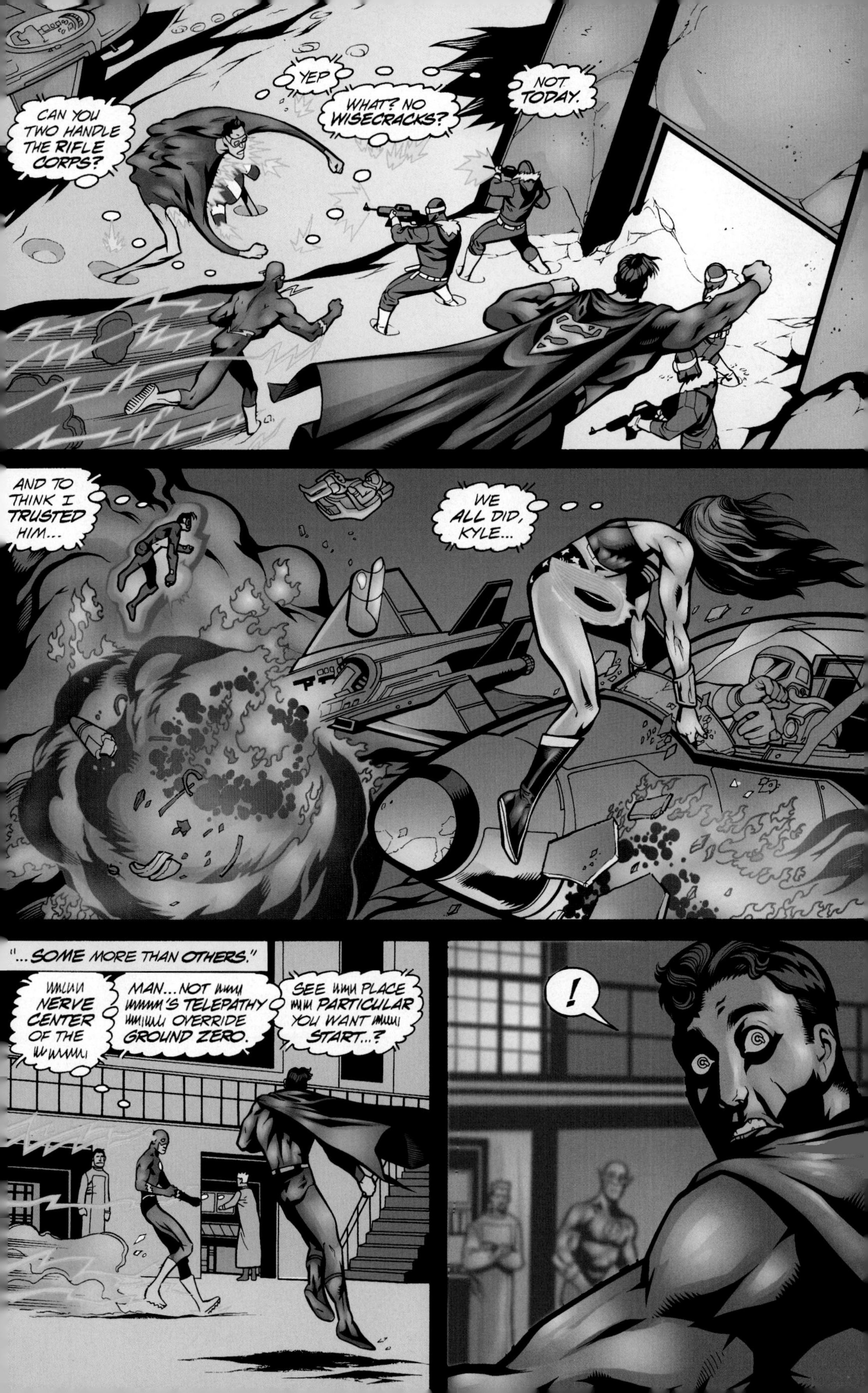
CAN YOU TWO HANDLE THE RIFLE CORPS?
YEP
WHAT? NO WISECRACKS?
NOT TODAY.
AND TO THINK I TRUSTED HIM...
WE ALL DID, KYLE...
"...SOME MORE THAN OTHERS."
NERVE CENTER OF THE
MAN...NOT 'S TELEPATHY OVERRIDE GROUND ZERO.
SEE PLACE PARTICULAR YOU WANT START...?
!

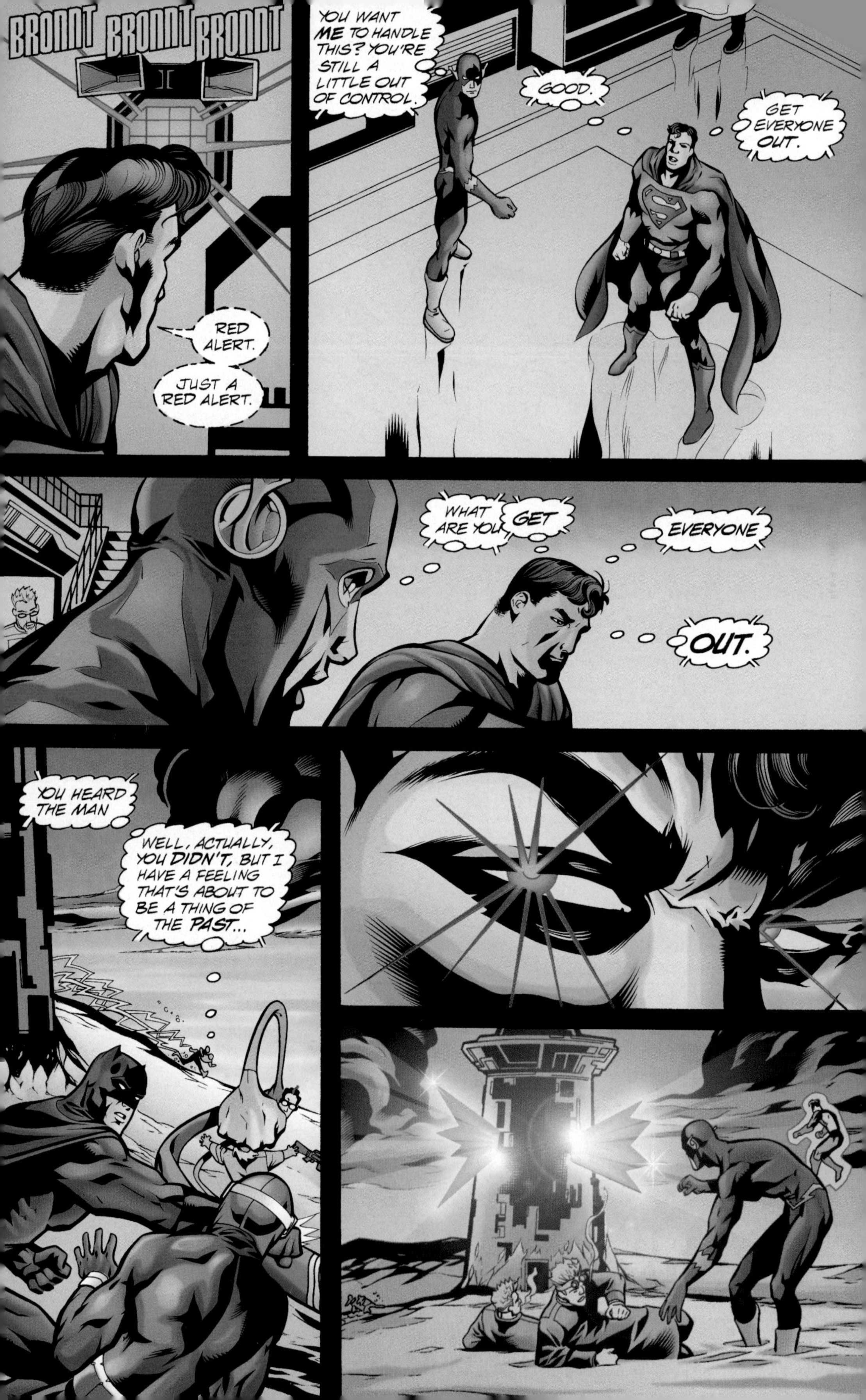
BRONNT BRONNT BRONNT
RED ALERT.
JUST A RED ALERT.
YOU WANT ME TO HANDLE THIS? YOU'RE STILL A LITTLE OUT OF CONTROL.
GOOD.
GET EVERYONE OUT.
WHAT ARE YOU
GET
EVERYONE
OUT.
YOU HEARD THE MAN
WELL, ACTUALLY, YOU DIDN'T, BUT I HAVE A FEELING THAT'S ABOUT TO BE A THING OF THE PAST...

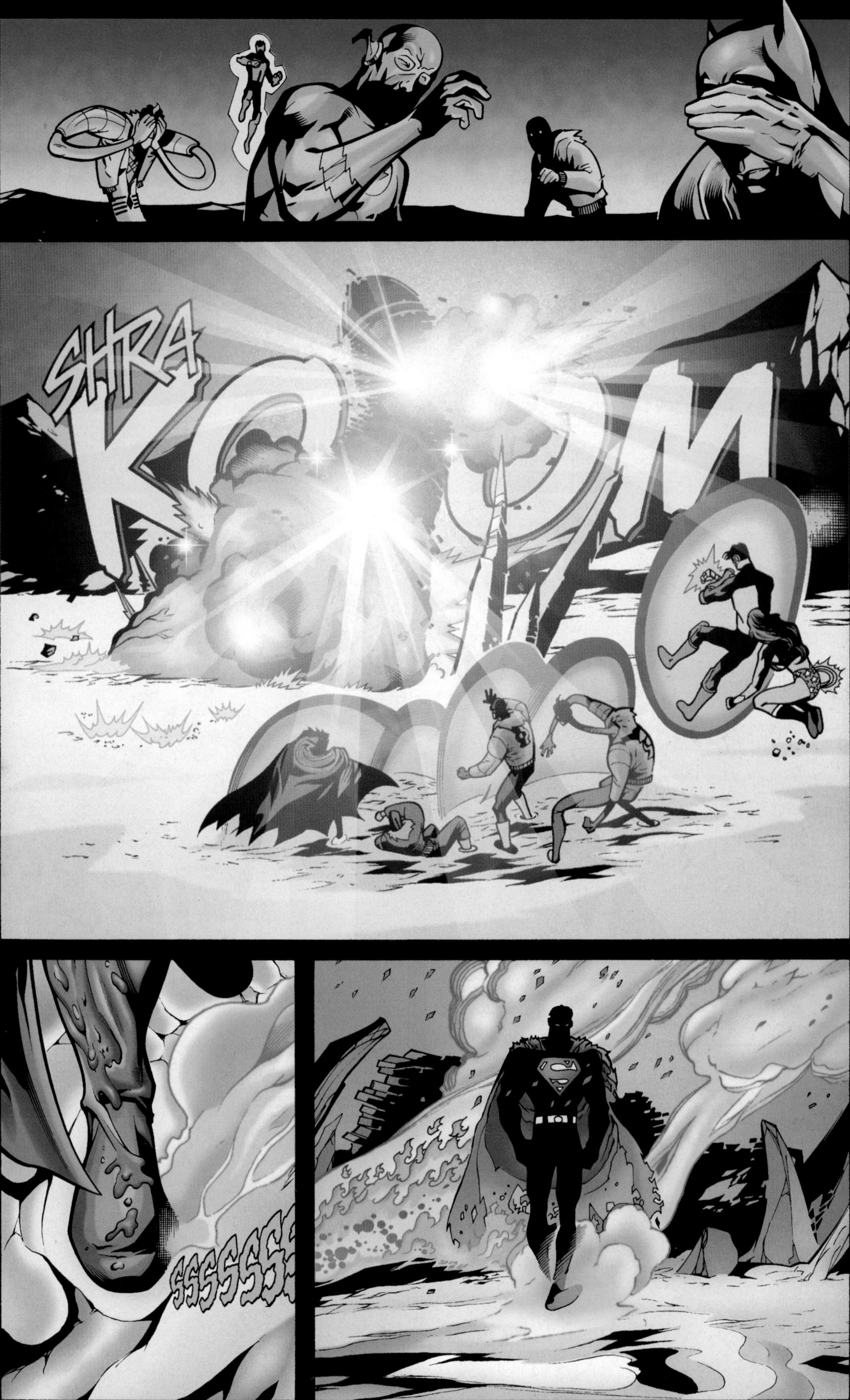
SHRA
SSSSSS

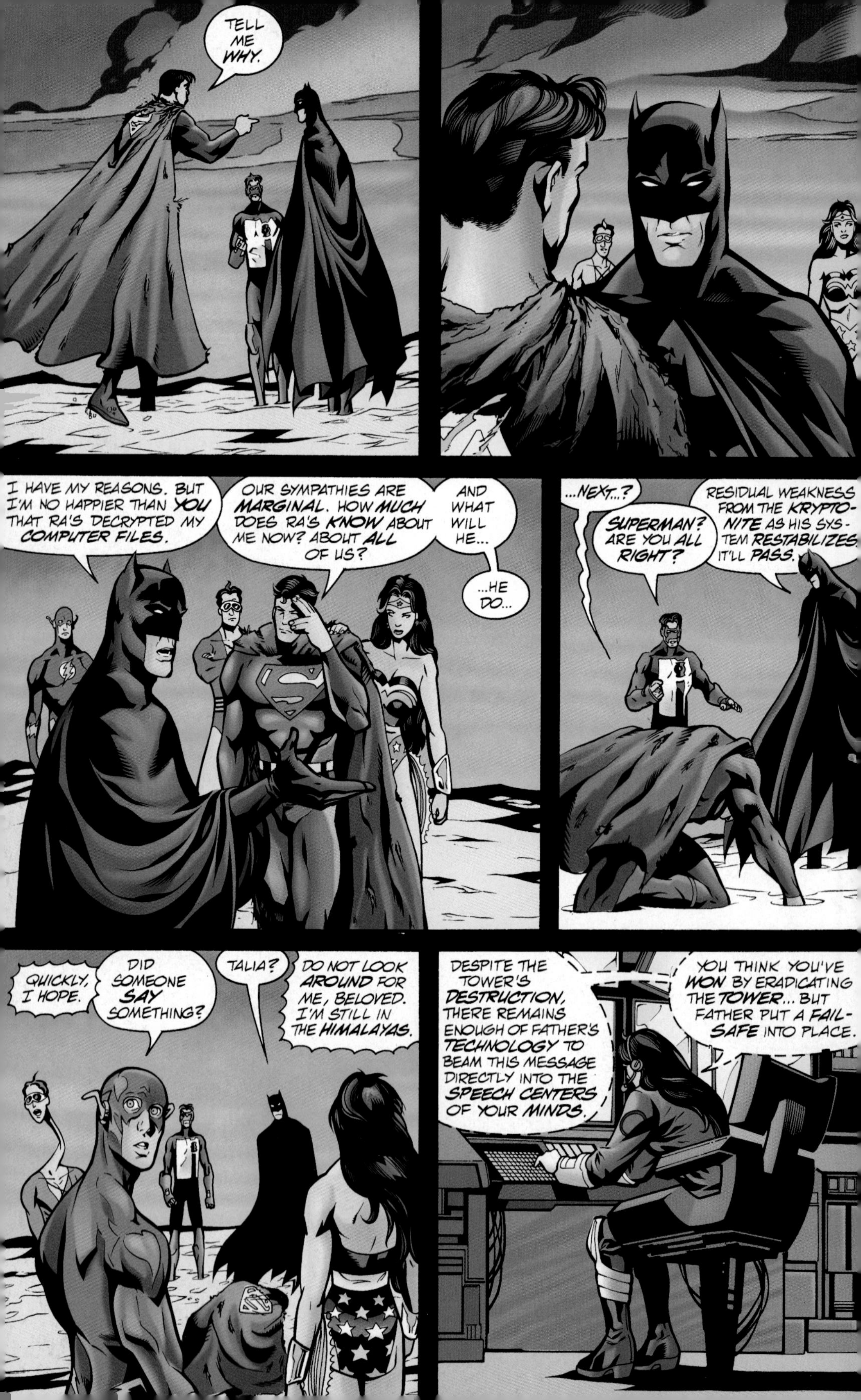
TELL ME WHY.
I HAVE MY REASONS. BUT I'M NO HAPPIER THAN YOU THAT RA'S DECRYPTED MY COMPUTER FILES.
OUR SYMPATHIES ARE MARGINAL. HOW MUCH DOES RA'S KNOW ABOUT ME NOW? ABOUT ALL OF US?
AND WHAT WILL HE...
...HE DO...
...NEXT...?
SUPERMAN? ARE YOU ALL RIGHT?
RESIDUAL WEAKNESS FROM THE KRYPTONITE AS HIS SYSTEM RESTABILIZES. IT'LL PASS.
QUICKLY, I HOPE.
DID SOMEONE SAY SOMETHING?
TALIA?
DO NOT LOOK AROUND FOR ME, BELOVED. I'M STILL IN THE HIMALAYAS.
DESPITE THE TOWER'S DESTRUCTION, THERE REMAINS ENOUGH OF FATHER'S TECHNOLOGY TO BEAM THIS MESSAGE DIRECTLY INTO THE SPEECH CENTERS OF YOUR MINDS.
YOU THINK YOU'VE WON BY ERADICATING THE TOWER... BUT FATHER PUT A FAIL-SAFE INTO PLACE.

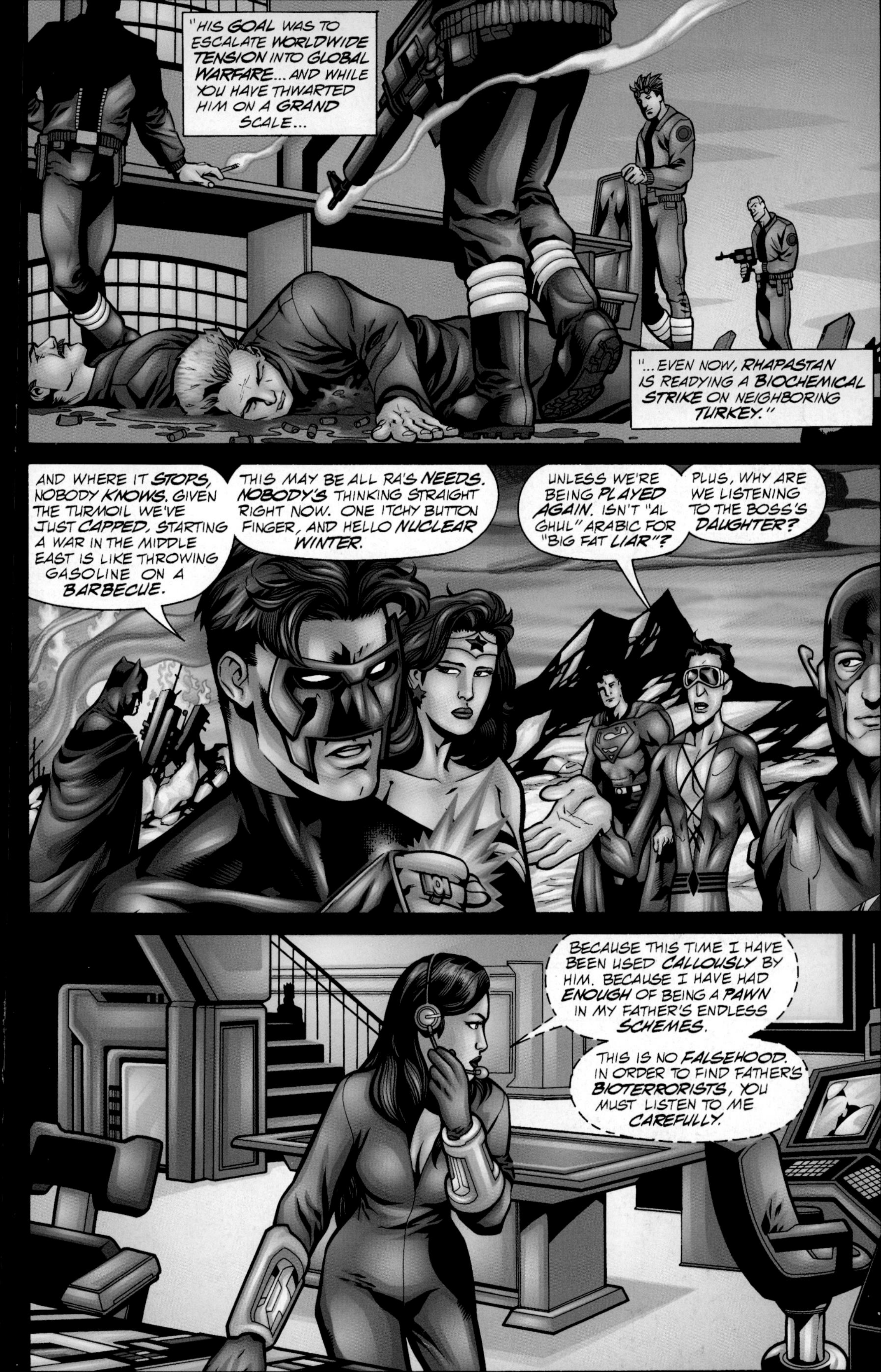
"HIS GOAL WAS TO ESCALATE WORLDWIDE TENSION INTO GLOBAL WARFARE... AND WHILE YOU HAVE THWARTED HIM ON A GRAND SCALE...
"...EVEN NOW, RHAPASTAN IS READYING A BIOCHEMICAL STRIKE ON NEIGHBORING TURKEY."
AND WHERE IT STOPS, NOBODY KNOWS. GIVEN THE TURMOIL WE'VE JUST CAPPED, STARTING A WAR IN THE MIDDLE EAST IS LIKE THROWING GASOLINE ON A BARBECUE.
THIS MAY BE ALL RA'S NEEDS. NOBODY'S THINKING STRAIGHT RIGHT NOW. ONE ITCHY BUTTON FINGER, AND HELLO NUCLEAR WINTER.
UNLESS WE'RE BEING PLAYED AGAIN. ISN'T "AL GHUL" ARABIC FOR "BIG FAT LIAR"?
PLUS, WHY ARE WE LISTENING TO THE BOSS'S DAUGHTER?
BECAUSE THIS TIME I HAVE BEEN USED CALLOUSLY BY HIM. BECAUSE I HAVE HAD ENOUGH OF BEING A PAWN IN MY FATHER'S ENDLESS SCHEMES.
THIS IS NO FALSEHOOD. IN ORDER TO FIND FATHER'S BIOTERRORISTS, YOU MUST LISTEN TO ME CAREFULLY.

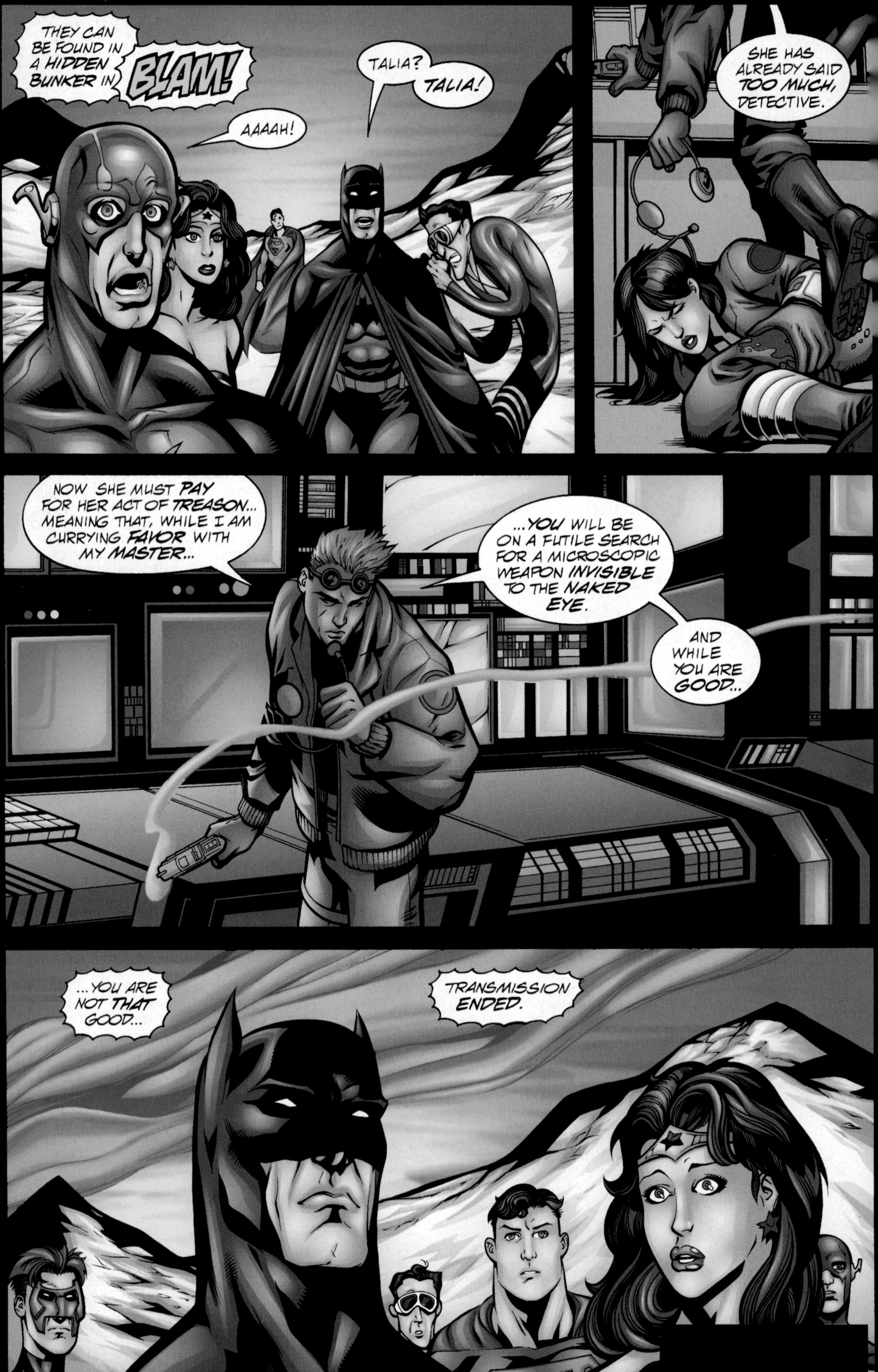
THEY CAN BE FOUND IN A HIDDEN BUNKER IN
BLAM!
AAAAH!
TALIA? TALIA!
SHE HAS ALREADY SAID TOO MUCH, DETECTIVE.
NOW SHE MUST PAY FOR HER ACT OF TREASON... MEANING THAT, WHILE I AM CURRYING FAVOR WITH MY MASTER...
...YOU WILL BE ON A FUTILE SEARCH FOR A MICROSCOPIC WEAPON INVISIBLE TO THE NAKED EYE.
AND WHILE YOU ARE GOOD...
...YOU ARE NOT THAT GOOD...
TRANSMISSION ENDED.
[redacted]

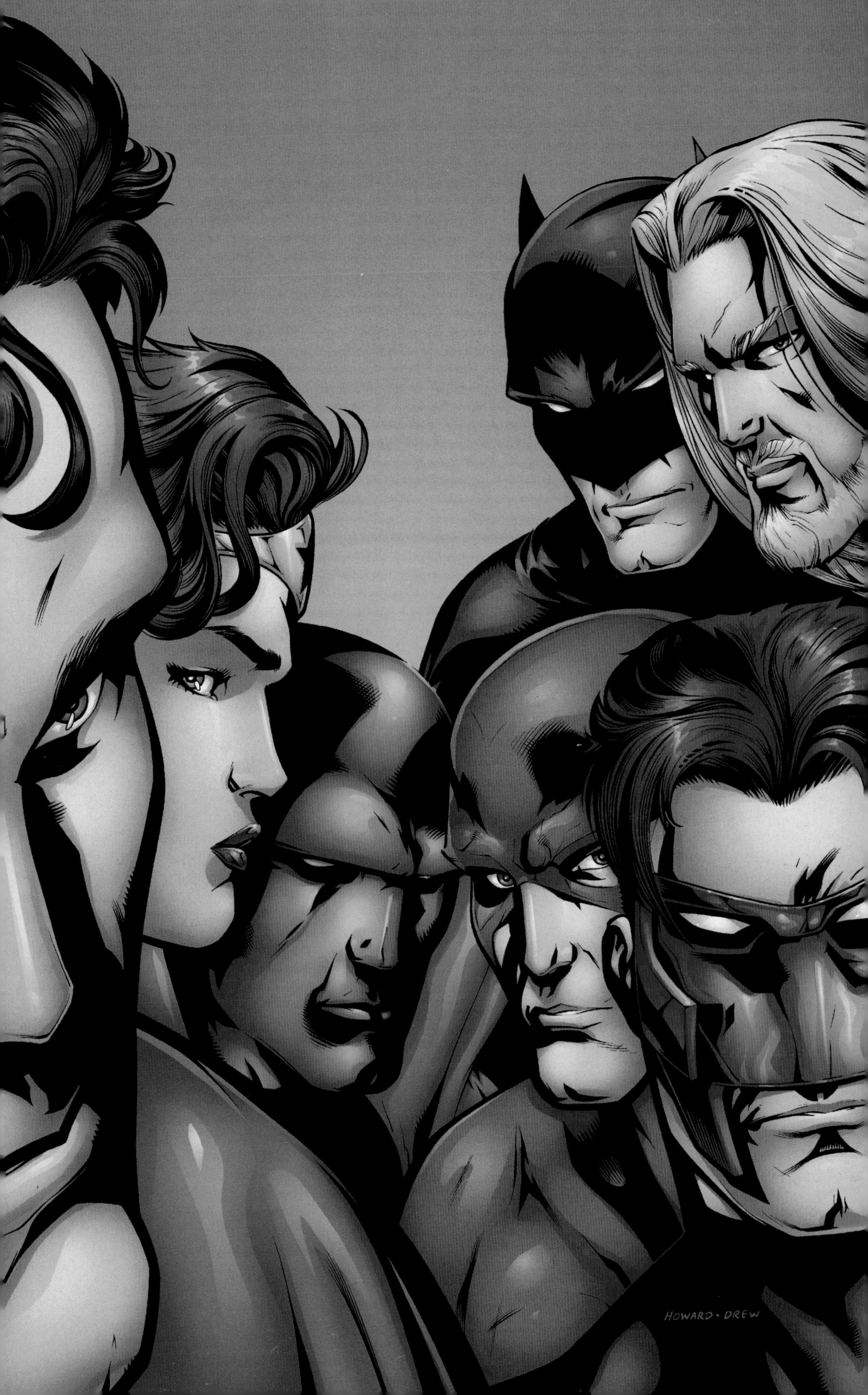
HOWARD • DREW

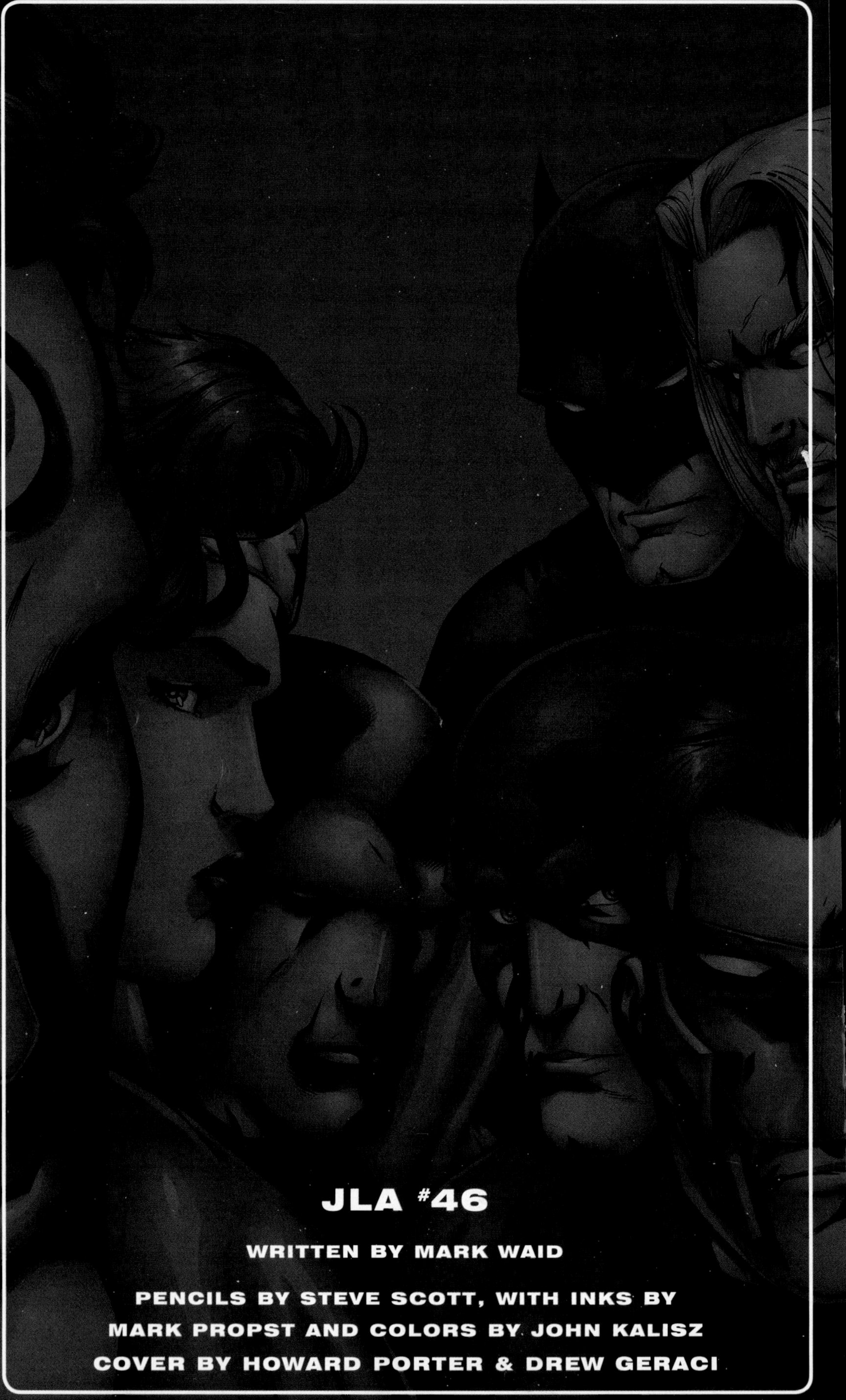

JLA #46

WRITTEN BY MARK WAID

PENCILS BY STEVE SCOTT, WITH INKS BY
MARK PROPST AND COLORS BY JOHN KALISZ
COVER BY HOWARD PORTER & DREW GERACI

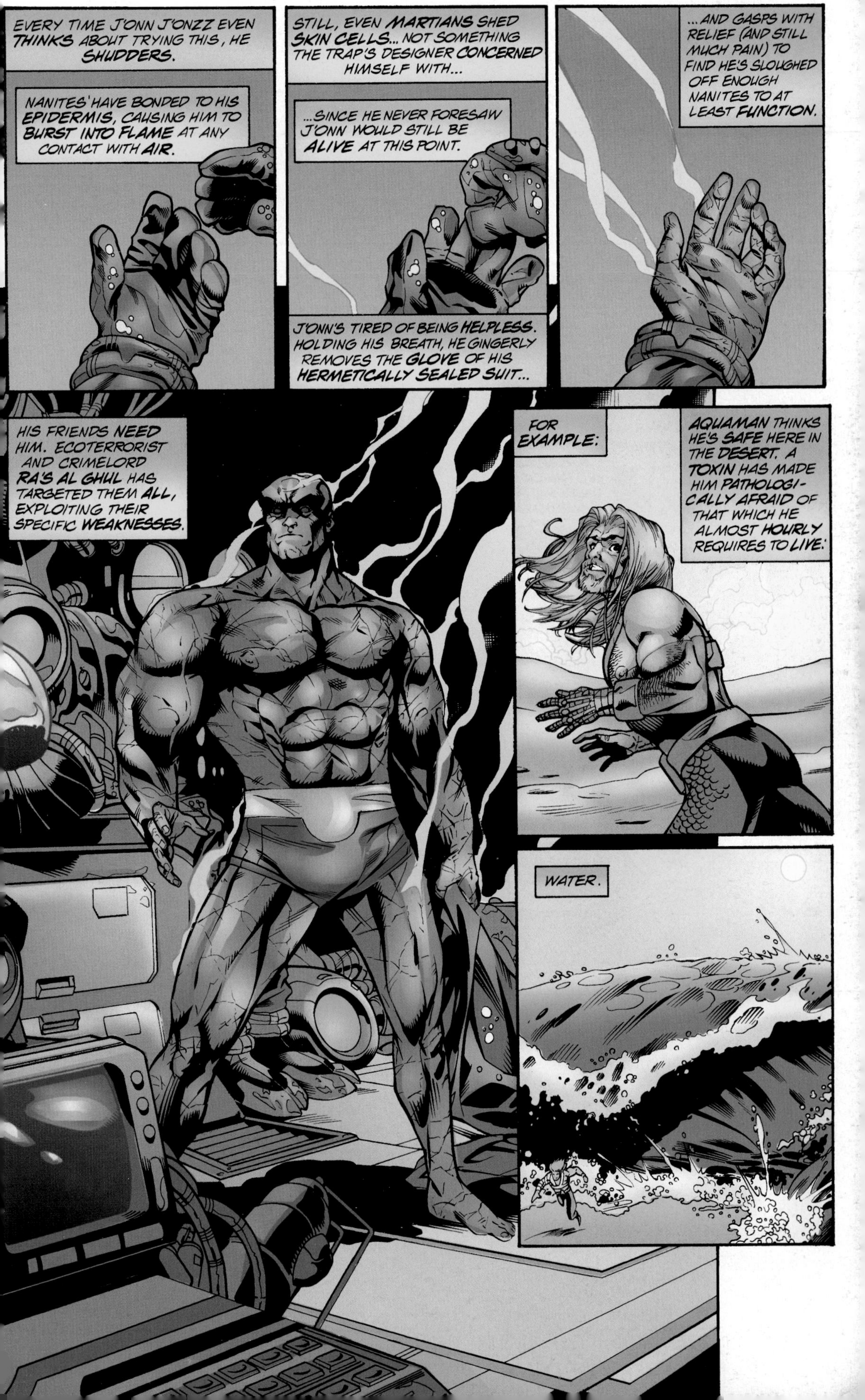
EVERY TIME J'ONN J'ONZZ EVEN THINKS ABOUT TRYING THIS, HE SHUDDERS.
NANITES HAVE BONDED TO HIS EPIDERMIS, CAUSING HIM TO BURST INTO FLAME AT ANY CONTACT WITH AIR.
STILL, EVEN MARTIANS SHED SKIN CELLS... NOT SOMETHING THE TRAP'S DESIGNER CONCERNED HIMSELF WITH...
...SINCE HE NEVER FORESAW J'ONN WOULD STILL BE ALIVE AT THIS POINT.
J'ONN'S TIRED OF BEING HELPLESS. HOLDING HIS BREATH, HE GINGERLY REMOVES THE GLOVE OF HIS HERMETICALLY SEALED SUIT...
...AND GASPS WITH RELIEF (AND STILL MUCH PAIN) TO FIND HE'S SLOUGHED OFF ENOUGH NANITES TO AT LEAST FUNCTION.
HIS FRIENDS NEED HIM. ECOTERRORIST AND CRIMELORD RA'S AL GHUL HAS TARGETED THEM ALL, EXPLOITING THEIR SPECIFIC WEAKNESSES.
FOR EXAMPLE:
AQUAMAN THINKS HE'S SAFE HERE IN THE DESERT. A TOXIN HAS MADE HIM PATHOLOGICALLY AFRAID OF THAT WHICH HE ALMOST HOURLY REQUIRES TO LIVE:
WATER.

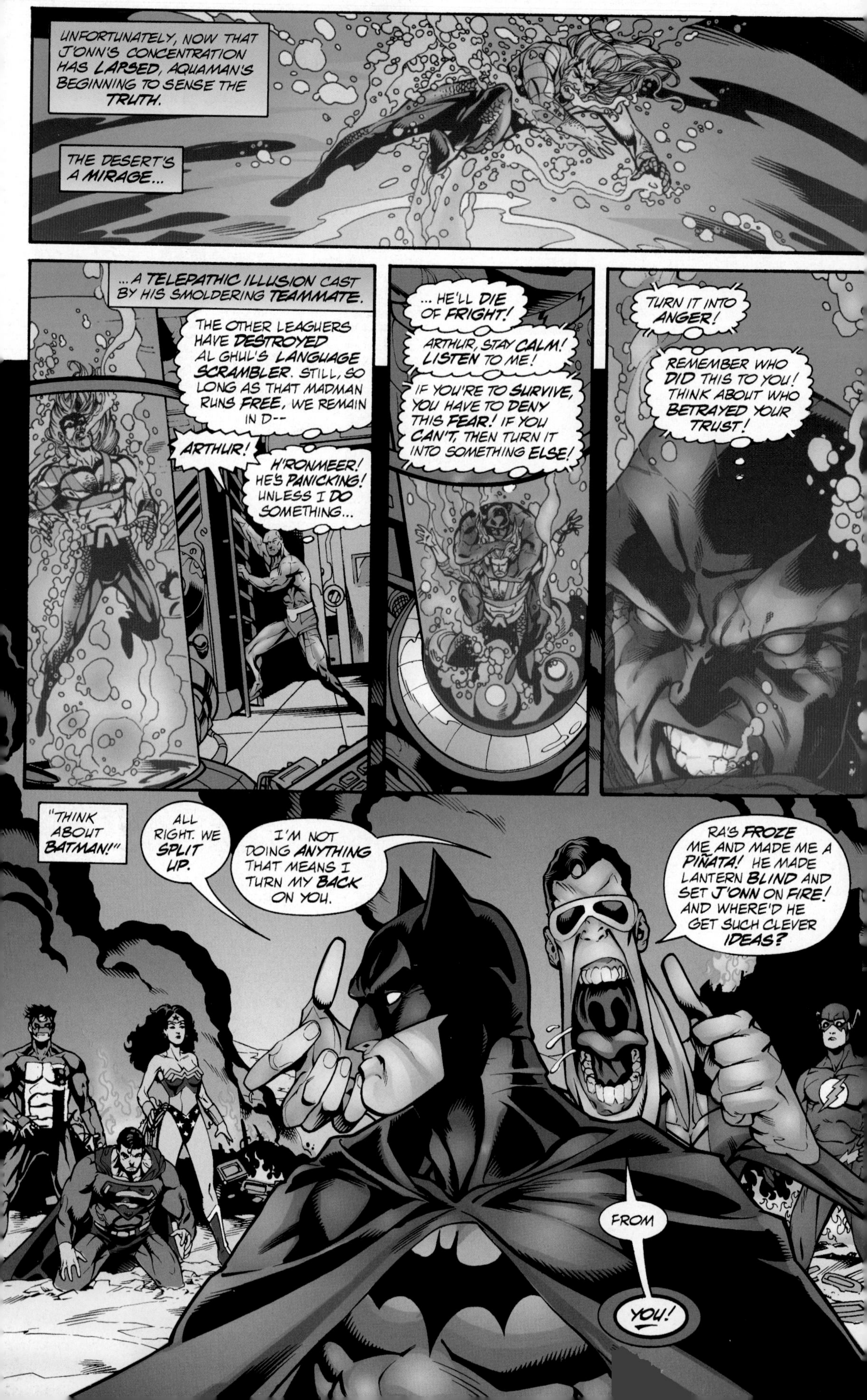
UNFORTUNATELY, NOW THAT J'ONN'S CONCENTRATION HAS LAPSED, AQUAMAN'S BEGINNING TO SENSE THE TRUTH.
THE DESERT'S A MIRAGE...
...A TELEPATHIC ILLUSION CAST BY HIS SMOLDERING TEAMMATE.
THE OTHER LEAGUERS HAVE DESTROYED AL GHUL'S LANGUAGE SCRAMBLER. STILL, SO LONG AS THAT MADMAN RUNS FREE, WE REMAIN IN D--
ARTHUR!
H'RONMEER! HE'S PANICKING! UNLESS I DO SOMETHING...
...HE'LL DIE OF FRIGHT!
ARTHUR, STAY CALM! LISTEN TO ME!
IF YOU'RE TO SURVIVE, YOU HAVE TO DENY THIS FEAR! IF YOU CAN'T, THEN TURN IT INTO SOMETHING ELSE!
TURN IT INTO ANGER!
REMEMBER WHO DID THIS TO YOU! THINK ABOUT WHO BETRAYED YOUR TRUST!
"THINK ABOUT BATMAN!"
ALL RIGHT. WE SPLIT UP.
I'M NOT DOING ANYTHING THAT MEANS I TURN MY BACK ON YOU.
RA'S FROZE ME AND MADE ME A PIÑATA! HE MADE LANTERN BLIND AND SET J'ONN ON FIRE! AND WHERE'D HE GET SUCH CLEVER IDEAS?
FROM
YOU!

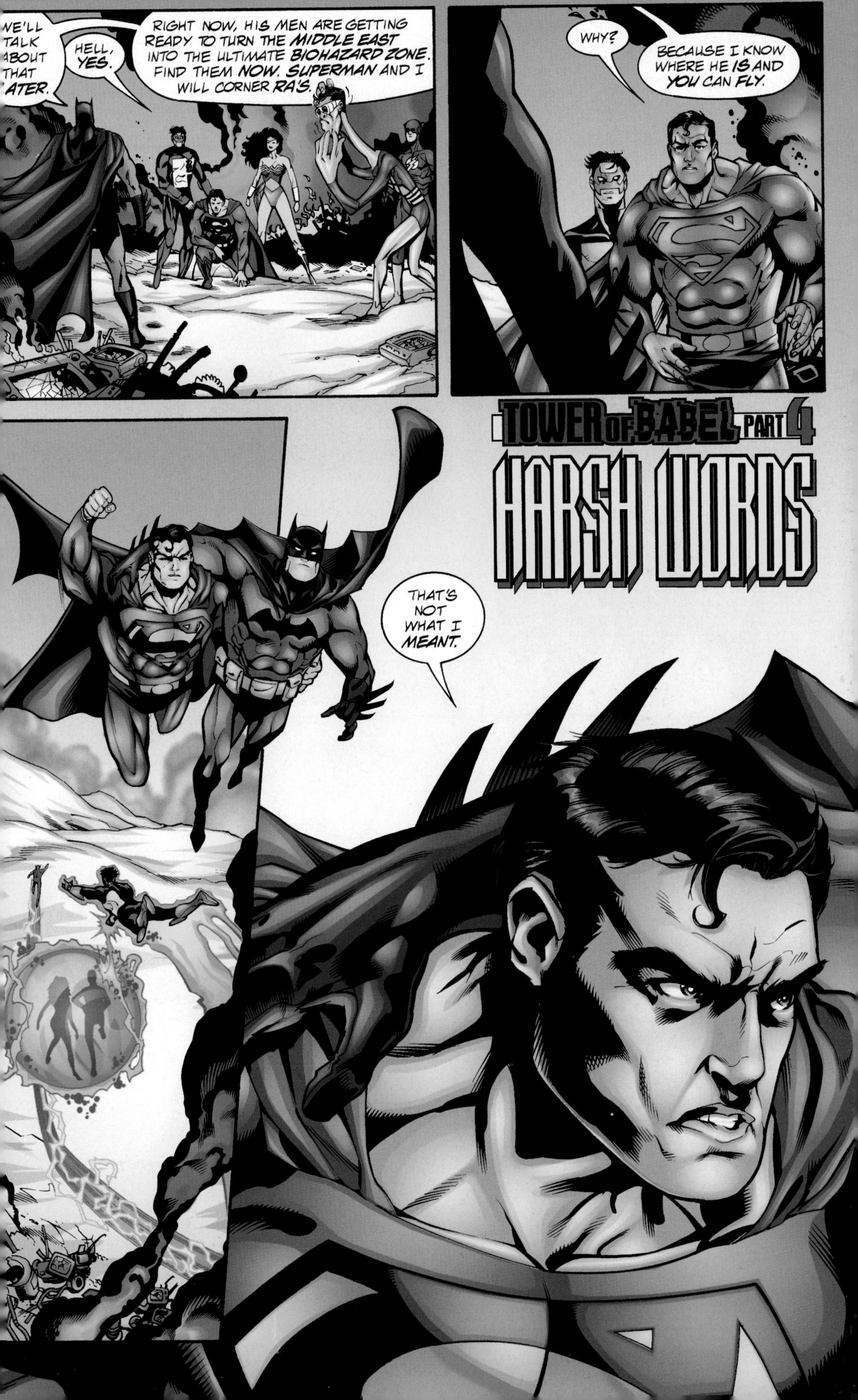

WE'LL TALK ABOUT THAT LATER.
HELL, YES.
RIGHT NOW, HIS MEN ARE GETTING READY TO TURN THE MIDDLE EAST INTO THE ULTIMATE BIOHAZARD ZONE. FIND THEM NOW. SUPERMAN AND I WILL CORNER RA'S.
WHY?
BECAUSE I KNOW WHERE HE IS AND YOU CAN FLY.
TOWER OF BABEL PART 4
HARSH WORDS
THAT'S NOT WHAT I MEANT.

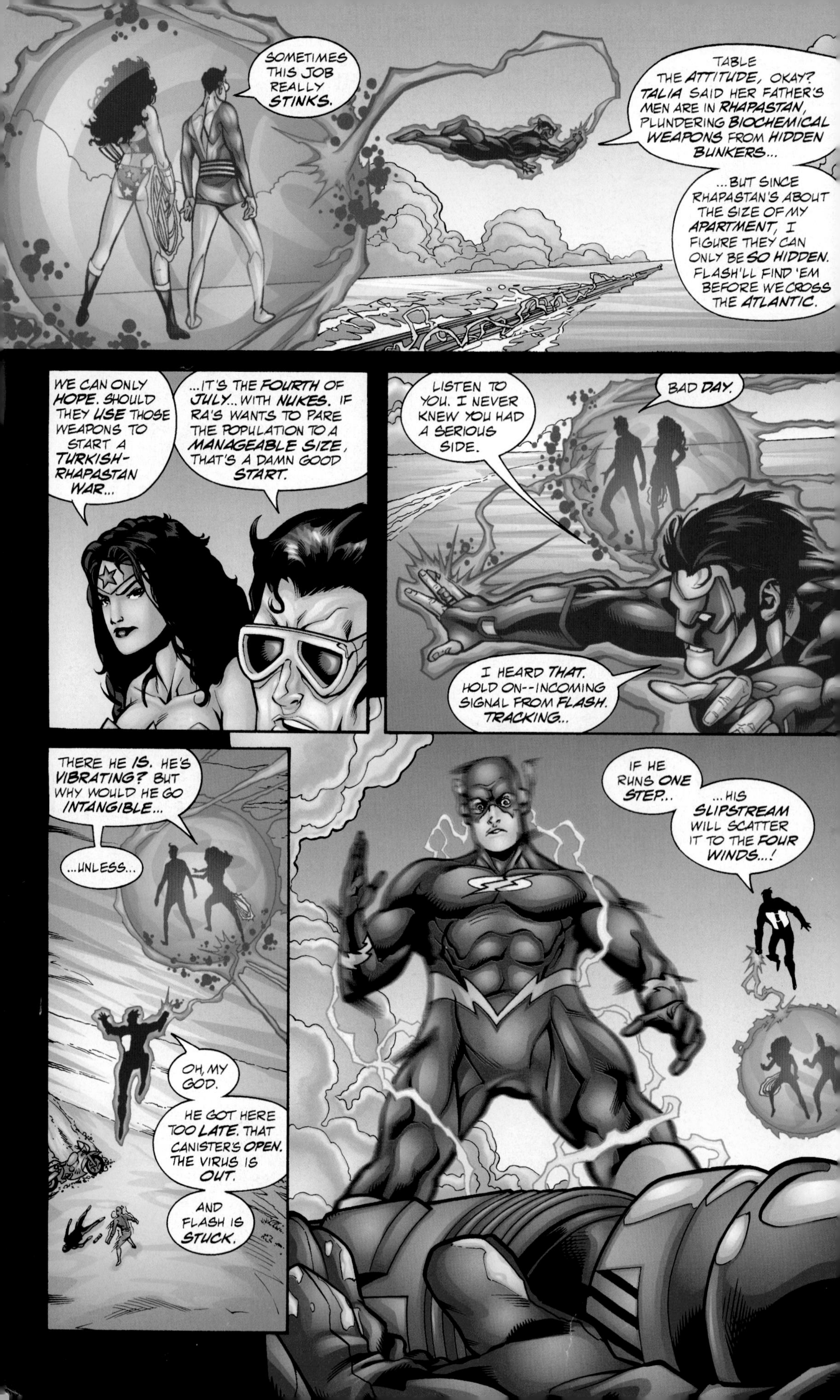
SOMETIMES THIS JOB REALLY STINKS.
TABLE THE ATTITUDE, OKAY? TALIA SAID HER FATHER'S MEN ARE IN RHAPASTAN, PLUNDERING BIOCHEMICAL WEAPONS FROM HIDDEN BUNKERS...
...BUT SINCE RHAPASTAN'S ABOUT THE SIZE OF MY APARTMENT, I FIGURE THEY CAN ONLY BE SO HIDDEN. FLASH'LL FIND 'EM BEFORE WE CROSS THE ATLANTIC.
WE CAN ONLY HOPE. SHOULD THEY USE THOSE WEAPONS TO START A TURKISH-RHAPASTAN WAR...
...IT'S THE FOURTH OF JULY...WITH NUKES. IF RA'S WANTS TO PARE THE POPULATION TO A MANAGEABLE SIZE, THAT'S A DAMN GOOD START.
LISTEN TO YOU. I NEVER KNEW YOU HAD A SERIOUS SIDE.
BAD DAY.
I HEARD THAT. HOLD ON--INCOMING SIGNAL FROM FLASH. TRACKING...
THERE HE IS. HE'S VIBRATING? BUT WHY WOULD HE GO INTANGIBLE...
...UNLESS...
OH, MY GOD.
HE GOT HERE TOO LATE. THAT CANISTER'S OPEN. THE VIRUS IS OUT.
AND FLASH IS STUCK.
IF HE RUNS ONE STEP...
...HIS SLIPSTREAM WILL SCATTER IT TO THE FOUR WINDS...!

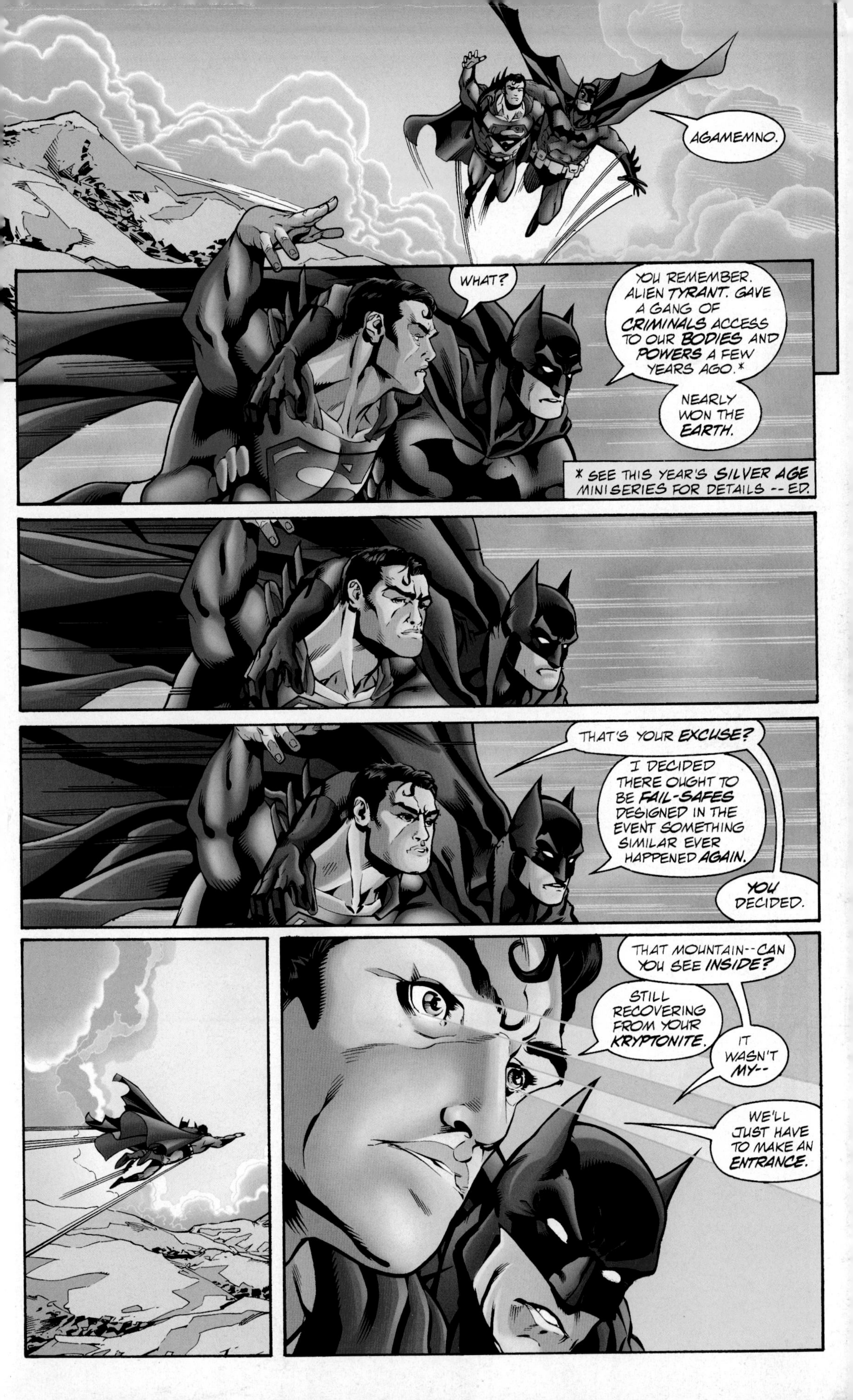
AGAMEMNO.
WHAT?
YOU REMEMBER. ALIEN TYRANT. GAVE A GANG OF CRIMINALS ACCESS TO OUR BODIES AND POWERS A FEW YEARS AGO.*
NEARLY WON THE EARTH.
* SEE THIS YEAR'S SILVER AGE MINISERIES FOR DETAILS --ED.
THAT'S YOUR EXCUSE?
I DECIDED THERE OUGHT TO BE FAIL-SAFES DESIGNED IN THE EVENT SOMETHING SIMILAR EVER HAPPENED AGAIN.
YOU DECIDED.
THAT MOUNTAIN--CAN YOU SEE INSIDE?
STILL RECOVERING FROM YOUR KRYPTONITE.
IT WASN'T MY--
WE'LL JUST HAVE TO MAKE AN ENTRANCE.

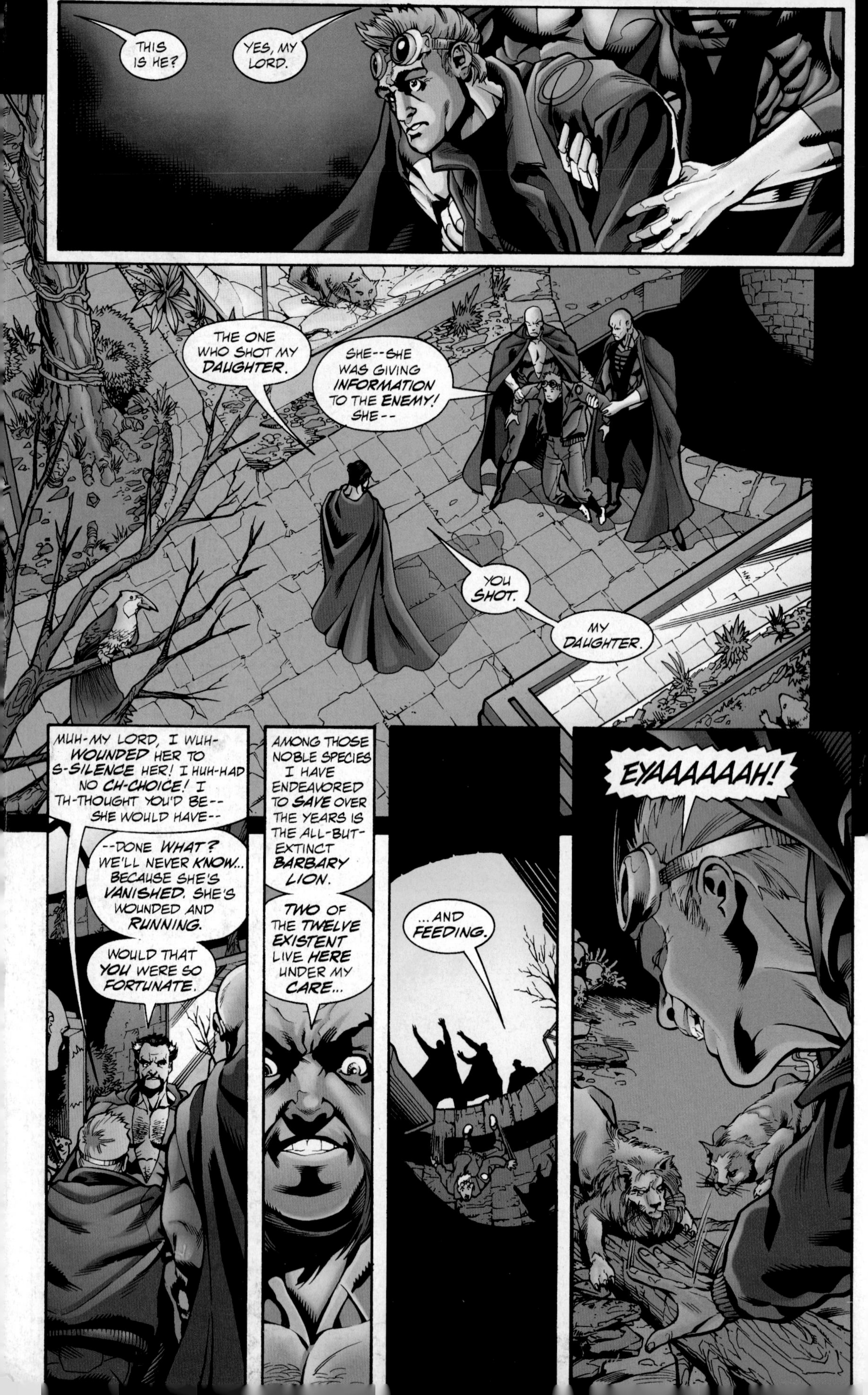
THIS IS HE?
YES, MY LORD.
THE ONE WHO SHOT MY DAUGHTER.
SHE--SHE WAS GIVING INFORMATION TO THE ENEMY! SHE--
YOU SHOT.
MY DAUGHTER.
MUH-MY LORD, I WUH-WOUNDED HER TO S-SILENCE HER! I HUH-HAD NO CH-CHOICE! I TH-THOUGHT YOU'D BE-- SHE WOULD HAVE--
--DONE WHAT? WE'LL NEVER KNOW... BECAUSE SHE'S VANISHED. SHE'S WOUNDED AND RUNNING.
WOULD THAT YOU WERE SO FORTUNATE.
AMONG THOSE NOBLE SPECIES I HAVE ENDEAVORED TO SAVE OVER THE YEARS IS THE ALL-BUT-EXTINCT BARBARY LION.
TWO OF THE TWELVE EXISTENT LIVE HERE UNDER MY CARE...
...AND FEEDING.
EYAAAAAAH!